THE
ROCK MUSIC
SOURCE BOOK

THE
ROCK MUSIC
SOURCE BOOK

BOB MACKEN
PETER FORNATALE
and BILL AYRES

ANCHOR BOOKS
ANCHOR PRESS/DOUBLEDAY
GARDEN CITY, NEW YORK
1980

The Anchor Books edition is the first publication of THE ROCK MUSIC SOURCE
   BOOK.
Anchor Books edition: 1980

ML
3534
M3

Credit for:
   The Critic for "Beginners' Guide"

$ 3936

Library of Congress Cataloging in Publication Data

Macken, Bob.
   The rock music source book.

   Bibliography: p. 641
   1. Rock music—Miscellanea. 2. Rock music—Themes, motives,
literary. I. Fornatale, Peter, joint author. II. Ayres, Bill, joint author.
III. Title.
ML3534.M3   784.5′4
ISBN: 0-385-14139-4
Library of Congress Catalog Card Number 78–1196

This book is dedicated to:

my mom and dad, whose love and encouragement enabled me to survive the trying times and make the happier times memorable. If love is an album, then you're the all-time "Greatest Hits," if thank you is a "single," then you're number one with a bullet!

Bob

my sons Peter Thomas, Mark Joseph and Steven John in the hope that rock and roll means as much to their lives as it does to mine.

Peter

my friends and partners Harry Chapin, Wray MacKay, Peter Mann, and Jeannie Ayres, with whom I share the journey into the mystery.

Bill

Acknowledgments

I would like to express my thanks and sincere gratitude to the following friends, who have supported and encouraged me over the years in the development of this project:

Bill Brown/WCBS-FM, Cathy Burney, Marci Ciamillo, Pat Cox, Jeanne Glynn and The Christophers, Hunter Village Inn, Pat Kelleher/RCA Records, Bob Liftin/Regent Sound Studios, Marian Nash, Tom Noonan/Billboard Publications, Bill Quinn and the Greenpoint Quinns and friends, Allan Rosenstein, Shooters Tavern/Hampton Bays, Rick Sklar/ABC Radio, Bruce Springsteen, Kathy Sullivan, and Kevin Treacy. From ABC-TV: Joe Adams, Greg Bogart, Joe Bush, Dave Eschelbacher, Jim Feeney, Stephanie Graf, Bill Herlihy, Al Kassel, Irene Largotta, Loy Nilsson, Ron Ogle, Ed Rossi, Fred Schuhmann, Joe Scibetta, Emily Tabacoff, George Talbot, Bill Waterbury, Jørn Winther.

Special thanks:

To WNEW-FM and its "World's Greatest Music Library"!

To Kevin "Charlie" Cannon, whose friendship, advice, and insanity always kept things rolling.

To my brother Kevin and sister Eileen, for your love and faith in me.

And to my lady, Debbie Macken, for her love and understanding.

Thank you all . . .
Bob

Thanks to:

Susan Fornatale, for endless hours of patience and understanding.

Dennis Elsas, for his initial efforts on behalf of this project, and to Steve Leeds for his forthcoming efforts on this project.

And to the great wall of music at WNEW-FM for countless amounts of information—all in alphabetical order!

Peter

Thanks to:

Pete Fornatale for opening my eyes to rock and roll many years ago.

Larry Berger of WPLJ-FM for many years of faith and encouragement.

Dave Marsh for many shared journeys back into the roots of rock and roll and forward into its future.

Jeannie, my love, my partner, my wife who puts up with most of my wall of records but loves Bruce.

Bill

And to Marie D. Brown, Bob Hutchins, and Tim McGinnis, whose support, encouragement, and patience were appreciated in the editing of this book.

Bob
Peter
Bill

Contents

10 *Contents*

PART ONE

"Hail! Hail! Rock and Roll!"

Beginners' Guide to Rock

Rock and roll is an inadequate umbrella term used to describe the single most influential unifying force for the rapidly multiplying numbers of media children. There are an estimated 300,000 professional and amateur rock groups performing in this country alone and countless millions more seeing, hearing, feeling, and sharing this music. Together, these people have developed an outlet to channel their creative energies.

The rock phenomenon has now cast its spell over an entire generation of young people from birth, not to mention the indelible mark it has left on the lives of countless "teen-agers" from the Elvis Presley fifties who are now pushing forty and raising kids who dig Kiss and Peter Frampton.

Let's see if we can put this generation gap business into perspective. The late Margaret Mead wrote in *Culture and Commitment,* "Even very recently, the elders could say, 'You know, I have been young, and you never have been old.' But today's young people can reply: 'You never have been young in the world I am young in, and you never can be. . . .' This break between generations is wholly new: it is planetary and universal."

In other words, the world has changed more rapidly in the last fifty years than in the previous thousand, and this period of our history happens to fall in the midst of an overwhelming cultural and sensory transition—one that has led to irreconcilable perceptual differences between the pre- and post-TV generations. Nobody asked for it to be this way, it just is. So why not try to make the best of the far-reaching consequences brought about by technological progression?

Why do most pre-rock adults have a difficult time accepting, let alone understanding, this music, while youngsters seem to thrive on it? I think I have a partial explanation for this dilemma. As anthropologist Ted Carpenter has pointed out, we must begin to recognize that all media are languages, complete with their own unique grammars and vocabularies. Think about the way most people learn their native tongues. It's an intuitive process that begins at birth, with the result that we are capable of communicating with others in our environment long before formal instruction begins. Then in high school we are presented with the opportunity to learn a second language.

Ah, now it's not such an easy matter. Our bias has been established and our ability to absorb a foreign tongue spontaneously has been severely checked. It is a formal and difficult process. Only by immersing ourselves in the foreign culture can we hope to grasp the idiosyncrasies of its language.

How does this apply to contemporary music? For young people, rock (and electronic media, for that matter) is a native tongue, an intuitive experience. For most adults, it is a second language, as trying and as difficult as Spanish I at Central High. Only by immersing themselves in this musical idiom can they hope to begin to appreciate it.

You can see evidence in all types of activity that the divisions separating young and old in this country are deep and wide, and haven't got a chance of being eliminated unless we find the key to some kind of mutual respect and understanding. For many, music is the most accessible "key," perhaps because the essence of its communication is nonverbal (more on this later). Now I'm not asking Grandma to go out and buy the new Stones LP, nor do I expect Lawrence Welk to be included at any of next year's rock concerts. I'm sure there's a happy medium somewhere between these two extremes. The point is that pride in one's own musical tradition and environmental conditioning is fine, but the reluctance to admit that other kinds of music and environments are valid is narrow-minded and destructive. For example, just because our environment does not allow for an understanding of the importance of the sitar to Indian culture does not mean that the sitar should be automatically discounted as an instrument of musical worth. You see, it's easy for people to recognize that American culture and Indian culture differ, but it's not so easy for people to realize that rapid technological growth created a whole counter culture inside the American environs with some differences that are just as marked as those between mainstream American culture and India's. But it's happening right under our noses and is, therefore a bit more difficult to perceive than if we had the chance to step aside and view it as an outsider.

It seems to me more than coincidental that Simon and Garfunkel's most popular LP is called "Bridge over Troubled Water," because these two, even more than the Beatles, did the most to bridge the musical gap in this country of any performers in recent memory. I think the reason for this is that Paul and Art are perfect examples of creative people caught in the midst of the overwhelming transition from a totally print-oriented culture to one in which print is forced to share the spotlight with the new electronic media. Somehow they make appropriate use of the new machinery while retaining references, devices, and techniques of the literary. The result is a blend that finds acceptance at both ends of the spectrum.

If you agree with my premise that music can serve as the lifeline between generations, a bridge over troubled water, so to speak, then it is time for a thumbnail sketch of the development of rock from its earliest beginnings up to the present:

Rock was controversial right from the start insofar as it was the offspring of a mixed marriage. Black rhythm and blues merged with white country and western music to produce a hip, free-wheeling sound that swept the country in the hands of performers like Bill Haley and the Comets, Buddy Holly and the Crickets, Chuck Berry, and Little Richard. The combination reflected the feelings and attitudes of the new postwar American teen-agers. They were hungry for an outlet which would acknowledge their existence and express their individuality. The advent of portable and transistor radios just at the dawn of the Age of Rock created a veritable communications network linking the various youth tribes of the global village. Film played its part as well. *Blackboard Jungle* put rock in theaters from coast to coast with its mind-blowing anthem, "Rock Around the Clock."

To be sure, the best-seller charts were still in large part dominated by Perry Como and Patti Page, but the stage had been set for a revolution that would rearrange the shape of American popular music. All it needed now was a leader.

Rock found that leader in a sensual, hip-swiveling Nashville ex-truck driver named Elvis Presley. It is easy to see why young people with an appetite for freedom were attracted to Elvis. He was loud, crude, and full of the vitality characteristic of youth in an affluent society. His impact was immediate and worldwide (stretching all the way to Liverpool, England, where four young men, who would have an impressive impact of their own later on, listened and learned). It was Elvis who singlehandedly set the precedents and opened the gates for the likes of Jerry Lee Lewis, Rick Nelson, and the Everly Brothers.

It was in these early years that rock began to prove just how much of a big business it could become and how large a consumer market young people represented.

Pioneered by Alan Freed and a handful of contemporaries, Top 40 radio stations flourished across the country. Befuddled television talent coordinators began booking every pop act in sight for the various variety shows. With a calculating finger on the pulsebeat of the youth culture, Dick Clark transformed a local Philadelphia dance show called *American Bandstand* into a network trend-setter and taste-maker. Ed Sullivan began booking weekly rock attractions (a practice which to the end remained an ingredient of the tried and true Sullivan formula). Small independent record labels stole some of the thunder from the previously untouchable big four (Capitol, Columbia, RCA Victor, and Decca). And big box office rock and roll shows filled auditoriums and theaters from coast to coast.

However, in spite of the phenomenal success of these early years and the brilliant foundation that they laid for the music that was to follow, the years '59–'63 almost saw the demise of rock as a musical or social force. Elvis and the Everly Brothers were in the Army and Marines, respectively. Buddy Holly had been killed in a plane crash. Chuck Berry spent some time behind bars. Little Richard had become a minister, and Jerry Lee Lewis was boycotted for marrying his thirteen-year-old cousin. On top of all this, the word "payola" crept into the American vocabulary. Payola referred to the practice of paying radio personalities in order to get the airplay so necessary to make a hit record and launch a career.

It was a dismal period for those of us who felt that rock had only just begun. The mediocrity continued through the early sixties with the Twist craze, as aging adults gyrated aimlessly in search of their lost youth, and the Peppermint Lounge in New York became a national landmark. One of the only rays of hope during these lean years came from a California-based group called the Beach Boys. Led by Brian Wilson, they singlehandedly developed a musical form that was uniquely American—the Southern California surfing craze-cum-youth celebration. Borrowing heavily from the blackest rhythm and blues melodies and chord progressions, the Beach Boys created a lily-white lyric environment whose impact is unsurpassed. "Surfin' U.S.A.," "Surfin' Safari," "Surf City" (a hit Wilson wrote for Jan and Dean), and "Surfer Girl" are as important to a complete understanding of American rock and roll as anything by Chuck Berry or the Everly Brothers.

The spark of creativity evident in groups like the Beach Boys kept the music alive through this slump period. No one knows the exact date that rock became significant again. The closest estimate puts it somewhere between February and August of 1964. That's when two giant steps toward maturity were taken almost simultaneously. First of all, the Beatles brought new life and respect to the somewhat tarnished reputation of rock, and, second, Bob Dylan proved that you could put meaningful lyrics and poetic imagery to a rock beat and reach a wider mass audience than ever before possible.

The British invasion reactivated all of the near dormant rock machinery. A New York disc jockey named Murray the K called himself the "fifth Beatle" and Top 40 radio stations began measuring the time in Beatle minutes. *Shindig* and *Hullabaloo* were two new network TV rock shows created to serve the revitalized youth market. *Help!* and *A Hard Day's Night* revolutionized the vocabulary of film. Any group with a British accent had it made. The Beatles, The Rolling Stones, The Dave Clark Five, Gerry and the Pacemakers, The Searchers, Herman's Hermits, The Kinks, and a host of others all had big hit records those first few months. When The Beatles made an appearance on the Sullivan show they attracted a viewing audience of seventy-three million people, nearly 45 percent of the entire population!

Now think about what was happening culturally in the United States at this time. The first generation of media children ever to hit the planet was coming into its own and on the lookout for an outlet to channel its new modes of perception. That outlet—rock and roll —has been the one medium of communication in which young people have been allowed to exert a unique influence. They learned the grammar and vocabulary of rock at a very tender age from radio, TV, records, etc. They are instinctively drawn to electric instruments because such instruments are a natural extension of our culture and environment. They write their own songs, arrange them, perform them, and then they go into the control room to engineer them. They know every facet of the language of popular music and they're doing creative, fresh, and exciting things with it.

With this background providing the setting, America's 1965 response to the British invasion was a massive counteroffensive which saw the emergence of such rock supertalents as John Sebastian (The Lovin' Spoonful), Paul Simon (Simon and Garfunkel), John Phillips (The Mamas and The Papas), Roger McGuinn (The

Byrds), and a new, more sophisticated Brian Wilson (The Beach Boys). They wrote lyrics that captured the authenticity of experience. The communication was immediate, one to one and relevant to contemporary concerns.

Rock had become the melting pot of all musical forms. To the basic mixture of rhythm and blues and country and western, it added folk and jazz chord progressions, baroque and modern harmony, art-song lyrics, and the rhythms of Indian ragas. In every instance, this healthy kind of experimentation has served to broaden the base of pop music and expand its outer limits to encompass new areas of awareness and communication.

The late '60s saw the development of a number of interesting phenomena that are still very much a part of the rock machinery:

In 1966, a young writer named Richard Goldstein became the rock critic for *New York* magazine and the *Village Voice,* paving the way for serious journals of rock criticism. *Rolling Stone* remains the most influential of these.

It was around this period, too, that "progressive" FM radio stations began springing up around the country. In contrast to AM, their approach was low-key, unhurried, and truthful. Though watered down by the markedly different political climate of the late '70s, a number of these stations continue to prosper in major markets across the United States.

Meanwhile, the marriage of rock and cinema was consummated in films like *The Graduate, Monterey Pop, Easy Rider, Alice's Restaurant,* and *Woodstock.* This trend grew stronger in the '70s, as evidenced by recent films like *American Graffiti, Tommy, Saturday Night Fever,* and *The Last Waltz,* etc.

For the most part, the '70s have been a cooling-off period. No new "Presley" or "Beatles" have emerged, but lots of excitement has been generated by the likes of Elton John, Fleetwood Mac, and Bruce Springsteen. Even without a focal point, however, one fact stands out above the rest. Contemporary popular music is the first totally developed, completely satisfying art form of the electronic age.

In preparing his book on pop music, *The Rock Story,* Jerry Hopkins conducted a poll. He asked young people from eight years to their middle twenties why they liked rock music. Nine out of ten said, "It makes me feel good."

That pretty much sums it up. The rock generation is definitely a *feel it* crowd. Their media orientation will not allow them to be detached or isolated (characteristics of print orientation). They demand participation and involvement, and woe to the print-oriented individual or institution who denies them this birthright. Rock's primary appeal is not on the lyric level. It is more nonverbal and tactile than aural. In fact, rock represents an entire life style—one which is becoming increasingly attractive to young people fed up with a world not too much to their liking and eager to experiment with new ways. Many of these young men and women give more of an actual damn about their music than anything else, including sex, religion, and politics. And that's no exaggeration. When you get right down to it, for them, rock is sex, rock is religion, and rock is politics.

As Plato put it, "Forms and rhythms in music are never changed without producing changes in the most important political forms and ways. The new style quietly insinuates itself into manners and customs and from there it assumes a greater force, goes on to attack laws and constitutions, displaying the utmost impudence until it ends by overthrowing everything, both in public and in private."

PETER FORNATALE

Rock: Values and Education

I. VALUES

"It's all in what you value."—George Harrison
"The whole system is based on the corruption of your ideals, on the watering down of things that are real."—Bruce Springsteen

That does not seem like a line from the Springsteen world of fast cars, Saturday-night pickups, and broken romances, but it is right at the heart of it. In fact, it is at the heart of the best of rock and roll, and so is Springsteen himself.

Trivialization and corruption of our ideals and values are always taking place in society. The worst of rock music panders to all of that and even acts as a vehicle for its apparent triumph. The beat of its music is the mindless droning of our attempts to escape the oppression of everyday living, only to find ourselves trapped in the hollow promise of diversion, a promise that never really delivers.

The best of rock does deliver, not only as an isolated musical entity, but as a driving life force that helps us to affirm our own existence, to feel good about ourselves, and, at the same time, to challenge both ourselves and the society in which we are living. To the extent that it helps us to do all of those things, rock and roll is a truly revolutionary music.

The two focal points of any revolution are the person and the society in which that person lives. The genuine personal revolution must help us to uncover our true centers and focus on accepting the good in ourselves, affirming our own value and doing battle with those fears and insecurities that make us want to maintain the status quo, however miserable it may be. The societal revolution must work to change those structures within the system which destroy life and reinforce oppression, self-hatred, and fear.

The question is, does rock and roll aid these two essential revolutionary processes? Does it help you to get past the debris that clutters up the surface of life and into your true center, or does it provide a kind of rhythm for bouncing around the surface, making you oblivious to the need to go any deeper? Does it look, not destructively, but critically, at the institutions of society, at the very processes and structures that control the lives of people? At this point, a further question arises. Is this asking too much of a very intense but limited means of communication? Will the answer come back, "I'm just a singer in a rock and roll band," or, "What can a poor boy do but play in a rock and roll band?"

In its best moments, rock and roll has been a positive force for the creation and reinforcement of personal values and real change in society. However, its greatest success has also led to the corruption and watering down of ideals about which Springsteen talks. This has happened in at least two stages.

1. Rock As Counter Culture

Culture is a conveyer of values and ideals. It is the atmosphere in which the "stuff of life" takes on specific form and meaning, and the channel through which it becomes accessible to us.

At one time—not so long ago—rock acted as a kind of "counter culture," challenging the boundaries of the dominant culture where it had become hypocritical and even unjust. At that point in its history, the main thrust of rock music was as a force for change, both on a personal level, in such things as sexual morality, drug use, or the pervasive consumptionistic, anti-environmental life style that most of us follow, and on a societal level, in opposition to the Vietnam War, racial injustice, and the oppressive economic problems of the poor.

Rock and roll provided much of the communicative power of the "counter culture," and, as such, was a force for change. Unfortunately, much of this power and dynamism has dissipated over the past ten years, partially because of a general stagnation within the larger culture and society, but also because rock itself has been co-opted. Its very success has been its own worst enemy. It has become a multi-billion-dollar industry. As Bruce Springsteen says ". . . the watering down of things that are real."

2. Rock As Alternate Culture

Rock is no longer "counter culture." Much of its most positive force has been absorbed into the dominant culture. However, it certainly is an important part of what could be called an "alternate culture."

Every age has had its childhood and teen-age heroes, but never before our age of electronic mass media has this whole mythology taken such definite and pervasive shape. It begins very early in the pre-teen years, with the Osmonds, the Fonz, and Farrah, pervades the teen-age years, and more and more frequently hangs on, at least in part, well into the twenties.

This "alternate culture" helps provide people with a whole series of identities as they grow up, and can be very helpful in developing a healthy self-identity. This is one of the positive reasons for so much preoccupation with the pop-rock culture. It gives a young person a frame of reference, something that creates self-definition and importance when family, school, and religion, the other major forces in a person's growth, are either silent or are seen as irrelevant or even negative.

The truth is, though, that the "alternate culture" itself has a very negative side. It tends to be a manipulative assault on a partially formed conscience and consciousness that helps to create homogenized, unreflective robots rather than thinking, feeling, believing people.

It does all of this by presenting stereotypes as real, then creating unrealistic expectations and escapist illusions, while at the same time encouraging both passivity and a kind of "me-first" attitude toward life that judges the value of things, people, and experiences by their ability to provide instant gratification. Its all-pervasive presence and its slick, media-created "non-events" and hyped-up superstars create a strange aura that is not itself reality but which masquerades as reality and is accepted as such by millions of people. Unfortunately, rock itself has become a highly profitable commodity. This puts tremendous commercial pressure on performers and writers to conform to the least common denominator. It drains the creative forces within and creates a kind of mask which often filters out the most authentic instincts of the music. The great paradox here is that music, the very force that has the power to help people create their best selves and relate more freely and authentically with each other, gets perverted.

Watch out, Bruce and Bob and Joni and Jackson and all you other "poets of the real" in rock. Schlock-rock is out to accomplish ". . . the corruption of your ideals . . ."—and ours—not only through the thematic content of the music, but by its musical quality and, even more, by the whole pervasive atmosphere of mediocrity upon which it survives and thrives.

There is an age-old controversy about whether music reflects the values of a society or whether it helps to create them. The former is more likely to be true, but here music plays another important role: as a reinforcer of values. This is especially true for young people. Rock music is always there. It becomes a kind of "aural horizon" within which everything else happens. Much of this, of course, is unreflective and unthematic. Therein lies the problem, and there also is the role of rock in education and the importance of education for the world and people of rock.

II. EDUCATION

"Teach your children well . . ." Crosby, Stills, Nash & Young
"Teach your teachers well." Macken, Fornatale, and Ayres

Our main reason for writing this book was to unearth the varied treasures, of both music and meaning, that are buried in the history of rock music. We hope it will be a tool for fans and musicians alike. We hope it will be a very special tool for teachers and students.

Rock is not primarily meant to be analyzed, dissected, and trampled to death, in an effort to get at some hidden inner meaning. It is rather meant to be heard and enjoyed. Nevertheless, there is a time and a place for reflecting on the words and themes of the music. There is real poetry in rock, poetry that is very close to the "stuff of life" in which we all need to be involved. The message of rock is an education in itself, and it can be a very positive force in the overall process of education. There are some key questions for teachers to keep in mind.

1. What is the overall effect of the self in the experience of rock music? What is the self that is revealed? Is it the superficial, unimaginative, escapist self or is it the best, the truest self? Songs as varied as "The Pretender" by Jackson Browne, "Hey Jude" by the Beatles, or "Won't Get Fooled Again" by The Who can help in this process of self-discovery. The further down the musical ladder, the more narcissistic and deadening the whole thing gets.

2. What is the thematic content of the music? Is it a challenge to live life more deeply or simply to give in to whatever is the easiest, least painful way to survive? "Let's All Boogie, All Night Long."

3. Does the quality of the music itself as well as its thematic content help to develop or dull the imagination? Compare, for example the vast wasteland of disco music with an average (not the best, just the average) Beatles song. One calls forth passive imitation, the other is much more likely to call forth creative, imaginative response.

There are also a number of cautions for teachers.

1. Rock will usually be seen by the students as *their* music, not the teachers'. Teachers should respect something that is not "their turf."

2. When the teacher is familiar and comfortable in the world of rock, the communication process with students is greatly enhanced; however, it is still primarily the music of the students.

3. If rock is seen as a means of propagandizing students, a way to get across "the message," whatever it is, the credibility of both teacher and message plummets to previously unknown depths.

4. Rock music, and particularly rock themes, can be a valuable bridge between the generations, a tool for dialogue in which both students and teachers share a journey of discovery, each bringing his or her own experience and knowledge. It may be that the teachers hate Kiss or some other fad of the day, and the students may never have heard of The Byrds or the Buffalo Springfield, but they might all like Neil Young or The Kinks.

5. Rock is best used in the education process when it is coming from the students, when they are making most of the choices of songs, artists, and themes. However, the teacher has a very active and important role to play here both as a guide and as a voice of supportive challenge. The teacher can use the theme as a vehicle for encouraging the reflective self-discovery and world-discovery process, starting with something that is very much a part of the students' lives.

BILL AYRES

PART TWO

Important Themes of Rock

How to Use the Themes

I. THE FIFTY PERSONAL, SOCIAL, AND POLITICAL THEMES

A. *The Choice of Themes*

When we started to write this book we had some four hundred themes in mind. We soon discovered that if we put such a large number into one volume, they would lead us out of our minds and lead you into a hernia. Instead, we chose fifty themes that reflect the deepest personal, social, and political concerns in our world and in the world of rock and roll. This meant that we had to hold some of the most popular "fun themes" like "Cars" and "Music" for Volume 2.

We found that many of the themes also had subthemes. We tried to include the most important and useful ones if there were enough songs to justify a separate listing. For example, the theme of "Working" also includes listings for "Unions," "Miners," "Secretaries," and "After Work Hours."

B. *The Structure of Each Theme*

The fifty personal, social, and political themes are listed in alphabetical order. Each theme has the following elements:

1. Definition:

There is a brief definition of each category that explains the types of songs that are included.

2. Related Categories:

Many songs have more than one message or meaning and can fit into more than one category. To find these songs and others, we have included a "Related Categories" listing which cross-references some additional themes that may be of further help.

3. Classics:

For each theme we selected some "Classic" songs, or songs that best represent the theme. These are the criteria we used for our "Classic" selections:

    a) the song deals *directly* and *predominantly* with the theme.

    b) it is *accessible* to the average record buyer.

    c) it is, in our view, *a good musical performance.*

    d) it says something *significant* about the theme.

We limited our selections to five in each theme or subtheme, although in many cases we could not find five songs that met all of our criteria. This was one of the most difficult parts of the book. We listened to records together and argued for hours about the relative merits of the songs. Now it is your turn. Good Luck!

4. Thematic Albums:

These are albums that deal entirely or at least primarily with one theme. They are frequently called concept albums, e.g., "Desperado" by the Eagles (Asylum) focuses on the theme of "Outlaws."

5. Definitive Songs:

Here we list songs that deal primarily with the theme. They are not all great songs, but each one might appeal to different people and meet different needs because of the way that it approaches the theme.

In a number of cases a song will be listed as a definitive song in more than one theme.

6. Reference Songs:

Most songs make references to more than one theme. It is virtually impossible to figure out all the references in these songs. We have included the most significant ones that make a partial or obvious reference.

7. Fill in the Blanks:

We kept including new songs in the book right up until the last minute. We were always convinced that the book would be judged incomplete and incompetent without the latest batch of songs. Finally our editors called a halt to our madness. However, no one need interfere with your madness. The blank spaces at the end of the listing for each theme are there for you to add new songs as well as those that you think we should have included in the first place.

8. Subthemes:

As mentioned earlier, some themes have subthemes. The subthemes follow the Fill in the Blanks section.

II. THE LOVE THEMES

A. *The Choice*

Love is the most popular theme in rock music, or in any other music, for that matter. Our problem was how to deal with the thousands of songs written about the various aspects of love. We decided to divide the love songs according to the different aspects of the experience itself. Starting with the "Looking for a Love" and "Like to Get to Know You" songs, we have listed twenty separate themes of love covering its important emotions, continuing right through to the "Happy Together" and "And I Love You So" songs.

B. *The Structure of Each Theme*

1. Title and Definition:

The title of each love theme is the title of a song that best summarizes what the theme is really about.

2. Choice Cuts:

We obviously could not make this an all-inclusive list, so we opted for two or three dozen of the best songs about each love theme. These are the criteria we used for our selections:

    a) the song deals directly and predominantly with the theme.

    b) it is accessible to the average record buyer.

    c) it is, in our view, a good musical performance.

    d) at least one version is recorded by a recognizable artist or band.

    e) it is a popular or fairly familiar song.

(N.B. There are no classic or reference songs, since we have tried to select the best all-around songs. There are some thematic albums that deal with love in general, and these albums are found at the beginning of the love section.)

III. THE SONGS

A. *The Choice of Songs*

The words that entered into our thoughts and conversations most often as we wrote this book were "arbitrary" and "paranoia." Our greatest paranoia was that we were being arbitrary in our choice of songs. Next on the list was that we left important songs out or had misinterpreted some of them. Many songs by Joni Mitchell, Bob Dylan, and the Moody Blues, among others, simply defy thematization. Some of these songs are great works of art, but we did not know where to put them. Who knows? Maybe they will appear in Volume 2 as a separate category.

There is bound to be a great deal of personal choice and subjective opinion in a book like this. We tried to minimize this by establishing the following criteria:

    a) we chose 1954 as the starting date for songs we would include. There are only a few exceptions to this.

    b) we tried to stay within the genre of rock music, realizing that there are many streams of rock that form the mainstream. We included notable "crossovers," i.e., records that had made it as hits even though they were not strictly rock: e.g., George Benson's

"Everything Must Change" or Johnny Cash's "A Boy Named Sue."

c) we included songs by artists who, although they are not rock performers, have significantly influenced rock music and have made significant statements about personal, social, or political issues, e.g., Pete Seeger and Woody Guthrie, Muddy Waters and B. B. King.

B. *The Structure of Each Song Listing*

Each entry consists of four parts, and is listed in the following manner:

1) The Song   2) The Artist or Band
3) The Record   4) The Record Label

for example:

I Can Hear Music   Beach Boys
"The 20/20 Album"   (Brother/Reprise)

(N.B. Some songs are contained on more than one album. When this occurs, we list as many additional albums as possible. These include "Greatest Hits" packages, "live" recordings, soundtrack albums, and compilation albums, i.e., albums containing songs from various artists.)

The symbol * indicates *Hard-to-find Songs/Albums*. This symbol will follow albums that are no longer listed in the record company catalogue and may be hard to find on the general market. We have listed these songs anyway because you may know someone who has them or you may have access through a good $.99 bin or "close-out albums" sale in your favorite record store. Record company catalogues are ever changing, so be prepared to add your own * as needed.

The symbol + indicates *Cover Version of Preceding Song*. Rock and roll is now in its third decade, and there has been some truly fine music in its short history. Many of the best songs are rerecorded by other artists in what are known as "cover" versions. We have listed the original version as well as any "cover" version that we know.

e.g.

Will You Still Love Me Tomorrow?   Carole King
  "Tapestry"   (Ode)
+Will You Still Love Me Tomorrow?   Dave Mason
  "Mariposa de Oro"   (Columbia)
    (same song)

If you see two songs with no marking, they are two completely different songs with the same title.

e.g.

Sittin' on a Fence	Rolling Stones
"Flowers"	(London)
Sittin' on a Fence	Poco
"Head over Heels"*	(ABC)

BOB MACKEN

AMERICA

America—the beautiful, the good, the bad, and the ugly.
Songs that portray various aspects of American society, through the eyes of its own people and through those of the world.

Related Categories: Ecology/Conservation, Freedom, Politics, Poverty, Protest/Revolution, War and Peace

+Same as Song Above
*Hard-to-find Songs/Albums

CLASSICS

America	Simon and Garfunkel
"Bookends"	(Columbia)
"Simon and Garfunkel's Greatest Hits"	(Columbia)
+America	Bert Sommer
"Inside Bert Sommer"*	(Eleuthera)
+America	Yes
"Yesterdays"	(Atlantic)
+America	Paul Simon
"Live Rhymin'"	(Columbia)
+America	The Nice
"Elegy"	(Mercury)
American Tune	Paul Simon
"There Goes Rhymin' Simon"	(Columbia)
"Live Rhymin'"	(Columbia)
"Greatest Hits, Etc."	(Columbia)
+American Tune	Starland Vocal Band
"Starland Vocal Band"	(Windsong)
Power and the Glory	Phil Ochs
"Chords of Fame"	(A&M)
"All the News That's Fit to Sing"	(Elektra)
+Power and the Glory	Pete Seeger
"God Bless the Grass"	(Columbia)
This Land Is Your Land	Woody Guthrie
"Woody Guthrie"	(Warner Brothers)
"Library of Congress"	(Elektra)
+This Land Is Your Land	Pete Seeger
"The World of Pete Seeger"	(Columbia)

CLASSICS

+This Land Is Your Land Peter, Paul and Mary
"Moving" (Warner Brothers)
"Live" (Warner Brothers)

+This Land Is Your Land Jim Croce
"Faces I've Been" (Lifesong)

+This Land Is Your Land Ramblin' Jack Elliott
"Hard Travelin'" (Fantasy)

+This Land Is Your Land The Limelighters
"Spirit of America" (RCA)

+This Land Is Your Land The Staple Singers
"Use What You Got" (Fantasy)

U. S. Blues Grateful Dead
"Mars Hotel" (Grateful Dead Records)
"Steal Your Face" (Grateful Dead Records)

DEFINITIVE SONGS

America Sammy Johns
"Sammy Johns"* (General Recording Corp.)

America My Home Buffy Sainte-Marie
"Sweet America"* (ABC)

America Squirm Nick Lowe
"Labour of Lust" (Columbia)

American City Suite Cashman and West
"A Song or Two"* (ABC/Dunhill)

American Dream Don Harrison Band
"Not Far from Free" (Mercury)

The American Dream Artie Kaplan
"Confessions of a Male Chauvinist (Hopi/Vanguard)
  Pig"*

The Americans Byron McGregor
"The Americans" (Westbound)

American Love Affair Tonio K
"Life in the Foodchain" (Full Moon/Epic)

American Mother Tyla Gang
"Moonproof" (Beserkley)

An American Trilogy Mickey Newberry
"Frisco Mabel Joy"* (Elektra)

36 *The Rock Music Source Book*

DEFINITIVE SONGS

+An American Trilogy
"Elvis Recorded Live at Madison
  Square Garden"
Elvis Presley
(RCA)

American Woman
"The Best of the Guess Who"
The Guess Who
(RCA)

America the Beautiful
"A Message from the People"
Ray Charles
(ABC)

America the Beautiful/The Times
  They Are a Changin'
"Spirit of '76"*
Spirit

(Mercury)

Amerika the Brave
"Hobo with a Grin"
Steve Harley
(Capitol)

Back in the U.S.A.
"Golden Decade"
Chuck Berry
(Chess)

+Back in the U.S.A.
"Back in the U.S.A."
MC 5
(Atlantic)

+Back in the U.S.A.
"Jonathan Richmond"
Jonathan Richmond
(Beserkley)

+Back in the U.S.A.
"Living in the U.S.A."
Linda Ronstadt
(Asylum)

+Back in the U.S.A.
"Roadwork"
Edgar Winter
(Epic)

Bicentennial
"T-Shirt"
Loudon Wainwright III
(Arista)

Bicentennial Blues
"The Whole Thing Started with Rock
  and Roll"*
Ray Manzarek
(Mercury)

The Big Country
"More Songs About Buildings and
  Food"
Talking Heads
(Sire)

Breakfast in America
"Breakfast in America"
Supertramp
(A&M)

Captain America
"Before the Salt"
Jimmy Buffett
(Barnaby)

City of New Orleans
"The Essential Steve Goodman"
Steve Goodman
(Buddah)

+City of New Orleans
"Judith"
Judy Collins
(Elektra)

+City of New Orleans
Arlo Guthrie

DEFINITIVE SONGS

"Hobo's Lullaby"	(Reprise)
"The Best of Arlo Guthrie"	(Reprise)
+City of New Orleans	John Denver
"Aerie"	(RCA)
Come Home America	Johnny Rivers
"L.A. Reggae"*	(United Artists)
Every Man a King	Randy Newman
"Good Old Boys"	(Reprise)
The Fiddle and the Drum	Joni Mitchell
"Clouds"	(Reprise)
Free in America	Ben Sidran
"Free in America"*	(Arista)
The Great American Eagle Tragedy	Earth Opera
"Earth Opera"*	(Elektra)
Growin' Up (in the U.S.A.)	Dan Hill
"Listen with Your Heart"*	(Columbia)
Hear Me Out	Stevie Wonder
"Songs in the Key of Life"	(Tamla)
I Could Be Singing	Arlo Guthrie
"Washington County"	(Reprise)
I'm So Bored with the U.S.A.	The Clash
"The Clash"	(Epic)
Just a Story from America	Elliott Murphy
"Just a Story from America"*	(Columbia)
Living in the U.S.A.	Stevie Miller
"Living in the U.S.A."	(Capitol)
"Anthology"	(Capitol)
The Man Who Built America	Horslips
"The Man Who Built America"	(DJM Records)
Miss America	Styx
"Grand Illusion"	(A&M)
Monster	Steppenwolf
"Steppenwolf's ABC Collection"	(ABC)
"Live Steppenwolf"	(ABC/Dunhill)
Mother Country	Bonnie Koloc
"You're Gonna Love Yourself in the Morning"*	(Ovation)
My Country 'Tis of Thy People You're Dying	Buffy Sainte-Marie
"The Best of Buffy Sainte-Marie"	(Vanguard)

DEFINITIVE SONGS

My Land Is a Good Land "The Best of Eric Andersen"	Eric Andersen (Vanguard)
+My Land Is a Good Land "God Bless the Grass"	Pete Seeger (Columbia)
Only in America "Greatest Hits"	Jay and the Americans (United Artists)
Orphans of Wealth "Tapestry"	Don McLean (United Artists)
Pastures of Plenty "Woody Guthrie"	Woody Guthrie (Warner Brothers)
Patriot Dream "Amigo"	Arlo Guthrie (Reprise)
Patriotic Flagwavin' Man "Babylon"	Dr. John (Atco)
The Patriot's Dream "Don Quixote"	Gordon Lightfoot (Reprise)
The Patriot Game "Whales and Nightingales"	Judy Collins (Elektra)
Prime Time "Prime Time"	Don McLean (Arista)
Promised Land "Golden Decade"	Chuck Berry (Chess)
+Promised Land "Moondog Matinee"	The Band (Capitol)
+Promised Land "Steal Your Face"	The Grateful Dead (Grateful Dead Records)
+Promised Land "Walking Man"	James Taylor (Warner Brothers)
+Promised Land "Johnny Rivers" (Superpak)	Johnny Rivers (United Artists)
Sail Away "Sail Away"	Randy Newman (Reprise)
+Sail Away "That's the Way It Is"	Harry Nilsson (RCA)
+Sail Away "Don't Cry Now"	Linda Ronstadt (Asylum)
+Sail Away "Darin 1936–1973"*	Bobby Darin (Motown)

DEFINITIVE SONGS

Save the Country "New York Tendaberry"	Laura Nyro (Columbia)
Show Yourself "Earth"	Jefferson Starship (Grunt)
Sigmund Freud's Interpretation of Albert Einstein in America "Little Criminals"	Randy Newman (Warner Brothers)
Sold American "Lasso from El Paso"*	Kinky Friedman (Epic)
Somewhere in America "Survivor"	Survivor (Atlantic)
Song for America "Song for America" "Two for the Show"	Kansas (Kirshner) (Kirshner)
Star-Spangled Banner (Instrumental) "Woodstock" (Soundtrack)	Jimi Hendrix (Cotillion)
+Star-Spangled Banner "Spirit of '76"*	Spirit (Mercury)
The Statue "Prime Time"	Don McLean (Arista)
Sweet America "Sweet America"*	Buffy Sainte-Marie (ABC)
Take It Where You Find It "Wave Length"	Van Morrison (Warner Brothers)
Talkin' Dust Bowl Blues "Dust Bowl Ballads" "Library of Congress"	Woody Guthrie (RCA) (Elektra)
That's America for Me "You're OK, I'm OK"	Billy Swan (A&M)
The Torn Flag "Now"	Pete Seeger (Columbia)
Two Hundred Years "Nashville" (Soundtrack)	Henry Gibson (ABC)
What Made America Famous? "Verities and Balderdash"	Harry Chapin (Elektra)
With God on Our Side "The Times They Are a Changin'"	Bob Dylan (Columbia)
+With God on Our Side (33 RPM E.P.)*	Manfred Mann (Ascot)

DEFINITIVE SONGS

+With God on Our Side   Joan Baez
  "The First Ten Years"   (Vanguard)
  "Joan Baez in Concert Part II"   (Vanguard)

  Your Flag Decal Won't Get You into   John Prine
    Heaven Anymore
  "John Prine"*   (Atlantic)

  Young Americans   David Bowie
  "Young Americans"   (RCA)
  "Changesonebowie"   (RCA)

REFERENCE SONGS

  All American Alien Boy   Ian Hunter
  "All American Alien Boy"   (Columbia)

  All American Man   Kiss
  "Kiss Alive II"   (Casablanca)

  America's Great National Pastime   The Byrds
  "The Best of the Byrds, Vol. II"   (Columbia)

  American Dreamer   Laura Nyro
  "Nested"*   (Columbia)

  American Girl   Tom Petty and the
                                                 Heartbreakers
  "Tom Petty and the Heartbreakers"   (Shelter)

+American Girl   Roger McGuinn
  "Thunderbyrd"   (Columbia)

  Angola   Ambrosia
  "Life Beyond L.A."   (Warner Brothers)

  Bless Me Miss America   Sam Neely
  "Sam Neely 2"*   (Capitol)

  Do Re Mi   Arlo Guthrie
  "A Tribute to Woody Guthrie"   (Warner Brothers)

  Draggin' Cross the U.S.A.   Roger McGuinn
  "Roger McGuinn"   (Columbia)

  House Un-American Blues Activity   Richard and Mimi Fariña
    Dreams
  "The Best of Richard and Mimi   (Vanguard)
    Fariña"

  Hungry Freaks, Daddy   The Mothers of Invention
  "Mothermania"   (Verve)

  I Stand Tall   The Dictators
  "Bloodbrothers"*   (Asylum)

REFERENCE SONGS

The Immigrant — Neil Sedaka
"Sedaka's Back" — (MCA)

I'm the Man That Builds the Bridges — Tom Paxton
"Ain't That News"* — (Elektra)

L'America — The Doors
"L.A. Woman" — (Elektra)

A Lifetime to Pay — Horslips
"Aliens" — (DJM Records)

My Country — The Impressions
"The Best Impressions" — (Curtom)

Philadelphia Freedom — Elton John
"Greatest Hits, Volume II" — (MCA)

Rockin' in the U.S.A. — Kiss
"Kiss Alive II" — (Casablanca)

Spirit of America — The Beach Boys
"Spirit of America" — (Capitol)
"Little Deuce Coupe" — (Capitol)

Stars and Stripes Forever (Instrumental) — Nitty Gritty Dirt Band
"Stars and Stripes Forever" — (United Artists)

Surfin' U.S.A. — The Beach Boys
"Endless Summer" — (Capitol)
"Surfin' U.S.A." — (Capitol)
"The Beach Boys in Concert" — (Brother/Reprise)

+Surfin' U.S.A. — Leif Garrett
"Leif Garrett" — (Atlantic)

Survivors — John Stewart
"Wingless Angels"* — (RCA)

YOUR ADDITIONAL SONGS

_____

_____

_____

_____

_____

APOCALYPTIC

Apocalyptic—a collision course toward cosmic cataclysm.
These are songs that have to do with imminent disaster or total destruction. Most are stories that are not historical but are rather a warning about the immediate future and what it may hold for us.

Related Categories: Death, Ecology

+Same as Song Above
*Hard-to-find Songs/Albums

CLASSICS

Bad Moon Rising	Creedence Clearwater Revival
"Chronicle"	(Fantasy)
"Green River"	(Fantasy)
Before the Deluge	Jackson Browne
"Late for the Sky"	(Asylum)
"No Nukes"	(Asylum)
Dance Band on the Titanic	Harry Chapin
"Dance Band on the Titanic"	(Elektra)
The End	The Doors
"The Doors"	(Elektra)
"Weird Scenes Inside the Gold Mine"	(Elektra)
+The End	Kevin Ayers
"June 1, 1974"	(Island)
A Hard Rain's Gonna Fall	Bob Dylan
"The Freewheelin' Bob Dylan"	(Columbia)
"Bob Dylan's Greatest Hits Vol. II"	(Columbia)
"Bangla Desh" (George Harrison)	(Apple)
+A Hard Rain's Gonna Fall	Joan Baez
"The First Ten Years"	(Vanguard)
+A Hard Rain's Gonna Fall	Leon Russell
"Leon Russell"	(Shelter)
+A Hard Rain's Gonna Fall	Pete Seeger
"The World of Pete Seeger"	(Columbia)
+A Hard Rain's Gonna Fall	Bryan Ferry
"These Foolish Things"*	(Atlantic)

CLASSICS

+A Hard Rain's Gonna Fall
"Use What You Got"
The Staple Singers
(Fantasy)

Very Last Day
"In the Wind"
Peter, Paul and Mary
(Warner Brothers)

DEFINITIVE SONGS

"A" Bomb in Wardour Street
"All Mod Cons"
The Jam
(Polydor)

+Bad Moon Rising
"The Session"
Jerry Lee Lewis
(Elektra)

Business As Usual
"Let There Be Music"
Orleans
(Asylum)

Crash on the Levee (Down in the
Flood)
"Basement Tapes"
Bob Dylan and The Band

(Columbia)

The Day the Earth Caught Fire
"The Day the Earth Caught Fire"
City Boy
(Atlantic)

Down in the Flood
"Bob Dylan's Greatest Hits Vol. II"
Bob Dylan
(Columbia)

Enough Time
"Black and White"*
The Stranglers
(Warner Brothers)

Eve of Destruction
"Eve of Destruction"*
(45 RPM Single)*
Barry McGuire
(ABC/Dunhill)
(ABC/Dunhill)

Fever Dream
"Mother Lode"
Loggins and Messina
(Columbia)

Five Years
"The Rise and Fall of Ziggy Stardust"
"Stage"
David Bowie
(RCA)
(RCA)

Full Speed Ahead
"Back to the Roots"
John Mayall
(Polydor)

Hard Times
"So Long, Harry Truman"
Danny O'Keefe
(Atlantic)

Homburg
"The Best of Procol Harum"
Procol Harum
(A&M)

In the Year 2525
"2525"*
Zager and Evans
(RCA)

Judgment Day
"Come and Get Your Redbone:
The Best of Redbone"
Redbone
(Epic)

DEFINITIVE SONGS

Living on the Fault Line "Living on the Fault Line"	The Doobie Brothers (Warner Brothers)
London Calling "London Calling"	The Clash (Epic)
Looking for a Hero "Night Lights"*	Elliott Murphy (RCA)
Miami 2017 "Turnstiles"	Billy Joel (Columbia)
New World "Grave New World" "The Best of Strawbs"	Strawbs (A&M) (A&M)
Oh Caritas "Catch Bull at Four"	Cat Stevens (A&M)
On the Road to Kingdom Come "On the Road to Kingdom Come"	Harry Chapin (Elektra)
Panic in the World "Drastic Plastic" "Best of and the Rest of Be Bop Deluxe"	Be Bop Deluxe (Harvest) (Harvest)
The Rock "Portrait Gallery"	Harry Chapin (Elektra)
Share the End "Anticipation"	Carly Simon (Elektra)
This Wheel's on Fire "The Basement Tapes"	Bob Dylan and The Band (Columbia)
+This Wheel's on Fire "Dr. Byrds & Mr. Hyde" "The Byrds Play Dylan"	The Byrds (Columbia) (Columbia)
+This Wheel's on Fire "Music from Big Pink" "Rock of Ages" "Anthology"	The Band (Capitol) (Capitol) (Warner Brothers)
+This Wheel's on Fire "Words and Music by Bob Dylan"	The Hollies (Epic)
+This Wheel's on Fire "Greatest Hits"	Ian and Sylvia (Vanguard)
Time Is Running Out "Steve Winwood"	Steve Winwood (Island)
Waiting for the End of the World "My Aim Is True"	Elvis Costello (Epic)

DEFINITIVE SONGS

While the City Sleeps   Chicago
"Chicago V"   (Columbia)

REFERENCE SONGS

Had Enough   The Who
"Who Are You"   (MCA)

I'm Scared   Burton Cummings
"Burton Cummings"   (Portrait)

Jesus on My Side   Leon Russell
"Americana"   (Paradise)

Love's in Need of Love Today   Stevie Wonder
"Songs in the Key of Life"   (Tamla)

Political Science   Randy Newman
"Sail Away"   (Reprise)

Shine On   Gene Cotton
"Save the Dancer"*   (Ariola/America)

Space Junk   Devo
"Q: Are We Not Men?   (Warner Brothers)
 A: We Are Devo!"

The Last Resort   The Eagles
"Hotel California"   (Asylum)

Wooden Ships   Crosby, Stills, Nash & Young
"Déjà Vu"   (Atlantic)
"Woodstock" (Soundtrack)   (Cotillion)
"So Far"   (Atlantic)

+Wooden Ships   Jefferson Airplane
"Volunteers"   (RCA)

YOUR ADDITIONAL SONGS

_____

_____

_____

_____

_____

BIG BUSINESS

Big Business—multinationals . . . conglomerates . . . agri-business . . . petrochemical oligopolies . . . rock and roll.
   Topics here range from big business corporations and their management to the ethics and attitudes of the big business world. (N.B. A subdivision of this category is "Automation.")

Related Categories: America, Money, Politics, Rat Race, Suburbia,
   Working

   +Same as Song Above
   *Hard-to-find Songs/Albums

CLASSICS

Masters of War "The Freewheelin' Bob Dylan"	Bob Dylan (Columbia)
+Masters of War "The World of Pete Seeger"	Pete Seeger (Columbia)
+Masters of War "Judy Collins ✕3"	Judy Collins (Elektra)
+Masters of War "Cher Sings the Hits"*	Cher (Springboard)
+Masters of War "Solo"	Don McLean (United Artists)
+Masters of War "Bag Full of War"	José Feliciano (RCA)
Mr. Business Man "The Very Best of Ray Stevens"	Ray Stevens (Janus)

DEFINITIVE SONGS

Cotton Growing Man "You Broke My Heart, So I Busted Your Jaw"	Spooky Tooth (A&M)
Dance Mr. Big "Deadly Nightshade"*	Deadly Nightshade (Phantom/RCA)
Fast Buck Freddie "Red Octopus" "Gold"	Jefferson Starship (Grunt) (Grunt)

DEFINITIVE SONGS

Funny Farm Blues "Song for Patty"*	Sammy Walker (Vanguard)
Good Business Man "Ferguslie Park"*	Stealers Wheel (A&M)
Let's Make A Deal "Free in America"*	Ben Sidran (Arista)
Liars "Goodnight Mrs. Calabash"	Ian Thomas Band (Chrysalis)
Madison Avenue "Greg Kihn Again"*	Greg Kihn (Beserkley)
Madison Avenue "Secrets"	Gil Scott-Heron (Arista)
Moneygoround "Lola vs. Powerman and the Moneygoround"	The Kinks (Reprise)
Money Won't Save You "Ellen McIlwaine"*	Ellen McIlwaine (United Artists)
Mr. Big Man "Sleepwalker"	The Kinks (Arista)
Mr. Penny Pincher "Hour of the Wolf"*	Steppenwolf (Epic)
On Behalf of the Entire Staff and Management "Cellophane Symphony"*	Tommy James and the Shondells (Roulette)
Power Man "Ooops . . . Wrong Planet"	Utopia (Bearsville)
Ring "Brother"*	Lon & Derrek Van Eaton (Apple)
Second-hand Car Spiv "Preservation Act 2"	The Kinks (Reprise)
Sell Sell "O Lucky Man"	Alan Price (Warner Brothers)
Step Right Up "Small Change"	Tom Waits (Asylum)
The Under Assistant West Coast Promotion Man "Out of Our Heads"	The Rolling Stones (London)
Wall Street Shuffle "100 CC"	10 CC (UK)

DEFINITIVE SONGS

"Sheet Music"   (UK)
We Deliver   The Miamis
"Live at Max's Kansas City"*   (Atlantic)
What Do You Want from Live?   The Tubes
"Live"   (A&M)

REFERENCE SONGS

Big Boss Man   The Grateful Dead
"Grateful Dead"   (Warner Brothers)
+Big Boss Man   John Hammond
"The Best of John Hammond"   (Vanguard)
+Big Boss Man   Jerry Lee Lewis
"The London Session"   (Mercury)
Big Bright Green Pleasure Machine   Simon and Garfunkel
"Parsley, Sage, Rosemary and Thyme"   (Columbia)
Cold Corporate Dealings   Mark and Clark Band
"Double Take"*   (Columbia)
Don't Look Now   Creedence Clearwater
                                             Revival
"More Gold"   (Fantasy)
"Willy and the Poor Boys"   (Fantasy)
He's Misstra Know-It-All   Stevie Wonder
"Innervisions"   (Tamla)
If Six Were Nine   Jimi Hendrix
"Axis Bold As Love"   (Reprise)
"Easy Rider" (Soundtrack)   (ABC/Dunhill)
+If Six Were Nine   Todd Rundgren
"Faithful"   (Bearsville)
Living in the Material World   George Harrison
"Living in the Material World"   (Apple)
Mr. Clean   The Jam
"All Mod Cons"   (Polydor)
No Money Down   Chuck Berry
"Golden Decade Vol. II"   (Chess)
+No Money Down   John Hammond
"The Best of John Hammond"   (Vanguard)
+No Money Down   Duane Allman
"An Anthology Vol. II"   (Capricorn)
+No Money Down   Dave Edmunds
"Subtle as a Flying Mallet"   (RCA)

REFERENCE SONGS

+No Money Down
"Thunderbox"

Humble Pie
(A&M)

Plastic Man
"Masterpiece"

The Temptations
(Gordy)

The Power of Gold

"Twin Sons of Different Mothers"

Dan Fogelberg and Tim
  Weisberg
(Full Moon/Epic)

Sue Me, Sue You Blues
"Living in the Material World"

George Harrison
(Apple)

Take the Money and Run
"Wind on the Water"

David Crosby/Graham Nash
(ABC)

Working for the Clampdown
"London Calling"

The Clash
(Epic)

YOUR ADDITIONAL SONGS

_____

_____

_____

_____

_____

Automation

CLASSICS

Feel like a Number

"Stranger in Town"

Bob Seger and the Silver
  Bullet Band
(Capitol)

DEFINITIVE SONGS

Automation Song
"All the News That's Fit to Sing"

Phil Ochs
(Elektra)

Hey (Rise of the Robots)
"Black and White"*

The Stranglers
(Warner Brothers)

DEFINITIVE SONGS

Machines "Presenting . . . Lothar and the Hand People"*	Lothar and the Hand People (Capitol)
Simple Hour Operation "Song for Patty"*	Sammy Walker (Vanguard)
Standing on the Edge of Town "Ramblin' Boy"	Tom Paxton (Elektra)

REFERENCE SONGS

Country Comforts "Tumbleweed Connection"	Elton John (MCA)
+Country Comforts "Gasoline Alley"	Rod Stewart (Mercury)

YOUR ADDITIONAL SONGS

_____

_____

_____

_____

_____

BROTHERHOOD

Brotherhood—". . . *smile on your brother.*"
   Statements about the way it should be, the fact that it isn't always, and encouragement to help it get there. Notice that most of these songs are nearly a decade old.

Related Categories: Friendship, War and Peace

   +Same as Song Above
    *Hard-to-find Songs/Albums

CLASSICS

All You Need Is Love	The Beatles
"Greatest Hits 1967–1970"	(Apple)
"Magical Mystery Tour"	(Capitol)
Get Together	The Youngbloods
"The Best of the Youngbloods"	(RCA)
"Ride the Wind"	(Warner Brothers)
"No Nukes"	(Asylum)
+Get Together	John Denver/The Chad Mitchell Trio
"Get Together"	(Mercury)
+Get Together	Anne Murray
"Snowbird"	(Capitol)
+Get Together	Jefferson Airplane
"Jefferson Airplane Takes Off"	(RCA)
He Ain't Heavy, He's My Brother	The Hollies
"The Hollies' Greatest Hits"	(Epic)
"He Ain't Heavy, He's My Brother"	(Epic)
"The Hollies Live"	(Columbia)
+He Ain't Heavy, He's My Brother	Neil Diamond
"Rainbow"	(MCA)
+He Ain't Heavy, He's My Brother	Olivia Newton-John
"Clearly Love"	(MCA)
Light Shine	Jesse Colin Young
"Light Shine"	(Warner Brothers)
Revival	The Allman Brothers
"Beginnings"	(Capricorn)

CLASSICS

+Revival   John Mayall
  "No More Interviews"   (DJM Records)

DEFINITIVE SONGS

  Abraham, Martin and John   Dion
  "Abraham, Martin and John"   (Laurie)
  "Sanctuary"*   (Warner Brothers)

+Abraham, Martin and John   Kenny Rogers
  "Love Lifted Me"   (United Artists)

+Abraham, Martin and John   Smokey Robinson & the
                                          Miracles
  "Anthology"   (Motown)

  All God's Children   Kenny Rogers
  "Transition"*   (Reprise)

  Amazing Air   The Lovin' Spoonful
  "Revelation: Revolution '69"*   (Kama Sutra)

  As   Stevie Wonder
  "Songs in the Key of Life"   (Tamla)

  Be on the Real Side   The Rascals
  "The Island of Real"*   (Columbia)

  Beautiful   Carole King
  "Tapestry"   (Ode)

  Beautiful People   Melanie
  "Four Sides of Melanie"*   (Buddah)
  "Leftover Wine"*   (Buddah)
  "Affectionately Melanie"*   (Buddah)
  "My First Album"*   (Buddah)
  "From the Beginning"   (ABC)

+Beautiful People   The Tokens
  "Both Sides Now"*   (Buddah)

  Because All Men Are Brothers   Peter, Paul and Mary
  "See What Tomorrow Brings"   (Warner Brothers)

  Believe in Humanity   Carole King
  "Fantasy"   (Ode)
  "Her Greatest Hits"   (Ode)

  Benedictus   Strawbs
  "Grave New World"   (A&M)
  "The Best of Strawbs"   (A&M)

  Black and White   Three Dog Night
  "Joy to the World"   (ABC/Dunhill)

DEFINITIVE SONGS

Blessed Are . . .   Simon and Garfunkel
"Sounds of Silence"   (Columbia)

The Chant   Lighthouse
"Peacing It All Together"*   (RCA)

Church   Stephen Stills
"Stephen Stills"   (Atlantic)

Close to It All   Melanie
"My First Album"*   (Buddah)
"Affectionately Melanie"*   (Buddah)
"Leftover Wine"*   (Buddah)

+Close to It All*   Dion
"You're Not Alone"   (Warner Brothers)

C'mon   Poco
"Deliverin'"   (Epic)
"The Very Best of Poco"   (Epic)

Courage of Love   Jerry Jeff Walker
"Five Years Gone"*   (Atco)

Crystal Blue Persuasion   Tommy James and the
                                           Shondells

"The Best of Tommy James and the
  Shondells"   (Roulette)

Day Is Done   Peter, Paul and Mary
"Ten Years Together"   (Warner Brothers)

The Day the World Gets 'Round   George Harrison
"Living in the Material World"   (Apple)

Every Kinda People   Robert Palmer
"Double Fun"   (Island)

Everybody Needs Love   Bloodstone
"Unreal"   (London)

Everyday People   Sly and the Family Stone
"Greatest Hits"   (Epic)
"Stand"   (Epic)

Everything Is Beautiful   Ray Stevens
"The Very Best of Ray Stevens"   (Janus)

Friendship Train   Gladys Knight and The Pips
"Anthology"   (Motown)

Full Measure   The Lovin' Spoonful
"The Best of the Lovin' Spoonful   (Kama Sutra)
  Vol. II"

DEFINITIVE SONGS

Games People Play	Joe South
"Joe South's Greatest Hits"	(Capitol)
"Introspect, the Songs of Joe South"	(Capitol)
Give a Damn	Spanky and Our Gang
"Spanky's Greatest Hits"	(Mercury)
"Anything You Choose"*	(Mercury)
+Give a Damn	Paul Stookey
"Paul And"*	(Warner Brothers)
Give a Hand, Take a Hand	Bee Gees
"Mr. Natural"	(RSO)
Give a Little Bit	Supertramp
"Even in the Quietest Moments"	(A&M)
Give Me Love	George Harrison
"The Best of George Harrison"	(Capitol)
"Living in the Material World"	(Apple)
Good Book	Melanie
"Good Book"*	(Buddah)
Hand of Man	Country Joe McDonald
"C. J. Fish"*	(Vanguard)
Harmony	Artie Kaplan
"Confessions of a Male Chauvinist Pig"*	(Hopi/Vanguard)
Heaven Is 10 Zillion Light Years Away	Stevie Wonder
"Fulfillingness' First Finale"	(Tamla)
Helping Hand	Dr. John
"Dr. John"*	(Trip)
He Was My Brother	Simon and Garfunkel
"Wednesday Morning 3 A.M."	(Columbia)
Hey Brother	Billy Preston
"That's the Way God Planned It"*	(Apple)
High on Love	Elliott Randall
"Elliott Randall's New York"*	(Kirshner)
I'd Like to Teach the World to Sing (45 RPM Single)*	The Hillside Singers (Metromedia)
"The Hillside Singers"*	(Metromedia)
If I Can Dream	Elvis Presley
"A Legendary Performer"	(RCA)
If I Had a Hammer	Peter, Paul and Mary

DEFINITIVE SONGS

"Ten Years Together"	(Warner Brothers)
"Peter, Paul and Mary"	(Warner Brothers)
"Live"	(Warner Brothers)
+If I Had a Hammer "The Essential Odetta"	Odetta (Vanguard)
+If I Had a Hammer "The Original Billy Preston . . . Soul'd Out"	Billy Preston (Crescendo)
+If I Had a Hammer "In the Wind"*	Jackie DeShannon (Imperial)
+If I Had a Hammer "Rivers Rocks The Folks"*	Johnny Rivers (Imperial)
+If I Had a Hammer "The World of Pete Seeger"	Pete Seeger (Columbia)
+If I Had a Hammer "Greatest Hits" "Reunion At Carnegie Hall"	The Weavers (Vanguard) (Vanguard)
If We Only Have Love "Sit Down Old Friend"*	Dion (Warner Brothers)
If Wishes Were Horses "J. F. Murphy and Salt"*	J. F. Murphy and Salt (Elektra)
Imagine "Shaved Fish" "Imagine"	John Lennon (Apple) (Apple)
+Imagine "Benny and Us"	Average White Band and Ben E. King (Atlantic)
In the Name of Love "Simple Things"	Carole King (Avatar)
Isn't It a Pity "All Things Must Pass"	George Harrison (Apple)
It's About Time "Sunflower"	The Beach Boys (Brother/Reprise)
John the Baptist "The Kids and Me"	Billy Preston (A&M)
Keep Love in Your Soul "Headin' Home"	Gary Wright (Warner Brothers)
Labyrinth "Simple Things"	Carole King (Avatar)

DEFINITIVE SONGS

Lay Down   Melanie
"Candles in the Rain"*   (Buddah)
"The Four Sides of Melanie"*   (Buddah)

Letter to Eve   Pete Seeger
"Now"   (Columbia)

Let the Happiness Begin   Lighthouse
"Peacing It All Together"*   (RCA)

Let Us All Get Together   Billy Preston
"That's the Way God Planned It"*   (Apple)

Let's Work Together   Canned Heat
"Live in Europe"   (United Artists)

+Let's Work Together   Climax Blues Band
"FM Live"   (Sire)

Lift Your Hearts to the Sun   Anne Murray
"High Prized Possession"   (Capitol)

Like a Seed   Kenny Rankin
"Like a Seed"   (Little David)

A Little Bit of Love   Free
"Best of Free"   (A&M)

Love, Peace and Happiness   The Chambers Brothers
"Greatest Hits"   (Columbia)
"Love, Peace and Happiness"*   (Columbia)

Love Among People   Peter Yarrow
"Love Songs"*   (Warner Brothers)

Love Comes to Everyone   George Harrison
"George Harrison"   (Dark Horse)

Love Is   Bill Withers
" 'Bout Love"   (Columbia)

Love Is Alive   Gary Wright
"The Dream Weaver"   (Warner Brothers)

Love Is the Answer   Utopia
"Oops . . . Wrong Planet"   (Bearsville)

+Love Is the Answer   England Dan and John
                                                    Ford Coley

"Dr. Heckell and Mr. Jive"   (Big Tree)
"Best of England Dan and John   (Big Tree)
    Ford Coley"

Love Is the Key   Ray Thomas
"From Mighty Oaks"   (Threshold)

DEFINITIVE SONGS

Love March
"Woodstock" (Soundtrack)
"Golden Butter—The Best of the Paul
   Butterfield Blues Band"

Paul Butterfield Blues Band
(Cotillion)
(Elektra)

Love's in Need of Love Today
"Songs in the Key of Life"

Stevie Wonder
(Tamla)

Love to the People
"No Place Like America Today"

Curtis Mayfield
(Curtom)

Love Train
"Live in London"
"Back Stabbers"

O'Jays
(Philadelphia International)
(Philadelphia International)

+Love Train
"The Three Degrees Live"

The Three Degrees
(Philadelphia International)

Make It Better
"Scratch Band"*

The Scratch Band
(Big Sound)

Maybe There's Another
"Brother"*

Lon & Derrek Van Eaton
(Apple)

Meeting in Africa
"Give Thankx"

Jimmy Cliff
(Warner Brothers)

Michael Row the Boat Ashore
"Pete Seeger"

Pete Seeger
(Columbia)

The Missionary
"Before the Salt"

Jimmy Buffett
(Barnaby)

My Sisters and Brothers
"Southern Winds"

Maria Muldaur
(Warner Brothers)

Oh Had I a Golden Thread
"The Essential Pete Seeger"

Pete Seeger
(Vanguard)

One Tin Soldier
"Coven"*

Coven
(Sunshine Snake/MGM)

+One Tin Soldier
"The Road Home"*

Peaceful Children
(ABC/Dunhill)

Peace Brother Peace
"In the Right Place"

Dr. John
(Atco)

Peace Brother Peace
"Soft and Soul"*
"Bill Medley"

Bill Medley
(MGM)
(MGM)

Peace Train
"Greatest Hits"
"Teaser and the Firecat"

Cat Stevens
(A&M)
(A&M)

DEFINITIVE SONGS

People Get Ready
"16 Greatest Hits"
The Impressions
(ABC/Dunhill)

+People Get Ready
"The Best of the Chambers Brothers"
"The Time Has Come Today"
"Live at Bill Graham's Fillmore East"
The Chambers Brothers
(Fantasy)
(Columbia)
(Columbia)

+People Get Ready
"Lady Soul"
Aretha Franklin
(Atlantic)

+People Get Ready
"Vanilla Fudge"*
Vanilla Fudge
(Atco)

People Got to Be Free
(45 RPM Single)
"Freedom's Suite"
The Young Rascals
(Atlantic)
(Atlantic)

+People Got to Be Free
"Castles in the Air"
Felix Cavaliere
(Epic)

Power of Love
"The Dream Weaver"
Gary Wright
(Warner Brothers)

Put a Little Love in Your Heart
"Put a Little Love in Your Heart"*
Jackie DeShannon
(Imperial)

+Put a Little Love in Your Heart
"The Best of the Isley Brothers"
The Isley Brothers
(Buddah)

Reach Out of the Darkness
(45 RPM Single)*
Friend and Lover
(Verve)

River of Jordan
"Peter"*
Peter Yarrow
(Warner Brothers)

The Seeds of Brotherhood
"The Best of Buffy Sainte-Marie,
 Vol. II"
Buffy Sainte-Marie
(Vanguard)

Share the Land
"The Best of the Guess Who"
The Guess Who
(RCA)

Sharin' Love
"All This for a Song"
The Guess Who
(Hilltak/Atlantic)

Shower the People
"In the Pocket"
"Greatest Hits"
James Taylor
(Warner Brothers)
(Warner Brothers)

Sing This All Together
"Their Satanic Majesties Request"
The Rolling Stones
(London)

Sit Down Old Friend
"Sit Down Old Friend"*
Dion
(Warner Brothers)

DEFINITIVE SONGS

Skinny Boy
"Chicago VII"

Chicago
(Columbia)

+Skinny Boy
"Skinny Boy"*

Robert Lamm
(Columbia)

Space Captain
"Mad Dogs and Englishmen"

Joe Cocker
(A&M)

That's the Way God Planned It
"That's the Way God Planned It"*
"Bangla Desh" (George Harrison)

Billy Preston
(Apple)
(Apple)

Together
"Together"*

The Illusion
(Steed)

Together and Free
"Gold Plated"

Climax Blues Band
(Sire)

Universal Love
"The Joneses"*

The Joneses
(Epic)

Universal Love
"Give Thankx"

Jimmy Cliff
(Warner Brothers)

Visions
"Innervisions"

Stevie Wonder
(Tamla)

Walk a Mile in My Shoes
"Joe South's Greatest Hits"

Joe South
(Capitol)

+Walk a Mile in My Shoes
"Another Time, Another Place"

Bryan Ferry
(Atlantic)

Wanted Man
"Give Thankx"

Jimmy Cliff
(Warner Brothers)

We Are Not Helpless
"Stephen Stills"

Stephen Stills
(Atlantic)

We Can Be Together
"The Worst of Jefferson Airplane"
"Volunteers"

Jefferson Airplane
(RCA)
(RCA)

We Got Love
"The Beach Boys in Concert"

The Beach Boys
(Brother/Reprise)

We Gotta All Get Together

Paul Revere and the Raiders
    Featuring Mark Lindsay

"All Time Greatest Hits"
"The Raiders Greatest Hits"

(Columbia)
(Columbia)

We Got to Live Together
"We Got to Live Together"*

Buddy Miles
(Mercury)

DEFINITIVE SONGS

We're All Playing in the Same Band "Inside Bert Sommer"*	Bert Sommer (Eleuthera)
We're All We Got "So Close"	Jake Holmes (Polydor)
We Shall Overcome "We Shall Overcome" "The World of Pete Seeger"	Pete Seeger (Columbia) (Columbia)
What's Going On "What's Going On"	Marvin Gaye (Tamla)
+What's Going On "What the World Needs Now Is Love"*	Tom Clay (Mowest)
What's This World Coming To "Chicago VI"	Chicago (Columbia)
What the World Needs Now Is Love "Dionne Warwick's Greatest Hits" "The Very Best of Dionne Warwick"	Dionne Warwick (Springboard) (United Artists)
+What the World Needs Now Is Love "The Time Has Come"	The Chambers Brothers (Columbia)
+What the World Needs Now Is Love "What the World Needs Now Is Love"*	Tom Clay (Mowest)
+What the World Needs Now Is Love "Hits of the 60's"	The Bachelors (London)
+What the World Needs Now Is Love "Don't Just Stand There"*	Patty Duke (United Artists)
+What the World Needs Now Is Love "Genesis"*	Delaney and Bonnie (Crescendo)
+What the World Needs Now Is Love "Marvin Gaye"	Marvin Gaye (Tamla)
+What the World Needs Now Is Love "The Best of Jackie DeShannon" "The Very Best of Jackie DeShannon"	Jackie DeShannon (Trip) (United Artists)
When the World Is at Peace "Backstabbers"	O'Jays (Philadelphia International)
Why Can't We Be Friends? "Greatest Hits"	War (United Artists)

DEFINITIVE SONGS

Wonderful World, Beautiful People	Jimmy Cliff
"Wonderful World, Beautiful People"	(A&M)
"In Concert: The Best of Jimmy Cliff"	(Island)

REFERENCE SONGS

America	Sammy Johns
"Sammy Johns"*	(General Recording Corp.)
Aquarius/Let the Sunshine In	The Fifth Dimension
"The Age of Aquarius"	(Soul City)
"Greatest Hits on Earth"	(Arista)
+Aquarius/Let the Sunshine In	The Undisputed Truth
"The Undisputed Truth"*	(Gordy)
+Aquarius	Various Artists
"Hair" (Soundtrack)	(RCA)
+Aquarius	Various Artists
"The Original Broadway Play"	(RCA)
Clouds of Sunshine	Jae Mason
"Tender Man"*	(Buddah)
Heavenly Music	Ray Charles
"True to Life"	(Atlantic)
I Wish You Peace	The Eagles
"One of These Nights"	(Asylum)
I Wonder Why	Billy Preston
"Music Is My Life"	(A&M)
People	Graham Central Station
"Graham Central Station"	(Warner Brothers)
Save the Planet	Edgar Winter
"White Trash"	(Epic)
Song for Judith (Open the Door)	Judy Collins
"Living"	(Elektra)
Sweet Music	Lon & Derrek Van Eaton
"Brother"*	(Apple)
Trying Times	Roberta Flack
"First Take"	(Atlantic)
Wake Up Everybody	Harold Melvin and the Blue Notes
"Wake Up Everybody"	(Philadelphia International)

REFERENCE SONGS

Whatever Happened to Love?   Tom Clay
"What the World Needs Now Is   (Mowest)
    Love"*

YOUR ADDITIONAL SONGS

_____

_____

_____

_____

_____

CHANGES

Changes—"all the changes"—in your heart and in your head, in your country and in your bed—"keep on changing."

Change is one of the constants of life. It can be personal, societal, or universal. Going through "changes" has also been the subject of some great music. (N.B. There are many songs that talk about changing political institutions and changes in love relationships. These songs are not included here, but are found in their respective categories.)

Related Categories: Children, Growing Up, Protest/Revolution,
  Self-Identity, Love

  +Same as Song Above
  *Hard-to-find Songs/Albums

CLASSICS

A Change Is Gonna Come "Moondog Matinee"	The Band (Capitol)
+A Change Is Gonna Come "I Never Loved a Man"	Aretha Franklin (Atlantic)
+A Change Is Gonna Come "Best of Otis Redding"	Otis Redding (Atco)
+A Change Is Gonna Come "Livin' Inside Your Love"	George Benson (Warner Brothers)
Changes "Chords of Fame"	Phil Ochs (A&M)
+Changes "Changes"*	Jim Glover and Jeanne Ray (Verve/Folkways)
The Times They Are a Changin' "The Times They Are a Changin'" "Bob Dylan's Greatest Hits" "Live at Budokan"	Bob Dylan (Columbia) (Columbia) (Columbia)
+The Times They Are a Changin' "Any Day Now"	Joan Baez (Vanguard)
+The Times They Are a Changin' "Beach Boys' Party"*	The Beach Boys (Capitol)
+The Times They Are a Changin' "Words and Music by Bob Dylan"*	The Hollies (Epic)
+The Times They Are a Changin' "Wednesday Morning 3 A.M."	Simon and Garfunkel (Columbia)

CLASSICS

+The Times They Are a Changin'
"The Byrds Play Dylan"

The Byrds
(Columbia)

+The Times They Are a Changin'
"No Nukes"

Carly Simon and Graham
Nash
(Asylum)

DEFINITIVE SONGS

All Things Must Pass
"All Things Must Pass"

George Harrison
(Apple)

As I See It Now
"As I See It Now"*

Melanie
(Neighborhood)

Bad Time
"Sinful"

Angel
(Casablanca)

Better Change
"Souvenirs"

Dan Fogelberg
(Epic)

Brave New World
"Donovan"

Donovan
(Arista)

Celeste
"In Concert"*

Donovan
(Epic)

+Celeste
"The Voice of Scott McKenzie"*

Scott McKenzie
(Ode)

Chameleon

Creedence Clearwater
Revival

"Pendulum"
"1970"

(Fantasy)
(Fantasy)

A Change Is Gonna Come
"The Best of Sam Cooke, Vol. II"

Sam Cooke
(RCA)

+A Change Is Gonna Come
"We Remember Sam Cooke"

The Supremes
(Motown)

Changes
"Changesonebowie"
"Hunky Dory"

David Bowie
(RCA)
(RCA)

Changes
"O Lucky Man"

Alan Price
(Warner Brothers)

Changes
"Motherlode"

Loggins and Messina
(Columbia)

Changes
"Shortest Stories"

Harry Chapin
(Elektra)

DEFINITIVE SONGS

Changes "Open Road"*	Donovan (Epic)
Changes "And Along Comes . . . the 　Association"*	The Association (Warner Brothers)
Changes "Welcome Home"	Carole King (Avatar)
Changes "We Sold Our Souls for Rock and 　Roll"	Black Sabbath (Warner Brothers)
Changes "If You Love Me Let Me Know"	Olivia Newton-John (MCA)
Changes "Great Grape"	Moby Grape (Columbia)
Changes "The Best of Ian and Sylvia"	Ian and Sylvia (Vanguard)
Changes "Cellophane Symphony"*	Tommy James and the 　Shondells (Roulette)
Changes "Lightfoot"	Gordon Lightfoot (United Artists)
Changes IV "Teaser and the Fire Cat"	Cat Stevens (A&M)
Changes in Latitudes, Changes In 　Attitudes "Changes in Latitudes/Changes in 　Attitudes"	Jimmy Buffett (ABC)
"You Had to Be There"	(ABC)
Change Is Gonna Come "Together Forever"	The Marshall Tucker Band (Capricorn)
Change Is Now "The Notorious Byrd Brothers"	The Byrds (Columbia)
Changing All Those Changes "Reminiscing"*	Buddy Holly (MCA)
Changing Horses "Souvenirs"	Dan Fogelberg (Epic)
Chasing Change "Gold Plated"	Climax Blues Band (Sire)

66   *The Rock Music Source Book*

Children of the World
"Children of the World"
The Bee Gees
(RSO)

The Circle Game
"Ladies of the Canyon"
"Miles of Aisles"
Joni Mitchell
(Reprise)
(Asylum)

+The Circle Game
"The Best of Buffy Sainte-Marie"
Buffy Sainte-Marie
(Vanguard)

+The Circle Game
"Classic Rush"
Tom Rush
(Elektra)

Everything Must Change
"In Flight"
George Benson
(Warner Brothers)

+Everything Must Change
"Bread and Roses"
Judy Collins
(Elektra)

Full Circle
"The Byrds"
The Byrds
(Asylum)

Go with Change
"The Fabulous Rhinestones"*
The Fabulous Rhinestones
(Just Sunshine Records)

Gonna Be a Change
"Ghost Town Parade"*
Les Dudek
(Columbia)

I Keep Changing
"Mr. Bojangles"
Jerry Jeff Walker
(Atco)

Meanings Will Change
"Paul and . . ."*
Paul Stookey
(Warner Brothers)

Mined
"Fear of Music"
Talking Heads
(Sire)

Reflections of My Life
"Reflections of My Life"*
Marmalade
(Deram)

Rings of Life
"Blue Sky—Night Thunder"
Michael Murphey
(Epic)

Secret Gardens
"True Stories and Other Dreams"
Judy Collins
(Elektra)

Seeds of Change
"Seeds"
Gallagher and Lyle
(A&M)

See the Changes
"CSN"
Crosby, Stills & Nash
(Atlantic)

Them Changes
"Them Changes"*
Buddy Miles
(Mercury)

Things Are Getting Better Now
"Hometown Frolics"*
Tommy West
(Lifesong)

DEFINITIVE SONGS

Things Change "Witness"*	Spooky Tooth (Island)
Thoroughfare Gap "Thoroughfare Gap"	Stephen Stills (Columbia)
Times Change "The Tufano and Giammarese Band"*	Tufano and Giammarese (Ode)
Times Have Changed "You Broke My Heart, So I Busted Your Jaw"	Spooky Tooth (A&M)
Waiting for the Change "Jonah"*	Jonah (20th Century Records)
When Seasons Change "America Today"*	Curtis Mayfield (Curtom)
Wind of Change "Wind of Change"	Peter Frampton (A&M)
Winds of Change "M.I.U. Album"	The Beach Boys (Brother/Reprise)
Winds of Change "Elan"	Firefall (Atlantic)
Winds of Change "Main Course" "Here at Last . . . Bee Gees Live"	The Bee Gees (RSO) (RSO)

REFERENCE SONGS

Changes "Really"	J. J. Cale (Cale/Shelter)
The Change Is Made "Horizontal"	The Bee Gees (ATCO)
The Chart Song "As I See It Now"*	Melanie (Neighborhood)
Father and Son "Tea for the Tillerman" "Greatest Hits"	Cat Stevens (A&M) (A&M)
+Father and Son "The Great Blind Degree"*	Richie Havens (Stormy Forest)
In My Life "Rubber Soul" "Love Songs"	The Beatles (Capitol) (Capitol)

REFERENCE SONGS

+In My Life
  "In My Life"   Judy Collins
                                        (Elektra)

+In My Life
  "Two Sides of the Moon"*   Keith Moon
                                        (MCA)

In These Changing Times
  "Anthology"   Four Tops
                                        (Motown)

That's Not Me
  "Pet Sounds"   The Beach Boys
                                        (Brother/Reprise)

Wheel of Fortune
  "Takin' It to the Streets"   The Doobie Brothers
                                        (Warner Brothers)

You Never Change
  "Minute by Minute"   The Doobie Brothers
                                        (Warner Brothers)

YOUR ADDITIONAL SONGS

_____

_____

_____

_____

_____

CHILDREN

*Children—we've all been there—some of us are still there (childlike)
and some of us have never grown up (childish).*

This category covers a lot of ground; from songs about particular children to attitudes about childhood. (N.B. Songs concerning the "Parent-Child Relationship" are listed as a subdivision.)

Related Categories: Changes, Fathers, Growing Up, Marriage, Mothers,
    Pregnancy, Schools/Educational Process

  +Same as Song Above
   *Hard-to-find Songs/Albums

CLASSICS

Forever Young "Planet Waves"	Bob Dylan (Asylum)
+Forever Young "From Every Stage"	Joan Baez (A&M)
+Forever Young "Reunion"	Peter, Paul and Mary (Warner Brothers)
Isn't She Lovely "Songs in the Key of Life"	Stevie Wonder (Tamla)
Oh Very Young "Catch Bull at Four"	Cat Stevens (A&M)
Teach Your Children "So Far" "Déjà Vu" "No Nukes"	Crosby, Stills, Nash & Young (Atlantic) (Atlantic) (Asylum)

THEMATIC ALBUMS

"Peter, Paul and Mommy"	Peter, Paul and Mary (Warner Brothers)
"Pete Seeger's Children's Concert"	Pete Seeger (Harmony/Columbia)
"Really Rosie"	Carole King (Ode)
"Save the Children"	The Intruders (Gamble)

THEMATIC ALBUMS

"Save the Children" (Soundtrack) Various Artists
 (Motown)

"Songs to Grow On Vol. 1" Woody Guthrie
 (Folkways)

"Songs to Grow On Vol. 2" Woody Guthrie
 (Folkways)

"Songs to Grow On Vol. 3" Woody Guthrie
 (Folkways)

"Songs to Grow On" Ramblin' Jack Elliott
 (Folkways)

DEFINITIVE SONGS

Adam and I Ray Thomas
"From Mighty Oaks"* (Threshold)

Baby Steve Forbert
"Jackrabbit Slim" (Nemperor)

Baby Tree Jefferson Starship
"Blows Against the Empire" (RCA)

Birth Comes to Us All The Good Rats
"Birth Comes to Us All" (Passport)

Black and White Three Dog Night
"Joy to the World" (ABC/Dunhill)

Blind Baby Al Kooper
"Naked Songs"* (Columbia)

Bundle of Sorrow, Bundle of Joy Kate and Anna McGarrigle
"Pronto Monto" (Warner Brothers)

Child of Innocence Kansas
"Masque" (Kirshner)

Child of Mine Carole King
"Writer" (Ode)

+Child of Mine Anne Murray
"Country" (Capitol)

Children Joe South
"Joe South's Greatest Hits" (Capitol)

Children, Children Wings
"London Town" (Capitol)

Children and All That Jazz Joan Baez
"Diamonds and Rust" (A&M)

DEFINITIVE SONGS

Children's Blues
"Wild and Recluse"*

Bonnie Koloc
(Epic)

Children Know
"Follow Your Heart"*

Sons of Champlin
(Capitol)

Children of the World
"Slow Down World"*

Donovan
(Epic)

Children One and All
"Grand Tour"

Rod McKuen
(Warner Brothers)

+Children One and All
"Mary"

Mary Travers
(Warner Brothers)

Child Whose Eyes I Am
"Mount Airy"*

Mount Airy
(Thimble)

Childsong
"Tap Root Manuscript"

Neil Diamond
(MCA)

Christian No
"El Mirage"*

Jimmy Webb
(Atlantic)

Christopher Robin
"The Four Sides of Melanie"*
"My First Album"*
"Affectionately Melanie"*

Melanie
(Buddah)
(Buddah)
(Buddah)

Cousin Kevin
"Tommy"

The Who
(MCA)

Daddy's Little Man
"At Home"

O. C. Smith
(Columbia)

Dancin' Boy
"Living Room Suite"

Harry Chapin
(Elektra)

Danny
"Words and Pictures"*

Bobby Goldsboro
(United Artists)

Day Is Done
"Ten Years Together"

Peter, Paul and Mary
(Warner Brothers)

Deliver Your Children
"London Town"

Wings
(Capitol)

Dooley Jones
"Pleasure and Pain"

Dr. Hook
(Capitol)

Dreams of a Child
"Dreams of a Child"

Burton Cummings
(Portrait/Epic)

Eli's Song
"Spirit"

John Denver
(RCA)

DEFINITIVE SONGS

Enter the Young
"The Association's Greatest Hits"

The Association
(Warner Brothers)

Eyes of a Child
"This Is the Moody Blues"
"To Our Children's Children's
 Children"

The Moody Blues
(Threshold)
(Threshold)

First Born
"J. F. Murphy and Salt"*

J. F. Murphy and Salt
(Elektra)

First Born
"Dancer with Bruised Knees"

Kate and Anna McGarrigle
(Warner Brothers)

Flowers Are Red
"Living Room Suite"

Harry Chapin
(Elektra)

For Baby (For Bobbie)
"John Denver's Greatest Hits"

John Denver
(RCA)

+For Baby (For Bobbie)
"The Peter, Paul and Mary Album"

Peter, Paul and Mary
(Warner Brothers)

Greatest Discovery
"Elton John"

Elton John
(MCA)

Hey Children
"Follow Your Heart"*

The Sons of Champlin
(Capitol)

Hey Little Tomboy
"M.I.U. Album"

The Beach Boys
(Brother/Reprise)

I'm a Boy
"Meaty Beaty Big and Bouncy"

The Who
(MCA)

I Am a Child
"Last Time Around"
"Retrospective"

Buffalo Springfield
(Atco)
(Atco)

+I Am a Child
"Decade"

Neil Young
(Reprise)

It's a Boy
"Tommy"

The Who
(MCA)

I Wanna Pick You Up
"Love You"

The Beach Boys
(Brother/Reprise)

I Was a Witness to a War
"New City"*

Blood, Sweat and Tears
(Columbia)

Jennifer's Rabbit
"The Compleat Tom Paxton"

Tom Paxton
(Elektra)

Julie Through the Glass
"Anticipation"

Carly Simon
(Elektra)

DEFINITIVE SONGS

Katy
"New Songs for Old Friends"*
Tom Paxton
(Reprise)

Kids These Days
"The Best of Tom Rush"
Tom Rush
(Columbia)

Let the Children Play
"Moonflower"
Santana
(Columbia)

Like Father, Like Son
"My Boy"*
Richard Harris
(ABC/Dunhill)

Little Girl
"Moving Finger"
The Hollies
(Epic)

Little Girls
"Love on a Shoe String"*
Kerry Chater
(Warner Brothers)

Little One
"Chicago XI"
Chicago
(Columbia)

Little Pink Pony
"Sit Down Old Friend"*
Dion
(Warner Brothers)

Loving My Children
"Sunset and Other Beginnings"
Melanie
(Neighborhood)

Lullaby for Nancy Carol
"The Best of Chuck Mangione"
Chuck Mangione
(A&M)

Magical Child
"Earth and Sky"
Graham Nash
(Capitol)

Mary Jane
"Goodnight Mrs. Calabash"*
Ian Thomas Band
(Chrysalis)

My Children
"Back to the Roots"
John Mayall
(Polydor)

My Name Is Jack
"You Are What You Eat"*
John Simon
(Columbia)

+My Name Is Jack
"The Best of Manfred Mann"
Manfred Mann
(Janus)

Nobody's Child
"In the Beginning"
"Ain't She Sweet"
The Beatles
(Polydor)
(Atco)

+Nobody's Child
"Puttin' on the Style"*
Lonnie Donegan
(United Artists)

Older Sister
"Hotcakes"
Carly Simon
(Elektra)

The Only Child
"The Pretender"
Jackson Browne
(Asylum)

DEFINITIVE SONGS

Pegasus
"Spirit"

John Denver
(RCA)

Pirate Ships
"Judith"

Judy Collins
(Elektra)

Pretty Little Martha
"Final Exam"

Loudon Wainwright III
(Arista)

Puff (The Magic Dragon)
"Ten Years Together"
"Moving"

Peter, Paul and Mary
(Warner Brothers)
(Warner Brothers)

Rock and Roll Baby
"The Best of the Stylistics"

The Stylistics
(Avco)

Save the Children
"Anthology"
"What's Goin' On?"

Marvin Gaye
(Motown)
(Tamla)

+Save the Children
"Save the Children"

The Intruders
(Gamble)

Scarlet Ribbons
(45 RPM Single)*
"Greatest Hits"

The Browns
(RCA)
(RCA)

+Scarlet Ribbons
"I'm Back and I'm Proud"*

Gene Vincent
(Elektra)

Sing Children Sing
"Sing Children Sing"*

Lesley Duncan
(Columbia)

Someone Keeps Calling My Name
"Portrait Gallery"

Harry Chapin
(Elektra)

Sons of . . .
"Colors of the Day/The Best of Judy
   Collins"

Judy Collins
(Elektra)

Song of a Sad Little Girl
"Just a Collection of Antiques and
   Curios"

Strawbs
(A&M)

St. Judy's Comet
"There Goes Rhymin' Simon"

Paul Simon
(Columbia)

Sweet Lovin'
"The Very Best of Poco"
"A Good Feeling to Know"

Poco
(Epic)
(Epic)

Then Came the Children
"Woodsmoke and Oranges"*

Paul Siebel
(Elektra)

DEFINITIVE SONGS

Think About the Children
"The Great Blind Degree"*
Richie Havens
(Stormy Forest)

Think About Your Children
(45 RPM Single)*
Mary Hopkins
(Apple)

This Is Our Child
"My Boy"*
Richard Harris
(ABC/Dunhill)

Tranquillo
"Boys in the Trees"
Carly Simon
(Elektra)

Welcome
"Listen with Your Heart"*
Dan Hill
(Columbia)

What Did You Learn in School Today?
"We Shall Overcome"
Pete Seeger
(Columbia)

+What Did You Learn in School Today?
"Ramblin' Boy"
Tom Paxton
(Elektra)

What Will There Be for the Children?
"Ain't It Something"*
James Talley
(Capitol)

When I Was a Child
"Native Sons"
Loggins and Messina
(Columbia)

When the Cookie Jar Is Empty
"Birchfield Nines"*
Michael Franks
(Warner Brothers)

Where Do the Children Play
"Tea for the Tillerman"
Cat Stevens
(A&M)

Wonderful Baby
"Homeless Brother"*
"Solo"
Don McLean
(United Artists)
(United Artists)

The World Beyond
"Words and Pictures"*
Bobby Goldsboro
(United Artists)

Zachary and Jennie
"Farewell Andromeda"
John Denver
(RCA)

REFERENCE SONGS

About the Children
"Things I Notice Now"*
Tom Paxton
(Elektra)

All God's Children
"Transition"*
Kenny Rogers
(Reprise)

All the Children Sing
"Hermit of Mink Hollow"
Todd Rundgren
(Bearsville)

Buy a Gun for Your Son
"Ain't That News"
Tom Paxton
(Elektra)

REFERENCE SONGS

Child for a Day "Izitso"	Cat Stevens (A&M)
A Child in These Hills "Saturate Before Using"	Jackson Browne (Asylum)
Children "America"	America (Warner Brothers)
Children of Night "Reborn to Be Wild"	Steppenwolf (Mums/Columbia)
Children of Rock and Roll "Natural Avenue"	John Lodge (Threshold)
Children of the Future "Children of the Future"	Steve Miller Band (Capitol)
Children of the Junks "Smile"	Laura Nyro (Columbia)
Children of the Universe "Flash"*	Flash (Capitol)
Children of the World "Children of the World"	The Bee Gees (RSO)
Daddy Don't Cry "How Great Thou Art" "Worldwide 50 Gold Hits"	Elvis Presley (RCA) (RCA)
Father to Son "Stolen Time"*	Lucy Simon (RCA)
For the Sake of the Children "Nashville" (Soundtrack)	Henry Gibson (ABC)
God Bless the Child "Blood, Sweat and Tears' Greatest Hits" "Blood, Sweat and Tears"	Blood, Sweat and Tears (Columbia) (Columbia)
+God Bless the Child "Richie Havens on Stage"*	Richie Havens (Stormy Forest)
Golden Child of God "Mirror"*	Emitt Rhodes (ABC/Dunhill)
Grown Ups Are Just Like Silly Children "When an Old Cricketer Leaves the Crease"*	Roy Harper (Chrysalis)
Happy Jack "A Quick One (Happy Jack)" "Meaty Beaty Big and Bouncy"	The Who (MCA) (MCA)

REFERENCE SONGS

If Children Had Wings "Endless Wire"	Gordon Lightfoot (Reprise)
Like a Child in Disguise "Patrick Moraz"*	Patrick Moraz (Atlantic)
Little Children	Billy J. Kramer and the Dakotas
"History of British Rock Vol. I" "Little Children"*	(Sire) (Imperial)
Love Child "Farewell"	The Supremes (Motown)
Me and Baby Brother "War's Greatest Hits"	War (United Artists)
Motherless Children "461 Ocean Blvd."	Eric Clapton (RSO)
Save the Life of My Child "Bookends"	Simon and Garfunkel (Columbia)
A Song for Julie "A Song for Julie"*	Jesse Colin Young (Warner Brothers)
Stay Young "Breakaway"	Gallagher and Lyle (A&M)
+Stay Young "Intakes"*	Rick Nelson (Epic)
Sweet Baby James "Sweet Baby James" "Greatest Hits"	James Taylor (Warner Brothers) (Warner Brothers)
+Sweet Baby James "Wrong End of the Rainbow"*	Tom Rush (Columbia)
Take Your Children Home "Take Your Children Home"	Phoebe Snow (Shelter)
Too Young to Feel This Old "Too Young to Feel This Old"*	McKendree Spring (Pye)
Watching Scotty Grow "10th Anniversary Album"	Bobby Goldsboro (United Artists)
Wild Children "Hard Nose the Highway"	Van Morrison (Warner Brothers)
+Wild Children "The End of the Beginning"	Richie Havens (A&M)
Working for the Children "KGB"*	KGB (MCA)

REFERENCE SONGS

You and Me Against the World "Greatest Hits"	Helen Reddy (Capitol)
You Must Have Been a Beautiful Baby (45 RPM Single)*	Dave Clark Five (Epic)

YOUR ADDITIONAL SONGS

_____

_____

_____

_____

_____

Parent-Child Relationships

CLASSICS

Cats in the Cradle "Verities and Balderdash" "Greatest Stories Live"	Harry Chapin (Elektra) (Elektra)
Father and Son "Tea for the Tillerman" "Greatest Hits"	Cat Stevens (A&M) (A&M)
+Father and Son "The Great Blind Degree"	Richie Havens (Stormy Forest)
She's Leaving Home "Sgt. Pepper's Lonely Hearts Club Band"	The Beatles (Capitol)
+She's Leaving Home "Room to Grow"*	Barnaby Bye (Atlantic)
+She's Leaving Home "Sgt. Pepper's Lonely Hearts Club Band" (Soundtrack)	The Bee Gees (RSO)
+She's Leaving Home "All Fly Home"	Al Jarreau (Warner Brothers)

CLASSICS

+She's Leaving Home   Bryan Ferry
 "All This and World War II"   (20th Century Records)

 Teach Your Children   Crosby, Stills, Nash & Young
 "Déjà Vu"   (Atlantic)
 "So Far"   (Atlantic)
 "Four Way Street"   (Atlantic)
 "No Nukes"   (Asylum)

+Teach Your Children   Richie Havens
 "The Great Blind Degree"*   (Stormy Forest)
 "Richie Havens on Stage"*   (Stormy Forest)

DEFINITIVE SONGS

 Adam Raised a Cain   Bruce Springsteen
 "Darkness on the Edge of Town"   (Columbia)

 Anastasia   Elliott Murphy
 "Just a Story from America"*   (Columbia)

 Born to the Breed   Judy Collins
 "Judith"   (Elektra)
 "The First Fifteen Years"   (Elektra)

 Child's Song   Murray McLauchlan
 "Only the Silence Remains"*   (Columbia)

+Child's Song   Tom Rush
 "The Best of Tom Rush"   (Columbia)
 "Tom Rush"   (Elektra)

+Child's Song   David Bromberg
 "Reckless Abandon"   (Fantasy)

 Cut My Hair   The Who
 "Quadrophenia"   (MCA)

 Doin' All the Right Things (the   Wet Willie
    Wrong Way)
 "Manorisms"   (Epic)

 Don't Blame the Children   Junior Walker and the All
                                        Stars
 "Anthology"   (Motown)

 Embrace Me You Child   Carly Simon
 "No Secrets"   (Elektra)

 Father to Son   Queen
 "Queen II"   (Elektra)

DEFINITIVE SONGS

Girls Don't Run Away "Alarm Clark"	Richie Havens (Stormy Forest)
Happy Mother's Day	David Peel and the Lower East Side
"Have a Marijuana"*	(Elektra)
I Can Never Go Home Anymore (45 RPM Single)*	The Shangri-las (Red Bird)
I'm Bugged at My Old Man "Summer Days and Summer Nights"	Beach Boys (Capitol)
Icarus "How Come the Sun"*	Tom Paxton (Reprise)
In the Shelter "Before the Salt"	Jimmy Buffett (Barnaby)
Janey's Blues "Janis Ian"	Janis Ian (Polydor)
Jimmy Jimmy "The Undertones"	The Undertones (Sire)
Kid "Pretenders"	Pretenders (Sire)
Let the Wind Carry Me "For the Roses"	Joni Mitchell (Reprise)
The Letter "Dean Friedman"*	Dean Friedman (Lifesong)
Lonely Boy "What's Wrong with This Picture?"	Andrew Gold (Asylum)
The Mayor of Candor Lied "Dance Band on the Titanic"	Harry Chapin (Elektra)
Memo to My Son "Sail Away"	Randy Newman (Reprise)
Momma "My First Album"*	Melanie (Buddah)
Mother "John Lennon/Plastic Ono Band"	John Lennon (Apple)
Mother "Barnstorm"	Barnstorm Featuring Joe Walsh (ABC/Dunhill)
+Mother "The Best of Joe Walsh"	Joe Walsh (ABC/Dunhill)

DEFINITIVE SONGS

My Idaho Home "Nashville" (Soundtrack) "Welcome"*	Ronee Blakely (ABC) (Warner Brothers)
The Nest "The Association"*	The Association (Warner Brothers)
Pulled Up "Talking Heads '77"	Talking Heads (Sire)
Rick Rack "Gerry Rafferty"	Gerry Rafferty (Visa)
The Runaway "American Roulette" "The O'Keefe Files"	Danny O'Keefe (Warner Brothers) (Atlantic)
The Runaway "Love on the Airwaves"	Gallagher and Lyle (A&M)
Runaway Child, Running Wild "Anthology—Tenth Anniversary Special"	The Temptations (Motown)
Sally Simpson "Tommy"	The Who (MCA)
Someday Never Comes "Chronicle"	Creedence Clearwater Revival (Fantasy)
Song for Patty "Song for Patty"*	Sammy Walker (Folkways)
Surrender "Heaven Tonight" "Cheap Trick at Budokan"	Cheap Trick (Epic) (Epic)
Too Old to Go 'Way Little Girl "Janis Ian"	Janis Ian (Polydor)
2000 Man "Their Satanic Majesties Request"	The Rolling Stones (London)
Trouble Child "Court and Spark"	Joni Mitchell (Asylum)
Waited So Long "No Secrets"	Carly Simon (Elektra)
Yackety-Yak "The Coasters' Greatest Hits"	The Coasters (Atco)
You Have to Be Carefully Taught "Stealin' Home"*	Ian Thomas Band (Mushroom)

DEFINITIVE SONGS

Younger Generation
"Everything Playing"*
"Best of the Lovin' Spoonful, Vol. II"

The Lovin' Spoonful
(Kama Sutra)
(Kama Sutra)

+Younger Generation
"John Sebastian Songbook"

John Sebastian
(Kama Sutra)

+Younger Generation
"Touch 'n Go with the Critters"*

The Critters
(Project 3)

Your Generation
"Generation X"*

Generation X
(Chrysalis)

Your Mama Don't Dance
"Loggins and Messina"
"On Stage"
"The Best of Friends"

Loggins and Messina
(Columbia)
(Columbia)
(Columbia)

REFERENCE SONGS

Back Seat of My Car
"Ram"

Paul and Linda McCartney
(Apple)

Black Sheep Boy
"The Best of Tim Hardin"

Tim Hardin
(Verve)

Brand New Day
"Al's Big Deal/Unclaimed
    Freight—An Al Kooper Anthology"

Al Kooper
(Columbia)

Drive All Night
"Just a Story from America"*

Elliott Murphy
(Columbia)

Girl, You'll be a Woman Soon
"Neil Diamond's Greatest Hits"
"Hot August Night"
"Gold"

Neil Diamond
(Bang)
(MCA)
(MCA)

Give Me a Reason Why
"Split Coconuts"

Dave Mason
(Columbia)

Harper
"Ramblin' Boy"

Tom Paxton
(Vanguard)

Her Father Didn't Like Me Anyway
"Gerry Rafferty"

Gerry Rafferty
(Visa)

I Think We're Alone Now

Tommy James and the
    Shondells

"The Best of Tommy James and the
    Shondells"

(Roulette)

REFERENCE SONGS

+I Think We're Alone Now
  "The Rubinoos"

The Rubinoos
(Beserkley)

+I Think We're Alone Now
  "Stateless"

Lena Lovich
(Stiff)

Let the Boy Rock and Roll
"Once upon a Time"

The Lovin' Spoonful
(Kama Sutra)

Mary Ain't Going Home
"Down in the Bunker"*

Steve Gibbons Band
(Polydor)

Save the Life of My Child
"Bookends"

Simon and Garfunkel
(Columbia)

Sea and Sand
"Quadrophenia"

The Who
(MCA)

Shilo
"Velvet Gloves and Spit"

Neil Diamond
(MCA)

Society's Child
"Janis Ian"

Janis Ian
(Polydor)

Why Don't They Let Us Fall in Love
"Look at Us"*

Sonny and Cher
(Atco)

YOUR ADDITIONAL SONGS

_____

_____

_____

_____

_____

COWBOYS/WILD WEST

Cowboys/Wild West—the great American fantasy—this time told with the help of electric *guitars.*

The American cowboy and his Wild West environment have long been a subject of fascination for painters, novelists, and film makers. Rock has its own storytelling way with the heroes and villains of the Wild West.

Related Categories: Guns, Indians, Outlaws/Criminals, Violence

+Same as Song Above
*Hard-to-find Songs/Albums

CLASSICS

Mammas Don't Let Your Babies . . .	Waylon Jennings and Willie Nelson
"Waylon and Willie"	(RCA)
+Mammas Don't Let Your Babies . . .	Tommy West
"Hometown Frolics"	(Lifesong)
+Mammas Don't Let Your Babies . . .	Waylon Jennings
"Greatest Hits"	(RCA)
+Mammas Don't Let Your Babies . . .	Willie Nelson
"The Electric Horseman" (Soundtrack)	(Columbia)
Theme for an Imaginary Western	Mountain
"Climbing"	(Windfall)
"The Best of Mountain"	(Columbia)

THEMATIC ALBUMS

"Desperado"	The Eagles (Asylum)
"Gypsy Cowboy"	New Riders of the Purple Sage (Columbia)
"Pat Garrett and Billy the Kid"	Bob Dylan (Columbia)

DEFINITIVE SONGS

Ballad of the Absent Mare
"Recent Songs"
Leonard Cohen
(Columbia)

Back in the Saddle
"Wild and Recluse"*
Bonnie Koloc
(Epic)

Billy (Cuts #1-4-7)
"Pat Garrett and Billy the Kid"
Bob Dylan
(Columbia)

Bitter Creek
"Desperado"
The Eagles
(Asylum)

Bronco Bill's Lament
"Don McLean"*
"Solo"
Don McLean
(United Artists)
(United Artists)

Buffalo Skinners
"One Night"
Arlo Guthrie
(Warner Brothers)

Cactus Cafe
"Jay Boy Adams"*
Jay Boy Adams
(Atlantic)

California Cowboy
"Love on the Wing"
Jesse Colin Young
(Warner Brothers)

Cattle Drive
"Tenth"
The Marshall Tucker Band
(Warner Brothers)

Cisco Kid
"Greatest Hits"
War
(United Artists)

Cosmic Cowboy
"Cosmic Cowboy Souvenir"*
Michael Murphey
(A&M)

+Cosmic Cowboy/Cosmic Breakdown
"Peaks Valleys Honky-Tonks & Alleys"
Michael Murphey
(Epic)

+Cosmic Cowboy
"Stars and Stripes Forever"
Nitty Gritty Dirt Band
(United Artists)

Covered Wagon
"So Long Harry Truman"*
Danny O'Keefe
(Atlantic)

Cowboy
"Live"
Randy Newman
(Reprise)

+Cowboy
"Nilsson Sings Newman"
Harry Nilsson
(RCA)

+Cowboy
"The Moth Confesses"*
Neon Philharmonic
(Warner Brothers)

Cowboy Angel
"Just a Stone's Throw Away"
Valerie Carter
(Columbia)

Cowboy Movie
"If I Only Could Remember My Name"
David Crosby
(Atlantic)

DEFINITIVE SONGS

Cowboy on the Run	Quicksilver Messenger Service
	(Capitol)
"Solid Silver"	
Cowboy's Delight	John Denver
"Spirit"	(RCA)
Cowboy Song	Thin Lizzy
"Jailbait"	(Mercury)
"Live and Dangerous"	(Mercury)
Cowboy Song	Arlo Guthrie
"Last of the Brooklyn Cowboys"	(Reprise)
Cowboy Trilogy	Tommy West
"Hometown Frolics"*	(Lifesong)
Dancin' Cowboys	The Bellamy Brothers
"You Can Get Crazy"	(Warner Brothers)
Days of '49	Bob Dylan
"Self-Portrait"	(Columbia)
Desert Cowboy	Lenny Le Blanc
"Hound Dog Man"*	(Big Tree)
Desert Skies	The Marshall Tucker Band
"Carolina Dreams"	(Capricorn)
Don't Fence Me In	Tommy West
"Hometown Frolics"*	(Lifesong)
+Don't Fence Me In	Mary McCaslin
"Old Friends"*	(Philo)
Doolin' Dalton	The Eagles
"Desperado"	(Asylum)
Dust on My Saddle	Seals and Crofts
"Diamond Girl"	(Warner Brothers)
El Paso	The Grateful Dead
"Steal Your Face"	(Grateful Dead Records)
Fire on the Mountain	The Marshall Tucker Band
"Searchin' for a Rainbow"	(Capricorn)
"Greatest Hits"	(Capricorn)
Frank and Jesse James	Warren Zevon
"Warren Zevon"	(Asylum)
Ghost Riders	Dennis Linde
"Under the Eye"*	(Monument)
Ghost Riders in the Sky	Mary McCaslin
"Prairie in the Sky"*	(Philo)

DEFINITIVE SONGS

Glendale Train	New Riders of the Purple Sage (Columbia)
"The Best of the New Riders of the Purple Sage"	
Gone with the Cowboys "Grand Tour"	Rod McKuen (Warner Brothers)
Gypsy Cowboy	New Riders of the Purple Sage
"Gypsy Cowboy"	(Columbia)
Happy Trails	Quicksilver Messenger Service
"Happy Trails"	(Capitol)
Honky Tonk Stardust Cowboy "Honky Tonk Stardust Cowboy"*	Jonathan Edwards (Atco)
Hoppy, Gene and Me "Hoppy, Gene and Me"	Roy Rogers (20th Century Records)
I'd Rather Be a Cowboy "Farewell Andromeda"	John Denver (RCA)
Jesse James "The Fish"*	Barry Melton (Fire-Sign)
The Kid "So Long Harry Truman"*	Danny O'Keefe (Atlantic)
King of the Cowboys "Too Stuffed to Jump"*	Amazing Rhythm Aces (ABC)
Knockin' on Heaven's Door "Pat Garrett and Billy the Kid" "Before the Flood" (with The Band)	Bob Dylan (Columbia) (Asylum)
+Knockin' on Heaven's Door "Roger McGuinn Band"	Roger McGuinn (Columbia)
+Knockin' on Heaven's Door (45 RPM Single)	Eric Clapton (RSO)
Ladies Love Outlaws "Ladies Love Outlaws"*	Tom Rush (Columbia)
The Last Cowboy "The Last Cowboy"*	Gallagher and Lyle (A&M)
Last of the Singing Cowboys "Running Like the Wind"	The Marshall Tucker Band (Warner Brothers)
Lily, Rosemary and the Jack of Hearts "Blood on the Tracks"	Bob Dylan (Columbia)

DEFINITIVE SONGS

+Lily, Rosemary and the Jack of Hearts   Joan Baez
  "From Every Stage"   (A&M)

Lonesome Cowboy   Elvis Presley
  "Worldwide 50 Gold Award Hits,   (RCA)
     Vol. 2"

Lonesome Cowboy Bill   The Velvet Underground
  "Loaded"   (Cotillion)
  "Live at Max's Kansas City"*   (Cotillion)

Lonesome Cowgirl   Randy Meisner
  "Randy Meisner"*   (Asylum)

Lonesome L.A. Cowboy   New Riders of the Purple
                                                  Sage
  "The Adventures of Panama Red"   (Columbia)

Me and My Uncle   Judy Collins
  "Golden Apples of the Sun"   (Elektra)

+Me and My Uncle   The Grateful Dead
  "The Grateful Dead"   (Warner Brothers)

Medley: Son of Bill Baety   Sir Douglas Quintet
  "Together After Five"*   (Smash)

My Heroes Have Always Been   Willie Nelson
     Cowboys
  "The Electric Horseman"   (Columbia)

Motel Cowboy   Loggins and Messina
  "Finale"   (Columbia)

Nine Hard Years   Jay Boy Adams
  "Jay Boy Adams"*   (Atlantic)

Panama Red   New Riders of the Purple
                                                  Sage
  "The Adventures of Panama Red"   (Columbia)

Pretty Boy Floyd   Woody Guthrie
  "Woody Guthrie"   (Warner Brothers)
  "Library of Congress"   (Elektra)

+Pretty Boy Floyd   Country Joe McDonald
  "Thinking of Woody"   (Vanguard)

+Pretty Boy Floyd   The Byrds
  "Sweetheart of the Rodeo"   (Columbia)

+Pretty Boy Floyd   Joan Baez
  "In Concert"   (Vanguard)

DEFINITIVE SONGS

+Pretty Boy Floyd
"Madrugada"*
Melanie
(Neighborhood)

Queen of the Rodeo
"New Arrangement"*
Jackie DeShannon
(Columbia)

Rocky Raccoon
"The Beatles" (The White Album)
The Beatles
(Apple)

+Rocky Raccoon
"Richie Havens on Stage"*
Richie Havens
(Stormy Forest)

Rodeo-deo
"A Man Must Carry On"
Jerry Jeff Walker
(MCA)

Rodeo Rider
"Swingtime in Springtime"*
Lew London
(Philo)

Roving Cowboy
"Words You Can Dance To"*
Steve Goodman
(Asylum)

Roy Rogers
"Goodbye Yellow Brick Road"
Elton John
(MCA)

Sage Brush Serenade
"Cantamos"
Poco
(Epic)

Singing Cowboy
"Reel to Reel"*
Love
(RSO)

Singing Cowboy

"Brujo"
New Riders of the Purple
Sage
(Columbia)

+Singing Cowboy
"Beau Brummels"*
Beau Brummels
(Warner Brothers)

So You Think You're a Cowboy
"The Electric Horseman"
Willie Nelson
(Columbia)

Someday Soon
"Who Knows Where the Time Goes"
Judy Collins
(Elektra)

Sutter's Mill

"Gypsy Cowboy"
New Riders of the Purple
Sage
(Columbia)

Sweet Baby James
"Sweet Baby James"
"Greatest Hits"
James Taylor
(Warner Brothers)
(Warner Brothers)

+Sweet Baby James
"Wrong End of the Rainbow"*
Tom Rush
(Columbia)

DEFINITIVE SONGS

Tapedeck in His Tractor
"Nashville" (Soundtrack)

Ronee Blakely
(ABC)

+Tapedeck in His Tractor
"Welcome"*

Ronee Blakely
(Warner Brothers)

Western Movies
(45 RPM Single)*

The Olympics
(Demon)

+Western Movies
"Peaks Valleys Honky-Tonks &
    Alleys"*

Michael Murphey
(Epic)

When I Was a Cowboy
"Greatest Hits"

Ian and Sylvia
(Vanguard)

+When I Was a Cowboy

Jim Kweskin and the Jug
    Band

"Garden of Joy"*

(Reprise)

When I Was a Cowboy
"Ralph McTell Live"

Ralph McTell
(Fantasy)

When the Cactus Is in Bloom
"Arlo Guthrie"

Arlo Guthrie
(Reprise)

Whoopee Ti Yi Ya
"How Late'll Ya Play Till?"

David Bromberg
(Fantasy)

Wild West Heroes
"Out of the Blue"

Electric Light Orchestra
(Jet)

Wild West Show
"Swans Against Sun"*

Michael Murphey
(Epic)

REFERENCE SONGS

Cowgirl in the Sand
"Decade"
"Everybody Knows This Is Nowhere"

Neil Young
(Reprise)
(Reprise)

Deep in the Motherlode
"Then There Were Three"

Genesis
(Atlantic)

Lily of the West
"Dylan"

Bob Dylan
(Columbia)

Rhinestone Cowboy
"Rhinestone Cowboy"

Glen Campbell
(Capitol)

This Old Cowboy
"Where We All Belong"
"Greatest Hits"

The Marshall Tucker Band
(Capricorn)
(Capricorn)

REFERENCE SONGS

Way Out West   The Dingoes
"Five Times the Sun"*   (A&M)

YOUR ADDITIONAL SONGS

_____

_____

_____

_____

_____

DEATH

Death—depressing, but inevitable.

Other than opera, which seems to have several during every perform-ance, popular music never really dealt with this subject adequately before the advent of rock. We are not sure whether rock has helped to break the taboo about death or whether the breaking of the taboo has allowed writers to deal with it. In either case, writers have covered the subject through songs ranging from the humorous to deeply moving poetry.

Related Categories: Old Age, Suicide, Violence, War and Peace: Victims of War

+Same as Song Above
*Hard-to-find Songs/Albums

CLASSICS

And When I Die
"The First Songs"*

Laura Nyro
(Columbia)

+And When I Die
"Blood, Sweat and Tears' Greatest
    Hits"

Blood, Sweat and Tears
(Columbia)

"Blood, Sweat and Tears"

(Columbia)

+And When I Die
"The Peter, Paul and Mary Album"

Peter, Paul and Mary
(Warner Brothers)

Forest Lawn
"Number 6"*

Tom Paxton
(Elektra)

+Forest Lawn
"Take Me to Tomorrow"

John Denver
(RCA)

Old Man
"Sail Away"

Randy Newman
(Reprise)

+Old Man
"Angel Clare"

Art Garfunkel
(Columbia)

DEFINITIVE SONGS

About to Die
"Home"

Procol Harum
(A&M)

Another Man
"The Last of the British Blues"

John Mayall
(ABC)

DEFINITIVE SONGS

The Art of Dying
"All Things Must Pass"
George Harrison
(Apple)

Barney
"Mac McAnally"*
Mac McAnally
(Ariola/America)

Beyond the Grave
"Time Honoured Ghosts"*
Barclay James Harvest
(Polydor)

Bluebird Is Dead
"On the Third Day"
Electric Light Orchestra
(Jet)

Bridges of God
"Silk Torpedo"
Pretty Things
(Swan Song)

Bummer
"Portrait Gallery"
Harry Chapin
(Elektra)

Bury My Body
"Animal Tracks"
The Animals
(ABKCO)

+Bury My Body
"Al's Big Deal/Unclaimed
    Freight—An Al Kooper Anthology"
Al Kooper
(Columbia)

But I Might Die Tonight
"Tea for the Tillerman"
Cat Stevens
(A&M)

Candle in the Wind
"Goodbye Yellow Brick Road"
Elton John
(MCA)

Can't Take It with You
"Enlightened Rogues"
Allman Brothers
(Capricorn)

Closer Everyday
"The Doobie Brothers"
The Doobie Brothers
(Warner Brothers)

Come Home Mama
"Silk Torpedo"
Pretty Things
(Swan Song)

Cool Water
"Burnt Lips"*
Leo Kottke
(Chrysalis)

Crucifixion
"Chords of Fame"
Phil Ochs
(A&M)

Dead Man's Dream
"Home"
Procol Harum
(A&M)

Death Don't Have No Mercy
"Hot Tuna"
Hot Tuna
(RCA)

Death Is Life
"Center of the Mind"*
Amboy Dukes
(Mainstream)

DEFINITIVE SONGS

Death Sound Blues
"The Life and Times of Country Joe
    and the Fish—from Haight-Ashbury
    to Woodstock"
Country Joe and the Fish
(Vanguard)

Death's Reply
"See"*
The Rascals
(Atlantic)

(Don't Fear) The Reaper
"Agents of Fortune"
Blue Oyster Cult
(Columbia)

Endless Sleep
"Burnt Lips"*
Leo Kottke
(Chrysalis)

Epitaph
"The Silver Tongued Devil and I"
Kris Kristofferson
(Monument)

Farewell My Friend
"Pacific Ocean Blue"
Dennis Wilson
(Caribou)

Fixin' to Die
"Bob Dylan"
Bob Dylan
(Columbia)

For a Dancer
"Late for the Sky"
Jackson Browne
(Asylum)

Fountain Avenue
"Albert Hammond"*
Albert Hammond
(Mums/Columbia)

Freddie's Dead
"Superfly"
Curtis Mayfield
(Curtom)

Friends Die Easy
"Track 5"*
"Second Thoughts"
McKendree Spring
(MCA)
(MCA)

The Grave
"American Pie"
Don McLean
(United Artists)

Gulliver
"Empty Sky"
Elton John
(MCA)

Hello Grandpa
"The Outsider"*
Tom Pacheco
(RCA)

He's Gone
"Europe '72"
The Grateful Dead
(Warner Brothers)

He Was My Brother
"Wednesday Morning 3 A.M."
Simon and Garfunkel
(Columbia)

The Highwayman
"I Ain't Marchin' Anymore"
Phil Ochs
(Elektra)

Hummingbird
"Matthew and Son"
Cat Stevens
(Deram)

DEFINITIVE SONGS

I Come and Stand at Every Door
"I Can See a New Day"

Pete Seeger
(Columbia)

+I Come and Stand at Every Door
"Fifth Dimension"

The Byrds
(Columbia)

I Don't Want to Die in an Air Disaster
"Albert Hammond"*

Albert Hammond
(Mums/CBS)

I Love the Dead
"Billion Dollar Babies"

Alice Cooper
(Warner Brothers)

(I Wish I Could) Hideaway

Creedence Clearwater
    Revival

"Pendulum"
"1970"

(Fantasy)
(Fantasy)

In My Dying Days
"Physical Graffiti"

Led Zeppelin
(Swan Song)

In My Time of Dying
"Bob Dylan"

Bob Dylan
(Columbia)

In the Quiet Morning
"Take Heart"*

Mimi Fariña and Tom Jans
(A&M)

Is It Today Lord?
"Grave New World"

Strawbs
(A&M)

It's All Right Now
"I'm Nearly Famous"

Cliff Richards
(Rocket Records)

Jimmy Newman
"The Compleat Tom Paxton"
"Number 6"

Tom Paxton
(Elektra)
(Elektra)

+Jimmy Newman
"Take Me to Tomorrow"

John Denver
(RCA)

Johnny Was
"Rastaman Vibration"

Bob Marley and the Wailers
(Island)

Kevin Barry
"Strangers and Cousins"

Pete Seeger
(Columbia)

The Killing of Georgie (Part I and II)
"A Night on the Town"

Rod Stewart
(Warner Brothers)

Knockin' on Heaven's Door
"Pat Garrett and Billy the Kid"
"Before the Flood" (with The Band)

Bob Dylan
(Columbia)
(Asylum)

+Knockin' on Heaven's Door
"Roger McGuinn Band"

Roger McGuinn
(Columbia)

DEFINITIVE SONGS

+Knockin' on Heaven's Door   Eric Clapton
  (45 RPM Single)   (RSO)

 Lady d'Arbanville   Cat Stevens
 "Mona Bone Jakon"   (A&M)

 The Last Shirt On   The Animals
 "Before We Were So Rudely   (United Artists)
    Interrupted"

 The Lonesome Death of Hattie Carroll   Bob Dylan
 "The Times They Are a Changin'"   (Columbia)

+The Lonesome Death of Hattie Carroll   Judy Collins
 "The Judy Collins Concert"   (Elektra)

 Long Black Veil   The Band
 "Music from Big Pink"   (Capitol)

+Long Black Veil   Johnny Cash
 "At Folsom Prison"   (Columbia)

+Long Black Veil   Joan Baez
 "Joan Baez in Concert Part II"   (Vanguard)

 Louise   Tom Paxton
 "How Come the Sun"*   (Reprise)

 Lucky Man   Emerson, Lake & Palmer
 "Emerson, Lake & Palmer"   (Cotillion)

 My Father Died   Lucy Simon
 "Lucy Simon"*   (RCA)

 My Mummy's Dead   John Lennon
 "John Lennon/Plastic Ono Band"   (Capitol)

 My Name Is Death   Incredible String Band
 "Relics of the Incredible   (Elektra)
    String Band"

 My Old Man   Steve Goodman
 "Say It in Private"*   (Asylum)

 Never Kill Another Man   Steve Miller Band
 "Steve Miller Band Number 5"   (Capitol)

 Night Games   Paul Simon
 "Still Crazy After All These Years"   (Columbia)

 No Headstone on My Grave   Jerry Lee Lewis
 "The Session"   (Mercury)

 The Old Laughing Lady   Neil Young
 "Decade"   (Reprise)

DEFINITIVE SONGS

Once Before I Die "The Eyes of an Only Child"*	Tom Jans (Columbia)
Pretty Polly "Who Knows Where the Time Goes"	Judy Collins (Elektra)
+Pretty Polly "Cardiff Rose"	Roger McGuinn (Columbia)
Red-Headed Wildflower "Sleeper Catcher"	Little River Band (Harvest)
Requiem for the Masses "The Association's Greatest Hits"	The Association (Warner Brothers)
Sam Stone "Prime Prine" "John Prine"	John Prine (Atlantic) (Atlantic)
+Sam Stone "Al's Big Deal/Unclaimed Freight—An Al Kooper Anthology" "Naked Songs"	Al Kooper (Columbia) (Columbia)
The Shortest Story "Greatest Stories Live"	Harry Chapin (Elektra)
Sniper "Sniper and Other Love Songs"	Harry Chapin (Elektra)
Song for Adam "Saturate Before Using"	Jackson Browne (Asylum)
Spirit in the Sky "Spirit in the Sky"*	Norman Greenbaum (Reprise)
Strange Affair "First Light"*	Richard and Linda Thompson (Chrysalis)
The Stranger "A Man Must Carry On"	Jerry Jeff Walker (MCA)
Tain't But Me One "Now"	Pete Seeger (Columbia)
'Til I Die "Surf's Up"	The Beach Boys (Brother/Reprise)
Tired Eyes "Tonight's the Night" "Decade"	Neil Young (Reprise) (Reprise)
Three Bells "Greatest Hits" (45 RPM Single)*	The Browns (RCA) (RCA)

DEFINITIVE SONGS

Tom Dooley "The Best of the Kingston Trio"	The Kingston Trio (Capitol)
+Tom Dooley "Rivers Rocks the Folks"*	Johnny Rivers (Imperial)
Travelin' Shoes "Waitress in a Donut Shop"	Maria Muldaur (Warner Brothers)
Waiting Hymn of the Republic "J. F. Murphy and Salt"*	J. F. Murphy and Salt (Elektra)
Watermark "Watermark"	Art Garfunkel (Columbia)
When I Lay My Burden Down "Hobos, Heroes and Other Clowns"*	Don Nix (Enterprise)
Where Have All the Flowers Gone? "Peter, Paul and Mary"	Peter, Paul and Mary (Warner Brothers)
+Where Have All the Flowers Gone? "The World of Pete Seeger"	Pete Seeger (Columbia)
+Where Have All the Flowers Gone? "Richie Havens on Stage"*	Richie Havens (Stormy Forest)
Where the Soul Never Dies "Motel Shot"	Delaney and Bonnie (Atco)
Who Killed Davey Moore? "The World of Pete Seeger" "We Shall Overcome"	Pete Seeger (Columbia) (Columbia)
Who Killed Norma Jean? "We Shall Overcome"	Pete Seeger (Columbia)
Will the Circle Be Unbroken "The Essential Ramblin' Jack Elliott"	Ramblin' Jack Elliott (Vanguard)
+Will the Circle Be Unbroken "The First Ten Years"	Joan Baez (Vanguard)
+Will the Circle Be Unbroken "Sunday Down South"*	Jerry Lee Lewis (Sun)
+Will the Circle Be Unbroken "Dirt, Silver and Gold"	The Nitty Gritty Dirt Band (United Artists)
+Will the Circle Be Unbroken "Reflection"*	Pentangle (Reprise)
+Will the Circle Be Unbroken "A Man Must Carry On"	Jerry Jeff Walker (MCA)
+Will the Circle Be Unbroken "Motel Shot"	Delaney and Bonnie (Atco)

DEFINITIVE SONGS

+Will the Circle Be Unbroken   Gregg Allman
  "Laid Back"   (Capricorn)

REFERENCE SONGS

  Abraham, Martin and John   Dion
  "Abraham, Martin and John"   (Laurie)
  "Sanctuary"   (Warner Brothers)

+Abraham, Martin, and John   Smokey Robinson & the
                                         Miracles
  "Anthology"   (Tamla)

  Alone Again (Naturally)   Gilbert O'Sullivan
  "Himself"   (MAM)

  Billy Dee   Kris Kristofferson
  "The Silver Tongued Devil and I"   (Monument)

  Blood on the Floor   Fleetwood Mac
  "Kiln House"   (Reprise)

  Bury Me Down by a River   The Bee Gees
  "Cucumber Castle"   (RSO)

  Corey's Coming   Harry Chapin
  "On the Road to Kingdom Come"   (Elektra)

  A Day in the Life   The Beatles
  "Sgt. Pepper's Lonely Hearts Club   (Capitol)
    Band"

+A Day in the Life   The Bee Gees
  "Sgt. Pepper's Lonely Hearts Club   (RSO)
    Band Soundtrack"

+A Day in the Life   War
                                         Featuring Eric Burdon
  "Love Is All Around"   (ABC)

  Don't Weep for Me   Joan Baez
  "The Best of Joan Baez"*   (Enus)

  Dyin' Crapshooter's Blues   David Bromberg
  "How Late'll Ya Play Till?"   (Fantasy)

  Dying to Live   Edgar Winter
  "White Trash"   (Epic)

  Everything I Own   Bread
  "The Best of Bread"   (Elektra)

  The Fuse   Jackson Browne
  "The Pretender"   (Asylum)

100   *The Rock Music Source Book*

Harper
"Ramblin' Boy"*
Tom Paxton
(Vanguard)

Hero and Heroine
"Hero and Heroine"
Strawbs
(A&M)

I'm Living in Shame
Diana Ross and the
    Supremes
"Anthology"
(Motown)

Jack's Friend
"The Outsider"*
Tom Pacheco
(RCA)

Leon
"One of the Boys"
Roger Daltrey
(MCA)

Life After Death
"You're Never Alone with a
    Schizophrenic"
Ian Hunter
(Chrysalis)

Long Nights
"Safety in Numbers"
Crack the Sky
(Lifesong)

Lucy
"Another Night"
The Hollies
(Epic)

The Moon Struck One
"Cahoots"
The Band
(Capitol)

Only a Pawn in Their Game
"The Times They Are a Changin'"
Bob Dylan
(Columbia)

On the Banks of the Ohio
"The Best of Joan Baez"*
Joan Baez
(Enus)

Ramblin' Boy
"Ramblin' Boy"
Tom Paxton
(Elektra)

Romeo Is Bleeding
"Blue Valentine"
Tom Waits
(Asylum)

Share the End
"Anticipation"
Carly Simon
(Elektra)

Sleep's Dark and Silent Gate
"The Pretender"
Jackson Browne
(Asylum)

Texas (When I Die)
"TNT"
Tanya Tucker
(MCA)

Texas Girl at the Funeral
    of Her Father
"Little Criminals"
Randy Newman

(Reprise)

That Smell
"Street Survivors"
Lynyrd Skynyrd
(MCA)

REFERENCE SONGS

Was I Right or Wrong	Lynyrd Skynyrd
"Lynyrd Skynyrd's First and . . . Last"	(MCA)
When I Die	Motherlode
"Motherlode"*	(Buddah)
When I'm Dead and Gone	McGuiness Flint
"McGuiness Flint"*	(Capitol)
A Young Man Is Gone	The Beach Boys
"Spirit of America"	(Capitol)
"Little Deuce Coupe"	(Capitol)

YOUR ADDITIONAL SONGS

_____

_____

_____

_____

_____

DIVORCE

Divorce—maybe not inevitable, but depressing.
Divorce has reached epidemic proportions in our time. These songs explore the causes, effects, and especially the feelings of the people before, during, and after. (N.B. Topics here also include separations, desertions, etc.)

Related Categories: Marriage, Love: "Babe I'm Gonna Leave You"

+Same as Song Above
*Hard-to-find Songs/Albums

CLASSICS

Husbands and Wives
"Golden Hits"

Roger Miller
(Smash)

+Husbands and Wives
"Rainbow"
"Stones"

Neil Diamond
(MCA)
(MCA)

+Husbands and Wives
"Goodnight Vienna"

Ringo Starr
(Apple)

+Husbands and Wives
"Pass the Chicken and Listen"*

The Everly Brothers
(RCA)

Little Girl
"Moving Finger"

The Hollies
(Epic)

Tears in the Morning
"Sunflower"

The Beach Boys
(Brother/Reprise)

You Better Sit Down Kids
"The Very Best of Cher"

Cher
(United Artists)

+You Better Sit Down Kids

"The Union Gap"*

Gary Puckett and the Union
  Gap
(Columbia)

DEFINITIVE SONGS

About the Children
"Things I Notice Now"*

Tom Paxton
(Elektra)

Alimony
"Show Time"
"Ry Cooder"

Ry Cooder
(Warner Brothers)
(Warner Brothers)

DEFINITIVE SONGS

All the Broken Children
"My Boy"*
Richard Harris
(ABC/Dunhill)

Already One
"Comes a Time"
Neil Young
(Reprise)

Alright for an Hour
"Atlantic Crossing"
Rod Stewart
(Warner Brothers)

Autumn of My Life
"Words and Pictures"*
Bobby Goldsboro
(United Artists)

Congratulations
"Paul Simon"
Paul Simon
(Columbia)

Father to Son
"Stolen Time"*
Lucy Simon
(RCA)

Fly Away
"Renunion in Central Park
Blues Project
(MCA)

Grounds for Separation
"Daryl Hall and John Oates"
Hall and Oates
(RCA)

Haitian Divorce
"Royal Scam"
"Greatest Hits"
Steely Dan
(ABC)
(ABC)

Hard Time for Lovers
"Hard Time for Lovers"
Judy Collins
(Elektra)

Legal Matter
"Meaty Beaty Big and Bouncy"
The Who
(MCA)

Mexican Divorce
"Paradise and Lunch"*
Ry Cooder
(Reprise)

+Mexican Divorce
"Nicolette"
Nicolette Larson
(Warner Brothers)

Quits
"So Long Harry Truman"*
Danny O'Keefe
(Atlantic)

+Quits
"Clear Sailing"*
Chris Hillman
(Asylum)

Sail On
"Midnight Magic"
Commodores
(Motown)

Sandra
"Barry Manilow II"
Barry Manilow
(Arista)

Sealed with a Traitor's Kiss
"Deadlines"
Strawbs
(Arista)

Separation Blues
"Patrick Sky"*
Patrick Sky
(Vanguard)

DEFINITIVE SONGS

Separation Ways	Elvis Presley
"Worldwide 50 Gold Award Hits, Vol. 1"	(RCA)
Someday Never Comes	Creedence Clearwater Revival
"Chronicle"	(Fantasy)
Stop in Nevada	Billy Joel
"Piano Man"	(Columbia)
Too Young to Feel This Old	McKendree Spring
"Too Young to Feel This Old"*	(Pye)
With Pen in Hand	Billy Vera
(45 RPM Single)*	(Atlantic)
+With Pen in Hand	Bobby Goldsboro
"10th Anniversary Album"	(United Artists)
"Honey"*	(United Artists)

REFERENCE SONGS

The Frying Pan	John Prine
"Diamonds in the Rough"*	(Atlantic)
Gasoline Alley Bred	The Hollies
"Moving Finger"	(Epic)
I'm Moving In by Myself	John Shine
"Songs for a Rainy Day"*	(Columbia)
On the Rocks	Loudon Wainwright III
"Unrequited"*	(Columbia)
Policeman	Chicago
"Chicago XI"	(Columbia)
River of Love	John Denver
"Farewell Andromeda"	(RCA)
Rotunda	Tom Rush
"Wrong End of the Rainbow"	(Columbia)
Take Time to Know Her	Percy Sledge
(45 RPM Single)*	(Atlantic)
"The Best of Percy Sledge"	(Atlantic)
There She Goes	John Prine
"Bruised Orange"*	(Asylum)
This Diamond Ring	Gary Lewis and the Playboys
"Golden Greats"	(Liberty)
"The Very Best of Gary Lewis and the Playboys"	(United Artists)

REFERENCE SONGS

+This Diamond Ring   Al Kooper
  "Act Like Nothing's Wrong"*   (United Artists)
  Three Flights Up   Don McLean
  "Tapestry"   (United Artists)
  "Solo"   (United Artists)

YOUR ADDITIONAL SONGS

_____

_____

_____

_____

_____

DRINKING

Drinking—when it's good it's very, very good, and when it's bad . . .
    The music covers both sides of this experience, from the sing-along drink-along song to the drag-along depression of alcoholism. Still other songs deal with the individual spirits: liquor, wine, beer, etc.

Related Categories: Working: After Work Hours

    +Same as Song Above
     *Hard-to-find Songs/Albums

CLASSICS

Alabama Song	The Doors
"The Doors"	(Elektra)
"Absolutely Live"	(Elektra)
Bottle of Wine	Tom Paxton
"Ain't That News"*	(Elektra)
+Bottle of Wine	Fireballs
(45 RPM Single)*	(Atco)
+Bottle of Wine	Judy Collins
"Golden Apples of the Sun"	(Elektra)
Margaritaville	Jimmy Buffett
"Changes in Latitudes, Changes in Attitudes"	(ABC)
"You Had to Be There"	(ABC)

DEFINITIVE SONGS

Ain't Gonna Make It	Jimmy Mack
"On the Corner"	(Big Tree)
Alcohol	Yesterday, Today and Tomorrow
"Yesterday, Today and Tomorrow"*	(London)
Alcohol	The Kinks
"Celluloid Heroes, Greatest Hits"	(RCA)
"Everybody's in Showbiz"	(RCA)
All the Way	Pure Prairie League
"Dance"	(RCA)
And the Wine Gets Better	Artie Kaplan
"Down by the Old Stream"*	(Paramount)

DEFINITIVE SONGS

The Anonymous Alcoholic "Bloody Tourist"	10 CC (Polydor)
Another Cheap Western "Peaks Valleys Honky-Tonks & Alleys"	Michael Murphey (Epic)
Another Try "Holiday" "America Live"	America (Warner Brothers) (Warner Brothers)
Arrested While Driving Drunk "Tejas"	ZZ Top (London)
Backslider's Wine "Peaks Valleys Honky-Tonks & Alleys" "Geronimo's Cadillac"	Michael Murphey (Epic) (Epic)
Bad Liver and a Broken Heart "Small Change"	Tom Waits (Asylum)
Bar Room Crystal Ball "Yellow Fever"	Hot Tuna (Grunt)
Bartender's Blues "J.T."	James Taylor (Columbia)
Beer Drinkers And Hell Raisers "The Best of ZZ Top"	ZZ Top (London)
The Beer Song "Swallowed Up in the Great American Heartland"*	Tom Pacheco (RCA)
Blue Bird Wine "Pieces of the Sky"	Emmylou Harris (Warner Brothers)
Blue Champagne "Manhattan Transfer"	Manhattan Transfer (Atlantic)
(Tonight) The Bottle Let Me Down "I've Always Been Crazy"	Waylon Jennings (RCA)
+Bottle Let Me Down "Pieces of the Sky"	Emmylou Harris (Warner Brothers)
Bottle of Red Wine "In Concert"	Derek and the Dominos (RSO)
Bring Another Bottle "Matthew and Son"	Cat Stevens (Deram)

DEFINITIVE SONGS

Champagne (and Wine)

Herman Brood and His Wild
  Romance
(Ariola/America)

"Herman Brood and His Wild
  Romance"

Champagne Jam
"Champagne Jam"
"Are You Ready"

Atlanta Rhythm Section
(Polydor)
(Polydor)

Champagne Rock and Roll
"Shine On"

Climax Blues Band
(Sire)

Cheap Tequila
"Still Alive and Well"

Johnny Winter
(Columbia)

Chug-a-Lug
"Golden Hits"

Roger Miller
(Smash)

Colorado Cool-Aid
"Johnny Paycheck's Greatest Hits
  Vol. II"

Johnny Paycheck
(Epic)

Copper Kettle
"In Concert"

Joan Baez
(Vanguard)

+Copper Kettle
"Self Portrait"

Bob Dylan
(Columbia)

Cracklin' Rosie
"Gold"
"Hot August Night"

Neil Diamond
(MCA)
(MCA)

Cruisin' and Boozin'
"Sammy Hagar"*

Sammy Hagar
(Capitol)

Down Drinking at the Bar
"Attempted Moustache"*

Loudon Wainwright III
(Columbia)

Drink All Day and Night
"The Place I Love"*

Splinter
(Dark Horse)

Drinkin' Blues
"Nothing but the Blues"

Johnny Winter
(Blue Sky)

Drinking Daddy's Wine
"The Second Coming"*

Jerry La Croix
(Mercury)

Drinking Man's Concerto
"Double Take"*

Mark and Clark
(Columbia)

Drinking Song
"Album II"

Loudon Wainwright III
(Columbia)

Drinking Wine Spodee O'Dee
"The Session"

Jerry Lee Lewis
(Mercury)

DEFINITIVE SONGS

+Drinking Wine Spodie Odie
"Te John Grease and Wolfman"
Charlie Daniels
(Buddah)

+Drinking Wine Spodie Odie
"Out of Their Skulls"*
The Pirates
(Warner Brothers)

Drunken Lady of the Morning
"Cosmic Cowboy Souvenir"*
Michael Murphey
(A&M)

Elderberry Wine
"Don't Shoot Me, I'm Only the Piano
    Player"
Elton John
(MCA)

Everything Gets Better When You're
    Drunk
"Rupert Holmes"*
Rupert Holmes

(Epic)

Feelin' Right
"Helluva Band"
Angel
(Casablanca)

Fine Champagne
"Yeah Yeah"*
Georgie Fame
(Imperial)

Gimme That Wine
"Brand New Day"*
Blood, Sweat and Tears
(Columbia)

Gimme That Wine
"Yeah Yeah"*
Georgie Fame
(Imperial)

Glass of Champagne
"Sailor"*
Sailor
(Epic)

The Glow
"The Glow"
Bonnie Raitt
(Warner Brothers)

God's Own Drunk
"Living and Dying in 3/4 Time"*
"You Had to Be There"
Jimmy Buffett
(ABC)
(ABC)

A Good Woman Likes to Drink with
    the Boys
"Marin County Line"
New Riders of the Purple
    Sage
(Columbia)

Have a Drink on Me
"Puttin' on the Style"*
Lonnie Donegan
(Monument)

Have Another Drink
"Soap Opera"
The Kinks
(RCA)

Hey Bartender
"Briefcase Full of Blues"
The Blues Brothers
(Atlantic)

Kentucky Moonshine
"Taking the Stage"
Pure Prairie League
(RCA)

DEFINITIVE SONGS

Kings and Queens
"Unrequited"

Loudon Wainwright III
(Columbia)

Letter That Johnny Walker Red
"Texas Gold"

Asleep at the Wheel
(Capitol)

Lightning Bar Blues
"Hobo's Lullaby"

Arlo Guthrie
(Reprise)

+Lightning Bar Blues
"Yeah"

Brownsville Station
(Big Tree)

Little Glass of Wine
"A Touch on the Rainy Side"*

Jesse Winchester
(Bearsville)

Mad Dog
"Holiday"

America
(Warner Brothers)

Million Dollar Bash
"Basement Tapes"

Bob Dylan and The Band
(Columbia)

Moonshine
"My Sporting Life"*

John Kay
(ABC)

Moonshine Man (b/w "Don't Go Out
    into the Rain")
(45 RPM Single)*
"Blaze"*

Herman's Hermits

(MGM)
(MGM)

Moonshine Whiskey
"Tupelo Honey"

Van Morrison
(Warner Brothers)

One Bourbon, One Scotch, and One
    Beer
"George Thorogood"

George Thorogood

(Rounder)

One Drink Too Many
"Sailor"*

Sailor
(Epic)

One Mint Julep
"History of Rhythm and Blues"
"Soul Years"

The Clovers
(Atlantic)
(Atlantic)

The Piano Has Been Drinking
"Small Change"

Tom Waits
(Asylum)

Please Daddy
"Farewell Andromeda"

John Denver
(RCA)

Red Red Wine
"Neil Diamond's Greatest Hits"

Neil Diamond
(Bang)

Rye Whiskey
"The Soul of a City Boy"

Jesse Colin Young
(Capitol)

DEFINITIVE SONGS

Sailor's Night on the Town "Sailor"*	Sailor (Epic)
San Gria Wine "Viva Terlingua"*	Jerry Jeff Walker (MCA)
Scotch and Soda "Kingston Trio's Greatest Hits" "Tom Dooley"	The Kingston Trio (Capitol) (Capitol)
+Scotch and Soda "Manhattan Transfer"	Manhattan Transfer (Atlantic)
She's Looking Better with Every Beer "New Riders"	New Riders of the Purple Sage (MCA)
Silver Horn "J. F. Murphy and Salt"*	J. F. Murphy and Salt (Elektra)
Slightly Drunk "Cool for Cats"	Squeeze (A&M)
Sloppy Drunk "How Late'll Ya Play Till?"	David Bromberg (Fantasy)
Social Disease "Goodbye Yellow Brick Road"	Elton John (MCA)
Sour Whiskey "Look to Your Heart"*	Dan Hill (Columbia)
Stoned "Orleans"*	Orleans (ABC)
Sunday Mornin' Comin' Down "Songs of Kristofferson"	Kris Kristofferson (Columbia)
Sweet Blindness "Eli and the 13th Confession"	Laura Nyro (Columbia)
+Sweet Blindness "Greatest Hits on Earth" "Stoned Soul Picnic"	The Fifth Dimension (Arista) (Soul City)
Tequila Sunrise "Their Greatest Hits 1971–1975" "Desperado"	The Eagles (Asylum) (Asylum)
To Beat the Devil "Me and Bobby McGee"	Kris Kristofferson (Monument)
Two More Bottles of Wine "Keeper of the Flame"	Delbert McClinton (Capricorn)

DEFINITIVE SONGS

+Two More Bottles of Wine — Emmylou Harris
"Quarter Moon in a Ten Cent Town" (Warner Brothers)
"Profile: Best of Emmylou Harris" (Warner Brothers)

W. Lee O'Daniel — James Talley
"Got No Bread, No Milk, No Honey"* (Capitol)

What Good Can Drinking Do — Janis Joplin
"Janis" (Soundtrack) (Columbia)

When Work Is Over — The Kinks
"Soap Opera" (RCA)

Whiskey — New Riders of the Purple Sage
"Gypsy Cowboy" (Columbia)

Whiskey — Charlie Daniels
"Volunteer Jam" (Capricorn)

Whiskey — Loggins and Messina
"Loggins and Messina" (Columbia)

Whiskey Headed Woman — Canned Heat
"Boogie with Canned Heat"* (Liberty)

Whiskey Man — The Who
"A Quick One (Happy Jack)" (MCA)

Whiskey Man — Aztec Two Step
"Two's Company"* (RCA)

Whiskey Train — Procol Harum
"Home" (A&M)

Whiskey Whiskey — Rita Coolidge
"The Lady's Not for Sale" (A&M)

White Lightning — Gene Vincent
"I'm Back and I'm Proud"* (Dandelion)

+White Lightning — Kate Taylor
"Kate Taylor"* (Cotillion)

Why Don't We Get Drunk (and Screw) — Jimmy Buffett
"A White Sports Coat and a Pink Crustacean" (ABC)
"You Had to Be There" (ABC)

The Wine Song — The Youngbloods
"The Best of the Youngbloods" (RCA)

DEFINITIVE SONGS

Wiped Out "Ace Frehley"*	Ace Frehley (Casablanca)

REFERENCE SONGS

Bed and a Bottle "Birth Comes to Us All"	The Good Rats (Passport/Arista)
The Best of All Possible Worlds "Me and Bobby McGee"	Kris Kristofferson (Monument)
Broke Again "Diamantina Cocktail"	Little River Band (Harvest)
C'mon Little Mama "All This for a Song"	The Guess Who (Hilltak/Atlantic)
Captain Jim's Drunken Dream "In the Pocket"	James Taylor (Warner Brothers)
Chug All Night "Eagles"	The Eagles (Asylum)
Cotton Growing Man "You Broke My Heart, So I Busted Your Jaw"	Spooky Tooth (A&M)
Cuban Crisis "Dog Days"	Atlanta Rhythm Section (Polydor)
Drunk on the Moon "The Heart of Saturday Night"	Tom Waits (Asylum)
Feeling Single, Seeing Double "Elite Motel"	Emmylou Harris (Warner Brothers)
The Fool "Before We Were So Rudely Interrupted"	The Animals (United Artists)
Georgia in a Jug "Johnny Paycheck's Greatest Hits, Vol. II"	Johnny Paycheck (Epic)
Good Friends and a Bottle of Wine "Weekend Warriors"	Ted Nugent (Epic)
Have a Good Time "Wet Willie"*	Wet Willie (Capricorn)
However Much I Booze "The Who by Numbers"	The Who (MCA/Track)
Indian Gin and Whiskey Dry "Idea"*	The Bee Gees (Atco)

REFERENCE SONGS

Jug of Wine
"Revelation: Revolution '69"*
The Lovin' Spoonful
(Kama Sutra)

Juke Joint Jump
"Hell Raisin'"
Elvin Bishop
(Capricorn)

Let's Go Get Stoned
"A Man and His Music"
Ray Charles
(ABC)

Let's Go to Town
"Sailor"*
Sailor
(Epic)

Louisville A.D.
"Michael Stanley"*
Michael Stanley
(Tumbleweed)

Margaritas
David Crosby/Graham Nash
(ABC)

"Whistle Down the Wire"

Midnight Creeper
"Hog Heaven"
Elvin Bishop
(Capricorn)

Moonshine Alley
"Release"*
Henry Gross
(Lifesong)

Picasso's Last Words
"Band on the Run"
Wings
(Capitol)

Pink Wine Sparkles in the Glass
"Wheatfield Soul"
The Guess Who
(RCA)

Potter's Field
"Foreign Affairs"
Tom Waits
(Asylum)

Raise Your Glass (to Foolish Me)
"Book Early"
City Boy
(Mercury)

Red Hot Women and Ice Cold Beer
New Riders of the Purple Sage
(MCA)

"Who Are Those Guys?"
Rollin'
"Good Old Boys"
Randy Newman
(Reprise)

Salt of the Earth
"Beggars Banquet"
The Rolling Stones
(London)

+Salt of the Earth
"Blessed Are"
Joan Baez
(Vanguard)

+Salt of the Earth
"Judith"
Judy Collins
(Elektra)

Send Me No Wine
"On the Threshold of a Dream"
The Moody Blues
(London)

REFERENCE SONGS

Sloop John B
"Pet Sounds"
"Good Vibrations—The Best of the Beach Boys"

The Beach Boys
(Capitol)
(Brother/Reprise)

+Sloop John B
"Greatest Hits"

The Weavers
(Vanguard)

+Sloop John B
"Puttin' on the Style"*

Lonnie Donegan
(United Artists)

+Sloop John B
"Eve of Destruction"*

Barry McGuire
(ABC/Dunhill)

+Sloop John B
"Paint Me a Picture"

Gary Lewis and the Playboys
(Liberty)

Spill the Wine

"Eric Burdon Declares War"

War
    Featuring Eric Burdon
(MGM)

+Spill the Wine
"The Best . . . Isley Brothers"
"Timeless"

The Isley Brothers
(Buddah)
(T-Neck)

Stoned Soul Picnic
"Eli and the 13th Confession"

Laura Nyro
(Columbia)

+Stoned Soul Picnic
"Greatest Hits on Earth"
"Stoned Soul Picnic"

The Fifth Dimension
(Arista)
(Soul City)

The Straight Life
"10th Anniversary Album"

Bobby Goldsboro
(United Artists)

Stranger
"Life on Earth"*

Artie Traum
(Rounder)

Strawberry Wine
"Stage Fright"

The Band
(Capitol)

Sweet Cherry Wine

"The Best of Tommy James and the Shondells"

Tommy James and the Shondells
(Roulette)

Talking Old Soldiers
"Tumbleweed Connection"

Elton John
(MCA)

Two Time Loser
"One Night Stands"

Fandango
(RCA)

Wasn't That a Party
"New Songs for Old Friends"*

Tom Paxton
(Reprise)

REFERENCE SONGS

What a Night "Book Early"	City Boy (Mercury)
Whiskey Rock-a-Roller "One More from the Road"	Lynyrd Skynyrd (MCA)
White Lightning Wine "Dreamboat Annie"	Heart (Mushroom)
Wine and Women "Stone Alone"	Bill Wyman (Rolling Stone Records)
Wino "Skynyrd's First . . . and Last"	Lynyrd Skynyrd (MCA)
Women and Drinkin' "Chirpin'"	The Persuasions (Elektra)
Yes I Guess They Oughta Name a Drink After You "Diamonds in the Rough"*	John Prine (Atlantic)

YOUR ADDITIONAL SONGS

_____

_____

_____

_____

_____

DRUGS

Drugs—everything from aspirin to OD.

These are the songs that are supposedly ruining the lives of America's youth. Interestingly enough, many more are against than for. (N.B. Subdivision categories are Heroin, Cocaine, Marijuana, and "The Pusher.")

+Same as Song Above
*Hard-to-find Songs/Albums

CLASSICS

Kicks	Paul Revere and the Raiders
	Featuring Mark Lindsay
"All-Time Greatest Hits"	(Columbia)
+Kicks	Nazz
"Nazz III"	(SGB/Atco)
+Kicks	Leif Garrett
"Same Goes for You"	(Atlantic)
Mother's Little Helper	The Rolling Stones
"Hot Rocks 1964–1971"	(London)
"Flowers"	(London)
"Through the Past, Darkly (Big Hits Vol. II)"	(London)
Purple Haze	Jimi Hendrix
"Smash Hits"	(Reprise)
"Are You Experienced?"	(Reprise)
"The Essential Jimi Hendrix"	(Reprise)
+Purple Haze	Dion
"Dion"*	(Laurie)
+Purple Haze	Roto Rooter
"Roto Rooter"*	(Vanguard)
White Rabbit	Jefferson Airplane
"The Worst of Jefferson Airplane"	(RCA)
"Surrealistic Pillow"	(RCA)
"Flight Log"	(RCA)
+White Rabbit	The Great Society
"Conspicuous Only in Its Absence"*	(Columbia)

THEMATIC ALBUMS

"Take a Trip with Me"* — Various Artists (Prestige)

"Tonight's the Night" — Neil Young (Reprise)

DEFINITIVE SONGS

The Acid Queen
"Tommy" — The Who (MCA)

+The Acid Queen
"Tommy" (Soundtrack) — Tina Turner (Polydor)

The Alphabet Song — David Peel and the Lower East Side (Elektra)

"Have a Marijuana"*

Amphetamine Annie
"Canned Heat"
"Boogie with Canned Heat" — Canned Heat (United Artists) (Liberty)

Angel Dust
"Secrets" — Gil Scott-Heron (Arista)

Apothecary
"Life Beyond L.A." — Ambrosia (Warner Brothers)

Artificial Energy
"The Notorious Byrd Brothers" — The Byrds (Columbia)

Banapple Gas
"Numbers" — Cat Stevens (A&M)

Brain Damage
"Welcome to Riddle Ridge"* — Brewer and Shipley (Capitol)

Codeine
"The Best of Buffy Sainte-Marie" — Buffy Sainte-Marie (Vanguard)

Donna/Hashish
"Hair—Original Broadway Play" — Various Artists (RCA)

+Donna/Hashish
"Hair" (Soundtrack) — Various Artists (RCA)

Dope Sucks
"Herman Brood and His Wild Romance" — Herman Brood and His Wild Romance (Ariola/America)

Double Vision
"Double Vision" — Foreigner (Atlantic)

Down the Road
"Down the Road" — Manassas (Stephen Stills) (Atlantic)

DEFINITIVE SONGS

Drug Stabbing Time
"Give 'Em Enough Rope"
The Clash
(Epic)

Eight Miles High
"Untitled"
"The Best of the Byrds"
The Byrds
(Columbia)
(Columbia)

+Eight Miles High
"The Best of Leo Kottke"
Leo Kottke
(Capitol)

+Eight Miles High
"Eight Miles High"
Golden Earring
(MCA)

Everything Put Together Falls Apart
"Paul Simon"
Paul Simon
(Columbia)

Freddie's Dead
"Superfly"
Curtis Mayfield
(Curtom)

From Your Own Back Yard
(45 RPM Single)*
"Born to Be with You" (Import)
Dion
(Warner Brothers)
(Phil Spector International)

Haywood
"Fantasy"
Carole King
(Ode)

Hurry Tomorrow
"Masterpiece"
The Temptations
(Gordy)

I'm Set Free
"Velvet Underground"*
The Velvet Underground
(MGM)

I Want to Get High

"The American Revolution"*
David Peel and the Lower
   East Side
(Elektra)

Josie
"Border Lord"
Kris Kristofferson
(Monument)

Julie's in the Drug Squad
"Give 'em Enough Rope"
The Clash
(Epic)

Lucy in the Sky with Diamonds
"Sgt. Pepper's Lonely Hearts Club
   Band"
The Beatles
(Capitol)

+Lucy in the Sky with Diamonds
"Greatest Hits, Vol. 2"
Elton John
(MCA)

+Lucy in the Sky with Diamonds
"Sgt. Pepper's Lonely Hearts Club
   Band Soundtrack"
Dianne Steinberg
(RSO)

Mr. Tambourine Man
"Bringing It All Back Home"
"Bob Dylan's Greatest Hits"
Bob Dylan
(Columbia)
(Columbia)

DEFINITIVE SONGS

+Mr. Tambourine Man — The Byrds
"Mr. Tambourine Man" (Columbia)
"Untitled" (Columbia)
"The Byrds' Greatest Hits" (Columbia)

+Mr. Tambourine Man — Johnny Rivers
"Rivers Rocks the Folks"* (Imperial)

+Mr. Tambourine Man — Judy Collins
"Recollections" (Elektra)

+Mr. Tambourine Man — John Denver/The Chad
 Mitchell Trio
"Beginnings" (Mercury)

+Mr. Tambourine Man — Melanie
"My First Album"* (Buddah)
"Four Sides of Melanie"* (Buddah)

+Mr. Tambourine Man — Kenny Rankin
"Mind Dusters"* (Mercury)

No No Song — Hoyt Axton
"Greatest Hits" (A&M)
"Road Songs"* (A&M)

+No No Song — Ringo Starr
"Blasts from Your Past" (Apple)

Opium Trail — Thin Lizzy
"Bad Reputation" (Mercury)

Overdose — AC/DC
"Let There Be Rock"* (Atco)

Sampaku — Michael Franks
"Tiger in the Rain" (Warner Brothers)

Sister Morphine — The Rolling Stones
"Sticky Fingers" (Rolling Stone Records)

Something Happened to Me Yesterday — The Rolling Stones
"Between the Buttons" (London)

Sonny Boy — Dion
"Dion"* (Laurie)

Take a Red — New Riders of the Purple
 Sage
"Marin County" (Columbia)

Tomorrow Never Knows — The Beatles
"Revolver" (Capitol)

DEFINITIVE SONGS

+T.N.K. (Tomorow Never Knows)   Phil Manzanera
"801 Live"   (Polydor)

Too High   Stevie Wonder
"Innervisions"   (Tamla)

Too Much Seconal   Edgar Winter
"Still Alive and Well"   (Epic)

White Punks on Dope   The Tubes
"What Do You Want From Live"   (A&M)

REFERENCE SONGS

All I Want Is Everything   Southside Johnny
"The Jukes"   (Mercury)

American Boy and Girl   Garland Jeffries
"American Boy and Girl"   (A&M)

Billy Dee   Kris Kristofferson
"The Silver Tongued Devil and I"   (Monument)

A Day in the Life   The Beatles
"Sgt. Pepper's Lonely Hearts Club   (Capitol)
   Band"
"The Beatles 1967–1970"   (Apple)

+A Day in the Life   Frankie Valli
"All This and World War II"   (20th Century-Fox)

+A Day in the Life   War
       Featuring Eric Burdon

"Love Is All Around"   (ABC)
Fresh Air   Quicksilver Messenger
     Service

"Anthology"   (Capitol)
"Just for Love"*   (Capitol)
Get High   Sons of Champlin
"Loosen Up Naturally"*   (Capitol)
I Can Get Off on You   Waylon Jennings and Willie
     Nelson

"Waylon and Willie"   (RCA)
I Wanna Be Sedated   The Ramones
"Road to Ruin"   (Sire)
Mayrowana   Pete Seeger
"Young vs. Old"   (Columbia)
Midnight Creeper   Elvin Bishop
"Hog Heaven"   (Capricorn)

REFERENCE SONGS

Naked Eye
"Odds and Sods"

The Who
(MCA/Track)

The Raid
"Stick to Me"

Graham Parker
(Mercury)

Undone
"The Best of The Guess Who"

The Guess Who
(RCA)

You Burned Yourself Out
"Rupert Holmes"*

Rupert Holmes
(Epic)

YOUR ADDITIONAL SONGS

_____

_____

_____

_____

_____

Heroin

CLASSICS

Heroin
"Velvet Underground"*
"The 1969 Velvet Underground Live"

The Velvet Underground
(MGM)
(Mercury)

+Heroin
"Rock and Roll Animal"

Lou Reed
(RCA)

The Needle and the Damage Done
"Decade"
"Harvest"

Neil Young
(Reprise)
(Reprise)

Sam Stone
"Prime Prine"
"John Prine"*

John Prine
(Atlantic)
(Atlantic)

+Sam Stone
"Al's Big Deal/Unclaimed
   Freight—An Al Kooper Anthology"
"Naked Songs"*

Al Kooper
(Columbia)

(Columbia)

DEFINITIVE SONGS

Been on a Train
"Christmas and the Beads of Sweat"

Laura Nyro
(Columbia)

Carmelita
"Warren Zevon"

Warren Zevon
(Asylum)

+Carmelita
"Simple Dreams"

Linda Ronstadt
(Asylum)

Cold Blue Steel and Sweet Fire
"For the Roses"

Joni Mitchell
(Reprise)

Cold Turkey
"Shaved Fish"

John Lennon
(Apple)

+Cold Turkey
"The Plastic Ono Band—Live Peace in Toronto 1969"

John Lennon
(Apple)

Coming Down
"Like a Seed"*

Kenny Rankin
(Little David)

Dead Flowers
"Sticky Fingers"

The Rolling Stones
(Rolling Stone Records)

+Dead Flowers

New Riders of the Purple Sage
(Columbia)

"Home, Home on the Road"

The Great Escape
"Champagne Jam"

Atlanta Rhythm Section
(Polydor)

Haywood
"Fantasy"

Carole King
(Ode)

I'm Waiting for the Man
"Live at Max's Kansas City"*

The Velvet Underground
(Cotillion)

+I'm Waiting for the Man
"Live—Take No Prisoners"

Lou Reed
(Arista)

Junkie's Lament
"In the Pocket"

James Taylor
(Warner Brothers)

The Needle and the Spoon
"One More from the Road"

Lynyrd Skynyrd
(MCA)

Needle of Death
"Family"*

Kenny Rankin
(Mercury)

A Night This Side of Dying
"Wrap Around Joy"

Carole King
(Ode)

Sheila
"Blue River"

Eric Andersen
(Columbia)

DEFINITIVE SONGS

Shootin' Dope   Garland Jeffries
"American Boy and Girl"   (A&M)
Signed D.C.   Love
"Love"*   (Elektra)
"Love Revisited"   (Elektra)
Stoned Junkie   Curtis Mayfield
"Curtis Live"   (Kama Sutra)
White Light, White Heat   The Velvet Underground
"White Light, White Heat"*   (Verve)
"Velvet Underground"   (MGM)
"The Velvet Underground"   (MGM)
+White Light, White Heat   Lou Reed
"Rock and Roll Animal"   (RCA)
+White Light, White Heat   Mick Ronson
"Play, Don't Worry"   (RCA)

REFERENCE SONGS

The End   Leo Sayer
"Here"   (Warner Brothers)
Me and Baby Jane   Leon Russell
"Carney"   (Shelter)
Tonight's the Night   Neil Young
"Tonight's the Night"   (Reprise)
"Decade"   (Reprise)
"Live Rust"   (Reprise)

YOUR ADDITIONAL SONGS

_____

_____

_____

_____

_____

Cocaine

CLASSICS

Cocaine "Running on Empty"	Jackson Browne (Asylum)
+Cocaine "Dave Van Ronk and the Hudson Dusters"*	Dave Van Ronk (Verve)
Cocaine Song "Troubadour"*	J. J. Cale (Shelter)
+Cocaine Song "Slow Hand"	Eric Clapton (RSO)

DEFINITIVE SONGS

Casey Jones "Workingman's Dead" "Skeletons from the Closet" "Steal Your Face"	The Grateful Dead (Warner Brothers) (Warner Brothers) (Grateful Dead Records)
Cocaine "Tom Rush"*	Tom Rush (Columbia)
Cocaine Blues "Van Ronk"*	Dave Van Ronk (Fantasy)
+Cocaine Blues "My Own House"	David Bromberg (Fantasy)
+Cocaine Blues "Looking Backwards to Tomorrow"*	Jeannie Lewis (Mainstream)
+Cocaine Blues "Johnny R. Cash" "Silver"	Johnny Cash (Columbia) (Columbia)
Cocaine Cowboys "Kid Blast"*	Kid Blast (Claridge Records)
Cocaine Drain "Power"	John Hall (Columbia)
Cocaine Elaine "Isis"*	Isis (Buddah)
Snow Blind Friend "ABC Collection" "Steppenwolf 7"	Steppenwolf (ABC) (ABC/Dunhill)

DEFINITIVE SONGS

Sweet Cocaine	Fred Neil
"The Other Side of This Life"*	(Capitol)
"Fred Neil"*	(Capitol)
"Everybody's Talkin' "	(Capitol)
Take a Whiff	The Byrds
"Untitled"	(Columbia)

REFERENCE SONGS

Ain't Nobody's Business	Taj Mahal
"Taj Mahal"	(Columbia)
Am I High	Asleep at the Wheel
"The Wheel"*	(Capitol)
Blues on the Ceiling	Fred Neil
"Bleeker Street"*	(Capitol)
Brother Bill	The Animals
"Before We Were So Rudely Interrupted"	(United Artists)
Buy and Sell	Laura Nyro
"The First Songs"	(Columbia)
Champagne Don't Hurt Me	Eric Von Schmidt
"Take a Trip with Me"* (Various Artists)	(Prestige)
Cocaine Blues	George Thorogood and the Destroyers
"Move It On Over"	(Rounder)
The Island Song	Marshall Chapman
"Jaded Virgin"*	(Epic)
Listen to Her Heart	Tom Petty and the Heartbreakers
"You're Gonna Get It"	(Shelter)
Moonlight Mile	The Rolling Stones
"Sticky Fingers"	(Rolling Stone Records)
Mr. Jones	Steve Gibbons
"Rolling On"*	(MCA)
The Road	Danny O'Keefe
"O'Keefe"*	(Sign Post)
+The Road	Jackson Browne
"Running on Empty"	(Asylum)

REFERENCE SONGS

Sailin' Shoes "Discover America"*	Van Dyke Parks (Warner Brothers)
+Sailin' Shoes "Waiting for Columbus"	Little Feat (Warner Brothers)
Short Days and Englishmen "The Best of P G & E"	Pacific Gas & Electric (Columbia)
Tired Eyes "Tonight's the Night" "Decade"	Neil Young (Reprise) (Reprise)

YOUR ADDITIONAL SONGS

_____

_____

_____

_____

_____

Marijuana

CLASSICS

Almost all of these songs are either silly or humorous stabs at marijuana or its use. All are good songs in their own right, but none, unfortunately, met our criteria to be recommended as a "classic" or significant song about "pot." We hope that by the time Volume Two appears, someone will have written one!

THEMATIC ALBUMS

"Have a Marijuana"*	David Peel and the Lower East Side (Elektra)
"Reefer Songs—Sixteen Original Classics"	(Stash Records)

DEFINITIVE SONGS

Bush Doctor
"Bush Doctor"

Peter Tosh
(Rolling Stone Records)

Commercial
"Spanky's Greatest Hits"
"Spanky and Our Gang"*

Spanky and Our Gang
(Mercury)
(Mercury)

Don't Bogart Me
"Easy Rider" (Soundtrack)

Fraternity of Man
(Dunhill)

+Don't Bogart That Joint
"Waiting for Columbus"

Little Feat
(Warner Brothers)

Henry

New Riders of the Purple
    Sage

"New Riders of the Purple Sage"

(Columbia)

Homegrown
"American Stars 'n Bars"

Neil Young
(Reprise)

I Got Some Marijuana

David Peel and the Lower
    East Side

"Have a Marijuana"*

(Elektra)

I Got Stoned and I Missed It
"Not Just Another Pretty Foot"

Jim Stafford
(MGM)

I Like Marijuana

David Peel and the Lower
    East Side

"Have a Marijuana"*

(Elektra)

Kaya
"Kaya"

Bob Marley and the Wailers
(Island)

Legalize It
"Legalize It"

Peter Tosh
(Columbia)

Legalize It

David Peel and the Lower
    East Side

"The American Revolution"*

(Elektra)

Marahuana
"Songs for the New Depression"

Bette Midler
(Atlantic)

Marijuana
"The Life and Times of Country Joe
    and the Fish—from Haight-Ashbury
    to Woodstock"

Country Joe and the Fish
(Vanguard)

Mary Jane
"Janis Joplin" (Soundtrack)

Janis Joplin
(Columbia)

One Paper Kid
"Guy Clark"*

Guy Clark
(Warner Brothers)

DEFINITIVE SONGS

One Toke over the Line "The Best . . . Brewer and Shipley"	Brewer and Shipley (Kama Sutra)
Papa Rolled His Own	Tommy James and the Shondells
"Cellophane Symphony"*	(Roulette)
Pledge of Allegiance	David Peel and the Lower East Side
"The American Revolution"*	(Elektra)
The Pot Smoker's Song "Velvet Gloves and Spit"	Neil Diamond (MCA)
Roll Your Own	Commander Cody and the Lost Planet Airmen
"Tales from the Ozone"*	(Warner Brothers)
Roll Your Own "The Fabulous Poodles"	The Fabulous Poodles (Epic)
Seeds and Stems	Commander Cody and the Lost Planet Airmen
"Lost in the Ozone"	(Paramount)
Shanty "Jonathan Edwards"*	Jonathan Edwards (Capricorn)
Take a Chance on the Viper	Jim Kweskin and the Jug Band
"Jim Kweskin and the Jug Band"*	(Vanguard)
Talking Cancer Blues "Van Ronk"*	Dave Van Ronk (Fantasy)
Twigs and Seeds "Nothing but a Breeze"*	Jesse Winchester (Bearsville)
Up in Smoke "Up in Smoke" (Soundtrack)	Cheech and Chong (Warner Brothers)
Wildwood Weed "Jim Stafford"	Jim Stafford (MGM)

REFERENCE SONGS

Along Comes Mary "The Association's Greatest Hits" "And Along Comes . . . The Association"*	The Association (Warner Brothers) (Warner Brothers)
The Alphabet Song	David Peel and the Lower East Side
"Have a Marijuana"*	(Elektra)

REFERENCE SONGS

Coming into Los Angeles	Arlo Guthrie
"The Best of Arlo Guthrie"	(Reprise)
"Woodstock" (Soundtrack)	(Cotillion)
Heighty-Hi	Lee Michaels
"Lee Michaels"*	(A&M)
Let's Go Get Stoned	Ray Charles
"A Man and His Music"	(ABC)
Let Me Ride	Bloodstone
"Unreal"	(London)
Long Haired Country Boy	Charlie Daniels
"Fire on the Mountain"	(Epic)
Mayrowana	Pete Seeger
"Young vs. Old"	(Columbia)
Midnight Creeper	Elvin Bishop
"Hog Heaven"	(Capricorn)
No No Song	Ringo Starr
"Blasts from Your Past"	(Apple)
+No No Song	Hoyt Axton
"Southbound"*	(A&M)
"Road Songs"*	(A&M)
Oh Jamaica	Country Joe McDonald
"Paradise with an Ocean View"*	(Fantasy)
Okie from Muskogee	Merle Haggard
"Merle Haggard's Greatest Hits"	(Capitol)
+Oakie from Meskogee	Phil Ochs
"Gunfight at Carnegie Hall"	(A&M)
+Okie from Muskogee	Teegarden and Van Winkle
"Teegarden and Van Winkle"*	(Westbound)
Outside of a Small Circle of Friends	Phil Ochs
"Chords of Fame"	(A&M)
Panama Red	New Riders of the Purple Sage
"The Best of the New Riders of the Purple Sage"	(Columbia)
"The Adventures of Panama Red"	(Columbia)
Rainy Day Women ♯12 & 35	Bob Dylan
"Bob Dylan's Greatest Hits"	(Columbia)
"Blonde on Blonde"	(Columbia)
Saddle Tramp	Charlie Daniels
"Saddle Tramp"	(Epic)

REFERENCE SONGS

Smokin' "Boston"	Boston (Epic)
Smokin' in the Boy's Room "Yeah"	Brownsville Station (Big Tree)
Stoned "Positive Vibrations"	Ten Years After (Columbia)
Stoned "Orleans"*	Orleans (ABC)
Talking Vietnam Pot Luck Blues "The Compleat Tom Paxton"	Tom Paxton (Elektra)
Tokin's "Steve Miller Band Number Five"	Steve Miller Band (Capitol)
Uneasy Rider "Honey in the Rock"*	Charlie Daniels (Epic)
You're a Viper "Dave Van Ronk and the Jug Stompers"*	Dave Van Ronk (Verve/Forecast)

YOUR ADDITIONAL SONGS

_____

_____

_____

_____

_____

"The Pusher"

CLASSICS

The Pusher "The ABC Collection" "Live Steppenwolf" "Early Steppenwolf"	Steppenwolf (ABC) (ABC/Dunhill) (ABC/Dunhill)

DEFINITIVE SONGS

Candy Man "Donovan P. Leitch"	Donovan (Janus)
Dealer/Spanish Rose "Inner Secrets"	Santana (Columbia)
Drug Dealer "The Reggie Knighton Band"*	The Reggie Knighton Band (Columbia)
I'm Waiting for the Man "1969 Velvet Underground Live" "Live at Max's Kansas City"	The Velvet Underground (Mercury) (Cotillion)
+I'm Waiting for the Man "Live—Take No Prisoners"	Lou Reed (Arista)
Important Exportin' Man "The Adventures of Panama Red"	New Riders of the Purple Sage (Columbia)
Look Out Johnny (There's a Monkey on Your Back) "Another Night"	The Hollies (Epic)
The Neighborhood Man "Mark-Almond 73"	The Mark-Almond Band (Columbia)
Rainy Day Man "James Taylor"*	James Taylor (Apple)
Uncle Charlie "Inside Bert Sommer"*	Bert Sommer (Eleuthera)

YOUR ADDITIONAL SONGS

_____

_____

_____

_____

_____

ECOLOGY/CONSERVATION

Ecology/Conservation—
"Where Do the Children Play?" cries Cat Stevens.
"Don't Go Near the Water" exhort the Beach Boys.
"Whose Garden Was This?" asks Tom Paxton.
"Nature's Disappearing" moans John Mayall.

This certainly seems to be the most important social concern for rock as we enter the '80s. These songs cover a wide range of problems and solutions. The pollution of our environment, the abuse of our natural resources, the question of nuclear waste, and man's insensitivity to endangered species are prime topics in this important category. (N.B. Songs pertaining to our most threatening ecological concern—control of nuclear energy—are listed with an (N) following the song title.)

+Same as Song Above
*Hard-to-find Songs/Albums

CLASSICS

Don't Go Near the Water "Holland"	The Beach Boys (Brother/Reprise)
Nature's Disappearing "U.S.A. Union"	John Mayall (Polydor)
Where Do the Children Play? "Tea for the Tillerman"	Cat Stevens (A&M)
Whose Garden Was This? "Tom Paxton 6"*	Tom Paxton (Elektra)
+Whose Garden Was This? "Whose Garden Was This?"	John Denver (RCA)
Wind on the Water "Wind on the Water"	David Crosby/Graham Nash (ABC)

THEMATIC ALBUMS

"Environment/Evolution"*	Ecology (Happy Tiger Records)
"God Bless the Grass"	Pete Seeger (Columbia)

DEFINITIVE SONGS

Air | Various Artists
"Hair" (Soundtrack) | (RCA)
"Hair—Original Broadway Play" | (RCA)

Beaks of Eagles (California Saga Part 2) | The Beach Boys
"Holland" | (Brother/Reprise)

Big Yellow Taxi | Joni Mitchell
"Ladies of the Canyon" | (Reprise)
"Miles of Aisles" | (Asylum)

+Big Yellow Taxi | Bob Dylan
"Dylan" | (Columbia)

Black Waters | Jean Ritchie
"None but One" | (Sire)

Bless Me Miss America | Sam Neely
"Sam Neely 2"* | (Capitol)

Blood on the Ice | Country Joe McDonald
"Goodbye Blues" | (Fantasy)

Blue Water | Poco
"Crazy Eyes" | (Epic)

Cement Octopus | Pete Seeger
"God Bless the Grass" | (Columbia)

The Clearwater | Pete Seeger
"Rainbow Race" | (Columbia)

Coyote | Country Joe McDonald
"Rock and Roll from Planet Earth" | (Fantasy)

Coyote, My Little Brother | Pete Seeger
"God Bless the Grass" | (Columbia)

Day in the Life of a Tree | The Beach Boys
"Holland" | (Brother/Reprise)

Don't Kill the Whale | Yes
"Tormato" | (Atlantic)

Earth Anthem | The Turtles
"Battle of the Bands"* | (White Whale)

Ecology Song | Stephen Stills
"Stephen Stills 2" | (Atlantic)

Farewell Fairbanks | Randy Edleman
"Farewell Fairbanks"* | (20th Century Records)

DEFINITIVE SONGS

Farewell to Tarwathie
"Colors of the Day/The Best of Judy
     Collins"

Judy Collins
(Elektra)

For What It's Worth
"The Muppet Show Two"

The Muppets
(Arista)

Garbage
"Circles and Seasons"

Pete Seeger
(Warner Brothers)

Garden of Eden

New Riders of the Purple
     Sage

"New Riders of the Purple Sage"

(Columbia)

Garden Song
"Circles and Seasons"

Pete Seeger
(Warner Brothers)

God Bless the Grass
"God Bless the Grass"

Pete Seeger
(Columbia)

Guns Guns Guns
"Rockin' "

The Guess Who
(RCA)

+Guns Guns Guns
"Dreams of a Child"

Burton Cummings
(Portrait)

I'm an American Child (on a Nuclear
     Pile) (N)
"Transcendence"

Shawn Phillips

(RCA)

I Don't Eat Animals
"Leftover Wine"*

Melanie
(Buddah)

The Japanese Song (Side 2, Cut 4)
"The Global Blues"

Danny O'Keefe
(Warner Brothers)

Keep Our Country Green
"Movin' On"

John Mayall
(Polydor)

King of Trees
"Buddah and the Chocolate Box"

Cat Stevens
(A&M)

The Land Will Roll On
"Swallowed Up in the Great American
     Heartland"*

Tom Pacheco
(RCA)

Last Lonely Eagle
"The Best of New Riders of the
     Purple Sage"

New Riders of the Purple
     Sage
(Columbia)

The Last Resort
"Hotel California"

The Eagles
(Asylum)

Little Blue Whale
"Goodbye Blues"

Country Joe McDonald
(Fantasy)

DEFINITIVE SONGS

Mercy Mercy Me (Ecology)　　　Marvin Gaye
"What's Going On"　　　(Tamla)
"Anthology"　　　(Motown)

The Most Beautiful World in the　　　Harry Nilsson
　　World
"Son of Schmilsson"　　　(RCA)

Mother　　　Chicago
"Chicago III"　　　(Columbia)

Mother Country　　　Bonnie Koloc
"You're Gonna Love Yourself in the　　　(Ovation)
　　Morning"*

Mother Earth　　　Tom Rush
"Merrimac County"*　　　(Columbia)

My Dirty Stream (Hudson River　　　Pete Seeger
　　Song)
"God Bless the Grass"　　　(Columbia)

Nature's Way　　　Spirit
"Twelve Dreams of Dr. Sardonicus"　　　(Epic)
"Spirit Live"　　　(Potato)

No More Nukes (N)　　　Avis Davis and Joy Rider
(45 RPM Single)*　　　(Monogram)

North Sea Oil　　　Jethro Tull
"Stormwatch"　　　(Chrysalis)

Oil on the Water　　　Randall's Island
"Rock and Roll City"*　　　(Polydor)

The Oil Song　　　Steve Forbert
(45 RPM Single)　　　(Columbia)

Only So Much Oil in the Ground　　　Tower of Power
"Urban Renewal"　　　(United Artists)

Pacific Ocean Blue　　　Dennis Wilson
"Pacific Ocean Blue"　　　(Caribou)

Paradise　　　The Everly Brothers
"Pass the Chicken and Listen"*　　　(RCA)

Plutonium Is Forever (N)　　　John Hall
"No Nukes"　　　(Asylum)

Pollution　　　The Chambers Brothers
"New Generation"　　　(Columbia)

Power (N)　　　John Hall
"Power"　　　(Columbia)
"No Nukes"　　　(Asylum)

DEFINITIVE SONGS

Pull the Damn Thing Down
"Rebel"

John Miles
(London)

Putting It Back
"Recycled"

Edgar Winter
(Blue Sky)

Richland, Washington (N)
"Ain't It Something"*

James Talley
(Capitol)

Rocky Mountain High
"John Denver's Greatest Hits"
"Rocky Mountain High"

John Denver
(RCA)
(RCA)

Sanctuary (N)
"American Dreams"

Jesse Colin Young
(Elektra)

Save the Planet
"Road Work"

Edgar Winter
(Epic)

Save the Whales
"Save the Whales"

Country Joe McDonald
(Fantasy)

Seventy Miles
"God Bless the Grass"

Pete Seeger
(Columbia)

Shut 'em Down (N)
"1980"

Gil Scott-Heron
(Arista)

Subway to the Country
"Subway to the Country"*

David Ackles
(Elektra)

Tapestry
"Tapestry"

Don McLean
(United Artists)

To the Last Whale
"Wind on the Water"
"The Best of David Crosby and
    Graham Nash"

David Crosby/Graham Nash
(ABC)
(ABC)

Town Square
"Pursuit of Happiness"*

Rupert Holmes
(Private Stock)

The Tree Song
"Swallowed Up in the Great American
    Heartland"*

Tom Pacheco
(RCA)

We're Running Out
"Albert Hammond"*

Albert Hammond
(Mums/CBS)

What Have They Done to the Rain?
"The History of the Searchers"
"The Golden Hour of the Searchers"

The Searchers
(Pye)
(Golden Hour)

+What Have They Done to the Rain?
"In Concert"

Joan Baez
(Vanguard)

DEFINITIVE SONGS

+What Have They Done to the Rain?   Marianne Faithful
  "Marianne Faithful"*   (London)

REFERENCE SONGS

  After the Gold Rush   Neil Young
  "Decade"   (Reprise)
  "After the Gold Rush"   (Reprise)
+After the Gold Rush   Prelude
  "After the Gold Rush"   (Island)
  Big Thirst   Jim Capaldi
  "Oh How We Danced"   (Island)
  The Faucets Are Dripping   Pete Seeger
  "God Bless the Grass"   (Columbia)
  Here We Are in the Years   Neil Young
  "Neil Young"   (Reprise)
  Let It Rain   Tom Pacheco
  "The Outsider"*   (RCA)
  Mother Nature   The Temptations
  "Anthology—Tenth Anniversary   (Motown)
    Special"
  My Rainbow Race   Pete Seeger
  "The World of Pete Seeger"   (Columbia)
  "Rainbow Race"   (Columbia)
  Nuclear Apathy (N)   Crack the Sky
  "Safety in Numbers"   (Lifesong)
  Paradise   John Prine
  "John Prine"*   (Atlantic)
  This Good Earth   Jim Dawson
  "The Essential Jim Dawson"   (Kama Sutra)
  Time Is Running Out   Steve Winwood
  "Steve Winwood"   (Island)
  What About Me   Quicksilver Messenger
                                             Service
  "What About Me"   (Capitol)
  "Anthology"   (Capitol)
+What About Me   Richie Havens
  "The Great Blind Degree"*   (Stormy Forest)
  Where Do We Go from Here?   The Band
  "Cahoots"   (Capitol)

REFERENCE SONGS

The World Beyond "Words and Pictures"*	Bobby Goldsboro (United Artists)
You and Me "Seventh Sojourn"	The Moody Blues (Threshold)

YOUR ADDITIONAL SONGS

_____

_____

_____

_____

_____

FATHERS

Fathers—some dead, some living, some loved, some despised, some willing and able, some caught by surprise.

These songs explore the complete range of feelings toward perhaps the most important man in our life . . . at least for a part of it. And don't forget, grandfathers are fathers too! Rock and roll writers have not forgotten, and their "grandfather" songs are included here.

Related Categories: Children, Divorce, Marriage, Mothers, Pregnancy

+Same as Song Above
*Hard-to-find Songs/Albums

CLASSICS

Danny's Song	Loggins and Messina
"Sittin' In"	(Columbia)
"The Best of Friends"	(Columbia)
"On Stage"	(Columbia)
+Danny's Song	Anne Murray
"Country"	(Capitol)
My Father	Judy Collins
"Colors of the Day/The Best of Judy Collins"	(Elektra)
My Father	Melanie
"Good Book"*	(Buddah)
Papa Was a Rolling Stone	The Temptations
"Anthology—Tenth Anniversary Special"	(Motown)
Younger Generation	The Lovin' Spoonful
"The Very Best of the Lovin' Spoonful"	(Kama Sutra)
"Everything Playing"*	(Kama Sutra)
+Younger Generation	John Sebastian
"John Sebastian Songbook"	(Kama Sutra)
+Younger Generation	The Critters
"Touch 'n Go with the Critters"*	(Project 3)

DEFINITIVE SONGS

Absentee Father	Killough and Eckley
"Killough and Eckley"*	(Epic)

DEFINITIVE SONGS

Adam and I
"From Mighty Oaks"

Ray Thomas
(Threshold)

Another Try
"Holiday"
"Live"

America
(Warner Brothers)
(Warner Brothers)

Can't Stop My Love for You
"Resolution"*

Andy Pratt
(Nemperor)

The Captain and the Kid
"Havana Daydream"
"You Had to Be There"
"Before the Salt"

Jimmy Buffett
(ABC)
(ABC)
(Barnaby)

Cat's in the Cradle
"Verities & Balderdash"

Harry Chapin
(Elektra)

Color Him Father
"Color Him Father"*
(45 RPM Single)*

The Winstons
(Metromedia)
(Metromedia)

+Color Him Father
"At Home"

O. C. Smith
(Columbia)

Come Home Mama
"Silk Torpedo"

Pretty Things
(Swan Song)

Daddy Don't Go
"Jennifer Warnes"

Jennifer Warnes
(Arista)

Daddy's Baby
"Walking Man"

James Taylor
(Warner Brothers)

Daddy's Tune
"The Pretender"

Jackson Browne
(Asylum)

Dear Father
"Yesterdays"

Yes
(Atlantic)

Don't Cry Daddy
"50 World Wide Gold Award Hits"

Elvis Presley
(RCA)

Earthquake in L.A.
"Reflection in a Mud Puddle"*

Dory Previn
(United Artists)

Embrace Me You Child
"No Secrets"

Carly Simon
(Elektra)

Fairweather Father
"Another Passenger"

Carly Simon
(Elektra)

Family Man
"In the Pocket"

James Taylor
(Warner Brothers)

DEFINITIVE SONGS

Father "Back to Earth"	Cat Stevens (A&M)
Father to Son "Stolen Time"*	Lucy Simon (RCA)
Father And Son "Tea for the Tillerman" "Greatest Hits"	Cat Stevens (A&M) (A&M)
+Father and Son "The Great Blind Degree"* "Richie Havens on Stage"*	Richie Havens (Stormy Forest) (Stormy Forest)
For My Father "Melanie"*	Melanie (Buddah)
Granddad "Memories"	John Mayall (Polydor)
Granddad "New Birth"*	New Birth (Buddah)
Grandpa Was a Carpenter "Sweet Revenge" "Prime Prine"	John Prine (Atlantic) (Atlantic)
Hello Grandpa "The Outsider"*	Tom Pacheco (RCA)
I Never Knew My Father "Lines on the Paper"*	Kate Wolf (Kaleidoscope)
Memo to Son "Sail Away"	Randy Newman (Warner Brothers)
My Daddy and Me "Something in My Life"	Tom Paxton (Private Stock)
My Father Died "Lucy Simon"*	Lucy Simon (RCA)
My Father's Room "The American Album"	Allan Taylor (United Artists)
My Father's Song "Lazy Afternoon"	Barbra Streisand (Columbia)
My Father's Shoes "Will o' the Wisp"	Leon Russell (Shelter)
My Old Man "Garden of Joy"*	Jim Kweskin and the Jug Band (Reprise)

DEFINITIVE SONGS

My Old Man "Mr. Bojangles"	Jerry Jeff Walker (Atco)
+My Old Man "Rhymes and Reasons"	John Denver (RCA)
My Old Man "Say It in Private"	Steve Goodman (Asylum)
My Old Man "New Boots and Panties"	Ian Dury (Arista)
Nothing's Too Good for My Little Girl "The Mamas and The Papas Golden Era Vol. II"	The Mamas and The Papas (ABC/Dunhill)
Patches "Soul Years"	Clarence Carter (Atco)
Please Daddy "Farewell Andromeda"	John Denver (RCA)
Ready or Not "For Everyman"	Jackson Browne (Asylum)
Rockin' Chair "A Man Must Carry On"	Jerry Jeff Walker (MCA)
See How the Years Have Gone By "Valdy"*	Valdy (A&M)
See Us When You Can "Goodnight Mrs. Calabash"*	Ian Thomas Band (Chrysalis)
So Long Dad "Live"	Randy Newman (Reprise)
+So Long Dad "Nilsson Sings Newman"	Harry Nilsson (RCA)
+So Long Dad "This Price Is Right"	Alan Price (London)
Song for My Father "Stay the Night"	Jane Olivor (Columbia)
Steamboat Row "Gerry Rafferty"	Gerry Rafferty (Visa)
Tangled Up Puppet "Portrait Gallery"	Harry Chapin (Elektra)
This Old Man "Crystal Ball"	Styx (A&M)
Watching Scotty Grow "10th Anniversary Album"	Bobby Goldsboro (United Artists)

DEFINITIVE SONGS

When I Was a Child   Loggins and Messina
"Native Sons"   (Columbia)

REFERENCE SONGS

Adam Raised a Cain   Bruce Springsteen
"Darkness on the Edge of Town"   (Columbia)

Alone Again, Naturally   Gilbert O'Sullivan
"Himself"   (MAM)

Angels Rejoiced   Nicolette Larson
"Nicolette"   (Warner Brothers)

A Boy Named Sue   Johnny Cash
"At San Quentin"   (Columbia)
"Greatest Hits"   (Columbia)

Daddy, Don't Live in That New York   Steely Dan
    City No More
"Katy Lied"   (ABC)

Dancin' Boy   Harry Chapin
"Living Room Suite"   (Elektra)

Everything I Own   Bread
"The Best of Bread"   (Elektra)

Factory   Bruce Springsteen
"Darkness on the Edge of Town"   (Columbia)

Father to Son   Queen
"Queen II"   (Elektra)

Humpty Dumpty   Joy of Cooking
"Closer to the Ground"*   (Capitol)

Marley Purt Drive   The Bee Gees
"Odessa"   (RSO)

Mother   John Lennon
"John Lennon/Plastic Ono Band"   (Apple)

My Daddy Knows Best   The Marvelettes
"Anthology"   (Motown)

To Daddy   Emmylou Harris
"Quarter Moon in a Ten Cent Town"   (Warner Brothers)
"Profile: Best of Emmylou Harris"   (Warner Brothers)

Will We Ever Find Our Fathers   Mary Travers
"It's in Every One of Us"*   (Chrysalis)

With My Daddy in the Attic   Dory Previn
"On My Way to Where?"*   (United Artists)

REFERENCE SONGS

The World Beyond   Bobby Goldsboro
"Words and Pictures"*   (United Artists)

YOUR ADDITIONAL SONGS

_____

_____

_____

_____

_____

FREEDOM

Freedom—just another word for . . .
Freedom means different things to different people, but in each of these songs there is a thread of continuity: the indomitable human spirit with its unquenchable thirst for personal and social freedom.

Related Categories: America, Injustice, Prisons, Protest/Revolution, Racism/Prejudice, Rat Race

+Same as Song Above
*Hard-to-find Songs/Albums

CLASSICS

Blowin' in the Wind	Bob Dylan
"The Freewheelin' Bob Dylan"	(Columbia)
"Bob Dylan's Greatest Hits"	(Columbia)
"Before the Flood" (with The Band)	(Asylum)
"Live at Budokan"	(Columbia)
+Blowin' in the Wind	Stevie Wonder
"Greatest Hits"	(Tamla)
+Blowin' in the Wind	Peter, Paul and Mary
"In the Wind"	(Warner Brothers)
"Ten Years Together"	(Warner Brothers)
"Peter, Paul and Mary in Concert"	(Warner Brothers)
+Blowin' in the Wind	Joan Baez
"Any Day Now"	(Vanguard)
"From Every Stage"	(A&M)
+Blowin' in the Wind	Jackie DeShannon
"In the Wind"*	(Imperial)
+Blowin' in the Wind	The Hollies
"Words and Music by Bob Dylan"*	(Epic)
+Blowin' in the Wind	Cher
"Cher Sings the Hits"*	(Springboard)
+Blowin' in the Wind	The Staple Singers
"Use What You Got"	(Fantasy)
Find the Cost of Freedom	Crosby, Stills, Nash & Young
"Four Way Street"	(Atlantic)
"So Far"	(Atlantic)

CLASSICS

Freedom	Richie Havens
"Woodstock" (Soundtrack)	(Cotillion)
"Richie Havens on Stage"*	(Stormy Forest)
If I Had a Hammer	Peter, Paul and Mary
"Peter, Paul and Mary"	(Warner Brothers)
"Ten Years Together"	(Warner Brothers)
+If I Had a Hammer	Odetta
"The Essential Odetta"	(Vanguard)
+If I Had a Hammer	Jackie DeShannon
"In the Wind"*	(Imperial)
+If I Had a Hammer	Johnny Rivers
"Rivers Rocks the Folks"*	(Imperial)
+If I Had a Hammer	Billy Preston
"The Original Billy Preston . . . Soul'd Out"	(Crescendo)
+If I Had a Hammer	Pete Seeger
"The World of Pete Seeger"	(Columbia)
+If I Had a Hammer	The Weavers
"Greatest Hits"	(Vanguard)
"Reunion At Carnegie Hall"	(Vanguard)
People Got to Be Free	The Young Rascals
"Freedom Suite"	(Atlantic)
(45 RPM Single)	(Atlantic)
+People Got to Be Free	Felix Cavaliere
"Castles in the Air"	(Epic)

THEMATIC ALBUMS

"Sometime in New York City"	John Lennon (Apple)
"The Times They Are a Changin'"	Bob Dylan (Columbia)

DEFINITIVE SONGS

Angela	John Lennon
"Sometime in New York City"	(Apple)
Badlands	Bruce Springsteen
"Darkness on the Edge of Town"	(Columbia)
Ballad of Easy Rider	The Byrds
"The Best of the Byrds Greatest Hits Vol. II"	(Columbia)

DEFINITIVE SONGS

"Easy Rider" (Soundtrack) — (ABC/Dunhill)

Be Free
"Finale" — Loggins and Messina
(Columbia)

Chimes of Freedom
"Another Side of Bob Dylan" — Bob Dylan
(Columbia)

+Chimes of Freedom
"The Byrds' Greatest Hits"
"Mr. Tambourine Man" — The Byrds
(Columbia)
(Columbia)

Don't Ever Take Away My Freedom
"Peter"* — Peter Yarrow
(Warner Brothers)

Easy to Be Free
"Rick Nelson in Concert" — Rick Nelson
(MCA)

Equal Rights
"Peter Tosh" — Peter Tosh
(Columbia)

Everybody's Got a Right to Live
"Now" — Pete Seeger
(Columbia)

Every Man Wants to Be Free
"Weeds"* — Brewer and Shipley
(Kama Sutra)

Ezy Ryder
"Cry of Love"
"The Essential Jimi Hendrix" — Jimi Hendrix
(Reprise)
(Reprise)

Fifty States of Freedom
"Tarkio"* — Brewer and Shipley
(Kama Sutra)

First Things First
"Stills" — Stephen Stills
(Columbia)

Free
"Chicago III" — Chicago
(Columbia)

Freeda People
"Mind Games" — John Lennon
(Apple)

Freedom
"The Isley's Greatest Hits"
"The Best . . . Isley Brothers" — The Isley Brothers
(T-Neck)
(Buddah)

Freedom Highway

"Encore" — Brian Auger and Julie
    Tippetts
(Warner Brothers)

Freedom's Star
"Serendipity Singers"* — Serendipity Singers
(Philips)

Free in America
"Free in America" — Ben Sidran
(Arista)

DEFINITIVE SONGS

Free the People "The Best of Delaney and Bonnie"	Delaney and Bonnie (Atco)
Good Morning Freedom "Blue Mink"*	Blue Mink (Philadelphia International)
Got to Be Free "Lola Versus Powerman and the Moneygoround"	The Kinks (Reprise)
Hear Me Out "Songs in the Key of Life"	Stevie Wonder (Tamla)
Hurricane "Desire"	Bob Dylan (Columbia)
I'm a Free Man "Clayton"*	David Clayton-Thomas (ABC)
If Dogs Run Free "New Morning"	Bob Dylan (Columbia)
I Feel Free "Best of Cream" "Fresh Cream"	Cream (RSO) (RSO)
If I Were Free "See What Tomorrow Brings"	Peter, Paul and Mary (Warner Brothers)
I Just Want to Be Free "Chicago III"	Chicago (Columbia)
I'm Free "Tommy" "Tommy" (Soundtrack)	The Who (MCA) (MCA)
I Shall Be Free "The Freewheelin' Bob Dylan"	Bob Dylan (Columbia)
It Isn't Nice "Fifth Album"	Judy Collins (Elektra)
I Wanna Be Free "The Monkees' Greatest Hits"	The Monkees (Arista)
I Wish I Knew How It Feels to Be Free "Rhymes and Reasons"	John Denver (RCA)
+I Wish I Knew How It Feels to Be Free "Mary"*	Mary Travers (Warner Brothers)
+I Wish I Knew How It Feels to Be Free "MacArthur Park"	Ray Charles (ABC)

DEFINITIVE SONGS

Justice "O Lucky Man"	Alan Price (Warner Brothers)
Let My People Be "TRB II"	The Tom Robinson Band (Harvest)
Links in the Chain "I Ain't Marching Anymore"	Phil Ochs (Elektra)
Maggie's Farm "Bob Dylan's Greatest Hits Vol. II" "Bringing It All Back Home"	Bob Dylan (Columbia) (Columbia)
+Maggie's Farm "Something Else Again"	Richie Havens (Stormy Forest)
Many a Mile to Freedom "Low Spark of High Heeled Boys"	Traffic (Island)
+Many a Mile to Freedom "Blowin' Away"	Joan Baez (A&M)
Mother Freedom "The Best of Bread"	Bread (Elektra)
Nigger Charlie "Music Is My Life"	Billy Preston (A&M)
Oh Freedom "We Shall Overcome"	Pete Seeger (Columbia)
Power in the Darkness "Power in the Darkness"	The Tom Robinson Band (Harvest)
Simple Man "Run with the Pack"	Bad Company (Swan Song)
Sing a Simple Song of Freedom (45 RPM Single)*	Tim Hardin (Columbia)
Someday We'll All Be Free "Benny and Us"	Average White Band and Ben E. King (Atlantic)
+Someday We'll All Be Free "The Best of Donny Hathaway"	Donny Hathaway (Atco)
Stone Free "Smash Hits"	Jimi Hendrix (Reprise)
T.V. Guide "Earth and Sky"	Graham Nash (Capitol)
To Be Free "Nomadness" "The Best of Strawbs"	Strawbs (A&M) (A&M)

DEFINITIVE SONGS

Waves of Freedom
"A Country Dream"*
What about Me

   Eric Andersen
   (Vanguard)
   Quicksilver Messenger
     Service

"What about Me"
"Anthology"

   (Capitol)
   (Capitol)

+What about Me
"The Great Blind Degree"*

   Richie Havens
   (Stormy Forest)

REFERENCE SONGS

Abraham, Martin and John
"Abraham, Martin and John"

   Dion
   (Laurie)

+Abraham, Martin and John

   Smokey Robinson & the
     Miracles

"Anthology"

   (Motown)

+Abraham, Martin and John
"Love Lifted Me"

   Kenny Rogers
   (United Artists)

Free Bird
"One More from the Road"
"Pronounced Leh-Nerd, Skin-Nerd"

   Lynyrd Skynyrd
   (MCA)
   (MCA)

Freedom Rider
"John Barleycorn Must Die"

   Traffic
   (United Artists)

Running to My Freedom
"Leo Sayer"

   Leo Sayer
   (Warner Brothers)

Why Can't I Be Free
"Twelve Dreams of Dr. Sardonicus"

   Spirit
   (Epic)

YOUR ADDITIONAL SONGS

_____

_____

_____

_____

_____

FRIENDSHIP

Friendship—winter, spring, summer, or fall, all you gotta do is call . . .
   Songs of "Brotherhood" praise the dreams of what ought to be among all people. These songs of "Friendship" embody the reality of what is among a very few treasured people.
   They reflect thoughts of great friendships and lost friendships; the times when you need a friend and when a friend needs you.

Related Categories: Brotherhood

   +Same as Song Above
   *Hard-to-find Songs/Albums

CLASSICS

Bridge over Troubled Water "Simon and Garfunkel's Greatest Hits"	Simon and Garfunkel (Columbia)
"Bridge over Troubled Water"	(Columbia)
+Bridge over Troubled Water "Live Rhymin'"	Paul Simon (Columbia)
+Bridge over Troubled Water "What the World Needs Now Is Love"*	Tom Clay (Mowest)
+Bridge over Troubled Water "Gimme Shelter"	Merry Clayton (Ode)
+Bridge over Troubled Water "Why Can't I Touch You"	Ronnie Dyson (Columbia)
+Bridge over Troubled Water "Quiet Fire"	Roberta Flack (Atlantic)
+Bridge over Troubled Water "Greatest Hits"	Aretha Franklin (Columbia)
+Bridge over Troubled Water "Standing Ovation"	Gladys Knight and the Pips (Soul)
+Bridge over Troubled Water "That's the Way It Is"	Elvis Presley (RCA)
+Bridge over Troubled Water "Sedaka Live in Australia"	Neil Sedaka (RCA)
+Bridge over Troubled Water "Let Me Be Your Woman"	Linda Clifford (RSO)

CLASSICS

Lean on Me "Still Bill" "The Best of Bill Withers"	Bill Withers (Sussex) (Sussex)
+Lean on Me "Edwin Hawkins Live"*	The Edwin Hawkins Singers (Buddah)
Thank You for Being a Friend "All This and Heaven Too"	Andrew Gold (Asylum)
With a Little Help from My Friends "Sgt. Pepper's Lonely Hearts Club Band"	The Beatles (Capitol)
+With a Little Help from My Friends "With a Little Help from My Friends" "Mad Dogs and Englishmen" "Joe Cocker's Greatest Hits"	Joe Cocker (A&M) (A&M) (A&M)
+With a Little Help from My Friends "Sgt. Pepper's Lonely Hearts Club Band Soundtrack"	Peter Frampton/The Bee Gees (RSO)
+With a Little Help from My Friends "The World of Ike and Tina Turner"	Ike and Tina Turner (United Artists)
You've Got a Friend "Tapestry" "Her Greatest Hits"	Carole King (Ode) (Ode)
+You've Got a Friend "Greatest Hits" "Mud Slide Slim and the Blue Horizon"	James Taylor (Warner Brothers) (Warner Brothers)
+You've Got a Friend "The Best of Donny Hathaway"	Donny Hathaway (Atco)
+You've Got a Friend "Roberta Flack and Donny Hathaway"	Roberta Flack and Donny Hathaway (Atlantic)
+You've Got a Friend "Talk It Over in the Morning"	Anne Murray (Capitol)

DEFINITIVE SONGS

Absent Friend "Nomadness"	Strawbs (A&M)

DEFINITIVE SONGS

All I Really Want to Do	Bob Dylan
"Bob Dylan's Greatest Hits, Vol. II"	(Columbia)
"Another Side of Bob Dylan"	(Columbia)
+All I Really Want to Do	The Byrds
"The Byrds' Greatest Hits"	(Columbia)
"Mr. Tambourine Man"	(Columbia)
+All I Really Want to Do	Cher
"Cher"*	(United Artists)
"Golden Hits"	(Sunset)
+All I Really Want to Do	The Hollies
"Words and Music by Bob Dylan"*	(Epic)
All My Friends	Danny O'Keefe
"American Roulette"	(Warner Brothers)
Backstreets	Bruce Springsteen
"Born to Run"	(Columbia)
Ballad of Frankie Lee and Judas Priest	Bob Dylan
"John Wesley Harding"	(Columbia)
Best Friend	Phil Cody
"Phil Cody"*	(Reprise)
Best Friends	Flo and Eddie
"Moving Targets"	(Columbia)
Best of Friends	Peter, Paul and Mary
"Reunion"	(Warner Brothers)
Best of Friends	Joan Baez
"Where Are You Now, My Son?"	(A&M)
Can We Still Be Friends	Todd Rundgren
"Hermit of Mink Hollow"	(Bearsville)
+Can We Still Be Friends	Robert Palmer
"Secrets"	(A&M)
The Closest Friends	Lucy Simon
"Lucy Simon"*	(RCA)
Count Me In	Gary Lewis and the Playboys
"The Very Best of Gary Lewis and the Playboys"	(United Artists)
"Golden Greats"*	(Liberty)
Dear Friend	Wings
"Wild Life"	(Apple)
Dear Friends	Queen
"Sheer Heart Attack"	(Elektra)

Do U No Hu Yor Phrenz R?
"Ginger Baker's Air Force 2"

Ginger Baker
(Atco)

Everybody Needs a Friend
"To the Heart"

The Mark-Almond Band
(ABC)

Feel No Fret
"Feel No Fret"

Average White Band
(Atlantic)

Fine Friends
"Fine Friends"*

Lesley Duncan
(Epic)

Forever
"Forever"

Orleans
(Infinity)

Friends
"Good Vibrations—The Best of the
    Beach Boys"
"Friends"

The Beach Boys
(Brother/Reprise)

(Brother/Reprise)

Friends
"Friends"

Elton John
(Paramount)

Friends
"The Best . . . Buzzy Linhart"

Buzzy Linhart
(Kama Sutra)

+Friends
"The Divine Miss M"
"Live at Last"

Bette Midler
(Atlantic)
(Atlantic)

Friends
"Inside Bert Sommer"*

Bert Sommer
(Eleuthera)

Friends
"Feather"*

Feather
(Columbia)

Friends
"The Best of Mark-Almond"

The Mark-Almond Band
(Blue Thumb)

Friends
"Giant for a Day"

Gentle Giant
(Capitol)

Friends Again
"Tarzana Kid"*

John Sebastian
(Reprise)

Friends Die Easy
"Second Thoughts"*
"Track 5"

McKendree Spring
(MCA)
(MCA)

Friends Last Longer
"No Accident"*

Driver
(A&M)

Friends with You
"Aerie"

John Denver
(RCA)

DEFINITIVE SONGS

+Friends with You   Starland Vocal Band
  "Late Night Radio"   (Windsong)

Hello Old Friend   Eric Clapton
  "No Reason to Cry"   (RSO)

Help!   The Beatles
  "The Beatles 1962–1966"   (Capitol)
  "Help!"   (Capitol)

+Help!   Henry Gross
  "Show Me to the Stage"*   (Lifesong)

How Many Friends   The Who
  "The Who By Numbers"   (MCA/Track)

I Believe in You   Gallagher and Lyle
  "Seeds"   (A&M)

I Just Want to Sing with My Friends   The Persuasions
  "I Just Want to Sing with My   (A&M)
    Friends"

If You Really Want to Be My Friend   The Rolling Stones
  "It's Only Rock and Roll"   (Rolling Stone Records)

It's So Nice to See an Old Friend   Minnie Riperton
  "Perfect Angel"   (Epic)

I Wish You Peace   The Eagles
  "One of These Nights"   (Asylum)

JB's Blues   David Crosby/Graham
     Nash

  "Whistlin' down the Wire"   (ABC)

Let It Be   The Beatles
  "Let It Be"   (Apple)
  "The Beatles 1967–1970"   (Apple)

+Let It Be   Joan Baez
  "Blessed Are . . ."   (Vanguard)

+Let It Be   John Denver
  "Poems, Prayers and Promises"   (RCA)

+Let It Be   Gladys Knight and the Pips
  "If I Were Your Woman"   (Soul)

+Let It Be   Dion
  "You're Not Alone"*   (Warner Brothers)

+Let It Be   Aretha Franklin
  "Aretha's Greatest Hits"   (Atlantic)

DEFINITIVE SONGS

+Let It Be
  "Fireworks"

José Feliciano
(RCA)

+Let It Be
  "Danny Kirwan"

Danny Kirwan
(DJM Records)

+Let It Be
  "All This and World War II"

Leo Sayer
(20th Century-Fox)

Let It Bleed
  "Let It Bleed"
  "More Hot Rocks (Big Hits and
      Fazed Cookies)"

The Rolling Stones
(London)
(London)

+Let It Bleed
  "Still Alive and Well"

Johnny Winter
(Columbia)

A Letter Sung to a Friend
  "Five Years Gone"*

Jerry Jeff Walker
(Atco)

Mr. Friend

Larry Graham and Graham
    Central Station
(Warner Brothers)

"My Radio Sure Sounds Good to Me"

My Best Friend
  "Surrealistic Pillow"

Jefferson Airplane
(RCA)

My Buddy
  "A Man Must Carry On"

Jerry Jeff Walker
(MCA)

My Friend
  "Sailor"

The Steve Miller Band
(Capitol)

No Friends Like Old Friends
  "From the Heartland"*

Becky Hobbs
(Tattoo/RCA)

Old Friends
  "Bookends"

Simon and Garfunkel
(Columbia)

+Old Friends
  "Richie Havens on Stage"*

Richie Havens
(Stormy Forest)

Old Friends
  "Old Friends"*

Mary McCaslin
(Philo)

People Love Each Other
  "Weeds"*

Brewer and Shipley
(Kama Sutra)

Ramblin' Boy
  "Ramblin' Boy"*

Tom Paxton
(Vanguard)

+Ramblin' Boy
  "Golden Apples of the Sun"

Judy Collins
(Elektra)

DEFINITIVE SONGS

Reach Out I'll Be There
"Greatest Hits"
"Anthology"

The Four Tops
(Motown)
(Motown)

+Reach Out I'll Be There
"Never Can Say Goodbye"

Gloria Gaynor
(MGM)

+Reach Out I'll Be There
"Ross"

Diana Ross
(Motown)

Remember Me My Friend
"Blue Jays"

Haywood and Lodge
(Threshold)

Sit Down Old Friend
"Sit Down Old Friend"*

Dion
(Warner Brothers)

Song for Adam
"Saturate Before Using"

Jackson Browne
(Asylum)

Song for a Friend Soon Gone
"Michael Stanley"*

Michael Stanley
(Tumbleweed)

Song for Judith
"Living"

Judy Collins
(Elektra)

That's What Friends Are For
"Fall into Spring"

Rita Coolidge
(A&M)

+That's What Friends Are For
"Words You Can Dance To"*

Steve Goodman
(Asylum)

What a Friend You Are
"Peace Will Come"*

Tom Paxton
(Reprise)

What Exactly Is a Friend?
"What Exactly Is a Friend?"*

Peter Cofield
(Metromedia)

Where Are all My Friends?

Harold Melvin and the Blue
    Notes

"To Be True"

(Philadelphia International)

Why Can't We Be Friends?
"Greatest Hits"

War
(United Artists)

Won't You Be My Friend
"I'm in You"

Peter Frampton
(A&M)

You Never Know Who Your Friends
    Are

Al Kooper

"You Never Know Who Your Friends
    Are"

(Columbia)

You're Life My Friend
"Let There Be Music"

Orleans
(Asylum)

DEFINITIVE SONGS

Your Friends   Richie Furay
"Dance a Little Light"   (Asylum)

REFERENCE SONGS

African Friend   Jimmy Buffett
"Son of a Son of a Sailor"   (ABC)

Farewell My Friend   Dennis Wilson
"Pacific Ocean Blue"   (Caribou)

Friends for the Sake of Convenience Dirty Angels
"Dirty Angels"   (A&M)

A Friend of Mine Is Going Blind   John Dawson Read
"A Friend of Mine Is Going Blind"   (Chrysalis)

Good Friend   Loggins and Messina
"Loggins and Messina"   (Columbia)

Hard to Be Friends   Kris Kristofferson
"Full Moon" (w/Rita Coolidge)   (A&M)

In Times Like These   Alan Price
"Between Today and Yesterday"*   (Warner Brothers)

Just a Friend   The Mark-Almond Band
"Other Peoples Rooms"   (Horizon/A&M)

The Killing of Georgie (Parts I and Rod Stewart
    II)
"A Night On The Town"   (Warner Brothers)

Lifesaver   Chicago
"Chicago VII"   (Columbia)

My Best Friend   The Marshall Tucker Band
"Running like the Wind"   (Capricorn)

Old Friend   Loudon Wainwright III
"Unrequited"*   (Columbia)

Omaha   Moby Grape
"Great Grape"   (Columbia)

Please Be My Friend/Take a Little   Dion
    Time
"Sanctuary"*   (Warner Brothers)

Reunions   Carly Simon
"Carly Simon"   (Elektra)

To All My Friends   Crabby Appleton
"Crabby Appleton"*   (Elektra)

REFERENCE SONGS

Whenever I Call You Friend Kenny Loggins
"Nightwatch" (Columbia)

+Whenever I Call You Friend Melissa Manchester
"Melissa Manchester" (Arista)

YOUR ADDITIONAL SONGS

_____

_____

_____

_____

_____

GROWING UP

Growing Up—we all do it—up to a point.

Growing up is a lifelong process. In some of us this topic evokes fond memories, in others great pain, and in most of us a little of both. These songs cover the entire span of time, from the early stages of growing up, to those songs reflecting back on particular moments in earlier days. (N.B. Songs about the turbulent and uncertain days of adolescence are found in the "Teen-Age Years/Adolescence" category.)

Related Categories: Changes, Children, Life, Mothers,
    Schools/Educational Process, Self-Identity

+Same as Song Above
 *Hard-to-find Songs/Albums

CLASSICS

At Seventeen "Between the Lines"	Janis Ian (Columbia)
The Circle Game "Ladies of the Canyon" "Miles of Aisles"	Joni Mitchell (Reprise) (Asylum)
+The Circle Game "The Best of Buffy Sainte-Marie"	Buffy Sainte-Marie (Vanguard)
+The Circle Game "Classic Rush" "Tom Rush"* "The Circle Game"	Tom Rush (Elektra) (Columbia) (Elektra)
+The Circle Game "Greatest Hits"	Ian and Sylvia (Vanguard)
+The Circle Game "Dave Van Ronk and the Hudson Dusters"*	Dave Van Ronk (Verve/Forecast)
Growin' Up "Greetings from Asbury Park, N.J."	Bruce Springsteen (Columbia)

THEMATIC ALBUMS

"Captain Fantastic and the Brown Dirt Cowboy"	Elton John (MCA)
"Quadrophenia"	The Who (MCA/Track)

DEFINITIVE SONGS

Acne Blues "The Last Cowboy"	Gallagher and Lyle (A&M)
Adam Raised a Cain "Darkness on the Edge of Town"	Bruce Springsteen (Columbia)
Against the Wind "Against the Wind"	Bob Seger and the Silver Bullet Band (Capitol)
All American Girl "Willard"*	John Stewart (Capitol)
All Grown Up "Showdown"	Gallagher and Lyle (A&M)
All My Choices "All My Choices"*	Mary Travers (Warner Brothers)
Almost Grown "Golden Decade"	Chuck Berry (Chess)
Almost Grown "What's Shakin' "*	The Lovin' Spoonful (Elektra)
Angie Baby "Live in London"	Helen Reddy (Capitol)
As I Come of Age "Stills"	Stephen Stills (Columbia)
+As I Come of Age "Energy"	The Pointer Sisters (Planet)
Baby Sitter "Portrait Gallery"	Harry Chapin (Elektra)
Back When My Hair Was Short "Gunhill Road"*	Gunhill Road (Kama Sutra)
Bad Boy "Can't Wait"*	Piper (A&M)
Bang Bang "Cher Superpak" "Cher's Greatest Hits" "The Very Best of Cher"	Cher (United Artists) (MCA) (United Artists)
+Bang Bang "The Chambers Brothers"	The Chambers Brothers (Columbia)
+Bang Bang "Vanilla Fudge"*	Vanilla Fudge (Atco)

DEFINITIVE SONGS

Banks of the Old Bandera
"Jerry Jeff"
Jerry Jeff Walker
(Elektra)

Barefoot Boys and Barefoot Girls
"New Arrangement"*
Jackie DeShannon
(Columbia)

Big Tree
"Ralph McTell Live"
Ralph McTell
(Fantasy)

Billy
"Sally Can't Dance"
Lou Reed
(RCA)

The Bomber

"The Best of the James Gang
   Featuring Joe Walsh"
The James Gang
   Featuring Joe Walsh
(ABC)

Born to the Breed
"Judith"
"The First Fifteen Years"
Judy Collins
(Elektra)
(Elektra)

The Boxer
"Simon and Garfunkel's Greatest
   Hits"
"Bridge over Troubled Water"
Simon and Garfunkel
(Columbia)

(Columbia)

+The Boxer
"Live Rhymin'"
Paul Simon
(Columbia)

+The Boxer
"Self Portrait"
Bob Dylan
(Columbia)

Boys in the Trees
"Boys in the Trees"
Carly Simon
(Elektra)

Brooklyn Roads
"Velvet Gloves and Spit"
Neil Diamond
(MCA)

Captain Jack
"Piano Man"
Billy Joel
(Columbia)

Carry Me
"Wind on the Water"
"The Best of David Crosby and
   Graham Nash"
David Crosby/Graham Nash
(ABC)
(ABC)

Carter Family
"No Secrets"
Carly Simon
(Elektra)

Catch Another Butterfly
"Rhymes and Reasons"
John Denver
(RCA)

City Liners
"Birth Comes to Us All"
The Good Rats
(Arista)

DEFINITIVE SONGS

Coat of Many Colors
"Pieces of the Sky"
Emmylou Harris
(Warner Brothers)

Coming Up the Hard Way
"Sleepless Nights"
Brooklyn Dreams
(Casablanca)

Coney Island Baby
"Coney Island Baby"
"Live—Take No Prisoners"
Lou Reed
(RCA)
(Arista)

Cotton Fields
"One Grain of Sand"
Odetta
(Vanguard)

+Cotton Fields
"20/20"
The Beach Boys
(Brother/Reprise)

+Cotton Fields

Creedence Clearwater
Revival

"Willy and the Poor Boys"
"1969"
(Fantasy)
(Fantasy)

+Cotton Fields
"Use What You Got"
The Staple Singers
(Fantasy)

Cut My Hair
"Quadrophenia"
The Who
(MCA)

Don't Be Denied
"Time Fades Away"
Neil Young
(Reprise)

Dreams Go By
"Greatest Stories Live"
"Portrait Gallery"
Harry Chapin
(Elektra)
(Elektra)

Dreams of a Child
"Dreams of a Child"
Burton Cummings
(Portrait)

Early Heroes of Our Lives
"Stolen Time"*
Lucy Simon
(RCA)

Easy Breezes
"Mark Farner"*
Mark Farner
(Atlantic)

Easy Then
"No Secrets"
Carly Simon
(Elektra)

Eighteen
"Alice Cooper's Greatest Hits"
"The Alice Cooper Show"
Alice Cooper
(Warner Brothers)
(Warner Brothers)

Enter the Young
"The Association's Greatest Hits"
The Association
(Warner Brothers)

Everyone's Gone to the Movies
"Katy Lied"
Steely Dan
(ABC)

DEFINITIVE SONGS

Everything Comes in Time
"Good for You Too"*
Toni Brown
(Capitol)

Father and Son
"Greatest Hits"
"Tea for the Tillerman"
Cat Stevens
(A&M)
(A&M)

+Father and Son
"The Great Blind Degree"*
Richie Havens
(Stormy Forest)

Feeling Better
"A Live Album"*
Holly Near
(Redwood)

Feel Older Now
"The Phlorescent Leech and Eddie"*
Flo and Eddie
(Reprise)

The First Mistake I Ever Made
"Two Years On"
The Bee Gees
(RSO)

First of May
"The Best of Bee Gees"
"Odessa"
"Gold"
The Bee Gees
(RSO)
(RSO)
(RSO)

Flowers Are Red
"Living Room Suite"
Harry Chapin
(Elektra)

Giving It All Away
"Just a Boy"
Leo Sayer
(Warner Brothers)

+Giving It All Away
"Daltrey"
Roger Daltrey
(MCA)

Goin' Back
"Nils Lofgren"
"Night After Night"
Nils Lofgren
(A&M)
(A&M)

+Goin' Back
"The Notorious Byrd Brothers"
The Byrds
(Columbia)

+Goin' Back
"Writer"
Carole King
(Ode)

Grandma's Feather Bed
"John Denver's Greatest Hits"
John Denver
(RCA)

Great White Horse
"Take Heart"*
Mimi Fariña and Tom Jans
(A&M)

Growin' Up
"Listen with Your Heart"*
Dan Hill
(Columbia)

Grown Up Wrong
"12×5"
The Rolling Stones
(London)

Grown Up Wrong
"Dirty Angels"
Dirty Angels
(A&M)

DEFINITIVE SONGS

Grownups "Hotcakes"	Carly Simon (Elektra)
Hair of Spun Gold "Janis Ian"	Janis Ian (Polydor)
Happiest Days of Our Lives/Another 　Brick in the Wall "The Wall"	Pink Floyd (Harvest)
Headmaster "School Boys in Disgrace"	The Kinks (RCA)
Hey Little Tomboy "M.I.U. Album"	The Beach Boys (Brother/Reprise)
Hoppy, Gene and Me "Hoppy, Gene and Me"	Roy Rogers (20th Century Records)
I Don't Know What I Want "Starting Over"	Raspberries (Capitol)
I May Be Young "Dean Friedman"*	Dean Friedman (Lifesong)
I'm Just a Kid "Abandoned Luncheonette"	Hall and Oates (Atlantic)
I'm the Greatest "Blasts from your Past" "Ringo"	Ringo Starr (Apple) (Apple)
In My Girlish Days "It Looks Like Snow"	Phoebe Snow (Columbia)
(I Used to Be a) Brooklyn Dodger "Return of the Wanderer"*	Dion (Lifesong)
I've Had Enough " 'Well, Well,' Said the Rocking 　Chair"	Dean Friedman (Lifesong)
I Was Only Joking "Foot Loose and Fancy Free"	Rod Stewart (Warner Brothers)
I Wish "Songs in the Key of Life"	Stevie Wonder (Tamla)
James "Turnstiles"	Billy Joel (Columbia)
Janey's Blues "Janis Ian"	Janis Ian (Polydor)
Jimmy and the Tough Guys "Louise Goffin"	Louise Goffin (Warner Brothers)

DEFINITIVE SONGS

Just a Kid "Survivor"	Randy Bachman (Polydor)
Juvenile Delinquent "Live at the El Macombo"*	April Wine (London)
King of Nothing "Seals and Crofts' Greatest Hits" "Unborn Child"	Seals and Crofts (Warner Brothers) (Warner Brothers)
Kodachrome "Greatest Hits, Etc." "There Goes Rhymin' Simon"	Paul Simon (Columbia) (Columbia)
Lather "The Worst of Jefferson Airplane" "Crown of Creation"	Jefferson Airplane (RCA) (RCA)
Lemon Tree "Ten Years Together" "Peter, Paul and Mary"	Peter, Paul and Mary (Warner Brothers) (Warner Brothers)
Little Billy "Odds and Sods"	The Who (MCA)
The Logical Song "Breakfast in America"	Supertramp (A&M)
Lonely Boy "What's Wrong with This Picture?"	Andrew Gold (Asylum)
Look at Me, Look at You "The Association"*	The Association (Warner Brothers)
Looking Back "Listen with Your Heart"*	Dan Hill (Columbia)
Looking for an Echo "32"*	Kenny Vance (Atlantic)
+Looking for an Echo "Chirpin' "	Persuasions (Elektra)
Loves Me Like a Rock "Greatest Hits, Etc." "There Goes Rhymin' Simon" "Live Rhymin' "	Paul Simon (Columbia) (Columbia) (Columbia)
+Loves Me Like a Rock "Coming at Ya"	The Persuasions (Flying Fish)
Main Street "Night Moves"	Bob Seger and the Silver Bullet Band (Capitol)

DEFINITIVE SONGS

Mama Tried "Grateful Dead"	The Grateful Dead (Warner Brothers)
Manhood "Dance Band on the Titanic"	Harry Chapin (Elektra)
Midtown American Main Street Gang "Return of the Wanderer"*	Dion (Lifesong)
Midwest Midnight "Stage Pass"	Michael Stanley Band (Epic)
Mirror Star "The Fabulous Poodles"	The Fabulous Poodles (Epic)
A Misspent Youth "Seeds"	Gallagher and Lyle (A&M)
Money to Burn (45 RPM Single)*	The Cyrkle (Columbia)
Mother "John Lennon/Plastic Ono Band"	John Lennon (Apple)
My Back Pages "Another Side of Bob Dylan" "Bob Dylan's Greatest Hits, Vol. II"	Bob Dylan (Columbia) (Columbia)
+My Back Pages "Younger than Yesterday" "The Byrds' Greatest Hits"	The Byrds (Columbia) (Columbia)
+My Back Pages "Words and Music by Bob Dylan"	The Hollies (Epic)
+My Back Pages "Elegy"	The Nice (Mercury)
My Eyes Adored You "Gold"	Frankie Valli (Private Stock)
My Father "Colors of the Day/The Best of Judy Collins"	Judy Collins (Elektra)
+My Father "Good Book"*	Melanie (Buddah)
My Idaho Home "Nashville" (Soundtrack) "Welcome"	Ronee Blakely (ABC) (Warner Brothers)
Night Moves	Bob Seger and the Silver Bullet Band

DEFINITIVE SONGS

"Night Moves"	(Capitol)
Older Sister	Carly Simon
"Hotcakes"	(Elektra)
On Growing Older	Strawbs
"Grave New World"	(A&M)
On the Corner	Brooklyn Dreams
"Brooklyn Dreams"	(Millennium)
On the Road	Bonnie Koloc
"Bonnie Koloc"*	(Ovation)
Puff (the Magic Dragon)	Peter, Paul and Mary
"Ten Years Together"	(Warner Brothers)
"Moving"	(Warner Brothers)
"Peter, Paul and Mary"	(Warner Brothers)
+Puff (the Magic Dragon)	Jackie DeShannon
"In the Wind"*	(Imperial)
Randolph and Me	Gallagher and Lyle
"Seeds"	(A&M)
Reelin' in the Years	Steely Dan
"Can't Buy a Thrill"	(ABC)
"Greatest Hits"	(ABC)
Rick Rack	Gerry Rafferty
"Gerry Rafferty"	(Visa)
Rock and Roll I Gave You	Kevin Johnson
(45 RPM Single)*	(UK)
Rock and Roll Never Forgets	Bob Seger and the Silver Bullet Band
"Night Moves"	(Capitol)
Rodeo Rider	Lou London
"Swingtime in Springtime"*	(Philo)
School Days	The Good Rats
"Birth Comes to Us All"	(Arista)
Secret Gardens	Judy Collins
"True Stories and Other Dreams"	(Elektra)
See How the Years Have Gone By	Valdy
"Valdy"*	(A&M)
Seems Like Only Yesterday	Jesse Winchester
"Nothing but a Breeze"	(Bearsville)
Shilo	Neil Diamond
"Velvet Gloves and Spit"	(MCA)

DEFINITIVE SONGS

Society's Child "Janis Ian"	Janis Ian (Polydor)
Solo "Just a Boy"	Leo Sayer (Warner Brothers)
Someday Never Comes	Creedence Clearwater Revival
"Chronicle"	(Fantasy)
Songs for Aging Children Come "Clouds"	Joni Mitchell (Reprise)
Stay Free "Give 'Em Enough Rope"	The Clash (Epic)
Street Corner Serenade "Manorisms"	Wet Willie (Epic)
Sugar Mountain "Decade" "Live Rust"	Neil Young (Reprise) (Reprise)
Summer in the Schoolyard "Book Early"	City Boy (Mercury)
Tangled Up Puppet "Portrait Gallery"	Harry Chapin (Elektra)
Tattoo "The Who Sellout"	The Who (MCA)
Teach Your Children "Déjà Vu" "So Far" "Four Way Street" "No Nukes"	Crosby, Stills, Nash & Young (Atlantic) (Atlantic) (Atlantic) (Asylum)
+Teach Your Children "The Great Blind Degree"* "Richie Havens on Stage"*	Richie Havens (Stormy Forest) (Stormy Forest)
Tenderness on the Block "Excitable Boy"	Warren Zevon (Asylum)
There Only Was One Choice "Dance Band on the Titanic"	Harry Chapin (Elektra)
This Girl Has Turned into a Woman "Torn Between Two Lovers"	Mary McGregor (Ariola/America)
This Girl Is a Woman Now	Gary Puckett and the Union Gap
"Gary Puckett and the Union Gap's Greatest Hits"	(Columbia)

DEFINITIVE SONGS

Ticking
"Caribou"
Elton John
(MCA)

Tinkerbell
"Still Here"
Ian Thomas Band
(Atlantic)

Trouble
"Spanky and Our Gang"*
Spanky and Our Gang
(Mercury)

Trouble Child
"Court and Spark"
Joni Mitchell
(Asylum)

Two Boys
"I Could Have Been a Sailor"
Peter Allen
(A&M)

Two Little Kids
"Golden Duets"
Peaches and Herb
(Date)

Typical American Boy
"Too Stuffed to Jump"*
Amazing Rhythm Aces
(ABC)

The Unicorn Song
"Reunion"
Peter, Paul and Mary
(Warner Brothers)

The Vicar's Daughter
"The Mighty Quinn"
Manfred Mann
(Mercury)

Waited So Long
"No Secrets"
Carly Simon
(Elektra)

Watching Scotty Grow
"10th Anniversary Album"
Bobby Goldsboro
(United Artists)

+Watching Scotty Grow
"Greatest Hits"
Mac Davis
(Columbia)

What Did You Learn in School
Today?
"We Shall Overcome"
Pete Seeger

(Columbia)

+What Did You Learn in School
Today?
"Ramblin' Boy"*
Tom Paxton

(Elektra)

Whatever Happened to Love
"What the World Needs Now Is Love"*
Tom Clay
(Mowest)

When I Grow Up
"Spirit of America"
"The Beach Boys Today"
"Dance, Dance, Dance"
The Beach Boys
(Capitol)
(Capitol)
(Capitol)

When I Was a Child
"Native Son"
Loggins and Messina
(Columbia)

DEFINITIVE SONGS

When I Was Young — Eric Burdon and the Animals (ABKCO)

"Best of Eric Burdon and the Animals Vol. II"

"Best of the Animals" — (ABKCO)

Who's Gonna Fry Your Eggs
"Love Is a Fire" — Country Joe McDonald (Fantasy)

Who's Gonna Take the Blame? — Smokey Robinson & the Miracles

"Anthology" — (Motown)

Why Can't I Be Like Other Girls?
"Jaded Virgin" — Marshall Chapman (Epic)

Wind Up
"Aqualung" — Jethro Tull (Chrysalis)

Wooden Spoon
"Moon Bathing"* — Lesley Duncan (MCA)

Yesterday When I Was Young
"Roy Clark's Greatest Hits" — Roy Clark (Dot/ABC)

Young Man's Blues
"Live at Leeds" — The Who (MCA)

Younger Generation
"The Very Best of the Lovin' Spoonful" — The Lovin' Spoonful (Kama Sutra)

"Everything Playing" — (Kama Sutra)

+Younger Generation
"John Sebastian Songbook" — John Sebastian (Kama Sutra)

You're a Big Boy Now
"John B. Sebastian"* — John Sebastian (Reprise)

You're a Big Girl Now
"The Best of the Stylistics" — The Stylistics (Avco)

REFERENCE SONGS

Almost Summer — Celebration Featuring Mike Love

"Almost Summer" — (MCA)

Angels Rejoiced
"Nicolette" — Nicolette Larson (Warner Brothers)

Ballad of Billy the Kid
"Piano Man" — Billy Joel (Columbia)

REFERENCE SONGS

Been There and Back — Garland Jeffreys
"One Eyed Jack" — (A&M)

Birds of a Feather — Joe South
"Joe South's Greatest Hits" — (Capitol)

Born in the 50's — The Police
"Outlandos d'Amour" — (A&M)

Born on the Bayou — Creedence Clearwater Revival

"Bayou Country" — (Fantasy)

Carrie Ann — The Hollies
"Greatest Hits" — (Epic)
"Hollies Live" — (Epic)

Child for a Day — Cat Stevens
"Izitso" — (A&M)

Crackerbox Palace — George Harrison
"33 and a ⅓" — (Dark Horse)

Dowdy Ferry Road — England Dan and John Ford Coley

"Dowdy Ferry Road" — (Big Tree)

Girl You'll Be a Woman Soon — Neil Diamond
"Neil Diamond's Greatest Hits" — (Bang)
"Gold" — (MCA)
"Hot August Night" — (MCA)

Grapefruit—Juicy Fruit — Jimmy Buffett
"A White Sports Coat and a Pink Crustacean" — (ABC)
"You Had to Be There" — (ABC)

Happy Jack — The Who
"A Quick One (Happy Jack)" — (MCA)

Helpless — Crosby, Stills, Nash & Young

"Déjà Vu" — (Atlantic)

+Helpless — Neil Young
"Decade" — (Reprise)
"The Last Waltz" (Soundtrack) — (Warner Brothers)

I'm a Boy — The Who
"Meaty Beaty Big and Bouncy" — (MCA)

Lost in the Supermarket — The Clash
"London Calling" — (Epic)

REFERENCE SONGS

Mama's Boy
"The Thorn in Mrs. Rose's Side"*
Biff Rose
(Buddah)

Molly
"Biff Rose"*
Biff Rose
(Buddah)

Momma
"Beautiful Loser"
Bob Seger
(Capitol)

My Momma's House
"Janis Ian"
Janis Ian
(Columbia)

Never Join the Fire Brigade
"I/You"*
Brian Protheroe
(Chrysalis)

That's the Way I've Always Heard It
    Should Be
Carly Simon

"The Best of Carly Simon, Vol. I"
"Carly Simon"
(Elektra)
(Elektra)

Time Fades Away
"Time Fades Away"
Neil Young
(Reprise)

To Be a Star
"Izitso"
Cat Stevens
(A&M)

Too Old to Rock and Roll
"Repeat. The Best of Jethro Tull.
    Vol. II"
Jethro Tull
(Chrysalis)

Twisted
"Court and Spark"
Joni Mitchell
(Asylum)

+Twisted
"Bette Midler"
Bette Midler
(Atlantic)

Younger Men Grow Older
"Alarm Clock"*
"Richie Havens on Stage"*
Richie Havens
(Stormy Forest)
(Stormy Forest)

YOUR ADDITIONAL SONGS

_____

_____

_____

_____

_____

HOPE/OPTIMISM

Hope/optimism—out of the darkness . . . you can make it if you try.
   Songs of encouragement: some from the depths of despair, others from the borders of loneliness and heartbreak. Whatever the circumstances, they all suggest that nothing is ever too bad. So don't give up, things always get better.

Related Categories: Brotherhood, Changes, Self-Identity

   +Same as Song Above
   *Hard-to-find Songs/Albums

CLASSICS

Hold Your Head Up "The Best of Argent—An Anthology"	Argent (Epic)
+Hold Your Head Up "Temptation"*	Marc Tanner (Elektra)
Let It Be "Let It Be" "The Beatles 1967–1970"	The Beatles (Apple) (Apple)
+Let It Be "Blessed Are . . ."	Joan Baez (Vanguard)
+Let It Be "Poems, Prayers and Promises"	John Denver (RCA)
+Let It Be "Fireworks"	José Feliciano (RCA)
+Let It Be "Danny Kirwan"	Danny Kirwan (DJM Records)
+Let It Be "Aretha's Greatest Hits"	Aretha Franklin (Atlantic)
+Let It Be "You're Not Alone"*	Dion (Warner Brothers)
+Let It Be "If I Were Your Woman"	Gladys Knight and the Pips (Soul)
+Let It Be "All This and World War II"	Leo Sayer (20th Century-Fox)
Long Promised Road "Surf's Up"	The Beach Boys (Brothers/Reprise)

CLASSICS

Out of the Darkness	David Crosby/Graham Nash
"Whistling Down the Wire"	(ABC)
"The Best of David Crosby and Graham Nash"	(ABC)
You Can Make It If You Try	Sly and the Family Stone
"Greatest Hits"	(Epic)
"Stand"	(Epic)

DEFINITIVE SONGS

Back on My Feet Again	The Babys
"Union Jacks"	(Chrysalis)
Badlands	Bruce Springsteen
"Darkness on the Edge of Town"	(Columbia)
Be Aware	The Mighty Diamonds
"Deeper Roots (Back to the Channel)"	(Virgin)
Be Positive	Elkie Brooks
"Shooting Star"	(A&M)
Big Man in Town	The Four Seasons
"Gold Vault of Hits"	(Philips)
"The Four Seasons Story"	(Private Stock)
Bottom to the Top	Joan Armatrading
"To the Limit"	(A&M)
Brand New Morning	Dion
"Sanctuary"*	(Warner Brothers)
Brighter Days	Loggins and Messina
"Mother Lode"	(Columbia)
Can't Keep a Good Man Down	Eddie Money
"Life for the Taking"	(Columbia)
Carry On	Crosby, Stills, Nash & Young
"Déjà Vu"	(Atlantic)
"Four Way Street"	(Atlantic)
Changes IV	Cat Stevens
"Teaser and the Firecat"	(A&M)
Crystal Blue Persuasion	Tommy James and the Shondells
"The Very Best of Tommy James and the Shondells"	(Roulette)

DEFINITIVE SONGS

Don't Be Sad 'Cause Your Sun Is Down	James Taylor
"In the Pocket"	(Warner Brothers)
Don't Look Back	Boston
"Don't Look Back"	(Epic)
Don't Stop	Fleetwood Mac
"Rumours"	(Reprise)
Everything's Coming Our Way	Santana
"Greatest Hits"	(Columbia)
Faith in Something Bigger	The Who
"Odds and Sods"	(MCA)
Feel No Fret	Average White Band
"Feel No Fret"	(Atlantic)
Getting Better	The Beatles
"Sgt. Pepper's Lonely Hearts Club Band"	(Capitol)
+Getting Better	Status Quo
"All This and World War II"	(20th Century-Fox)
+Getting Better	Peter Frampton/The Bee Gees
"Sgt. Pepper's Lonely Hearts Club Band Soundtrack"	(RSO)
The Good Times Are Coming	Mama Cass
"Mama's Big Ones—Her Greatest Hits"	(ABC/Dunhill)
Hey Jude	The Beatles
"The Beatles 1967–1970"	(Apple)
"Hey Jude"	(Apple)
+Hey Jude	Duane Allman
"An Anthology"	(Capricorn)
+Hey Jude	Wilson Pickett
"The Best of Wilson Pickett Vol. II"	(Atlantic)
+Hey Jude	The Brothers Johnson
"All This and World War II"	(20th Century-Fox)
Hold On	John Lennon
"John Lennon"	(Apple)
Hold On	Dan Hill
"Hold On"*	(20th Century Records)
I Believe	The Young Rascals
"The Young Rascals"	(Atlantic)

DEFINITIVE SONGS

+I Believe (45 RPM Single)	The Bachelors (London)
I Can See a New Day "I Can See a New Day"	Pete Seeger (Columbia)
I Can See Clearly Now "Johnny Nash's Greatest Hits"	Johnny Nash (Columbia)
+I Can See Clearly Now "True to Life"	Ray Charles (Atlantic)
I Shall Be Released "Bob Dylan's Greatest Hits"	Bob Dylan (Columbia)
+I Shall Be Released "Music from Big Pink" "The Last Waltz" (Soundtrack)	The Band (Capitol) (Warner Brothers)
+I Shall Be Released "Words and Music by Bob Dylan"*	The Hollies (Epic)
+I Shall Be Released "From Every Stage" "Any Day Now"	Joan Baez (A&M) (Vanguard)
+I Shall Be Released "Dimensions"*	Box Tops (Bell)
+I Shall Be Released (45 RPM Single)*	Coven (Bell)
+I Shall Be Released "Rick Nelson in Concert"	Rick Nelson (MCA)
+I Shall Be Released "Late Again"	Peter, Paul and Mary (Warner Brothers)
+I Shall Be Released "With a Little Help from My Friends"	Joe Cocker (A&M)
I Will Survive "Love Tracks"	Gloria Gaynor (Polydor)
If I Can Dream "A Legendary Performer" "Worldwide 50 Gold Award Hits, Vol. 1"	Elvis Presley (RCA) (RCA)
I'm Gonna Use What I Got, to Get What I Want "Wonderful World, Beautiful People"	Jimmy Cliff (A&M)
I'm Not Down "London Calling"	The Clash (Epic)

DEFINITIVE SONGS

The Impossible Dream
"Anthology—Tenth Anniversary
  Special"
The Temptations
(Motown)

It All Comes Together
"Dreams of a Child"
Burton Cummings
(Portrait)

It Don't Come Easy
"Bangla Desh" (George Harrison)
"Blasts from Your Past"
Ringo Starr
(Apple)
(Apple)

It's Never Too Late
"The ABC Collection"
Steppenwolf
(ABC)

Just One Victory
"A Wizard a True Star"
Todd Rundgren
(Bearsville)

+Just One Victory
"The Handsome Devils"*
Hello People
(ABC)

Keep a Goin'
"Nashville" (Soundtrack)
Henry Gibson
(ABC)

Keep on Pushing
"The Impressions' Big Sixteen"
The Impressions
(ABC)

Keep on Trying
"Burning for You"
Strawbs
(Oyster/Polydor)

Keep Your Dream Alive
"Shivers in the Night"*
Andy Pratt
(Nemperor)

Laughing at Life
"Swingtime in Springtime"*
Lew London
(Philo)

Light Shine
"Light Shine"
Jesse Colin Young
(RCA)

Living in Hope
"The Rutles"
The Rutles
(Warner Brothers)

Love Is Gonna Come at Last
"Airwaves"
Badfinger
(Elektra)

Morning Has Broken
"Greatest Hits"
"Teaser and the Firecat"
Cat Stevens
(A&M)
(A&M)

Mountain Song
"Ian Tamblyn"*
Ian Tamblyn
(Cream)

Move On
"Inner Secrets"
Santana
(Columbia)

Move On Up
"Curtis"
Curtis Mayfield
(Curtom)

DEFINITIVE SONGS

New and Different Way
"Oasis"

Jimmy Messina
(Columbia)

New Day, New World Coming
"Let's Clean Up the Ghetto"

Billy Paul
(Philadelphia International)

New World Coming
"Mama's Big Ones—Her Greatest
  Hits"

Mama Cass
(ABC/Dunhill)

One of These Days
"Elite Hotel"
"Profile: The Best of Emmylou
  Harris"

Emmylou Harris
(Warner Brothers)
(Warner Brothers)

Ooh Child
(45 RPM Single)*
"Five Stairsteps and Cubie"

Five Stairsteps and Cubie
(Buddah)
(Buddah)

+Ooh Child
"Mixed Bag 2"*

Richie Havens
(Stormy Forest)

+Ooh Child
"Just a Stone's Throw Away"

Valerie Carter
(Columbia)

+Ooh Child
"Let's Clean Up the Ghetto"

Dee Dee Sharp Gamble
(Philadelphia International)

+Ooh Child
"Second Time Around"

The Spinners
(Atlantic)

Optimism Blues
"Motion"

Allen Toussaint
(Warner Brothers)

Pack Up Your Troubles
"Nobody's Fool"

Slade
(Polydor)

Peace Train
"Greatest Hits"
"Teaser and the Firecat"

Cat Stevens
(A&M)
(A&M)

Pick Myself Up
"Bush Doctor"

Peter Tosh
(Rolling Stone Records)

A Place in the Sun
"Greatest Hits"

Stevie Wonder
(Tamla)

+A Place in the Sun
"Groovin'"

The Young Rascals
(Atlantic)

The Promised Land
"Darkness on the Edge of Town"

Bruce Springsteen
(Columbia)

Raindrops Keep Falling on My Head
"The Very Best of B. J. Thomas"

B. J. Thomas
(United Artists)

DEFINITIVE SONGS

Reach
"Waking and Dreaming"

Orleans
(Asylum)

Rose Colored Glasses
"Starting Over"

Raspberries
(Capitol)

Shinin' Brightly

Bob Seger and the Silver
    Bullet Band

"Against the Wind"

(Capitol)

Shower the People
"Greatest Hits"
"In the Pocket"

James Taylor
(Warner Brothers)
(Warner Brothers)

Smile Please
"Fulfillingness' First Finale"

Stevie Wonder
(Tamla)

Someday We'll All Be Free

Average White Band and
    Ben E. King

"Benny and Us"

(Atlantic)

Things Are Getting Better Now
"Hometown Frolics"*

Tommy West
(Lifesong)

Things Get Better
"On Tour"

Delaney and Bonnie
(Atco)

Things Will Be Better
"The Byrds"

The Byrds
(Asylum)

Time for Us
"Cate Brothers"*

Cate Brothers
(Asylum)

To Try for the Sun
"Donovan P. Litch"*

Donovan
(Janus)

Up
"Grand Tour"

Rod McKuen
(Warner Brothers)

Way Over Yonder
"Tapestry"

Carole King
(Ode)

We're Gonna Make It
"Music Is My Life"

Billy Preston
(A&M)

Yes We Can
"The Pointer Sisters"
"Live at the Opera House"

The Pointer Sisters
(Blue Thumb)
(Blue Thumb)

You Can Get It if You Really Want
"In Concert: The Best Of Jimmy
    Cliff"

Jimmy Cliff
(Island)

You Can Make It if You Try
"Rolling Stones"

The Rolling Stones
(London)

DEFINITIVE SONGS

You've Got to Believe   Pierce Arrow
"Pierce Arrow"*   (Columbia)

REFERENCE SONGS

Beginning to See the Light   The Velvet Underground
"Velvet Underground"*   (MGM)
"Live at Max's Kansas City"*   (Cotillion)
"1969 Velvet Underground Live"   (Mercury)

Ding Dong   George Harrison
"Dark Horse"   (Dark Horse)

Easy to Be Free"   Rick Nelson
"Rick Nelson in Concert"   (MCA)

Feelin' Stronger Everyday   Chicago
"Chicago IX Greatest Hits"   (Columbia)
"Chicago VI"   (Columbia)

Happiness Runs   Donovan
"Barabajagal"   (Epic)

Hyperdrive   Jefferson Starship
"Dragon Fly"   (Grunt)
"Gold"   (Grunt)

New Beginnings   Strawbs
"Deadlines"   (Arista)

You Have to Make It Through This   Van Morrison
   World
"A Period of Transition"   (Warner Brothers)

You'll Make It Someday   Mark and Clark Band
"Double Take"*   (Columbia)

You'll Make It Through   Mike Pinder
"The Promise"*   (Threshold)

YOUR ADDITIONAL SONGS

_____

_____

_____

_____

_____

HUNGER

Hunger—of the belly, not the soul or the heart

There are over *half a billion people* in the world today who are mal-nourished (a polite word for starving) and yet there are very few songs that even mention hunger. Why? Funny you should ask that. That is the name of an organization that Harry Chapin and Bill Ayres founded in 1975 to deal with the problem. For more information write to World Hunger Year (WHY), Box 1975, Garden City, New York 11530.

Related Categories: Poverty

+Same as Song Above
 *Hard-to-find Songs/Albums

CLASSICS

Bangla Desh	George Harrison
"Bangla Desh"	(Apple)
"The Best of George Harrison"	(Apple)
Shortest Stories	Harry Chapin
"Shortest Stories"	(Elektra)

DEFINITIVE SONGS

East Texas Red	Woody Guthrie
"Library of Congress"	(Elektra)
Grocery Store Blues	Arlo Guthrie
"Amigo"	(Reprise)
Harvest for the World	The Isley Brothers
"Harvest for the World"	(T-Neck/Epic)
Orphans of Wealth	Don McLean
"Tapestry"	(United Artists)
Them Belly Full (But We Were Hungry)	Bob Marley and the Wailers
"Live"	(Island)
"Natty Dread"	(Island)
Too Many People	Paul McCartney
"Ram"	(Apple)
A Truly Good Song	Gulliver
"Gulliver"*	(Elektra)

DEFINITIVE SONGS

We're All in This Together
"Wrap Around Joy"

Carole King
(Ode)

You Can Eat Dog Food
"New Songs from the Briarpatch"*

Tom Paxton
(Vanguard)

REFERENCE SONGS

Banquet
"For the Roses"

Joni Mitchell
(Asylum)

Bread
"Hermit of Mink Hollow"

Todd Rundgren
(Bearsville)

The Breadline
"Golden Butter/The Best of the
 Paul Butterfield Blues Band"

Paul Butterfield Blues Band
(Elektra)

Doubling

Pete Seeger

(This was originally a public service announcement that developed into a song. If you know what album it can be found on, please write and tell us!)

Feed the Children
"Up and Up"

Tom Paxton
(Mountain Railroad
 Records)

God Knows I'm Good
"Space Oddity"

David Bowie
(RCA)

If There's a God in Heaven
"Blue Moves"

Elton John
(MCA)

In the Ghetto
"Worldwide 50 Gold Award Hits,
 Vol. 1"

Elvis Presley
(RCA)

+In the Ghetto
"Greatest Hits"

Mac Davis
(Columbia)

I Want to Live
"I Want to Live"

John Denver
(RCA)

Jarrow Song
"Between Today and Yesterday"*

Alan Price
(Warner Brothers)

Population
"So Close, So Very Far To Go"

Jake Holmes
(Polydor)

The Robber
"Pierce Arrow"

Pierce Arrow
(Columbia)

Sufferin' in the Land
"Wonderful World, Beautiful People"

Jimmy Cliff
(A&M)

REFERENCE SONGS

Time Is Running "Stevie Wonder"	Stevie Wonder (Island)
Village Ghetto Land "Songs in the Key of Life"	Stevie Wonder (Tamla)

YOUR ADDITIONAL SONGS

_____

_____

_____

_____

_____

INDIANS

Indians—as in cowboys and . . .

The first Americans have found their way into the world of rock and roll largely through the efforts of people like Buffy Sainte-Marie, Michael Murphey, Redbone, and others. Not only have they written about Indians, but also they have given their time and talents to try to right some of the wrongs suffered by them.

Related Categories: Cowboys/Wild West, Injustice

+Same as Song Above
*Hard-to-find Songs/Albums

CLASSICS

Now That the Buffalo Is Gone "The Best of Buffy Sainte-Marie"	Buffy Sainte-Marie (Vanguard)
Wooden Indian "Poems, Prayers and Promises"	John Denver (RCA)

THEMATIC ALBUMS

"Pepper's Pow-Wow"*	Jim Pepper (Embryo)
"Native North American Child . . . An Odyssey"	Buffy Sainte-Marie (Vanguard)
"Wovoka"	Redbone (Epic)

DEFINITIVE SONGS

Apache Woman "Stone Alone"	Bill Wyman (Rolling Stone Records)
Ballad of Ira Hayes "Dylan"	Bob Dylan (Columbia)
+Ballad of Ira Hayes "Johnny Cash's Greatest Hits"	Johnny Cash (Columbia)
+Ballad of Ira Hayes "Lasso from El Paso"*	Kinky Friedman (Epic)
+Ballad of Ira Hayes "Patrick Sky"*	Patrick Sky (Vanguard)

DEFINITIVE SONGS

Before You Came
"Songbird"
Jesse Colin Young
(Warner Brothers)

Chant: Thirteenth Hour
"Come and Get Your Redbone—The
  Best of Redbone"
Redbone
(Epic)

Chant Wovoka
"Wovoka"
Redbone
(Epic)

Cherokee Bend
"Cold on the Shoulder"
Gordon Lightfoot
(Reprise)

Cherokee Fiddle
"Flowing Free Forever"
Michael Murphey
(Epic)

Cheyenne Anthem
"Leftoverture"
Kansas
(Kirshner)

Coyote
"Rock and Roll Music from Planet
  Earth"
Country Joe McDonald
(Fantasy)

Don't Go Near the Indians
(45 RPM Single)*
Rex Allen
(Mercury)

Drums
"Pepper's Pow-Wow"*
Jim Pepper
(Embryo)

Fast War Dance
"Pepper's Pow-Wow"*
Jim Pepper
(Embryo)

Geronimo's Cadillac
"Life Machine"
Hoyt Axton
(A&M)

+Geronimo's Cadillac
"Geronimo's Cadillac"
"Peaks Valleys Honky-Tonks & Alleys"
Michael Murphey
(A&M)
(Epic)

+Geronimo's Cadillac
"Stage Door Johnnies"*
Claire Hamill
(Konk)

Ghost Dance
"Easter"
Patti Smith
(Arista)

Half Breed
"Cher's Greatest Hits"
Cher
(MCA)

He's an Indian Cowboy
"Moonshot"*
Buffy Sainte-Marie
(Vanguard)

Indian Brown
"In Time"
Reneé Armand
(Windsong)

Indian Man
"Midnight Wind"
Charlie Daniels
(Epic)

DEFINITIVE SONGS

Indian Prayer "Mixed Bag 2"*	Richie Havens (Stormy Forest)
Indian Reservation	Paul Revere and the Raiders Featuring Mark Lindsay
"All Time Greatest Hits"	(Columbia)
Indian Sunset "Madman Across the Water"	Elton John (MCA)
+Indian Sunset "Mary"*	Mary Travers (Warner Brothers)
Indian Wedding "More of Roy Orbison's Greatest Hits"	Roy Orbison (Monument)
Indian Woman from Wichita "Ladies Love Outlaws"	Tom Rush (Columbia)
Liquid Truth "Wovoka"	Redbone (Epic)
Medicine Man "Blue Sky, Night Thunder"	Michael Murphey (Epic)
My Country 'Tis of Thy People You're Dying "The Best of Buffy Sainte-Marie"	Buffy Sainte-Marie (Vanguard)
Niji Trance "Come and Get Your Redbone—The Best of Redbone"	Redbone (Epic)
Pocahontas "Rust Never Sleeps"	Neil Young (Reprise)
Renegade "Swans Against the Sun"	Michael Murphey (Epic)
The Renegade "Ian and Sylvia"	Ian and Sylvia (Vanguard)
Rock Stomp Indian Style "Pepper's Pow-Wow"*	Jim Pepper (Embryo)
Slow War Dance "Pepper's Pow-Wow"*	Jim Pepper (Embryo)
Soldier Blue "She Used to Wanna Be a Ballerina"	Buffy Sainte-Marie (Vanguard)
Squaw Song "Pepper's Pow-Wow"*	Jim Pepper (Embryo)

DEFINITIVE SONGS

Ten Little Indians
"The Beach Boys"*

The Beach Boys
(Pickwick)

War Paint and Indian Feathers
"Cherished"

Cher
(Warner Brothers)

White Man
"A Day at the Races"

Queen
(Elektra)

Witchi-tai-to
"Weeds"*
"The Best . . . Brewer and Shipley"

Brewer and Shipley
(Kama Sutra)
(Kama Sutra)

+Witchi-tai-to
"Pepper's Pow-Wow"*

Jim Pepper
(Embryo)

Wovoka
"Wovoka"
"Come and Get Your Redbone—The
Best of Redbone"

Redbone
(Epic)
(Epic)

REFERENCE SONGS

Apache (Instrumental)
"Roots of British Rock"

The Shadows
(Sire)

+Apache (Instrumental)
(45 RPM Single)*

Jorgen Ingmann
(Atco)

Broken Promises
"A Live Album"*

Holly Near
(Redwood)

General Custer
"How Come the Sun"*

Tom Paxton
(Reprise)

The Last Resort
"Hotel California"

The Eagles
(Asylum)

Live and Let Die
"Forever Changes"

Love
(Elektra)

Mr. Custer
(45 RPM Single)*

Larry Verne
(Era)

Peace Pipe
"Together"*

The Illusion
(Steed)

With God on Our Side
"The Times They Are a Changin'"

Bob Dylan
(Columbia)

+With God on Our Side
(33⅓ RPM E.P.)*

Manfred Mann
(Ascot)

REFERENCE SONGS

+With God on Our Side   Joan Baez
  "The First Ten Years"   (Vanguard)
  "Joan Baez in Concert Part II"   (Vanguard)

YOUR ADDITIONAL SONGS

_____

_____

_____

_____

_____

INJUSTICE

Injustice—when justice doesn't prevail . . . even worse, when people have come to accept injustice as justice.

The basis of injustice is the violation of a person's rights. There are as many kinds of injustice as there are situations in life. These songs focus on some of the most striking social and political injustices in our society —e.g., racial injustice, prisons and the judicial system and other structures, attitudes and laws that prevent people from exercising their own personal freedom and basic human rights. (N.B. The actual topics here vary greatly, as do their related categories.)

Related Categories: Freedom, Indians, Police, Poverty, Prisons,
    Racism/Prejudice, War and Peace: Victims of War, Women's
    Identity/Liberation

+Same as Song Above
 *Hard-to-find Songs/Albums

CLASSICS

Justice "O Lucky Man"	Alan Price (Warner Brothers)
Living for the City "Innervisions"	Stevie Wonder (Tamla)
+Living for the City "Sweet Rhode Island Red"	Ike and Tina Turner (United Artists)
+Living for the City "It's a Heartache"	Bonnie Tyler (RCA)
The Lonesome Death of Hattie Carroll "The Times They Are a Changin'"	Bob Dylan (Columbia)
+The Lonesome Death of Hattie Carroll "The Judy Collins Concert"	Judy Collins (Elektra)
Ohio "Decade" "Journey Through the Past"	Neil Young (Reprise) (Reprise)
+Ohio "So Far" "Four Way Street"	Crosby, Stills, Nash & Young (Atlantic) (Atlantic)
Respectable "Tapestry"	Don McLean (United Artists)

THEMATIC ALBUMS

"Sometime in New York City"	John Lennon (Apple)
"The Times They Are a Changin' "	Bob Dylan (Columbia)

DEFINITIVE SONGS

Angela "Sometime in New York City"	John Lennon (Apple)
Attica State "Sometimes in New York City"	John Lennon (Apple)
Bad Boy "Mac McAnally"	Mac McAnally (Ariola/America)
The Ballad of Johnny Strozier "Song for Patty"*	Sammy Walker (Vanguard)
Ballad of Sacco and Vanzetti "From Every Stage"	Joan Baez (A&M)
Ballad of William Worthy "All the News That's Fit to Sing"	Phil Ochs (Elektra)
Blowin' in the Wind "Bob Dylan's Greatest Hits" "The Freewheelin' Bob Dylan" "Before the Flood" (with The Band) "Live at Budokan"	Bob Dylan (Columbia) (Columbia) (Asylum) (Columbia)
+Blowin' in the Wind "Ten Years Together" "In the Wind" "Peter, Paul and Mary"	Peter, Paul and Mary (Warner Brothers) (Warner Brothers) (Warner Brothers)
+Blowin' in the Wind "Words and Music by Bob Dylan"*	The Hollies (Epic)
+Blowin' in the Wind "From Every Stage"	Joan Baez (A&M)
+Blowin' in the Wind "Greatest Hits"	Stevie Wonder (Tamla)
+Blowin in the Wind "Cher Sings the Hits"*	Cher (Springboard)
Blue Murder "TRB Two"	The Tom Robinson Band (Harvest)
Chicago "Songs for Beginners"	Graham Nash (Atlantic)

DEFINITIVE SONGS

+Chicago

"Four Way Street"

+Chicago
"The Best of David Crosby and
Graham Nash"

The Death of Stephen Biko
"Heroes"

Equal Rights
"Equal Rights"

Framed
"Bill Haley's Scrapbook"

+Framed
"A New Age"

+Framed
"My Own Way to Rock"

+Framed
"Up in Smoke"

Geronimo's Cadillac
"Peaks Valleys Honky-Tonks & Alleys"
"Geronimo's Cadillac"

+Geronimo's Cadillac
"Life Machine"

+Geronimo's Cadillac
"Stage Door Johnnies"*

Give Ireland Back to the Irish
(45 RPM Single)

Goodman, Schwerner and Chaney
"Things I Notice Now"

He Was My Brother
"Wednesday Morning 3 A.M."

High Sheriff of Hazard
"Ramblin' Boy"

The Hubbardville Store
"Tramps and Hawks"*

Hurricane
"Desire"

Crosby, Stills, Nash &
Young
(Atlantic)

David Crosby/Graham Nash
(ABC)

Tom Paxton
(Vanguard)

Peter Tosh
(Columbia)

Bill Haley
(Kama Sutra)

Canned Heat
(United Artists)

Burton Cummings
(Portrait/CBS)

Cheech and Chong
(Warner Brothers)

Michael Murphey
(Epic)
(A&M)

Hoyt Axton
(A&M)

Claire Hamill
(Konk)

Wings
(Apple)

Tom Paxton
(Elektra)

Simon and Garfunkel
(Columbia)

Tom Paxton
(Elektra)

Jim Ringer
(Philo)

Bob Dylan
(Columbia)

DEFINITIVE SONGS

If I Had a Hammer — Peter, Paul and Mary
"Ten Years Together" (Warner Brothers)
"Peter, Paul and Mary" (Warner Brothers)
"Peter, Paul and Mary in Concert" (Warner Brothers)

+If I Had a Hammer — Odetta
"Odetta" (Vanguard)

+If I Had a Hammer — Billy Preston
"The Original Billy Preston . . . (Crescendo)
Soul'd Out"

+If I Had a Hammer — Pete Seeger
"The World of Pete Seeger" (Columbia)

+If I Had a Hammer — The Weavers
"Greatest Hits" (Vanguard)
"Reunion at Carnegie Hall" (Vanguard)

+If I Had a Hammer — Johnny Rivers
"Rivers Rocks the Folks"* (Imperial)

+If I Had a Hammer — Jackie DeShannon
"In the Wind"* (Imperial)

Joe Hill — Joan Baez
"From Every Stage" (A&M)
"Woodstock" (Soundtrack) (Cotillion)

Joe Hill — Phil Ochs
"Tape from California" (A&M)

John Sinclair — John Lennon
"Sometime in New York City" (Apple)

Joshua Gone Barbados — Tom Rush
"Classic Rush" (Columbia)

Justice Don't Be Slow — Steppenwolf
"Slow Flux" (Mums/Columbia)

The Justice Game — Buzzy Linhart
"Pussy Cats Can Go Far"* (Atco)

Kevin Barry — Pete Seeger
"Strangers and Cousins" (Columbia)

The Law Is For the Protection of the — Kris Kristofferson
People
"Me and Bobby McGee" (Monument)

Links in the Chain — Phil Ochs
"I Ain't Marchin' Anymore" (Elektra)

DEFINITIVE SONGS

Maggie's Farm	Bob Dylan
"Bob Dylan's Greatest Hits Vol. II"	(Columbia)
"Bringing It All Back Home"	(Columbia)
+Maggie's Farm	Richie Havens
"Something Else Again"	(Stormy Forest)
Mrs. Clara Sullivan's Letter	Pete Seeger
"I Can See a New Day"	(Columbia)
My Country 'Tis of Thy People You're Dying	Buffy Sainte-Marie
"The Best of Buffy Sainte-Marie"	(Vanguard)
My Crime	Canned Heat
"Boogie with Canned Heat"	(Liberty)
Nigger Charlie	Billy Preston
"Music Is My Life"	(A&M)
1913 Massacre	Woody Guthrie
"Library of Congress"	(Elektra)
+1913 Massacre	Arlo Guthrie
"Hobo's Lullaby"	(Reprise)
+1913 Massacre	Jack Elliot
"A Tribute to Woody Guthrie"	(Warner Brothers)
Now That the Buffalo Is Gone	Buffy Sainte-Marie
"The Best of Buffy Sainte-Marie"	(Vanguard)
Only a Pawn in Their Game	Bob Dylan
"The Times They Are a Changin'"	(Columbia)
Packed Up and Left	Mac McAnally
"Mac McAnally"	(Ariola/America)
Percy's Song	Arlo Guthrie
"Washington County"	(Reprise)
Sorry Mr. Harris	The Tom Robinson Band
"TRB Two"	(Harvest)
Southern Man	Neil Young
"After the Gold Rush"	(Reprise)
"Decade"	(Reprise)
+Southern Man	Crosby, Stills, Nash & Young
"Four Way Street"	(Atlantic)
Speed Trap	Hoyt Axton
"Life Machine"	(A&M)
Sufferin' in the Land	Jimmy Cliff
"Wonderful World, Beautiful People"	(A&M)

DEFINITIVE SONGS

Talking Birmingham Jam
"I Ain't Marching Anymore"

Phil Ochs
(Elektra)

Testimony of a Dying Lady
"Song for Patty"*

Sammy Walker
(Vanguard)

Those Three Are on My Mind
"Strangers and Cousins"

Pete Seeger
(Columbia)

Uneasy Rider
"Honey in the Rock"

Charlie Daniels
(Kama Sutra)

Victor Jara
"Amigos"

Arlo Guthrie
(Warner Brothers)

Washington Square
"Strangers and Cousins"

Pete Seeger
(Columbia)

We Didn't Know
"Ain't That News"

Tom Paxton
(Elektra)

What About Me

Quicksilver Messenger
    Service

"What About Me"
"Anthology"

(Capitol)
(Capitol)

+What About Me
"The Great Blind Degree"*

Richie Havens
(Stormy Forest)

What Made America Famous?
"Verities And Balderdash"

Harry Chapin
(Elektra)

REFERENCE SONGS

The Laws Must Change
"Turning Point"

John Mayall
(Polydor)

Murder in My Heart for the Judge
"Great Grape"

Moby Grape
(Columbia)

+Murder in My Heart for the Judge
"Harmony"

Three Dog Night
(ABC/Dunhill)

YOUR ADDITIONAL SONGS

_____

_____

_____

_____

_____

LIFE

Life—from both sides now.

Not surprisingly, this is a topic in which the poetry of rock is at its best: celebrating life, reflecting on its meaning, questioning its uncertainties, and dreaming of a better life ahead.

Related Categories: Changes, Growing Up, Hope/Optimism, Self-Identity

+Same as Song Above
*Hard-to-find Songs/Albums

CLASSICS

Both Sides Now	Judy Collins
"Colors of the Day/The Best of Judy Collins"	(Elektra)
"Wildflowers"	(Elektra)
+Both Sides Now	Joni Mitchell
"Clouds"	(Reprise)
"Miles of Aisles"	(Asylum)
+Both Sides Now	Dave Van Ronk
"Dave Van Ronk and the Hudson Dusters"	(Vanguard)
+Both Sides Now	Neil Diamond
"Gold"	(MCA)
"Touching You, Touching Me"	(MCA)
"Rainbow"	(MCA)
+Both Sides Now	The Tokens
"Both Sides Now"*	(Buddah)
+Both Sides Now	Tom Clay
"What the World Needs Now Is Love"*	(Mowest)
+Both Sides Now	Dion
"Dion"*	(Laurie)
+Both Sides Now	Rod McKuen
"Alone"*	(Warner Brothers)
+Both Sides Now	Pete Seeger
"Young vs. Old"	(Columbia)

CLASSICS

Circle	Harry Chapin
"Sniper and Other Love Songs"	(Elektra)
"Greatest Stories Live"	(Elektra)
Poems, Prayers and Promises	John Denver
"Poems, Prayers and Promises"	(RCA)
"John Denver's Greatest Hits"	(RCA)
Secret o' Life	James Taylor
"J.T."	(Columbia)
We May Never Pass This Way Again	Seals and Crofts
"Seals and Crofts' Greatest Hits"	(Warner Brothers)
"Diamond Girl"	(Warner Brothers)

THEMATIC ALBUMS

"Days of Future Passed"	Moody Blues
	(London)

DEFINITIVE SONGS

Alfie	Dionne Warwick
"The Very Best of Dionne Warwick"	(United Artists)
All Things Must Pass	George Harrison
"All Things Must Pass"	(Apple)
Against the Wind	Bob Seger and the Silver Bullet Band
"Against the Wind"	(Capitol)
As I Come of Age	Stephen Stills
"Stills"	(Atlantic)
+As I Come of Age	The Pointer Sisters
"Energy"	(Planet)
Attics of My Life	The Grateful Dead
"American Beauty"	(Warner Brothers)
Big Parade	Ian Thomas Band
"Goodnight Mrs. Calabash"*	(Chrysalis)
The Balance	The Moody Blues
"Question of Balance"	(Threshold)
Caravan	Utopia
"Adventures in Utopia"	(Bearsville)
Circles	Ten Years After
"Cricklewood Green"	(Deram)

DEFINITIVE SONGS

The Circle Game	Joni Mitchell
"Ladies of the Canyon"	(Reprise)
"Miles of Aisles"	(Asylum)
+The Circle Game	Buffy Sainte-Marie
"The Best of Buffy Sainte-Marie"	(Vanguard)
+The Circle Game	Tom Rush
"Classic Rush"	(Columbia)
"Tom Rush"*	(Columbia)
"The Circle Game"	(Elektra)
+The Circle Game	Dave Van Ronk
"Dave Van Ronk and the Hudson Dusters"	(Verve/Forecast)
+The Circle Game	Ian and Sylvia
"Greatest Hits"	(Vanguard)
Complications	Steve Forbert
"Jackrabbit Slim"	(Nemperor)
Crazy Circles	Bad Company
"Desolation Angels"	(Swan Song)
Damned If You Do	Jesse Winchester
"Let the Rough Side Drag"	(Bearsville)
A Day in the Life	The Beatles
"Sgt. Pepper's Lonely Hearts Club Band"	(Capitol)
+A Day in the Life	War
	Featuring Eric Burdon
"Love Is All Around"	(ABC)
+A Day in the Life	The Bee Gees
"Sgt. Pepper's Lonely Hearts Club Band Soundtrack"	(RSO)
Days Are Short	Arlo Guthrie
"Hobo's Lullaby"	(Reprise)
Desperate Falls	Eric Carmen
"Change of Heart"	(Arista)
Everything Comes and Goes	Jim Dawson
"Elephants in the Rain"*	(RCA)
First of May	The Bee Gees
"Best of Bee Gees"	(RSO)
"Gold"	(RSO)
"Odessa"	(RSO)
Forty Without Fear	Rod McKuen
"Back to Carnegie Hall"	(Warner Brothers)

DEFINITIVE SONGS

Fourteen Today
"Sometimes When We Touch"
Dan Hill
(20th Century Records)

Full Circle
"The Byrds"
The Byrds
(Asylum)

Giving It All Away
"Just a Boy"
Leo Sayer
(Warner Brothers)

Goin' Back
"Writer"
Carole King
(Ode)

+Goin' Back
"The Notorious Byrd Brothers"
The Byrds
(Asylum)

+Goin' Back
"Nils Lofgren"
"Night After Night"
Nils Lofgren
(A&M)
(A&M)

Hard Life
"First under the Wire"
Little River Band
(Capitol)

Hard Life/Giving It All Away
"Daltrey"
Roger Daltrey
(Track)

I Found a Reason
"Loaded"
The Velvet Underground
(Cotillion)

I Know Now
"Bare Wires"
John Mayall
(London)

In My Life
"Rubber Soul"
The Beatles
(Capitol)

+In My Life
"Colors of the Day"/The Best of
Judy Collins
Judy Collins
(Elektra)

+In My Life
"Just a Boy"
Leo Sayer
(Warner Brothers)

+In My Life
"Two Sides of the Moon"*
Keith Moon
(MCA)

Isn't Life Strange
"Seventh Sojourn"
"This Is the Moody Blues"
Moody Blues
(Threshold)
(Threshold)

It's Life
"Hat Trick"
America
(Warner Brothers)

It's My Life
"Best of the Animals"
The Animals
(ABKCO)

It's My Life
"Saddle Tramp"
Charlie Daniels
(Epic)

It Takes Time
"Tenth"
The Marshall Tucker Band
(Warner Brothers)

DEFINITIVE SONGS

It Was a Very Good Year
"Portfolio"

Richie Havens
(Stormy Forest)

+It Was a Very Good Year
"It Ain't Me Babe"*

The Turtles
(White Whale)

I Want to Live
"I Want to Live"

John Denver
(RCA)

I Was Educated by Myself
"The End of the Beginning"

Richie Havens
(A&M)

Laughing at Life
"Swingtime in Springtime"*

Lew London
(Philo)

Lemon Tree
"Ten Years Together"
"Peter, Paul and Mary"

Peter, Paul and Mary
(Warner Brothers)
(Warner Brothers)

Life
"Greatest Hits"

Sly and the Family Stone
(Epic)

Life
"Something in My Life"*
"Up And Up"

Tom Paxton
(Private Stock)
(Mountain Railroad
  Records)

Life
"Rudy the Fifth"

Rick Nelson
(MCA)

Life for the Taking
"Life for the Taking"

Eddie Money
(Columbia)

Life Goes On
"Fresh Air"*

Fresh Air
(Columbia)

Life Has Its Ups and Downs
"Back to My Roots"

Solomon Burke
(Chess)

Life Is But a Dream
"Runaround Sue"*

Dion
(Laurie)

Life Is a Carnival
"Cahoots"
"Rock of Ages"
"The Last Waltz"
"Anthology"

The Band
(Capitol)
(Capitol)
(Warner Brothers)
(Capitol)

Life Is a Gamble
"Skullduggery"*

Steppenwolf
(Epic)

Life Is a Game
"L.A. Reggae"*

Johnny Rivers
(United Artists)

Life Is Just a Passing Parade
"Oneness"

Devadip Carlos Santana
(Columbia)

DEFINITIVE SONGS

Life Is So Good "JD"	John Denver (RCA)
Living and the Dying "Elephant in the Rain"*	Jim Dawson (RCA)
Man on a Fish "Birth Comes to Us All"	The Good Rats (Arista)
Moving in Stereo "The Cars"	The Cars (Elektra)
My Back Pages "Bob Dylan's Greatest Hits Vol. II" "Another Side of Bob Dylan"	Bob Dylan (Columbia) (Columbia)
+My Back Pages "The Byrds' Greatest Hits" "Younger Than Yesterday"	The Byrds (Columbia) (Columbia)
+My Back Pages "Words and Music by Bob Dylan"*	The Hollies (Epic)
+My Back Pages "Elegy"	The Nice (Mercury)
Nothing Is Your Own "Lonewolf"	Michael Murphey (Epic)
The Other Side of This Life "The Other Side of This Life"*	Fred Neil (Capitol)
+The Other Side of This Life "Animalism" "Best of Eric Burdon and the Animals, Vol. II"	The Animals (MGM) (ABKCO)
Part of the Plan "Souvenirs"	Dan Fogelberg (Epic)
Patterns "Parsley, Sage, Rosemary and Thyme"	Simon and Garfunkel (Columbia)
Poems, Prayers and Promises "John Denver's Greatest Hits" "Poems, Prayers and Promises"	John Denver (RCA) (RCA)
Prime Time "Prime Time"	Don McLean (Arista)
Question of Balance "This Is the Moody Blues" "Question of Balance"	The Moody Blues (Threshold) (Threshold)

DEFINITIVE SONGS

Reflections
"Reflections"*
Marmalade
(London)

Rings of Life
"Blue Sky, Night Thunder"
Michael Murphey
(Epic)

The Road to Utopia
"Adventures in Utopia"
Utopia
(Bearsville)

Run for Home
"Back and Fourth"
Lindisfarne
(Atco)

Running on Empty
"Running on Empty"
Jackson Browne
(Asylum)

Send in the Clowns
"Judith"
Judy Collins
(Elektra)

+Send in the Clowns
"Lou Rawls Live"
Lou Rawls
(Philadelphia International)

Shades of Gray
"Refocus"
"The Greatest Hits of the Monkees"
"Headquarters"*
The Monkees
(Arista)
(Arista)
(Colgems)

Simple Things
"Simple Things"
Carole King
(Avatar)

Sit Down Young Stranger
"If You Could Read My Mind"
Gordon Lightfoot
(Reprise)

Snake Eyes
"City Lights"
Dr. John
(Horizon/A&M)

Someday Never Comes

"Chronicle"
Creedence Clearwater
Revival
(Fantasy)

Song for the Life
"A Man Must Carry On"
Jerry Jeff Walker
(MCA)

Songs to Aging Children Come
"Clouds"
Joni Mitchell
(Reprise)

Spinning Wheel
"Blood, Sweat and Tears' Greatest
Hits"
"Blood, Sweat and Tears"
Blood, Sweat and Tears
(Columbia)

(Columbia)

Tapestry
"Tapestry"
"Her Greatest Hits"
Carole King
(Ode)
(Ode)

DEFINITIVE SONGS

That's the Way Life Goes
"Wonderful World, Beautiful People"

Jimmy Cliff
(A&M)

There But for Fortune
"Chords of Fame"
"Phil Ochs in Concert"

Phil Ochs
(A&M)
(Elektra)

+There But for Fortune
"Joan Baez"
"The First Ten Years"

Joan Baez
(Vanguard)
(A&M)

+There But for Fortune
"Cher"*

Cher
(United Artists)

These Days
"For Everyman"

Jackson Browne
(Asylum)

+These Days
"Laid Back"

Gregg Allman
(Capricorn)

+These Days
"Valley Hi"

Ian Matthews
(Elektra)

They'll Make You Cry
"The Best of the Beau Brummels"

The Beau Brummels
(Vault)

This Door Swings Both Ways
"Herman's Hermits XX—Their
  Greatest Hits"
"Both Sides of Herman's Hermits"*

Herman's Hermits
(ABKCO)

(MGM)

This Is the Way
"My Boy"*

Richard Harris
(ABC/Dunhill)

This Side of Paradise
"Roaring Silence"

Manfred Mann
(Warner Brothers)

The Thoughts of Emerlist Davjack
"The Thoughts of Emerlist Davjack"
"Autumn to Spring"*

The Nice
(Mercury)
(Charisma/Buddah)

Time in a Bottle
"Photographs and Memories"
"Time in a Bottle"

Jim Croce
(ABC)
(Lifesong)

Touch and Go
"Singles"

Rupert Holmes
(Epic)

Watching the River Run
"The Best of Friends"
"Full Sail"

Loggins and Messina
(Columbia)
(Columbia)

What a Life
"Love and Other Bruises"*

Air Supply
(Columbia)

DEFINITIVE SONGS

What Is Life?	George Harrison
"The Best of George Harrison"	(Dark Horse)
"All Things Must Pass"	(Apple)
When I Was Young	The Animals
"Best of the Animals"	(ABKCO)
The Wind	Cat Stevens
"Teaser and the Firecat"	(A&M)
Within You, Without You	The Beatles
"Sgt. Pepper's Lonely Hearts Club Band"	(Capitol)
Wonder Why We Ever Go Home	Jimmy Buffett
"Changes in Attitudes, Changes in Latitudes"	(ABC)
"You Had to Be There"	(ABC)
World	The Bee Gees
"Best of Bee Gees"	(RSO)
"Horizontal"	(RSO)
Yesterday When I Was Young	Roy Clark
"Roy Clark's Greatest Hits"	(Dot/ABC)
Young and Free	Sam Neely
"Sam Neely Two"*	(Capitol)
Younger Men Grow Older	Richie Havens
"Richie Havens on Stage"*	(Stormy Forest)
"Alarm Clock"*	(Stormy Forest)

REFERENCE SONGS

Amateur Hour	Joe Jackson
"I'm the Man"	(A&M)
Carry Me	David Crosby/Graham Nash
"Whistling Down the Wire"	(ABC)
"The Best of David Crosby and Graham Nash"	(ABC)
Changes in Latitudes, Changes in Attitudes	Jimmy Buffett
"Changes in Latitudes, Changes in Attitudes"	(ABC)
"You Had to Be There"	(ABC)
Dreidel	Don McLean
"Don McLean"*	(United Artists)
"Solo"	(United Artists)

REFERENCE SONGS

Everyday of My Life
"Diamantina Cocktail"
Little River Band
(Harvest)

Great Expectations
"Eric Carmen"
Eric Carmen
(Arista)

Life
"Izitso"
Cat Stevens
(A&M)

Live Life
"Misfits"
The Kinks
(Arista)

My Way
"Live in Concert"
Elvis Presley
(RCA)

Ob La Di, Ob La Da
"The Beatles" (White Album)
"The Beatles 1967–1970"
The Beatles
(Apple)
(Apple)

San Diego Serenade
"The Heart of Saturday Night"*
Tom Waits
(Asylum)

+San Diego Serenade
"Be True to You"
Eric Andersen
(Arista)

Sweet Seasons
"Music"
Carole King
(Ode)

Time and Life
"Deadlines"
Strawbs
(Arista)

We'll Be Together
"Terry Cashman"*
Terry Cashman
(Lifesong)

YOUR ADDITIONAL SONGS

_____

_____

_____

_____

_____

LONELINESS

Loneliness—one is the loneliest number . . . even when you are number one.

Being alone can be a beautiful experience, when you choose it. This is more aptly called solitude. Loneliness is not usually chosen. It is that aching kind of emptiness that accompanies those times in life when you are without family, friends, or the person that you love most.

Related Categories: Divorce, Outcasts/Hobos, Self-Identity,
   Love: "Babe I'm Gonna Leave You",
   Love: "I Still Miss Someone",
   Love: "Darling Be Home Soon"

+Same as Song Above
*Hard-to-find Songs/Albums

CLASSICS

All by Myself "Eric Carmen"	Eric Carmen (Arista)
Alone Again, Naturally "Himself"	Gilbert O'Sullivan (MAM)
Eleanor Rigby "The Beatles 1962–1966" "Revolver"	The Beatles (Capitol) (Capitol)
+Eleanor Rigby "Mixed Bag"*	Richie Havens (Stormy Forest)
+Eleanor Rigby "Twenty-Fifth Anniversary"	Ray Charles (ABC)
+Eleanor Rigby "MacArthur Park"	Four Tops (Motown)
+Eleanor Rigby "Vanilla Fudge"*	Vanilla Fudge (Atco)
+Eleanor Rigby "Joan"*	Joan Baez (Vanguard)
+Eleanor Rigby "Teegarden and Van Winkle"*	Teegarden and Van Winkle (Westbound)
+Eleanor Rigby "Whose Garden Was This?"	John Denver (RCA)

CLASSICS

+Eleanor Rigby
"Two Sides of Gene Chandler"

Gene Chandler
(Brunswick)

+Eleanor Rigby
"Live at the Fillmore West"

Aretha Franklin
(Atlantic)

+Eleanor Rigby   •
"Ecology"

Rare Earth
(Rare Earth)

+Eleanor Rigby
"Do Your Thing"

Jackie Wilson
(Brunswick)

Lonely People
"History of America"

America
(Warner Brothers)

THEMATIC ALBUMS

"Lonewolf"

Michael Murphey
(Epic)

"Nighthawks at the Diner"

Tom Waits
(Asylum)

DEFINITIVE SONGS

Absent Friend
"Nomadness"

Strawbs
(A&M)

Accidentally Like a Martyr
"Excitable Boy"

Warren Zevon
(Asylum)

After Hours
"Velvet Underground"*
"Live at Max's Kansas City"
"The Velvet Underground"

The Velvet Underground
(MGM)
(Cotillion)
(MGM)

All Is Loneliness
"Janis Joplin in Concert"

Janis Joplin
(Columbia)

Alone
"New Blood"*

Blood, Sweat and Tears
(Columbia)

Alone Tonight
"Not Far from Free"*

Don Harrison Band
(Mercury)

Alone Too Long
"Hall and Oates"

Hall and Oates
(RCA)

Am I Blue?
"It's Only Love"

Rita Coolidge
(A&M)

Are You Lonesome Tonight?
"Worldwide 50 Gold Award Hits,
    Vol. 1"

Elvis Presley
(RCA)

DEFINITIVE SONGS

As Tears Go By
"Hot Rocks 1964–1971"
"December's Children"

The Rolling Stones
(London)
(London)

+As Tears Go By
"Marianne Faithful's Greatest Hits"

Marianne Faithful
(London)

Better Place to Be
"Sniper and Other Love Songs"

Harry Chapin
(Elektra)

Blackness of the Night
"New Masters"

Cat Stevens
(Deram)

Blue
"Blue"
"Miles of Aisles"

Joni Mitchell
(Reprise)
(Asylum)

Blue Moon
(45 RPM Single)*

Marcels
(Colpix)

+Blue Moon
"Self Portrait"

Bob Dylan
(Columbia)

The Blues Are Just a Bad Dream
"James Taylor"

James Taylor
(Apple)

Captain Jack
"Piano Man"

Billy Joel
(Columbia)

Don't Let Me Be Lonely
"One Man Dog"
"Greatest Hits"

James Taylor
(Warner Brothers)
(Warner Brothers)

Don't Let the Sun Catch You Crying
"Gerry and the Pacemakers' Greatest
Hits"
"Don't Let the Sun Catch You
Crying"

Gerry and the Pacemakers
(Laurie)

(Laurie)

+Don't Let the Sun Catch You Crying
"This Is Jackie DeShannon"*

Jackie DeShannon
(Imperial)

Don't Let the Sun Go Down on Me
"Caribou"
"Greatest Hits"

Elton John
(MCA)
(MCA)

+Don't Let the Sun Go Down on Me
"The Three Degrees Live"

The Three Degrees
(Philadelphia International)

Do You Know How It Feels
"The Gilded Palace of Sin"

The Flying Burrito Brothers
(A&M)

Early Morning Rain
"The Very Best of Gordon Lightfoot"

Gordon Lightfoot
(United Artists)

DEFINITIVE SONGS

+ Early Morning Rain
"Ten Years Together"
"See What Tomorrow Brings"

Peter, Paul and Mary
(Warner Brothers)
(Warner Brothers)

+ Early Morning Rain
"Self Portrait"

Bob Dylan
(Columbia)

Empty Chairs
"American Pie"

Don McLean
(United Artists)

Everybody's Lonely
"Heads and Tales"

Harry Chapin
(Elektra)

Falling
"Monkey Island"

J. Geils Band
(Atlantic)

First Night Alone Without You
"Home Plate"

Bonnie Raitt
(Warner Brothers)

Fly Away
"John Denver's Greatest Hits Vol. II"
"Windsong"

John Denver
(RCA)
(RCA)

Frisco Depot
"Frisco Mabel Joy"*

Mickey Newberry
(Elektra)

Good Time Charlie's Got the Blues
"O'Keefe"
"The O'Keefe Files"

Danny O'Keefe
(Signpost)
(Warner Brothers)

Heartsong
"Randy Meisner"*

Randy Meisner
(Asylum)

Heartbreak Hotel
"Worldwide 50 Gold Award Hits,
Vol. 1"

Elvis Presley
(RCA)

+ Heartbreak Hotel
"June 1, 1974"

Kevin Ayers
(Island)

+ Heartbreak Hotel
"Genesis"

Delaney and Bonnie
(Capricorn)

+ Heartbreak Hotel
"Sha Na Na"

Sha Na Na
(Kama Sutra)

He Lives Alone
"On My Way to Where"*

Dory Previn
(United Artists)

Help Me Make It Through the Night
"Me and Bobby McGee"

Kris Kristofferson
(Monument)

+ Help Me Make It Through the Night
"Blessed Are"

Joan Baez
(Vanguard)

+ Help Me Make It Through the Night
"Anthology"

Gladys Knight and The Pips
(Motown)

DEFINITIVE SONGS

+Help Me Make It Through the Night Rod McKuen
"Cycles"* (Buddah)

+Help Me Make It Through the Night Willie Nelson
"Willie Nelson Sings Kris (Columbia)
   Kristofferson"

+Help Me Make It Through the Night Elvis Presley
"Welcome To My World" (RCA)

Hey There Lonely Girl Eddie Holman
(45 RPM Single)* (ABC)

Homeward Bound Simon and Garfunkel
"Simon and Garfunkel's Greatest (Columbia)
   Hits"

"Parsley, Sage, Rosemary and Thyme" (Columbia)

+Homeward Bound Paul Simon
"Live Rhymin'" (Columbia)

+Homeward Bound David Clayton-Thomas
"Clayton"* (ABC)

I Ain't Blue Bonnie Raitt
"Bonnie Raitt" (Warner Brothers)

I Am a Rock Simon and Garfunkel
"Simon and Garfunkel's Greatest (Columbia)
   Hits"

"Sounds of Silence" (Columbia)

+I Am a Rock The Hollies
"Bus Stop"* (Imperial)

I'm So Afraid Fleetwood Mac
"Fleetwood Mac" (Reprise)

I'm So Lonesome I Could Cry B. J. Thomas
"The Very Best of B. J. Thomas" (United Artists)

I Don't Want to Be Alone Tonight Dr. Hook
"Pleasure and Pain" (Capitol)

Let Me Be Lonely Janis Ian
"Miracle Row" (Columbia)

Living Alone Phil Everly
"Living Alone" (Elektra)

Loneliness Horslips
"The Man Who Built America" (DJM Records)

Loneliness Jim Glover
"Changes"* (Verve/Folkways)

DEFINITIVE SONGS

Loneliness Is Just a Word
"Chicago III"
Chicago
(Columbia)

Lonely
"Closing Time"
Tom Waits
(Asylum)

Lonely at the Top
"Sail Away"
Randy Newman
(Warner Brothers)

Lonely Avenue
"Before We Were So Rudely
    Interrupted"
The Animals
(United Artists)

Lonely Boy
"Vintage Years 1957–1961"
Paul Anka
(Sire)

Lonely Boy
"What's Wrong with This Picture"
Andrew Gold
(Asylum)

Lonely Days, Lonely Nights
"Two Years On"
The Bee Gees
(RSO)

Lonely Girl
" '73"
The Mark-Almond Band
(Columbia)

Lonely Hours
"A Giant of Rock and Roll"*
Ronnie Hawkins
(Monument)

Lonely Man
"Worldwide 50 Gold Award Hits,
    Vol. 2"
Elvis Presley
(RCA)

Lonely Sea
"Surfin' U.S.A."
The Beach Boys
(Capitol)

The Lonely Side
"Beau Brummels"*
Beau Brummels
(Warner Brothers)

Lonely Woman
"Eli and the 13th Confession"
Laura Nyro
(Columbia)

Loners
"Lonewolf"*
Michael Murphey
(Epic)

Lonesome and a Long Way from
    Home
"Motel Shot"
Delaney and Bonnie

(Atco)

Lonesome Gal
"I'm in Love"*
Rory Block
(Blue Goose)

Lonesome Tears
"Holly in the Hills"*
Buddy Holly
(MCA)

DEFINITIVE SONGS

Lonesome Town
"A Giant of Rock and Roll"*
Ronnie Hawkins
(Monument)

+Lonesome Town
"Ricky Nelson"
Rick Nelson
(United Artists)

Long and Winding Road
"Let It Be"
"Love Songs"
The Beatles
(Apple)
(Apple)

+Long and Winding Road
"Standing Ovation"
Gladys Knight and The Pips
(Soul)

+Long and Winding Road
"Come On Over"
Olivia Newton-John
(MCA)

+Long and Winding Road
"All This and World War II"
Leo Sayer
(20th Century-Fox)

Lost and Lonely
"Gimme Some Neck"
Ron Woods
(Columbia)

Many Rivers to Cross
"Wonderful World, Beautiful People"
Jimmy Cliff
(A&M)

+Many Rivers to Cross
"Prisoner in Disguise"
Linda Ronstadt
(Asylum)

+Many Rivers to Cross
"Before We Were So Rudely
　Interrupted"
The Animals
(United Artists)

Marcie
"Joni Mitchell"
Joni Mitchell
(Reprise)

A Most Peculiar Man
"Sounds of Silence"
Simon and Garfunkel
(Columbia)

Mr. Lonely
"Bobby Vinton's Greatest Hits"
"Autumn Memories"*
Bobby Vinton
(Epic)
(Epic)

A Nice Boy Like Me
"Trying to Get That Feeling Again"
Barry Manilow
(Arista)

Oh Lonesome Me
"After the Gold Rush"
Neil Young
(Reprise)

+Oh Lonesome Me
"So Fine"
Loggins and Messina
(Columbia)

One Lonely Room
"Songwriter"*
Justin Hayward
(Threshold)

DEFINITIVE SONGS

Only Alone
"Back and Fourth"
Lindisfarne
(Atco)

The Only Living Boy in New York
"Bridge over Troubled Water"
Simon and Garfunkel
(Columbia)

Only the Blues
"Cosmic Wheels"*
Donovan
(Epic)

Only the Lonely
"The Very Best of Roy Orbison"
Roy Orbison
(Monument)

Out on the Weekend
"Harvest"
Neil Young
(Reprise)

Piano Man
"Piano Man"
Billy Joel
(Columbia)

Policeman
"Chicago XI"
Chicago
(Columbia)

Rainy Night in Georgia
"Best of Brook Benton"
Brook Benton
(Atco)

Running Dry
"Everybody Knows This Is Nowhere"
Neil Young
(Reprise)

Sailing Nights
"Beautiful Loser"
Bob Seger
(Capitol)

See the Funny Little Clown
"10th Anniversary Album"
Bobby Goldsboro
(United Artists)

Shadow and Me
"Americana"
Leon Russell
(Paradise)

Sittin' on the Dock of the Bay
"The Best of Otis Redding"
"Sittin' on the Dock of the Bay"
Otis Redding
(Atco)
(Volt)

+Sittin' on the Dock of the Bay
"All Fly Home"
Al Jarreau
(Warner Brothers)

+Sittin' on the Dock of the Bay
"Hickory Holler Revisited"
O. C. Smith
(Columbia)

Six-Thirty Sunday Morning
"Taught by Experts"
Peter Allen
(A&M)

So Hard Living Without You
"New Days"*
Airwaves
(A&M)

Solitaire
"Greatest Hits"
Neil Sedaka
(Rocket Records)

+Solitaire
"Stay the Night"
Jane Olivor
(Warner Brothers)

DEFINITIVE SONGS

Sorrow "Peter, Paul and Mary"	Peter, Paul and Mary (Warner Brothers)
So Sad "Golden Hits of the Everly Brothers"	The Everly Brothers (Warner Brothers)
So Sad "Dark Horse"	George Harrison (Dark Horse)
The Sun Ain't Gonna Shine Anymore "The History of British Rock"	Walker Brothers (Sire)
There's a Lot of Lonely People Tonight "Short Stories"	Harry Chapin (Elektra)
There's a Place "Introducing the Beatles" (45 RPM Single)*	The Beatles (Vee Jay) (Vee Jay)
There Must Be Someone "Ballad of Easy Rider"	The Byrds (Columbia)
These Days "For Everyman"	Jackson Browne (Asylum)
+These Days "Laid Back"	Gregg Allman (Capricorn)
+These Days "Valley Hi"*	Ian Mathews (Elektra)
Those Lonely, Lonely Nights "Gumbo"	Dr. John (Atco)
Three Flights Up "Tapestry" "Solo"	Don McLean (United Artists) (United Artists)
Tonight I Feel So Far Away from Home "Alive on Arrival"	Steve Forbert (Nemperor)
Victoria Dines Alone "Morning Again"*	Tom Paxton (Elektra)
Virginia Avenue "Closing Time"	Tom Waits (Asylum)
Walkin' the Streets Alone "Long Hard Ride"	The Marshall Tucker Band (Capricorn)
We All Have to Be Alone "Thoroughbred"	Carole King (Ode)

DEFINITIVE SONGS

We've Got Tonight

"Stranger in Town"
Bob Seger and the Silver Bullet Band
(Capitol)

Why Should I Be So Lonely
"I'm in Love"*
Rory Block
(Blue Goose)

A Woman Left Lonely
"Pearl"
Janis Joplin
(Columbia)

+A Woman Left Lonely
"Queen of the Night"
Maggie Bell
(Atlantic)

Yellow Cat
"Rhymes and Reasons"
John Denver
(RCA)

Yesterday
"Love Songs"
"The Beatles 1962–1966"
"Yesterday . . . And Today"
The Beatles
(Capitol)
(Capitol)
(Capitol)

+Yesterday
"Wings Over America"
Wings
(Capitol)

+Yesterday
"Go Away from My World"*
Marianne Faithful
(London)

+Yesterday
"Listen"
Ray Charles
(ABC)

Yesterday's Music
"Queen of the Night"
Maggie Bell
(Atlantic)

Young Girl Blues
"In Concert"
"Mellow Yellow"
Donovan
(Epic)
(Epic)

You're Only Lonely
"You're Only Lonely"
J. D. Souther
(Columbia)

You're Telling Me
"Between Today and Yesterday"*
Alan Price
(Warner Brothers)

REFERENCE SONGS

Alone
"Second Gold Vault of Hits"
The Four Seasons
(Philips)

Another Day
"Wings Greatest"
Wings
(Capitol)

Boredom
"Everything Playing"*
The Lovin' Spoonful
(Kama Sutra)

REFERENCE SONGS

The Boxer "Bridge over Troubled Water" "Simon and Garfunkel's Greatest Hits"	Simon and Garfunkel (Columbia) (Columbia)
+The Boxer "Self Portrait"	Bob Dylan (Columbia)
+The Boxer "Live Rhymin'"	Paul Simon (Columbia)
Bridge over Troubled Water "Bridge over Troubled Water" "Simon and Garfunkel's Greatest Hits"	Simon and Garfunkel (Columbia) (Columbia)
Bridge over Troubled Water "Live Rhymin'"	Paul Simon (Columbia)
+Bridge over Troubled Water "What the World Needs Now Is Love"*	Tom Clay (Mowest)
+Bridge over Troubled Water "Gimme Shelter"	Merry Clayton (Ode)
+Bridge over Troubled Water "Why Can't I Touch You"	Ronnie Dyson (Columbia)
+Bridge over Troubled Water "Quiet Fire"	Roberta Flack (Atlantic)
+Bridge over Troubled Water "Greatest Hits"	Aretha Franklin (Columbia)
+Bridge over Troubled Water "Standing Ovation"	Gladys Knight and The Pips (Soul)
+Bridge over Troubled Water "That's the Way It Is"	Elvis Presley (RCA)
+Bridge over Troubled Water "Sedaka Live in Australia"	Neil Sedaka (RCA)
+Bridge over Troubled Water "Let Me Be Your Woman"	Linda Clifford (RSO)
Coming Down Again "Goats Head Soup"	The Rolling Stones (Rolling Stone Records)
Hard Life "Daltrey"	Roger Daltrey (MCA/Track)
Helpless "Déjà Vu"	Crosby, Stills, Nash & Young (Atlantic)

REFERENCE SONGS

+Helpless   Neil Young
"Decade"   (Reprise)
"The Last Waltz" (Soundtrack)   (Warner Brothers)

I Am a Lonesome Hobo   Bob Dylan
"John Wesley Harding"   (Columbia)

I'm Blowin' Away   Bonnie Raitt
"Home Plate"   (Warner Brothers)

+I'm Blowin' Away   American Flyer
"Spirit of a Woman"   (United Artists)

+I'm Blowin' Away   Linda Ronstadt
"Living in the U.S.A."   (Asylum)

+I'm Blowin' Away   Joan Baez
"Blowin' Away"   (Portrait)

I Won't Be Hangin' 'Round   Linda Ronstadt
"Linda Ronstadt"   (Capitol)

Is It Really Love at All?   Eric Andersen
"The Best Songs"   (Arista)

+Is It Really Love at All?   Jericho Harp
"Jericho Harp"*   (United Artists)

I've Been Lonely Too Long   The Young Rascals
"Time Peace"   (Atlantic)
"Collection"   (Atlantic)

+I've Been Lonely Too Long   Richie Furay
"I Still Have Dreams"   (Asylum)

Please Send Me Someone to Love   The Animals
"Before We Were So Rudely   (United Artists)
   Interrupted"

Sad Young Man   Strawbs
"Hero and Heroine"   (A&M)

Someone Saved My Life Tonight   Elton John
"Captain Fantastic and the Brown   (MCA)
   Dirt Cowboy"

Stay the Night   Jane Olivor
"Stay the Night"   (Warner Brothers)

Stella Blue   The Grateful Dead
"Wake of the Flood"   (Grateful Dead Records)

Tired of Being Alone   Al Green
"Al Green's Greatest Hits"   (Hi)

REFERENCE SONGS

Winter Has Me in Its Grip   Don McLean
"Homeless Brother"*   (United Artists)

YOUR ADDITIONAL SONGS

_____

_____

_____

_____

_____

MARRIAGE

Marriage—Something old, something new
Something borrowed, something blue.

These songs about marriage cover a lot of ground, much like marriage itself. We have divided this topic into four clearly defined sections:

1. Getting Married—and the ceremony itself
2. Happily Married (too few songs here)
3. Unhappily Married (too many songs here)
4. Adultery (there'll always be songs here)

Related Categories: Divorce, Fathers, Mothers, Pregnancy, Sexuality,
   Love: "And I Love You So"

+Same as Song Above
 *Hard-to-find Songs/Albums

YOUR ADDITIONAL SONGS

_____

_____

_____

_____

_____

Getting Married

CLASSICS

Wedding Bell Blues "Greatest Hits on Earth"	The Fifth Dimension (Arista)
+Wedding Bell Blues "First Songs"	Laura Nyro (Columbia)
Wedding Song "Paul And"*	Paul Stookey (Warner Brothers)

THEMATIC ALBUMS

"Wedding Album"
Leon and Mary Russell
(Warner Brothers)

DEFINITIVE SONGS

Be My Wife
"Low"
David Bowie
(RCA)

The Bells
"Gonna Take a Miracle"
Laura Nyro and Labelle
(Columbia)

Big Bad Bill Is Sweet William Now
"Jazz"
Ry Cooder
(Warner Brothers)

+Big Bad Bill Is Sweet William Now
"Champagne Charlie"
Leon Redbone
(Warner Brothers)

Bride of 1945
"Woodsmoke and Oranges"*
Paul Siebel
(Elektra)

Chapel of Love
(45 RPM Single)*
Dixie Cups
(Red Bird)

+Chapel of Love
"Let It Be Written"*
Ellie Greenwich
(Verve)

+Chapel of Love
"15 Big Ones"
The Beach Boys
(Brother/Reprise)

+Chapel of Love
"The Divine Miss M"
Bette Midler
(Atlantic)

Church Bells May Ring
(45 RPM Single)*
Five Willows
(Melba)

Country Pie
"Celebration"
Celebration
(Pacific Arts)

Dammit Janet
"The Rocky Horror Picture Show"
  (Soundtrack)
Various Artists
(Ode)

Emaline
"Back in Your Life"
Jonathan Richmond
(Beserkley)

For Me and My Gal
"A Little Touch of Schmilsson"
Harry Nilsson
(RCA)

Future Mrs. 'Awkins
"Both Sides of Herman's Hermits"*
Herman's Hermits
(MGM)

Girl I Want to Marry You
"Love, Lost and Found"*
Jay and the Techniques
(Smash)

DEFINITIVE SONGS

Goodbye Old Buddies
"Get Closer"
Seals and Crofts
(Warner Brothers)

Guide for the Married Man
"Happy Together Again"
The Turtles
(Sire)

Hawaiian Wedding Song
"Elvis in Concert"
Elvis Presley
(RCA)

Here Comes My Wife
"Very Young and Early Songs"
Cat Stevens
(Deram)

Hey Paula
(45 RPM Single)*
Paul and Paula
(Philips)

I'd Like to Take You Home
"See"*
The Rascals
(Atlantic)

I Hear Bells
(45 RPM Single)*
The Del-Vikings
(Dot)

I Never Will Marry
"Roses and Sunshine"
Nana Mouskouri
(Cachet)

I Wish That We Were Married
(45 RPM Single)*
Ronnie and the Hi-Lites
(Joy)

I Would Marry You Today
"Inner Views"*
Sonny Bono
(Atco)

I'm Gonna Get Married
"Mr. Personality's Fifteen Hits"
Lloyd Price
(ABC/Paramount)

+I'm Gonna Get Married
(45 RPM Single)*
Lou Christie
(Buddah)

I'm So Young
"Dance, Dance, Dance"
"The Beach Boys Today"
The Beach Boys
(Capitol)
(Capitol)

If You Wanna Be Happy
(45 RPM Single)
Jimmy Soul
(S.P.Q.R.)

+If You Wanna Be Happy
"Stone Alone"
Bill Wyman
(Rolling Stone Records)

+If You Wanna Be Happy
"Randy Meisner"*
Randy Meisner
(Asylum)

Indian Wedding
"More of Roy Orbison's Greatest
    Hits"
Roy Orbison
(Monument)

John Riley
"First Ten Years"
Joan Baez
(Vanguard)

DEFINITIVE SONGS

+John Riley
"Fifth Dimension"
The Byrds
(Columbia)

+John Riley
"Maid of Constant Sorrow"
Judy Collins
(Elektra)

Just Got Married
"Born Again"
Randy Newman
(Warner Brothers)

Let the Bells Keep Ringing
"The Vintage Years 1957–1961"
Paul Anka
(Sire)

Mail Order Annie
"Short Stories"
Harry Chapin
(Elektra)

Makin' Whoopee
"A Man and His Music"
Ray Charles
(ABC)

Marriage Madness
"Back to the Roots"
John Mayall
(Polydor)

The Married Life
"Made in Chicago"
The Buckinghams
(Columbia)

Monday Morning
"A Song Will Rise"
Peter, Paul and Mary
(Warner Brothers)

Not Too Young to Get Married

"Phil Spector's Greatest Hits"
Bob B. Soxx and the Blue
Jeans
(Warner-Spector)

Oh Happy Day
"That's Enough for Me"*
Peter Yarrow
(Warner Brothers)

Peggy Sue Got Married
"The Buddy Holly Story"
Buddy Holly
(MCA)

Proposal
"My Boy"*
Richard Harris
(ABC/Dunhill)

Roll Georgia
"Pacific Gas & Electric
  Starring Charles Allen"
Pacific Gas & Electric
(ABC/Dunhill)

Semi-Detached Suburban Mr. James
"The Mighty Quinn"
Manfred Mann
(Mercury)

She Moved Through the Fair
"Watermark"
Art Garfunkel
(Columbia)

Something Blue
"Deadly Nightshade"*
Deadly Nightshade
(Phantom/RCA)

DEFINITIVE SONGS

Sportin' Life "Tarzana Kid"*	John Sebastian (Reprise)
Starting a New Life "Tupelo Honey"	Van Morrison (Warner Brothers)
Tell Me Who I'll Marry "Golden Apples of the Sun"	Judy Collins (Elektra)
The $1000 Wedding "Grievous Angel"	Gram Parsons (Reprise)
Today (June Song) "If Love Is Real"*	Randy Edleman (Arista)
Today I Met the Boy I'm Gonna Marry "Phil Spector's Greatest Hits"	Darlene Love (Warner-Spector)
+Today I Met the Boy I'm Gonna Marry "Let It Be Written"*	Ellie Greenwich (Verve)
To the Aisle "American Graffiti" (Soundtrack)	Five Satins (MCA)
The Wedding (45 RPM Single)*	Julie Rogers (Mercury)
The Wedding (45 RPM Single)*	Solitaires (Old Town)
Wedding Bells "Country Class"	Jerry Lee Lewis (Mercury)
Wedding Blues "I Can Help"	Billy Swan (Monument)
Wedding Day in Funeralville "Common Sense"*	John Prine (Atlantic)
Wedding Dress "Reflection"	Pentangle (Reprise)
Wedding in White "Ian Tamblyn"	Ian Tamblyn (Cream)
The Wedding Song "Quiet Storm"	Smokey Robinson (Tamla)
Wedding Song "Planet Waves"	Bob Dylan (Asylum)
+Wedding Song "Fire and Fleet and Candlelight"*	Buffy Sainte-Marie (Vanguard)

DEFINITIVE SONGS

The Wedding Song
"Booker T. and Priscilla"

Booker T. and Priscilla
(A&M)

Wedding Song
"Outlasting the Blues"

Arlo Guthrie
(Warner Brothers)

Wedding Song
"Suite for Late Summer"*

Dion
(Warner Brothers)

We've Only Just Begun
"Classics"

Paul Williams
(A&M)

+We've Only Just Begun
"Singles"

The Carpenters
(A&M)

We'll Run Away
"All Summer Long"

The Beach Boys
(Capitol)

What Do I Keep
"Sunset and Other Beginnings"

Melanie
(Neighborhood)

White on White
(45 RPM Single)*

Danny Williams
(United Artists)

Yes My Darling
"Fats Domino"

Fats Domino
(United Artists)

You and Me
"Life Is Like That"*

Tom Chapin
(Fantasy)

You Never Can Tell
"Golden Decade—Vol. II"

Chuck Berry
(Chess)

+You Never Can Tell
"Luxury Liner"
"Profile: Best of Emmylou Harris"

Emmylou Harris
(Warner Brothers)
(Warner Brothers)

+You Never Can Tell
"So Fine"

Loggins and Messina
(Columbia)

REFERENCE SONGS

Ain't Gonna Do It
"Cookin' with Fats"

Fats Domino
(United Artists)

All My Friends Are Getting Married
"Skyhooks"

Skyhooks
(Mercury)

Anniversary Song
"Oh How We Danced"

Jim Capaldi
(Island)

Apples, Peaches, Pumpkin Pie
(45 RPM Single)

Jay and the Techniques
(Smash)

REFERENCE SONGS

Boy with the Moon and Star "Catch Bull at Four"	Cat Stevens (A&M)
Can't You Hear My Heartbeat "Herman's Hermits XX—Their Greatest Hits" "Herman's Hermits on Tour"*	Herman's Hermits (ABKCO) (MGM)
Dear Doctor "Beggars Banquet"	The Rolling Stones (London)
Do Wah Diddy Diddy "The Manfred Mann Album" "The Best of Manfred Mann" "The History of British Rock"	Manfred Mann (Ascot) (Janus) (Sire)
+Do Wah Diddy Diddy "What's Wrong with This Picture?"	Andrew Gold (Asylum)
+Do Wah Diddy Diddy "Puttin' on the Dog"	Hound (Columbia)
Follow Me "John Denver's Greatest Hits"	John Denver (RCA)
+Follow Me "Mary"*	Mary Travers (Warner Brothers)
I'm Gonna Be King "New Masters"	Cat Stevens (Deram)
I'm Henry VIII, I Am "Herman's Hermits XX—Their Greatest Hits" "Herman's Hermits on Tour"*	Herman's Hermits (ABKCO) (MGM)
I Knew the Bride "Get It"	Dave Edmunds (Swan Songs)
I'll Be Your Lover Too "His Band and Street Choir"	Van Morrison (Warner Brothers)
It's Gonna Work Out Fine "The Best of Manfred Mann"	Manfred Mann (Janus)
Jessica "Diamond Girl"	Seals and Crofts (Warner Brothers)
The Lady Came from Baltimore "The Best of Tim Hardin"	Tim Hardin (Verve)
Let's Get Married "Greatest Hits"	Al Green (Hi)

REFERENCE SONGS

Let the Music Begin "Victim of Romance"*	Michelle Phillips (A&M)
Love Me Tender "50 World Wide Gold Award Hits"	Elvis Presley (RCA)
+Love Me Tender "Living in the U.S.A."	Linda Ronstadt (Asylum)
+Love Me Tender "Someone Is Standing Outside"	Bill Medley (MGM)
+Love Me Tender "King Does the King's Things"	Albert King (Stax)
+Love Me Tender "B. J. Thomas' Greatest Hits"	B. J. Thomas (Scepter)
+Love Me Tender "Warm and Tender Soul"	Percy Sledge (Atlantic)
My Sweet Lady "Poems, Prayers and Promises" "John Denver's Greatest Hits Vol. II"	John Denver (RCA) (RCA)
No Dough "People Like Us"	The Mamas and The Papas (ABC/Dunhill)
Ooh Girl "The Reggie Knighton Band"*	The Reggie Knighton Band (Columbia)
Pamela Brown "The Best of Leo Kottke"	Leo Kottke (Capitol)
Pledging My Love "The Giant of Rock and Roll"*	Ronnie Hawkins (Monument)
Sailor "Smiler"	Rod Stewart (Mercury)
So Good Together "Andy Kim's Greatest Hits"	Andy Kim (Steed)
So Long Dad "Randy Newman Live"	Randy Newman (Reprise)
+So Long Dad "Nilsson Sings Newman"	Harry Nilsson (RCA)
+So Long Dad "This Price Is Right"	Alan Price (Parrot)
South Coast "Peaks Valleys Honky-Tonks & Alleys"	Michael Murphey (Epic)

228 *The Rock Music Source Book*

Spend Your Life with Me "Let It Flow"	Dave Mason (Columbia)
Sue's Gotta Be Mine "The Vintage Years"	Del Shannon (Sire)
That's The Way I Always Heard It Should Be	Carly Simon
"Carly Simon"	(Elektra)
"The Best of Carly Simon Vol. I"	(Elektra)
Things I'd Like to Say "Revelations"*	The New Colony Six (Mercury)
True Fine Love "Book of Dreams" "Greatest Hits 1974–1978"	The Steve Miller Band (Capitol) (Capitol)
Wedding in Cherokee County "Good Old Boys"	Randy Newman (Reprise)
Where Were You (on Our Wedding Day)	Lloyd Price
"Mr. Personality's Fifteen Hits"	(ABC/Paramount)
Worst That Could Happen "Brooklyn Bridge"*	Brooklyn Bridge (Buddah)
Wouldn't It Be Nice "Pet Sounds" "Good Vibrations—Best of the Beach Boys"	The Beach Boys (Capitol) (Brother/Reprise)
"Live in London" "The Beach Boys in Concert"	(Capitol) (Brother/Reprise)
You Send Me "This Is Sam Cooke"	Sam Cooke (RCA)
+You Send Me "Fly Like an Eagle"	The Steve Miller Band (Capitol)
+You Send Me "Smiler"	Rod Stewart (Mercury)
+You Send Me "Lady's Choice"*	Bonnie Bramlett (Capricorn)
+You Send Me "We Remember Sam Cooke"	The Supremes (Motown)
+You Send Me "Nicolette"	Nicolette Larson (Warner Brothers)

YOUR ADDITIONAL SONGS

_____

_____

_____

_____

_____

Happily Married

CLASSICS

Little Green Apples "O. C. Smith's Greatest Hits"	O. C. Smith (Columbia)
+Little Green Apples "Golden Greats"	Roger Miller (Mercury)
+Little Green Apples "Honey"*	Bobby Goldsboro (United Artists)
Ob La Di, Ob La Da "The Beatles" (White Album) "The Beatles 1967–1970"	The Beatles (Apple) (Apple)
Ruby Jean and Billy Lee "Diamond Girl"	Seals and Crofts (Warner Brothers)

DEFINITIVE SONGS

Ain't Nobody Else Like You "Mama's Big Ones—Her Greatest Hits"	Mama Cass (ABC/Dunhill)
Always Be Together "Worlds Away"	Pablo Cruise (A&M)
By Surprise "Reunion"	Peter, Paul and Mary (Warner Brothers)
Danny's Song "The Best of Friends" "Sittin' In" "Loggins and Messina on Stage"	Loggins and Messina (Columbia) (Columbia) (Columbia)
+Danny's Song "Country"	Anne Murray (Capitol)
Dreams Go By "Greatest Stories Live"	Harry Chapin (Elektra)
Fifty Years "Let Me Live in Your Life"	Ben E. King (Atlantic)
Friend, Lover, Woman, Wife "Greatest Hits"	Mac Davis (Columbia)
+Friend, Lover, Woman, Wife "At Home"	O. C. Smith (Columbia)
+Friend, Lover, Woman, Wife "Tonight I'm Singing Just for You"	Country Joe McDonald (Vanguard)

DEFINITIVE SONGS

Good Hearted Woman
"Pass the Chicken and Listen"*
The Everly Brothers
(RCA)

+Good Hearted Woman
"Greatest Hits"
Waylon Jennings
(RCA)

Hand It to You
"High and Outside"
Steve Goodman
(Elektra)

I Do It for Your Love
"Greatest Hits Etc."
"Still Crazy After All These Years"
Paul Simon
(Columbia)
(Columbia)

Kisses Sweeter Than Wine
"Greatest Hits"
The Weavers
(Vanguard)

My Wife
"Who's Next"
The Who
(MCA)

Old Father Time
"That's Enough for Me"*
Peter Yarrow
(Warner Brothers)

Poem for My Little Lady
"Transition"*
Kenny Rogers
(Reprise)

Queen of '59
"Streetheart"*
Dion
(Warner Brothers)

Sarah Jane
"Dylan"
Bob Dylan
(Columbia)

Wedding Song
"Outlasting the Blues"
Arlo Guthrie
(Warner Brothers)

Working Man's Woman

"Brujo"
New Riders of the Purple
Sage
(Columbia)

YOUR ADDITIONAL SONGS

_____

_____

_____

_____

_____

Unhappily Married

CLASSICS

The Arrangement "Ladies of the Canyon"	Joni Mitchell (Reprise)
Husbands and Wives "Golden Greats"	Roger Miller (Mercury)
+Husbands and Wives "Goodnight Vienna"	Ringo Starr (Apple)
+Husbands and Wives "Stones" "Rainbow"	Neil Diamond (MCA) (MCA)
+Husbands and Wives "Pass the Chicken and Listen"*	The Everly Brothers (RCA)

DEFINITIVE SONGS

Away Away "Between Today and Yesterday"	Alan Price (Warner Brothers)
The Ballad of Lucy Jordan "Broken English"	Marianne Faithful (Island)
Band of Gold "Band of Gold"	Freda Payne (Invictus)
Chain of Fools "Aretha's Greatest Hits"	Aretha Franklin (Atlantic)
Dissatisfied Man "Words and Pictures"*	Bobby Goldsboro (United Artists)
Dogtown "Heads and Tales"	Harry Chapin (Elektra)
Dreams of the Everyday Housewife "Young Girl"*	Gary Puckett and the Union Gap (Columbia)
+Dreams of the Everyday Housewife (45 RPM Single)	Glen Campbell (Capitol)
Everyday Another Hair Turns to Grey "The Mighty Quinn"	Manfred Mann (Mercury)
Fairweather Father "Another Passenger"	Carly Simon (Elektra)
The Great American Marriage "You Never Know Who Your Friends Are"*	Al Kooper (Columbia)

DEFINITIVE SONGS

Housewife "Americana"	Leon Russell (Paradise)
I've Lost You "Worldwide 50 Gold Award Hits, Vol. 1"	Elvis Presley (RCA)
I Need Me to Be for Me "Reunion"	Peter, Paul and Mary (Warner Brothers)
I Stayed Away Too Long "Pousette Dart Band 3"	Pousette Dart Band (Capitol)
Jody Girl	Bob Seger and the Silver Bullet Band
"Live Bullet" "Beautiful Loser"	(Capitol) (Capitol)
Let's Hang On "Gold Vault of Hits" "The Four Seasons Story"	The Four Seasons (Philips) (Private Stock)
Love Don't Live Here Anymore	Kris Kristofferson and Rita Coolidge (A&M)
"Natural Act"	
A Lover's Plea "Life in the Foodchain"	Tonio K (Epic)
Maggie "Words and Pictures"*	Bobby Goldsboro (United Artists)
Marriage (Excerpt) "Confessions of a Male Chauvinist Pig"*	Artie Kaplan (Hopi/Vanguard)
Motions of Love "Two Man Band"*	Splinter (Dark Horse)
Much Too Much "Ancient Medicine"	Baby Grand (Arista)
My Husband Got No Courage in Him "Silly Sisters"*	Silly Sisters (Chrysalis)
992 Arguments "Back Stabbers"	O'Jays (Philadelphia International)
Only Women Bleed "The Alice Cooper Show"	Alice Cooper (Warner Brothers)
+Only Women Bleed "Deep in the Night"	Etta James (Warner Brothers)
On the Rocks "Unrequited"*	Loudon Wainwright III (Columbia)

DEFINITIVE SONGS

Perfect Lady Housewife "Moving Finger"	The Hollies (Epic)
Red Wine at Noon "Joy of Cooking"*	Joy of Cooking (Capitol)
Rock Me at Home "I Came to Dance"	Nils Lofgren (A&M)
Rotunda "Wrong End of the Rainbow"*	Tom Rush (Columbia)
Sadly Sorta Like a Soap Opera "Jackrabbit Slim"	Steve Forbert (Nemperor)
See Her Run "Rag 'n Roll Revue"*	Cathy Chamberlain (Warner Brothers)
(She's a Housewife) No More Rock and Roll "Too Young to Feel This Old"*	McKendree Spring (Pye)
She Was So Young "Falling in Love Again"	David Gates (Elektra)
The Smokey Life "Recent Songs"	Leonard Cohen (Columbia)
Started Out Fine "A Live Album"*	Holly Near (Redwood)
Thirteen "No Second Chance"	Charlie (Janus)
Through the Eyes of Grace "Don't Cry Out Loud"	Melissa Manchester (Arista)
Too Young to Be Married "Moving Finger" "Hollies Live"	The Hollies (Epic) (Epic)
Train Off the Track "Three-Way Mirror"*	Livingston Taylor (Epic)
Wastin' Our Time "Native Sons"	Loggins and Messina (Columbia)
We Grew Up a Little Bit "Dance Band on the Titanic"	Harry Chapin (Elektra)
Weekdays "Fantasy"	Carole King (Ode)
Winner Take All "You Can Know Everything I Am"*	Holly Near (Redwood)

DEFINITIVE SONGS

With This Ring
"I Just Want to Sing with My
   Friends"

The Persuasions
(A&M)

You Don't Bring Me Flowers
"Greatest Hits Vol. II"

Barbra Streisand
(Columbia)

+You Don't Bring Me Flowers
"You Don't Bring Me Flowers"

Neil Diamond
(Columbia)

REFERENCE SONGS

The Dangling Conversation
"Parsley, Sage, Rosemary and Thyme"

Simon and Garfunkel
(Columbia)

Isis
"Desire"

Bob Dylan
(Columbia)

Lucille
"Ten Years of Gold"

Kenny Rogers
(United Artists)

Take Me Back Wife
"Sam Neely Two"

Sam Neely
(Capitol)

YOUR ADDITIONAL SONGS

_____

_____

_____

_____

_____

Adultery

CLASSICS

If Loving You Is Wrong
"Foot Loose and Fancy Free"

Rod Stewart
(Warner Brothers)

+If Loving You Is Wrong
"Bonded"

The Chambers Brothers
(Avco)

+If Loving You Is Wrong
"His California Album"

Bobby Bland
(ABC/Dunhill)

CLASSICS

+If Loving You Is Wrong   Barbara Mandrell
 (45 RPM Single)   (ABC)

+If Loving You Is Wrong   Millie Jackson
 "Live and Uncensored"   (Polydor)

DEFINITIVE SONGS

The Agony and the Ecstasy   Smokey Robinson & the
                                    Miracles
"Smokin'"   (Tamla)

Alcohol   The Kinks
"Everybody's in Showbiz"   (RCA)

Asking Too Much of You   The Marshall Tucker Band
"Forever Together"   (Capricorn)

Beware of Young Girls   Dory Previn
"On My Way to Where"*   (Warner Brothers)

Bye Bye Baby   The Four Seasons
"Gold Vault of Hits"   (Philips)
"The Four Seasons Story"   (Private Stock)

Dark End of the Street   Ry Cooder
"Show Time"   (Warner Brothers)

+Dark End of the Street   The Flying Burrito Brothers
"The Gilded Palace of Sin"   (A&M)

Daytime Friends   Kenny Rogers
"Ten Years Gold"   (Reprise)

Desperately   The Pets
"Wet Behind the Ears"   (Arista)

For the Sake of the Children   Henry Gibson
"Nashville" (Soundtrack)   (ABC)

Geraldine and John   Joe Jackson
"I'm the Man"   (A&M)

Half Way to Heaven   Harry Chapin
"Verities and Balderdash"   (Elektra)

Have You Ever Loved a Woman   Derek and the Dominoes
"Layla and Other Love Songs"   (RSO)
"In Concert"   (RSO)

I Heard You've Been Laying with My New Riders of the Purple
 Old Lady   Sage
"Oh What a Mighty Time"   (Columbia)

DEFINITIVE SONGS

Just Now It Feels So Right
"A Touch on the Rainy Side"*
Jesse Winchester
(Bearsville)

Listen to the Clock on the Wall
"Back Stabbers"
O'Jays
(Philadelphia International)

Look What I Got
"Boz Scaggs"
Boz Scaggs
(Atlantic)

The Love You Gave Away
"Moving Targets"
Flo and Eddie
(Columbia)

The Married Men
"Against the Grain"
Phoebe Snow
(Columbia)

+The Married Man
"The Roches"
The Roches
(Warner Brothers)

Me and Mrs. Jones
"Live in Europe"
"360 Degrees of Billy Paul"
"The Best of Billy Paul"
Billy Paul
(Philadelphia International)
(Philadelphia International)
(Philadelphia International)

Midnight Confessions
"The ABC Collection"
The Grass Roots
(ABC)

Much Too Much
"Ancient Medicines"
Baby Grand
(Arista)

No Tell Lover
"Hot Streets"
Chicago
(Columbia)

Not a Woman, Not a Child
"Tracks on Wax 4"
Dave Edmunds
(Swan Song)

Out of Hand
"Eyes of an Only Child"*
Tom Jans
(Columbia)

Outside Woman
"Unreal"
Bloodstone
(London)

Pretty Princess
"Native Sons"
Loggins and Messina
(Columbia)

Rodrigo, Rita and Elaine
"The Amazing Rhythm Aces"
Amazing Rhythm Aces
(ABC)

Saddle Up the Palominos
"American Stars and Bars"
Neil Young
(Reprise)

She Was So Young
"Falling in Love Again"
David Gates
(Elektra)

Slippery When It's Wet
"Commodores' Greatest Hits"
The Commodores
(Motown)

DEFINITIVE SONGS

Southern Woman	Styx
"Best of Styx"	(Wooden Nickel/RCA)
Storybook Children	Billy Vera
"Out of the Darkness"*	(Midland International)
Take a Letter Maria	R. B. Greaves
(45 RPM Single)	(Atco)
+Take a Letter Maria	New Riders of the Purple Sage
	(Columbia)
"Oh What a Mighty Time"	
Terminal	Rupert Holmes
"Widescreen"*	(Epic)
Willy Ruby	Elizabeth Barraclough
"Elizabeth Barraclough"*	(Bearsville)
Why Did You Wait to Tell Me?	Mary MacGregor
"Torn Between Two Lovers"	(Ariola/America)
Your Husband, My Wife	Brooklyn Bridge
(45 RPM Single)*	(Buddah)
"The Second Brooklyn Bridge"*	(Buddah)

REFERENCE SONGS

Holiday Romance	The Kinks
"Soap Opera"	(RCA)
Long Black Veil	The Band
"Music from Big Pink"	(Capitol)
+Long Black Veil	Joan Baez
"Joan Baez in Concert Part II"	(Vanguard)
+Long Black Veil	Johnny Cash
"At Folsom Prison"	(Columbia)
Love on a Shoestring	Renee Armand
"In Time"	(Windsong)
Lucille	Kenny Rogers
"Ten Years of Gold"	(Reprise)
Mr. Pleasant	The Kinks
"Kink Kronikles"	(RCA)
Ruby, Don't Take Your Love to Town	Kenny Rogers
"Ten Years of Gold"	(United Artists)

REFERENCE SONGS

"The First Edition '69"*   (Reprise)
Take Time to Know Her   Percy Sledge
(45 RPM Single)*   (Atlantic)
"The Best of Percy Sledge"   (Atlantic)

YOUR ADDITIONAL SONGS

_____

_____

_____

_____

_____

MONEY

Money—some say it's the root of all evil; others say it's the root of rock and roll.

The record industry is the largest money-making entertainment medium (four billion dollars in 1979). Some artists have chosen not only to make money but to reflect on its meaning in their lives and ours. The scope of this category is wide-ranging, from those who have money to those who wish they did. (N.B. Songs about taxes are listed in a separate subcategory.)

Related Categories: Big Business, Poverty, Rat Race, Suburbia, Working

+Same as Song Above
*Hard-to-find Songs/Albums

CLASSICS

It's Money That I Love	Randy Newman
"Born Again"	(Warner Brothers)
It's Only Money	Argent
"The Best of Argent—An Anthology"	(Epic)
"In Deep"	(Epic)
Money	The Lovin' Spoonful
"The Best of the Lovin' Spoonful Vol. II"	(Kama Sutra)
"The Best . . . Lovin' Spoonful"	(Kama Sutra)
"Once Upon a Time"	(Kama Sutra)
"Everything Playing"	(Kama Sutra)
Money	Barrett Strong
"Motown Story"	(Motown)
Money	The Beatles
"Second Album"	(Capitol)
"Rock and Roll"	(Capitol)
+Money	The Rolling Stones
"More Hot Rocks (Big Hits and Fazed Cookies)"	(London)
+Money	Jerry Lee Lewis
"Original Golden Hits Vol. II"	(Sun)
+Money	Smokey Robinson & the Miracles
"From the Beginning . . ."	(Tamla)

CLASSICS

+Money   Diana Ross
  "An Evening with Diana Ross"   (Motown)

+Money   John Lennon
  "The Plastic Ono Band—Live Peace   (Capitol)
    in Toronto 1969"

+Money   Junior Walker and the All
                                                Stars
  "Anthology"   (Motown)

+Money   The Flying Lizards
  "The Flying Lizards"   (Virgin)

Money   Pink Floyd
  "Dark Side of the Moon"   (Harvest)

DEFINITIVE SONGS

Blue Money   Van Morrison
  "His Band and His Street Choir"   (Warner Brothers)

Cold Hard Cash   Greg Kihn
  "Next of Kihn"   (Beserkley)

The Day the Dollar Died   Peter Tosh
  "Mystic Man"   (Rolling Stone Records)

Easy Money   Rickie Lee Jones
  "Rickie Lee Jones"   (Warner Brothers)

+Easy Money   Lowell George
  "Thanks I'll Eat It Here"   (Warner Brothers)

+Easy Money   Ian Lloyd
  "Goose Bumps"   (Atlantic)

For the Love of Money   O'Jays
  "Ship Ahoy"   (Philadelphia International)

Free Money   Patti Smith
  "Horses"   (Arista)

Gimme Your Money Please   Bachman-Turner Overdrive
  "Bachman-Turner Overdrive"   (Mercury)
  "Best of B.T.O. . . . (So Far)"   (Mercury)

Greenback Dollar   The Dillards
  "Decade Waltz"   (Flying Fish)

+Greenback Dollar   The Kingston Trio
  (45 RPM Single)*   (Capitol)

+Greenback Dollar   Jim Croce
  "Faces I've Seen"   (Lifesong)

DEFINITIVE SONGS

I Give You Money "Frampton Comes Alive"	Peter Frampton (A&M)
I Makes Money "Mr. Bojangles"	Jerry Jeff Walker (Atco)
Insufficient Funds "Reunion"*	Country Joe McDonald (Fantasy)
It's Only Money "Night Life"	Thin Lizzy (Vertigo)
It's Only Money "For Earth Below"	Robin Trower (Chrysalis)
Lose Your Money (45 RPM Single)*	The Moody Blues (London)
Low Budget "Low Budget"	The Kinks (Arista)
Luxury's Lap "High and Outside"	Steve Goodman (Elektra)
Midas Man "Novella"	Renaissance (Sire)
Money "Smile"	Laura Nyro (Columbia)
Money "Zephyr National"*	Tom Fogarty (Fantasy)
Money "Straight Up"*	Badfinger (Apple)
Money Can't Save Your Soul "Looking In"	Savoy Brown (Parrot)
Money Honey "Close Up the Honky Tonks"	The Flying Burrito Brothers (A&M)
Money Honey "Greatest Hits"	Little Richard (Trip)
Money Honey "Alvin Lee in Flight"	Alvin Lee (Columbia)
Money Honey "Twenty-Four Original Hits"	The Drifters (Atlantic)
+Money Honey "Elvis Presley"	Elvis Presley (RCA)
+Money Honey "Into the Purple Valley"	Ry Cooder (Reprise)
+Money Honey "Tom Rush"	Tom Rush (Elektra)

DEFINITIVE SONGS

Money Man
"All Pink Inside"

Frijid Pink
(Fantasy)

Money Money
"Mars Hotel"

The Grateful Dead
(Grateful Dead Records)

Money, Money, Money
"Arrival"

ABBA
(Atco)

The Moneygoround
"Lola Versus Powerman and the
    Moneygoround"

The Kinks
(Reprise)

Money Machine
"In the Pocket"

James Taylor
(Warner Brothers)

Money Talks
"Preservation Act II"

The Kinks
(RCA)

Money Talks
"Cool Cool Penguin"

The Penguins
(Dooto)

Money to Burn
(45 RPM Single)*

Cyrkle
(Columbia)

Money Won't Save You
"Music Maker"

Jimmy Cliff
(Reprise)

+Money Won't Save You
"Ellen McIlwaine"

Ellen McIlwaine
(United Artists)

Music for Money
"Pure Pop for Now People"

Nick Lowe
(Columbia)

Pity the Rich
"Pity the Rich"*

Pierce Arrow
(Columbia)

Put the Money Down
"Odds and Sods"

The Who
(MCA/Track)

Rich Get Richer
"Survival"

O'Jays
(Philadelphia International)

Rich Man
"Rich Man"

Climax Blues Band
(Sire)

Silas Stingy
"The Who Sell Out"

The Who
(MCA/Track)

Take the K.A.S.H
"The Wonderful World of Wreckless
    Eric"

Wreckless Eric
(Stiff)

Take the Money and Run
"Fly Like an Eagle"
"Greatest Hits 1974–1978"

Steve Miller Band
(Capitol)
(Capitol)

DEFINITIVE SONGS

Take the Money and Run
"Wind on the Water"

David Crosby/Graham Nash
(ABC)

Viva la Money
"Motion"

Allen Toussaint
(Warner Brothers)

Where Is the Money
"Snake, Rattle and Roll"

Crawler
(Epic)

You Got Money
"Crawler"

Crawler
(Epic)

You Never Give Me Your Money
"Abbey Road"

The Beatles
(Apple)

+You Never Give Me Your Money
"Sgt. Pepper's Lonely Hearts Club
Band Soundtrack"

Various Artists
(RSO)

+You Never Give Me Your Money

Wil Malone and Lou
Reizner

"All This and World War II"

(20th Century-Fox)

REFERENCE SONGS

Ain't Got No Money

Bob Seger and the Silver
Bullet Band

"Stranger in Town"

(Capitol)

Brother, Can You Spare a Dime
"See What Tomorrow Brings"

Peter, Paul and Mary
(Warner Brothers)

+Brother, Can You Spare a Dime
"Judith"

Judy Collins
(Elektra)

+Brother, Can You Spare a Dime
"Spanky and Our Gang"*

Spanky and Our Gang
(Mercury)

+Brother, Can You Spare a Dime
"Slim Chance"

Ronnie Lane
(A&M)

+Brother, Can You Spare a Dime
"Greatest Hits"

The Weavers
(Vanguard)

+Brother Can You Spare a Dime?
"Rag 'n Roll Revue"*

Cathy Chamberlain
(Warner Brothers)

Busted
"A Man and His Music"

Ray Charles
(ABC)

Can't Buy Me Love
"The Beatles 1962–1966"
"'A Hard Day's Night' (Soundtrack)"
"The Beatles at the Hollywood Bowl"

The Beatles
(Capitol)
(United Artists)
(Capitol)

REFERENCE SONGS

Everyday I Have to Cry
"Jerry Lee Lewis"

Jerry Lee Lewis
(Elektra)

Fast Buck Freddie
"Red Octopus"
"Gold"

Jefferson Starship
(Grunt)
(Grunt)

First I Look at the Purse
"Full House"

J. Geils Band
(Atlantic)

Gas Money
"Happy Together Again"

The Turtles
(Sire)

Green Tambourine
"The Lemon Pipers"*

The Lemon Pipers
(Buddah)

+Green Tambourine
"Both Sides Now"*

The Tokens
(Buddah)

I Don't Want Your Money
"Chicago III"

Chicago
(Columbia)

If I Had a Billion Dollars
"J Is for Jump"*

Jo Mama
(Atlantic)

In for a Penny
"Nobody's Fool"

Slade
(Warner Brothers)

Justice
"O Lucky Man"

Alan Price
(Warner Brothers)

Liars
"Goodnight Mrs. Calabash"

Ian Thomas Band
(Chrysalis)

Living in the Material World
"Living in the Material World"

George Harrison
(Apple)

Making Money in Chile
"Country Joe"*

Country Joe McDonald
(Vanguard)

Million Dollar Bash
"The Basement Tapes"

Bob Dylan and The Band
(Columbia)

Money Down
"Side 3"

Raspberries
(Capitol)

Money Honey
"Greatest Hits"

Bay City Rollers
(Arista)

Money Won't Change You
"Lady Soul"

Aretha Franklin
(Atlantic)

My Mama's House
"Janis Ian"

Janis Ian
(Columbia)

Nickel Song
"The Four Sides of Melanie"*
"Good Book"*

Melanie
(Buddah)
(Buddah)

REFERENCE SONGS

No Money Down "Golden Decade Vol. II"	Chuck Berry (Chess)
+No Money Down "The Best of John Hammond"	John Hammond (Vanguard)
+No Money Down "Thunderbox"	Humble Pie (A&M)
+No Money Down "Subtle as a Flying Mallet"	Dave Edmunds (RCA)
+No Money Down "An Anthology, Vol. II"	Duane Allman (Capricorn)
The Power of Gold "Twin Sons of Different Mothers"	Dan Fogelberg and Tim Weisberg (Full Moon/Epic)
Rich Man "The Statue Makers of Hollywood"	Alpha Band (Arista)
Sign Your Life Away "The Barbecue Of Deville"*	Hoodoo Rhythm Devils (Blue Thumb)
Speed Trap "Life Machine"	Hoyt Axton (A&M)
Sue Me, Sue You Blues "Living in the Material World"	George Harrison (Apple)
When the Money Runs Out "Here"	Leo Sayer (Warner Brothers)
You Can't Buy Love "Sinful"	Angel (Casablanca)

YOUR ADDITIONAL SONGS

_____

_____

_____

_____

_____

Taxes

CLASSICS

Taxman   The Beatles
"Revolver"   (Capitol)
"Rock and Roll"   (Capitol)

+Taxman   George Harrison
"The Best of George Harrison"   (Apple)

+Taxman   Black Oak Arkansas
"Live Mutha"   (Atlantic)

DEFINITIVE SONGS

The Hold Up   David Bromberg
"David Bromberg"   (Columbia)

Me and the I.R.S.   Johnny Paycheck
"Take This Job and Shove It"   (Epic)
"Johnny Paycheck's Greatest Hits"   (Epic)

My Friend Peter   Strawbs
"Deep Cuts"   (Polydor)

Sunny Afternoon   The Kinks
"The Kink Kronikles"   (RCA)
"The Live Kinks"   (Reprise)

Taxman   The Guess Who
"All This for a Song"   (Hilltak/Atlantic)

Taxman (Mister Thief)   Cheap Trick
"Cheap Trick"   (Epic)

Taxman Blues   John Mayall
"New Year, New Band, New   (ABC)
    Company"

When the Taxman Comes   Murray McLauchlan
"Hard Rock Town"   (True North)

YOUR ADDITIONAL SONGS

_____

_____

_____

_____

_____

MOTHERS

Mothers—"loves me like a rock."

Much like their counterparts in the "Fathers" category, these songs explore the complete range of feelings toward perhaps the most important woman in our life . . . at least for a part of it. And, again like their male counterparts, grandmothers are mothers too, and "grandmother" songs are included here.

Related Categories: Children, Divorce, Fathers, Marriage, Pregnancy

+Same as Song Above
*Hard-to-find Songs/Albums

CLASSICS

I'll Always Love My Mother	The Intruders
"Philadelphia Classics"	(Philadelphia International)
"Save the Children"	(Gamble)
To Daddy	Emmylou Harris
"Quarter Moon in a Ten Cent Town"	(Warner Brothers)
"Profile: Best of Emmylou Harris"	(Warner Brothers)

DEFINITIVE SONGS

Coat of Many Colors	Emmylou Harris
"Pieces of the Sky"	(Warner Brothers)
Don't Worry Mother	The McCoys
(45 RPM Single)*	(Bang)
For My Mother	Dean Friedman
"Dean Friedman"*	(Lifesong)
I'm Living in Shame	Diana Ross and the Supremes
"Anthology"	(Motown)
The Loser in the End	Queen
"Queen II"	(Elektra)
Loves Me Like a Rock	Paul Simon
"Greatest Hits, Etc."	(Columbia)
"There Goes Rhymin' Simon"	(Columbia)
"Live Rhymin'"	(Columbia)
+Loves Me Like a Rock	The Persuasions
"Coming at Ya"	(Flying Fish)

DEFINITIVE SONGS

Ma
"Masterpiece"

The Temptations
(Gordy)

Mama
"The Very Best of B. J. Thomas"

B. J. Thomas
(United Artists)

Mama
"Live in London"

Helen Reddy
(Capitol)

Mama's Getting Love
"Shiver in the Night"

Andy Pratt
(Nemperor)

Mama's Song
"Put a Little Love in Your Heart"*

Jackie DeShannon
(Imperial)

Mama Tried
"Grateful Dead"

The Grateful Dead
(Warner Brothers)

Momma
"Beautiful Loser"

Bob Seger
(Capitol)

Momma, Momma
"My First Album"*

Melanie
(Buddah)

Mother
"John Lennon/Plastic Ono Band"

John Lennon
(Apple)

Mother Dear
"Equinox"

Styx
(A&M)

Mother of a Miner's Child
"Old Dan's Records"

Gordon Lightfoot
(Reprise)

My Mama
"Mirriam"

Jessi Colter
(Capitol)

My Mummy's Dead
"The Plastic Ono Band—Live Peace in
    Toronto 1969"

John Lennon
(Apple)

Passing Thing
"Get Closer"

Seals and Crofts
(Warner Brothers)

Sadie
"The Best of the Spinners"

The Spinners
(Atlantic)

The Sweetest Gift
"Prisoner in Disguise"

Linda Ronstadt
(Asylum)

When I See Mommy I Feel Like a
    Mummy
"Shiny Beast"*

Captain Beefheart

(Warner Brothers)

Your Mother Should Know
"Magical Mystery Tour"

The Beatles
(Capitol)

REFERENCE SONGS

Alone Again (Naturally)	Gilbert O'Sullivan
"Himself"	(MAM)
Grandma's Hands	Bill Withers
"The Best of Bill Withers"	(Sussex)
Have You Seen Your Mother	The Rolling Stones
"More Hot Rocks (Big Hits and	(London)
Fazed Cookies)"	
"Flowers"	(London)
+Have You Seen Your Mother, Baby?	The Records
"The Records"	(Virgin)
Hey Grandma	The Move
"The Best of the Move"	(A&M)
I'm the Only Hell (Mama Ever	Johnny Paycheck
Raised)	
"Johnny Paycheck's Greatest Hits	(Epic)
Vol. II"	
Little Old Lady	New Riders of the Purple
	Sage
"Oh What a Mighty Time"	(Columbia)
Little Old Lady from Pasadena	Jan and Dean
"Gotta Take That One Last Ride"	(United Artists)
Mama Gets High	Blood, Sweat and Tears
"B,S&T; 4"*	(Columbia)
Mama Open Up	Flo and Eddie
"Moving Targets"	(Columbia)
Mama Said	The Shirelles
"The Very Best of the Shirelles"	(United Artists)
+Mama Said	Melanie
"Sunset and Other Beginnings"	(Neighborhood)
Mama's Boy	Biff Rose
"The Thorn in Mrs. Rose's Side"*	(Buddah)
Mama Told Me Not to Come	Randy Newman
"Live"	(Reprise)
+Mama Told Me Not to Come	Three Dog Night
"Golden Biscuits"	(ABC/Dunhill)
Mother	Chicago
"Chicago III"	(Columbia)
Mother	Pink Floyd
"The Wall"	(Harvest)

REFERENCE SONGS

Mother and Child Reunion	Paul Simon
"Greatest Hits, Etc."	(Columbia)
"Paul Simon"	(Columbia)
"Live Rhymin' "	(Columbia)
+Mother and Child Reunion	Johnny Rivers
"L.A. Reggae"	(United Artists)
+Mother and Child Reunion	Randy California
"Kapt. Kopter and the Twirley Birds"*	(Epic)
Mother in Law	Herman's Hermits
"Introducing Herman's Hermits"*	(MGM)
Motherless Children	Eric Clapton
"461 Ocean Blvd."	(RSO)
Mother of Love	Nitty Gritty Dirt Band
"Dream"	(United Artists)
Mother's Little Helper	The Rolling Stones
"Hot Rocks"	(London)
"Flowers"	(London)
My Mammy	The Happenings
(45 RPM Single)*	(B. T. Puppy)
Shortnin' Bread	The Beach Boys
"The Beach Boys L.A. (Light Album)"	(Caribou)
Too Old to Go 'Way Little Girl	Janis Ian
"Janis Ian"	(Polydor)

YOUR ADDITIONAL SONGS

_____

_____

_____

_____

_____

OLD AGE

Old age—we will all get there someday—if we are lucky.

Rock writers have given us a few moving portraits of old people and the many problems they encounter. Hunger, financial worry, "keeping busy," forced retirement, loneliness, and "our children who forget us" are among important topics covered here.

Some songs are written through the persona of the "old person," who passes down advice and warning to the next generation of potential "senior citizens." It will be interesting to see as rock and its writers grow older if this rather small body of music increases.

Related Categories: Fathers (for Grandfathers), Life, Mothers (for Grandmothers)

+Same as Song Above
*Hard-to-find Songs/Albums

CLASSICS

Hello in There	John Prine
"Prime Prine"	(Atlantic)
"John Prine"*	(Atlantic)
+Hello in There	Bette Midler
"The Divine Miss M"	(Atlantic)
"Live at Last"	(Atlantic)
+Hello in There	Joan Baez
"Diamonds and Rust"	(A&M)
Old Friends	Simon and Garfunkel
"Bookends"	(Columbia)
+Old Friends	Richie Havens
"Richie Havens on Stage"*	(Stormy Forest)
When I'm Sixty-four	The Beatles
"Sgt. Pepper's Lonely Hearts Club Band"	(Capitol)
+When I'm Sixty-four	Various Artists
"Sgt. Pepper's Lonely Hearts Club Band Soundtrack"	(RSO)
+When I'm Sixty-four	Keith Moon
"All This and World War II"	(20th Century-Fox)

DEFINITIVE SONGS

Abandoned Luncheonette	Hall and Oates
"Abandoned Luncheonette"	(Atlantic)

DEFINITIVE SONGS

Barney
"Mac McAnally"

Mac McAnally
(Ariola/America)

The Captain and the Kid
"Before the Salt"
"You Had to Be There"

Jimmy Buffett
(Barnaby)
(ABC)

Clarence
"David Pomeranz"*

David Pomeranz
(Arista)

Daisy a Day
"Daisy a Day"*

Jud Strunk
(MGM)

Desperados Waiting for a Train
"Old Number 1"*

Guy Clark
(RCA)

+Desperados Waiting for a Train
"Ladies Love Outlaws"

Tom Rush
(Columbia)

Don't Cry Old Man
"Aftertones"

Janis Ian
(Columbia)

Dutchman
"Somebody Else's Troubles"*
"The Essential Steve Goodman"

Steve Goodman
(Buddah)
(Buddah)

+Dutchman
"Lifesong"*

Cashman and West
(ABC)

Fate of Man
(45 RPM Single)*

Glen Campbell
(Capitol)

Ghosts
"Born Again"

Randy Newman
(Warner Brothers)

Grandma's Hands
"The Best of Bill Withers"

Bill Withers
(Sussex)

Grandpa Was a Carpenter
"Sweet Revenge"*
"Prime Prine"

John Prine
(Atlantic)
(Atlantic)

He Went to Paris
"You Should Have Been There"

Jimmy Buffett
(ABC)

Holy Mother, Aging Father
"Sammy Johns"*

Sammy Johns
(GRC)

Jesse Tucker
"Swallowed Up in the Great American
    Heartland"*

Tom Pacheco
(RCA)

Lonely Old People
"Venus and Mars"

Paul McCartney
(Capitol)

DEFINITIVE SONGS

Look What the Years Have Done
"Hobos, Heroes, and Street Corner
   Clowns"*

Don Nix
(Enterprise/Stax)

Madge
"Steven Bishop"

Steven Bishop
(ABC)

Maggie
"Ladies Love Outlaws"

Tom Rush
(Columbia)

Man on a Fish
"Birth Comes to Us All"

The Good Rats
(Arista)

Old Folks
"Whose Garden Was This?"

John Denver
(RCA)

Old Folks
"Everything's Playing"*
"The Best of the Lovin' Spoonful
   Vol. II"

The Lovin' Spoonful
(Kama Sutra)
(Kama Sutra)

Old Folks Boogie
"Time Loves a Hero"
"Waiting for Columbus"

Little Feat
(Warner Brothers)
(Warner Brothers)

The Old Laughing Lady
"Neil Young"

Neil Young
(Reprise)

Old Man
"Forever Changes"

Love
(Elektra)

Old Man
"Sail Away"

Randy Newman
(Reprise)

+Old Man
"Angel Clare"

Art Garfunkel
(Columbia)

Old Man
"Decade"
"Harvest"

Neil Young
(Reprise)
(Reprise)

Old Mister Time
"Bloody Tourist"

10 CC
(Polydor)

Old People
"Let's Clean Up the Ghetto"

Archie Bell
(Philadelphia International)

Old Time Woman
"A Live Album"*

Holly Near
(Redwood)

Pass It On
"Running Like the Wind"

The Marshall Tucker Band
(Warner Brothers)

Razor Face
"Madman Across the Water"

Elton John
(MCA)

DEFINITIVE SONGS

See How the Years Have Gone By
"Escape from Babylon"*

Martha Velez
(Sire)

Shady Acres
"For All the Seasons of Your Mind"*

Janis Ian
(Verve)

Sixty Years On
"Elton John"

Elton John
(MCA)

Streets of London
"Spiral Staircase"
"Ralph McTell Live"

Ralph McTell
(20th Century Records)
(Fantasy)

Sunset of Your Life
"Miracle Row"

Janis Ian
(Columbia)

This Old Man
"Crystal Ball"

Styx
(A&M)

Through the Eyes of Grace
"Don't Cry Out Loud"

Melissa Manchester
(Arista)

Victoria Dines Alone
"Morning Again"*

Tom Paxton
(Elektra)

REFERENCE SONGS

Bag Lady
"Hermit of Mink Hollow"

Todd Rundgren
(Bearsville)

Beans, Bacon and Gravy
"Hard Times"*

Peter Yarrow
(Warner Brothers)

Don't Let It Bring You Down
"After the Gold Rush"

Neil Young
(Reprise)

Everybody Needs a Friend
"To the Heart"*

The Mark-Almond Band
(ABC)

Hitchhiker
"Spirit"

John Denver
(RCA)

I Pity the Mother and the Father
"Burning the Ballroom Down"

Amazing Rhythm Aces
(ABC)

Laughed at Him
"Sweet Thursday"

Sweet Thursday
(Great Western
  Gramophone)

Little Old Lady

New Riders of the Purple
  Sage

"Oh What a Mighty Time"

(Columbia)

REFERENCE SONGS

Little Old Lady from Pasadena   Jan and Dean
"Gotta Take That One Last Ride"   (United Artists)

The Miners' Strike   Pete Fowler
(45 RPM Single)*   (Oval)

Mr. Bojangles   Jerry Jeff Walker
"A Man Must Carry On"   (MCA)
"Mr. Bojangles"   (Atco)
"Five Years Gone"   (Atco)

+Mr. Bojangles   Nitty Gritty Dirt Band
"Dirt, Silver And Gold"   (United Artists)

+Mr. Bojangles   David Bromberg
"Demon in Disguise"   (Columbia)

+Mr. Bojangles   John Denver
"Whose Garden Was This?"   (RCA)

+Mr. Bojangles   Jim Stafford
"Jim Stafford"   (MGM)

+Mr. Bojangles   Neil Diamond
"Touching You, Touching Me"   (MCA)
"Rainbow"   (MCA)

+Mr. Bojangles   Bob Dylan
"Dylan"   (Columbia)

+Mr. Bojangles   Harry Nilsson
"Harry"   (RCA)

Old Man Took   America
"Holiday"   (Warner Brothers)
"America Live"   (Warner Brothers)

Shopping Bag Ladies   Dean Friedman
" 'Well, Well,' said the Rocking   (Lifesong)
    Chair"*

Streets of London   Ralph McTell
"Spiral Staircase"*   (20th Century Records)

Talking Old Soldiers   Elton John
"Tumbleweed Connection"   (MCA)

Tenterfield Saddler   Peter Allen
"It's Time for Peter Allen"   (A&M)

We All Get Old   Ron Woods
"Gimme Some Neck"   (Columbia)

Younger Men Grow Older   Richie Havens
"Alarm Clock"*   (Stormy Forest)
"Richie Havens on Stage"*   (Stormy Forest)

YOUR ADDITIONAL SONGS

_____

_____

_____

_____

_____

OUTCASTS/HOBOS

Outcasts/hobos—all of the songs, some of the singers.

There have always been and probably always will be those people who live and operate on the fringe of society. Some are there by choice, others by hard luck, and still others by the prejudice and injustice of society.

They have traditionally been a fertile source of inspiration for all the arts, especially rock and roll. Rock deals with the whole range of people in this situation and the reasons and circumstances why they are there.

Related Categories: Injustice, Loneliness, Poverty, Racism/Prejudice

+Same as Song Above
*Hard-to-find Songs/Albums

CLASSICS

Hobo's Lullaby "Library of Congress"	Woody Guthrie (Elektra)
+Hobo's Lullaby "The World of Pete Seeger"	Pete Seeger (Columbia)
+Hobo's Lullaby "Hobo's Lullaby"	Arlo Guthrie (Reprise)
+Hobo's Lullaby "A Tribute to Woody Guthrie"	Joan Baez (Warner Brothers)
King of the Road "Golden Greats"	Roger Miller (Smash)
+King of the Road "Nightflight to Venus"	Boney M (Sire)
Mr. Bojangles "Mr. Bojangles" "Five Years Gone"* "A Man Must Carry On"	Jerry Jeff Walker (Atco) (Atco) (MCA)
+Mr. Bojangles "Dirt, Silver and Gold"	Nitty Gritty Dirt Band (United Artists)
+Mr. Bojangles "Jim Stafford"	Jim Stafford (MGM)
+Mr. Bojangles "Demon in Disguise"	David Bromberg (Columbia)
+Mr. Bojangles "Whose Garden Was This?"	John Denver (RCA)

CLASSICS

+Mr. Bojangles   Neil Diamond
  "Touching You, Touching Me"   (MCA)
  "Rainbow"   (MCA)

+Mr. Bojangles   Bob Dylan
  "Dylan"   (Columbia)

+Mr. Bojangles   Harry Nilsson
  "Harry"   (RCA)

  Streets of London   Ralph McTell
  "Streets of London"   (Fantasy)
  "Ralph McTell Live"   (Fantasy)

THEMATIC ALBUMS

  "John Wesley Harding"   Bob Dylan
       (Columbia)

DEFINITIVE SONGS

  Ace   Jimmy Buffett
  "Before the Salt"   (Barnaby)

  Bag Lady   Todd Rundgren
  "Hermit of Mink Hollow"   (Bearsville)

  Ballad of Ira Hayes   Bob Dylan
  "Dylan"   (Columbia)

+Ballad of Ira Hayes   Johnny Cash
  "Johnny Cash's Greatest Hits"   (Columbia)

+Ballad of Ira Hayes   Kinky Friedman
  "Lasso from El Paso"*   (Epic)

+Ballad of Ira Hayes   Patrick Sky
  "Patrick Sky"*   (Vanguard)

  Beat the Devil   Kris Kristofferson
  "Me and Bobby McGee"   (Monument)

  Billy the Bum   John Prine
  "Diamonds in the Rough"*   (Atlantic)

  Brother, Can You Spare a Dime?   Peter, Paul and Mary
  "See What Tomorrow Brings"   (Warner Brothers)

+Brother, Can You Spare a Dime?   Judy Collins
  "Judith"   (Elektra)

+Brother, Can You Spare a Dime?   Spanky and Our Gang
  "Spanky and Our Gang"*   (Mercury)

DEFINITIVE SONGS

+Brother, Can You Spare a Dime?
"Slim Chance"
Ronnie Lane
(A&M)

+Brother, Can You Spare a Dime?
"Greatest Hits"
The Weavers
(Vanguard)

The Bum
"Waking and Dreaming"
Orleans
(Asylum)

Davey the Fat Boy
"Live"
Randy Newman
(Reprise)

Deportee
"Arlo Guthrie"
Arlo Guthrie
(Reprise)

+Deportee
"Judy Collins ⅓3"
"A Tribute to Woody Guthrie"
Judy Collins
(Elektra)
(Warner Brothers)

+Deportee
"Ballad of Easy Rider"
The Byrds
(Columbia)

Grapes of Wrath
"Midnight Wind"
Charlie Daniels
(Epic)

Hard Luck Joe
"Words and Pictures"*
Bobby Goldsboro
(United Artists)

Hard Travelin'
"Woody Guthrie"
Woody Guthrie
(Warner Brothers)

Hobo in My Mind
"New Songs for Old Friends"
Tom Paxton
(Reprise)

Hobo Jungle
"Northern Lights, Southern Cross"
The Band
(Capitol)

Hobo's Mandolin
"Ladies Love Outlaws"
Tom Rush
(Columbia)

The Hobo Song
"Bruised Orange"*
John Prine
(Asylum)

Home from the Forest
"The Way I Feel"
Gordon Lightfoot
(United Artists)

Homeless Brother
"Homeless Brother"*
"Solo"
Don McLean
(United Artists)
(United Artists)

Honkey Red
"Only the Silence Remains"*
Murray McLauchlan
(Columbia)

I Ain't Got No Home
"Song for Patty"*
Sammy Walker
(Vanguard)

DEFINITIVE SONGS

I Am a Lonesome Hobo "John Wesley Harding"	Bob Dylan (Columbia)
Jimmy the Fiddler "Swallowed Up in the Great American Heartland"*	Tom Pacheco (RCA)
John Gary "Adjoining Suite"*	Aztec Two Step (RCA)
Junkman "Breezy Stories"	Danny O'Keefe (Atlantic)
Last, Lonely and Wretched "Blessed Are"	Joan Baez (Vanguard)
Little Beggar Man "Greatest Hits"	Ian and Sylvia (Vanguard)
+Little Beggar Man "One Night"	Arlo Guthrie (Warner Brothers)
Little Brown Jug "Giant for a Day"	Gentle Giant (Capitol)
Lonely Hobo Lullaby "Another Night"	The Hollies (Epic)
The Loner "Live Rust" "Neil Young" "Decade"	Neil Young (Warner Brothers) (Reprise) (Reprise)
+The Loner "Illegal Stills"	Stephen Stills (Columbia)
Magic Mirror "Carney"	Leon Russell (Shelter)
Midnight Rider "Laid Back"	Gregg Allman (Capricorn)
+Midnight Rider "An Anthology—Vol. II"	Duane Allman (Capricorn)
+Midnight Rider "The Road Goes On Forever"	The Allman Brothers (Capricorn)
+Midnight Rider "Thoroughfare Gap"	Stephen Stills (Columbia)
Old Joe "The American Album"*	Allan Taylor (United Artists)

DEFINITIVE SONGS

Old Man Sleeping on the Bowery
"Willy Nile"

Willy Nile
(Arista)

Ramblin' Boy
"Ramblin' Boy"
"The Compleat Tom Paxton"

Tom Paxton
(Elektra)
(Elektra)

+Ramblin' Boy
"Golden Apples of the Sun"

Judy Collins
(Elektra)

Rambling Round (Your City)
"Library of Congress"

Woody Guthrie
(Elektra)

+Ramblin' Round (Your City)
"Linda Ronstadt"

Linda Ronstadt
(Capitol)

+Rambling Round (Your City)
"Tribute to Woody Guthrie"

Odetta
(Warner Brothers)

Shopping Bag Ladies
" 'Well, Well,' said the Rocking
    Chair"*

Dean Friedman
(Lifesong)

Shopping Bag Lady
"Life Lines"

Richard Supa
(Epic)

Shopping Bag People
"Sense of Direction"

Climax Blues Band
(Sire)

Song to J.C.B.
"The Best of Eric Andersen"

Eric Andersen
(Vanguard)

Strawberry Flats
"Little Feat"

Little Feat
(Warner Brothers)

Taxi Dancer
"John Cougar"

John Cougar
(Riva)

There's Nothin' Soft About Hard
    Times
"Before the Salt"

Jimmy Buffett

(Barnaby)

The Watchman's Gone
"Sundown"

Gordon Lightfoot
(Reprise)

Wait
"Jackrabbit Slim"

Steve Forbert
(Nemperor)

Wino
"Skynyrd's First . . . and Last"

Lynyrd Skynyrd
(MCA)

YOUR ADDITIONAL SONGS

OUTLAWS/CRIMINALS

Outlaws/criminals—bad guys seen sometimes as good guys, and occasionally good guys portrayed as bad guys.

From the Wild West to Watergate, these songs cover many different kinds of outlaws and criminals. Rock writers attempt to tell not only what they did, but why they did it. This fascination with the image of outlaws may stem from the fact that until recently many figures in the rock music world were considered to be musical as well as moral outlaws. "We Are All Outlaws In the Eyes of America" cried the Jefferson Airplane in their 1969 song "We Can Be Together." (N.B. Organized crime and gangster types are listed as a subdivision.)

Related Categories: Cowboys/Wild West, Police, Violence: Guns

+Same as Song Above
*Hard-to-find Songs/Albums

CLASSICS

Have Mercy on the Criminal "Don't Shoot Me I'm Only the Piano Player"	Elton John (MCA)
John Wesley Harding "John Wesley Harding"	Bob Dylan (Columbia)
Pretty Boy Floyd "Woody Guthrie" "Library of Congress"	Woody Guthrie (Warner Brothers) (Elektra)
+Pretty Boy Floyd "Thinking of Woody"*	Country Joe McDonald (Vanguard)
+Pretty Boy Floyd "Sweetheart of the Rodeo"	The Byrds (Columbia)
+Pretty Boy Floyd "In Concert"	Joan Baez (Vanguard)
+Pretty Boy Floyd "Madrugada"	Melanie (Neighborhood)
Smackwater Jack "Tapestry" "Her Greatest Hits"	Carole King (Ode) (Ode)
+Smackwater Jack "J Is for Jump"*	Jo Mama (Atlantic)

THEMATIC ALBUMS

"Desperado"	The Eagles (Asylum)
"Gypsy Cowboy"	New Riders of the Purple Sage (Columbia)
"Pat Garrett and Billy the Kid"	Bob Dylan (Columbia)

DEFINITIVE SONGS

Bad Eyed Bill "A Little Bit More"	Dr. Hook (Capitol)
Bad Man's Blunder "The Best of the Kingston Trio"	The Kingston Trio (Capitol)
Ballad of a Well Known Gun "Tumbleweed Connection"	Elton John (MCA)
The Ballad of Crafty Jack "Firing on All Six"*	Lone Star (Columbia)
Billy (Cuts ⅓1-4-7) "Pat Garrett and Billy the Kid"	Bob Dylan (Columbia)
Billy John "Mirage"	Richie Havens (A&M)
Billy the Kid "Te John, Grease and Wolfman"	Charlie Daniels (Kama Sutra)
Bitter Creek "Desperado"	The Eagles (Asylum)
Black Magic Gun "Ladies Love Outlaws"	Tom Rush (Columbia)
Bonnie and Clyde (45 RPM Single)*	Georgie Fame (Epic)
Bushwackers "Urban Renewal"*	J. F. Murphy (ABC/Dunhill)
The Day That Curly Bill Shot Down Crazy Sam McGee "Hollies"	The Hollies (Epic)
Cocaine Blues "Move It On Over"	George Thorogood and the Destroyers (Rounder)

DEFINITIVE SONGS

Doolin' Dalton "Desperado"	The Eagles (Asylum)
Drifter's Escape "John Wesley Harding"	Bob Dylan (Columbia)
Dust on My Saddle "Diamond Girl"	Seals and Crofts (Warner Brothers)
El Diablo "Tejas"	ZZ Top (London)
El Paso "Steal Your Face"	The Grateful Dead (Grateful Dead Records)
Frank and Jesse James "Warren Zevon"	Warren Zevon (Asylum)
Gimme Some Water "Life for the Taking"	Eddie Money (Columbia)
Gimme Your Money Please "Bachman-Turner Overdrive" "Best of B.T.O. . . . (So Far)"	Bachman-Turner Overdrive (Mercury) (Mercury)

Glendale Train
 	
"New Riders of the Purple Sage"
"The Best of the New Riders of the
  Purple Sage"
	New Riders of the Purple
	  Sage
	(Columbia)
	(Columbia)

Gunslinger "Mink DeVille"	Mink DeVille (Capitol)
Gunsmoke "Gunsmoke"	The Outlaws (Arista)
Hey Joe "Smash Hits" "Are You Experienced?"	Jimi Hendrix (Reprise) (Reprise)
+Hey Joe "Realization"* "Johnny Rivers" (Superpak)	Johnny Rivers (United Artists) (United Artists)
+Hey Joe (45 RPM Single)*	The Leaves (Columbia)
+Hey Joe "Love"	Love (Elektra)
+Hey Joe "Spirit of '76"	Spirit (Mercury)

DEFINITIVE SONGS

+Hey Joe	Wilson Pickett
"The Best of Wilson Pickett Vol. II"	(Atlantic)
Hurry Sundown	The Outlaws
"Hurry Sundown"	(Arista)
"Bring It Back Alive"	(Arista)
I Ain't Living Long Like This	Emmylou Harris
"Quarter Moon in a Ten Cent Town"	(Warner Brothers)
I Fought the Law	Bobby Fuller Four
"Oldies but Goodies, Volume 9"	(Original Sound)
(45 RPM Single)*	(Mustang)
+I Fought the Law	The Demons
"The Demons"*	(Mercury)
+I Fought the Law	Ducks Deluxe
"Don't Mind Rockin' Tonight"	(RCA)
+I Fought the Law	Kris Kristofferson and Rita Coolidge
"Natural Act"	(A&M)
+I Fought the Law	The Clash
"The Clash"	(Epic)
I'm an Outlaw	Dan Hicks
"It Happened One Bite"	(Warner Brothers)
I Shot the Sheriff	Eric Clapton
"461 Ocean Blvd."	(RSO)
+I Shot the Sheriff	Bob Marley and the Wailers
"Burnin'"	(Island)
"Live"	(Island)
Jesse James	Barry Melton
"The Fish"*	(Fire-Sign)
John Hardy	George Thorogood and the Destroyers
"George Thorogood and the Destroyers"	(Rounder)
Johnny Too Bad	Le Blanc and Carr
"Midnight Wind"	(Big Tree)
Ladies Love Outlaws	Tom Rush
"Ladies Love Outlaws"	(Columbia)
+Ladies Love Outlaws	The Everly Brothers
"Pass the Chicken and Listen"*	(Atlantic)

DEFINITIVE SONGS

+Ladies Love Outlaws   Waylon Jennings
  "Greatest Hits"   (RCA)
Lily, Rosemary, and the Jack of   Bob Dylan
  Hearts
  "Blood on the Tracks"   (Columbia)
+Lily, Rosemary, and the Jack of   Joan Baez
  Hearts
  "From Every Stage"   (A&M)
Lion in the Park   Bill Chinnock
  "Badlands"   (Atlantic)
Little Criminals   Randy Newman
  "Little Criminals"   (Reprise)
Machine Gun Kelly   James Taylor
  "Mud Slide Slim and the Blue   (Warner Brothers)
  Horizon"
The Man Who Shot Liberty Valance   Gene Pitney
  "Greatest Hits of All Time"   (Musicor)
+The Man Who Shot Liberty Valance   The Royal Guardsmen
  "Snoopy Versus the Red Baron"   (Laurie)
Midnight Rider   Gregg Allman
  "Laid Back"   (Capricorn)
+Midnight Rider   Duane Allman
  "An Anthology—Vol. II"   (Capricorn)
+Midnight Rider   The Allman Brothers
  "The Road Goes On Forever"   (Capricorn)
+Midnight Rider   Stephen Stills
  "Thoroughfare Gap"   (Columbia)
Outlaw   Tom Paxton
  "Up and Up"   (Mountain Railroad
                                             Records)
Outlaw Blues   Bob Dylan
  "Bringing It All Back Home"   (Columbia)
+Outlaw Blues   Great Society
  "Conspicuous Only by Their   (Columbia)
  Absence"*
Outlaw Man   The Eagles
  "Desperado"   (Asylum)
+Outlaw Man   David Blue
  "Nice Baby and the Angel"*   (Asylum)

DEFINITIVE SONGS

The Outsider
"You're Never Alone with a
   Schizophrenic"

Ian Hunter
(Chrysalis)

Outskirts
"French Kiss"

Bob Welch
(Capitol)

Poncho and Lefty
"Luxury Liner"

Emmylou Harris
(Warner Brothers)

Potter's Field
"Foreign Affairs"

Tom Waits
(Asylum)

Renegade
"Pieces of Eight"

Styx
(A&M)

Rider in the Rain
"Little Criminals"

Randy Newman
(Reprise)

Ringo
(45 RPM Single)*

Lorne Greene
(RCA)

Rocky Raccoon
"The Beatles" (White Album)

The Beatles
(Apple)

+Rocky Raccoon
"Richie Havens on Stage"*

Richie Havens
(Stormy Forest)

Run Red Run
"Sixteen Greatest Hits"

The Coasters
(Trip)

Rusty Gun
"Grin"

Grin
(Epic)

The Sheriff
"Trilogy"

Emerson, Lake & Palmer
(Cotillion)

Shotgun Rider
"Freeways"

Bachman-Turner Overdrive
(Mercury)

Shotgun Riders
"The Winters Brothers Band"*

The Winters Brothers
(Atco)

Silver Eagle
"Sold American"

Kinky Friedman
(Vanguard)

Sinister Purpose

Creedence Clearwater
   Revival

"Green River"
"1969"

(Fantasy)
(Fantasy)

Small Change Got Rained On
"Small Change"

Tom Waits
(Asylum)

Smuggler's Song
"Kate Taylor"

Kate Taylor
(Columbia)

DEFINITIVE SONGS

Somebody "Monkey Island"	J. Geils Band (Atlantic)
Somewhere They Can't Find Me "Sounds of Silence"	Simon and Garfunkel (Columbia)
Songs the Minstrel Sang "Endless Wire"	Gordon Lightfoot (Reprise)
Stagger Lee "Live on the Queen Mary" "Rock and Roll Gumbo"	Professor Longhair (Harvest) (French Blue Star)
+Stagger Lee "Dave Van Ronk"	Dave Van Ronk (Fantasy)
+Stagger Lee "Taj Mahal"	Taj Mahal (Columbia)
+Stagger Lee "Jump for Joy"*	Jim Kweskin (Vanguard)
+Stagger Lee "You Make Me Feel So Good"*	The McCoys (Bang)
+Stagger Lee "Meanwhile at the Whiskey A Go-Go"*	Johnny Rivers (Imperial)
+Stagger Lee "Mr. Personality's Fifteen Hits"	Lloyd Price (ABC/Paramount)
+Stagger Lee "The Best of Wilson Pickett Vol. II"	Wilson Pickett (Atlantic)
+Stagger Lee "The History of the Righteous Brothers"	The Righteous Brothers (MGM)
+Stagger Lee "The Best of PG and E"	Pacific Gas & Electric (Columbia)
+Stagger Lee "Somewhere"*	P. J. Proby (Liberty)
+Stagger Lee "Shakedown Street"	The Grateful Dead (Arista)
+Stagger Lee "September Morn"	Neil Diamond (Columbia)
+Stack-o-Lee "Gumbo"	Dr. John (Atco)
Stone Cold Crazy "Sheer Heart Attack"	Queen (Elektra)

DEFINITIVE SONGS

Take a Message to Mary
"Self Portrait".
Bob Dylan
(Columbia)

Take the Money and Run
"Fly Like an Eagle"
"Greatest Hits 1974–1978"
Steve Miller Band
(Capitol)
(Capitol)

Traveling Man
"Bandit in a Bathing Suit"
David Bromberg
(Fantasy)

Turnpike Tom
"The Essential Steve Goodman"
Steve Goodman
(Buddah)

Wednesday Morning 3 A.M.
"Wednesday Morning 3 A.M."
Simon and Garfunkel
(Columbia)

With a Gun
"Pretzel Logic"
Steely Dan
(ABC)

Young Wesley
"How Late'll Ya Play Till?"
David Bromberg
(Fantasy)

REFERENCE SONGS

Are They Gonna Make Us Outlaws
Again?
"Try Like the Devil"*
James Talley

(Capitol)

Ballad of Billy the Kid
"Piano Man"
Billy Joel
(Columbia)

Blood on the Floor
"Kiln House"
Fleetwood Mac
(Reprise)

Heroes and Villains
"Smiley Smile"
"Good Vibrations—The Best of the
Beach Boys"
The Beach Boys
(Brother/Reprise)
(Brother/Reprise)

The Lady Came from Baltimore
"The Best of Tim Hardin"
Tim Hardin
(Verve)

Lido Beach
"Silk Degrees"
Boz Scaggs
(Columbia)

Mrs. Delion's Lament
"Reckless Abandon"
David Bromberg
(Fantasy)

The Robber
"Pierce Arrow"
Pierce Arrow
(Columbia)

Rock and Roll Outlaws
"Rock and Roll Outlaws"
Foghat
(Bearsville)

REFERENCE SONGS

Shotgun	Junior Walker and the All Stars
"Anthology"	(Motown)
Sniper	Harry Chapin
"Sniper and Other Love Songs"	(Elektra)
Stealing at the Seven-Eleven	The New Commander Cody Band
"Rock and Roll Again"	(Arista)
Thieves and Robbers	Dog Soldier
"Dog Soldier"*	(United Artists)

YOUR ADDITIONAL SONGS

_____

_____

_____

_____

_____

Gangsters/Organized Crime

CLASSICS

The Big Gangster	O'Jays
"Let's Clean Up the Ghetto"	(Philadelphia International)
Mack the Knife	Bobby Darin
"The Bobby Darin Story"	(Atco)
"Darin—1936–1973"*	(Motown)
+Mack the Knife	Cathy Chamberlain
"Rag 'n Roll Revue"*	(Warner Brothers)
+Mack the Knife	Dave Van Ronk
"Rag Time Jug Stompers"*	(Mercury)
+Mack the Knife	Lou Christie
"Lou Christie"*	(Three Brothers)

DEFINITIVE SONGS

Al Capone
(45 RPM Single)*
Prince Buster
(Blue Beat)

Chicago
"Here"
Leo Sayer
(Warner Brothers)

Con Man
"Mad Love"
Golden Earring
(MCA)

Dealer/Spanish Rose
"Inner Secrets"
Santana
(Columbia)

Gangster on the Loose
"Tall Tales"
Richard Supa
(Polydor)

Gino
"Birth Comes to Us All"
The Good Rats
(Arista)

Gino (The Manager)
"Daryl Hall and John Oates"
Hall and Oates
(RCA)

The Jimmy Hoffa Memorial
    Building Blues
"The Global Blues"
Danny O'Keefe

(Warner Brothers)

Joey
"Desire"
Bob Dylan
(Columbia)

Let the Cement Dry
"Rag 'n Roll Revue"*
Cathy Chamberlain
(Warner Brothers)

Meeting Across the River
"Born to Run"
Bruce Springsteen
(Columbia)

The Night Chicago Died
(45 RPM Single)
Paper Lace
(Mercury)

Nobody's Leavin' Here Tonight
"Coven"
Coven
(MGM)

A Piece of the Action
"Broken Heart"
The Babys
(Chrysalis)

REFERENCE SONGS

Back When the Bands Played in
    Ragtime
"Mystic Line"
Phil Everly

(Pye)

Small Change Got Rained On
"Small Change"
Tom Waits
(Asylum)

Somebody
"Monkey Island"
J. Geils Band
(Atlantic)

YOUR ADDITIONAL SONGS

_____

_____

_____

_____

_____

POLICE

Police—a few for them, most against them.

This has always been a touchy subject for the world of rock. The wide variety of songs here deal with law and order, resentment of authority, and the *enforcement* of the law. (N.B. This category includes sheriffs, rangers, detectives, the national guard, correction officers, and state troopers.)

Related Categories: Cowboys/Wild West, Injustice, Outlaws/Criminals, Prisons, Protest/Revolution

+Same as Song Above
*Hard-to-find Songs/Albums

CLASSICS

Policeman	Chicago
"Chicago XI"	(Columbia)

DEFINITIVE SONGS

Blue Murder	The Tom Robinson Band
"TRB II"	(Harvest)
Bodyguard	The Mighty Diamond
"Deeper Roots (Back to the Channel)"	(Virgin)
Brass Knuckles	Rupert Holmes
"Rupert Holmes"	(Epic)
Buzz the Fuzz	Biff Rose
"A Thorn in Mrs. Rose's Side"*	(Buddah)
Conversation with a Cop	Fanny
"Fanny"*	(Reprise)
Doo Doo Doo Doo Doo (Heartbreaker)	The Rolling Stones
"Made in the Shade"	(Rolling Stone Records)
"Goats Head Soup"	(Rolling Stone Records)
Framed	Canned Heat
"A New Age"*	(United Artists)
+Framed	Burton Cummings
"My Own Way to Rock"	(Portrait)

DEFINITIVE SONGS

+Framed   Bill Haley
  "Bill Haley's Scrapbook"   (Kama Sutra)

+Framed   Cheech and Chong
  "Up in Smoke"   (Warner Brothers)

G-Man Hoover   Van Dyke Parks
  "Discover America"*   (Warner Brothers)

Good Old Boy   Charlie Daniels
  "Midnight Wind"   (Epic)

Here Comes a Cop   David Peel and the Lower
                                                East Side
  "Have a Marijuana"*   (Elektra)

High Sheriff of Hazard   Tom Paxton
  "Ramblin' Boy"   (Elektra)

Highway Patrol   The Reggie Knighton Band
  "The Reggie Knighton Band"   (Columbia)

I Fought the Law   Bobby Fuller Four
  (45 RPM Single)*   (Mustang)
  "Oldies But Goodies, Volume 9"   (Original sound)

+I Fought the Law   The Demons
  "The Demons"*   (Mercury)

+I Fought the Law   Ducks Deluxe
  "Don't Mind Rockin' Tonight"   (RCA)

+I Fought the Law   Kris Kristofferson and Rita
                                                Coolidge
  "Natural Act"   (A&M)

+I Fought the Law   The Clash
  "The Clash"   (Epic)

I Shot the Sheriff   Eric Clapton
  "461 Ocean Blvd."   (RSO)

+I Shot the Sheriff   Bob Marley and the Wailers
  "Burnin' "   (Island)
  "Live"   (Island)

Jolly Coppers on Parade   Randy Newman
  "Little Criminals"   (Warner Brothers)

The Law Is for the Protection of the   Kris Kristofferson
  People
  "Me and Bobby McGee"   (Monument)

Laws and Order   The Tom Robinson Band
  "TRB II"   (Harvest)

DEFINITIVE SONGS

Lincoln Park Pirates
"Somebody Else's Troubles"*
"The Essential Steve Goodman"

Steve Goodman
(Buddah)
(Buddah)

Murphy
"New Arrangement"*

Jackie DeShannon
(Columbia)

My Crime
"Boogie with Canned Heat"*

Canned Heat
(Liberty)

The Night Chicago Died
(45 RPM Single)

Paper Lace
(Mercury)

Oink, Oink

David Peel and the Lower
   East Side

"The American Revolution"*

(Elektra)

Ordinary Man
"Birth Comes to Us All"

The Good Rats
(Arista)

Police and Thieves
"The Clash"

The Clash
(Epic)

+Police and Thieves
"Rockers" (Soundtrack)

Various Artists
(Mango)

Police Man
"Stiff Lives"*

Larry Wallis
(Stiff)

Police, Police
"Red Tape"

Atlanta Rhythm Section
(Polydor)

Prove It
"Marquee Moon"

Television
(Elektra)

Public Servant
"Reggie Knighton"*

The Reggie Knighton Band
(Columbia)

Rubber Bullets
"10 CC"
"Greatest Hits 1972–78"

10 CC
(UK)
(Polydor)

The Sheriff
"Trilogy"

Emerson, Lake & Palmer
(Cotillion)

Sic 'Em Pigs
"Cook Book"

Canned Heat
(Liberty)

Speed Trap
"Life Machine"

Hoyt Axton
(A&M)

Traffic Cop
"Unreal"

Bloodstone
(London)

Washington Square
"3 Saints 4 Sinners and 6 Others"*

Pete Seeger
(Folk Odyssey/CBS)

REFERENCE SONGS

Back When the Bands Played in
  Ragtime
"Mystic Line"

Phil Everly

(Pye)

Bad Man's Blunder
"The Best of the Kingston Trio"

The Kingston Trio
(Capitol)

Can't It All Be Love
"If Love Is Real"*

Randy Edleman
(Arista)

Charley's Girl
"Coney Island Baby"

Lou Reed
(RCA)

Cops of the World
"Phil Ochs in Concert"

Phil Ochs
(Elektra)

Detective Man
"Detective"

Detective
(Swan Song)

Ex-Offender
"Blondie"

Blondie
(Private Stock)

Glad to Be Gay
"Power in the Darkness"

The Tom Robinson Band
(Harvest)

Goodbye Yer Honor
"Alive and Kickin' "*

Kingfish
(United Artists)

Good Morning Judge
"Live"
"Deceptive Bends"

10 CC
(Mercury)
(Mercury)

I'm an Outlaw
"It Happened One Bite"

Dan Hicks
(Warner Brothers)

The Laws Must Change
"The Turning Point"

John Mayall
(Polydor)

Living for the City
"Innervisions"

Stevie Wonder
(Tamla)

+Living for the City
"It's a Heartache"

Bonnie Tyler
(RCA)

Lost in the Flood
"Greetings from Asbury Park, N.J."

Bruce Springsteen
(Columbia)

Lovely Rita
"Sgt. Pepper's Lonely Hearts Club
  Band"

The Beatles
(Capitol)

Man You Never Saw
"Power in the Darkness"

The Tom Robinson Band
(Harvest)

Murder in My Heart for the Judge
"Great Grape"

Moby Grape
(Columbia)

REFERENCE SONGS

+Murder in My Heart for the Judge
"Harmony"
Three Dog Night
(Dunhill/ABC)

Night Patrol
"Lonewolf"
Michael Murphey
(Epic)

Ohio
"So Far"
"Four Way Street"
Crosby, Stills, Nash & Young
(Atlantic)
(Atlantic)

+Ohio
"Decade"
"Journey Through the Past"
Neil Young
(Reprise)
(Reprise)

Piggies
"The Beatles" (White Album)
The Beatles
(Apple)

The Raid
"Stick to Me"
Graham Parker
(Mercury)

Rangers at Midnight
"Animal Notes"*
Crack the Sky
(Lifesong)

State of the Union
"Chicago V"
Chicago
(Columbia)

Ticking
"Caribou"
Elton John
(MCA)

Traveling Man
"Bandit in a Bathing Suit"
David Bromberg
(Fantasy)

Watching the Detectives
"Elvis Costello"
Elvis Costello
(Columbia)

Who Are the Brain Police
"Freak Out"
"Mothermania—The Best of the
Mothers"
The Mothers of Invention
(Verve)
(Verve)

YOUR ADDITIONAL SONGS

_____

_____

_____

_____

_____

POLITICS

Politics . . . promises, promises.

There has always been a political dimension to rock. In the early sixties, rock and folk rock were used as a platform to express opinions about the government and the political process. Today, rock music and its writers still act in that same "watchdog" capacity, expressing concern over the different roles the government undertakes.

Because of the wide range of topics that "Politics" covers, this category has been divided into four sections:

1. Politicians
2. Elections
3. Government and Its Established System
4. Specific Political Events

Related Categories: America, Big Business, Freedom, Injustice, Protest/Revolution

   +Same as Song Above
   *Hard-to-find Songs/Albums

Thematic Albums: Although they are not specifically thematic albums, the subject of POLITICS appears consistently in the early recordings of Bob Dylan, Joan Baez, Phil Ochs, Tom Paxton, Pete Seeger, et al.

YOUR ADDITIONAL SONGS

_____

_____

_____

_____

_____

Politicians

This first section deals with the politician as an individual and as a part of the political process. If the song is about a specific politician, his or her name will appear in parentheses after the song title.

Songs about Richard Nixon are found in a separate listing at the end of this section.

CLASSICS

Abraham, Martin and John	Dion
"Abraham, Martin and John"	(Laurie)
"Sanctuary"*	(Warner Brothers)
+Abraham, Martin and John	Smokey Robinson & the Miracles
"Anthology"	(Motown)
+Abraham, Martin and John	Kenny Rogers
"Love Lifted Me"	(United Artists)
Gimme Some Truth	John Lennon
"Imagine"	(Apple)
+Gimme Some Truth	Generation X
"Generation X"*	(Chrysalis)
Harry Truman	Chicago
"Chicago VIII"	(Columbia)
I Wanna Grow Up and Be a Politician	The Byrds
"The Best of the Byrds Greatest Hits, Vol. II"	(Columbia)
"Byrdmaniax"	(Columbia)

DEFINITIVE SONGS

Abie Baby/Fourscore (Abraham Lincoln)	Various Artists
"Hair" (Soundtrack)	(RCA)
Ballad of a Thin Man	Bob Dylan
"Highway 61 Revisited"	(Columbia)
Big Brother	Stevie Wonder
"Talking Book"	(Tamla)
Ché (Che Guevara)	Judy Collins
"True Stories and Other Dreams"	(Elektra)
Crazy Words (George Washington)	Jim Kweskin and the Jug Band
"The Best of Jim Kweskin and the Jug Band"	(Vanguard)
Dear Mrs. Roosevelt	Bob Dylan
"Tribute to Woody Guthrie"	(Warner Brothers)

DEFINITIVE SONGS

Elected	Alice Cooper
"Greatest Hits"	(Warner Brothers)
"Billion Dollar Babies"	(Warner Brothers)
FDR in Trinidad (Franklin Delano Roosevelt)	Van Dyke Parks
"Discover America"*	(Warner Brothers)
Foreign Policy (John Kennedy)	The Buckinghams
"Made in Chicago"	(Columbia)
Fortunate Son	Creedence Clearwater Revival
"Chronicle"	(Fantasy)
"Willy and the Poor Boys"	(Fantasy)
The Gettysburg Address (Abraham Lincoln)	Lord Buckley
"The Best of Lord Buckley"*	(Elektra)
G-Man Hoover (J. Edgar Hoover)	Van Dyke Parks
"Discover America"*	(Warner Brothers)
He Was a Friend of Mine (John Kennedy)	The Byrds
"The Best of the Byrds Greatest Hits, Vol. II"	(Columbia)
Howdido	Woody Guthrie
"Woody Guthrie"	(Warner Brothers)
Kingfish (Huey Long)	Randy Newman
"Good Old Boys"	(Reprise)
L.B.J. (Lyndon Johnson)	Various Artists
"Hair" (Soundtrack)	(RCA)
Louisiana 1927 (Calvin Coolidge)	Randy Newman
"Good Old Boys	(Reprise)
Love Me, I'm a Liberal	Phil Ochs
"Chords of Fame"	(A&M)
"Phil Och's in Concert"	(Elektra)
Lyndon Johnson Told the Nation	Tom Paxton
"Ain't That News"*	(Elektra)
Message to the Politician	David Amram
"Subway Night"*	(RCA)
A Mind of My Own	Strawbs
"Nomadness"	(A&M)
Mr. Blue	Tom Paxton
"The Compleat Tom Paxton"	(Elektra)

DEFINITIVE SONGS

+Mr. Blue/White Bones of Allende
   "New Songs from the Briarpatch"*
Tom Paxton
(Vanguard)

+Mr. Blue
   "Clear Light"*
Clear Light
(Elektra)

Mr. President (Have Pity on the
      Working Man)
   "Good Old Boys"
Randy Newman

(Reprise)

Mr. Rockefeller (Nelson)
   "Songs for the New Depression"
   "Live at Last"
Bette Midler
(Atlantic)
(Atlantic)

Nobody Left to Crown
   "Mirage"
Richie Havens
(A&M)

Nutted by Reality (Fidel Castro)
   "Pure Pop for Now People"
Nick Lowe
(Columbia)

Politician
   "Goodbye"
   "Wheels of Fire"
Cream
(RSO)
(RSO)

The Politician (A Man of Many
      Words)
   "Good for You Too"*
Tony Wilson

(Capitol)

Promise the Wind (Jimmy Carter)
   "Fire in the Wind"
John Stewart
(RSO)

Redneck (Lester Maddox)
   "Good Old Boys"
Randy Newman
(Reprise)

Same Old Wine
   "Sittin' In"
Loggins and Messina
(Columbia)

So Long Harry Truman
   "So Long Harry Truman"
   "The O'Keefe Files"
Danny O'Keefe
(Atlantic)
(Atlantic)

Tell Me Why You Like Roosevelt
   "Learn to Love It"*
Jesse Winchester
(Bearsville)

That Was the President (John
      Kennedy)
   "I Ain't Marchin' Anymore"
Phil Ochs

(Elektra)

Uncle Ho (Ho Chi Minh)
   "Rainbow Race"*
Pete Seeger
(Columbia)

Vote for Me
   "Chicago XI"
Chicago
(Columbia)

DEFINITIVE SONGS

Waist Deep in the Big Muddy (Lyndon Johnson)	Pete Seeger
"Waist Deep in the Big Muddy"	(Columbia)
War Song (George McGovern)	Neil Young and Graham Nash
(45 RPM Single)*	(Warner Brothers)
We Want a Rock and Roll President	The Dynomites
(45 RPM Single)*	(Epic)
What If We Say (American Dreams Suite)	Jesse Colin Young
"American Dream"	(Elektra)

REFERENCE SONGS

Fool's Overture (Winston Churchill)	Supertramp
"Even in the Quietest Moments"	(A&M)
The Mayor of Candor Lied	Harry Chapin
"On the Road to Kingdom Come"	(Elektra)
Lincoln Freed Me Today	Joan Baez
"Blessed Are"	(Vanguard)
Little Hitler	Nick Lowe
"Pure Pop for Now People"	(Columbia)
On the Road to Kingdom Come	Harry Chapin
"On the Road to Kingdom Come"	(Elektra)
Rockefeller Square	Jimmy Buffett
"Before the Salt"	(Barnaby)
Veracruz (Woodrow Wilson)	Warren Zevon
"Excitable Boy"	(Asylum)

YOUR ADDITIONAL SONGS

_____
_____
_____
_____
_____

RICHARD NIXON

A President of many firsts: the first to visit China, the first to say "I am not a crook," and the first to resign as President of the United States. He is also the first President and political figure to be the object of enough songs to warrant his own listing.

DEFINITIVE SONGS

Editorial	Paul Davis
"I Go Crazy"*	(Warner Brothers)
Here's to the State of Richard Nixon	Phil Ochs
"Chords of Fame"	(A&M)
If I Had a Friend Like Rose Mary Woods	Bill Horowitz
"Lies, Lies, Lies"*	(ESP)
Presidential Rag	Arlo Guthrie
"Arlo Guthrie"	(Reprise)
Super Bird (Tricky Dick)	Country Joe McDonald
"The Life and Times of Country Joe McDonald—from Haight-Ashbury to Woodstock"	(Vanguard)
Tricia, Tell Your Daddy	Andy Kim
"Greatest Hits"	(Steed)

REFERENCE SONGS

Campaigner	Neil Young
"Decade"	(Reprise)
Ohio	Crosby, Stills, Nash & Young
"So Far"	(Atlantic)
"Four Way Street"	(Atlantic)
+Ohio	Neil Young
"Decade"	(Reprise)
"Journey Through the Past"	(Reprise)
Use the Power	Johnny Rivers
"L.A. Reggae"*	(United Artists)
You Haven't Done Nothing Yet	Stevie Wonder
"Fulfillingness' First Finale"	(Tamla)
Young Americans	David Bowie
"Young Americans"	(RCA)
"Changesonebowie"	(RCA)

YOUR ADDITIONAL SONGS

_____

_____

_____

_____

_____

Elections

CLASSICS

Elected   Alice Cooper
"Alice Cooper's Greatest Hits"   (Warner Brothers)
"Billion Dollar Babies"   (Warner Brothers)
Vote for Me   Chicago
"Chicago XI"   (Columbia)

DEFINITIVE SONGS

Beehive State   Randy Newman
"Randy Newman"   (Reprise)
+Beehive State   Harry Nilsson
"Nilsson Sings Newman"   (RCA)
+Beehive State   The Doobie Brothers
"The Doobie Brothers"   (Warner Brothers)
Convention '72   The Delegates
(45 RPM Single)*   (Mainstream)
Election Blues   Canned Heat
"New Age"*   (United Artists)
Election Year Rag   Steve Goodman
"The Essential . . . Steve Goodman"   (Buddah)
Snoopy for President   Royal Guardsmen
(45 RPM Single)*   (Laurie)
Use the Power   Johnny Rivers
"L.A. Raggae"*   (United Artists)

YOUR ADDITIONAL SONGS

_____

_____

_____

_____

_____

Government and Its Established System

Big brother and the establishment, control and regulation, bureaucracy and red tape, FBI and CIA, all the clichés that have become associated with our government's function down through the years.

CLASSICS

Big Brother
"Talking Book"

Stevie Wonder
(Tamla)

State of the Union
"Chicago V"

Chicago
(Columbia)

DEFINITIVE SONGS

A Apolitical Blues
"Sailing Shoes"

Little Feat
(Warner Brothers)

Ballad of William Worthy
"All the News That's Fit to Sing"

Phil Ochs
(Elektra)

Bring Back the Chair
"New Songs from the Briarpatch"

Tom Paxton
(Vanguard)

Children of Night
"Slow Flux"

Steppenwolf
(Mums/Columbia)

Contact in Red Square
"Plastic Letters"

Blondie
(Chrysalis)

Cops of the World
"Phil Ochs in Concert"

Phil Ochs
(Elektra)

DEFINITIVE SONGS

49 Bye Byes/America's Children "Four Way Street"	Crosby, Stills, Nash & Young (Atlantic)
Here Come the People in Grey "Muswell Hillbillies"	The Kinks (RCA)
I Could Be Singing "Washington County"	Arlo Guthrie (Reprise)
In the 80's "Earth and Sky"	Graham Nash (Capitol)
It's Alright "Native Sons"	Loggins and Messina (Columbia)
Knock on the Door "All the News That's Fit to Sing"	Phil Ochs (Elektra)
Love Me, I'm a Liberal "Chords of Fame" "Phil Ochs in Concert"	Phil Ochs (A&M) (Elektra)
The Merry Minuet "The Best of the Kingston Trio"	The Kingston Trio (Capitol)
Mr. Blue "Morning Again"*	Tom Paxton (Elektra)
+Mr. Blue/White Bones of Allende "New Songs from the Briarpatch"*	Tom Paxton (Vanguard)
+Mr. Blue "Clear Light"*	Clear Light (Elektra)
On the Border "On the Border"	The Eagles (Asylum)
Peacemaker "Native Sons"	Loggins and Messina (Columbia)
Political Science "Sail Away"	Randy Newman (Reprise)
Reality "Deeper Roots (Back to the Channel)"	The Mighty Diamonds (Virgin)
Respectable "Tapestry"	Don McLean (United Artists)
Rules and Regulations "Donovan in Concert"*	Donovan (Epic)
Secret Agent Man "Johnny Rivers" (Superpak)	Johnny Rivers (United Artists)

DEFINITIVE SONGS

A Simple Desultory Philippic
"Parsley, Sage, Rosemary and Thyme"
Simon and Garfunkel
(Columbia)

Sorry Mr. Harris
"TRB II"
The Tom Robinson Band
(Harvest)

Spys
"Born Again"
Randy Newman
(Warner Brothers)

Subterranean Homesick Blues
"Bringing It All Back Home"
Bob Dylan
(Columbia)

+Subterranean Homesick Blues
"Michael Stanley"*
Michael Stanley
(Tumbleweed)

T.V. Guide
"Earth and Sky"
Graham Nash
(Capitol)

Talkin' Watergate Blues
"New Songs from the Briarpatch"*
Tom Paxton
(Vanguard)

The Times They Are a Changin'
"The Times They Are a Changin'"
"Bob Dylan's Greatest Hits"
"Live at Budokan"
Bob Dylan
(Columbia)
(Columbia)
(Columbia)

+The Times They Are a Changin'
"Any Day Now"
Joan Baez
(Vanguard)

+The Times They Are a Changin'
"Words and Music by Bob Dylan"*
The Hollies
(Epic)

+The Times They Are a Changin'
"Beach Boys' Party"
The Beach Boys
(Capitol)

+The Times They Are a Changin'
"Wednesday Morning 3 A.M."
Simon and Garfunkel
(Columbia)

+The Times They Are a Changin'
"The Byrds Play Dylan"
The Byrds
(Columbia)

+The Times They Are a Changin'

"No Nukes"
Carly Simon and Graham Nash
(Asylum)

Undercover Man
"Recycled"
Edgar Winter
(Blue Sky)

Volunteers
"The Worst of the Jefferson Airplane"
"Volunteers"
Jefferson Airplane
(RCA)
(RCA)

Washington A.C./D.C.
"Christ Child"*
Christ Child
(Buddah)

DEFINITIVE SONGS

What About Me

Quicksilver Messenger
Service

"Anthology"
"What about Me"

(Capitol)
(Capitol)

+What About Me
"The Great Blind Degree"*

Richie Havens
(Stormy Forest)

With God on Our Side
"The Times They Are a Changin'"

Bob Dylan
(Columbia)

+With God on Our Side
(45 RPM E.P.)*

Manfred Mann
(Ascot/H.M.V.)

+With God on Our Side
"The First Ten Years"
"Joan Baez in Concert Part 2"

Joan Baez
(Vanguard)
(Vanguard)

REFERENCE SONGS

Daily News
"Ramblin' Boy"*

Tom Paxton
(Elektra)

Eve of Destruction
(45 RPM Single)*
"Eve of Destruction"*

Barry McGuire
(ABC/Dunhill)
(ABC/Dunhill)

Foreign Policy
"Made in Chicago"

The Buckinghams
(Columbia)

Man You Never Saw
"Power in the Darkness"

The Tom Robinson Band
(Harvest)

The House Un-American Dream
"The Best of Richard and Mimi
    Fariña"

Richard and Mimi Fariña
(Vanguard)

My Country 'Tis of Thy People
    You're Dying
"The Best of Buffy Sainte-Marie"

Buffy Sainte-Marie

(Vanguard)

Reds in My Bed
"Bloody Tourists"

10 CC
(Polydor)

Seven O'Clock News/Silent Night
"Parsley, Sage, Rosemary and Thyme"

Simon and Garfunkel
(Columbia)

The Undercover Man
"Skip Battin"*

Skip Battin
(Signpost)

YOUR ADDITIONAL SONGS

_____

_____

_____

_____

_____

Specific Political Events

Our country has played an important part in many historical events and crises. Some of these have been documented by rock writers.

CLASSICS

It was not practical to select "classic" songs for this category, since each song is special and unique to its own subject matter.

DEFINITIVE SONGS

Black Day in July (Detroit Riots)
"The Very Best of Gordon Lightfoot"

Gordon Lightfoot
(United Artists)

Chicago (1968 Democratic
   Convention)
"Songs for Beginners"

Graham Nash

(Atlantic)

+Chicago
"Four Way Street"

Crosby, Stills, Nash & Young
(Atlantic)

+Chicago
"The Best of David Crosby and
   Graham Nash"

David Crosby/Graham Nash
(ABC)

Days of Decision (Cuban Crisis)
"Chords of Fame"
"I Ain't Marchin' Anymore"

Phil Ochs
(A&M)
(Elektra)

How I Spent My Summer Vacation
   (1968 Democratic Convention)
"The Street Giveth . . ."*

Cat Mother and the All
   Night Newsboys
(Polydor)

DEFINITIVE SONGS

It Could Have Been Me (Kent—Jackson State)	Holly Near
"A Live Album"*	(Redwood)
Jackson—Kent Blues	Steve Miller Band
"Steve Miller Band Number 5"	(Capitol)
Last Train to Nuremberg (World War II)	Pete Seeger
"The World of Pete Seeger"	(Columbia)
Ohio (Kent State)	Crosby, Stills, Nash & Young
"Four Way Street"	(Atlantic)
"So Far"	(Atlantic)
+Ohio (Kent State)	Neil Young
"Decade"	(Reprise)
"Journey Through the Past"	(Reprise)
Prologue/Someday (August 29, 1968) (1968 Democratic Convention)	Chicago
"Chicago Transit Authority"	(Columbia)
Ride Captain Ride (Pueblo Crisis)	Blues Image
"Open"	(Atco)
Santo Domingo	Phil Ochs
"Chords of Fame"	(A&M)
"Phil Ochs in Concert"	(Elektra)
Talkin' Cuban Crisis	Phil Ochs
"All the News That's Fit to Sing"	(Elektra)
Talkin' Watergate Blues	Tom Paxton
"New Songs from the Briarpatch"*	(Vanguard)
Trouble Coming Everyday (Watts Riots)	Mothers of Invention
"Freak Out"	(Verve)

YOUR ADDITIONAL SONGS

_____

_____

_____

_____

_____

POVERTY

Poverty—busted flat in Baton Rouge . . . or anywhere else, for that matter.

These songs refer to conditions of poverty suffered by individuals and families both in rural areas and the inner city. Not surprisingly these are the very places that gave birth to rock and roll. Isn't it ironic that the richest entertainment medium of our time sprang from black rhythm and blues and white country and western music, whose creators were primarily poor people?

Related Categories: Hunger, Money, Outcasts/Hobos, Racism/Prejudice, Urban/City Life, Working

+Same as Song Above
*Hard-to-find Songs/Albums

CLASSICS

Brother, Can You Spare a Dime? "See What Tomorrow Brings"	Peter, Paul and Mary (Warner Brothers)
+Brother, Can You Spare a Dime? "Judith"	Judy Collins (Elektra)
+Brother, Can You Spare a Dime? "Spanky and Our Gang"*	Spanky and Our Gang (Mercury)
+Brother, Can You Spare a Dime? "Rag 'n Roll Revue"	Cathy Chamberlain (Warner Brothers)
+Brother, Can You Spare a Dime? "Slim Chance"	Ronnie Lane (A&M)
+Brother, Can You Spare a Dime? "Greatest Hits"	The Weavers (Vanguard)
Orphans of Wealth "Tapestry"	Don McLean (United Artists)

THEMATIC ALBUMS

"Let's Clean Up the Ghetto"	Philadelphia All Stars (Philadelphia International)

DEFINITIVE SONGS

Bag Lady "Hermit of Mink Hollow"	Todd Rundgren (Bearsville)

DEFINITIVE SONGS

Ballad of Hollis Brown
"The Times They Are a Changin'"
Bob Dylan
(Columbia)

Bangla Desh
"Bangla Desh"
"The Best of George Harrison"
George Harrison
(Apple)
(Apple)

Beans, Bacon and Gravy
"Hard Times"*
Peter Yarrow
(Warner Brothers)

Better Wages, Better Days
"The Movies"*
The Movies
(Arista)

Billy the Bum
"Diamonds in the Rough"*
John Prine
(Atlantic)

The Breadline
"Golden Butter/The Best of the Paul
    Butterfield Blues Band"
Paul Butterfield Blues Band
(Elektra)

Busted
"A Man and His Music"
Ray Charles
(ABC)

Circle of Steel
"Sundown"
Gordon Lightfoot
(Reprise)

Cloud Nine
"Anthology—Tenth Anniversary
    Special"
The Temptations
(Motown)

Coat of Many Colors
"Pieces of the Sky"
Emmylou Harris
(Warner Brothers)

The Dole Song

"Fame and Price . . . Together"*
Alan Price and Georgie
    Fame
(Warner Brothers)

Face of Appalachia
"Tarzana Kid"*
John Sebastian
(Reprise)

Family Tree
"Family Tree"
The Staple Singers
(Warner Brothers)

From Stanton Station
"Looking Glass"
Looking Glass
(Epic)

Ghetto
"Graham Central Station"
Graham Central Station
(Warner Brothers)

Ghetto
"The Original Delaney and Bonnie"
Delaney and Bonnie
(Elektra)

+Ghetto
"The First Ten Years"
Joan Baez
(Vanguard)

DEFINITIVE SONGS

The Ghetto "The Best of Donny Hathaway"	Donny Hathaway (Atco)
Ghetto Child "The Spinners"	The Spinners (Atlantic)
Give a Damn "Without Rhyme or Reason"* "Spanky's Greatest Hits"	Spanky and Our Gang (Mercury) (Mercury)
+Give a Damn "Paul and . . ."	Paul Stookey (Warner Brothers)
Grocery Store Blues "Amigo"	Arlo Guthrie (Reprise)
Hard Times "Arlo Guthrie"	Arlo Guthrie (Reprise)
Hard Times "So Long Harry Truman"	Danny O'Keefe (Atlantic)
Hard Times, Come Again No More "Shot Through the Heart"	Jennifer Warnes (Arista)
Help the Poor "Live at the Regal"	B. B. King (ABC)
Hobo Jungle "Northern Lights, Southern Cross"	The Band (Capitol)
Hobo's Lullaby "Library of Congress"	Woody Guthrie (Elektra)
+Hobo's Lullaby "Hobo's Lullaby"	Arlo Guthrie (Reprise)
+Hobo's Lullaby "The World of Pete Seeger"	Pete Seeger (Columbia)
+Hobo's Lullaby "Tribute to Woody Guthrie"	Joan Baez (Warner Brothers)
Hobo's Mandolin "Ladies Love Outlaws"	Tom Rush (Columbia)
The Hobo Song "Bruised Orange"*	John Prine (Asylum)
Home from the Forest "The Way I Feel"	Gordon Lightfoot (United Artists)
Homeless Brother "Homeless Brother"* "Solo"	Don McLean (United Artists) (United Artists)

DEFINITIVE SONGS

Honky Red "Only the Silence Remains"*	Murray McLauchlan (True North)
How Can a Poor Man Stand Such Times and Live "Randy Newman"	Randy Newman (Reprise)
+How Can a Poor Man Stand Such Times and Live "Show Time"	Ry Cooder (Warner Brothers)
The Hubbardville Store "Tramps and Hawks"*	Jim Ringer (Philo)
I Ain't Got No Home "Song for Patty"*	Sammy Walker (Vanguard)
I Am a Lonesome Hobo "John Wesley Harding"	Bob Dylan (Columbia)
In the Ghetto "Worldwide 50 Gold Award Hits, Vol. 1"	Elvis Presley (RCA)
+In the Ghetto "Greatest Hits"	Mac Davis (Columbia)
Jack's Friend "The Outsider"*	Tom Pacheco (RCA)
The Jarrow Song "Between Today and Yesterday"	Alan Price (Warner Brothers)
A Job of Work "Ramblin' Boy"*	Tom Paxton (Elektra)
Junkman "Breezy Stories"	Danny O'Keefe (Atlantic)
King of the Road "Golden Greats"	Roger Miller (Mercury)
+King of the Road "Nightflight to Venus"	Boney M (Sire)
Laid Off "A Live Album"*	Holly Near (Redwood)
Last, Lonely and Wretched "Blessed Are"	Joan Baez (Vanguard)
Let's Clean Up the Ghetto "Let's Clean Up the Ghetto" (Various Artists)	All Stars (Philadelphia International)
Little Beggarman "Greatest Hits"	Ian and Sylvia (Vanguard)

DEFINITIVE SONGS

+Little Beggarman
"One Night"

Arlo Guthrie
(Warner Brothers)

Little Ghetto Boy
"Live"

Donny Hathaway
(Atlantic)

Loan Me a Dime
"An Anthology"

Duane Allman
(Capricorn)

+Loan Me a Dime
"Boz Scaggs"

Boz Scaggs
(Atlantic)

Lonely Tenement
"David Johansen"

David Johansen
(Blue Sky)

The Love of the Common People
"Rhymes and Reasons"

John Denver
(RCA)

Mother of a Miner's Child
"Old Dan's Records"

Gordon Lightfoot
(Reprise)

Mr. Welfare Man
"Give, Get, Take and Have"

Curtis Mayfield
(Curtom)

Old Men Sleeping on the Bowery
"Willy Nile"

Willy Nile
(Arista)

Old Joe
"American Album"*

Allan Taylor
(United Artists)

Rich Man, Poor Man
"Late Again"

Peter, Paul and Mary
(Warner Brothers)

Shopping Bag Ladies
" 'Well, Well,' said the Rocking
    Chair"*

Dean Friedman
(Lifesong)

Shopping Bag Lady
"Life Lines"*

Richard Supa
(Epic)

Shopping Bag People
"Sense of Direction"

Climax Blues Band
(Sire)

Slum Baby
(45 RPM Single)*

Booker T. and the MG's
(Stax)

Slums
"Live"

Donny Hathaway
(Atlantic)

Streets of London
"Streets of London"
"Ralph McTell Live"

Ralph McTell
(Fantasy)
(Fantasy)

That's What I Want to Hear
"I Ain't Marchin' Anymore"*

Phil Ochs
(Elektra)

DEFINITIVE SONGS

There's Nothin' Soft About Hard Times	Jimmy Buffett
"Before the Salt"	(Barnaby)
Things Goin' On	Lynyrd Skynyrd
"Skynyrd's First . . . and Last"	(MCA)
Unemployment	Steve Goodman
"Words We Can Dance To"*	(Asylum)
Unemployment Blues	Force of Nature
"Force of Nature"*	(Philadelphia International)
Village Ghetto Land	Stevie Wonder
"Songs in the Key of Life"	(Tamla)
Wait	Steve Forbert
"Jackrabbit Slim"	(Nemperor)
We're Gonna Move	Elvis Presley
"Worldwide 50 Gold Award Hits, Vol. 2"	(RCA)
Welfare Mother	Neil Young
"Rust Never Sleeps"	(Reprise)
Welfare Song	The Beach Boys
"Surf's Up"	(Brother/Reprise)
Welfare Symphony	Carole King
"Fantasy"	(Ode)
Why I Sing the Blues	B. B. King
"Live and Well"	(ABC)
The World Is a Ghetto	War
"Greatest Hits"	(United Artists)
"The World Is a Ghetto"	(United Artists)

REFERENCE SONGS

Ain't That Nothing	Billy Preston
"Music Is My Life"	(A&M)
Are They Gonna Make Us Outlaws Again?	James Talley
"Trying Like the Devil"*	(Capitol)
Black Friday	Steely Dan
"Katy Lied"	(ABC)
The Bum	Orleans
"Waking and Dreaming"	(Asylum)

REFERENCE SONGS

Down in the Boondocks (45 RPM Single)*	Billy Joe Royal (Columbia)
+Down in the Boondocks "Nightwatch"*	Kenny Loggins (Columbia)
I'm Living in Shame	Diana Ross and the Supremes
"Anthology"	(Motown)
Love Child	Diana Ross and the Supremes
"Anthology"	(Motown)
Mercedes Benz "Pearl"	Janis Joplin (Columbia)
Mr. Bojangles "Mr. Bojangles" "Five Years Gone"* "A Man Must Carry On"	Jerry Jeff Walker (Atco) (Atco) (MCA)
+Mr. Bojangles "Demon in Disguise"	David Bromberg (Columbia)
+Mr. Bojangles "Dirt, Silver and Gold"	Nitty Gritty Dirt Band (United Artists)
+Mr. Bojangles "Whose Garden Was This?"	John Denver (RCA)
+Mr. Bojangles "Jim Stafford"	Jim Stafford (MGM)
+Mr. Bojangles "Touching You, Touching Me" "Rainbow"	Neil Diamond (MCA) (MCA)
+Mr. Bojangles "Dylan"	Bob Dylan (Columbia)
+Mr. Bojangles "Harry"	Harry Nilsson (RCA)
Old Mister Time "Bloody Tourist"	10 CC (Polydor)
Poets of the West Virginia Mines "Ain't It Somethin' "*	James Talley (Capitol)
Poor Side of Town "The Very Best of Johnny Rivers"	Johnny Rivers (United Artists)
+Poor Side of Town "Up, Up and Away"	The Fifth Dimension (Soul City)

REFERENCE SONGS

Poverty Train
. "Eli and the 13th Confession"

Laura Nyro
(Columbia)

Prodigal Son
"Beggars Banquet"

The Rolling Stones
(London)

Rag Doll
"Rag Doll"
"Gold Vault of Hits"
"The Four Seasons Story"

The Four Seasons
(Philips)
(Philips)
(Private Stock)

+Rag Doll
"Live at Last"

Steeleye Span
(Chrysalis)

Tobacco Road
"Greatest Hits"

Nashville Teens
(London)

+Tobacco Road
"Psychedelic Lollipop"*

Blues Magoos
(Mercury)

+Tobacco Road
"Jefferson Airplane Takes Off"

Jefferson Airplane
(RCA)

+Tobacco Road
"The Best of Spooky Tooth"

Spooky Tooth
(Island)

Waiting for a Train
"Real Live"

John Sebastian
(Kama Sutra)

YOUR ADDITIONAL SONGS

_____

_____

_____

_____

_____

PREGNANCY

Pregnancy—ready and willing or already and unwilling.
The sentiments expressed in this category vary as greatly, as do the circumstances in which the sentiments were first expressed.

Related Categories: Children, Fathers, Marriage, Mothers

+Same as Song Above
*Hard-to-find Songs/Albums

CLASSICS

Ready or Not "For Everyman"	Jackson Browne (Asylum)
Think I'm Gonna Have a Baby "Hot Cakes"	Carly Simon (Elektra)
When a Man Needs a Woman "Friends"	The Beach Boys (Capitol)

DEFINITIVE SONGS

Ballad of the Unborn Child "My Boy"*	Richard Harris (ABC/Dunhill)
A Child Is Coming "Blows Against the Empire"	Jefferson Starship (RCA)
Cinderella "Firefall"	American Flyer (United Artists)
Don't Make Me Pregnant "Marshall"	Marshall Chapman (Epic)
Good Lady of Toronto	Kenny Rogers and the First Edition
"Transition"*	(Reprise)
Having My Baby "Times of Your Life"	Paul Anka (United Artists)
I Think We Fell in Love Too Fast "Endless Flight"	Leo Sayer (Warner Brothers)
Question of Birth "Suite for Susan"	Tim Hardin (Columbia)
Runs in the Family "The Roches"	The Roches (Warner Brothers)

DEFINITIVE SONGS

See Us When You Can
"Goodnight Mrs. Calabash"

Ian Thomas Band
(Chrysalis)

Sister's Coming Home
"Blue Kentucky Girl"

Emmylou Harris
(Warner Brothers)

That's How Things Go Down
"Fantasy"

Carole King
(Ode)

Too Young to Be Married
"Moving Finger"
"Hollies Live"

The Hollies
(Epic)
(Epic)

Unborn Lullaby
"Ollie Moggus"*

Bob Hinkle
(Ampex)

REFERENCE SONGS

All My Friends Are Getting Married
"Skyhooks"

Skyhooks
(Mercury)

Barefoot and Pregnant
"To the Limit"

Joan Armatrading
(A&M)

Big Betty
"The Mighty Quinn"

Manfred Mann
(Mercury)

Boy with the Moon and Star
"Catch Bull at Four"

Cat Stevens
(A&M)

Crow on the Cradle
"Golden Apples of the Sun"

Judy Collins
(Elektra)

Danny's Song
"The Best of Friends"
"Sittin' In"
"Loggins and Messina"

Loggins and Messina
(Columbia)
(Columbia)
(Columbia)

+Danny's Song
"Country"

Anne Murray
(Capitol)

Old Time Woman
"A Live Album"*

Holly Near
(Redwood)

One Mint Julep
(45 RPM Single)*
"History of Rhythm and Blues"
"Soul Years"

The Clovers
(Atlantic)
(Atlantic)
(Atlantic)

Roy
"Slides"*

Richard Harris
(ABC/Dunhill)

10 O'Clock and All Is Well
"Judy Collins #3"

Judy Collins
(Elektra)

REFERENCE SONGS

Up the Junction   Squeeze
"Cool for Cats"   (A&M)

YOUR ADDITIONAL SONGS

_____

_____

_____

_____

_____

PRISONS

Prisons—outside looking in . . . at the inside looking out.
Rock has always been concerned with freedom, both personal and social. These songs deal with the absence of and yearning for freedom. In theory the present system is supposed to rehabilitate the prisoner and restore his freedom. In reality it contains and dehumanizes him. These songs focus on the system itself, and on the prisoner, often the victim of its injustice.

Related Categories: Freedom, Injustice

+Same as Song Above
*Hard-to-find Songs/Albums

CLASSICS

Attica State	John Lennon
"Sometime in New York City"	(Apple)
Inside Looking Out	The Animals
"Best of Eric Burdon and the Animals Vol. II"	(ABKCO)
"Best of the Animals"	(ABKCO)
+Inside Looking Out	Grand Funk Railroad
"Live Album"	(Capitol)
"Mark, Don and Mel"	(Capitol)
Prison Trilogy	Joan Baez
"Joan C. Baez"	(A&M)
"Come from the Shadows"	(A&M)
San Quentin	Johnny Cash
"At San Quentin"	(Columbia)

THEMATIC ALBUMS

"At Folsom Prison"	Johnny Cash (Columbia)
"At San Quentin"	Johnny Cash (Columbia)
"Live in Cook County Jail"	B. B. King (ABC)
"Short Eyes" (Soundtrack)	Curtis Mayfield (Curtom)

DEFINITIVE SONGS

Angela "Sometime in New York City"	John Lennon (Apple)
Back Against the Wall "Short Eyes"	Curtis Mayfield (Curtom)
Back on the Street "Oops . . . Wrong Planet"	Utopia (Bearsville)
Ballad of Caryl Chessman (45 RPM Single)*	Ronnie Hawkins (Monument)
Born in a Prison "Sometime in New York City"	John Lennon (Apple)
Break It Down "Short Eyes" (Soundtrack)	Curtis Mayfield (Curtom)
California Prison Blues "T-Shirt"*	Loudon Wainwright III (Arista)
Care of Cell 44 "Odessy and Oracle"*	The Zombies (Epic)
Celia "All the News That's Fit to Sing"	Phil Ochs (Elektra)
Chain Gang "This Is Sam Cooke"	Sam Cooke (RCA)
+Chain Gang (Medley) "The Faces I've Been"*	Jim Croce (Lifesong)
+Chain Gang "We Remember Sam Cooke"	The Supremes (Motown)
+Chain Gang "Best of Otis Redding"	Otis Redding (Atco)
+Chain Gang "Manufacturers of Soul"	Jackie Wilson (Brunswick)
+Chain Gang "Peaks Valleys Honky-Tonks & Alleys"	Michael Murphey (Epic)
Cocaine Blues "Move It On Over"	George Thorogood (Rounder)
Columbus, Georgia Stockade "Woody Guthrie"	Woody Guthrie (Warner Brothers)
County Jail Blues "No Reason to Cry"	Eric Clapton (RSO)
David's Song "David's Album"	Joan Baez (Vanguard)

DEFINITIVE SONGS

The Death of Stephen Biko "Heroes"*	Tom Paxton (Vanguard)
Easy Times "Living"	Judy Collins (Elektra)
11 Months and 29 Days "Johnny Paycheck's Greatest Hits Vol. II"	Johnny Paycheck (Epic)
Empty Sky "Empty Sky"	Elton John (MCA)
Folsom Prison Blues "At Folsom Blues"	Johnny Cash (Columbia)
+Folsom Prison Blues "Greatest Hits"	Carl Perkins (Columbia)
From the Prison "Something Else Again"*	Richie Havens (MGM)
George Jackson (45 RPM Single)*	Bob Dylan (Columbia)
Hollaway Jail "Muswell Hillbillies"	The Kinks (RCA)
The Hostage "Peace Will Come"*	Tom Paxton (Reprise)
+The Hostage "True Stories and Other Dreams"	Judy Collins (Elektra)
Hurricane "Desire"	Bob Dylan (Columbia)
I Fought the Law "Oldies But Goodies, Volume 9" (45 RPM Single)	Bobby Fuller 4 (Original sound) (Mustang)
+I Fought the Law "The Demons"	The Demons (Mercury)
+I Fought the Law "Don't Mind Rockin' Tonight"	Ducks Deluxe (RCA)
+I Fought the Law "Natural Act"	Kris and Rita (A&M)
+I Fought the Law "The Clash"	The Clash (Epic)
I Shall Be Released "Bob Dylan's Greatest Hits"	Bob Dylan (Columbia)

DEFINITIVE SONGS

+I Shall Be Released
  "Music from Big Pink"
  "The Last Waltz" (Soundtrack)
  The Band
  (Capitol)
  (Warner Brothers)

+I Shall Be Released
  "Words and Music by Bob Dylan"*
  The Hollies
  (Epic)

+I Shall Be Released
  "From Every Stage"
  "Any Day Now"
  Joan Baez
  (A&M)
  (Vanguard)

+I Shall Be Released
  "Dimensions"*
  The Box Tops
  (Bell)

+I Shall Be Released
  (45 RPM Single)*
  Coven
  (Bell)

+I Shall Be Released
  "Rick Nelson in Concert"
  Rick Nelson
  (MCA)

+I Shall Be Released
  "Late Again"
  Peter, Paul and Mary
  (Warner Brothers)

+I Shall Be Released
  "With a Little Help from My
    Friends"
  Joe Cocker
  (A&M)

I'll Kiss the World Goodbye
  "Really"
  J. J. Cale
  (Cale/Shelter)

In the Jailhouse Now
  "The World of Johnny Cash"
  Johnny Cash
  (Columbia)

+In the Jailhouse Now
  "Guy Clark"
  Guy Clark
  (Warner Brothers)

Iron Lady
  "I Ain't Marchin' Anymore"
  Phil Ochs
  (Elektra)

I've Gotta Get a Message to You
  "Gold"
  "Best of the Bee Gees"
  "Idea"
  The Bee Gees
  (RSO)
  (RSO)
  (RSO)

+I've Gotta Get a Message to You
  "Leah Kunkel"*
  Leah Kunkel
  (Columbia)

Jail Bird Love Song
  "Having a Wonderful Time"*
  Geoff Muldaur
  (Reprise)

Jail Guitar Doors
  "The Clash"
  The Clash
  (Epic)

Jailbreak
  "Jailbreak"
  "Live and Dangerous"
  Thin Lizzy
  (Mercury)
  (Warner Brothers)

DEFINITIVE SONGS

Jailhouse Rock
"50 World Wide Gold Award Hits"
Elvis Presley
(RCA)

+Jailhouse Rock
"Beck-Ola"
Jeff Beck
(Epic)

+Jailhouse Rock
"Coven"*
Coven
(MGM)

+Jailhouse Rock
"The Best of Sha Na Na"
Sha Na Na
(Kama Sutra)

+Jailhouse Rock
"Fandango"
ZZ Top
(London)

John Sinclair
"Sometime in New York City"
John Lennon
(Apple)

Life in Prison
"Sweetheart of the Rodeo"
The Byrds
(Columbia)

New Colorado Blues
"Closer to the Ground"*
Joy of Cooking
(Capitol)

Parchman's Farm
"Te John, Grease and Wolfman"
Charlie Daniels
(Kama Sutra)

+Parchman's Farm
"The Last of the British Blues"
"Blues Breakers"
John Mayall
(ABC)
(London)

+Parchman's Farm
"Seventh Son"
Mose Allison
(Prestige)

+Parchman's Farm
"Johnny Rivers" (Superpak)
Johnny Rivers
(United Artists)

+Parchman's Farm
"About Blues"
John Winter
(Janus)

Peat Bog Soldiers
"Strangers and Cousins"
Pete Seeger
(Columbia)

Percy's Song
"Washington County"
Arlo Guthrie
(Reprise)

+Percy's Song
"Unhalfbricking"
Fairport Convention
(Polydor)

The Prisoner
"Wild Tales"
Graham Nash
(Atlantic)

+The Prisoner
"One of the Boys"
Roger Daltrey
(MCA/Track)

Prisoner's Song
(45 RPM Single)*
Fats Domino
(Imperial)

DEFINITIVE SONGS

Raise Your Glass (to Foolish Me)
"Book Early"

City Boy
(Mercury)

Riot in Cell Block Nine
(45 RPM Single)*

The Robins
(Spark)

+Riot in Cell Block Nine

Commander Cody and the
Lost Planet Airmen
(Paramount)

"Live from Deep in the Heart of
Texas"

The Rock
"The Rock"*

Frankie Miller
(Chrysalis)

Rubber Bullets
"100 CC"
"10 CC"
"Greatest Hits 1972–1978"

10 CC
(UK)
(UK)
(Polydor)

Seven Long Years
"Shakin' All Over"*

The Guess Who
(Springboard)

Shackles and Chains
"Hobo's Lullaby"

Arlo Guthrie
(Reprise)

Sister Woman Sister
"You Can Know Who I Am"*

Holly Near
(Redwood)

Starkville City Jail
"At San Quentin"

Johnny Cash
(Columbia)

Take a Message to Mary
"Self Portrait"

Bob Dylan
(Columbia)

Thirty Days in the Hole
"Smokin'"

Humble Pie
(A&M)

The Tijuana Jail
"The Best of the Kingston Trio"

The Kingston Trio
(Capitol)

Waiting for the Worms
"The Wall"

Pink Floyd
(Harvest)

When You Get Outside
"Down in the Bunker"

Steve Gibbons Band
(Polydor)

Wichita Jail
"Saddle Tramp"

Charlie Daniels
(Epic)

Yazoo City Jail
"Basement Tapes"

Bob Dylan and The Band
(Columbia)

REFERENCE SONGS

Alcatraz
"Leon Russell"

Leon Russell
(Shelter)

REFERENCE SONGS

Band on the Run	Wings
"Band on the Run"	(Apple)
"Wings Over America"	(Capitol)
Bring Back the Chair	Tom Paxton
"New Songs from the Briarpatch"*	(Vanguard)
Christmas Card from a Hooker in Minnesota	Tom Waits
"Blue Valentine"	(Asylum)
Cry Myself to Sleep	Del Shannon
"The Vintage Years"	(Sire)
Fifteen Months	Joan Baez
"Blessed Are"	(Vanguard)
Five Minutes More	Rick Nelson
"Intakes"*	(Epic)
Georgia	Boz Scaggs
"Silk Degrees"	(Columbia)
Go Down Old Hannah	Pete Seeger
"I Can See a New Day"	(Columbia)
The Hangman's Knee	Jeff Beck
"Beck-Ola"	(Epic)
I Ain't Living Long Like This	Emmylou Harris
"Quarter Moon in a Ten Cent Town"	(Warner Brothers)
I Ain't Scared of Your Jail	Pete Seeger
"We Shall Overcome"	(Columbia)
John Hardy	George Thorogood
"George Thorogood"*	(Rounder)
Mr. Bojangles	Jerry Jeff Walker
"Mr. Bojangles"	(Atco)
"Five Years Gone"*	(Atco)
"A Man Must Carry On"	(MCA)
+Mr. Bojangles	David Bromberg
"Demon in Disguise"	(Columbia)
+Mr. Bojangles	Neil Diamond
"Touching You, Touching Me"	(MCA)
"Rainbow"	(MCA)
+Mr. Bojangles	Bob Dylan
"Dylan"	(Columbia)
+Mr. Bojangles	Harry Nilsson
"Harry"	(RCA)

REFERENCE SONGS

+Mr. Bojangles
"Dirt, Silver and Gold"

Nitty Gritty Dirt Band
(United Artists)

+Mr. Bojangles
"Whose Garden Was This?"

John Denver
(RCA)

+Mr. Bojangles
"Jim Stafford"

Jim Stafford
(MGM)

A New Life
"A New Life"

The Marshall Tucker Band
(Capricorn)

The Night I Get Out of Jail

Ten Wheel Drive with
  Genya Ravan

"Peculiar Friends"

(Polydor)

Rotten Peaches
"Madman Across the Water"

Elton John
(MCA)

The Sweetest Gift
"Prisoner in Disguise"

Linda Ronstadt
(Asylum)

There But for Fortune
"Chords of Fame"
"Phil Ochs in Concert"

Phil Ochs
(A&M)
(Elektra)

+There But for Fortune
"First Ten Years"

Joan Baez
(Vanguard)

+There But for Fortune
"Cher"

Cher
(United Artists)

Years Behind Bars
"Peaks Valleys Honky-Tonks &
  Alleys"

Michael Murphey
(Epic)

YOUR ADDITIONAL SONGS

_____

_____

_____

_____

_____

PROSTITUTION

Prostitution—can't buy you love.

The world's oldest profession has not escaped the pen of the rock writer. The topic is explored with emphasis on the reasons and circumstances of prostitution (i.e., drug problems, the need for quick money, "the teen-age runaway," etc.).

Related Categories: Poverty, Sexuality, Urban/City Life

+Same as Song Above
*Hard-to-find Songs/Albums

CLASSICS

Cindy's Crying/Hooker "The Compleat Tom Paxton"	Tom Paxton (Elektra)
House of the Rising Son "Best of the Animals" "The Animals"*	The Animals (ABKCO) (MGM)
+House of the Rising Son "Bob Dylan"	Bob Dylan (Columbia)
+House of the Rising Son "Joan Baez"	Joan Baez (Vanguard)
+House of the Rising Son "A Little Bit of Liverpool"	The Supremes (Motown)
+House of the Rising Son "The Best of the Chambers Brothers"	The Chambers Brothers (Fantasy)
+House of the Rising Son "The Essential Jack Elliot"	Ramblin' Jack Elliot (Vanguard)
+House of the Rising Son (45 RPM Single)	Frijid Pink (London)
+House of the Rising Son "Deep Are the Roosts"	Tracey Nelson (Prestige)
+House of the Rising Son "Greatest Hits"	The Weavers (Vanguard)
+House of the Rising Son "Great Fatsby"*	Leslie West (Phantom)
+The House of the Rising Son "The House of the Rising Son"	Santa Esmeralda (Casablanca)

DEFINITIVE SONGS

Alice
"The Hoople"
Mott the Hoople
(Columbia)

Cracked Actor
"Aladdin Sane"
David Bowie
(RCA)

Easy Money
"Rickie Lee Jones"
Rickie Lee Jones
(Warner Brothers)

+Easy Money
"Thanks I'll Eat It Here"
Lowell George
(Warner Brothers)

+Easy Money
"Goose Bumps"
Ian Lloyd
(Atlantic)

The Fire Down Below

"Night Moves"
Bob Seger and the Silver
    Bullet Band
(Capitol)

+The Fire Down Below
"Rough Roadshow"
Tina Turner
(United Artists)

42nd Street
"Piper"*
Piper
(A&M)

Gertrude
"Driftin' Way of Life"*
Jerry Jeff Walker
(Vanguard)

Honky Tonk Downstairs
"Poco"
Poco
(Epic)

House of Blue Lights
"House of Blue Lights"*
Don Covay
(Atco)

The Hustler
"Too Late to Cry"
Widow Maker
(United Artists)

Island Girl
"Rock of the Westies"
"Greatest Hits Vol. II"
Elton John
(MCA)
(MCA)

Josie
"Border Lord"
Kris Kristofferson
(Monument)

Lovely Lubina
"Firing on All Six"*
Lone Star
(Columbia)

Lucretia
"Tall Tales"
Richard Supa
(Polydor)

The Minnesota Strip
"Blood Brothers"
The Dictators
(Elektra)

Painted Ladies
"Ian Thomas"*
Ian Thomas
(Janus)

DEFINITIVE SONGS

Pammie's on a Bummer
"Inner Views"*
Sonny Bono
(Atco)

Pasties and a "G" String
"Small Change"
Tom Waits
(Asylum)

Pro Girl
"Janis Ian"
Janis Ian
(Polydor)

Readers Wives
"Tracks on Wax 4"
Dave Edmunds
(Swan Song)

Roxanne
"Outlandos d'Amour"
The Police
(A&M)

Runner in the Rain
"Ancient Medicine"
Baby Grand
(Arista)

Shouts Across the Streets
"Shouts Across the Streets"*
Alan Price
(Polydor)

Sisters of Mercy
"The Best Of"
Leonard Cohen
(Columbia)

+Sisters of Mercy
"Wildflowers"
Judy Collins
(Elektra)

+Sisters of Mercy
"Dion"*
Dion
(Laurie)

Sleazy Love
"A Song"
Neil Sedaka
(Elektra)

Stephanie
"The Essential Jim Dawson"
Jim Dawson
(Kama Sutra)

Sweet Cream Ladies
"Super Hits"
Box Tops
(Bell)

Sweet Fast Hooker Blues
"Buffy"
Buffy Sainte-Marie
(MCA)

Sweet Painted Ladies
"Goodbye Yellow Brick Road"
Elton John
(MCA)

Truck Stop Girl
"Untitled"
The Byrds
(Columbia)

Une Nuit à Paris
"The Original Soundtrack"
10 CC
(Mercury)

You're So Static
"Caribou"
Elton John
(MCA)

REFERENCE SONGS

The Boxer	Simon and Garfunkel
"Bridge over Troubled Water"	(Columbia)
"Simon and Garfunkel's Greatest Hits"	(Columbia)
+The Boxer	Bob Dylan
"Self-Portrait"	(Columbia)
+The Boxer	Paul Simon
"Live Rhymin'"	(Columbia)
Christmas Card from a Hooker in Minnesota	Tom Waits
"Blue Valentine"	(Asylum)
Honky Tonk Woman	The Rolling Stones
"Hot Rocks 1964–1971"	(London)
"Through the Past Darkly (Big Hits Vol. II)"	(London)
"Love You Live"	(Rolling Stone Records)
+Honky Tonk Woman	Elton John
"11-17-70"	(MCA)
+Honky Tonk Woman	Rick Nelson
"Rudy the Fifth"	(MCA)
+Honky Tonk Woman	Gram Parsons
"Sleepless Nights"	(A&M)
+Honky Tonk Woman	Joe Cocker
"Mad Dogs and Englishmen"	(A&M)
+Honky Tonk Woman	Humble Pie
"Eat It"	(A&M)
+Honky Tonk Woman	Jebadiah
"Rock 'n Soul"	(Epic)
Ladies of the Night	Leon Russell
"Americana"	(Paradise)
Main Street	Bob Seger and the Silver Bullet Band
"Night Moves"	(Capitol)
Men Who Love Women Who Love Men	Steve Goodman
"High and Outside"	(Elektra)
Miracle Row/Maria	Janis Ian
"Miracle Row"	(Columbia)

REFERENCE SONGS

Penicillin Penny
"Belly Up"

Dr. Hook
(Columbia)

Single Man's Dilemma
"One of the Boys"

Roger Daltrey
(MCA)

Who's Gonna Take the Blame?

Smokey Robinson & the
    Miracles

"Anthology"

(Motown)

YOUR ADDITIONAL SONGS

_____

_____

_____

_____

_____

PROTEST/REVOLUTION

Protest/Revolution—an old friend from the dusty archives

Rock itself is revolutionary music. It has always been a q̶
ever, whether rock effects change or change affects rock. In ̶ ̶ ̶̶nhood
it is a little of both. Most of these songs aim to change the political establishment either by force of reason or reason of force.

Related Categories: America, Changes, Freedom, Injustice, Politics,
   Racism/Prejudice, Violence, War and Peace

   +Same as Song Above
   *Hard-to-find Songs/Albums

CLASSICS

For What It's Worth	Buffalo Springfield
"Retrospective"	(Atco)
"Buffalo Springfield"	(Atco)
Power to the People	John Lennon
"Shaved Fish"	(Apple)
Revolution	The Beatles
"The Beatles" (White Album)	(Apple)
"The Beatles 1967–1970"	(Apple)
Something in the Air	Thunderclap Newman
"Hollywood Dream"*	(MCA/Track)
"History of British Rock Vol. 2"	(Sire)
"Strawberry Statement"	(MGM)
Won't Get Fooled Again	The Who
"Who's Next"	(MCA/Track)
"The Kids Are Alright" (Soundtrack)	(MCA)

Thematic Albums: Although they are not specifically thematic albums,
the subject of Protest/Revolution appears consistently in the early recordings of Bob Dylan, Joan Baez, Phil Ochs, Tom Paxton, Pete Seeger,
et al.

DEFINITIVE SONGS

All Right All Night	The Tom Robinson Band
"TRB II"	(Harvest)
Anarchy in the U.K.	Sex Pistols
"Never Mind the Bollocks, Here's the Sex Pistols"	(Warner Brothers)

INITIVE SONGS

Ché	Judy Collins
"True Stories and Other Dreams"	(Elektra)
Chicago	Graham Nash
"Songs for Beginners"	(Atlantic)
+Chicago	Crosby, Stills, Nash & Young
"Four Way Street"	(Atlantic)
+Chicago	David Crosby/Graham Nash
"The Best of David Crosby and Graham Nash"	(ABC)
Children of the Revolution	T-Rex
(45 RPM Single)*	(Reprise)
Exodus	Bob Marley and the Wailers
"Exodus"	(Island)
"Babylon by Bus"	(Island)
Fight the Power	The Isley Brothers
"The Isley's Greatest"	(T-Neck/Epic)
Five to One	The Doors
"Waiting for the Sun"	(Elektra)
"Weird Scenes Inside the Gold Mine"	(Elektra)
Fortunate Son	Creedence Clearwater Revival
"Willy and the Poor Boys"	(Fantasy)
"1969"	(Fantasy)
49 Bye Byes/America's Children	Crosby, Stills, Nash & Young
"Four Way Street"	(Atlantic)
God Save the Queen	Sex Pistols
"Never Mind the Bollocks, Here's the Sex Pistols"	(Warner Brothers)
Guns of Brixton	The Clash
"London Calling"	(Epic)
I-Feel-Like-I'm-Fixin'-to-Die-Rag	Country Joe McDonald
"I-Feel-Like-I'm-Fixin'-to-Die-Rag"	(Vanguard)
"The Life and Times of Country Joe and The Fish from Haight-Ashbury to Woodstock"	(Vanguard)
"More American Graffiti"	(MCA)
In the 80's	Graham Nash
"Earth and Sky"	(Capitol)

DEFINITIVE SONGS

Jackson—Kent Blues
"Steve Miller Band Number Five"

Steve Miller Band
(Capitol)

Kick Out the Jams
"Kick Out the Jams"*

MC 5
(Elektra)

The Laws Must Change
"The Turning Point"

John Mayall
(Polydor)

Let's Burn Down the Cornfields
"It Ain't Easy"

Long John Baldry
(Warner Brothers)

Long Time Gone
"Crosby, Stills & Nash"

Crosby, Stills & Nash
(Atlantic)

Marat/Sade
"In My Life"

Judy Collins
(Elektra)

Ohio
"So Far"
"Four Way Street"

Crosby, Stills, Nash & Young
(Atlantic)
(Atlantic)

+Ohio
"Decade"
"Journey Through the Past"

Neil Young
(Reprise)
(Reprise)

The Old Revolution
"Songs from a Room"

Leonard Cohen
(Columbia)

Pig's Head
"Weeds"*

Brewer and Shipley
(Kama Sutra)

The Power and the Glory
"Book of Invasions"

Horslips
(DJM Records)

Power in the Darkness
"Power in the Darkness"

The Tom Robinson Band
(Harvest)

Prelude/Angry Young Man
"Turnstiles"

Billy Joel
(Columbia)

Rebel Music (3 o'clock roadblock)
"Natty Dread"
"Babylon by Bus"

Bob Marley and the Wailers
(Island)
(Island)

Revelation: Revolution '69
"Revelation: Revolution '69"

The Lovin' Spoonful
(Kama Sutra)

Revolution
"Natty Dread"
"Live"

Bob Marley and the Wailers
(Island)
(Island)

Revolution Blues
"On the Beach"

Neil Young
(Reprise)

DEFINITIVE SONGS

Revolutionary Ways "Together after Five"*	Sir Douglas Quintet (Mercury)
A Rumblin' in the Land "Ramblin' Boy"*	Tom Paxton (Elektra)
Stand Up and Fight "Give Thankx"	Jimmy Cliff (Warner Brothers)
State of the Union "Chicago V"	Chicago (Columbia)
Stop! I Don't Want to Hear It Anymore "RPM"* (Soundtrack)	Melanie (Bell)
Student Demonstration Time "Surf's Up"	The Beach Boys (Brother/Reprise)
Tear the Walls Down "Fifth Album"	Judy Collins (Elektra)
That's What I Want to Hear "I Ain't Marching Anymore"	Phil Ochs (Elektra)
There's Anger in the Land "Late Again"	Peter, Paul and Mary (Warner Brothers)
The Times They Are a Changin' "The Times They Are a Changin'" "Bob Dylan's Greatest Hits" "Live at Budokan"	Bob Dylan (Columbia) (Columbia) (Columbia)
+The Times They Are a Changin' "Words and Music by Bob Dylan"	The Hollies (Epic)
+The Times They Are a Changin' "Any Day Now"	Joan Baez (Vanguard)
+The Times They Are a Changin' "Beach Boys' Party Album"	The Beach Boys (Capitol)
+The Times They Are a Changin' "Wednesday Morning 3 A.M."	Simon and Garfunkel (Columbia)
+The Times They Are a Changin' "The Byrds Play Dylan"	The Byrds (Columbia)
+The Times They Are a Changin' "No Nukes"	Carly Simon and Graham Nash (Asylum)
Up Against the Wall "Power in the Darkness"	The Tom Robinson Band (Harvest)

DEFINITIVE SONGS

Use the Power "Stamp Album"	Climax Blues Band (Sire)
Victor Jara "Amigos"	Arlo Guthrie (Warner Brothers)
Volunteers "The Worst of the Jefferson Airplane" "Volunteers" "Woodstock"	Jefferson Airplane (RCA) (RCA) (Cotillion)
Wasn't Born to Follow "The Best of the Byrds Greatest Hits, Vol. II" "The Notorious Byrd Brothers"	The Byrds (Columbia) (Columbia)
We Can Be Together "The Worst of the Jefferson Airplane" "Volunteers"	Jefferson Airplane (RCA) (RCA)
We Can Change the World "Songs for Beginners"	Graham Nash (Atlantic)
We're Not Gonna Take It "Tommy" "Woodstock"	The Who (MCA/Track) (Cotillion)
We Shall Overcome "We Shall Overcome" "The World of Pete Seeger"	Pete Seeger (Columbia) (Columbia)
+We Shall Overcome "Joan Baez in Concert Part II"	Joan Baez (Vanguard)
+We Shall Overcome "Newport Folk Festival"	Freedom Singers (Vanguard)
What About Me "Anthology" "What About Me"	Quicksilver Messenger Service (Capitol) (Capitol)
+What About Me "Great Blind Degree"*	Richie Havens (Stormy Forest)
When I'm Gone "Chords of Fame" "Phil Ochs in Concert"	Phil Ochs (A&M) (Elektra)
When a Solution Comes "Preservation Act 2"	The Kinks (RCA)

DEFINITIVE SONGS

When the Music's Over	The Doors
"Weird Scenes Inside the Gold Mine"	(Elektra)
"Strange Days"	(Elektra)
White Riot	The Clash
"The Clash"	(Epic)
Wild in the Street	Garland Jeffreys
"Ghost Writer"	(A&M)

REFERENCE SONGS

Ain't Gonna Take It	The Tom Robinson Band
"Power in the Darkness"	(Harvest)
Change of Guard	Steely Dan
"Can't Buy a Thrill"	(ABC)
Days of Decision	Phil Ochs
"I Ain't Marchin' Anymore"	(Elektra)
Dialogue (Parts 1 & 2)	Chicago
"Chicago V"	(Columbia)
How I Spent My Summer Vacation (1968 Democratic Convention)	Cat Mother and the All Night Newsboys
"The Street Giveth . . ."*	(Polydor)
I'd Love to Change the World	Ten Years After
"The Classic Performances of Ten Years After"	(Columbia)
Move Over	Steppenwolf
"Sixteen Greatest Hits"	(ABC/Dunhill)
"ABC Collection"	(ABC)
Pushing Too Hard	Seeds
"The Seeds"*	(GNP)
Ride the Tiger	Jefferson Starship
"Dragonfly"	(Grunt)
"Gold"	(Grunt)
Stand	Sly and the Family Stone
"Greatest Hits"	(Epic)
"Stand"	(Epic)
Street Man	Brooklyn Dreams
"Sleepless Nights"	(Casablanca)
Time	The Chambers Brothers
"Greatest Hits"	(Columbia)
"Time Has Come Today"	(Columbia)

REFERENCE SONGS

Victor Jara
"Amigos

Arlo Guthrie
(Warner Brothers)

Vigilante Man
"Library of Congress"

Woody Guthrie
(Elektra)

+Vigilante Man
"A Tribute to Woody Guthrie"

Richie Havens
(Warner Brothers)

YOUR ADDITIONAL SONGS

_____

_____

_____

_____

_____

RACISM/PREJUDICE

Racism/prejudice—rock and roll . . . rhythm and blues . . . race music.

Rock and roll music has many sources—country, jazz, folk, pop, classical, gospel, etc.—but its real roots are in the rhythm and blues of the '40s and '50s, which was actually called "race music." In the early '60s, many songs of the folk revival focused on the continuing racial discrimination and prejudice that existed in our society. Many of these songs went on to become "anthems" of the civil rights movement.

In the following songs, rock acknowledges its black roots by exploring the social as well as personal dimensions of the relations between the races in America and elsewhere. (N.B. Songs about bigoted/narrow minded people are listed here separately.)

Related Categories: Brotherhood, Injustice, Poverty, Protest/Revolution, Urban/City Life, Working

+Same as Song Above
*Hard-to-find Songs/Albums

CLASSICS

Living for the City "Innervisions"	Stevie Wonder (Tamla)
+Living for the City "It's a Heartache"	Bonnie Tyler (RCA)
+Living for the City/For the Love of Money "The Three Degrees Live"	The Three Degrees (Philadelphia International)
Only a Pawn in Their Game "The Times They Are a Changin'"	Bob Dylan (Columbia)

THEMATIC ALBUMS

"Equal Rights"	Peter Tosh (Columbia)

DEFINITIVE SONGS

Africa Unite "Survival"	Bob Marley and the Wailers (Island)
African "Equal Rights"	Peter Tosh (Columbia)

DEFINITIVE SONGS

Apartheid
"Equal Rights"
Peter Tosh
(Columbia)

Backlash Blues
"Now"
Pete Seeger
(Columbia)

The Ballad of a Crystal Man
"Donovan P. Leitch"*
Donovan
(Janus)

Ballad of Hollis Brown
"The Times They Are a Changin'"
Bob Dylan
(Columbia)

Birmingham Sunday
"Joan Baez 5"
Joan Baez
(Vanguard)

Black and White
"Joy to the World"
Three Dog Night
(ABC/Dunhill)

Black Day in July
"The Very Best of Gordon Lightfoot"
Gordon Lightfoot
(United Artists)

Black Man
"Songs in the Key of Life"
Stevie Wonder
(Tamla)

Black Messiah
"Misfits"
The Kinks
(Arista)

Blowin' in the Wind
"The Freewheelin' Bob Dylan"
"Before the Flood" (with The Band)
"Bob Dylan's Greatest Hits"
Bob Dylan
(Columbia)
(Asylum)
(Columbia)

+Blowin' in the Wind
"Ten Years Together"
Peter, Paul and Mary
(Warner Brothers)

+Blowin' in the Wind
"Greatest Hits"
Stevie Wonder
(Tamla)

+Blowin' in the Wind
"Words and Music by Bob Dylan"
The Hollies
(Epic)

+Blowin' in the Wind
"From Every Stage"
Joan Baez
(A&M)

+Blowin' in the Wind
"Cher Sings the Hits"*
Cher
(Springboard)

+Blowin' in the Wind
"Whales and Nightingales"
Judy Collins
(Elektra)

Brother Louie
"About Us"
Stories
(Kama Sutra)

+Brother Louie
"Ten Greatest Hits"
Hot Chocolate
(Big Tree)

DEFINITIVE SONGS

Bummer
"Portrait Gallery"
Harry Chapin
(Elektra)

Choice of Colors
"The Best Impressions"
The Impressions
(Curtom)

The Cities Are Burning
"Now"
Pete Seeger
(Columbia)

Colored Spade
"Hair" (Soundtrack)
Various Artists
(RCA)

Cotton Needed Pickin' So Bad
"Now"
Pete Seeger
(Columbia)

The Death of Stephen Biko
"Heroes"
Tom Paxton
(Vanguard)

Dirty White Boy
"Head Games"
Foreigner
(Atlantic)

Doesn't Make It Right
"The Specials"
The Specials
(Chrysalis)

Don't Call Me Nigger, Whitey
"Stand"
Sly and the Family Stone
(Epic)

Down at Tube Station at Midnight
"All Mod Cons"
The Jam
(Polydor)

Down by the Riverside
"Waist Deep in the Big Muddy"
Pete Seeger
(Columbia)

Dreadlock Holiday
"Bloody Tourists"
10 CC
(Polydor)

Ellis Dee
"Before the Salt"
Jimmy Buffett
(Barnaby)

Equal Rights
"Equal Rights"
Peter Tosh
(Columbia)

Everybody's Got a Right to Live
"Now"
Pete Seeger
(Columbia)

Everyday People
"Greatest Hits"
"Stand"
Sly and the Family Stone
(Epic)
(Epic)

Fayette County
"3 Saints, 4 Sinners and 6 Others"*
Pete Seeger
(Folk Odyssey)

Goodman, Schwerner and Chaney
"Ain't That News"
Tom Paxton
(Elektra)

Harlem
"The Best of Bill Withers"
Bill Withers
(Sussex)

DEFINITIVE SONGS

The Harlem Song "Together"*	Country Joe McDonald (Vanguard)
Harriet Tubbman "Kate Taylor"*	Kate Taylor (Columbia)
+He Was My Brother "Wednesday Morning, 3 A.M."	Simon and Garfunkel (Columbia)
Heaven Is Ten Zillion Light Years Away "Fulfillingness' First Finale"	Stevie Wonder (Tamla)
Here's to the State of Mississippi "I Ain't Marchin' Anymore"	Phil Ochs (Elektra)
Hurricane "Desire"	Bob Dylan (Columbia)
I Ain't Scared of Your Jail "We Shall Overcome"	Pete Seeger (Columbia)
I'm Black/Ain't Got No "Hair" (Soundtrack)	Various Artists (RCA)
If You Miss Me at the Back of the Bus "We Shall Overcome"	Pete Seeger (Columbia)
In the Ghetto "Worldwide 50 Gold Award Hits, Vol. 1"	Elvis Presley (RCA)
+In the Ghetto "Greatest Hits"	Mac Davis (Columbia)
In the Heat of Summer "I Ain't Marchin' Anymore"	Phil Ochs (Elektra)
Jack of Diamonds "Jay Boy Adams"*	Jay Boy Adams (Atlantic)
Keep on Pushing "The Impressions' Big Sixteen"	The Impressions (ABC)
The Klan "Somethin' Else Again"*	Richie Havens (MGM)
Kute Klux Klan "Love Bomb"	Bobby Braddock (Elektra)
Lincoln Freed Me Today "Blessed Are"	Joan Baez (Vanguard)
The Lonesome Death of Hattie Carroll "The Times They Are a Changin'"	Bob Dylan (Columbia)

DEFINITIVE SONGS

+The Lonesome Death of Hattie Carroll   (Judy Collins
  "The Judy Collins Concert"   (Elektra)

Mary Ain't Going Home   Steve Gibbons Band
  "Down in the Bunker"   (Polydor)

McCarthy's Day   Dan Hill
  "Longer Fuse"   (20th Century Records)

Medgar Evers' Lullaby   Judy Collins
  "The Judy Collins Concert"   (Elektra)

Message from a Black Man   The Temptations
  "Puzzle People"   (Motown)

Mighty Mighty Spade and Whitey   The Impressions
  "The Best Impressions"   (Curtom)

Move On Up   Curtis Mayfield
  "Curtis"   (Curtom)

Mr. You're a Better Man Than I   Jeff Beck
  "Shapes of Things"*   (Springboard)

My Country   The Impressions
  "The Best Impressions"   (Curtom)

Nigger Charlie   Billy Preston
  "Music Is My Life"   (A&M)

Niggers in the Woods   Pacific Gas & Electric
                                             Starring Charles Allen
  "Pacific Gas & Electric   (ABC/Dunhill)
    Starring Charles Allen"

Oh Freedom   Pete Seeger
  "We Shall Overcome"   (Columbia)

Oh Lord, Why Lord   Los Pop Tops
  (45 RPM Single)*   (Calla)

One Brother Short   The Mighty Diamonds
  "Deeper Roots" (Back to the   (Virgin)
    Channel)

Opposites   Eric Clapton
  "There's One in Every Crowd"   (RSO)

Oxford Town   Bob Dylan
  "The Freewheelin' Bob Dylan"   (Columbia)

Packed Up and Left   Mac McAnally
  "Mac McAnally"   (Ariola/America)

Rednecks   Randy Newman
  "Good Old Boys"   (Reprise)

DEFINITIVE SONGS

Right on Brothers and Sisters	Junior Walker and the All Stars
"Rainbow Funk"	(Soul)
Safe European Home	The Clash
"Give 'em Enough Rope"	(Epic)
Say It Loud, I'm Black and I'm Proud	James Brown
"Soul Classics"	(Polydor)
Slave	Elton John
"Honky Chateau"	(MCA)
Slavery Days	Burning Spear
"Live"	(Island)
Society's Child	Janis Ian
"Janis Ian"	(Polydor)
Talking Birmingham Jam	Phil Ochs
"I Ain't Marchin' Anymore"	(Elektra)
They Ain't Making Jews Like Jesus Anymore	Kinky Friedman
"Kinky Friedman"	(ABC)
Thirsty Boots	Eric Andersen
"The Best of Eric Andersen"	(Vanguard)
+Thirsty Boots	John Denver
"I Want to Live"	(RCA)
+Thirsty Boots	Judy Collins
"Fifth Album"	(Elektra)
Too Many Martyrs	Phil Ochs
"Chords of Fame"	(A&M)
"All the News That's Fit to Sing"	(Elektra)
Trouble Coming Everyday	Mothers of Invention
"Freak Out"	(Verve)
War	Bob Marley and the Wailers
"Rastaman Vibration"	(Island)
"Babylon by Bus"	(Island)
We're a Winner	The Impressions
"Impressions' Sixteen Greatest Hits"	(ABC)
We Shall Overcome	Pete Seeger
"We Shall Overcome"	(Columbia)
"The World of Pete Seeger"	(Columbia)
+We Shall Overcome	Joan Baez
"In Concert"	(Vanguard)

DEFINITIVE SONGS

We the People Who Are Darker Than the Blues	Curtis Mayfield
"Live"	(Curtom)
What's That I Hear	Phil Ochs
"All the News That's Fit to Sing"	(Elektra)
White Boy Blues	Felix Pappalardi
"Don't Worry, Ma"	(A&M)
Why I Sing the Blues	B. B. King
"Live and Well"	(ABC/Stateside)
Why Oh	Garland Jeffreys
"Ghost Writer"	(A&M)
Word Game	Stephen Stills
"Stephen Stills 2"	(Atlantic)

REFERENCE SONGS

Black Girl	Long John Baldry
"It Ain't Easy"*	(Warner Brothers)
Black Pearl	Sonny Charles
"Phil Spector's Greatest Hits"	(Warner-Spector)
General Store	Don McLean
"Tapestry"	(United Artists)
Go Down Old Hannah	Pete Seeger
"I Can See a New Day"	(Columbia)
Hard Times	Curtis Mayfield
"America Today"*	(Curtom)
It Isn't Nice	Judy Collins
"Fifth Album"	(Elektra)
The Klan	Richie Havens
"Something Else Again"*	(MGM)
The Law Is for the Protection of the People	Kris Kristofferson
"Me and Bobby McGee"	(Monument)
Links in the Chain	Phil Ochs
"I Ain't Marchin' Anymore"	(Elektra)
Rednecks	Randy Newman
"Good Old Boys"	(Reprise)
Talking Birmingham Jam	Phil Ochs
"I Ain't Marchin' Anymore"	(Elektra)

REFERENCE SONGS

Texan Love Song   Elton John
"Don't Shoot Me I'm Only the Piano   (MCA)
    Player"
Way Back Home   Junior Walker and the All
                                                 Stars
"Anthology"   (Motown)

YOUR ADDITIONAL SONGS

_____

_____

_____

_____

_____

Bigoted/Narrow Minded People

CLASSICS

Southern Man   Neil Young
"Decade"   (Reprise)
"After the Gold Rush"   (Reprise)
+Southern Man   Crosby, Stills, Nash & Young
"Four Way Street"   (Atlantic)
+Southern Man   Merry Clayton
"Merry Clayton"   (Ode)

THEMATIC ALBUMS

Good Old Boys   Randy Newman
                                             (Reprise)

DEFINITIVE SONGS

Do You Remember the Americans   Manassas (Stephen Stills)
"Down the Road"   (Atlantic)

332   *The Rock Music Source Book*

DEFINITIVE SONGS

Drug Store Truck Driving Man "The Best of the Byrds, Greatest Hits Vol. II"	The Byrds (Columbia)
"Dr. Byrds and Mr. Hyde"	(Columbia)
Drug Store Truck Driving Man "Woodstock" (Soundtrack)	Joan Baez (Cotillion)
General Store "Tapestry"	Don McLean (United Artists)
Okie "Songs That Made America Famous"*	Patrick Sky (Adelphi Records)
Okie from Muskogee "The Best of Merle Haggard"	Merle Haggard (Capitol)
+Oakie from Meskogee "Gunfight at Carnegie Hall"	Phil Ochs (A&M)
+Okie from Muskogee "Teegarden and Van Winkle"*	Teegarden and Van Winkle (Atlantic)
Only a Pawn in Their Game "The Times They Are a Changin'"	Bob Dylan (Columbia)
Rednecks "Good Old Boys"	Randy Newman (Reprise)
Talking Birmingham Jam "I Ain't Marchin' Anymore"	Phil Ochs (Elektra)
Texan Love Song "Don't Shoot Me I'm Only the Piano Player"	Elton John (MCA)
The Klan "Something Else Again"*	Richie Havens (MGM)
The Law Is for the Protection of the People "Me and Bobby McGee"	Kris Kristofferson (Monument)
They Ain't Making Jews Like Jesus Anymore "Kinky Friedman"*	Kinky Friedman (ABC)
Uneasy Rider "Uneasy Rider" "Honey in the Rock"*	Charlie Daniels (Epic) (Kama Sutra)
Up Against the Wall Redneck "A Man Must Carry On"	Jerry Jeff Walker (MCA)

DEFINITIVE SONGS

+Up Against the Wall Redneck

New Riders of the Purple Sage
(Columbia)

"Oh What a Mighty Time"

We Reserve the Right to Refuse Service to You
"Sold American"*

Kinky Friedman

(Vanguard)

What Made America Famous
"Verities and Balderdash"

Harry Chapin
(Elektra)

REFERENCE SONGS

Ballad of Easy Rider
"The Best of the Byrds, Greatest Hits Vol. II"

The Byrds
(Columbia)

"Easy Rider" (Soundtrack)

(ABC/Dunhill)

Bring Back the Chair
"New Songs from the Briarpatch"*

Tom Paxton
(Vanguard)

Everyday People
"Greatest Hits"
"Stand"

Sly and the Family Stone
(Epic)
(Epic)

Gimme Three Steps
"One More from the Road"

Lynyrd Skynyrd
(MCA)

In Rain in Spring
"Jay Boy Adams"*

Jay Boy Adams
(Atlantic)

My Crime
"Boogie with Canned Heat"*

Canned Heat
(Liberty)

Red Neck Fiddlin' Man
"Midnight Wind"

Charlie Daniels
(Epic)

Red Neck Friend
"For Everyman"

Jackson Browne
(Asylum)

Rise Up Easy Rider
"Weeds"*

Brewer and Shipley
(Kama Sutra)

Signs
(45 RPM Single)*

Five Man Electrical Band
(Lionel)

Swallowed Up in the Great American Heartland
"Swallowed Up in the Great American Heartland"*

Tom Pacheco

(RCA)

YOUR ADDITIONAL SONGS

_____

_____

_____

_____

_____

RAT RACE

Rat race—traffic jams and subway cars, nine to five then "after work" bars.

Songs about all those people chained to desks, clocks, jammed highways and crowded trains, hating every minute of it, and worse still, justifying it as the price to be paid for the great American dream.

Related Categories: Big Business, Money, Suburbia, Working

+Same as Song Above
*Hard-to-find Songs/Albums

CLASSICS

Moving Out (Anthony's Song) "The Stranger"	Billy Joel (Columbia)
Mr. Businessman "The Very Best of Ray Stevens"	Ray Stevens (Janus)
Traffic Jam "J.T."	James Taylor (Columbia)

THEMATIC ALBUMS

"Muswell Hillbillies"	The Kinks (RCA)
"Soap Opera"	The Kinks (RCA)
"Split"*	Groundhogs (United Artists)

DEFINITIVE SONGS

Ball of Confusion "Anthology—Tenth Anniversary Special"	The Temptations (Motown)
+Ball of Confusion "The Undisputed Truth"	The Undisputed Truth (Gordy)
+Ball of Confusion "Involved"	Edwin Starr (Gordy)
The Beat Goes On "The Best of Sonny and Cher"	Sonny and Cher (Atco)

DEFINITIVE SONGS

+The Beat Goes On
"The Beat Goes On"*
Vanilla Fudge
(Atco)

Big Bright Green Pleasure Machine
"Parsley, Sage, Rosemary and Thyme"
Simon and Garfunkel
(Columbia)

Bus Rider
"The Best of The Guess Who"
The Guess Who
(RCA)

Dog Eat Dog
"Let There Be Rock"*
AC/DC
(Atco)

Dreidel
"Don McLean"*
"Solo"
Don McLean
(United Artists)
(United Artists)

Family Man
"Worlds Away"
Pablo Cruise
(A&M)

Fast Buck Freddie
"Red Octopus"
"Gold"
Jefferson Starship
(Grunt)
(Grunt)

Feel like a Number

"Stranger in Town"
Bob Seger and the Silver
   Bullet Band
(Capitol)

Five O'Clock World
(45 RPM Single)*
"The Vogues' Greatest Hits"
The Vogues
(Co and Ce Records)
(Reprise)

Georgie on the Freeway
"Tom Paxton"
Tom Paxton
(Elektra)

Hard Rock Town
"Hard Rock Town"
Murray McLauchlan
(True North)

High Pressured Living
"Moving On"
John Mayall
(Polydor)

Just a Story from America
"Just a Story from America"*
Elliott Murphy
(Columbia)

Let's Make a Deal
"Free in America"
Ben Sidran
(Arista)

Living in the Material World
"Living in the Material World"
George Harrison
(Apple)

Look Over Your Shoulder
"O Lucky Man"
Alan Price
(Warner Brothers)

Madison Avenue
"Greg Kihn Again"
Greg Kihn
(Beserkley)

DEFINITIVE SONGS

Madison Avenue Blues
"Street Action"

Bachman-Turner Overdrive
(Mercury)

Mean Old World
"The Second Coming"*

Jerry LaCroix
(Mercury)

Money
"Smile"

Laura Nyro
(Columbia)

Mr. Penny Pincher
"Hour of the Wolf"*

Steppenwolf
(Epic)

Nine to Five
"A Soap Opera"

The Kinks
(RCA)

One Way Road to Hell
"Road Food"

The Guess Who
(RCA)

The Ostrich
"Rest in Peace"
"Steppenwolf"

Steppenwolf
(ABC/Dunhill)
(ABC/Dunhill)

Peace of Mind
"Boston"

Boston
(Epic)

Plastic Man
"Masterpiece"

The Temptations
(Gordy)

Prisons on the Road
"Back to the Roots"

John Mayall
(Polydor)

Rat Race
"Joneses"*

Joneses
(Epic)

Rat Race
"Rastaman Vibration"
"Babylon by Bus"

Bob Marley and the Wailers
(Island)
(Island)

Rats
"Lola Versus Powerman and the
    Moneygoround"

The Kinks
(Reprise)

Richard Cory
"Sounds of Silence"

Simon and Garfunkel
(Columbia)

+Richard Cory
"Wings Over America"

Wings
(Capitol)

+Richard Cory

Them
    Featuring Van Morrison

"Backtrackin' "

(London)

Rush Hour Blues
"Soap Opera"

The Kinks
(RCA)

DEFINITIVE SONGS

Sell Sell
"O Lucky Man"

Alan Price
(Warner Brothers)

Slowdown
"Stranger in the City"

John Miles
(London)

Slow Down World
"Slow Down World"*

Donovan
(Epic)

Step Right Up
"Small Change"

Tom Waits
(Asylum)

Street in the City

Pete Townsend and Ronnie
Lane

"Rough Mix"

(MCA)

Taking Care of Business
"Best of B.T.O. . . . (So Far)"
"Bachman-Turner Overdrive II"

Bachman-Turner Overdrive
(Mercury)
(Mercury)

Twentieth Century Man
"Muswell Hillbillies"

The Kinks
(RCA)

Wall Street Shuffle
"10 CC"

10 CC
(UK)

We All Wanna Boogie
"Mirage"

Richie Havens
(A&M)

Well Respected Man
"Golden Hour of the Kinks"
"The Kinks' Greatest Hits"
"The Live Kinks"

The Kinks
(Pye)
(Reprise)
(Reprise)

Why Are People Like That
"The Muddy Waters Woodstock
    Album"

Muddy Waters
(Chess)

Work
"Here"

Leo Sayer
(Warner Brothers)

You're the Man
"Anthology"

Marvin Gaye
(Tamla)

Young Turks
"Terry Cashman"*

Terry Cashman
(Lifesong)

REFERENCE SONGS

Animal Zoo
"Twelve Dreams of Dr. Sardonicus"
"Spirit Live"

Spirit
(Epic)
(Potato)

REFERENCE SONGS

Ballad of John and Yoko — The Beatles
"The Beatles 1967–1970" — (Apple)
"Hey Jude" — (Apple)

Big City Cat — Steve Forbert
"Alive on Arrival" — (Nemperor)

Cat's in the Cradle — Harry Chapin
"Verities and Balderdash" — (Elektra)
"Greatest Stories—Live" — (Elektra)

Funny Farm Blues — Sammy Walker
"Song for Patty"* — (Vanguard)

Georgie on the Freeway — Tom Paxton
"Tom Paxton" — (Elektra)

Get Off My Cloud — The Rolling Stones
"Hot Rocks 1964–1971" — (London)
"December's Children (and Everybody's)" — (London)
"Got Live If You Want It" — (London)

+Get Off My Cloud — Alexis Korner
"Get Off My Cloud"* — (Columbia)

Gotta Get Up — Harry Nilsson
"Nilsson Schmillsson" — (RCA)

Have Another Drink — The Kinks
"A Soap Opera" — (RCA)

Hiding Place — Ray Stevens
"Be Your Own Best Friend" — (Warner Brothers)

Hollywood — Chicago
"Chicago VI" — (Columbia)

Human Being Blues — Skip Battin
"Skip Battin"* — (Signpost)

I'm Not Gonna Let It Bother Me Tonight — Atlanta Rhythm Section
"Champagne Jam" — (Polydor)

In the Crowd — The Jam
"All Mod Cons" — (Polydor)

It's a Crazy World — Mac McAnally
"Mac McAnally"* — (Ariola/America)

It's a Hard Life — Seeds
"The Seeds"* — (GNP)

REFERENCE SONGS

It's A Mad, Mad, Mad, Mad World "The Very Best of the Shirelles"	The Shirelles (United Artists)
Just Another Nervous Wreck "Breakfast in America"	Supertramp (A&M)
Look Through Any Window "The Very Best of the Hollies"	The Hollies (United Artists)
Making Love "Shine On"	Climax Blues Band (Sire)
Pieces of Eight "Pieces of Eight"	Styx (A&M)
Rainbow End "Alan Price"*	Alan Price (United Artists)
Satisfaction "Hot Rocks 1964–1971"	The Rolling Stones (London)
+Satisfaction "Otis Blue" "Otis Redding Live in Europe" "The History of Otis Redding"	Otis Redding (Volt) (Volt) (Volt)
+Satisfaction "Q: Are We Not Men? A: We Are Devo!"	Devo (Warner Brothers)
+Satisfaction "The Troggs"	The Troggs (Pye)
Subterranean Homesick Blues "Bringing It All Back Home"	Bob Dylan (Columbia)
+Subterranean Homesick Blues "Michael Stanley"*	Michael Stanley (Tumbleweed)
Two-Faced World "Orleans"*	Orleans (ABC)
Up on the Roof "Twenty-Four Original Hits"	The Drifters (Atlantic)
+Up on the Roof "Writer"	Carole King (Ode)
+Up on the Roof "Christmas and the Beads of Sweat"	Laura Nyro (Columbia)
+Up on the Roof "Flag"	James Taylor (Columbia)
+Up on the Roof "A Scratch in the Sky"*	Cryan Shames (Columbia)

REFERENCE SONGS

Victim of Society   Spirit
"Spirit of '76"*   (Mercury)

YOUR ADDITIONAL SONGS

_____

_____

_____

_____

_____

RELIGIOUS SONGS

Religion—"God gave rock and roll to you" . . . *thank you, God!*
Rock has been highly critical of organized religion, and yet it contains many moving statements of faith, cries for help and forgiveness, prayers of praise and thanksgiving to God in general, and to Jesus Christ in particular. Because of the vast nature and many aspects of "religion," this category has been subdivided into five sections:

1. Religion/Prayer
2. God/Lord
3. Jesus Christ
4. Anti-Institutional Religion
5. Alternative Forms of Prayer, Worship and Meditation

Related Categories: Brotherhood

+Same as Song Above
*Hard-to-find Songs/Albums

THEMATIC ALBUMS

"Amazing Grace"	Aretha Franklin (Atlantic)
"Before My Heart Finds Out"	Gene Cotton (Ariola/America)
"The Edward Hawkins Singers"	The Edwin Hawkins Singers (Buddah)
"From Art of the Past"	The Kingsmen (Heartwarming)
"His Hand in Mine"	Elvis Presley (RCA)
"Holy Bible, the Old and New Testament"	The Statler Brothers (Mercury)
"How Great Thou Art"	Elvis Presley (RCA)
"Lady Is a Child"	Reba (Greentree Records)
"Mass in F Minor"*	The Electric Prunes (Reprise)
"Mirriam"	Jessi Colter (Capitol)

THEMATIC ALBUMS

"The Prodigal"   Reba
                                  (Greentree Records)

"Promised Land"   Elvis Presley
                                  (RCA)

"Slow Train Coming"   Bob Dylan
                                  (Columbia)

"We Believe"   Mylon
                                  (Cotillion)

"Wings to Fly"   Jeannie C. Reilly
                                  (Heartwarming)

"You Got Me Running"   Gene Cotton
                                  (ABC)

YOUR ADDITIONAL SONGS

_____

_____

_____

_____

_____

Religion/Prayer

CLASSICS

Amazing Grace   Judy Collins
"Whales and Nightingales"   (Elektra)
"Colors of the Day/Best of Judy   (Elektra)
    Collins"
+Amazing Grace   Aretha Franklin
"Amazing Grace"   (Atlantic)
+Amazing Grace   Joan Baez
"From Every Stage"   (A&M)

CLASSICS

+Amazing Grace | Jonathan Richman and the Modern Lovers
"Jonathan Richman" | (Beserkley)

Day by Day | Godspell
"Godspell" | (Arista)

Give Me Strength | Eric Clapton
"461 Ocean Blvd." | (RSO)

People Get Ready | The Impressions
"The Impressions' Sixteen Greatest" | (ABC)

+People Get Ready | The Chambers Brothers
"The Time Has Come" | (Columbia)
"The Best of the Chambers Brothers" | (Fantasy)
"Live at Bill Graham's Fillmore East" | (Columbia)

+People Get Ready | Aretha Franklin
"Lady Soul" | (Atlantic)

+People Get Ready | Vanilla Fudge
"Vanilla Fudge"* | (Atco)

+People Get Ready | Sonny Terry & Brownie McGee
"Sonny & Brownie" | (A&M)

+People Get Ready | Burning Spear
"Man in the Hills" | (Island)

+People Get Ready | Jonathan Edwards
"Sailboat" | (Warner Brothers)

+People Get Ready | The Persuasions
"Street Corner Symphony" | (Capitol)

+People Get Ready | Kenny Rankin
"Silver Morning" | (Little David)

Year of Sunday | Seals and Crofts
"Year of Sunday" | (Warner Brothers)

DEFINITIVE SONGS

A Glimpse of Heaven | Strawbs
"The Best of Strawbs" | (A&M)
"From the Witchwood" | (A&M)

Amen | The Impressions
"The Impressions' Sixteen Greatest" | (ABC)

+Amen | Johnny Cash
"Orange Blossom Special" | (Columbia)

DEFINITIVE SONGS

Awaiting on You All   George Harrison
"Bangla Desh"   (Apple)
"All Things Must Pass"   (Apple)

Benedictus   Strawbs
"Grave New World"   (A&M)
"The Best of Strawbs"   (A&M)

Benedictus   Simon and Garfunkel
"Wednesday Morning 3 A.M."   (Columbia)

Blessed   Simon and Garfunkel
"Sounds of Silence"   (Columbia)

Change My Way   Bob Dylan
"Slow Train Coming"   (Columbia)

Children of Abraham   Arlo Guthrie
"Arlo Guthrie"   (Reprise)

The Christian   Jimmy Buffett
"Before the Salt"   (Barnaby)

The Christian Life   The Byrds
"Sweetheart of the Rodeo"   (Columbia)

Christopher, Mr. Christopher   Styx
"Man of Miracles"   (Wooden Nickel/RCA)

Cry for Mary   Byron Keith Dougherty
"Let My Heart Be My Home"*   (Fantasy)

Crying in the Chapel   Sonny Till and the Orioles
"American Graffiti"   (MCA)

+Crying in the Chapel   Elvis Presley
"Worldwide 50 Gold Award Hits,   (RCA)
   Vol. 1"

+Crying in the Chapel   Don McLean
"Homeless Brother"   (United Artists)

Daniel and the Sacred Harp   The Band
"Stage Fright"   (Capitol)
"Anthology"   (Capitol)

Do Right to Me   Bob Dylan
"Slow Train Coming"   (Columbia)

Dominique   The Singing Nun
"The Singing Nun"*   (Philips)
(45 RPM Single)*   (Philips)

Early in the Morning   Peter, Paul and Mary
"Peter, Paul and Mary"   (Warner Brothers)

The Euphrates   Seals and Crofts
"Summer Breeze"   (Warner Brothers)

DEFINITIVE SONGS

Every Christian Lion Hearted Man "Bee Gees First"	The Bee Gees (Atco)
Glad to See You Got Religion "Album I"	Loudon Wainwright III (Atlantic)
Glory, Glory "Byrdmaniax"	The Byrds (Columbia)
Go Down Moses "Arlo Guthrie"	Arlo Guthrie (Reprise)
Good Gospel Music "Pacific Gas & Electric featuring Charles Allen"	Pacific Gas & Electric Featuring Charles Allen (ABC/Dunhill)
Good Christian Soldier "The Silver Tongued Devil and I"	Kris Kristofferson (Monument)
Good Shepherd "Volunteers"	Jefferson Airplane (RCA)
Gospel Changes "Poems, Prayers and Promises"	John Denver (RCA)
Gospel Plow "Bob Dylan"	Bob Dylan (Columbia)
Gospel Ship "Joan Baez in Concert"	Joan Baez (Vanguard)
Harbor for My Soul "Geronimo's Cadillac"	Michael Murphey (A&M)
The Gospel Singer "Shine On"	Climax Blues Band (Sire)
(Go) Tell It on the Mountain "In the Wind"	Peter, Paul and Mary (Warner Brothers)
Healing River "I Can See a New Day"	Pete Seeger (Columbia)
Heaven Help Us All "Blessed Are"	Joan Baez (Vanguard)
Holy Roller "Paradise with an Ocean View"*	Country Joe McDonald (Fantasy)
Holy Water "You Broke My Heart, So I Busted Your Jaw"	Spooky Tooth (A&M)
If I Had My Way "Peter, Paul and Mary"	Peter, Paul and Mary (Warner Brothers)

DEFINITIVE SONGS

+(If I Had My Way) "Samson and Delilah"
The Grateful Dead

"Terrapin Station"
(Arista)

I'm Scared
"Burton Cummings"
Burton Cummings
(Portrait)

I Saw the Light
"Living by the Days"*
Don Nix
(Elektra)

Job's Tears
"Relics of the Incredible String Band"
Incredible String Band
(Elektra)

John the Baptist
"Blood, Sweat and Tears 4"*
Blood, Sweat and Tears
(Columbia)

Just a Closer Walk with Thee
"The Best of the Chambers Brothers"
The Chambers Brothers
(Fantasy)

Kumbaya
"Joan Baez in Concert"
Joan Baez
(Vanguard)

Kyrie Eleison
"Mass in F Minor"*
The Electric Prunes
(Reprise)

Let It Go
"Mirriam"*
Jessi Colter
(Capitol)

Lo and Behold
"Sweet Baby James"
James Taylor
(Warner Brothers)

+Lo and Behold/Jesus Is Just Alright
"Sister Kate"*
Kate Taylor
(Cotillion)

Lonesome Valley

"Together in Concert"
Pete Seeger and Arlo Guthrie
(Warner Brothers)

Lord I'm Amazed
"Down Home"*
Sam Neely
(A&M)

The Lord's Prayer
"Life Mask"*
Roy Harper
(Harvest)

+The Lord's Prayer
"Sister Janet Mead"*
Sister Janet Mead
(A&M)

+The Lord's Prayer
(45 RPM Single b/w Little Saint Nick)
The Beach Boys
(Capitol)

Man Came into Egypt
"Moving"
Peter, Paul and Mary
(Warner Brothers)

DEFINITIVE SONGS

Mary "The Best of Buffy Sainte-Marie Vol. II"	Buffy Sainte-Marie (Vanguard)
Michael Row the Boat Ashore "The Highway Men"	The Highway Men (United Artists)
+Michael Row the Boat Ashore "Johnny Rivers Rocks the Folks"*	Johnny Rivers (Imperial)
+Michael Row the Boat Ashore "Now"	Pete Seeger (Columbia)
+Michael Row the Boat Ashore "Greatest Hits"	The Weavers (Vanguard)
+Michael Row the Boat Ashore "Let It Be Me"	The Lettermen (Capitol)
"Moses"—The Prophets "Bush Doctor"	Peter Tosh (Rolling Stone Records)
Oh What a Beautiful City "I Can See a New Day"	Pete Seeger (Columbia)
Old Time Religion "Ain't It Something"*	James Talley (Capitol)
Passing Through "Anniversary Special"	Earl Scruggs (Columbia)
A Piece of the Rock "Thorn on the Rose"*	Even Stevens (Elektra)
Preacher Man "Preacher Man"*	The Impressions (Curtom)
Put Your Hand in the Hand (45 RPM Single)*	Ocean (Kama Sutra)
+Put Your Hand in the Hand "Country"	Anne Murray (Capitol)
+Put Your Hand in the Hand "Blessed Are"	Joan Baez (Vanguard)
+Put Your Hand in the Hand "Elvis—Now"	Elvis Presley (RCA)
Redemption "Blood, Sweat and Tears 4"*	Blood, Sweat and Tears (Columbia)
Rivers of Babylon "Hasten Down the Wind"	Linda Ronstadt (Asylum)
+Rivers of Babylon "Nightflight to Venus"	Boney M (Sire)

DEFINITIVE SONGS

River Jordan
"Janis"
Janis Joplin
(Columbia)

River of Jordan
"Peter"*
Peter Yarrow
(Warner Brothers)

Rock Me on the Water
"Saturate Before Using"
Jackson Browne
(Asylum)

+Rock Me on the Water
"A Retrospective"
Linda Ronstadt
(Capitol)

+Rock Me on the Water
"Johnny Rivers" (Superpak)
Johnny Rivers
(United Artists)

Rock of Ages
"Motel Shot"
Delaney and Bonnie
(Atco)

Sail My Soul
"Stealin' Home"
Ian Matthews
(Mushroom)

Serve Somebody
"Slow Train Coming"
Bob Dylan
(Columbia)

Silent Eyes
"Still Crazy After All These Years"
Paul Simon
(Columbia)

Sing Hallelujah
"Golden Apples of the Sun"
Judy Collins
(Elektra)

Sister Marie
"Of Cabbages and Kings"*
Chad and Jeremy
(Columbia)

Sister Mary Ryan
"Personal Belongings"
Dave Loggins
(Vanguard)

Slow Train Coming
"Slow Train Coming"
Bob Dylan
(Columbia)

Swing Low, Sweet Chariot
"There's One in Every Crowd"
Eric Clapton
(RSO)

+Swing Low, Sweet Chariot
"From Every Stage"
Joan Baez
(A&M)

Turn, Turn, Turn
"The World of Pete Seeger"
Pete Seeger
(Columbia)

+Turn, Turn, Turn
"Turn, Turn, Turn"
"The Byrds' Greatest Hits"
The Byrds
(Columbia)
(Columbia)

+Turn, Turn, Turn
"Recollections"
Judy Collins
(Elektra)

Valley to Pray
"Washington County"
Arlo Guthrie
(Reprise)

DEFINITIVE SONGS

Very Last Day "In the Wind"	Peter, Paul and Mary (Warner Brothers)
Wake Up "Slow Train Coming"	Bob Dylan (Columbia)
When I Lay My Burden Down "Hoboes, Heroes and Street Corner Clowns"*	Don Nix (Enterprise/Stax)
Will the Circle Be Unbroken "The Essential Ramblin' Jack Elliott"	Ramblin' Jack Elliott (Vanguard)
+Will the Circle Be Unbroken "The First Ten Years"	Joan Baez (Vanguard)
+Will the Circle Be Unbroken "Sunday Down South"*	Jerry Lee Lewis (Sun)
+Will the Circle Be Unbroken "Dirt, Silver and Gold"	The Nitty Gritty Dirt Band (United Artists)
+Will the Circle Be Unbroken "Reflection"*	Pentangle (Reprise)
+Will the Circle Be Unbroken "A Man Must Carry On"	Jerry Jeff Walker (MCA)
+Will the Circle Be Unbroken "Motel Shot"	Delaney and Bonnie (Atco)
+Will the Circle Be Unbroken "Laid Back"	Gregg Allman (Capricorn)

REFERENCE SONGS

Brother Love's Traveling Salvation Show	Neil Diamond
"Gold"	(MCA)
"Hot August Night"	(MCA)
"Neil Diamond"	(MCA)
Burn Down the Mission "Tumbleweed Connection"	Elton John (MCA)
Christopher Robin "My First Album"*	Melanie (Buddah)
Joseph and Joe "J.D."	John Denver (RCA)
Morning Train "Moving"	Peter, Paul and Mary (Warner Brothers)

REFERENCE SONGS

Son of a Preacher Man	Jackie DeShannon
(45 RPM Single)*	(Liberty)
"The Very Best of Jackie	(United Artists)
DeShannon"	
Where to Now St. Peter?	Elton John
"Tumbleweed Connection"	(MCA)

YOUR ADDITIONAL SONGS

_____

_____

_____

_____

_____

God/Lord

CLASSICS

Father of Night	Bob Dylan
"New Morning"	(Columbia)
Have a Talk with God	Stevie Wonder
"Songs in the Key of Life"	(Tamla)
My Sweet Lord	George Harrison
"The Best of George Harrison"	(Apple)
"All Things Must Pass"	(Apple)
"Bangla Desh"	(Apple)
+My Sweet Lord	Richie Havens
"Richie Havens on Stage"*	(Stormy Forest)
+My Sweet Lord	Flo and Eddie
"Illegal, Immortal and Fattening"	(Columbia)

DEFINITIVE SONGS

All in All	Al Green
"The Belle Album"	(Hi)

DEFINITIVE SONGS

Awaiting on You All   George Harrison
"All Things Must Pass"   (Apple)
"Bangla Desh"   (Apple)

Bury My Body   Al Kooper
"Al's Big Deal/Unclaimed   (Columbia)
  Freight—An Al Kooper Anthology"

Cry for Mary   Brian Keith Dougherty
"Let My Heart Be My Home"*   (Fantasy)

Crying in the Chapel   Sonny Till and the Orioles
"American Graffiti"   (MCA)

+Crying in the Chapel   Elvis Presley
"Worldwide 50 Gold Award Hits,   (RCA)
  Vol. 1"

+Crying in the Chapel   Don McLean
"Homeless Brother"   (United Artists)

Day by Day   Godspell
"Godspell"   (Arista)

Dear Lord   Thin Lizzy
"Bad Reputation"   (Mercury)

Dear Lord   Willy Nile
"Willy Nile"   (Arista)

Early in the Morning   Peter, Paul and Mary
"Peter, Paul and Mary"   (Warner Brothers)

Freddie's Walkin'   Chuck Mangione
"The Best of Chuck Mangione"   (Mercury)

Full Force Gail   Van Morrison
"Into the Music"   (Warner Brothers)

Give Me Strength   Eric Clapton
"461 Ocean Blvd."   (RSO)

God   Ian Hunter
"All American Alien Boy"   (Columbia)

God   David Peel and the Lower
                                          East Side
"The American Revolution"*   (Elektra)

God Don't Own a Car   Jimmy Buffett
"Before the Salt"   (Barnaby)

God Fearing Man   Steppenwolf
"At Your Birthday Party"*   (ABC/Dunhill)

DEFINITIVE SONGS

God, If I Only Could Write You a Love Song	Jessi Colter
"Mirriam"*	(Capitol)
God I Love You	Jessi Colter
"Mirriam"*	(Capitol)
God Is Love	Marvin Gaye
"What's Going On?"	(Tamla)
God Loves You	Billy Preston
"Music Is My Life"	(A&M)
Goin' Down the Road	The Grateful Dead
"The Grateful Dead"	(Warner Brothers)
+Goin' Down the Road	Delaney and Bonnie
"Motel Shot"	(Atco)
The Good Lord Loves You	Neil Diamond
"September Morn"	(Columbia)
He	The Righteous Brothers
"Soul and Inspiration"	(Verve)
He Gives Us All His Love	Randy Newman
"Sail Away"	(Reprise)
Hear My Cry	Lon & Derrek Van Eaton
"Brother"*	(Apple)
Heaven Is Ten Zillion Light Years Away	Stevie Wonder
"Fulfillingness' First Finale"	(Tamla)
Helpless	Russ Ballard
"At the Third Stroke"*	(Epic)
He's Got the Whole World in His Hands	Laurie London
"Roots of British Rock"	(Sire)
How Do the Fools Survive	The Doobie Brothers
"Minute by Minute"	(Warner Brothers)
How Great Thou Art	Elvis Presley
"Elvis in Concert"	(RCA)
"How Great Thou Art"	(RCA)
Hymn	Peter, Paul and Mary
"Late Again"	(Warner Brothers)
Hymn	Barclay James Harvest
"Gone to Earth"*	(Polydor)

DEFINITIVE SONGS

I Believe in the Man in the Sky "Worldwide 50 Gold Award Hits, Vol. 2"	Elvis Presley (RCA)
I Believe in You "Slow Train"	Bob Dylan (Columbia)
I Love the Lord "Extension of Man"	Donny Hathaway (Atlantic)
I Walk with the Lord "Book of Numbers" (Soundtrack)	Sonny Terry and Brownie McGee (Brut/Buddah)
I'm Scared "Burton Cummings"	Burton Cummings (Portrait)
If I Ever Needed Someone "His Band and Street Choir"	Van Morrison (Warner Brothers)
Intone My Servant "Diamond Girl"	Seals and Crofts (Warner Brothers)
Just a Closer Walk with Thee "The Best of the Chambers Brothers"	The Chambers Brothers (Fantasy)
+Just a Closer Walk with Thee "David's Album"	Joan Baez (Vanguard)
Keep on Searching "Hopes, Wishes, Promises"	Ray Thomas (Threshold)
Kumbaya "Joan Baez in Concert"	Joan Baez (Vanguard)
Land o' Free Love and Goodbyes "Numbers"	Cat Stevens (A&M)
Let It Shine "Long May You Run"	The Stills-Young Band (Reprise)
Let Us Go into the House of the Lord "The Edwin Hawkins Singers"* "Let Us Go into the House of the Lord"*	The Edwin Hawkins Singers (Buddah) (Buddah)
The Lord "Cucumber Castle"*	The Bee Gees (Atco)
Lord Don't Move That Mountain "The Edwin Hawkins Singers"*	The Edwin Hawkins Singers (Buddah)
Lord Have Mercy on My Soul "Best of Black Oak Arkansas"	Black Oak Arkansas (Atlantic)
Lord I'm Amazed "Down Home"*	Sam Neely (A&M)

DEFINITIVE SONGS

Lord Is It Mine? "Breakfast in America"	Supertramp (A&M)
The Lord Loves the One "Living in the Material World"	George Harrison (Apple)
The Lord's Prayer "Life Mask"*	Roy Harper (Harvest)
+The Lord's Prayer "Sister Janet Mead"*	Sister Janet Mead (A&M)
+The Lord's Prayer (45 RPM Single b/w Little Saint Nick)	The Beach Boys (Capitol)
Lord's Song "Pousette Dart Band 3"	Pousette Dart Band (Capitol)
Lovin' You "The Belle Album"	Al Green (Hi)
Master, Master "Mirriam"*	Jessi Colter (A&M)
Mighty Maker "I've Got a Reason"	Richie Furay (Asylum)
Music's My Life "Music Is My Life"	Billy Preston (A&M)
My God "Keys to the Country"*	Barefoot Jerry (Monument)
My Mama "Mirriam"*	Jessi Colter (Capitol)
Now Let Us Enter into the House of the Lord "Love, Devotion, Surrender"	John McLaughlin/Santana (Columbia)
O God of Loveliness "Jennifer Warnes"	Jennifer Warnes (Arista)
Oh Lord, Why Lord (45 RPM Single)*	Los Pop Tops (Calla)
People Get Ready "The Impressions' Sixteen Greatest"	The Impressions (ABC)
+People Get Ready "The Time Has Come" "The Best of the Chambers Brothers" "Live at Bill Graham's Fillmore East"	The Chambers Brothers (Columbia) (Columbia) (Columbia)
+People Get Ready "Lady Soul"	Aretha Franklin (Atlantic)

DEFINITIVE SONGS

+People Get Ready
"Vanilla Fudge"*
Vanilla Fudge
(Atco)

+People Get Ready

"Sonny & Brownie"
Sonny Terry & Brownie
  McGee
(A&M)

+People Get Ready
"Man in the Hills"
Burning Spear
(Island)

+People Get Ready
"Sailboat"*
Jonathan Edwards
(Warner Brothers)

+People Get Ready
"Street Corner Symphony"
The Persuasions
(Capitol)

+People Get Ready
"Silver Morning"
Kenny Rankin
(Little David)

A Piece of the Rock
"Thorn on the Rose"*
Even Stevens
(Elektra)

Prayer
"Hog Heaven"*
Hog Heaven
(Roulette)

Prepare Ye the Way of the Lord
"Godspell"
Godspell
(Arista)

Presence of the Lord
"Blind Faith"
Blind Faith
(Atco)

+Presence of the Lord
"In Concert"
Derek and the Dominoes
(RSO)

+Presence of the Lord
"Eric Clapton's Rainbow Concert"
Eric Clapton
(RSO)

Rolling Hills
"Into the Music"
Van Morrison
(Warner Brothers)

Sail into Tomorrow
"Clearly Love"
Olivia Newton-John
(MCA)

Shine a Light
"Exile on Main Street"
The Rolling Stones
(Rolling Stone Records)

Soldier of the Cross
"Accept No Substitute"*
Delaney and Bonnie
(Elektra)

Someone to Believe In
"The Promise"*
Mike Pinder
(Threshold)

Sunshine Embrace

"Pacific Gas & Electric
  Featuring Charles Allen"*
Pacific Gas & Electric
  Featuring Charles Allen
(ABC/Dunhill)

DEFINITIVE SONGS

Thank God
"The Statue Makers of Hollywood"*
Alpha Band
(Arista)

Thank You Lord
"Rudy the Fifth"
Rick Nelson
(MCA)

Thank You Lord
"All Things Must Pass"
George Harrison
(Apple)

Thank You Lord
"Spirit of '76"*
Spirit
(Mercury)

That's the Way God Planned It
"That's the Way God Planned It"*
"Bangla Desh" (George Harrison)
Billy Preston
(Apple)
(Apple)

There Ain't No Room
"Mirriam"*
Jessi Colter
(Capitol)

To My Father's House
"Let Us Go into the House of the
Lord"
The Edwin Hawkins Singers
(Buddah)

Trust in the Lord
"Keep on Smiling"*
Wet Willie
(Capricorn)

Wade in the Water
"Live at Bill Graham's Fillmore East"
The Chambers Brothers
(Columbia)

Wake Me
"Learn to Love It"*
Jesse Winchester
(Bearsville)

We Thank You
"Bursting at the Seams"
Strawbs
(A&M)

When the Lord Closes the Door (He
Opens a Little Window)
"Kinky Friedman"
Kinky Friedman

(ABC)

Without the Lord
"Brother"*
Lon & Derrek Van Eaton
(Apple)

REFERENCE SONGS

All God's Lonely Children

"Transition"*
Kenny Rogers and the First
Edition
(Reprise)

Bed and a Bottle
"Birth Comes to Us All"
The Good Rats
(Arista)

Closer Everyday
"The Doobie Brothers"
The Doobie Brothers
(Warner Brothers)

REFERENCE SONGS

Everything Is Going to Be Alright
"Teegarden and Van Winkle"*

Teegarden and Van Winkle
(Bellaphon)

God Bless the Child
"Blood, Sweat and Tears Greatest
    Hits"

Blood, Sweat and Tears
(Columbia)

"Blood, Sweat and Tears"

(Columbia)

+God Bless the Child
"Richie Havens on Stage"*

Richie Havens
(Stormy Forest)

God Gave Rock and Roll to You
"The Best of Argent . . . An
    Anthology"

Argent
(Epic)

"In Deep"

(Epic)

God Is Alive, Magic Is Afoot
"The Best of Buffy Sainte-Marie"

Buffy Sainte-Marie
(Vanguard)

God Knows I Love You
"To Bonnie from Delaney"

Delaney and Bonnie
(Atco)

God Knows I'm Good
"Space Oddity"

David Bowie
(RCA)

God, Love and Rock and Roll
"Teegarden and Van Winkle"*

Teegarden and Van Winkle
(Westbound)

God Only Knows
"Pet Sounds"

The Beach Boys
(Capitol)

"Good Vibrations—Best of the Beach
    Boys"

(Brother/Reprise)

+God Only Knows
"I'm Glad You're Here"

Neil Diamond
(Columbia)

God Only Knows
"Simple Things"

Carole King
(Avatar)

God's Children
"Kink Kronikles"

The Kinks
(RCA)

In the Lap of the Gods
"Sheer Heart Attack"

Queen
(Elektra)

Is It Today Lord?
"Grave New World"

Strawbs
(A&M)

Mercedes Benz
"Pearl"

Janis Joplin
(Columbia)

One Love/People Get Ready
"Exodus"

Bob Marley and the Wailers
(Island)

REFERENCE SONGS

Please Send Me Someone to Love "Before We Were So Rudely Interrupted"	The Animals (United Artists)
Sailing	The Sutherland Brothers and Quiver
"Lifeboat"	(Island)
+Sailing "Atlantic Crossing"	Rod Stewart (Warner Brothers)
+Sailing "Blowin' Away"	Joan Baez (Portrait)
+Sailing "Long Misty Days"	Robin Trower (Chrysalis)
Thank God for You Baby "The Best of P G & E"	Pacific Gas & Electric (Columbia)
Thank the Lord for the Night Time "Neil Diamond's Greatest Hits"	Neil Diamond (Bang)
Too Late for Prayin' "Sundown"	Gordon Lightfoot (Reprise)
Traveling Prayer "Piano Man"	Billy Joel (Columbia)
Valley to Pray "Washington County"	Arlo Guthrie (Reprise)
With God on Our Side "The Times They Are a Changin'"	Bob Dylan (Columbia)
+With God on Our Side "First Ten Years"	Joan Baez (Vanguard)
+With God on Our Side (33 RPM E.P.)*	Manfred Mann (Ascot/HMV)

YOUR ADDITIONAL SONGS

_____

_____

_____

_____

_____

Jesus Christ

THEMATIC ALBUMS

"Godspell" (original cast) — Various Artists (Arista)

"Godspell" (Soundtrack) — Various Artists (Arista)

"Jesus Christ Superstar" (original Broadway cast) — Various Artists (MCA)

"Jesus Christ Superstar" (original London cast) — Various Artists (MCA)

"Jesus Christ Superstar" (Soundtrack) — Various Artists (MCA)

CLASSICS

Amen
"The Impressions' Sixteen Greatest" — The Impressions (ABC)

+Amen
"Orange Blossom Special" — Johnny Cash (Columbia)

Jesus Christ Superstar
"Jesus Christ Superstar" (original Broadway cast) — Various Artists (MCA)

+Jesus Christ Superstar
"Jesus Christ Superstar" (original London cast) — Various Artists (MCA)

+Jesus Christ Superstar
"Jesus Christ Superstar" (Soundtrack) — Various Artists (MCA)

O Happy Day
"O Happy Day" — The Edwin Hawkins Singers (Buddah)

+O Happy Day
"From Every Stage" — Joan Baez (A&M)

DEFINITIVE SONGS

About to Die
"Home" — Procol Harum (A&M)

Ballad of a Carpenter
"I Ain't Marchin' Anymore" — Phil Ochs (Elektra)

Can You See Him
"Off the Shelf"* — Batdorf and Rodney (Atlantic)

DEFINITIVE SONGS

The Christian Life
"Sweetheart Of The Rodeo"
The Byrds
(Columbia)

Consider Me
"Mirriam"*
Jessi Colter
(Capitol)

Dear Jesus
"After the Gold Rush"
Prelude
(Island)

Everybody
"Diamonds in the Rough"*
John Prine
(Atlantic)

The Finale
"Godspell"
Godspell
(Arista)

Groovin' with Jesus
"Thunderbox"
Humble Pie
(A&M)

Help Me Jesus
"Sing Children Sing"*
Lesley Duncan
(Columbia)

High on Jesus
"Sold American"*
Kinky Friedman
(Epic)

Hymn
"Late Again"
Peter, Paul and Mary
(Warner Brothers)

I Heard the Voice of Jesus
"The Edwin Hawkins Singers"*
"Let Us Go into the House of the
    Lord"*
The Edwin Hawkins Singers
(Buddah)
(Buddah)

I Told Jesus
"First Take"
Roberta Flack
(Atlantic)

Jesus
"Southwest"*
Herb Pedersen
(Epic)

Jesus
"Velvet Underground"*
The Velvet Underground
(MGM)

Jesus
"Buddah and the Chocolate Box"
Cat Stevens
(A&M)

Jesus
"America Today"*
Curtis Mayfield
(Curtom)

Jesus
"Queen"
Queen
(Elektra)

Jesus Broke the Wild Horses
"Airborne"
The Flying Burrito Brothers
(Columbia)

Jesus Build a Fence Around Me
"More Than Before"
The Persuasions
(A&M)

DEFINITIVE SONGS

Jesus Came Down "Lake"	Lake (Columbia)
Jesus Children of America "Innervisions"	Stevie Wonder (Tamla)
Jesus Christ "Woody Guthrie"	Woody Guthrie (Warner Brothers)
+Jesus Christ "A Tribute to Woody Guthrie"	Arlo Guthrie (Warner Brothers)
Jesus Hearted People "Third Annual Pipe Dream"	Atlanta Rhythm Section (Polydor)
Jesus Is a Soul Man "Johnny Rivers" (Superpak)	Johnny Rivers (United Artists)
Jesus Is Just Alright "The Best of the Byrds Greatest Hits, Vol. II"	The Byrds (Columbia)
"Ballad of Easy Rider"	(Columbia)
+Jesus Is Just Alright "Best of the Doobies"	The Doobie Brothers (Warner Brothers)
Jesus Is Waiting "Call Me"	Al Green (Hi)
Jesus Lover of My Soul "The Edwin Hawkins Singers" "Let Us Go into the House of the Lord"	The Edwin Hawkins Singers (Buddah) (Buddah)
Jesus Met the Woman at the Well "Live in Concert"	Peter, Paul and Mary (Warner Brothers)
Jesus on My Side "Americana"	Leon Russell (Paradise)
Jesus Once Again "Herb Pedersen"*	Herb Pedersen (Epic)
Jesus on the Main Line "Show Time"	Ry Cooder (Warner Brothers)
Jesus Save Me "Willie and the Lapdog"*	Gallagher and Lyle (A&M)
Jesus Was a Crossmaker "Romany"	The Hollies (Epic)
Make the Devil Mad (Turn On to Jesus) "Kinky Friedman"*	Kinky Friedman (ABC)

DEFINITIVE SONGS

My Jesus Told Me So
"The Marshall Tucker Band"

The Marshall Tucker Band
(Capricorn)

People Call Me Jesus
"Mac McAnally"

Mac McAnally
(Ariola/America)

Rainbow
"Shiver in the Night"

Andy Pratt
(Nemperor)

Take My Hand

Kenny Rogers and the First
   Edition

"Transition"*

(Reprise)

Talkin' About Jesus
"Motel Shot"

Delaney and Bonnie
(Atco)

Touched the Hem of His Garment
"Naked Songs"*

Al Kooper
(Columbia)

+Touched the Hem of His Garment
"I Just Want to Sing with My Friends"

The Persuasions
(A&M)

Tramp on the Street
"Late Again"

Peter, Paul and Mary
(Warner Brothers)

+(The) Tramp on the Street
"David's Album"

Joan Baez
(Vanguard)

Traveling On for Jesus
"Kate and Anna McGarrigle"

Kate and Anna McGarrigle
(Warner Brothers)

Wake Me
"Learn to Love It"*

Jesse Winchester
(Bearsville)

Way Out Jesus
"Sammy Johns"*

Sammy Johns
(General Recording
   Corporation)

We've Been Told
"There's One in Every Crowd"

Eric Clapton
(RSO)

Which Side?
"Outlasting the Blues"

Arlo Guthrie
(Warner Brothers)

You Can Tell the World
"Wednesday Morning 3 A.M."

Simon and Garfunkel
(Columbia)

REFERENCE SONGS

Color TV Blues
"Prime Time"

Don McLean
(Arista)

Diamonds in the Rough
"Diamonds in the Rough"*

John Prine
(Atlantic)

REFERENCE SONGS

Did Jesus Have a Baby Sister?
"Dory Previn"*
Dory Previn
(Warner Brothers)

Far Away Eyes
"Some Girls"
The Rolling Stones
(Rolling Stone Records)

Is He Coming at All?
"The Main Refrain"*
Wendy Waldman
(Warner Brothers)

Jesus Just Left Chicago
"The Best of ZZ Top"
ZZ Top
(London)

Joyful Resurrection
"Tom Fogerty"
Tom Fogerty
(Fantasy)

Letter to Jesus
"Take Heart"*
Mimi Fariña and Tom Jans
(A&M)

Lo and Behold
"Sweet Baby James"
James Taylor
(Warner Brothers)

Lo and Behold/Jesus Is Just Alright
"Sister Kate"*
Kate Taylor
(Cotillion)

The Man in Question
"The Essential . . . Jim Dawson"
Jim Dawson
(Kama Sutra)

Natural Man
"Sit Down Old Friend"*
Dion
(Warner Brothers)

Railroad Angels
"Don't Worry, Ma"
Felix Pappalardi
(A&M)

Spirit in the Sky
"Spirit in the Sky"*
Norman Greenbaum
(Reprise)

Starlight
"Wrong End of the Rainbow"*
Tom Rush
(Columbia)

Sweet Jesus
"Time Honoured Ghost"*
Barclay James Harvest
(Polydor)

YOUR ADDITIONAL SONGS

_____

_____

_____

_____

_____

Anti-Institutional Religion

CLASSICS

Hymn 43	Jethro Tull
"Aqualung"	(Reprise)

THEMATIC ALBUMS

"Aqualung" (Side 2, "My God")	Jethro Tull
	(Reprise)

DEFINITIVE SONGS

Benediction	Stealers Wheel
"Right or Wrong"*	(A&M)
"The Best of Stealers Wheel"	(A&M)
Canons of Christianity	Phil Ochs
"Phil Ochs in Concert"	(Elektra)
Catechism Wednesday	George Gerdes
"Sons of Obituary"*	(United Artists)
Cathedral	Crosby, Stills & Nash
"Crosby, Stills & Nash"	(Atlantic)
(I Don't Wanna Be No) Catholic Boy	The Dead Boys
"We Have Come for Your Children"	(Sire)
Don't Ask Me Questions	Graham Parker
"Howlin' Wind"	(Mercury)
"The Parkerilla"	(Mercury)
Ester's First Communion	Dory Previn
"On My Way to Where"*	(Warner Brothers)
God	John Lennon
"John Lennon/Plastic Ono Band"	(Apple)
God's Song	Randy Newman
"Sail Away"	(Reprise)
+God's Song	Tracey Nelson
"Homemade Songs"*	(Flying Fish)
Good for God	Harry Nilsson
"Duit On Mon Dei"	(RCA)
Heaven	Talking Heads
"Fear of Music"	(Sire)
Hymn	Peter, Paul and Mary
"Late Again"	(Warner Brothers)
My God	Jethro Tull
"Aqualung"	(Reprise)

DEFINITIVE SONGS

New Christ Cardiac Hero "Janis Ian"	Janis Ian (Polydor)
No Strangers in Paradise "Lines"	Charlie (Janus)
Oh My Soul "One-Eyed Jack"	Garland Jeffreys (A&M)
Poke at the Pope "Open Road"*	Donovan (Epic)
Reverend Posey	Gary Puckett and the Union Gap
"Incredible"*	(Columbia)
The Second Sitting for the Last Supper "The Original Soundtrack"	10 CC (Mercury)
Wind Up "Aqualung"	Jethro Tull (Reprise)

REFERENCE SONGS

Church "Three Hearts"	Bob Welch (Capitol)
Louie the Hook vs. the Preacher "O'Keefe"	Danny O'Keefe (Signpost)
On the Road to Kingdom Come "On the Road to Kingdom Come"	Harry Chapin (Elektra)
Stand Firm "Bush Doctor"	Peter Tosh (Rolling Stone Records)
Where to Now St. Peter "Tumbleweed Connection"	Elton John (MCA)

YOUR ADDITIONAL SONGS

_____

_____

_____

_____

_____

Alternative Forms of Prayer, Worship, and Meditation

CLASSICS

We did not pick any classic songs here. The individuality and personal nature of each song remains unique to its own subject matter.

THEMATIC ALBUMS

"The Radha Krishna Temple"

The Radha Krishna Temple
(Apple)

DEFINITIVE SONGS

Abdul 'l Baha
"Year of Sunday"

Seals and Crofts
(Warner Brothers)

Babaji
"Even in the Quietest Moments"

Supertramp
(A&M)

Blind Feeling
"The Dreamer Weaver"

Gary Wright
(Warner Brothers)

Children of the Half-Light

"Dr. Heckle and Mr. Jive"

England Dan and John Ford
    Coley
(Big Tree)

Creation
"Bush Doctor"

Peter Tosh
(Rolling Stone Records)

East of Ginger Trees
"Summer Breeze"

Seals and Crofts
(Warner Brothers)

Guru
"Unrequited"*

Loudon Wainwright III
(Columbia)

Hare Krishna
"Hair" (Soundtrack)

Various Artists
(RCA)

+Hare Krishna
"Universal Consciousness"

Alice Coltrane
(Impulse)

Hare Krishna Mantra
"The Radha Krishna Temple"

The Radha Krishna Temple
(Apple)

He Come Down
"Carl and the Passions, So Tough"

The Beach Boys
(Brother/Reprise)

Is It "He" (Jai Sri Krishna)
"Dark Horse"

George Harrison
(Dark Horse)

Maya Love
"Dark Horse"

George Harrison
(Dark Horse)

DEFINITIVE SONGS

My Sweet Lord	George Harrison
"All Things Must Pass"	(Apple)
"Bangla Desh"	(Apple)
"The Best of George Harrison"	(Apple)
+My Sweet Lord	Richie Havens
"Richie Havens on Stage"*	(Stormy Forest)
+My Sweet Lord	Flo and Eddie
"Illegal, Immortal, and Fattening"	(Columbia)
Parvardigar	Pete Townsend
"Who Came First"	(MCA)
The Prisoner	England Dan and John Ford Coley
"Nights Are Forever"	(Big Tree)
Seven Valleys	Seals and Crofts
"Seals and Crofts I and II"	(Warner Brothers)
Something Very Special	Gary Wright
"Touch and Go"	(Warner Brothers)
Transcendental Meditation	The Beach Boys
"Friends"	(Brother/Reprise)

REFERENCE SONGS

Dream Weaver	Gary Wright
"Dream Weaver"	(Warner Brothers)
Inner Light	The Beatles
"The Beatles/Rarities"	(Capitol)
(45 RPM Single)	(Capitol)
Instant Karma	John Lennon
"Shaved Fish"	(Apple)
Om	Moody Blues
"In Search of the Lost Chord"	(London)
Within You, Without You	The Beatles
"Sgt. Pepper's Lonely Hearts Club Band"	(Capitol)

YOUR ADDITIONAL SONGS

_____

_____

_____

_____

_____

SCHOOLS/EDUCATIONAL PROCESS

Schools/educational process—from "Blackboard Jungle" to "Welcome Back Kotter."

The songs here explore all levels of learning, grammar school through post-graduate, as well as the individual students, teachers, and their activities. Some are serious, some are very silly, but each of them reflects a part of the picture.

Related Categories: Growing Up, Teen-age Years/Adolescence

+Same as Song Above
*Hard-to-find Songs/Albums

CLASSICS

Be True to Your School	The Beach Boys
"Endless Summer"	(Capitol)
"Little Deuce Coupe"	(Capitol)
Rock and Roll High School	The Ramones
"Rock and Roll High School"	(Sire)
Old Schoolyard	Cat Stevens
"Izitso"	(A&M)
School's Out	Alice Cooper
"Alice Cooper's Greatest Hits"	(Warner Brothers)
"The Alice Cooper Show"	(Warner Brothers)
What Did You Learn in School Today?	Tom Paxton
"Ramblin' Boy"	(Vanguard)
+What Did You Learn in School Today?	Pete Seeger
"We Shall Overcome"	(Columbia)

THEMATIC ALBUMS

"Rock and Roll High School" (Soundtrack)	The Ramones (Sire)
"Schoolboys in Disgrace"	The Kinks (RCA)

DEFINITIVE SONGS

Abigail Beecher (Our History Teacher) (45 RPM Single)*	Freddie Cannon (Warner Brothers)

DEFINITIVE SONGS

Alma Mater
"School's Out"
Alice Cooper
(Warner Brothers)

Are You Going My Way
"Cookin' with Fats"
Fats Domino
(United Artists)

Art School
"In the City"
The Jam
(Polydor)

Art School Credentials
"Not Far from Free"*
Don Harrison Band
(Mercury)

Back to School
"The Simms Brothers Band"
The Simms Brothers
(Elektra)

Back to School Days
"Howlin' Wolf"
"The Parkerilla"
Graham Parker
(Mercury)
(Mercury)

+Back to School Days
"Get It"
Dave Edmunds
(Swan Song)

Beauty School Dropout
"Grease" (Soundtrack)
Frankie Avalon
(RSO)

Charlie Brown
"Sixteen Greatest Hits"
"The Coasters' Greatest Hits"
The Coasters
(Trip)
(Atco)

Disco Tech
"Welcome Home"
Carole King
(Avatar)

The Dean and I
"10 CC"
10 CC
(UK)

Education
"Blue Jug"*
Blue Jug
(Capricorn)

Education
"Schoolboys in Disgrace"
The Kinks
(RCA)

Final Exam
"Final Exam"
Loudon Wainwright III
(Arista)

Flowers Are Red
"Living Room Suite"
Harry Chapin
(Elektra)

Girls School
(45 RPM Single)
Wings
(Capitol)

Goin' Through School and Love
"Rock On"
Raydio
(Arista)

Graduation Day
(45 RPM Single)
The Arbors
(Columbia)

DEFINITIVE SONGS

+Graduation Day "Freshmen Favorites"	The Four Freshmen (Capitol)
+Graduation Day "Spirit of America" "Beach Boys in Concert"	The Beach Boys (Capitol) (Capitol)
Graduation's Here (45 RPM Single)* "The Very Best of the Fleetwoods"	The Fleetwoods (Dolton) (United Artists)
Happiest Days of Our Lives/ Another Brick in the Wall "The Wall"	Pink Floyd (Harvest)
Harper Valley P.T.A. "Greatest Hits"	Jeannie C. Riley (Plantation)
Headmaster "Schoolboys in Disgrace"	The Kinks (RCA)
High School "Rock and Roll High School" "Back in the U.S.A."*	MC 5 (Sire) (Atlantic)
High School Confidential "The Session"*	Jerry Lee Lewis (Mercury)
High School Dance "Something Special" "Best of the Sylvers"	The Sylvers (Capitol) (Capitol)
High School History "Desire Wire"	Cindy Bullens (United Artists)
High School Star "Take It to the Max"	Aka the Max Demian (RCA)
Jack the Idiot Dunce "Schoolboys in Disgrace"	The Kinks (RCA)
The Last Assembly "Schoolboys in Disgrace"	The Kinks (RCA)
Little Lou "Legendary Masters"	Eddie Cochran (United Artists)
Moments to Remember "The Vogues' Greatest Hits"	The Vogues (Reprise)
+Moments to Remember "Rock On"*	Four Lads (Columbia)
My Old Yearbook "Song for Patty"*	Sammy Walker (Vanguard)

DEFINITIVE SONGS

New Girl in School "Gotta Take That One Last Ride"	Jan and Dean (United Artists)
The Old School "Pursuit of Happiness"*	Rupert Holmes (Private Stock)
Poisoning the Students' Minds "Young vs. Old"	Pete Seeger (Columbia)
Pom Pom Play Girl "Fun Fun Fun" "Shutdown Vol. II"	The Beach Boys (Capitol) (Capitol)
Rock and Roll High School "Rock and Roll High School" "End of the Century"	The Ramones (Sire) (Sire)
+Getting Better "All This and World War II"	Status Quo (20th Century Records)
Roses Are Red "Greatest Hits" (45 RPM Single)	Bobby Vinton (Epic) (Epic)
School "Crime of the Century"	Supertramp (A&M)
School Boy Crush "Person to Person"	Average White Band (Atlantic)
School Days "Golden Decade" "Chuck Berry's Greatest Hits"	Chuck Berry (Chess) (Chess)
+School Days "Home, Home on the Road"	New Riders of the Purple Sage (Columbia)
+School Days "Keepin' the Summer Alive"	The Beach Boys (CBS)
School Days "Loudon Wainwright III"*	Loudon Wainwright III (Atlantic)
School Days "Schoolboys in Disgrace"	The Kinks (RCA)
+School Days "Explore Your Mind"	Al Green (Hi)
School Days "Birth Comes to Us All"	The Good Rats (Arista)
School Days "All Pink Inside"*	Frijid Pink (Fantasy)

DEFINITIVE SONGS

School Days "The Runaways"	The Runaways (Mercury)
School Days "God Bless the Starjets"	Starjets (Columbia)
School Drag "Dirty Angels"	Dirty Angels (A&M)
School Girl "Argent"	Argent (Epic)
School Is Out "Pick of the Radio Good Guys"	Gary U. S. Bonds (Laurie)
+School Is Out "Show Time"	Ry Cooder (Warner Brothers)
School Is Out "Matthew and Son"	Cat Stevens (Deram)
School Mam "No More Heroes"*	Stranglers IV (A&M)
Slides "Slides"*	Richard Harris (ABC/Dunhill)
Smokin' in the Boys' Room "Yeah"	Brownsville Station (Big Tree)
Status Back Baby "Absolutely Free"	The Mothers of Invention (Verve)
Student Demonstration Time "Surf's Up"	The Beach Boys (Brother/Reprise)
Swinging School (45 RPM Single)*	Bobby Rydell (Cameo)
Teacher "Benefit" "M.U. The Best of Jethro Tull"	Jethro Tull (Chrysalis) (Chrysalis)
Teacher "Christ Child"*	Christ Child (Buddah)
Teacher I Need You "Don't Shoot Me, I'm Only the Piano Player"	Elton John (MCA)
Teacher's Pet (45 RPM Single)*	Frankie Avalon (Chancellor)
Teacher, Teacher "There Was a Time"	Gene Chandler (Brunswick)

DEFINITIVE SONGS

Teenage Jail "The Long Run"	The Eagles (Asylum)
To Sir with Love (45 RPM Single)* "To Sir with Love" "To Sir with Love" (Soundtrack)	Lulu (Epic) (Epic) (United Artists)
Waiting in School "Ricky Nelson"	Rick Nelson (United Artists)
Welcome Back "Welcome Back"	John Sebastian (Reprise)
When Will the School Start Laughing "Back to Carnegie Hall"	Rod McKuen (Warner Brothers)
Wild and Hot "Sinful"	Angel (Casablanca)

REFERENCE SONGS

Advertisement in the *Voice* "Ratcity in Blue"*	The Good Rats (Ratcity/Platinum)
All American Girl "Willard"*	John Stewart (Capitol)
All My Choices "All My Choices"*	Mary Travers (Warner Brothers)
Almost Summer "Almost Summer"	Celebration (MCA)
Carrie Ann "The Hollies' Greatest Hits" "Hollies Live"	The Hollies (Epic) (Columbia)
Chemistry Class "Armed Forces"	Elvis Costello (Columbia)
Coney Island Baby "Coney Island Baby" "Live—Take No Prisoners"	Lou Reed (RCA) (Arista)
Dance, Dance, Dance "Spirit of America" "Dance, Dance, Dance" "The Beach Boys Today"	The Beach Boys (Capitol) (Capitol) (Capitol)
Day of the Locusts "New Morning"	Bob Dylan (Columbia)

REFERENCE SONGS

Getting Better   The Beatles
"Sgt. Pepper's Lonely Hearts Club   (Capitol)
    Band"

Public Animal #9   Alice Cooper
"School's Out"   (Warner Brothers)

+Getting Better   Peter Frampton, The Bee
                                                    Gees
"Sgt. Pepper's Lonely Hearts Club   (RSO)
    Band Soundtrack"

Gonna Have a Good Good Time   Livingston Taylor
"Three Way Mirror"*   (Epic)

Good Morning Little School Girl   Muddy Waters
"I'm Ready"   (Blue Sky)
"Folk Singer"   (Chess)

+Good Morning Little School Girl   Ten Years After
"The Classic Performances of Ten   (Columbia)
    Years After"
"Ssssh"   (Deram)

+Good Morning Little School Girl   Paul Butterfield Blues Band
"What's Shakin' "   (Elektra)

+Good Morning Little School Girl   Taj Mahal
"Taj Mahal"   (Columbia)

Grown Up Wrong   Dirty Angels
"Dirty Angels"   (A&M)

Hand Bags and Glad Rags   Rod Stewart
"The Best of Rod Stewart"   (Mercury)
"The Rod Stewart Album"   (Mercury)

It's Raining on Prom Night   Cindy Bullen
"Grease" (Soundtrack)   (RSO)

It's Summertime   The Jamies
(45 RPM Single)*   (Epic)

I Was Educated by Myself   Richie Havens
"The End of the Beginning"   (A&M)

I Wish   Stevie Wonder
"Songs in the Key of Life"   (Tamla)

James   Billy Joel
"Turnstiles"   (Columbia)

Kodachrome   Paul Simon
"Greatest Hits Etc."   (Columbia)
"There Goes Rhymin' Simon"   (Columbia)

REFERENCE SONGS

Mary of the Fourth Form	The Boomtown Rats
"The Boomtown Rats"	(Columbia)
Me and Julio Down by the School Yard	Paul Simon
"Greatest Hits Etc."	(Columbia)
"Paul Simon"	(Columbia)
"Live Rhymin'"	(Columbia)
Mirror Star	The Fabulous Poodles
"The Fabulous Poodles"	(Epic)
My Old School	Steely Dan
"Count Down to Ecstasy"	(ABC)
"Greatest Hits"	(ABC)
The Ostrich	Steppenwolf
"Rest in Peace"*	(ABC/Dunhill)
"Steppenwolf"	(ABC/Dunhill)
Stay Free	The Clash
"Give 'em Enough Rope"	(Epic)
Summer in the Schoolyard	City Boy
"Book Early"	(Mercury)
Surfin' U.S.A.	The Beach Boys
"Surfin' U.S.A."	(Capitol)
"Endless Summer"	(Capitol)
+Surfin' U.S.A.	Leif Garrett
"Leif Garrett"	(Atlantic)
Victim of Romance	Moon Martin
"Shots from a Cold Nightmare"	(Capitol)
We May Never Pass This Way Again	Seals and Crofts
"Greatest Hits"	(Warner Brothers)
"Diamond Girl"	(Warner Brothers)
Wind Up	Jethro Tull
"Aqualung"	(Chrysalis)
Wonderful World	Sam Cooke
"This Is Sam Cooke"	(RCA)
+Wonderful World	Herman's Hermits
"Herman's Hermits XX—Their Greatest Hits"	(ABKCO)
+Wonderful World	Kenny Vance
"Vance 32"*	(Atlantic)
+Wonderful World	David Bromberg
"Midnight on the Wind"	(Columbia)

REFERENCE SONGS

+Wonderful World   Art Garfunkel
  "Watermark"   (Columbia)
+Wonderful World   The Supremes
  "We Remember Sam Cooke"   (Motown)
  "A Little Bit of Liverpool"   (Motown)
+Wonderful World   Otis Redding
  "Otis Blue"   (Volt)
+Wonderful World   Bryan Ferry
  "Another Time, Another Place"   (Atlantic)

YOUR ADDITIONAL SONGS

_____

_____

_____

_____

_____

SELF-IDENTITY

Self-identity—I am, I said . . . but I did not believe it.
Other than love, this is probably the most important theme in rock.
The quest for self-identity with its many struggles, achievements, and disappointments is treated by the rock writers with humor, understanding, anger, and desperation.

Related Categories: Changes, Growing Up, Hope/Optimism, Life,
   Loneliness, Women's Identity/Liberation

+Same as Song Above
*Hard-to-find Songs/Albums

CLASSICS

Be Yourself "Songs for Beginners"	Graham Nash (Atlantic)
Garden Party "Garden Party"	Rick Nelson (MCA)
On the Road to Find Out "Tea for the Tillerman"	Cat Stevens (A&M)

DEFINITIVE SONGS

Ain't No Backing Up Now "Ain't No Backing Up Now"*	Isis (Buddah)
Anyway, Anyhow, Anywhere "Meaty Beaty Big and Bouncy"	The Who (MCA)
Attitude Dancing "Playing Possum" "Best of Carly Simon Vol. I"	Carly Simon (Elektra) (Elektra)
Baby the Rain Must Fall "Baby the Rain Must Fall"	Glenn Yarborough (RCA)
Badlands "Darkness on the Edge of Town"	Bruce Springsteen (Columbia)
Be Free "Mother Lode"	Loggins and Messina (Columbia)
Be True to You "The Best Songs" "Be True to You"	Eric Andersen (Arista) (Arista)

DEFINITIVE SONGS

Be Your Own Best Friend
"Be Your Own Best Friend"
Ray Stevens
(Warner Brothers)

(Be Yourself) Be Real
"Naked Songs"*
Al Kooper
(Columbia)

Beautiful
"Tapestry"
Carole King
(Ode)

Blazin' Your Own Trail
"You Can Tune a Piano, But You
    Can't Tuna Fish"
REO Speedwagon
(Epic)

Breakaway
"Spirit of America"
The Beach Boys
(Capitol)

Dare to Be Different
"Donovan"*
Donovan
(Arista)

Dear Abbie
"Prime Prine"
John Prine
(Atlantic)

Desert Skies
"Carolina Dreams"
The Marshall Tucker Band
(Capricorn)

Don't Let Me Be Misunderstood
"Best of the Animals"
"Animal Tracks"
The Animals
(ABKCO)
(ABKCO)

+Don't Let Me Be Misunderstood   .
"Santa Esmeralda"
Santa Esmeralda
(Casablanca)

.+Don't Let Me Be Misunderstood
"With a Little Help from My Friends"
Joe Cocker
(A&M)

+Don't Let Me Be Misunderstood

"Encore"
Brian Auger and Julie
    Tippets
(Warner Brothers)

Do What You Want, Be What You
    Are
"Bigger Than Both of Us"
Hall and Oates

(RCA)

Everybody Is a Star

"Greatest Hits"
Sly and the Family
    Stone
(Epic)

+Everybody Is a Star
"Energy"
The Pointer Sisters
(Elektra)

Everybody's Talking
"Aerial Ballet"
"Greatest Hits"
"Midnight Cowboy" (Soundtrack)
Harry Nilsson
(RCA)
(RCA)   .
(United Artists)

DEFINITIVE SONGS

+Everybody's Talking   Fred Neil
  "Everybody's Talking"   (Capitol)
  "Other Side of This Life"*   (Capitol)
  "Fred Neil"*   (Capitol)

+Everybody's Talking   Spanky and Our Gang
  "Spanky's Greatest Hits"   (Mercury)

+Everybody's Talking   Harold Melvin
  "Let's Clean Up the Ghetto"   (Philadelphia International)

+Everybody's Talking   Neil Diamond
  "Touching You, Touching Me"   (MCA)
  "Rainbow"   (MCA)

+Everybody's Talking   Bill Withers
  "The Best of Bill Withers"   (Sussex)

Exactly Who You Are   Mirabai
  "Mirabai"*   (Swan Song)

A Face in the Crowd   The Kinks
  "Soap Opera"   (RCA)

Finally Got Myself Together   The Impressions
  "Finally Got Myself Together"*   (Curtom)

Flowers Never Bend with the Rainfall   Simon and Garfunkel
  "Parsley, Sage, Rosemary and Thyme"   (Columbia)

The Fool on the Hill   The Beatles
  "Magical Mystery Tour"   (Capitol)
  "The Beatles 1967–1970"   (Capitol)

Fooling Yourself   Styx
  "The Grand Illusion"   (A&M)

Free as the Morning Sun   Devadip Carlos Santana
  "Oneness"   (Columbia)

Free Yourself, Be Yourself   Brothers Johnson
  "Right on Time"   (A&M)

Get It Together   Country Joe McDonald
  "Rock and Roll Music from Planet   (Fantasy)
    Earth"

Go Where You Wanna Go   The Mamas and The Papas
  "Sixteen of Their Greatest Hits"   (ABC/Dunhill)
  "If You Can Believe Your Eyes and   (ABC/Dunhill)
    Ears"

Head Up High   The Velvet Underground
  "Loaded"   (Cotillion)

DEFINITIVE SONGS

Hold On* "John Lennon/Plastic Ono Band"	John Lennon (Apple)
Hold Out "TRB II"	The Tom Robinson Band (Harvest)
I Am a Rock "Simon and Garfunkel's Greatest Hits"	Simon and Garfunkel (Columbia)
"Sounds of Silence"	(Columbia)
I'm Coming Home Again "Jaded Virgin"	Marshall Chapman (Polydor)
I Am, I Said "Gold"	Neil Diamond (MCA)
"Hot August Night"	(MCA)
I Believe in Myself "Urban Renewal"	Tower of Power (Warner Brothers)
I Can Feel You Crying "Headin' Home"	Gary Wright (Warner Brothers)
I Could Have Been a Sailor "I Could Have Been a Sailor"	Peter Allen (A&M)
If You Believe "George Harrison"	George Harrison (Dark Horse)
If You Could See the World Through My Eyes "Resolution"*	Andy Pratt (Nemperor)
I'm Easy "Nashville" (Soundtrack)	Keith Carradine (ABC)
Instant Karma "Shaved Fish"	John Lennon (Apple)
I'm Gonna Be King "New Masters"	Cat Stevens (Deram)
I'm OK "Pieces of Eight"	Styx (A&M)
I'm So Anxious "The Jukes"	Southside Johnny (Mercury)
I Got Life "Hair" (original Broadway cast)	Various Artists (RCA)
+I Got Life "Hair" (original cast)	Various Artists (RCA)
I Got Life "Hair" (Soundtrack)	Various Artists (RCA)

(I've Been) Searching So Long — Chicago (Columbia)
"Chicago IX—Chicago's Greatest Hits"

"Chicago VII" — (Columbia)

I've Got a Name — Jim Croce (ABC)
"Photographs and Memories" (ABC)
"I've Got a Name" (ABC)

I Know There's an Answer — The Beach Boys (Capitol)
"Pet Sounds"

I Know Who I Am — Tommy James and the Shondells (Roulette)

"Cellophane Symphony"*

I Need Me to Be for Me — Peter, Paul and Mary (Warner Brothers)
"Reunion"

Isn't It Nice — The Hollies (Epic)
"Moving Finger"

I Think I Found Myself — Eric Carmen (Arista)
"Boats Against the Current"

If You Were Wondering — Peter Allen (A&M)
"I Could Have Been a Sailor"

It's My Life — The Animals (ABKCO)
"Best of the Animals"

It's My Way — Buffy Sainte-Marie (Vanguard)
"The Best of Buffy Sainte-Marie"

It's Your Life — Andy Kim (Steed)
"Greatest Hits"

It's Your Thing — The Isley Brothers (T-Neck)
"The Isleys' Greatest Hits" (T-Neck)
"Timeless"

James — Billy Joel (Columbia)
"Turnstiles"

Just Imagine — The Illusion (Steed)
"The Illusion"*

Keep Yourself Alive — Queen (Elektra)
"Queen"

Laugh at Me — Sonny and Cher (Atco)
"The Best of Sonny and Cher"

+Laugh at Me — Mott the Hoople (Atlantic)
"Mott the Hoople"

DEFINITIVE SONGS

Let Yourself Go
"America Dreams"

Rubicon
(20th Century-Fox)

Living for Me
"American Boy and Girl"

Garland Jeffreys
(A&M)

Looking for Space
"Windsong"
"John Denver's Greatest Hits Vol. II"

John Denver
(RCA)
(RCA)

Looking Out for Number One
"Best of B.T.O. . . . (So Far)"

Bachman-Turner Overdrive
(Mercury)

Look to Your Soul
"Realization"*
"A Touch of Gold"

Johnny Rivers
(United Artists)
(United Artists)

Make Your Own Kind of Music
"Mama's Big Ones—Her Greatest Hits"

Mama Cass
(ABC/Dunhill)

Marathon Man
"Boats Against the Current"

Eric Carmen
(Arista)

Misunderstood

"Rough Mix"

Pete Townsend and Ronnie Lane
(MCA)

My Judgement Day
"At the Third Stroke"*

Russ Ballard
(Epic)

My Own Man
"Savage Return"

Savoy Brown
(London)

My Way
"Elvis Presley in Concert"

Elvis Presley
(RCA)

Native Son
"Native Sons"

Loggins and Messina
(Columbia)

Netherlands
"Netherlands"

Dan Fogelberg
(Full Moon/Epic)

New Rooms
"Dory Previn"*

Dory Previn
(Warner Brothers)

No Man's Land

"Against the Wind"

Bob Seger and the Silver Bullet Band
(Capitol)

Peace of Mind
"Boston"

Boston
(Epic)

Perceive It
"Sunset and Other Beginnings"*

Melanie
(Neighborhood)

DEFINITIVE SONGS

A Place in the Sun
"A Place in the Sun"
Pablo Cruise
(A&M)

Poems, Prayers and Promises
"John Denver's Greatest Hits"
"Poems, Prayers and Promises"
John Denver
(RCA)
(RCA)

Poor People
"O Lucky Man"
Alan Price
(Warner Brothers)

The Promised Land
"Darkness on the Edge of Town"
Bruce Springsteen
(Columbia)

The Real Me
"Quadrophenia"
The Who
(MCA/Track)

Remember Who You Are
"Back on the Right Track"
Sly Stone
(Warner Brothers)

Respect Yourself
"The Best of the Staple Singers"
The Staple Singers
(Stax)

Round the Bend
"Blue River"
Eric Andersen
(Columbia)

Sally
"Still Here"*
Ian Thomas Band
(Atlantic)

Shades of Gray
"The Monkees' Greatest Hits"
"The Best of the Monkees"
"Headquarters"*
The Monkees
(Arista)
(Arista)
(Colgems)

Shot in the Dark
"Adventures in Utopia"
Utopia
(Bearsville)

Simple Things
"Simple Things"
Carole King
(Avatar)

So Many Paths
"Sleeper Catcher"
Little River Band
(Harvest)

Songs for the Life
"A Man Must Carry On"
Jerry Jeff Walker
(MCA)

Stand
"Headin' Home"
Gary Wright
(Warner Brothers)

The Stranger
"The Stranger"
Billy Joel
(Columbia)

Take Me for What I'm Worth
"The History of the Searchers"
"The Golden Hour of the Searchers"
The Searchers
(Pye)
(Golden Hour)

Take Off Your Mask
"Peter"*
Peter Yarrow
(Warner Brothers)

DEFINITIVE SONGS

Taking Out Time
"Here We Go 'Round the Mulberry
 Bush"
Spencer Davis Group
(United Artists)

Thank You
"Greatest Hits"
Sly and the Family
 Stone
(Epic)

+Thank You
"Stop the World We Wanna Get On"*
Hearts of Stone
(Motown)

That's Not Me
"Pet Sounds"
The Beach Boys
(Capitol)

These Are Not My People
"Joe South's Greatest Hits"
Joe South
(Capitol)

Thinkin'
"Alive on Arrival"
Steve Forbert
(Nemperor)

This Is Your Life
"Commodores' Greatest Hits"
Commodores
(Motown)

Trust Yourself
"John Hall"
John Hall
(Asylum)

Tuesday's Dead
"Teaser and the Firecat"
Cat Stevens
(A&M)

Twisted
"Court and Spark"
Joni Mitchell
(Reprise)

+Twisted
"Bette Midler"
Bette Midler
(Atlantic)

Up to Yourself
"Passin' Thru"
The James Gang
(ABC)

Wake Up and Live
"Survival"
Bob Marley and the Wailers
(Island)

What's Exactly the Matter with Me?"
"Eve of Destruction"*
Barry McGuire
(ABC/Dunhill)

What's Important to You
"Shiver in the Night"
Andy Pratt
(Nemperor)

What Kinda Guy
"Alive on Arrival"
Steve Forbert
(Nemperor)

Who Am I?
"The Life and Times of Country Joe
 and the Fish From Haight-Ashbury
 to Woodstock"
Country Joe McDonald
(Vanguard)

DEFINITIVE SONGS

Who Are You
"Who Are You"

The Who
(MCA)

Who I Really Am
"The Don Harrison Band"

Don Harrison Band
(Atlantic)

Why Can't I Be Like Other Girls
"Jaded Virgin"

Marshall Chapman
(Epic)

Within You, Without You
"Sgt. Pepper's Lonely Hearts Club
    Band"

The Beatles
(Capitol)

Words from the Wise
"Giant for a Day"

Gentle Giant
(Capitol)

You Are Yourself
"Daltrey"

Roger Daltrey
(MCA/Track)

You've Been Around Too Long
"Fantasy"

Carole King
(Ode)

Your Own Man
"The Fish"*

Barry Melton
(Firesign)

REFERENCE SONGS

Couldn't Get It Right
"Gold Plated"

Climax Blues Band
(Sire)

Crippled Inside
"Imagine"

John Lennon
(Apple)

Desperate Fools
"Change of Heart"

Eric Carmen
(Arista)

Do Anything You Wanna Do
"Life on the Line"

Eddie and the Hot Rods
(Island)

Easy
"Commodores' Greatest Hits"
"Commodores"

Commodores
(Motown)
(Motown)

Faking It
"Bookends"

Simon and Garfunkel
(Columbia)

Father and Son
"Tea for the Tillerman"
"Greatest Hits"

Cat Stevens
(A&M)
(A&M)

+Father and Son
"The Great Blind Degree"*

Richie Havens
(Stormy Forest)

REFERENCE SONGS

Fixing a Hole
"Sgt. Pepper's Lonely Hearts Club
    Band"

The Beatles
(Capitol)

+Fixing a Hole
"Sgt. Pepper's Lonely Hearts Club
    Band Soundtrack"

George Burns
(RSO)

Flowers Are Red
"Living Room Suite"

Harry Chapin
(Elektra)

The Grand Illusion
"The Grand Illusion"

Styx
(A&M)

Happiness Runs
"Barabajagal"

Donovan
(Epic)

I Stand Tall
"Bloodbrothers"

The Dictators
(Elektra)

In My Room
"Endless Summer"
"The Beach Boys in Concert"

The Beach Boys
(Capitol)
(Capitol)

In the Beginning
"On the Threshold of a Dream"
"This Is the Moody Blues"

The Moody Blues
(Deram)
(Threshold)

Just the Way You Are
"The Stranger"

Billy Joel
(Columbia)

+Just the Way You Are
"The Man"

Barry White
(20th Century Records)

Live Life
"Misfits"

The Kinks
(Arista)

Look in the Mirror
"Bare Wires"

John Mayall
(London)

Magic Mirror
"Carney"

Leon Russell
(Shelter)

Man in the Mirror
"Captured Angel"

Dan Fogelberg
(Full Moon/Epic)

Patterns
"Parsley, Sage, Rosemary and Thyme"

Simon and Garfunkel
(Columbia)

Stand
"Greatest Hits"
"Stand"

Sly and the Family Stone
(Epic)
(Epic)

Take It Easy
"Their Greatest Hits 1971–1975"
"Eagles"

The Eagles
(Asylum)
(Asylum)

REFERENCE SONGS

+Take It Easy
  "For Everyman"

Jackson Browne
(Asylum)

YOUR ADDITIONAL SONGS

_____

_____

_____

_____

_____

SEXUALITY

Sexuality—more about the choice and attitudes . . . than the perform-ance.

The wide variety of "sex" songs made it difficult to divide up this cate-gory. We finally decided to select songs about sexual attitudes and prefer-ence.

1. Virginity/First Time
2. Masturbation
3. One-night Stands
4. Alternative Sexual Preferences

(N.B. For even further categorization, songs about "one-night stands" within marriage are listed in the "Marriage" section under "Adultery." In addition, songs about intimate lovemaking are found in the section "Twenty Emotions and Themes of Love" under "Feel Like Makin' Love.")

Related Categories: Growing Up, Self-Identity, Teen-age
 Years/Adolescence

 +Same as Song Above
 *Hard-to-find Songs/Albums

YOUR ADDITIONAL SONGS

_____

_____

_____

_____

_____

Virginity/First Time

CLASSICS

| Only the Good Die Young | Billy Joel |
| "The Stranger" | (Columbia) |

CLASSICS

Waited So Long   Carly Simon
"No Secrets"   (Elektra)

DEFINITIVE SONGS

The Baby Sitter   Harry Chapin
"Portrait Gallery"   (Elektra)

Back Seat Baby   Cathy Chamberlain
"Rag 'n Roll Revue"*   (Warner Brothers)

December 1963 (Oh What a Night)   The Four Seasons
"Who Loves You"   (Warner Brothers)

Don't Touch Me There   The Tubes
"What Do You Want from Live"   (A&M)

Donna   Various Artists
"Hair" (Soundtrack)   (RCA)

Duncan   Paul Simon
"Paul Simon"   (Columbia)
"Greatest Hits Etc."   (Columbia)

First Affair   Artie Traum
"Life on Earth"*   (Rounder)

Fixture in the Park   Kate and Anna McGarrigle
"Pronto Monto"   (Warner Brothers)

Jefftown Creek   Head East
"Head East Live"   (A&M)

Look at Me, I'm Sandra Dee   Olivia Newton-John
"Grease" (Soundtrack)   (RSO)

Morning Girl   Neon Philharmonic
"The Moth Confesses"*   (Warner Brothers)

Paradise by the Dashboard Light   Meat Loaf
"Bat Out of Hell"   (Epic)

Shake It Up   Trigger
"Trigger"   (Casablanca)

Sweet Surrender   Robert Gordon with Link
                                        Wray
"Robert Gordon with Link Wray"   (RCA)

This Girl Has Turned into a Woman   Mary MacGregor
"Torn Between Two Lovers"   (Ariola/America)

Tonight's the Night   Rod Stewart
"Night on the Town"   (Warner Brothers)

DEFINITIVE SONGS

Underneath the Moon "Seductive Reasoning"*	Maggie and Terre Roche (Columbia)
Up in Lily's Room "Adjoining Suite"	Aztec Two Step (RCA)
Wiser Than You "If You Knew Suzi . . ."	Suzi Quatro (RSO)

REFERENCE SONGS

Dr. Jimmy "Quadrophenia"	The Who (MCA)
For Beginners Only "Rupert Holmes"	Rupert Holmes (Epic)
God of Thunder "Double Platinum"	Kiss (Casablanca)
Good Girls Don't "Get the Knack"	The Knack (Capitol)
The Grove of Eglantine "Best of Styx"	Styx (Wooden Nickel/RCA)
It's Different for Girls "I'm the Man"	Joe Jackson (A&M)
Just the Wanting "Not Shy"	Walter Egan (Columbia)
Let's Go "Candy-O"	The Cars (Elektra)
She Shook Me Cold "The Man Who Sold the World"	David Bowie (RCA)

YOUR ADDITIONAL SONGS

_____

_____

_____

_____

_____

Masturbation

CLASSICS

Imaginary Lover	Atlanta Rhythm Section
"Champagne Jam"	(Polydor)
"Are You Ready?"	(Polydor)

DEFINITIVE SONGS

Five Finger Exercise	Christ Child
"Christ Child"*	(Buddah)
Makin' Love on the Phone	Suzanne Fellini
"Suzanne Fellini"	
Pictures of Lily	The Who
"Magic Bus"	(MCA/Track)
"Meaty Beaty Big and Bouncy"	(MCA/Track)
Sometimes a Fantasy	Billy Joel
"Glass House"	(Columbia)
Touching Me, Touching You	Squeeze
"Cool for Cats"	(A&M)
Young Girl's Blues	Donovan
"Mellow Yellow"	(Epic)
"Donovan in Concert"	(Epic)

REFERENCE SONGS

Captain Jack	Billy Joel
"Piano Man"	(Columbia)
Midwest Midnight	Michael Stanley
"Stage Pass"	(Epic)
Sodomy	Various Artists
"Hair" (original Broadway cast)	(RCA)
+Sodomy	Various Artists
"Hair" (original cast)	(RCA)
+Sodomy	Various Artists
"Hair" (Soundtrack)	(RCA)
You Can't Go Home with Your Hard-On	Leonard Cohen
"Death of a Ladies' Man"	(Warner Brothers)

YOUR ADDITIONAL SONGS

_____

_____

_____

_____

_____

One-Night Stands

CLASSICS

Better Place to Be "Sniper and Other Love Songs" "Greatest Stories—Live"	Harry Chapin (Elektra) (Elektra)
Love Song to a Stranger "From Every Stage"	Joan Baez (A&M)
Third Rate Romance "Late Night Radio"	Starland Vocal Band (Windsong)
+Third Rate Romance "Stacked Deck"	Amazing Rhythm Aces (ABC)
+Third Rate Romance "Learn to Love It"*	Jesse Winchester (Bearsville)

DEFINITIVE SONGS

All Through the Night "Starting Over"	Raspberries (Capitol)
Baby You Sure Look Good to Me Tonight "Spirit"	John Denver (RCA)
The Beautiful Strangers "Grand Tour"	Rod McKuen (Warner Brothers)
The Blond in the Blue T-Bird "Not Shy"	Walter Egan (Columbia)
Boy I Really Tied One On "Aftertones"	Janis Ian (Columbia)

DEFINITIVE SONGS

Chevy Van
"The Van" (Soundtrack)
Sammy John
(Warner Brothers)

Come On By
"My Own Way to Rock"
Burton Cummings
(Portrait)

Don't Say Nothing
"Rock and Roll Again"
New Commander Cody Band
(Arista)

Early Morning Strangers
"Barry Manilow 2"
Barry Manilow
(Arista)

First Affair
"Life on Earth"*
Artie Traum
(Rounder)

Gypsy in Flight
"Ringo the Fourth"
Ringo Starr
(Atlantic)

Help Me Make It Through the Night
"Me and Bobby McGee"
Kris Kristofferson
(Monument)

+Help Me Make It Through the Night
"Blessed Are"
Joan Baez
(Vanguard)

+Help Me Make It Through the Night
"Anthology"
Gladys Knight and The Pips
(Motown)

+Help Me Make It Through the Night
"Cycles"
Rod McKuen
(Buddah)

+Help Me Make It Through the Night
"Let Me Be There"
Olivia Newton-John
(MCA)

+Help Me Make It Through the Night
"Welcome to My World"
Elvis Presley
(RCA)

+Help Me Make It Through the Night
"Willie Nelson Sings Kris Kristofferson"
Willie Nelson
(Columbia)

I'll Be Your Baby Tonight
"John Wesley Harding"
Bob Dylan
(Columbia)

+I'll Be Your Baby Tonight
"Snow Bird"
Anne Murray
(Capitol)

+I'll Be Your Baby Tonight
"The Lady's Not for Sale"
Rita Coolidge
(A&M)

+I'll Be Your Baby Tonight
"A Retrospective"
Linda Ronstadt
(Capitol)

I Was Only Telling a Lie
"J.T."
James Taylor
(Columbia)

DEFINITIVE SONGS

Let's Spend the Night Together | The Rolling Stones
"Hot Rocks 1964–1971" | (London)
"Flowers" | (London)

+Let's Spend the Night Together | Smith
"A Group Called Smith"* | (ABC/Dunhill)

+Let's Spend the Night Together | Jerry Garcia
"Compliments of Garcia" | (Round)

+Let's Spend the Night Together | David Bowie
"Aladdin Sane" | (RCA)

+Let's Spend the Night Together | Fire and Rain
"Living Together" | (20th Century Records)

+Let's Spend the Night Together | Joe Simon
"Joe Simon, Today" | (Spring)

+Let's Spend the Night Together | Tina Turner
"Acid Queen" | (United Artists)

+Let's Spend the Night Together | Muddy Waters
"Electric Mud" | (Chess)

Lightning Love Affair | The Rubinoos
"Back to the Drawing Board" | (Beserkley)

Liza, Light the Candle | Eric Andersen
"Be True to You" | (Arista)

Love Me Tonight | Head East
"Flat As a Pancake" | (A&M)
"Head East Live" | (A&M)

Love the One You're with | Crosby, Stills, Nash
 | & Young
"Four Way Street" | (Atlantic)

+Love the One You're with | Stephen Stills
"Stephen Stills" | (Atlantic)
"Still Stills . . . The Best of Stephen | (Atlantic)
 Stills"

+Love the One You're with | The Isley Brothers
"The Best . . . Isley Brothers" | (T-Neck)

Make Love to You | Stills/Young Band
"Long May You Run" | (Warner Brothers)

Morning After | Deaf School
"English Boys" | (Warner Brothers)

Norwegian Wood | The Beatles
"Rubber Soul" | (Capitol)
"Love Songs" | (Capitol)

DEFINITIVE SONGS

An Old Song "Avalanche"*	Eric Andersen (Warner Brothers)
One Night Stand "Windfall"	Rick Nelson (MCA)
One Night Stand "Michael Kenny"	Michael Kenny (Tom Cat/RCA)
One Night Stand "A Song"	Neil Sedaka (Elektra)
One Night Stand "Two Sides of the Moon"	Keith Moon (MCA)
One Night Stand "One Night Stand"	Fandango (RCA)
Oowotonite "Live at the El Macambo"	April Wine (London)
The Photographer "Circles and Seasons"	Pete Seeger (Warner Brothers)
Real Good Time "Stage Pass"	Michael Stanley Band (Epic)
Sharing the Night Together "Pleasure and Pain"	Dr. Hook (Capitol)
Single Man's Dilemma "One of the Boys"	Roger Daltrey (MCA)
Someone to Lay Down Beside Me "Hasten Down the Wind"	Linda Ronstadt (Asylum)
+Someone to Lay Down Beside Me "Karla Bonoff"	Karla Bonoff (Columbia)
Traveling Boy "Life Goes On"	Paul Williams (A&M)
+Traveling Boy "Angel Clare"	Art Garfunkel (Columbia)
Until the Real Thing Comes Along "Like an Old Fashioned Waltz"	Sandy Denny (Island)
+Until the Real Thing Comes Along "The Ravens"	The Ravens (Savoy/Arista)
We've Got Tonight "Stranger in Town"	Bob Seger and the Silver Bullet Band (Capitol)

REFERENCE SONGS

Down to You "Court and Spark"	Joni Mitchell (Reprise)
Holiday Romance "A Soap Opera"	The Kinks (RCA)
Hotels and One Night Stands "Janis Ian"	Janis Ian (Columbia)
I Wake Up Slow "We're Children of Coincidence and Harpo Marx"*	Dory Previn (Warner Brothers)
Last Summer "Blondes Have More Fun"	Rod Stewart (Warner Brothers)
She Loves to Hear the Music "It's Time for Peter Allen"	Peter Allen (A&M)
+She Loves to Hear the Music "She Loves to Hear the Music"	Sylvia Sims (A&M)
Stay Awhile (45 RPM Single)*	The Bells (Polydor)
Take Me Home with You "Melanie"*	Melanie (Buddah)
Tonight I'll Be Staying Here with You "Nashville Skyline"	Bob Dylan (Columbia)
Why Don't We Get Drunk (and Screw) "A White Sports Coat and a Pink Crustacean"	Jimmy Buffett (ABC)
"You Had to Be There"	(ABC)
Will You Still Love Me Tomorrow? "Tapestry"	Carole King (Ode)
+Will You Still Love Me Tomorrow? "The Very Best of the Shirelles"	The Shirelles (United Artists)
+Will You Still Love Me Tomorrow? "Cher Sings the Hits"*	Cher (Springboard)
+Will You Still Love Me Tomorrow? (45 RPM Single) "Mariposa de Oro"	Dave Mason (Columbia) (Columbia)
+Will You Still Love Me Tomorrow? "A Retrospective"	Linda Ronstadt (Capitol)
+Will You Still Love Me Tomorrow? "Quiet Fire"	Roberta Flack (Atlantic)

REFERENCE SONGS

+Will You Still Love Me Tomorrow?   Four Seasons
  "The Four Seasons Story"   (Private Stock)

+Will You Still Love Me Tomorrow?   Rod McKuen
  "Sleep Warm"*   (Warner Brothers)

+Will You Still Love Me Tomorrow?   Smokey Robinson & the
                                             Miracles
  "Smokey"   (Tamla)

+Will You Still Love Me Tomorrow?   Michael Stanley Band
  "Stagepass"   (Epic)

YOUR ADDITIONAL SONGS

_____   _____

_____   _____

_____   _____

_____   _____

_____

Alternative Sexual Preferences

CLASSICS

Glad to Be Gay   The Tom Robinson Band
"Power in the Darkness"   (Harvest)

The Killing of Georgie   Rod Stewart
"A Night on the Town"   (Warner Brothers)

Lola   The Kinks
"Kink Kronikles"   (Reprise)
"Lola Versus Powerman and the   (Reprise)
  Moneygoround"

Walk on the Wild Side   Lou Reed
"Transformer"   (RCA)
"Live—Take No Prisoners"   (Arista)

DEFINITIVE SONGS

All the Young Girls Love Alice   Elton John
"Goodbye Yellow Brick Road"   (MCA)

DEFINITIVE SONGS

The Alter Boy and the Thief
"Blown Away"
Joan Baez
(A&M)

Anita O.J.
"Heroes"
Tom Paxton
(Vanguard)

Anita's Crusaders
(45 RPM Single)*
Ron Kauffman
(Miami Victory Records)

Baby Face
"Sally Can't Dance"
Lou Reed
(RCA)

Black Angel
"TRB II"
The Tom Robinson Band
(Harvest)

Bobbi and Maria
"Ain't No Backing Up Now"*
Isis
(Buddah)

Cherry Poppin'
"How I Spent My Vacation"
Mitch Ryder
(Seeds and Stems)

Closet Man
"Living Without Your Love"
Dusty Springfield
(United Artists)

Crossing Over the Road
"TRB II"
The Tom Robinson Band
(Harvest)

David Watts
"Something Else By The Kinks"
The Kinks
(Reprise)

+David Watts
"All Mod Cons"
The Jam
(Polydor)

Down in the City
"Down in the Bunker"
Steve Gibbons Band
(Polydor)

Earache My Eye
"Up in Smoke"
Cheech and Chong
(Warner Brothers)

Hollywood Babies
"Com'n Back for More"*
David Blue
(Asylum)

Hurricane Anita
(45 RPM Single)*
Lynn Friggel
(Miami Victory Records)

I Was Born That Way
(45 RPM Single)*
Carl Bean
(Motown)

The Jon
"How I Spent My Vacation"
Mitch Ryder
(Seeds and Stems)

Lady Stardust
"The Rise and Fall of Ziggy Stardust"
"Stage"
David Bowie
(RCA)
(RCA)

DEFINITIVE SONGS

My Roommate
"Cruisin' "

Village People
(Casablanca)

Out of the Wardrobe
"Misfits"

The Kinks
(Arista)

Paradise George
"Fearless"

Tim Curry
(A&M)

Queen Bitch
"Hunky Dory"
"Stage"

David Bowie
(RCA)
(RCA)

Rebel, Rebel
"Diamond Dogs"
"Changesonebowie"

David Bowie
(RCA)
(RCA)

Rosie
"How Cruel"

Joan Armatrading
(A&M)

S&M
" 'Well, Well,' Said the Rocking
    Chair"*

Dean Friedman
(Lifesong)

Sweet Thing
"Diamond Dog"

David Bowie
(RCA)

Sweet Transvestite

"Dr. Frank N. Furter" (Tim
    Curry)

"The Rocky Horror Picture Show"
    (Soundtrack)

(Ode)

Untitled
"Unrequited"*

Loudon Wainwright III
(Columbia)

When the Whip Comes Down
"Some Girls"

The Rolling Stones
(Rolling Stone Records)

Y.M.C.A.
"Cruisin' "
"Live and Sleazy"

The Village People
(Casablanca)
(Casablanca)

REFERENCE SONGS

Better Decide Which Side You're On
"Power in the Darkness"

The Tom Robinson Band
(Harvest)

Half a Man
"Born Again"

Randy Newman
(Warner Brothers)

Long Hot Summer
"Power in the Darkness"

The Tom Robinson Band
(Harvest)

REFERENCE SONGS

Men Who Love Women Who Love   Steve Goodman
    Men
"High and Outside"   (Elektra)
Width of a Circle   David Bowie
"The Man Who Sold the World"   (RCA)

YOUR ADDITIONAL SONGS

_____

_____

_____

_____

_____

STARDOM

Stardom—hopeful . . . happening . . . has-been.
The fantasy of stardom is often far different from the reality. These songs talk about stardom in all of its stages: the struggle, the achievement, the glory and/or disenchantment, and, for some, the loss.

Related Categories: Hope/Optimism, Money, Self-Identity

+Same as Song Above
*Hard-to-find Songs/Albums

CLASSICS

Celluloid Heroes	The Kinks
"Celluloid Heroes"	(RCA)
"Everybody's in Showbiz"	(RCA)
Legend in Your Own Time	Carly Simon
"The Best of Carly Simon Vol. I"	(Elektra)
"Anticipation"	(Elektra)
Lonely at the Top	Randy Newman
"Sail Away"	(Reprise)
On Broadway	The Drifters
"Sixteen Greatest Hits"	(Trip)
"Twenty-Four Original Hits"	(Atlantic)
+On Broadway	The Dave Clark Five
"Return"*	(Epic)
+On Broadway	Eric Carmen
"Eric Carmen"	(Arista)
+On Broadway	George Benson
"Weekend in L.A."	(Warner Brothers)
+On Broadway	The Vogues
"Till"*	(Reprise)
+On Broadway	Barry Mann
"Lay It All Out"*	(Columbia)
So You Wanna Be a Rock and Roll Star	The Byrds
"The Byrds' Greatest Hits"	(Columbia)
"Younger Than Yesterday"	(Columbia)
"Untitled"	(Columbia)

CLASSICS

+So You Wanna Be a Rock and Roll Star	The Royal Guardsmen
"Return of the Red Baron"	(Laurie)
+So You Wanna Be a Rock and Roll Star	Black Oak Arkansas
"The Best of Black Oak Arkansas"	(Atco)
+So You Want to Be a Rock and Roll Star	Nazareth
"Nazareth"	(Warner Brothers)
+So You Wanna Be a Rock and Roll Star	Patti Smith
"Wave"	(Arista)

DEFINITIVE SONGS

A-1 on the Jukebox	Dave Edmunds
"Tracks on Wax 4"	(Swan Song)
Act Naturally	The Beatles
"Yesterday and Today"	(Capitol)
Ain't He a Genius	Jimmy Buffett
"Before the Salt"	(Barnaby)
All the World Is a Stage	Slade
"Nobody's Fool"	(Warner Brothers)
American Beauty Rose	The Movies
"The Movies"*	(Arista)
Another Pop Star's Life	Flo and Eddie
"Flo and Eddie"	(Warner Brothers)
Attila's Blues	The Guess Who
"Road Food"*	(RCA)
Autograph	Kinky Friedman
"Kinky Friedman"*	(ABC)
Ballad of Mott	Mott the Hoople
"Greatest Hits"	(Columbia)
Bronco Bill's Lament	Don McLean
"Don McLean"*	(United Artists)
"Solo"	(United Artists)
Candle in the Wind	Elton John
"Goodbye Yellow Brick Road"	(MCA)
Child Star	T-Rex
"Tyrannosaurus Rex (A Beginning)"	(A&M)

DEFINITIVE SONGS

Company Man "Flag"	James Taylor (Columbia)
Do You Know the Way to San Jose? "The Very Best of Dionne Warwick"	Dionne Warwick (United Artists)
Don't Wait Too Long "Three Hearts"	Bob Welch (Capitol)
Drive My Car "Yesterday and Today"	The Beatles (Capitol)
The Entertainer "Streetlife Serenade"	Billy Joel (Columbia)
+The Entertainer "Live in London"	Helen Reddy (Capitol)
Everybody Is a Star "Greatest Hits"	Sly and the Family Stone (Epic)
+Everybody Is a Star "Energy"	The Pointer Sisters (Planet)
Everybody's a Star (Starmaker) "A Soap Opera"	The Kinks (RCA)
Everybody's Goin' Hollywood "American Gypsies"*	Galdston and Thom (Warner Brothers)
Everybody's Making It But Me "Bankrupt"	Dr. Hook (Capitol)
Everything "Eric Carmen"	Eric Carmen (Arista)
Fame "Young Americans" "Changesonebowie" "Stage"	David Bowie (RCA) (RCA) (RCA)
Fame and Fortune "Worldwide 50 Gold Award Hits, Vol. 2"	Elvis Presley (RCA)
Faster "George Harrison"	George Harrison (Dark Horse)
For the Roses "For the Roses"	Joni Mitchell (Asylum)
Gonna Be a Star "Rock On"	David Essex (Columbia)
Good Night Mrs. Calabash "Good Night Mrs. Calabash"*	Ian Thomas (Janus)

DEFINITIVE SONGS

The Great Hall of Fame "Tall Tales"*	Richard Supa (Polydor)
Hey Mister, That's Me Up on the Juke Box "Mud Slide Slim and the Blue Horizon"	James Taylor (Warner Brothers)
+Hey Mister, That's Me Up on the Juke Box "Prisoner in Disguise"	Linda Ronstadt (Asylum)
Hollywood "Down Two Then Left"	Boz Scaggs (Columbia)
Hollywood Dream ⚡1 & 2 "Hollywood Dream"*	Thunderclap Newman (MCA/Track)
Hollywood Heckle and Jive "Dr. Heckle and Mr. Jive"	England Dan and John Ford Coley (Big Tree)
Hollywood Hopeful "T-Shirt"*	Loudon Wainwright III (Arista)
Hollywood Lady "A Song"	Neil Sedaka (Elektra)
Hollywood Sue "Blue Ridge Mountain Skyline"*	Sammy Walker (Warner Brothers)
Honey Pie "The Beatles" (White Album)	The Beatles (Apple)
Hooray for Hollywood "Motion"*	Geoff Muldaur (Reprise)
I Wanna Be a Star "People Like Us"	The Mamas and The Papas (ABC/Dunhill)
Idol "Blue Moves"	Elton John (MCA)
I'm a Star "Survivors"	Randy Bachman (Polydor)
I'm Going to Be a Teenage Idol "Don't Shoot Me I'm Only the Piano Player"	Elton John (MCA)
I'm Nearly Famous "I'm Nearly Famous"	Cliff Richards (Rocket)
In Hollywood "Live and Sleazy"	Village People (Casablanca)

DEFINITIVE SONGS

James Dean "On the Border"	The Eagles (Asylum)
Jingle "Letting Go"*	Lori Lieberman (Millennium)
King of Hollywood "The Long Run"	The Eagles (Asylum)
Let's Get the Show on the Road "Stage Pass"	Michael Stanley (Epic)
Life in the Fast Lane "Hotel California"	The Eagles (Asylum)
Life's Been Good "FM" (Soundtrack) "But Seriously, Folks"	Joe Walsh (MCA) (Asylum)
Long Way to the Top "High Voltage"	AC/DC (Atco)
Make It All So Real "Jackrabbit Slim"	Steve Forbert (Nemperor)
Most of Us Are Sad "Eagles"	The Eagles (Asylum)
Name Up in Lights "New Directions"	The Meters (Warner Brothers)
New Age "Loaded"	The Velvet Underground (Cotillion)
On Broadway Tonight "Rag Doll"*	The Four Seasons (Philips)
Overnight Sensation "Starting Over"	Raspberries (Capitol)
Overnight Sensation "Phil Cody"*	Phil Cody (Reprise)
Peg "Aja" "Steely Dan's Greatest Hits"	Steely Dan (ABC) (ABC)
Pop Star "Mona Bone Jakon"	Cat Stevens (A&M)
Quiet Please, There's a Lady on Stage (For Judy Garland) "It's Time for Peter Allen"	Peter Allen (A&M)
Revue "Cool for Cats"	Squeeze (A&M)

DEFINITIVE SONGS

Right Profile "London Calling"	The Clash (Epic)
Rock and Roll Baby "The Best of the Stylistics"	The Stylistics (Avco)
Rock and Roll I Gave You the Best Years of My Life (45 RPM Single)	Kevin Johnson (UK)
Rock It to the Stars "No Accident"*	Driver (A&M)
See You on the Other Side "The Doctor Is In"	Ben Sidran (Arista)
Send the Man Over "Cherished"	Cher (Warner Brothers)
She's a Star "Tryin' to Get the Feeling Again"	Barry Manilow (Arista)
She's in the Toothpaste Commercial "Thorn on the Rose"*	Even Stevens (Elektra)
Shining Star "Spirit" "Earth, Wind and Fire's Greatest Hits"	Earth, Wind and Fire (Columbia) (Columbia)
Shooting Star "Straight Shooter"	Bad Company (Swan Song)
The Show Must Go On "Joy to the World"	Three Dog Night (ABC)
+The Show Must Go On "Leo Sayer"	Leo Sayer (Warner Brothers)
A Showman's Life "A Touch on the Rainy Side"*	Jesse Winchester (Bearsville)
Sitting in My Hotel "Everybody's in Show Biz"	The Kinks (RCA)
Somewhere in Hollywood "10 CC"	10 CC (UK)
So You Are a Star "Hollywood Situation"*	Hudson Brothers (Warner Brothers)
Stage Door "Songwriter"	Justin Hayward (Deram)
Stage Door Johnnies "Stage Door Johnnies"*	Claire Hamill (Konk)

DEFINITIVE SONGS

Star	Nazareth
"No Mean City"	(A&M)
Star	Stealers Wheel
"Ferguslie Park"*	(A&M)
"The Best of Stealers Wheel"	(A&M)
Star	David Bowie
"The Rise and Fall of Ziggy Stardust and the Spiders from Mars"	(RCA)
"Stage"	(RCA)
Star	The Hollies
"Hollies Live"	(Epic)
Star in the Dust	Walter Egan
"Not Shy"	(Columbia)
A Star in the Ghetto	Average White Band and Ben E. King
"Benny and Us"	(Atlantic)
Star Tripper	Harry Chapin
"Portrait Gallery"	(Elektra)
Starmaker	Judy Collins
"Hard Times for Lovers"	(Elektra)
Stars	Janis Ian
"Stars"	(Columbia)
Sunset People	Donna Summers
"Bad Girls"	(Casablanca)
Superstar	The Temptations
"Anthology—Tenth Anniversary Special"	(Motown)
Superstars	Styx
"The Grand Illusion"	(A&M)
Survivor	Randy Bachman
"Survivor"	(Polydor)
Teenage Idol	Rick Nelson
"Ricky Nelson" (Anthology)	(United Artists)
Teenage Idol	Keith Moon
"Two Sides of the Moon"	(MCA)
To Be a Star	Cat Stevens
"Izitso"	(A&M)
To Be Someone	The Jam
"All Mod Cons"	(Polydor)

DEFINITIVE SONGS

Top of the Pops "Everybody's in Show Biz" "Lola Versus Powerman and the Moneygoround"	The Kinks (RCA) (Reprise)
Tough Guys "Ratcity in Blue"*	The Good Rats (Ratcity/Platinum)
Until We Meet Again "Chesapeake Juke Box Band"*	Chesapeake Juke Box Band (Green Bottle Records)
Vicious Circle "The Fabulous Rhinestones"*	The Fabulous Rhinestones (Just Sunshine Records)
Virginia Days' Ragtime Memories "The Collage"*	The Collage (Smash)
Wanna Be a Rock and Roll Star "Eddie Money"	Eddie Money (Columbia)
(A) Well Known Has-Been "Slowdown World"*	Donovan (Epic)
Yesterday's Heroes "Greatest Hits"	Bay City Rollers (Arista)
Your Favorite Entertainer "Phil Cody"*	Phil Cody (Reprise)

REFERENCE SONGS

Citizen Kane "Byrdmaniax" "The Best of the Byrds Greatest Hits, Vol. II"	The Byrds (Columbia) (Columbia)
The Comedian "We're Children of Coincidence and Harpo Marx"*	Dory Previn (Warner Brothers)
Diana "Tender Man"*	Jae Mason (Buddah)
Emma "Ten Greatest Hits"	Hot Chocolate (Big Tree)
Green Tambourine "Green Tambourine"*	The Lemon Pipers (Buddah)
+Green Tambourine "Both Sides Now"	The Tokens (Buddah)
Hotels and One Night Stands "Janis Ian"	Janis Ian (Columbia)

REFERENCE SONGS

Last of the Singing Cowboys
"Running Like the Wind"
The Marshall Tucker Band
(Capricorn)

Ooh Girl
"The Reggie Knighton Band"*
The Reggie Knighton Band
(Columbia)

The Prize
"Good Book"*
Melanie
(Buddah)

Recognition
"Detection"
Detective
(Swan Song)

Riders to the Night
"Live"
Barry Manilow
(Arista)

Rosalinda's Eyes
"52nd Street"
Billy Joel
(Columbia)

Spooky Lady's Revenge
"Easter Island"
Kris Kristofferson
(Monument)

Star Baby
"Road Food"*
The Guess Who
(RCA)

Star Collector
"Pisces, Aquarius, Capricorn and
    Jones Ltd."*
The Monkees
(Colgems)

Star Star
"Goats Head Soup"
The Rolling Stones
(Rolling Stone Records)

Starstruck
"Village Green Preservation Society"
The Kinks
(RCA)

Sunrise on Sunset
"The Hollywood Starz"*
The Hollywood Starz
(Arista)

YOUR ADDITIONAL SONGS

_____

_____

_____

_____

SUBURBIA

Suburbia—the American dream . . . or nightmare.
Rock and roll today is largely supported by the dollars of suburbanites, yet most of these songs focus more on the negative aspects of suburban living.

Related Categories: Big Business, Marriage: Unhappily Married, Money, Rat Race, Working

+Same as Song Above
*Hard-to-find Songs/Albums

CLASSICS

Little Boxes "The World of Pete Seeger"	Pete Seeger (Columbia)
Movin' Out (Anthony's Songs) "The Stranger"	Billy Joel (Columbia)
Pleasant Valley Sunday "The Monkees' Greatest Hits" "Pisces, Aquarius, Capricorn and Jones Ltd."*	The Monkees (Arista) (Colgems)

THEMATIC ALBUMS

"Arthur"	The Kinks (Reprise)
"A Soap Opera"	The Kinks (RCA)
"Village Green Preservation Society"	The Kinks (Reprise)

DEFINITIVE SONGS

Blame It on the Rolling Stones "Me and Bobby McGee"	Kris Kristofferson (Monument)
Bright Suburban Mr. and Mrs. Clean "Together"*	Country Joe McDonald (Vanguard)
Captain Jack "Piano Man"	Billy Joel (Columbia)

DEFINITIVE SONGS

Don't Let the Joneses Get You Down "Anthology—Tenth Anniversary Special"	The Temptations (Motown)
The Great Suburban Showdown "Streetlife Serenade"	Billy Joel (Columbia)
Janey's Blues "Janis Ian"	Janis Ian (Polydor)
Just a Story from America "Just a Story from America"*	Elliott Murphy (Columbia)
A Lifetime to Pay "Aliens"	Horslips (DJM Records)
Mr. Clean "All Mod Cons"	The Jam (Polydor)
Mr. Penny Pincher "Hour of the Wolf"*	Steppenwolf (Epic)
Mr. Pleasant "Kink Kronikles"	The Kinks (RCA)
The Other Man's Grass Is Always Greener "The Other Man's Grass Is Always Greener"	Petula Clark (Warner Brothers)
Proper Ornaments of Life "Kites Are Fun"*	Free Design (Project)
Rockin' Shopping Center "Jonathan Richman and the Modern Lovers"	Jonathan Richman and the Modern Lovers (Beserkley)
Shangri-la "Kink Kronikles" "Arthur"	The Kinks (Reprise) (Reprise)
Village Green "Village Green Preservation Society"	The Kinks (RCA)
Village Green Preservation Society "Village Green Preservation Society"	The Kinks (RCA)
Weekend Song "Streetlife Serenade"	Billy Joel (Columbia)
Well Respected Man "The Kinks' Greatest Hits" "The History of the Kinks Vol. II"	The Kinks (Reprise) (Pye)

DEFINITIVE SONGS

+Well Respected Man
"Hits of the 60's"

The Bachelors
(London)

+Well Respected Man

Gary Lewis and the
Playboys

"Hits Again"

(Liberty)

Where Did All My Friends Go?
"The Eyes of an Only Child"*

Tom Jans
(Columbia)

You Make It All Worthwhile
"A Soap Opera"

The Kinks
(RCA)

REFERENCE SONGS

The American Dream
"Confessions of a Male Chauvinist
    Pig"*

Artie Kaplan
(Hopi/Vanguard)

The Arrangement
"Ladies of the Canyon"

Joni Mitchell
(Reprise)

Family Man
"Worlds Away"

Pablo Cruise
(A&M)

Funny Farm Blues
"Song for Patty"*

Sammy Walker
(Vanguard)

Living in the Material World
"Living in the Material World"

George Harrison
(Apple)

Night of the Living Dead
"American Boy and Girl"

Garland Jeffreys
(A&M)

Look Through Any Window
"The Very Best of the Hollies"

The Hollies
(United Artists)

Makin' Love
"Shine On"

Climax Blues Band
(Sire)

19th Nervous Breakdown
"Hot Rocks 1964–1971"
"Flowers"

The Rolling Stones
(London)
(London)

Plastic Man
"Masterpiece"

The Temptations
(Motown)

Sign Your Life Away
"The Barbecue of Deville"

Hoo Doo Rhythm Aces
(Blue Thumb)

Small Town Talk
"Rick Danko"

Rick Danko
(Arista)

+Small Town Talk
"Rising Son"

Yvonne Elliman
(RSO)

REFERENCE SONGS

Step Right Up	Tom Waits
"Small Change"	(Asylum)
Sunny Afternoon	The Kinks
"Kink Kronikles"	(RCA)
U.M.C.	Bob Seger and the Silver Bullet Band
"Live Bullet"	(Capitol)
"Seven"	(Capitol)
We're a Happy Family	The Ramones
"Rocket to Russia"	(Sire)

YOUR ADDITIONAL SONGS

_____

_____

_____

_____

_____

SUICIDE

Suicide 30,000 in the United States last year.
  These are moving portraits of tragic suicidal situations. There are also a few humorous looks at what has become a very serious problem in our society today, especially among young people.

Related Categories: Death, Loneliness

  +Same as Song Above
  *Hard-to-find Songs/Albums

CLASSICS

Fire and Rain "Sweet Baby James" "Greatest Hits"	James Taylor (Warner Brothers) (Warner Brothers)
+Fire and Rain "Poems, Prayers and Promises"	John Denver (RCA)
+Fire and Rain "Snowbound"	Anne Murray (Capitol)
+Fire and Rain "The Best . . . Isley Brothers"	The Isley Brothers (Buddah)
+Fire and Rain "Standing Ovation"	Gladys Knight and The Pips (Soul)
+Fire and Rain "Homegrown"*	Johnny Rivers (United Artists)
+Fire and Rain "Communication"	Bobby Womack (United Artists)
A Most Peculiar Man "Sounds of Silence"	Simon and Garfunkel (Columbia)
Richard Cory "Sounds of Silence"	Simon and Garfunkel (Columbia)
+Richard Cory "Wings over America"	Wings (Capitol)
+Richard Cory	Them Featuring Van Morrison
"Backtrackin' "	(London)

DEFINITIVE SONGS

Accidental Suicide "Back to the Roots"	John Mayall (Polydor)
The Ballad of Lucy Jordan "Broken English"	Marianne Faithful (Island)
Barbara Allen "The World of Pete Seeger"	Pete Seeger (Columbia)
The Bed "Berlin"	Lou Reed (RCA)
Come Jeff "Back to Carnegie Hall"	Rod McKuen (Warner Brothers)
Emma "Ten Greatest Hits"	Hot Chocolate (Big Tree)
The End "Here"	Leo Sayer (Warner Brothers)
Endless Sleep "Innuendo"	Danny Kortchmar (Asylum)
Insanity Comes Quietly to the Structured Mind "For All the Seasons of Your Mind"	Janis Ian (Polydor)
I Think I'm Gonna Kill Myself "Don't Shoot Me I'm Only the Piano Player"	Elton John (MCA)
Life Goes On "Sleep Walker"	The Kinks (Arista)
Living in an Island "The Boomtown Rats"	The Boomtown Rats (Columbia)
Ode to Billy Joe "Ode to Billy Joe"	Bobbie Gentry (Capitol)
The Quiet Room "From the Inside"	Alice Cooper (Warner Brothers)
Reach Out "Take Heart"*	Mimi Fariña and Tom Jans (A&M)
Rock and Roll Suicide "The Rise and Fall of Ziggy Stardust and the Spiders from Mars"	David Bowie (RCA)
Save the Life of My Child "Bookends"	Simon and Garfunkel (Columbia)

DEFINITIVE SONGS

Scarred and Scared
"Blondes Have More Fun"
Rod Stewart
(Warner Brothers)

Someone's Final Song
"Blue Moves"
Elton John
(MCA)

Song for Adam
"Saturate Before Using"
Jackson Browne
(Asylum)

Song for Martin
"True Stories and Other Dreams"
Judy Collins
(Elektra)

Suicide
"Live and Dangerous"
Thin Lizzy
(Warner Brothers)

Suicide
"If You Knew Suzi . . ."
Suzi Quatro
(RSO)

Suicide Man
"Wonderworld"
Uriah Heep
(Warner Brothers)

Suicide Sal
"Suicide Sal"
Maggie Bell
(Swan Song)

Suicide Song
"Album II"*
Loudon Wainwright III
(Atlantic)

Sylvia
"Ralph McTell Live"
Ralph McTell
(Fantasy)

10 O'Clock and All Is Well
"Judy Collins #3"
Judy Collins
(Elektra)

Wait by the Water
"Dreams of a Child"
Burton Cummings
(Portrait)

Yer Blues
"The Beatles" (The White Album)
The Beatles
(Apple)

+Yer Blues
"The Plastic Ono Band—Live Peace in Toronto 1969"
John Lennon
(Apple)

REFERENCE SONGS

Candle in the Wind
"Goodbye Yellow Brick Road"
Elton John
(MCA)

I'm Not Gonna Let It Bother Me
"Champagne Jam"
Atlantic Rhythm Section
(Polydor)

Me and Baby Jane
"Carney"
Leon Russell
(Shelter)

Panic in Detroit
"Aladdin Sane"
David Bowie
(RCA)

REFERENCE SONGS

Phil

"Heroes"

Prison Trilogy

"Come from the Shadows"

Street in the City

"Rough Mix"

Tenth Floor Clown

"The Shirts"

Tom Paxton

(Vanguard)

Joan Baez

(A&M)

Peter Townsend and Ronnie
     Lane

(MCA)

The Shirts

(Capitol)

YOUR ADDITIONAL SONGS

_____

_____

_____

_____

_____

TEEN-AGE YEARS/ADOLESCENCE

Teen-age years/adolescence—the wild and the innocent, doin' the bad-boy shuffle.

The focus here is on the life-style rather than the process of growing up. As a matter of fact, rock has done more to create this life-style and the cult that has grown up around it than any other force on youth in history.

Related Categories: Changes, Growing Up, Schools/Educational Process, Violence

+Same as Song Above
*Hard-to-find Songs/Albums

CLASSICS

Blinded by the Light "Greetings from Asbury Park, N.J."	Bruce Springsteen (Columbia)
+Blinded by the Light "The Roaring Silence"	Manfred Mann (Warner Brothers)
Eighteen "Love It to Death" "Alice Cooper's Greatest Hits" "The Alice Cooper Show"	Alice Cooper (Warner Brothers) (Warner Brothers) (Warner Brothers)
I Don't Know What I Want "Starting Over"	Raspberries (Capitol)
My Generation "My Generation" "Live at Leeds"	The Who (MCA) (MCA)
+My Generation (45 RPM Single)	Patti Smith (Arista)

THEMATIC ALBUMS

"Quadrophenia"	The Who (MCA/Track)

DEFINITIVE SONGS

All Grown Up "Bionic Gold"*	Phillip Rambow (Big Sound)

DEFINITIVE SONGS

All the Kids on the Street
"Hollywood Starz"*

Hollywood Starz
(Arista)

All the Young Dudes
"Greatest Hits"
"Mott the Hoople Live"
"All the Young Dudes"

Mott the Hoople
(Columbia)
(Columbia)
(Columbia)

+All the Young Dudes
"Live Without a Net"

Angel
(Casablanca)

Bad Boy
"Beatles VI"
"Rock and Roll"

The Beatles
(Capitol)
(Capitol)

Bad Boy
"Can't Wait"*

Piper
(A&M)

Certain Kind of Fool
"Desperado"

The Eagles
(Asylum)

Cool Down Boy
"Ghost Writer"

Garland Jeffreys
(A&M)

Cut My Hair
"Quadrophenia"

The Who
(MCA)

Dark Eyed Johnny
"Round the Back"*

Cafe Jacques
(Columbia)

Department of Youth
"Welcome to My Nightmare"

Alice Cooper
(Atlantic)

Dr. Jimmy
"Quadrophenia"

The Who
(MCA)

Don't Push Me Around
"Live at the El Macombo"*

April Wine
(London)

Doo Doo Doo Doo Doo
 (Heartbreaker)
"Goats Head Soup"
"Made in the Shade"

The Rolling Stones

(Rolling Stone Records)
(Rolling Stone Records)

Down on the Corner

"Willy and the Poor Boys"
"1969"

Creedence Clearwater
 Revival
(Fantasy)
(Fantasy)

The E Street Shuffle
"The Wild, the Innocent and the E
 Street Shuffle"

Bruce Springsteen
(Columbia)

422   *The Rock Music Source Book*

Eddie
"The Rocky Horror Picture Show" (Soundtrack)

"Dr. Scott" (Jonathan Adams)
(Ode)

Fight from the Inside
"News of the World"

Queen
(Elektra)

5:15
"Quadrophenia"

The Who
(MCA)

Fooling Yourself
"Grand Illusion"

Styx
(A&M)

Growin' Up
"Greetings from Asbury Park, N.J."

Bruce Springsteen
(Columbia)

Guilty
"Alice Cooper Goes to Hell"

Alice Cooper
(Warner Brothers)

I'm a Boy
"Meaty Beaty Big and Bouncy"

The Who
(MCA)

In the Crowd
"All Mod Cons"

The Jam
(Polydor)

Johnny Hold Back
"No Second Chance"*

Charlie
(Janus)

Juvenile Delinquent
"Live at the El Macombo"

April Wine
(London)

Juvenile Song
"Birth Comes to Us All"

The Good Rats
(Arista)

The Kids Are Alright
"My Generation"
"Meaty Beaty Big and Bouncy"

The Who
(MCA)
(MCA)

+The Kids Are Alright
"Two Sides of the Moon"

Keith Moon
(MCA)

+The Kids Are Alright
"Teenage Depression"

Eddie and The Hot Rods
(Island)

King of the Nighttime World
"Kiss Alive II"

Kiss
(Casablanca)

Leave the Kids Alone
"Widowmaker"*

Widowmaker
(United Artists)

A Misspent Youth
"Seeds"

Gallagher and Lyle
(A&M)

Not a Woman, Not a Child
"Tracks on Wax 4"

Dave Edmunds
(Swan Song)

DEFINITIVE SONGS

One of the Boys
"One of the Boys"
Roger Daltrey
(MCA/Track)

Problem Child
"Stick to Me"
Graham Parker
(Mercury)

Problem Child
"Let There Be Rock"*
"If You Want Blood"
AC/DC
(Atco)
(Atlantic)

Rat Trap
"The Boomtown Rats"
The Boomtown Rats
(Columbia)

Runaway Child, Running Wild
"Anthology—Tenth Anniversary
  Special"
The Temptations
(Motown)

Saturday Night's Alright for Fighting
"Goodbye Yellow Brick Road"
"Greatest Hits"
Elton John
(MCA)
(MCA)

Street Boys
"Love on the Airwaves"
Gallagher and Lyle
(A&M)

Street Fight
"Mark Farner"*
Mark Farner
(Atlantic)

Street Kids
"Rock of the Westies"
Elton John
(MCA)

Teenage Crutch
"The Shirts"
The Shirts
(Capitol)

Teenage Lobotomy
"Rocket to Russia"
The Ramones
(Sire)

That's No Way to Spend Your Youth
"Give 'em Enough Rope"
The Clash
(Epic)

Ticking
"Caribou"
Elton John
(MCA)

To Try for the Sun
"Donovan P. Leitch"
Donovan
(Janus)

Tough Kid
"How I Spent My Vacation"
Mitch Ryder
(Seeds and Stems)

Trouble Boys
"Tracks on Wax 4"
Dave Edmunds
(Swan Song)

Twenty-One
"Desperado"
The Eagles
(Asylum)

Wild Age
"Bad Luck in Dancing School"
Warren Zevon
(Asylum)

DEFINITIVE SONGS

Wild and Hot
"Sinful"

Angel
(Casablanca)

Wild East
"You're Never Alone with a
    Schizophrenic"

Ian Hunter
(Chrysalis)

Wild Youth
"Generation X"*

Generation X
(Chrysalis)

Yakety Yak
"The Coasters' Early Years"
"Sixteen Greatest Hits"

The Coasters
(Atlantic)
(Trip)

Youth, Youth
"Generation X"*

Generation X
(Chrysalis)

REFERENCE SONGS

Born in Chicago
"Golden Butter/The Best of the Paul
    Butterfield Blues Band"
"The Paul Butterfield Band"

Paul Butterfield Blues Band
(Elektra)

(Elektra)

It's Hard to Be a Saint in the City
"Greetings from Asbury Park, N.J."

Bruce Springsteen
(Columbia)

Little Billy
"Odds and Sods"

The Who
(MCA)

On the Corner
"Brooklyn Dreams"

Brooklyn Dreams
(Millennium)

Street Fighting Man
"Hot Rocks 1964–1971"
"Beggars Banquet"

The Rolling Stones
(London)
(London)

+Street Fighting Man
"The Best of Rod Stewart"

Rod Stewart
(Mercury)

Street Man
"Sleepless Nights"

Brooklyn Dreams
(Casablanca)

Sure the Boy Was Green
"Aliens"

Horslips
(DJM Records)

Tenth Avenue Freeze-Out
"Born to Run"

Bruce Springsteen
(Columbia)

Trouble
"Spanky and Our Gang"*

Spanky and Our Gang
(Mercury)

REFERENCE SONGS

Wild Child	The Doors
"13"	(Elektra)
"Soft Parade"	(Elektra)

YOUR ADDITIONAL SONGS

_____

_____

_____

_____

_____

URBAN/CITY LIFE

Urban/city life—the symbol of our imagination, sophistication, and degradation, side by side.

Not songs about specific cities, e.g. New York or Los Angeles *per se*, but rather songs about some positive and mostly negative aspects of city living.

Related Categories: America, Poverty, Rat Race, Working

+Same as Song Above
*Hard-to-find Songs/Albums

CLASSICS

Give a Damn "Spanky's Greatest Hits" "Without Rhyme or Reason"*	Spanky and Our Gang (Mercury) (Mercury)
In the Ghetto "Worldwide 50 Gold Award Hits"	Elvis Presley (RCA)
+In the Ghetto "Greatest Hits"	Mac Davis (Columbia)
Summer in the City "The Best . . . Lovin' Spoonful" "The Very Best of the Lovin' Spoonful"	The Lovin' Spoonful (Kama Sutra) (Kama Sutra)
+Summer in the City "Almost Summer" (Soundtrack)	Celebration (MCA)
+Summer in the City "Guess Who"	B. B. King (ABC)

THEMATIC ALBUMS

"Between Today and Yesterday"	Alan Price (Warner Brothers)
"Let's Clean Up the Ghetto"	Philadelphia All Stars (Philadelphia International)

DEFINITIVE SONGS

Abandoned City "Oops, Wrong Planet"	Utopia (Bearsville)

DEFINITIVE SONGS

Animal Zoo
"Twelve Dreams of Dr. Sardonicus"
"Spirit Live"

Spirit
(Epic)
(Potato)

Badi-Da
"The Other Side of This Life"*
"Fred Neil"*
"Everybody's Talking"

Fred Neil
(Capitol)
(Capitol)
(Capitol)

Big City Cat
"Alive on Arrival"

Steve Forbert
(Nemperor)

Black Day in July
"The Very Best of Gordon Lightfoot"

Gordon Lightfoot
(United Artists)

Born in Chicago
"Golden Butter/The Best of the Paul
   Butterfield Blues Band"
"The Paul Butterfield Band"

Paul Butterfield Blues Band
(Elektra)

(Elektra)

Cities
"Fear of Music"

Talking Heads
(Sire)

The Cities Are Burning
"Now"

Pete Seeger
(Columbia)

Citiest People
"Candles in the Rain"*

Melanie
(Buddah)

City

"City"

Roger McGuinn and Chris
   Hillman
(Capitol)

The City
"The Best of the Mark-Almond Band"

The Mark-Almond Band
(Blue Thumb)

The City
"The American Album"

Allan Taylor
(United Artists)

City Boy
"American Dreams"

Jesse Colin Young
(Elektra)

City in Heat
"Desmond Child and Rouge"

Desmond Child and Rouge
(Capitol)

City Junkies
"Manassas"

Manassas (Stephen Stills)
(Atlantic)

City Kids
"American Boys and Girls"

Garland Jeffreys
(A&M)

City Life
"Harry Nilsson"

Harry Nilsson
(RCA)

DEFINITIVE SONGS

City Lights
"Between Today and Yesterday"
Alan Price
(Warner Brothers)

City Lights
"City Lights"
Dr. John
(Horizon/A&M)

City Liners
"Birth Comes to Us All"
The Good Rats
(Arista)

City Music
"James Montgomery Band"*
James Montgomery
(Island)

City Sunday Morning Day
"Life Lines"*
Richard Supa
(Epic)

Concrete Jungle
"Babylon by Bus"
Bob Marley and the Wailers
(Island)

+Concrete Jungle
"The Specials"
The Specials
(Chrysalis)

Daughters and Sons
"Peacing It All Together"*
Lighthouse
(RCA)

Dirty City

"Reach for the Sky"
Sutherland Brothers and
    Quiver
(Columbia)

Does This Bus Stop at 82nd Street?
"Greetings from Asbury Park, N.J."
Bruce Springsteen
(Columbia)

Downtown
"Petula Clark's Greatest Hits"
Petula Clark
(Warner Brothers)

+Downtown
"The B-52's"
The B-52's
(Warner Brothers)

Down to the City
"The Fabulous Rhinestones"*
The Fabulous Rhinestones
(Just Sunshine Records)

The Faucets Are Dripping
"God Bless the Grass"
Pete Seeger
(Columbia)

Garden in the City
"Garden in the City"*
Melanie
(Buddah)

Ghetto
"Accept No Substitute"*
Delaney and Bonnie
(Elektra)

+Ghetto
"First Ten Years"
Joan Baez
(Vanguard)

Ghetto
"Graham Central Station"
Graham Central Station
(Warner Brothers)

Hard to Be a Saint in the City
"Greetings from Asbury Park, N.J."
Bruce Springsteen
(Columbia)

DEFINITIVE SONGS

Harlem "The Best of Bill Withers"	Bill Withers (Sussex)
Heart of the City "Tracks on Wax 4"	Dave Edmunds (Swan Song)
+Heart of the City "Pure Pop for Now People"	Nick Lowe (Columbia)
Incident on 57th Street "The Wild, the Innocent and the E Street Shuffle"	Bruce Springsteen (Columbia)
Inner City Blues "What's Goin' On" "Anthology"	Marvin Gaye (Tamla) (Motown)
In the City "In the City"	The Jam (Polydor)
In the City "Te John, Grease and Wolfman"	Charlie Daniels (Kama Sutra)
In the City "The Warriors"	Joe Walsh (A&M)
+In the City "The Long Run"	The Eagles (Asylum)
In the Heat of Summer "I Ain't Marchin' Anymore"	Phil Ochs (Elektra)
Jungleland "Born to Run"	Bruce Springsteen (Columbia)
Let's Clean Up the Ghetto "Let's Clean Up the Ghetto"	Philadelphia All-Stars (Philadelphia International)
Little Ghetto Boy "Live"	Donny Hathaway (Atlantic)
Living for the City "Innervisions"	Stevie Wonder (Tamla)
+Living for the City "It's a Heartache"	Bonnie Tyler (RCA)
+Living for the City/For the Love of Money "The Three Degrees Live"	The Three Degrees (Philadelphia International)
Nathan La Franeer "Joni Mitchell"	Joni Mitchell (Reprise)
Neon Rainbow "Super Hits"	Box Tops (Bell)

DEFINITIVE SONGS

Night in the City
"Joni Mitchell"

Joni Mitchell
(Reprise)

No Mean City
"No Mean City"

Nazareth
(A&M)

Outlaw
"Badlands"

Bill Chinnock
(Atlantic)

Rat Trap
"The Boomtown Rats"

The Boomtown Rats
(Columbia)

Razor Blade Alley
"One Step Beyond"

Madness
(Sire)

Shadow Break
"Got No Breeding"

Jules and the Polar Bears
(Columbia)

The Sleepy City
"Metamorphosis"

The Rolling Stones
(London)

Slums
"Donny Hathaway Live"

Donny Hathaway
(Atlantic)

Small Change Got Rained On
"Small Change"

Tom Waits
(Asylum)

Somebody's City
"The Place I Love"*

Splinter
(Dark Horse)

Something in the City Changes People
"Chicago VI"

Chicago
(Columbia)

Stranger in the City
"Stranger in the City"

John Miles
(London)

Street Fight
"Mark Farner"*

Mark Farner
(Atlantic)

Street Fire
"School's Out"

Alice Cooper
(Warner Brothers)

Street Kids
"Rock of the Westies"

Elton John
(MCA)

Street Life
"Beautiful Noise"

Neil Diamond
(Columbia)

Streetlife Serenaders
"Janis Ian"

Janis Ian
(Columbia)

Struggle in Darkness
"Eyes of an Only Child"*

Tom Jans
(Columbia)

Too Hot
"The Specials"

The Specials
(Chrysalis)

DEFINITIVE SONGS

Tracks Run Through the City
"Five Years Gone"*

Jerry Jeff Walker
(Atco)

Urban Renewal
"Urban Renewal"*

Murphy's Law
(ABC)

Village Ghetto Land
"Songs in the Key of Life"

Stevie Wonder
(Tamla)

Westside Pow Wow
"Desmond Child and Rouge"

Desmond Child and Rouge
(Capitol)

Wild Hot Summer Nights
"Detective"

Detective
(Swan Song)

Wild in the Street
"Ghost Writer"

Garland Jeffreys
(A&M)

The World Is a Ghetto
"Greatest Hits"
"The World Is a Ghetto"

War
(United Artists)
(United Artists)

World of Pain
"Disraeli Gears"

Cream
(RSO)

Youngblood
"Rickie Lee Jones"

Rickie Lee Jones
(Warner Brothers)

REFERENCE SONGS

Aye Colorado
"Urban Desire"

Genya Ravan
(20th Century Records)

Big Brother
"Talking Book"

Stevie Wonder
(Tamla)

Big City
"Spitfire"

Jefferson Starship
(Grunt)

Calcutta Monsoon
"Garland Jeffreys"*

Garland Jeffreys
(Atlantic)

Devil Wind
"Three Hearts"

Bob Welch
(Capitol)

Doo Doo Doo Doo Doo
  (Heartbreaker)
"Goats Head Soup"
"Made in the Shade"

The Rolling Stones

(Rolling Stone Records)
(Rolling Stone Records)

Down in the City
"Down in the Bunker"

Steve Gibbons Band
(Polydor)

REFERENCE SONGS

Down on the Corner	Creedence Clearwater Revival
"Chronicle"	(Fantasy)
"Willy and the Poor Boys"	(Fantasy)
Eastern Avenue River Railway Blues	Jerry Jeff Walker
"Jerry Jeff"	(Elektra)
Fool for the City	Foghat
"Foghat Live"	(Bearsville)
"Fool for the City"	(Bearsville)
The Ghost of Saturday Night	Tom Waits
"The Heart of Saturday Night"	(Asylum)
I'm the Urban Spaceman	Bonzo Dog Band
"The Doughnut in Granny's Greenhouse"*	(Imperial)
In the Street Today	The Jam
"This Is the Modern World"	(Polydor)
Junkman	Danny O'Keefe
"Breezy Stories"	(Atlantic)
Lawd, I'm Just a Country Boy in This Great Big City	Sir Douglas Quintet
"Mendocino"	(Mercury)
The Loner	Neil Young
"Decade"	(Reprise)
"Neil Young"	(Reprise)
"Live Rust"	(Warner Brothers)
+The Loner	Stephen Stills
"Illegal Stills"	(Columbia)
+The Loner	Richie Havens
"Mixed Bag II"*	(Stormy Forest)
Long Way Home	Dan Fogelberg
"Home Free"	(Columbia)
Lost in the Flood	Bruce Springsteen
"Greetings from Asbury Park, N.J."	(Columbia)
Love Child	Diana Ross and The Supremes
"Anthology"	(Motown)
Love in the City	The Turtles
"Turtle Soup"*	(White Whale)
Mack the Knife	Bobby Darin
"The Bobby Darin Story"	(Atco)

REFERENCE SONGS

+Mack the Knife
"Rag and Roll Revue"

Cathy Chamberlain
(Warner Brothers)

+Mack the Knife
"Rag Time Jug Stompers"*

Dave Van Ronk
(Mercury)

+Mack the Knife
"Lou Christie"*

Lou Christie
(Three Brothers)

Mainstreet

"Night Moves"

Bob Seger and the Silver
    Bullet Band
(Capitol)

Motor City Is Burning
"Kick Out the Jams"*

MC 5
(Elektra)

Night in the City
"Out of the Blue"

Electric Light Orchestra
(Jet)

On the Corner
"Brooklyn Dreams"

Brooklyn Dreams
(Millennium)

Out in the Cold
"Heroes and Heroines"

Strawbs
(A&M)

Outside of a Small Circle of Friends
"Chords of Fame"
"Pleasures of the Harbor"

Phil Ochs
(A&M)
(A&M)

Reachin' Out
"Sense of Direction"

Climax Blues Band
(Sire)

Street Boys
"Love on the Airways"

Gallagher and Lyle
(A&M)

Street Corner Serenade
"Manorisms"

Wet Willie
(Epic)

Street in the City

"Rough Mix"

Pete Townsend and Ronnie
    Lane
(MCA/Track)

Street Life
"Greatest Hits"

Roxy Music
(Atco)

Sweet Johanna
"Levon Helm"

Levon Helm
(ABC)

The Sweetest One
"Urban Desire"

Genya Ravan
(20th Century Records)

Taking It to the Streets
"Taking It to the Streets"
"Best of the Doobies"

The Doobie Brothers
(Warner Brothers)
(Warner Brothers)

REFERENCE SONGS

Tenth Avenue Freeze-Out
"Born to Run"

Bruce Springsteen
(Columbia)

We Gotta Get Out of This Place
"Best of the Animals"

The Animals
(MGM)

+We Gotta Get Out of This Place
"Stage Door Johnnies"*

Claire Hamill
(Konk)

+We Gotta Get Out of This Place
"Some Enchanted Evening"

Blue Oyster Cult
(Columbia)

We're All We've Got
"So Close, So Very Far to Go"

Jake Holmes
(Polydor)

YOUR ADDITIONAL SONGS

_____

_____

_____

_____

_____

VIOLENCE

Violence 40,000 murders, 900,000 assaults last year in the United States.
Some tragic stories, some funny stories, some statements about violence, and some reporting about real incidents. (N.B. Songs about guns are listed as a sub-theme.)

Related Categories: Cowboys/Wild West, Outlaws/Criminals,
    Protest/Revolution, Suicide, War and Peace

  +Same as Song Above
   *Hard-to-find Songs/Albums

CLASSICS

Sniper	Harry Chapin
"Sniper and Other Love Songs"	(Elektra)
Sympathy for the Devil	The Rolling Stones
"Hot Rocks 1964–1971"	(London)
"Beggars Banquet"	(London)
"Love You Live"	(Rolling Stone Records)
+Sympathy for the Devil	Bryan Ferry
"These Foolish Things"	(Atco)

DEFINITIVE SONGS

"A" Bomb in Wardour Street	The Jam
"All Mod Cons"	(Polydor)
Bad, Bad Leroy Brown	Jim Croce
"Photographs and Memories"	(ABC)
Bad Company	Bad Company
"Bad Company"	(Swan Song)
Bad Moon Rising	Creedence Clearwater Revival
"Chronicle"	(Fantasy)
"Green River"	(Fantasy)
+Bad Moon Rising	Jerry Lee Lewis
"The Session"	(Mercury)
The Ballad of Charles Whitman	Kinky Friedman
"Sold American"*	(Vanguard)
Belfast Cowboy	Pretty Things
"Silk Torpedo"	(Swan Song)

DEFINITIVE SONGS

Black Day in July
"The Very Best of Gordon Lightfoot"
Gordon Lightfoot
(United Artists)

Black September/Belfast
"Mason Profit"*
Mason Profit
(Warner Brothers)

Blow It Up
"Christ Child"*
Christ Child
(Buddah)

Blue Murder
"TRB II"
The Tom Robinson Band
(Harvest)

Born in Chicago
"Golden Butter/The Best of the Paul
    Butterfield Blues Band"
"The Paul Butterfield Band"
Paul Butterfield Blues Band
(Elektra)

(Elektra)

A Boy Named Sue
"San Quentin"
"Johnny Cash's Greatest Hits Vol. II"
Johnny Cash
(Columbia)
(Columbia)

Breaking Glass
"Pure Pop for Now People"
Nick Lowe
(Columbia)

Bummer
"Portrait Gallery"
Harry Chapin
(Elektra)

Crash Street Kids
"The Hoople"
Mott the Hoople
(Columbia)

Doo Doo Doo Doo Doo
    (Heartbreaker)
"Goats Head Soup"
"Made in the Shade"
The Rolling Stones

(Rolling Stone Records)
(Rolling Stone Records)

Down in the Tube Station at Midnight
"All Mod Cons"
The Jam
(Polydor)

Fight from the Inside
"News of the World"
Queen
(Elektra)

Gang War Blues
"Slow Flux"
Steppenwolf
(Mums/Columbia)

Gino
"Birth Comes to Us All"
The Good Rats
(Arista)

Good Old Boy
"Midnight Wind"
Charlie Daniels
(Epic)

Harry Simms
"Circles and Seasons"
Pete Seeger
(Warner Brothers)

Headknocker
"Foreigner"
Foreigner
(Atlantic)

DEFINITIVE SONGS

House Burning Down "Electric Ladyland" "The Essential Jimi Hendrix"	Jimi Hendrix (Reprise) (Reprise)
In the Street Today "This Is the Modern World"	The Jam (Polydor)
I've Seen an Old Fighter "Easter Island"	Kris Kristofferson (Monument)
I Was a Witness to a War "New City"	Blood, Sweat, and Tears (Columbia)
Killer Without a Cause "Bad Reputation"	Thin Lizzy (Mercury)
The Killing of Georgie "A Night on the Town"	Rod Stewart (Warner Brothers)
The Knack "Cool for Cats"	Squeeze (A&M)
Kung Fu Fighting "Sweet Exorcist"	Curtis Mayfield (Curtom)
Lead On, I'll Follow (Belfast '71) "American Album"*	Allan Taylor (United Artists)
Lost in the Flood "Greetings from Asbury Park, N.J."	Bruce Springsteen (Columbia)
Lou Marsh "All the News That's Fit to Sing"	Phil Ochs (Elektra)
Massacre "Live and Dangerous"	Thin Lizzy (Warner Brothers)
Midnight Blue "Taking It Easy"	Seals and Crofts (Warner Brothers)
Morning Final "Agents of Fortune"	Blue Oyster Cult (Columbia)
Mr. Charlie "Europe '72"	The Grateful Dead (Warner Brothers)
Nice Man Jack "Zaragon"	John Miles (Arista)
Pavanne "First Light"	Richard and Linda Thompson (Island)
Pig's Head "Weeds"	Brewer and Shipley (Kama Sutra)

DEFINITIVE SONGS

Problem Child	AC/DC
"Let There Be Rock"	(Atco)
"If You Want Blood"	(Atlantic)
Psycho Killer	Talking Heads
"Talking Heads 77"	(Sire)
Revolution Blues	Neil Young
"On the Beach"	(Reprise)
Roland the Headless Thompson Gunner	Warren Zevon
"Excitable Boy"	(Asylum)
Romeo Is Bleeding	Tom Waits
"Blue Valentine"	(Asylum)
Rough and Ready	Garland Jeffreys
"Ghost Writer"	(A&M)
Running Gun Blues	David Bowie
"The Man Who Sold the World"	(RCA)
San Quentin	Johnny Cash
"At San Quentin"	(Columbia)
Saturday Night's Alright for Fighting	Elton John
"Greatest Hits"	(MCA)
"Goodbye Yellow Brick Road"	(MCA)
Smackwater Jack	Carole King
"Tapestry"	(Ode)
"Her Greatest Hits"	(Ode)
+Smackwater Jack	Jo Mama
"J Is for Jump"*	(Atlantic)
Son of Sam	The Dead Boys
"We Have Come for Your Children"	(Sire)
Stepping Razor	Peter Tosh
"Equal Rights"	(Columbia)
Street Fight	Mark Farner
"Mark Farner"*	(Atlantic)
Street Fight	David Essex
"Rock On"	(Atlantic)
Street Fighting Man	The Rolling Stones
"Hot Rocks 1964–1971"	(London)
"Beggars Banquet"	(London)
+Street Fighting Man	Rod Stewart
"The Best of Rod Stewart"	(Mercury)

DEFINITIVE SONGS

Street Fire "School's Out"	Alice Cooper (Warner Brothers)
Street Kids "Rock of the Westies"	Elton John (MCA)
Sunday Bloody Sunday "Sometime in New York City"	John Lennon (Apple)
Ticking "Caribou"	Elton John (MCA)
Trouble Boys "Tracks on Wax 4"	Dave Edmunds (Swan Song)
Warrior "Jailbreak" "Live and Dangerous"	Thin Lizzy (Mercury) (Warner Brothers)
Who Killed Davey Moore? "The World of Pete Seeger" "We Shall Overcome"	Pete Seeger (Columbia) (Columbia)
Wild Hot Summer Nights "Detective"	Detective (Swan Song)
Wild in the Streets "Garland Jeffreys"	Garland Jeffreys (A&M)
Wild Man "Sanctuary"	J. Geils Band (EMI)
You Don't Mess Around with Jim "You Don't Mess Around with Jim" "Photographs and Memories—His Greatest Hits"	Jim Croce (ABC) (ABC)

REFERENCE SONGS

Coming After Me* "Flamingo"*	Flaming Groovies (Kama Sutra)
Down by the River "Everyone Knows This Is Nowhere" "Decade"	Neil Young (Reprise) (Reprise)
+Down by the River "McKendree Spring Three"*	McKendree Spring (MCA)
Make the Headlines "Steelyard Blues" (Soundtrack)	Various Artists (Warner Brothers)
Panic in the Street "Aladdin Sane"	David Bowie (RCA)

REFERENCE SONGS

Sex and Violence
"Lothar and the Hand People"*

Lothar and the Hand People
(Capitol)

Taking It to the Streets
"Taking It to the Streets"
"Best of the Doobies"

The Doobie Brothers
(Warner Brothers)
(Warner Brothers)

Two Lovely Black Eyes
"Both Sides of Herman's Hermits"*

Herman's Hermits
(MGM)

YOUR ADDITIONAL SONGS

_____

_____

_____

_____

_____

Guns

CLASSICS

We did not pick any classic songs here, as each song is unique to its own particular story and subject matter.

DEFINITIVE SONGS

Ballad of a Well-known Gun
"Tumbleweed Connection"

Elton John
(MCA)

Black Magic Gun
"Ladies Love Outlaws"

Tom Rush
(Columbia)

Buy a Gun for Your Son
"Ain't That News"

Tom Paxton
(Elektra)

Don't Take Your Guns to Town
"Johnny Cash's Greatest Hits Vol. I"

Johnny Cash
(Columbia)

For What It's Worth
"The Muppets II"

The Muppets
(Arista)

Go for Your Guns
"Go for Your Guns"

The Isley Brothers
(T-Neck)

DEFINITIVE SONGS

Guns
"Fear"*
John Cale
(Island)

Guns
"Moving Targets"
Flo and Eddie
(Columbia)

Guns, Guns, Guns
"Rockin' "
The Guess Who
(RCA)

+Guns, Guns, Guns
"Dreams of a Child"
Burton Cummings
(Portrait)

Guns of Brixton
"London Calling"
The Clash
(Epic)

Guns on the Roof
"Give 'em Enough Rope"
The Clash
(Epic)

I'm Gonna Get Me a Gun
"Matthew and Son"
Cat Stevens
(Deram)

I Shot the Sheriff
"461 Ocean Blvd."
Eric Clapton
(RSO)

+I Shot the Sheriff
"Live"
"Burnin' "
Bob Marley and the Wailers
(Island)
(Island)

I Want to Kill You
David Peel and the Lower
   East Side

"The American Revolution"*
(Elektra)

Machine Gun Kelly
"Mud Slide Slim and the Blue
   Horizon"
James Taylor
(Warner Brothers)

Medley: Son of Bill Baety
"Together After Five"*
Sir Douglas Quintet
(Mercury)

Mr. Charlie
"Europe '72"
The Grateful Dead
(Warner Brothers)

Roland the Headless Thompson
   Gunner
"Excitable Boy"
Warren Zevon

(Asylum)

Rubber Bullets
"Greatest Hits 1972–78"
"10 CC"
10 CC
(Polydor)
(Mercury)

Running Gun Blues
"The Man Who Sold the World"
David Bowie
(RCA)

Shot Gun Rider
"Freeways"
Bachman-Turner Overdrive
(Mercury)

DEFINITIVE SONGS

Shot Gun Riders
"The Winters Brothers Band"*

The Winters Brothers
(Atco)

Small Change Got Rained On
"Small Change"

Tom Waits
(Asylum)

Tommy Gun
"Give 'em Enough Rope"

The Clash
(Epic)

Watch My .38

Commander Cody and the
Lost Planet Airmen
(Paramount)

"Hot Licks, Cold Steel and Truckers'
Favorites"

With a Gun
"Pretzel Logic"

Steely Dan
(ABC)

REFERENCE SONGS

Born in Chicago
"Golden Butter/The Best of the Paul
Butterfield Blues Band"
"The Paul Butterfield Band"

Paul Butterfield Blues Band
(Elektra)

(Elektra)

Drop Your Guns
"Live at the El Macombo"

April Wine
(London)

For What It's Worth
"Buffalo Springfield"
"Retrospective"

Buffalo Springfield
(Atco)
(Atco)

Gimme Back My Bullets
"Gimme Back My Bullets"
"Gold and Platinum"

Lynyrd Skynyrd
(MCA)
(MCA)

Gunslinger
"Mink DeVille"

Mink DeVille
(Capitol)

Gunsmoke
"Hurry Sundown"

The Outlaws
(Arista)

I Had to Shoot That Rabbit
"How Come the Sun"*

Tom Paxton
(Reprise)

Jealous Gun
"I Came to Dance"

Nils Lofgren
(A&M)

The Men Behind the Guns
"I Ain't Marchin' Anymore"

Phil Ochs
(Elektra)

My Father's Gun
"Tumbleweed Connection"

Elton John
(MCA)

REFERENCE SONGS

Revolution Blues   Neil Young
"On the Beach"   (Reprise)

Rusty Gun   Grin
"All Out"   (Spindizzy)

Saturday Night Special   Lynyrd Skynyrd
"One More from the Road"   (MCA)

Shotgun   Junior Walker and the All
                                       Stars
"Anthology"   (Motown)

YOUR ADDITIONAL SONGS

_____

_____

_____

_____

_____

WAR AND PEACE

War and peace—rock and roll did help to "give peace a chance."

During the sixties, this was one of the most important themes to evolve in rock. As the Vietnam War ended, so did this genre of music. However, the effects of these songs are still with us, much like the effects of war itself.

Since the nature of the title "War and Peace" is so broad, we have separated it into four sections:

1. War/Soldiers
2. Peace
3. The Draft
4. Victims of War

Related Categories: America, Brotherhood, Freedom, Injustice, Politics

+Same as Song Above
*Hard-to-find Songs/Albums

THEMATIC ALBUMS

"War, War, War"*   Country Joe McDonald
                                    (Vanguard)

YOUR ADDITIONAL SONGS

_____

_____

_____

_____

_____

War/Soldiers

From the American Revolution to the present day, declared wars to undeclared wars, buck privates to the commander in chief.

CLASSICS

Handsome Johnny "Mixed Bag"* "Richie Havens on Stage"*	Richie Havens (MGM) (Stormy Forest)
Masters of War "The Freewheelin' Bob Dylan"	Bob Dylan (Columbia)
+Masters of War "The World of Pete Seeger"	Pete Seeger (Columbia)
+Masters of War "Cher Sings the Hits"*	Cher (Springboard)
+Masters of War "Judy Collins ✕3"	Judy Collins (Elektra)
+Masters of War "Bag Full of Soul"	José Feliciano (RCA)
+Masters of War "Solo"	Don McLean (United Artists)
Sky Pilot	Eric Burdon and the Animals (MGM)
"The Best of Eric Burdon and the Animals Vol. III" "The Twain Shall Meet"*	(MGM)
Universal Soldier "The Best of Buffy Sainte-Marie"	Buffy Sainte-Marie (Vanguard)
+Universal Soldier "Like It Is" "Early Treasures"	Donovan (Hickory) (Bell)
The War Is Over "Chords of Fame" "Tape from California"	Phil Ochs (A&M) (A&M)
+The War Is Over "Third Annual Pipe Dream"	Atlanta Rhythm Section (Polydor)

DEFINITIVE SONGS

American Boy Soldiers "The Edgar Broughton Band"*	The Edgar Broughton Band (Capitol)
An Untitled Protest "Together"*	Country Joe and The Fish (Vanguard)
The "A" Team (45 RPM Single)*	Sgt. Barry Sadler (RCA)

DEFINITIVE SONGS

Back from Korea
"Memories"

John Mayall
(Polydor)

The Ballad of a Crystal Man
"Donovan P. Leitch"*

Donovan
(Janus)

Ballad of Lieutenant William Calley
(45 RPM Single)*

"C" Company
(Plantation)

Ballad of the Fort Hood Three
"Young vs. Old"

Pete Seeger
(Columbia)

Ballad of the Green Berets
"Ballad of the Green Berets"
"More American Graffiti"

Sgt. Barry Sadler
(RCA)
(MCA)

Belfast Cowboy
"Silk Torpedo"

Pretty Things
(Swan Song)

Blood and Glory
"Gerry Rafferty"

Gerry Rafferty
(Visa)

The Box
"Poems, Prayers and Promises"

John Denver
(RCA)

Bring Them Home
"Young vs. Old"

Pete Seeger
(Columbia)

Broken Barricades
"Broken Barricades"

Procol Harum
(A&M)

Butcher's Tale
"Time of the Season"

The Zombies
(Epic)

Carnal Questions
"The Gist of Gemini"

Gino Vanelli
(A&M)

Carolina Soldier Boy
"Blue Ridge Mountain Skyline"*

Sammy Walker
(Warner Brothers)

Cruel War
"Peter, Paul and Mary"

Peter, Paul and Mary
(Warner Brothers)

+Cruel War
"Cher Vol. II"

Cher
(United Artists)

The Dove
"Judy Collins ⅗3"

Judy Collins
(Elektra)

Dr. Mudd
"Sabotage/Live"

John Cale
(A&M)

English Civil War
"Give 'em Enough Rope"

The Clash
(Epic)

The Fiddle and the Drum
"Clouds"

Joni Mitchell
(Reprise)

DEFINITIVE SONGS

The Fighting Line "Memories"	John Mayall (Polydor)
For Years? "What the World Needs Now Is Love"*	Tom Clay (Mowest)
G.I. Blues "G.I. Blues"	Elvis Presley (RCA)
Hero from the War "Willard"*	John Stewart (Capitol)
Hot Youth "Hobo with a Grin"	Steve Harley (Capitol)
I Ain't Marchin' Anymore "Chords of Fame" "I Ain't Marching Anymore"	Phil Ochs (A&M) (A&M)
I Don't Wanna Be a Soldier "Imagine"	John Lennon (Apple)

I-Feel-Like-I'm-Fixin'-to-Die-Rag
"The Life and Times of Country Joe
   and the Fish—from Haight-
   Ashbury to Woodstock"
"Woodstock" (Soundtrack)
"I-Feel-Like-I'm-Fixin'-to-Die-Rag"
	Country Joe and the Fish
	(Vanguard)
	
	(Cotillion)
	(Vanguard)

In the Navy "Live and Sleazy"	Village People (Casablanca)
The Iron Man "Things I Notice Now"*	Tom Paxton (Elektra)
Is There Anybody Here? "Chords of Fame" "Phil Ochs in Concert"	Phil Ochs (A&M) (Elektra)
Jimmy Newman "The Compleat Tom Paxton" "Tom Paxton No. 6"*	Tom Paxton (Elektra) (Elektra)
+Jimmy Newman "Take Me to Tomorrow"	John Denver (RCA)
Jungle Work "Bad Luck Streak in Dancing School"	Warren Zevon (Asylum)
Kevin Barry "Strangers and Cousins"	Pete Seeger (Columbia)
Land of Hope and Glory "One Step Beyond"	Madness (Sire)

DEFINITIVE SONGS

Lead On, I'll Follow (Belfast '71)
"The American Album"*
Allan Taylor
(United Artists)

Letter from Vietnam
"Ballad of the Green Beret"
Sgt. Barry Sadler
(RCA)

Life During Wartime
"Fear of Music"
Talking Heads
(Sire)

Llewellyn

New Riders of the Purple Sage
(Columbia)

"Marin County Line"

Lyndon Johnson Told the Nation
"Ain't That News"*
Tom Paxton
(Elektra)

Massacre
"Live and Dangerous"
Thin Lizzy
(Warner Brothers)

The Men Behind the Guns
"I Ain't Marchin' Anymore"
Phil Ochs
(Elektra)

Mercenaries (Ready for War)
"Sabotage/Live"
John Cale
(A&M)

Military Madness
"Songs for Beginners"
Graham Nash
(Atlantic)

The Missionary
"Before the Salt"
Jimmy Buffett
(Barnaby)

Mr. Lonely
"Greatest Hits"
Bobby Vinton
(Epic)

Navy Blue
(45 RPM Single)*
Diane Renay
(20th Century Records)

No Man Can Find the War
"Goodbye and Hello"*
Tim Buckley
(Elektra)

Old Forgotten Soldier
"Pussy Cats"
Harry Nilsson
(RCA)

Oliver's Army
"Armed Forces"
Elvis Costello
(Columbia)

One More Parade
"All the News That's Fit to Sing"
Phil Ochs
(Elektra)

The Partisan
"The Best Of"
Leonard Cohen
(Columbia)

Peat Bog Soldiers
"Strangers and Cousins"
Pete Seeger
(Columbia)

P.T. 109
"Johnny Horton's Greatest Hits"
Johnny Horton
(Columbia)

DEFINITIVE SONGS

Readjustment Blues "Aerie"	John Denver (RCA)
Remember the Alamo "Donovan P. Leitch"	Donovan (Janus)
Roland the Headless Thompson Gunner "Excitable Boy"	Warren Zevon (Asylum)
Rumours of War "Mystic Man"	Peter Tosh (Rolling Stone)
Saigon Bride "Joan"	Joan Baez (Vanguard)
Silent Night "New Songs from the Briarpatch"	Tom Paxton (Vanguard)
Sink the Bismarck "Johnny Horton's Greatest Hits"	Johnny Horton (Columbia)
Soldier "Twelve Dreams of Dr. Sardonicus"	Spirit (Epic)
Soldier "Decade" "Journey Through the Past"	Neil Young (Reprise) (Reprise)
Soldier Blue "She Used to Want to Be a Ballerina"*	Buffy Sainte-Marie (Vanguard)
Soldier Boy "The Very Best of the Shirelles"	The Shirelles (United Artists)
Soldier of Fortune "Bad Reputation"	Thin Lizzy (Mercury)
Soldier of Fortune "Stormbringer"	Deep Purple (Warner Brothers)
Soldiers "Mud Slide Slim and the Blue Horizon"	James Taylor (Warner Brothers)
Spanish Bombs "London Calling"	The Clash (Epic)
Stop the War "Involved"	Edwin Starr (Gordy)
Summer of My Life "The Gist of Gemini"	Gino Vanelli (A&M)

DEFINITIVE SONGS

Take the Star Out of the Window   John Prine
"Diamonds in the Rough"*   (Atlantic)

Talking Ben Tre   Pete Seeger
"Now"   (Columbia)

Talking Vietnam   Phil Ochs
"All the News That's Fit to Sing"   (Elektra)

Talking Vietnam Pot Luck Blues   Tom Paxton
"The Compleat Tom Paxton"   (Elektra)

This Is It   Kenny Loggins
"Keep the Fire"   (Columbia)

3-5-0-0   Various Artists
"Hair" (original Broadway cast)   (RCA)

+3-5-0-0   Various Artists
"Hair" (original cast)   (RCA)

+3-5-0-0   Various Artists
"Hair" (Soundtrack)   (RCA)

To Hell with War   Prelude
"After the Gold Rush"*   (Island)

To Susan on the West Coast Waiting   Donovan
"Barabajagal"   (Epic)

To the War   Gino Vanelli
"The Gist of Gemini"   (A&M)

The Unknown Soldier   The Doors
"Waiting for the Sun"   (Elektra)
"13"   (Elektra)

The Veterans' Big Parade   Dory Previn
"On My Way to Where"*   (United Artists)

War   Bob Marley and the Wailers
"Rastaman Vibration"   (Island)

War   Edwin Starr
"Greatest Hits"   (Gordy)
"Involved"   (Gordy)

+War   The Temptations
"Psychedelic Shack"   (Gordy)

The War Drags On   Donovan
"Like It Is"   (Hickory)

War Games   The Lovin' Spoonful
"Revelation: Revolution '69"*   (Kama Sutra)

War Song   Neil Young/Graham Nash
(45 RPM Single)*   (Warner Brothers)

DEFINITIVE SONGS

The War Suite
"The Gist of Gemini"

Gino Vanelli
(A&M)

War Widow
"War, War, War"*

Country Joe McDonald
(Vanguard)

What's Going On
"What's Going On"
"Anthology"

Marvin Gaye
(Tamla)
(Tamla)

+What's Going On
"Portfolio"*

Richie Havens
(Stormy Forest)

+What's Going On
"What the World Needs Now Is
   Love"*

Tom Clay
(Mowest)

White Boots Marching in a Yellow
   Land
"Tape from California"

Phil Ochs

(A&M)

The Willing Conscript
"Ain't That News"

Tom Paxton
(Elektra)

With God on Our Side
"The Times They Are a Changin'"

Bob Dylan
(Columbia)

+With God on Our Side
(33⅓ RPM E.P.)*

Manfred Mann
(Ascot)

+With God on Our Side
"First Ten Years"
"Joan Baez in Concert Part II"

Joan Baez
(Vanguard)
(Vanguard)

Yes Sir, No Sir
"Arthur"

The Kinks
(Reprise)

Zor and Zam
"The Monkees' Greatest Hits"

The Monkees
(Arista)

REFERENCE SONGS

Ain't That Nothing
"Music Is My Life"

Billy Preston
(A&M)

Battle of New Orleans
"Johnny Horton's Greatest Hits"

Johnny Horton
(Columbia)

+Battle of New Orleans
"Keys to the Country"*

Barefoot Jerry
(Monument)

+Battle of New Orleans
"Stars and Stripes Forever"

Nitty Gritty Dirt Band
(United Artists)

REFERENCE SONGS

Boogie Woogie Bugle Boy | Bette Midler
"The Divine Miss M" | (Atlantic)
"Live at Last" | (Atlantic)

Bring the Boys Home | Freda Payne
(45 RPM Single)* | (Invictus)

Broken Promises | Holly Near
"You Can Know Who I Am"* | (Redwood)

Coming Home Soldier | Bobby Vinton
"Bobby Vinton's Greatest Hits" | (Epic)

Eve of Destruction | Barry McGuire
"Eve of Destruction"* | (ABC/Dunhill)

Last Night I Had the Strangest Dream | Pete Seeger
"The World of Pete Seeger" | (Columbia)

+Last Night I Had the Strangest Dream | Simon and Garfunkel
"Wednesday Morning 3 A.M." | (Columbia)

+Last Night I Had the Strangest Dream | Arlo Guthrie
"One Night" | (Warner Brothers)

Long Live Our Love | The Shangri-las
(45 RPM Single) | (Red Bird)

Mercenary | Harry Chapin
"Dance Band on the Titanic" | (Elektra)

Political Science | Randy Newman
"Sail Away" | (Reprise)

Post World War II Blues | Al Stewart
"Past, Present and Future" | (Janus)

The Sinking of the *Reuben James* | Pete Seeger
"The World of Pete Seeger" | (Columbia)

Tank | The Stranglers
"Black and White"* | (Warner Brothers)

Toy Soldier | The Four Seasons
(45 RPM Single)* | (Philips)
"Gold Vault of Hits" | (Philips)

War | Bob Marley and the Wailers
"Babylon by Bus" | (Island)
"Rastaman Vibration" | (Island)

War Child | Jethro Tull
"War Child" | (Chrysalis)

REFERENCE SONGS

| Your Flag Decal Won't Get You into Heaven Anymore | John Prine |
| "John Prine"* | (Atlantic) |

YOUR ADDITIONAL SONGS

_____

_____

_____

_____

_____

Peace

They're called "Peace" songs. They could more accurately be called "pleas for peace."

CLASSICS

Give Peace a Chance	John Lennon
"Shaved Fish"	(Apple)
"The Plastic Ono Band—Live Peace in Toronto 1969"	(Apple)
+Give Peace a Chance (45 RPM Single)*	Hot Chocolate (Harvest)
+Give Peace a Chance "Leon Russell"	Leon Russell (Shelter)
Peace Train	Cat Stevens
"Greatest Hits"	(A&M)
"Teaser and the Firecat"	(A&M)
Peace Will Come	Melanie
"Four Sides of Melanie"*	(Buddah)
"Leftover Wine"*	(Buddah)
"From the Beginning: Twelve Great Performances"	(ABC)

DEFINITIVE SONGS

Aquarius
"Hair" (original Broadway cast)
Various Artists
(RCA)

+Aquarius
"Hair" (original cast)
Various Artists
(RCA)

+Aquarius
"Hair" (Soundtrack)
Various Artists
(RCA)

+Aquarius
"The Age of Aquarius"
"Greatest Hits on Earth"
The Fifth Dimension
(Soul City)
(Bell)

+Aquarius
"The Undisputed Truth"
The Undisputed Truth
(Gordy)

The Dove
"Judy Collins #3"
Judy Collins
(Elektra)

Give Me Love
"The Best of George Harrison"
"Living in the Material World"
George Harrison
(Apple)
(Apple)

I Wish You Peace
"One of These Nights"
The Eagles
(Asylum)

Last Night I Had the Strangest Dream
"The World of Pete Seeger"
Pete Seeger
(Columbia)

+Last Night I Had the Strangest Dream
"Wednesday Morning 3 A.M."
Simon and Garfunkel
(Columbia)

+Last Night I Had the Strangest Dream
"One Night"
Arlo Guthrie
(Warner Brothers)

Peace
"O'Jays Meet the Moments"
O'Jays
(Stang)

Peace Brother Peace
"In the Right Place"
Dr. John
(Atco)

Peace Brother Peace
"Soft and Soul"*
"Bill Medley"
Bill Medley
(MGM)
(MGM)

Peace by Peace
"Crabby Appleton"*
Crabby Appleton
(Elektra)

Peace Holy Peace
"War of the Gods"
Billy Paul
(Philadelphia International)

Peacemaker
"Native Sons"
Loggins and Messina
(Columbia)

Peacemaker
"The Free Electrical Band"
Albert Hammond
(Mums/Columbia)

DEFINITIVE SONGS

Peace on You "Peace on You"	Roger McGuinn (Columbia)
Peace Song "On the Road"	Jesse Colin Young (Warner Brothers)
Peace Will Come "Peace Will Come"*	Tom Paxton (Reprise)
Peaceful Children "The Road Home"*	Peaceful Children (ABC/Dunhill)
The Side of a Hill "The Paul Simon Songbook"	Paul Simon (Columbia)
Song of Peace "Morning Glory"*	Mary Travers (Warner Brothers)
We Got to Have Peace "Roots"	Curtis Mayfield (Curtom)
When the World's at Peace "Back Stabbers" "Live in London"	O'Jays (Philadelphia International) (Philadelphia International)

YOUR ADDITIONAL SONGS

_____

_____

_____

_____

_____

The Draft

Songs of comment and protest on the Selective Service System, more commonly called the "The Draft."

CLASSICS

Draft Dodger Rag "Chords of Fame" "I Ain't Marchin' Anymore"	Phil Ochs (A&M) (Elektra)
+Draft Dodger Rag "Dangerous Songs?"	Peter Seeger (Columbia)

DEFINITIVE SONGS

Draft Morning	The Byrds
"The Notorious Byrd Brothers"	(Columbia)
Draft Resister	Steppenwolf
"Monster"*	(ABC/Dunhill)
For What Was Gained	Eric Andersen
"Avalanche"*	(Warner Brothers)
Goodbye	Wadsworth Mansion
"Wadsworth Mansion"*	(Sussex/Duddah)
Greetings This Is Uncle Sam	The Vadliers
"Sixteen Original Big Hits"	(Tamla)
Hey Mr. Draft Board	David Peel and the Lower East Side
"The American Revolution"*	(Elektra)
I Ain't Marchin' Anymore	Phil Ochs
"Chords of Fame"	(A&M)
"I Ain't Marchin' Anymore"	(Elektra)
My Uncle	The Flying Burrito Brothers
"The Gilded Palace of Sin"	(A&M)
The Willing Conscript	Tom Paxton
"Ain't That News"	(Elektra)

REFERENCE SONGS

Alice's Restaurant (the second half of the song)	Arlo Guthrie
"Alice's Restaurant"	(Reprise)
"The Best of Arlo Guthie"	(Reprise)
Boogie Woogie Bugle Boy	Bette Midler
"Divine Miss M"	(Atlantic)
"Live at Last"	(Atlantic)
The Great Mandella	Peter, Paul and Mary
"1700"	(Warner Brothers)
I Have Decided to Join the Air Force	The Bee Gees
"Idea"	(RSO)
I-Feel-Like-I'm-Fixin'-to-Die-Rag	Country Joe and the Fish
"The Life and Times of Country Joe and the Fish—from Haight-Ashbury to Woodstock"	(Vanguard)
"Woodstock" (Soundtrack)*	(Cotillion)
"I-Feel-Like-I'm-Fixin'-to-Die-Rag"	(Vanguard)
"More American Graffiti"	(MCA)

REFERENCE SONGS

Lyndon Johnson Told the Nation	Tom Paxton
"Ain't That News"	(Elektra)
What's the Difference	Scott McKenzie
"The Voice of Scott McKenzie"*	(Ode)

YOUR ADDITIONAL SONGS

_____

_____

_____

_____

_____

Victims Of War

The widows, parents, and friends of the dead, maimed, and "missing in action," each one a victim of war.

CLASSICS

Ballad of Ira Hayes	Bob Dylan
"Dylan"	(Columbia)
+Ballad of Ira Hayes	Johnny Cash
"Johnny Cash's Greatest Hits"	(Columbia)
+Ballad of Ira Hayes	Kinky Friedman
"Lasso from El Paso"*	(Epic)
+Ballad of Ira Hayes	Patrick Sky
"Patrick Sky"*	(Vanguard)
Jimmy Newman	Tom Paxton
"The Compleat Tom Paxton"	(Elektra)
"Tom Paxton No. 6"*	(Elektra)
+Jimmy Newman	John Denver
"Take Me to Tomorrow"	(RCA)
Sam Stone	John Prine
"Prime Prine"	(Atlantic)
"John Prine"*	(Atlantic)

CLASSICS

+Sam Stone	Al Kooper
"Al's Big Deal/Unclaimed	(Columbia)
Freight—An Al Kooper Anthology"	
"Naked Songs"*	(Columbia)
The Unknown Soldier	The Doors
"13"	(Elektra)
"Waiting for the Sun"	(Elektra)
Where Have All the Flowers Gone?	Peter, Paul and Mary
"Peter, Paul and Mary"	(Warner Brothers)
+Where Have All the Flowers Gone?	Pete Seeger
"The World of Pete Seeger"	(Columbia)
+Where Have All the Flowers Gone?	Johnny Rivers
"The Very Best of Johnny Rivers"	(United Artists)
+Where Have All the Flowers Gone?	Richie Havens
"Richie Havens on Stage"*	(Stormy Forest)
+Where Have All the Flowers Gone?	The Kingston Trio
"The Best of the Kingston Trio"	(Capitol)
+Where Have All the Flowers Gone?	Joan Baez
"Farewell, Angelina"	(Vanguard)
+Where Have All the Flowers Gone?	The Chambers Brothers
"New Time, New Day"	(Columbia)
+Where Have All the Flowers Gone?	Earth, Wind and Fire
"Last Days and Time"	(Columbia)

DEFINITIVE SONGS

Ballad of Penny Evans	Steve Goodman
"The Essential Steve Goodman"	(Buddah)
"Somebody Else's Troubles"*	(Buddah)
Born on the Fourth of July	Tom Paxton
"New Songs from the Briarpatch"*	(Vanguard)
Come Away Melinda	Kenny Rankin
"Mind Dusters"	(Mercury)
+Come Away Melinda	Judy Collins
"Judy Collins #3"	(Elektra)
An Empty Glass	Sgt. Barry Sadler
(45 RPM Single)*	(RCA)
For What Was Gained	Eric Andersen
"Avalanche"*	(Warner Brothers)

DEFINITIVE SONGS

Fox Hole
"Adventure"
Television
(Elektra)

Golden Ribbons
"Loggins and Messina"
"Loggins and Messina on Stage"
Loggins and Messina
(Columbia)
(Columbia)

The Grave
"American Pie"
Don McLean
(United Artists)

Hero from the War
"Willard"*
John Stewart
(Capitol)

He Went to Paris
"You Had to Be There"
Jimmy Buffett
(ABC)

He Wore the Green Beret
(45 RPM Single)*
Lesley Miller
(RCA)

I Come and Stand at Every Door
"I Can See a New Day"
Pete Seeger
(Columbia)

+I Come and Stand at Every Door
"Fifth Dimension"
The Byrds
(Columbia)

Jackknife Johnny
"From the Inside"
Alice Cooper
(Warner Brothers)

Letter from the Front
"Love Beach"
Emerson, Lake & Palmer
(Atlantic)

Lucky Man
"Emerson, Lake & Palmer"
Emerson, Lake & Palmer
(Cotillion)

Massacre
"Live and Dangerous"
Thin Lizzy
(Warner Brothers)

Mrs. McGrath
"I Can See a New Day"
Pete Seeger
(Columbia)

Ruby Don't Take Your Love to Town
"Ten Years of Gold"
"The First Edition '69"*
Kenny Rogers
(United Artists)
(Reprise)

Soldier
"Illegal Stills"
Stephen Stills
(Columbia)

The Soldier's Tale
"Deep Cuts"
Strawbs
(A&M)

Some Mother's Son
"Arthur"
The Kinks
(Reprise)

The Victors
"What the World Needs Now Is
    Love"*
Tom Clay
(Mowest)

DEFINITIVE SONGS

Vietnam   Jimmy Cliff
"Wonderful World, Beautiful People"   (A&M)

Waiting Hymn of the Republic   J. F. Murphy and Salt
"J. F. Murphy and Salt"   (Elektra)

When Morning Breaks   Tom Paxton
"Ramblin' Boy"*   (Elektra)

Where Are You Now?   Joan Baez
"Where Are You Now?"   (A&M)

The Wife of the Soldier   Steeleye Span
"Storm Force Ten"   (Chrysalis)

REFERENCE SONGS

Bummer   Harry Chapin
"Portrait Gallery"   (Elektra)

Daniel   Elton John
"Don't Shoot Me I'm Only the Piano   (MCA)
    Player"
"Greatest Hits"   (MCA)

Gone the Rainbow   Peter, Paul and Mary
"Moving"   (Warner Brothers)

Requiem for the Masses   The Association
"The Association's Greatest Hits"   (Warner Brothers)

Rosalee   David Forman
"David Forman"*   (Arista)

Toy Soldier   The Four Seasons
"Gold Vault of Hits"   (Philips)

War Widow   Country Joe McDonald
"War, War, War"   (Vanguard)

YOUR ADDITIONAL SONGS

WOMEN'S IDENTITY/LIBERATION

Women's identity/liberation—"under my thumb" . . . *no more.*
    As sexist as rock music generally is, it has still provided a large body of songs that deal with women's rights in society, business, family, and interpersonal relationships. (N.B. Sexist/chauvinist songs are listed in a separate subcategory.)

Related Categories: Marriage, Mothers, Pregnancy, Prostitution,
    Self-Identity, Working

    +Same as Song Above
    *Hard-to-find Songs/Albums

CLASSICS

I Am Woman	Helen Reddy
"Helen Reddy's Greatest Hits"	(Capitol)
"I Am Woman"	(Capitol)
You Don't Own Me	Lesley Gore
"Golden Hits of Lesley Gore"	(Mercury)

THEMATIC ALBUMS

"Changing Woman"	Buffy Sainte-Marie
	(Vanguard)

DEFINITIVE SONGS

All My Choices	Mary Travers
"All My Choices"*	(Warner Brothers)
Better to Find Out for Yourself	Buffy Sainte-Marie
"The Best of Buffy Sainte-Marie"	(Vanguard)
Dance Mr. Big, Dance	Deadly Nightshade
"Deadly Nightshade"*	(Phantom/RCA)
Did Jesus Have a Baby Sister?	Dory Previn
"Dory Previn"*	(Warner Brothers)
Do Right Woman, Do Right Man	Aretha Franklin
"Aretha's Greatest Hits"	(Atlantic)
+Do Right Woman, Do Right Man	Phoebe Snow
"Against the Grain"	(Columbia)

DEFINITIVE SONGS

Even It Up
"Bebe Le Strange"
Heart
(Epic)

Everything Comes in Time
"Good for You Too"*
Toni Brown
(MCA)

Fairweather Father
"Another Passenger"
Carly Simon
(Elektra)

Free the Lady
"Sweet America"*
Buffy Sainte-Marie
(ABC)

The Girl You Think You See
"Anticipation"
Carly Simon
(Elektra)

Good News (for the Lady)
"It's in Everyone of Us"*
Mary Travers
(Chrysalis)

Hard Working Woman
"Intoxication"*
Rory Block
(Chrysalis)

High Flying Woman
"Deadly Nightshade"*
Deadly Nightshade
(Phantom/RCA)

I'm a Woman
Jim Kweskin and the Jug
   Band

"The Best of Jim Kweskin and the Jug
   Band"
(Vanguard)

+I'm a Woman
"Waitress in a Doughnut Shop"
Maria Muldaur
(Warner Brothers)

I Wanna Be an Engineer
"Circles and Seasons"
Pete Seeger
(Warner Brothers)

Liberated Girls Don't Cry
"Clayton"
David Clayton-Thomas
(ABC)

Liberated Woman
"Rear View Mirror"
Starland Vocal Band
(Windsong)

Liberation Rag
"Slow Down World"
Donovan
(Epic)

Men Smart, Women Smarter
"Some People Can Do What They
   Like"
Robert Palmer
(Island)

Messing Around with the Wrong
   Woman
"John Hall"
John Hall

(Asylum)

My Old Lady
"Dance Band on the Titanic"
Harry Chapin
(Elektra)

DEFINITIVE SONGS

Only Time Will Tell "Joy of Cooking"	Joy of Cooking (Capitol)
Only Women Bleed "The Alice Cooper Show"	Alice Cooper (Warner Brothers)
+Only Women Bleed "Deep in the Night"	Etta James (Warner Brothers)
Ramble Just Like You "Ellen McIlwaine"	Ellen McIlwaine (United Artists)
Right On Sister "Power in the Darkness"	The Tom Robinson Band (Harvest)
See Her Run "Rag 'n Roll Revue"*	Cathy Chamberlain (Warner Brothers)
Sister, O Sister "Sometime in New York City"	John Lennon (Apple)
Slave "Playing Possum"	Carly Simon (Elektra)
Why Can't I Be Like Other Girls? "Jaded Virgin"	Marshall Chapman (Epic)
Why Do Little Girls "Living Room Suite"	Harry Chapin (Elektra)
Woman Is the Nigger of the World "Sometime in New York City" "Shaved Fish"	John Lennon (Apple) (Apple)
The Women "Cruisin'"	Village People (Casablanca)
Words of Love "Sixteen of Their Greatest"	The Mamas and The Papas (Dunhill)
+Words of Love "Mama's Big Ones—Her Greatest Hits"	Mama Cass (ABC/Dunhill)
You Don't Know "Hand in Glove"*	Terry Garthwaite (Fantasy)

REFERENCE SONGS

Barefoot and Pregnant "To the Limit"	Joan Armatrading (A&M)
Brando "Dory Previn"*	Dory Previn (Warner Brothers)

REFERENCE SONGS

Free to Be You and Me	Marlo Thomas and Various Artists
"Free to Be You and Me"	(Arista)

YOUR ADDITIONAL SONGS

_____

_____

_____

_____

_____

Sexism/Chauvinism

CLASSICS

Under My Thumb	The Rolling Stones
"Aftermath"	(London)
"Hot Rocks 1964–1971"	(London)
+Under My Thumb	Jebadiah
"Rock 'n Soul"	(Epic)
+Under My Thumb	Del Shannon
"Vintage Years"	(Sire)
+Under My Thumb	Hounds
"Puttin' on the Dog"	(Columbia)
The Wanderer	Dion and the Belmonts
"Runaround Sue"*	(Laurie)
"Dion's Greatest Hits"	(Laurie)
"Reunion—Live at Madison Square Garden"	(Warner Brothers)
+The Wanderer	The Beach Boys
"Beach Boys in Concert"	(Capitol)
+The Wanderer	Leif Garrett
"Leif Garrett"	(Atlantic)

DEFINITIVE SONGS

Ain't That Just like a Woman "Cookin' with Fats"	Fats Domino (United Artists)
Bad Boy "Mac McAnally"	Mac McAnally (Ariola/America)
Beware Brother Beware "Reckless Abandon"	David Bromberg (Fantasy)
Born a Woman (45 RPM Single)	Nick Lowe (Columbia)
Caught with the Meat in Your Mouth "Young, Loud and Snotty"	Dead Boys (Sire)
Dancing in the Nude "Martin Mull"*	Martin Mull (Capricorn)
Fat Bottomed Girls "Jazz"	Queen (Elektra)
Fooled Around and Fell in Love "Raisin' Hell" "Struttin' My Stuff"	Elvin Bishop (Capricorn) (Capricorn)
For Lovin' Me "The Very Best of Gordon Lightfoot"	Gordon Lightfoot (United Artists)
+For Lovin' Me "Ten Tears Together"	Peter, Paul and Mary (Warner Brothers)
Get Your Biscuits in the Oven and Buns in the Bed "Sold American"*	Kinky Friedman (Vanguard)
A Gift "Coney Island Baby"	Lou Reed (RCA)
Girls, Girls, Girls "The American Revolution"*	David Peel and the Lower East Side (Elektra)
I'm a Man "The Yardbirds' Greatest Hits"	The Yardbirds (Epic)
I Need Lunch "Young, Loud and Snotty"	Dead Boys (Sire)
If You Can't Give Me Love "If You Knew Suzi . . ."	Suzi Quatro (RSO)
It's a Man's World "Soul Classics"	James Brown (Polydor)
Love 'Em and Leave 'Em "Rock and Roll Over"	Kiss (Casablanca)

DEFINITIVE SONGS

Melody Fair
"Odessa"

The Bee Gees
(RSO)

Rufus Was a Titman
"Unrequited"*

Loudon Wainwright III
(Columbia)

Shiny Stockings
"Dreams of a Child"

Burton Cummings
(Portrait)

Sixty Minute Man
"The Session"

Jerry Lee Lewis
(Mercury)

Some Girls
"Some Girls"

The Rolling Stones
(Rolling Stone Records)

Tush
"The Best of ZZ Top"

ZZ Top
(London)

Women
"Head Games"

Foreigner
(Atlantic)

YOUR ADDITIONAL SONGS

_____

_____

_____

_____

_____

WORKING

Working—some do, some don't, some can't, some won't.

Positive and Negative songs about various kinds of work, working conditions, and unemployment. (N.B. Because of the complexity and scope of "Working," the category has been subdivided into the following sections):

1. Working/Jobs and the Worker
2. Unions
3. Miners
4. Secretaries
5. After Work Hours

Related Categories: Big Business, Money, Poverty, Rat Race, Suburbia

+Same as Song Above
 *Hard-to-find Songs/Albums

YOUR ADDITIONAL SONGS

_____

_____

_____

_____

_____

Working/Jobs and the Worker

CLASSICS

Factory "Darkness on the Edge of Town"	Bruce Springsteen (Columbia)
Maggie's Farm "Bob Dylan's Greatest Hits Vol. II" "Bringing It All Back Home"	Bob Dylan (Columbia) (Columbia)
+Maggie's Farm "Something Else Again"*	Richie Havens (MGM)

CLASSICS

Salt of the Earth "Beggars Banquet"	The Rolling Stones (London)
+Salt of the Earth "Blessed Are"	Joan Baez (Vanguard)
+Salt of the Earth "Judith"	Judy Collins (Elektra)
+Salt of the Earth "Songs"	Rotary Connection (Cadet Concept)

THEMATIC ALBUMS

"A Soap Opera"	The Kinks (RCA)

DEFINITIVE SONGS

Automation Song "All the News That's Fit to Sing"	Phil Ochs (Elektra)
Away Away "Between Today and Yesterday"	Alan Price (Warner Brothers)
Back in the Old Routine "Burning for You"	Strawbs (A&M)
Better Wages, Better Days "The Movies"*	The Movies (Arista)
Big Boss Man "The Grateful Dead"	The Grateful Dead (Warner Brothers)
+Big Boss Man "The Best of John Hammond"	John Hammond (Vanguard)
+Big Boss Man "The London Session"	Jerry Lee Lewis (Mercury)
Blue Collar	Bachman-Turner Overdrive (Mercury)
"Best of B.T.O. . . . (So Far)"	(Mercury)
Blue Collar Man "Pieces of Eight"	Styx (A&M)
Brand New Day "The Original Soundtrack"	10 CC (Mercury)
Brother Trucker "Flag"	James Taylor (Columbia)
Bus Rider "The Best of the Guess Who"	The Guess Who (RCA)

DEFINITIVE SONGS

But I Might Die Tonight "Tea for the Tillerman"	Cat Stevens (A&M)
Clean Up Woman "The Soul Years"	Betty Wright (Atlantic)
Commercial "Spanky's Greatest Hits"	Spanky and Our Gang (Mercury)
Crossroads "The Way I Feel"	Gordon Lightfoot (United Artists)
Don't Look Now	Creedence Clearwater Revival
"More Creedence Gold" "Willy and the Poor Boys"	(Fantasy) (Fantasy)
Family Man "Worlds Away"	Pablo Cruise (A&M)
Feel Like a Number	Bob Seger and the Silver Bullet Band
"Stranger in Town"	(Capitol)
Fieldworker	David Crosby/Graham Nash
"Wind on the Water"	(ABC)
Five O'Clock World "The Vogues' Greatest Hits"	The Vogues (Reprise)
Forty Hours "Trying Like the Devil"*	James Talley (Capitol)
Friday "I'm the Man"	Joe Jackson (A&M)
Get a Job (45 RPM Single) "American Graffiti"	The Silhouettes (Ember) (MCA)
Got a Job	Smokey Robinson & the Miracles
"Anthology"	(Tamla)
Hard Luck Story "Rock of the Westies"	Elton John (MCA)
Hard Travelin' "Woody Guthrie"	Woody Guthrie (Warner Brothers)
Hard Work "Hard Work"*	John Handy (ABC)

DEFINITIVE SONGS

Hump Day
"Contents Dislodged During
   Shipment"

Tin Huey
(Warner Brothers)

I Ain't Working
"Not Just Another Pretty Foot"

Jim Stafford
(MGM)

I Can't Wait to Get Off Work
"Small Change"

Tom Waits
(Asylum)

I've Been Working
"It's Too Late to Stop Now"
"His Band and Street Choir"

Van Morrison
(Warner Brothers)
(Warner Brothers)

+I've Been Working

"Live Bullet"

Bob Seger and the Silver
   Bullet Band
(Capitol)

A Job of Work
"Ramblin' Boy"*

Tom Paxton
(Elektra)

Just Got Paid
"The Best of ZZ Top"

ZZ Top
(London)

King Harvest (Has Surely Come)
"The Band"
"Rock of Ages"
"Anthology"

The Band
(Capitol)
(Capitol)
(Capitol)

Kitty
"New Masters"

Cat Stevens
(Deram)

Lazy Bones
"Leon Redbone"

Leon Redbone
(Warner Brothers)

Little People
"Peacing It All Together"*

Lighthouse
(RCA)

Luxury
"It's Only Rock and Roll"

The Rolling Stones
(Rolling Stone Records)

Matthew and Son
"Matthew and Son"
"Cat's Cradle"

Cat Stevens
(Deram)
(Deram)

Millworker
"Flag"

James Taylor
(Columbia)

Mr. President (Have Pity on the
   Working Man)
"Good Old Boys"

Randy Newman

(Reprise)

Mr. Sellack
"The Roches"

The Roches
(Warner Brothers)

DEFINITIVE SONGS

Night Shift
"Rastaman Vibration"
Bob Marley and the Wailers
(Island)

Nine to Five
"A Soap Opera"
The Kinks
(RCA)

Oklahoma U.S.A.
"Muswell Hillbillies"
The Kinks
(RCA)

Pay Day Blues

"Last Train to Hicksville"
Dan Hicks and His Hot
  Licks
(Blue Thumb)

The Promised Land
"Darkness on the Edge of Town"
Bruce Springsteen
(Columbia)

Rush Hour Blues
"A Soap Opera"
The Kinks
(RCA)

Salesman
"Pisces, Aquarius, Capricorn and
  Jones Ltd."
The Monkees
(Colgems)

Sixteen Tons
"Tennessee Ernie Ford's Greatest
  Hits"
Tennessee Ernie Ford
(Capitol)

+Sixteen Tons
"Greatest Hits"
The Weavers
(Vanguard)

+Sixteen Tons
"Don Harrison"*
Don Harrison Band
(Atlantic)

Smokey Factory Blues
"Slow Flux"
Steppenwolf
(Mums/Columbia)

Someday I'll Build a Boat
"Song for a Friend"
Jon Mark
(Columbia)

Standing on the Edge of Town
"Ramblin' Boy"*
Tom Paxton
(Elektra)

Sunshine
"Jonathan Edwards"*
Jonathan Edwards
(Capricorn)

Take This Job and Shove It
"Take This Job and Shove It"
"Johnny Paycheck's Greatest Hits
  Vol. II"
Johnny Paycheck
(Epic)
(Epic)

Taking Care of Business
"Best of B.T.O. . . . (So Far)"
"Bachman-Turner Overdrive 2"
Bachman-Turner Overdrive
(Mercury)
(Mercury)

Theme from "Car Wash"
"Car Wash" (Soundtrack)
Rose Royce
(MCA)

DEFINITIVE SONGS

Unemployed
"Words You Can Dance To"*
Steve Goodman
(Asylum)

Washer Woman
"Levon Helm and the RCO All Stars"
Levon Helm
(ABC)

Way Out West
"Five Times the Sun"
The Dingoes
(A&M)

Weekend Song
"Streetlife Serenade"
Billy Joel
(Columbia)

We Gotta Get Out of This Place
"Best Of the Animals"
The Animals
(ABKCO)

+We Gotta Get Out of This Place
"Stage Door Johnnies"*
Claire Hamill
(Konk)

+We Gotta Get Out of This Place
"Some Enchanted Evening"
Blue Oyster Cult
(Columbia)

Welcome to the Working Week
"My Aim Is True"
Elvis Costello
(Columbia)

Well Respected Man
"The Kinks' Greatest Hits"
"The Live Kinks"
"The History of the Kinks Vol. II"
The Kinks
(Reprise)
(Reprise)
(Pye)

+Well Respected Man
"Hits of the 60's"
The Bachelors
(London)

+Well Respected Man
"Hits Again"
Gary Lewis and the Playboys
(Liberty)

When Work Is Over
"Soap Opera"
The Kinks
(RCA)

Work All Week
(45 RPM Single)
The Mekons
(Virgin)

William Brown
"Born Again"
Randy Newman
(Warner Brothers)

Workin' Man
"Utopia"
Utopia
(Kent)

Working All Day
"Three Friends"
Gentle Giant
(Columbia)

Working at the Car Wash Blues
"Photographs and Memories"
Jim Croce
(ABC)

Working Class Hero
"John Lennon/Plastic Ono Band"
John Lennon
(Apple)

DEFINITIVE SONGS

+Working Class Hero
"Broken English"

Marianne Faithful
(Island)

+Working Class Hero
"Full Bloom"

Tommy Roe
(Monument)

Working for the Clampdown
"London Calling"

The Clash
(Epic)

Working for the Man
"More of Roy Orbison's Greatest
Hits"

Roy Orbison
(Monument)

Working Girls
"English Boys/Working Girls"

Deaf School
(Warner Brothers)

Working in the Vineyard
"Let the Rough Side Drag"*

Jesse Winchester
(Warner Brothers)

The Working Man

Creedence Clearwater
Revival

"Creedence Clearwater Revival"

(Fantasy)

Working Man's Woman

New Riders of the Purple
Sage

"Brujo"

(Columbia)

Work
"Here"

Leo Sayer
(Warner Brothers)

Work Shy
"The Fabulous Poodles"

The Fabulous Poodles
(Epic)

The Work Song
"Maria Muldaur"

Maria Muldaur
(Warner Brothers)

Work to Do
"The Isley Brothers' Greatest"
"Timeless"

The Isley Brothers
(T-Neck)
(T-Neck)

+Work to Do
"Average White Band"

Average White Band
(Atlantic)

REFERENCE SONGS

Celtic Rock
"Open Road"*

Donovan
(Epic)

Factory Girl
"Beggars Banquet"

The Rolling Stones
(London)

The Frying Pan
"Diamonds in the Rough"*

John Prine
(Atlantic)

REFERENCE SONGS

A Hard Day's Night   The Beatles
"A Hard Day's Night" (Soundtrack)   (United Artists)

+A Hard Day's Night   The Supremes
"A Little Bit of Liverpool"   (Motown)
"Anthology"   (Motown)

+A Hard Day's Night   John Mayall
"Notice to Appear"   (ABC)

Just a Story from America   Elliott Murphy
"Just a Story from America"*   (Columbia)

Manura Manyah   Pete Seeger
"Strangers and Cousins"   (Columbia)

On Behalf of the Entire Staff and   Tommy James and the
    Management   Shondells
"Cellophane Symphony"*   (Roulette)

The Pretender   Jackson Browne
"The Pretender"   (Asylum)

Proud Mary   Creedence Clearwater
                                                Revival

"Bayou Country"   (Fantasy)
"Chronicle"   (Fantasy)

+Proud Mary   Ike and Tina Turner
"Working Together"   (Liberty)
"The Very Best of Ike and Tina   (United Artists)
    Turner"

+Proud Mary   Spiral Staircase
"More Today Than Yesterday"   (Columbia)

Shoe Salesman   Alice Cooper
"Easy Action"   (Warner Brothers)

Shoe Shine Boy   Eddie Kendricks
"For You"   (Motown)

Shoeshine Boy   Gerry Rafferty
"Gerry Rafferty"   (Visa)

Singing the Blues   Eric Clapton
"There's One in Every Crowd"   (RSO)

Steve Forbert's Midsummer Night's   Steve Forbert
    Toast
"Alive on Arrival"   (Nemperor)

Summertime Blues   Eddie Cochran
"Legendary Masters No. 4" ·   (United Artists)

REFERENCE SONGS

+Summertime Blues "Vincebus Eruptum"*	Blue Cher (Philips)
+Summertime Blues "Live at Leeds"	The Who (MCA/Track)
+Summertime Blues "The Beach Boys"	The Beach Boys (Pickwick)
+Summertime Blues "Clearly Love"	Olivia Newton-John (MCA)
+Summertime Blues "Robert Gordon with Link Wray"	Robert Gordon with Link Wray (RCA)
Take a Letter Maria (45 RPM Single)	R. B. Greaves (Atco)
+Take a Letter Maria "Oh What a Mighty Time"	New Riders of the Purple Sage (Columbia)
Tenth Floor Clown "The Shirts"	The Shirts (Capitol)
Terminal "Widescreen"*	Rupert Holmes (Epic)
Wichita Lineman "Glen Campbell's Greatest Hits"	Glen Campbell (Capitol)
You Make It All Worthwhile "Soap Opera"	The Kinks (RCA)

YOUR ADDITIONAL SONGS

_____

_____

_____

_____

_____

Unions

Songs about unions, strikes, and management/labor relations.

CLASSICS

Joe Hill	Joan Baez
"Woodstock" (Soundtrack)	(Cotillion)
"One Day at a Time"	(Vanguard)
"From Every Stage"	(A&M)
Part of the Union	Strawbs
"Bursting at the Seams"	(A&M)
"The Best of Strawbs"	(A&M)

DEFINITIVE SONGS

Better World	Woody Guthrie
"Woody Guthrie"	(Warner Brothers)
The Closed Shop (Fact)	Barclay James Harvest
"Barclay James Harvest XII"	(Polydor)
Get Back in Line	The Kinks
"Kink Kronikles"	(Reprise)
"Lola Versus Powerman and the Moneygoround"	(Reprise)
Harry Simms	Pete Seeger
"Circles and Seasons"	(Warner Brothers)
High Sheriff of Hazard	Tom Paxton
"Ramblin' Boy"*	(Elektra)
Joe Hill	Phil Ochs
"Tape from California"	(A&M)
Joshua Gone Barbados	Tom Rush
"Classic Rush"	(Columbia)
King Harvest (Has Surely Come)	The Band
"The Band"	(Capitol)
"Rock of Ages"	(Capitol)
"Anthology"	(Capitol)
Links on the Chain	Phil Ochs
"I Ain't Marchin' Anymore"	(Elektra)
1913 Massacre	Arlo Guthrie
"Hobo's Lullaby"	(Reprise)
Pastures of Plenty	Woody Guthrie
"Woody Guthrie"	(Warner Brothers)
Talking Unions	Pete Seeger
"Pete Seeger's Greatest Hits"	(Columbia)
Union Maid	Pete Seeger and Judy Collins
"A Tribute to Woody Guthrie"	(Warner Brothers)

DEFINITIVE SONGS

Union Man
"Cate Brothers"

Cate Brothers
(Asylum)

Victor Jara
"Amigos"

Arlo Guthrie
(Warner Brothers)

Which Side Are You On
"The Essential Pete Seeger"

Pete Seeger
(Columbia)

YOUR ADDITIONAL SONGS

_____

_____

_____

_____

_____

Miners

Tales of the miners and the mines of America.

CLASSICS

Sixteen Tons
"Tennessee Ernie Ford's Greatest
    Hits"

Tennessee Ernie Ford
(Capitol)

+Sixteen Tons
"Greatest Hits"

The Weavers
(Vanguard)

+Sixteen Tons
"Don Harrison Band"*

Don Harrison Band
(Atlantic)

DEFINITIVE SONGS

Appalachian Coal Miner's Son
"Blue Ridge Mountain Skyline"*

Sammy Walker
(Warner Brothers)

Bells of Rhymney
"The Byrds' Greatest Hits"
"Mr. Tambourine Man"

The Byrds
(Columbia)
(Columbia)

DEFINITIVE SONGS

+Bells of Rhymney   Pete Seeger
  "The World of Pete Seeger"   (Columbia)
  "Pete Seeger's Greatest Hits"   (Columbia)

+Bells of Rhymney   Judy Collins
  "Recollections"   (Elektra)

+Bells of Rhymney   Cher
  "All I Really Want to Do"*   (Imperial)

Big Bad John   Jimmy Dean
  "Jimmy Dean's Greatest Hits"   (Columbia)

Calico Silver   Michael Murphey
  "Geronimo's Cadillac"   (A&M)

Coal Miner's Daughter   Sissy Spacek
  "Coal Miner's Daughter"   (MCA)
    (Soundtrack)

Coal Tattoo   Judy Collins
  "The Judy Collins Concert"   (Elektra)

Dirty Business   New Riders of the Purple
                                                       Sage
  "New Riders of the Purple Sage"   (Columbia)

Faces of Appalachia   John Sebastian
  "Tarzana Kid"*   (Reprise)

Green Rolling Hills   Emmylou Harris
  "Quarter Moon in a Ten Cent Town"   (Warner Brothers)

The Miner's Song   Pete Fowler
  (45 RPM Single)*   (Oval)

Mother of a Miner's Child   Gordon Lightfoot
  "Old Dan's Records"   (Reprise)

Mrs. Clara Sullivan's Letter   Pete Seeger
  "I Can See a New Day"   (Columbia)

New York Mining Disaster 1941   The Bee Gees
  "Best of Bee Gees"   (RSO)
  "Bee Gees' First"   (Atco)
  "Bee Gees' Gold"   (RSO)

Poet of the West Virginia Mines   James Talley
  "Ain't It Something"*   (Capitol)

Red Wing Black Bird   Judy Collins
  "Judy Collins in Concert"   (Elektra)

Steamboat Row   Gerry Rafferty
  "Gerry Rafferty"   (Visa)

DEFINITIVE SONGS

Sweet Guinevere "Endless Wire"	Gordon Lightfoot (Reprise)
Which Side Are You On "Pete Seeger's Greatest Hits"	Pete Seeger (Columbia)
Working in a Coal Mine "New Orleans Jazz and Heritage Festival"*	Lee Dorsey (Island)
+Working in a Coal Mine "Just Fly"	Pure Prairie League (RCA)

REFERENCE SONGS

Brave Mountaineer "Don Quixote"	Gordon Lightfoot (Reprise)
Don't Look Now	Creedence Clearwater Revival
"More Creedence Gold" "Willy and the Poor Boys"	(Fantasy) (Fantasy)
Hills of West Virginia "I Ain't Marchin' Anymore"	Phil Ochs (Elektra)

YOUR ADDITIONAL SONGS

_____

_____

_____

_____

_____

Secretaries

The secretaries . . . the vital and underestimated part of every office and business.

DEFINITIVE SONGS

Dance Mr. Big, Dance "Deadly Nightshade"*	Deadly Nightshade (Phantom/RCA)

DEFINITIVE SONGS

Disco   Elliot Lurie
"Elliot Lurie"*   (Epic)

Nasty Secretary   Joy Rider and Avis Davis
(45 RPM Single)   (Monogram)

She Loves to Hear the Music   Peter Allen
"It's Time for Peter Allen"   (A&M)

+She Loves to Hear the Music   Sylvia Sims
"She Loves to Hear the Music"   (A&M)

Take a Letter Maria   R. B. Greaves
(45 RPM Single)   (Atco)

+Take a Letter Maria   New Riders of the Purple
                                             Sage
"Oh What a Mighty Time"   (Columbia)

REFERENCE SONGS

Halfway to Heaven   Harry Chapin
"Verities and Balderdash"   (Elektra)

I Wanna Be an Engineer   Pete Seeger
"Circles & Seasons"   (Warner Brothers)

Working Girls   Deaf School
"English Boys/Working Girls"   (Warner Brothers)

YOUR ADDITIONAL SONGS

_____

_____

_____

_____

_____

After Work Hours

The time of the day many people think about most during work hours.

CLASSICS

Night	Bruce Springsteen
"Born to Run"	(Columbia)

DEFINITIVE SONGS

Five O'Clock World	The Vogues
"The Vogues' Greatest Hits"	(Reprise)
A Hard Day's Night	The Beatles
" 'A Hard Day's Night' (Soundtrack)"	(United Artists)
+A Hard Day's Night	The Supremes
"A Little Bit of Liverpool"	(Motown
"Anthology"	(Motown)
+A Hard Day's Night	John Mayall
"Notice to Appear"	(ABC)
The Heart of Saturday Night	Tom Waits
"The Heart of Saturday Night"	(Asylum)
+The Heart of Saturday Night	Dion
"Return of the Wanderer"	(Lifesong)
I Can't Wait to Get Off Work	Tom Waits
"Small Change"	(Asylum)
I Know a Place	Petula Clark
"Greatest Hits"	(Warner Brothers)
Kitty	Cat Stevens
"New Masters"	(Deram)
Nighttime	Tommy Roe
"It's Now Winter's Day"*	(ABC)
Nighttime	J. Geils
"Love Stinks"	(EMI/America)
Quitting Time	The Roches
"The Roches"	(Warner Brothers)
Racing in the Streets	Bruce Springsteen
"Darkness on the Edge of Town"	(Columbia)
The Promised Land	Bruce Springsteen
"Darkness on the Edge of Town"	(Columbia)
Sara Monday	Ian Tamblyn
"Ian Tamblyn"*	(Cream)
Weekend Song	Billy Joel
"Streetlife Seranade"	(Columbia)
When Work Is Over	The Kinks
"Soap Opera"	(RCA)

DEFINITIVE SONGS

You Make It All Worthwhile	The Kinks
"Soap Opera"	(RCA)

REFERENCE SONGS

Another Saturday Night	Sam Cooke
"This Is Sam Cooke"	(RCA)
+Another Saturday Night	Cat Stevens
"Greatest Hits"	(A&M)
The Fever	Southside Johnny and the Asbury Jukes
"I Don't Want to Go Home"	(Epic)
+The Fever	Allan Rich
"Glass Heart"	(Columbia)
Gimme Some Lovin'	The Spencer Davis Group
"The Best of the Spencer Davis Group"	(Island)
"Spencer Davis' Greatest Hits"	(United Artists)
+Gimme Some Lovin'	Steve Winwood
"Winwood"	(United Artists)
+Gimme Some Lovin'	Rubicon
"American Dreams"	(20th Century-Fox)
+Gimme Some Lovin'	Olivia-Newton John
"Totally Hot"	(MCA)
Have Another Drink	The Kinks
"Soap Opera"	(RCA)
Here Comes the Night	The Beach Boys
"Wild Honey"	(Brother/Reprise)
"The Beach Boys' L.A. Album"	(Caribou)
Just Got Paid	ZZ Top
"The Best of ZZ Top"	(London)
Rip It Up	Little Richard
"Little Richard's Greatest Hits"	(Trip)
"All Time Greatest"	(Specialty)
+Rip It Up	The Everly Brothers
"The Everly Brothers Greatest Hits"	(Barnaby)
+Rip It Up	Commander Cody and the Lost Planet Airmen
"Hot Licks, Cold Steel and Truckers' Favorites"	(Paramount)

REFERENCE SONGS

+Rip It Up
"I'll Be There"*

Gerry and the Pacemakers
(Laurie)

+Rip It Up
"Golden Hits"

Bill Haley and the Comets
(MCA)

+Rip It Up
"Elvis"

Elvis Presley
(RCA)

Shoeshine Boy
"Gerry Rafferty"

Gerry Rafferty
(Visa)

Talk to Me

Southside Johnny and the
   Asbury Jukes

"Hearts of Stone"

(Epic)

Until the Night
"52nd Street"

Billy Joel
(Columbia)

Up on the Roof
"Writer"

Carole King
(Ode)

+Up on the Roof
"Twenty-Four Original Hits"
"Sixteen Greatest Hits"

The Drifters
(Atlantic)
(Trip)

+Up on the Roof
"Christmas and the Beads of Sweat"

Laura Nyro
(Columbia)

+Up on the Roof
"A Scratch in the Sky"*

Cryan Shames
(Columbia)

+Up on the Roof
"Flag"

James Taylor
(Columbia)

YOUR ADDITIONAL SONGS

_____

_____

_____

_____

_____

TWENTY EMOTIONS AND THEMES OF LOVE

Related Categories: Children, Divorce, Friendship, Loneliness, Marriage

+Same as Song Above
*Hard-to-find Songs/Albums

The Cast, in Order of Appearance
"Looking for a Love"
"Like to Get to Know You"
"Feel Like Makin' Love"
"Fallin' in Love"
"I Want You"
"How Can I Be Sure?"
"Don't Mess Up a Good Thing"/"We Can Work It Out"
"Torn Between Two Lovers"
"Love Hurts"
"Unrequited Love"
"Babe I'm Gonna Leave You" (partings)
"I Don't Wanna See You Again" (bitter partings)
"Please Don't Go" (unwilling partings)
"I Still Miss Someone"
"Darling Be Home Soon" (temporarily apart)
"Back Together Again"
"Here I Go Again" (love on the rebound)
"It's So Nice to See Old Friends" (reunion of old lovers)
"Yesterday"/"Memories of Love"
"Lessons Learned"
"Happy Together"
"And I Love You So" (ballad love songs)

THEMATIC ALBUMS

"Love Songs"	The Beatles (Capitol)
"Time in a Bottle (Greatest Love Songs)"	Jim Croce (Lifesong)
"Suite for Susan Moore and Damion"*	Tim Hardin (Columbia)
"Heart Like a Wheel"	Linda Ronstadt (Asylum)

THEMATIC ALBUMS

"Mad Love"	Linda Ronstadt (Asylum)
"Torn Between Two Lovers"	Mary MacGregor (Ariola/America)
"My Boy"*	Richard Harris (ABC/Dunhill)
"A Little Touch of Schmilsson"	Harry Nilsson (RCA)

YOUR ADDITIONAL SONGS

_____

_____

_____

_____

_____

"Looking for a Love"

Another Night "Another Night"	The Hollies (Epic)
Attractive Female Wanted "Blondes Have More Fun"	Rod Stewart (Warner Brothers)
Dream Lover "Bobby Darin Story"	Bobby Darin (Atco)
+Dream Lover "A Giant of Rock and Roll"*	Ronnie Hawkins (Monument)
+Dream Lover "Highly Prized Possessions"	Anne Murray (Capitol)
+Dream Lover "McKinley Mitchell"*	McKinley Mitchell (Chimneyville)
+Dream Lover "Dion Sings the Fifteen Million Sellers"	Dion (Laurie)

"Looking for a Love"   (cont.)

+Dream Lover (45 RPM Single)	Rick Nelson (Epic)
Everyday "Twenty Golden Hits" "The Buddy Holly Story"	Buddy Holly (MCA) (MCA)
+Everyday "Playing Favorites"	Don McLean (United Artists)
+Everyday "Everyday"	Becky Hobbs (Tattoo)
+Everyday "Aerie"	John Denver (RCA)
Hard Headed Woman "Tea for the Tillerman" "Greatest Hits"	Cat Stevens (A&M) (A&M)
Heart of Gold "Decade" "Harvest"	Neil Young (Reprise) (Reprise)
If He's Ever Near "Hasten Down the Wind"	Linda Ronstadt (Asylum)
+If He's Ever Near "Karla Bonoff"	Karla Bonoff (Columbia)
In and Out of Love	Diana Ross and the Supremes
"Diana Ross and the Supremes' Greatest Hits" "Anthology"	(Motown) (Motown)
Looking for a Lady "Home Free"	Dan Fogelberg (Epic)
Looking for a Love "Bobby Womack's Greatest Hits"	Bobby Womack (United Artists)
+Looking for a Love "More Than Before"	The Persuasions (A&M)
+Looking for a Love "Full House" (Live)	J. Geils Band (Atlantic)
+Looking for a Love "Playmates"	Small Faces (Atlantic)
Looking for a Love "Zuma"	Neil Young (Reprise)

"Looking for a Love"   (cont.)

Looking for Another Pure Love "Talking Book"	Stevie Wonder (Tamla)
Looking for the Right One "Breakaway"	Art Garfunkel (Columbia)
+Looking for the Right One "Bish"	Steven Bishop (ABC)
Love Me Somebody "Run with the Pack"	Bad Company (Swan Song)
Need a Lady "Living on the Fault Line"	The Doobie Brothers (Warner Brothers)
One of These Nights "One of These Nights" "Their Greatest Hits 1971–1975"	The Eagles (Asylum) (Asylum)
Sunday Kind of Love "The Original Rock and Roll Show" "Remember How Great Vol. III"	The Harptones (Gold Disc) (Columbia)
+A Sunday Kind of Love "Wonder Where I'm Bound"*	Dion (Laurie)
+Sunday Kind of Love "Inside"	Kenny Rankin (Little David)
Walking in the Rain "Phil Spector's Greatest Hits"	Ronettes (Warner-Spector)
+Walking in the Rain "Wax Museum"*	Jay and the Americans (United Artists)
When Will I Be Loved "The Everly Brothers' Original Greatest Hits"	The Everly Brothers (Barnaby/CBS)
+When Will I Be Loved "Greatest Hits" "Heart Like a Wheel"	Linda Ronstadt (Asylum) (Asylum)
+When Will I Be Loved "Mystic Line"*	Phil Everly (Pye)
+When Will I Be Loved "Tanya Tucker"	Tanya Tucker (MCA)
You Can't Hurry Love "Anthology" "The Supremes' Greatest Hits"	The Supremes (Motown) (Motown)

YOUR ADDITIONAL SONGS

_____

_____

_____

_____

_____

"Like to Get to Know You"

All Right Now	Free
"Best of Free"	(A&M)
"Free Live"	(A&M)
"Fire and Water"	(A&M)
Ariel	Dean Friedman
"Dean Friedman"*	(Lifesong)
Da Doo Ron Ron	The Crystals
"Phil Spector's Greatest Hits"	(Warner-Spector)
+Da Doo Ron Ron	Ian Matthews
"Tigers Will Survive"	(Mercury)
+Da Doo Ron Ron	Roger C. Reale
"Bionic Gold"*	(Big Sound)
+Da Doo Ron Ron	The Chiffons
"Everything You Always Wanted to Know"	(Laurie)
+Da Doo Ron Ron	Laverne & Shirley
"Laverne & Shirley Sing"	(Atco)
Haven't We Met?	Kenny Rankin
"Silver Morning"	(Little David)
Hello I Love You	The Doors
"13"	(Elektra)
"Waiting for the Sun"	(Elektra)
I Met Him on a Sunday	The Shirelles
"The Very Best of the Shirelles"	(United Artists)
+I Met Him on a Sunday	Laura Nyro
"Gonna Take a Miracle"	(Columbia)

"Like to Get to Know You"   (cont.)

I'm Into Something Good "Herman's Hermits XX—Their Greatest Hits"	Herman's Hermits (ABKCO)
"Introducing Herman's Hermits"	(ABKCO)
I'm Just a Kid "Abandoned Luncheonette"	Hall and Oates (Atlantic)
I Never Talk to Strangers "Broken Blossom"	Bette Midler (Atlantic)
+I Never Talk to Strangers "Foreign Affairs"	Tom Waits (Asylum)
I Saw Her Standing There "Meet the Beatles" "Rock and Roll"	The Beatles (Capitol) (Capitol)
+I Saw Her Standing There (45 RPM Single, b/w Philadelphia Freedom)	Elton John (MCA)
+I Saw Her Standing There "Suicide Sal"	Maggie Bell (Swan Song)
+I Saw Her Standing There "What Do You Want From Live"	The Tubes (A&M)
+I Saw Her Standing There "Three Hearts"	Bob Welch (Capitol)
Like to Get to Know You "Spanky's Greatest Hits"	Spanky and Our Gang (Mercury)
Oh! Pretty Woman "The Very Best of Roy Orbison"	Roy Orbison (Monument)
Sharing the Night Together "Pleasure and Pain"	Dr. Hook (Capitol)
Strangers in the Night "Songs for the New Depression"	Bette Midler (Atlantic)
Then He Kissed Me "Phil Spector's Greatest Hits"	Crystals (Warner-Spector)
+Then He Kissed Me "Let It Be Written, Let It Be Sung"*	Ellie Greenwich (Verve)
+Then He Kissed Me "Look At Us"*	Sonny and Cher (Atco)
+Then He Kissed Me "Bionic Gold"*	The Scratch Band (Big Sound)

"Like to Get to Know You"   (cont.)

+Then I Kissed Her   Kiss
  "Love Gun"   (Casablanca)
+Then I Kissed Her   The Beach Boys
  "Summer Days"   (Capitol)
+Then I Kissed Her   Bob Welch
  "Three Hearts"   (Capitol)

YOUR ADDITIONAL SONGS

_____

_____

_____

_____

_____

"Feel Like Makin' Love"

  Afternoon Delight   Starland Vocal Band
  "Starland Vocal Band"   (Windsong)
  Crazy Love   Van Morrison
  "Moondance"   (Warner Brothers)
+Crazy Love   Rita Coolidge
  "Rita Coolidge"   (A&M)
+Crazy Love   The Isley Brothers
  "Sixteen Greatest Hits"   (Trip)
+Crazy Love   Helen Reddy
  "I Don't Know How to Love Him"   (Capitol)
  Cuddle Up   The Beach Boys
  "Carl and the Passions"   (Brother/Reprise)
  Feel Like Makin' Love   Roberta Flack
  "Feel Like Makin' Love"   (Atlantic)
+Feel Like Makin' Love   Gladys Knight and The Pips
  "Second Anniversary"   (Buddah)

"Feel Like Makin' Love"   (cont.)

Feel Like Makin' Love "Straight Shooter"	Bad Company (Swan Song)
For Old Times Sake "Boys in the Trees"	Carly Simon (Elektra)
I Dig Love "All Things Must Pass"	George Harrison (Apple)
I Love Making Love to You "Sweet Soul Music"	José Feliciano (RCA)
+I Love Making Love to You "Allman and Woman"	Gregg Allman and Cher (Warner Brothers)
I'm in the Mood for Love "Fats Domino"	Fats Domino (United Artists)
+I'm in the Mood for Love "Since I Fell For You"	Lenny Welch (Columbia)
+I'm in the Mood for Love "Yeah Yeah"	Georgie Fame (Imperial)
+I'm in the Mood for Love "Let's Fall in Love"	Peaches and Herb (Date)
Lay Lady Lay "Nashville Skyline"	Bob Dylan (Columbia)
+Lay Lady Lay "Road Songs"	Hoyt Axton (A&M)
+Lay Lady Lay "The Best . . . Isley Brothers"	The Isley Brothers (Buddah)
+Lay Lady Lay "Four Sides of Melanie"*	Melanie (Buddah)
A Little Bit More "A Little Bit More"	Dr. Hook (Capitol)
Look Me in the Eyes "Playing Possum"	Carly Simon (Elektra)
Lovin' You "Perfect Angel"	Minnie Riperton (Epic)
Make Yourself Comfortable "Broken Blossom"	Bette Midler (Atlantic)
Moondance "Moondance"	Van Morrison (Warner Brothers)
+Moondance "Hand in Glove"	Terry Garthwaite (Fantasy)

"Feel Like Makin' Love"   (cont.)

More and More "Playing Possum"	Carly Simon (Elektra)
Ready "Buddah and the Chocolate Box"	Cat Stevens (A&M)
The Right Thing to Do "No Secrets"	Carly Simon (Elektra)
Right Time of the Night "Jennifer Warnes"	Jennifer Warnes (Arista)
Sleep Song "Song for Beginners"	Graham Nash (Atlantic)
Stay Awhile "Fly Little White Dove"	The Bells (Polydor)

YOUR ADDITIONAL SONGS

_____

_____

_____

_____

_____

"Fallin' in Love"

All Shook Up "Worldwide 50 Gold Award Hits"	Elvis Presley (RCA)
+All Shook Up "Suzi Quatro"	Suzi Quatro (Bell)
+All Shook Up "Fringe Benefit"*	Fringe Benefit (Capricorn)
+All Shook Up "Beck-Ola"	Jeff Beck (Epic)
Betcha By Golly, Wow "The Best of the Stylistics"	The Stylistics (Avco)

"Fallin' in Love"   (cont.)

Can't Help Falling in Love "Worldwide 50 Gold Award Hits"	Elvis Presley (RCA)
+Can't Help Falling in Love "Dylan"	Bob Dylan (Columbia)
+Can't Help Falling in Love "Patti Rice"*	Patti Rice (H&L Records)
+Can't Help Falling in Love "Fabulous"	The Stylistics (H&L Records)
+Can't Help Falling in Love "You Were on My Mind"*	We Five (A&M)
Could It Be I'm Falling in Love "The Spinners" "The Best of the Spinners"	The Spinners (Atlantic) (Atlantic)
Do Wah Diddy Diddy "The Best of Manfred Mann" "History of British Rock" "The Manfred Mann Album"*	Manfred Mann (Janus) (Sire) (Ascot)
+Do Wah Diddy Diddy "What's Wrong with This Picture?"	Andrew Gold (Asylum)
+Do Wah Diddy Diddy Puttin' on the Dog"*	Hound (Columbia)
Do You Want to Know a Secret? "Introducing the Beatles"	The Beatles (Vee Jay)
+Do You Want to Know a Secret? "History of British Rock Vol. III" "Little Children"*	Billy J. Kramer (Sire) (Imperial)
Don't Want to Live Without "Worlds Away"	Pablo Cruise (A&M)
Fallin' in Love "Fallin' in Love"	Hamilton, Joe Frank and Reynolds (Dunhill)
Fallin' in Love "Souther, Hillman and Furay"	Souther, Hillman and Furay (Asylum)
Fooled Around and Fell in Love "Raisin' Hell" "Struttin' My Stuff"	Elvin Bishop (Capricorn) (Capricorn)
For Once in My Life "Greatest Hits"	Stevie Wonder (Tamla)

"Fallin' in Love"   (cont.)

+For Once in My Life
  "Anthology"

Four Tops
(Motown)

+For Once in My Life
  "Live"

Glen Campbell
(Capitol)

+For Once in My Life
  "Anthology"

Gladys Knight and The Pips
(Motown)

+For Once in My Life
  "Once I Loved"

Esther Satterfield
(A&M)

+For Once in My Life
  "It's All Part of Love"

Jackie Wilson
(Brunswick)

+For Once in My Life
  "More Today Than Yesterday"

Spiral Staircase
(Columbia)

Happy Man
"Chicago VII"

Chicago
(Columbia)

Help Me
"Court and Spark"

Joni Mitchell
(Asylum)

I Believe (When I Fall in Love)
"Talking Book"

Stevie Wonder
(Tamla)

+I Believe (When I Fall in Love)
  "Frampton's Camel"

Peter Frampton
(A&M)

+I Believe (When I Fall in Love)
  "Breakaway"

Art Garfunkel
(Columbia)

It's So Easy
"Golden Greats"
"The Buddy Holly Story"

Buddy Holly
(MCA)
(MCA)

+It's So Easy
  "Simple Dreams"

Linda Ronstadt
(Asylum)

+It's So Easy
  "Hoppkorv"

Hot Tuna
(RCA)

+It's So Easy
  "The Buddy Holly Story"
    (Soundtrack)

Gary Busey
(Epic)

I've Just Seen a Face
"Rubber Soul"

The Beatles
(Capitol)

+I've Just Seen a Face
  "One Night"

Arlo Guthrie
(Warner Brothers)

+I've Just Seen a Face
  "Memories"*

Bonnie Bramlett
(Capricorn)

"Fallin' in Love"   (cont.)

+I've Just Seen a Face
  "Wings over America"

Wings
(Capitol)

Just One Look
  (45 RPM Single)

Dori Troy
(Atlantic)

+Just One Look
  "Here I Go Again"*
  "The Very Best of the Hollies"
  "Hollies Live"

The Hollies
(Imperial)
(United Artists)
(Epic)

+Just One Look
  "Living in the U.S.A."

Linda Ronstadt
(Asylum)

+Just One Look
  "Victim of Romance"*

Michelle Phillips
(A&M)

+Just One Look
  "Go For Broke"

Ian Matthews
(Columbia)

+Just One Look
  "England's Greatest Hit Makers"

Marianne Faithful
(London)

+Just One Look
  "Love Songs"

Anne Murray
(Capitol)

Mad Love
  "Mad Love"

Linda Ronstadt
(Asylum)

Why Do Fools Fall in Love?
  "American Hot Wax" (Soundtrack)

The Chesterfields
(A&M)

+Why Do Fools Fall in Love?
  "Spirit of America"

The Beach Boys
(Capitol)

+Why Do Fools Fall in Love?
  (45 RPM Single)

Frankie Lymon
(Ace)

With Your Love
  "Spitfire"
  "Gold"

Jefferson Starship
(Grunt)
(Grunt)

You Didn't Have to Be So Nice
  "The Very Best of the Lovin'
    Spoonful"
  "The John Sebastian Songbook"

The Lovin' Spoonful
(Kama Sutra)

(Kama Sutra)

You Got to Me
  "Neil Diamond's Greatest Hits"

Neil Diamond
(Bang)

You Showed Me
  "Happy Together Again"

The Turtles
(Sire)

+You Showed Me
  "Preflyte"

The Byrds
(Columbia)

YOUR ADDITIONAL SONGS

_____

_____

_____

_____

_____

"I Want You"

All I Have to Do Is Dream "The Very Best of the Everly Brothers"	The Everly Brothers (Warner Brothers)
+All I Have to Do Is Dream "In Dreams"	Roy Orbison (Monument)
+All I Have to Do Is Dream "Dream"	Nitty Gritty Dirt Band (United Artists)
+All I Have to Do Is Dream "Lucy Simon"*	Lucy Simon (RCA)
+All I Have to Do Is Dream "Rogue Waves"	Terry Reid (Capitol)
All I Want "Blue"	Joni Mitchell (Reprise)
Be My Baby "Phil Spector's Greatest Hits"	Ronettes (Warner-Spector)
+Be My Baby "The Golden Hour of the Searchers Vol. II"	The Searchers (Golden Hour)
+Be My Baby "Andy Kim's Greatest Hits"	Andy Kim (Steed)
+Be My Baby "Let It Be Written, Let It Be Sung"*	Ellie Greenwich (Verve)
+Be My Baby "Shaun Cassidy"	Shaun Cassidy (Warner Brothers)
Earth Angel (45 RPM Single) "Original Gold Soul"	The Penguins (Dootone) (Mercury)

"I Want You" (cont.)

For Your Love	The Yardbirds
"For Your Love"	(Epic)
"The Yardbirds' Greatest Hits"	(Epic)
+For Your Love	Fleetwood Mac
"Mystery to Me"	(Reprise)
+For Your Love	Gary Lewis and the Playboys
"A Session with Gary Lewis and the Playboys"*	(Liberty)
Foxy Lady	Jimi Hendrix
"Are You Experienced?"	(Reprise)
"Smash Hits"	(Reprise)
From Me to You	The Beatles
"Introducing the Beatles"*	(Vee Jay)
"The Beatles 1962–1966"	(Capitol)
+From Me to You	The Swallows
"Ain't She Sweet" (The Beatles)	(Atco)
+From Me to You	Del Shannon
"Vintage Years"	(Sire)
Go My Way	Gordon Lightfoot
"Summer Side of Life"	(Reprise)
Hey Baby	Bruce Channel
(45 RPM Single)*	(Smash)
+Hey Baby	Ringo Starr
"Rotogravure"	(Atlantic)
+Hey Baby	José Feliciano
"Greatest Hits of José Feliciano"	(RCA)
I'd Like to Know You Better	Carole King
"Thoroughbred"	(Ode)
I Wanna Be Your Man	The Beatles
"Meet the Beatles"	(Capitol)
+I Wanna Be Your Man	The Rolling Stones
(45 RPM Single b/w Not Fade Away)	(London)
+I Wanna Be Your Man	The Swallows
"Ain't She Sweet" (The Beatles)	(Atco)
I Want You	Bob Dylan
"Blonde on Blonde"	(Columbia)
"Bob Dylan's Greatest Hits"	(Columbia)
"Live At Budokan"	(Columbia)

"I Want You" (cont.)

+I Want You
  "Cher Sings the Hits"*

Cher
(Springboard)

I Want You
  "Double Platinum"

Kiss
(Casablanca)

I Want You, I Need You, I Love You
  "Worldwide 50 Gold Award Hits"

Elvis Presley
(RCA)

Just to Be Close to You
  "Commodores' Greatest Hits"
  "Hot Tracks"

Commodores
(Motown)
(Motown)

Love Me Do
  "Introducing the Beatles"
  "The Beatles 1962–1966"

The Beatles
(Vee Jay)
(Apple)

Sooner or Later
  "Their Greatest Hits"
  "The ABC Collection"

The Grass Roots
(ABC/Dunhill)
(ABC)

Tell Me What You See
  "Beatles VI"
  "Love Songs"

The Beatles
(Capitol)
(Capitol)

Thunder Road
  "Born to Run"

Bruce Springsteen
(Columbia)

Where You Lead
  "Tapestry"

Carole King
(Ode)

+Where You Lead
  "Sister Kate"*

Kate Taylor
(Cotillion)

With a Girl Like You
  "Vintage Troggs"
  "History of British Rock Vol. II"

The Troggs
(Sire)
(Sire)

Wonderful World
  "This Is Sam Cooke"

Sam Cooke
(RCA)

+Wonderful World
  "Herman's Hermits XX—Their
    Greatest Hits"

Herman's Hermits
(ABKCO)

+Wonderful World
  "Vance Thirty-Two"*

Kenny Vance
(Atlantic)

+Wonderful World
  "Midnight Wind"

David Bromberg
(Columbia)

+Wonderful World
  "Watermark"

Art Garfunkel
(Columbia)

"I Want You" (cont.)

+Wonderful World   The Supremes
  "A Little Bit of Liverpool"   (Motown)
  "We Remember Sam Cooke"   (Motown)

+Wonderful World   Otis Redding
  "Otis Blue"   (Volt)

+Wonderful World   Bryan Ferry
  "Another Time, Another Place"   (Atco)

YOUR ADDITIONAL SONGS

_____

_____

_____

_____

_____

"How Can I Be Sure?"

Did You Ever Have to Make Up Your   The Lovin' Spoonful
  Mind?
  "The Very Best of the Lovin'   (Kama Sutra)
  Spoonful"
  "The Best . . . Lovin' Spoonful"   (Kama Sutra)

How   John Lennon
  "Imagine"   (Apple)

+How   Helen Reddy
  "Helen Reddy"   (Capitol)

How Can I Be Sure?   The Young Rascals
  "Time Peace"   (Atlantic)
  "Groovin' "   (Atlantic)

+How Can I Be Sure?   Helen Reddy
  "I Don't Know How to Love Him"   (Capitol)

I Believe in You   Neil Young
  "Decade"   (Reprise)
  "After the Gold Rush"   (Reprise)

"How Can I Be Sure?"   (cont.)

+I Believe in You
  "Don't Cry Now"

Linda Ronstadt
(Asylum)

+I Believe in You
  "Rita Coolidge"

Rita Coolidge
 (A&M)

I Don't Know How to Love Him
  "I Don't Know How To Love Him"
  "Jesus Christ Superstar"

Yvonne Elliman
(Polydor)
(Decca)

+I Don't Know How to Love Him
  "I Don't Know How to Love Him"
  "Helen Reddy's Greatest Hits"

Helen Reddy
(Capitol)
(Capitol)

I'm Not in Love
  "10 CC"
  "Greatest Hits 1972–78"

10 CC
(U.K.)
(Polydor)

+I'm Not in Love
  "Happy 'Bout the Whole Thing"

Dee Dee Sharp
(Philadelphia International)

+I'm Not in Love
  "The End of the Beginnings"

Richie Havens
 (A&M)

I Second That Emotion

Smokey Robinson & the
  Miracles

  "Greatest Hits Vol. II"
  "Anthology"
  "Smokin'"

(Tamla)
(Motown)
(Tamla)

It's Now or Never
  "Worldwide 50 Gold Award Hits"
  "Elvis in Concert"

Elvis Presley
(RCA)
(RCA)

It's Up to You
  "Back Home Again"

John Denver
(RCA)

A Lover's Question
(45 RPM Single)

Clyde McPhatter
(Atlantic)

+A Lover's Question
  "So Fine"

Loggins and Messina
(Columbia)

+A Lover's Question
  "Wax Museum"*

Jay and the Americans
(United Artists)

Make Up Your Mind
  "Bloodshot"

J. Geils Band
(Atlantic)

She's Still a Mystery to Me
  "The Best of the Lovin' Spoonful
    Vol. II"

The Lovin' Spoonful
(Kama Sutra)

"How Can I Be Sure?"   (cont.)

"The Very Best of the Lovin' Spoonful"	(Kama Sutra)
"Everything Playing"*	(Kama Sutra)
Shoop Shoop Song (It's in His Kiss) (45 RPM Single)*	Betty Everett (Vee Jay)
"First Generation"	(Buddah)
+Shoop Shoop Song (It's in His Kiss) "Kate Taylor"	Kate Taylor (Columbia)
Sitting on a Fence "Head over Heels"*	Poco (ABC)
Sitting on a Fence "Flowers"	The Rolling Stones (London)
Surfer Girl "Endless Summer" "In Concert" "Surfer Girl"	The Beach Boys (Capitol) (Brother/Reprise) (Capitol)
Take It or Leave It "Boats Against the Current"	Eric Carmen (Arista)
Tired of Waiting "The Kinks' Greatest Hits" "The History of the Kinks Vol. II"	The Kinks (RCA) (Pye)
+Tired of Waiting "The Flock"*	The Flock (Columbia)
+Tired of Waiting "If You Knew Suzi . . ."	Suzi Quatro (RSO)
Try Too Hard "Glad All Over Again"	The Dave Clark Five (Epic)

YOUR ADDITIONAL SONGS

_____

_____

_____

_____

_____

"Don't Mess Up a Good Thing"/"We Can Work It Out"

Bad Weather "The Very Best of Poco" "From the Inside"*	Poco (Epic) (Epic)
+Bad Weather "Rising Son"	Yvonne Elliman (RSO)
Best of My Love "Their Greatest Hits 1971–1975" "On the Border"	The Eagles (Asylum) (Asylum)
+Best of My Love "Rising Son"*	Yvonne Elliman (RSO)
+Best of My Love "You Are So Beautiful"	Tanya Tucker (Columbia)
Break Up to Make Up "The Best of the Stylistics"	The Stylistics (Avco)
Can't You See "Marshall Tucker Band" "Greatest Hits"	The Marshall Tucker Band (Capricorn) (Capricorn)
Cold as Ice "Foreigner"	Foreigner (Atlantic)
Don't Be Cruel "Worldwide 50 Gold Award Hits"	Elvis Presley (RCA)
+Don't Be Cruel "I Can Help"	Billy Swan (Monument)
+Don't Be Cruel "In Flight"	Alvin Lee (Columbia)
+Don't Be Cruel "Monsters"	Jerry Lee Lewis (Sun)
Don't Mess Up a Good Thing "Laid Back"	Gregg Allman (Capricorn)
Dreams "Rumours"	Fleetwood Mac (Reprise)
For No One "Revolver" "Love Songs"	The Beatles (Capitol) (Apple)
Get Closer "Get Closer"	Seals and Crofts (Warner Brothers)
Growing Away from Me "Music"	Carole King (Ode)

"Don't Mess Up a Good Thing"/"We Can Work It Out"   (cont.)

Half a Chance "Another Passenger"	Carly Simon (Elektra)
Hasten Down the Wind "Hasten Down the Wind"	Linda Ronstadt (Asylum)
+Hasten Down the Wind "Warren Zevon"	Warren Zevon (Asylum)
I Heard It Through the Grapevine "Anthology"	Marvin Gaye (Motown)
+I Heard It Through the Grapevine "Cosmo's Factory" "Chronicle"	Creedence Clearwater Revival (Fantasy) (Fantasy)
+I Heard It Through the Grapevine "Anthology"	Gladys Knight and The Pips (Motown)
+I Heard It Through the Grapevine "Grand Slam"	Rare Earth (Rare Earth)
+I Heard It Through the Grapevine "A Luxury You Can Afford"	Joe Cocker (Asylum)
+I Heard It Through the Grapevine "Full Moon"	Kris Kristofferson and Rita Coolidge (A&M)
I Heard It Through the Grapevine "Cloud Nine"	The Temptations (Gordy)
+I Heard It Through the Grapevine "Person to Person"	Average White Band (Atlantic)
Late for the Sky "Late for the Sky"	Jackson Browne (Asylum)
Losing Touch "Even Now"	Barry Manilow (Arista)
Monday Morning "Fleetwood Mac"	Fleetwood Mac (Reprise)
Nothing at All "Daryl Hall and John Oates"	Hall and Oates (RCA)
Sign Language "No Reason to Cry"	Eric Clapton (RSO)
Sorry Seems to Be the Hardest Word "Blue Moves" "Greatest Hits, Volume 2"	Elton John (MCA) (MCA)
Suspicious Minds "Worldwide 50 Gold Award Hits"	Elvis Presley (RCA)

"Don't Mess Up a Good Thing"/"We Can Work It Out"   (cont.)

+Suspicious Minds
  "B. J. Thomas"
       B. J. Thomas
       (Springboard)

+Suspicious Minds
  "The Outlaws"
       Waylon Jennings
       (RCA)

Talking in Your Sleep
  "Summer Side of Life"
       Gordon Lightfoot
       (Reprise)

Tenderness
  "There Goes Rhymin' Simon"
       Paul Simon
       (Columbia)

This Masquerade
  "Best of Leon"
  "Carney"
       Leon Russell
       (Shelter)
       (Shelter)

+This Masquerade
  "Breezin'"
       George Benson
       (Warner Brothers)

+This Masquerade
  "I Am Woman"
       Helen Reddy
       (Capitol)

Tightrope
  "Best of Leon"
  "Carney"
       Leon Russell
       (Shelter)
       (Shelter)

Tonight
  "Blue Moves"
       Elton John
       (MCA)

We Can Work It Out
  "The Beatles 1962–1966"
  "Yesterday and Today"
       The Beatles
       (Capitol)
       (Capitol)

+We Can Work It Out
  "Phonogenic, Not Just Another Pretty
    Face"
       Melanie
       (Midsong International)

+We Can Work It Out
  "Greatest Hits Vol. II"
       Stevie Wonder
       (Tamla)

+We Can Work It Out
  "Street Rats"
       Humble Pie
       (A&M)

+We Can Work It Out
  "All This and World War II"
    (Soundtrack)
       The Four Seasons
       (20th Century-Fox)

Woman Woman

  "Gary Puckett and the Union Gap's
    Greatest Hits"
  "Woman Woman"
       Gary Puckett and the Union
       Gap
       (Columbia)

       (Columbia)

YOUR ADDITIONAL SONGS

_____

_____

_____

_____

_____

"Torn Between Two Lovers"

(N.B. Songs involving married people are listed in "Unhappily Married" and "Adultery.")

Anna "Introducing the Beatles"	The Beatles (Vee Jay)
+Anna "Thunderbox"	Humble Pie (A&M)
Baby's in Black "Beatles' '65"	The Beatles (Capitol)
Conversation "Ladies of the Canyon"	Joni Mitchell (Reprise)
Daytime Friend "Ten Years of Gold"	Kenny Rogers (United Artists)
Frankie and Johnny "This Is Sam Cooke"	Sam Cooke (RCA)
+Frankie and Johnny "Frankie and Johnny" (Soundtrack)	Elvis Presley (RCA)
+Frankie and Johnny "Golden Greats of Jerry Lee Lewis"	Jerry Lee Lewis (Sun)
+Frankie and Johnny "Putting on the Style"	Lonnie Donegan (United Artists)
Hey Joe "Are You Experienced?" "Smash Hits"	Jimi Hendrix (Reprise) (Reprise)
+Hey Joe "Fifth Dimension"	The Byrds (Columbia)

"Torn Between Two Lovers"   (cont.)

+Hey Joe	Johnny Rivers
"Realization"	(United Artists)
"Johnny Rivers" (Superpak)	(United Artists)
+Hey Joe	The Leaves
(45 RPM Single)*	(Columbia)
"Nuggets: Original Artyfacts from the First Psychedelic Era 1965–1968"	(Sire)
+Hey Joe	Love
"Love"*	(Elektra)
+Hey Joe	Spirit
"Spirit of '76"	(Mercury)
Him or Me, What's It Gonna Be?	Paul Revere and the Raiders
"All Time Greatest Hits"	(Columbia)
I Honestly Love You	Peter Allen
"It's Time for Peter Allen"	(A&M)
+I Honestly Love You	Olivia Newton-John
"If You Love Me, Let Me Know"	(MCA)
+I Honestly Love You	Bobby Womack
"Road of Life"	(Arista)
+I Honestly Love You	The Staple Singers
"Family Tree"	(Warner Brothers)
I Looked Away	Derek and the Dominos
"Layla"	(RSO)
Lily, Rosemary and the Jack of Hearts	Bob Dylan
"Blood on the Tracks"	(Columbia)
+Lily, Rosemary and the Jack of Hearts	Joan Baez
"From Every Stage"	(A&M)
Lying Eyes	The Eagles
"Their Greatest Hits 1971–1975"	(Asylum)
"One of These Nights"	(Asylum)
My Girl Bill	Jim Stafford
"Jim Stafford"	(MGM)
Rocky Raccoon	The Beatles
"The Beatles" (White Album)	(Apple)
+Rocky Raccoon	Richie Havens
"Richie Havens on Stage"*	(Stormy Forest)
Run Like a Thief	Bonnie Raitt
"Home Plate"	(Warner Brothers)

"Torn Between Two Lovers"   (cont.)

Stagger Lee	Lloyd Price
"Sixteen Greatest Hits"	(Trip)
"The ABC Collection"	(ABC)
"Mr. Personality's Fifteen Greatest Hits"	(ABC)
Stagger Lee	Professor Longhair
"Live on the Queen Mary"	(Harvest)
"Rock and Roll Gumbo"	(French Blue Star)
+Stagger Lee	Wilson Pickett
"The Best of Wilson Pickett Vol. II"	(Atlantic)
+Stagger Lee	The Righteous Brothers
"The History of the Righteous Brothers"	(MGM)
+Stagger Lee	Dave Van Ronk
"Dave Van Ronk"*	(Fantasy)
+Stagger Lee	Taj Mahal
"Taj Mahal"	(Columbia)
+Stagger Lee	Jim Kweskin
"Jump for Joy"*	(Vanguard)
+Stagger Lee	The McCoys
"You Make Me Feel So Good"*	(Bang)
+Stagger Lee	Johnny Rivers
"Meanwhile at the Whiskey A Go-Go"*	(Imperial)
+Stagger Lee	Pacific Gas & Electric
"The Best of P G & E"	(Columbia)
+Stagger Lee	Neil Diamond
"September Morn"	(Columbia)
+Stagger Lee	P. J. Proby
"Somewhere"*	(Liberty)
+Stagger Lee	The Grateful Dead
"Shakedown Street"	(Arista)
+Stack-o-Lee	Dr. John
"Gumbo"	(Atco)
That's When Your Heartaches Begin	Elvis Presley
"Worldwide 50 Gold Award Hits"	(RCA)
Three Hearts	Bob Welch
"Three Hearts"	(Capitol)

"Torn Between Two Lovers"　(cont.)

Torn Between Two Lovers "Torn Between Two Lovers"	Mary MacGregor (Ariola/America)
Triad "Four Way Street"	Crosby, Stills, Nash & Young (Atlantic)
+Triad "Crown of Creation"	Jefferson Airplane (RCA)
Where Is the Love? "The Best of Donny Hathaway"	Donny Hathaway (Atlantic)

YOUR ADDITIONAL SONGS

_____

_____

_____

_____

_____

"Love Hurts"

Crying in the Rain "The Very Best of the Everly 　Brothers"	The Everly Brothers (Warner Brothers)
+Crying in the Rain "Rock and Roll Forever"*	Flash Cadillac (Epic)
Feelings "Feelings"	Morris Alpert (RCA)
+Feelings "Traveling at the Speed of Thought"	O'Jays (Philadelphia International)
First Cut Is the Deepest "New Masters"	Cat Stevens (Deram)
+First Cut Is the Deepest "The Legendary Christine Perfect 　Album"	Christine Perfect (Sire)
+First Cut Is the Deepest "A Night on the Town"	Rod Stewart (Warner Brothers)

"Love Hurts"   (cont.)

How Can You Mend a Broken Heart "Gold"	The Bee Gees (RSO)
+How Can You Mend a Broken Heart "Love Songs"*	Peter Yarrow (Warner Brothers)
+How Can You Mend a Broken Heart "Greatest Hits"	Al Green (Hi)
Hurt "In Concert"	Elvis Presley (RCA)
The Hurt "Foreigner"	Cat Stevens (A&M)
Hurts So Bad	Little Anthony and the Imperials
"The Very Best of Little Anthony and the Imperials"	(United Artists)
+Hurt So Bad "Mad Love"	Linda Ronstadt (Asylum)
I Don't Want to Talk About It "Atlantic Crossing"	Rod Stewart (Warner Brothers)
I Go to Pieces "Vintage Years"	Del Shannon (Sire)
+I Go to Pieces "The History of British Rock" "Peter and Gordon's Greatest Hits"	Peter and Gordon (Sire) (Capitol)
+I Go to Pieces "Fool Around"	Rachel Sweet (Stiff)
I'm Blowin' Away "Home Plate"	Bonnie Raitt (Warner Brothers)
+I'm Blowin' Away "Spirit of a Woman"	American Flyer (United Artists)
+I'm Blowin' Away "Living in the U.S.A."	Linda Ronstadt (Asylum)
+I'm Blowin' Away "Blowin' Away"	Joan Baez (Portrait)
It Hurts to Be in Love "Greatest Hits of All Time"	Gene Pitney (Musicor)
+It Hurts to Be in Love "Randy Meisner"*	Randy Meisner (Asylum)
It's a Heartache "It's a Heartache"	Bonnie Tyler (RCA)

"Love Hurts"   (cont.)

It's Over "The Very Best of Roy Orbison"	Roy Orbison (Monument)
I Wish It Would Rain "I Wish It Would Rain" "Anthology—Tenth Anniversary Special"	The Temptations (Gordy) (Motown)
+I Wish It Would Rain "Hobo with a Grin"	Steve Harley (Capitol)
+I Wish It Would Rain "Anthology"	Gladys Knight and The Pips (Motown)
+I Wish It Would Rain "Safety Zone"	Bobby Womack (United Artists)
+I Wish It Would Rain "Coast to Coast"	Rod Stewart (Mercury)
+I Wish It Would Rain "A New Time—A New Day"	The Chambers Brothers (Columbia)
Jealousy "Jazz"	Queen (Elektra)
Laughing "The Best of the Guess Who" "Canned Wheat"	The Guess Who (RCA) (RCA)
Love Has No Pride "Greatest Hits" "Don't Cry Now"	Linda Ronstadt (Asylum) (Asylum)
+Love Has No Pride "Give It Up"	Bonnie Raitt (Warner Brothers)
+Love Has No Pride "Fall into Spring"	Rita Coolidge (A&M)
+Love Has No Pride "American Flyer"	American Flyer (United Artists)
+Love Has No Pride "Libby Titus"	Libby Titus (Columbia)
+Love Has No Pride "Love Songs"*	Peter Yarrow (Warner Brothers)
Love Hurts "The All Time Greatest Hits of Roy Orbison"	Roy Orbison (Monument)
+Love Hurts "Nazareth's Greatest Hits"	Nazareth (A&M)

"Love Hurts"   (cont.)

+Love Hurts
  "Short Cut Draw Blood"

Jim Capaldi
(Island)

+Love Hurts
  "Everly Brothers Original Greatest
    Hits"

The Everly Brothers
(Barnaby/CBS)

+Love Hurts
  "Jennifer Warnes"

Jennifer Warnes
(Arista)

+Love Hurts
  "Grievous Angel"

Gram Parsons
(Reprise)

Love Is a Hurtin' Thing
  "Cloud Nine"

The Temptations
(Gordy)

Love Is a Hurtin' Thing
  "The Best from Lou Rawls"

Lou Rawls
(Capitol)

Mr. Blue
  "American Hot Wax" (Soundtrack)

Timmy and the Tulips
(A&M)

+Mr. Blue
  "Demon in Disguise"

David Bromberg
(Columbia)

Needles and Pins
  "Meet the Searchers"*
  "The History of the Searchers"
  "The Golden Hour of the Searchers"
  "The History of British Rock"

The Searchers
(Kapp)
(Pye)
(Golden Hour)
(Sire)

+Needles and Pins
  "The Very Best of Cher"

Cher
(United Artists)

+Needles and Pins
  "The Very Best of Jackie
    DeShannon"

Jackie DeShannon
(United Artists)

+Needles and Pins
  "Road to Ruin"

The Ramones
(Sire)

+Needles and Pins
  "This Diamond Ring"*

Gary Lewis and the Playboys
(Liberty)

+Needles and Pins
  (45 RPM Single)

Smokie
(RSO)

Operator
  "Photographs and Memories"
  "Time in a Bottle"

Jim Croce
(ABC)
(Lifesong)

Ordinary Pain
  "Songs in the Key of Life"

Stevie Wonder
(Tamla)

Sad Lisa
  "Tea for the Tillerman"

Cat Stevens
(A&M)

"Love Hurts" (cont.)

Silence Is Golden	The Tremeloes
"History of British Rock Vol. II"	(Sire)
+Silence Is Golden	The Four Seasons
"Born to Wander"*	(Philips)
"Gold Vault of Hits"	(Philips)
Stand Tall	Burton Cummings
"Burton Cummings"	(Portrait)
Tears on My Pillow	Little Anthony and the Imperials
"The Very Best of Little Anthony and the Imperials"	(United Artists)
+Tears on My Pillow	Sha Na Na
"Grease" (Soundtrack)	(RSO)
These Eyes	The Guess Who
"The Best of the Guess Who"	(RCA)
"Wheatfield Soul"	(RCA)
+These Eyes	Junior Walker and the All Stars
"Anthology"	(Motown)
Tracks of My Tears	Smokey Robinson & the Miracles
"Greatest Hits Vol. II"	(Tamla)
"Smokin' "	(Tamla)
"Anthology"	(Motown)
+Tracks of My Tears	Linda Ronstadt
"Prisoner in Disguise"	(Asylum)
"Greatest Hits"	(Asylum)
+Tracks of My Tears	Johnny Rivers
"A Touch of Gold"	(Liberty)
+Tracks of My Tears	Gladys Knight and The Pips
"Anthology"	(Motown)
+Tracks of My Tears	Mighty Diamonds
"Ice on Fire"	(Virgin)
Try and Love Again	The Eagles
"Hotel California"	(Asylum)
Walk On By	Dionne Warwick
"The Very Best of Dionne Warwick"	(United Artists)
+Walk On By	Average White Band
"Feel No Fret"	(Atlantic)

"Love Hurts"   (cont.)

+Walk On By "Experience Gloria Gaynor"	Gloria Gaynor (MGM)
+Walk On By "Mitch Ryder Sings the Hits"	Mitch Ryder (New Voice)
Yes It Is "Love Songs" "Beatles VI"	The Beatles (Capitol) (Capitol)
You've Got to Hide Your Love Away "Love Songs" "'Help!' (Soundtrack)"	The Beatles (Capitol) (Capitol)
+You've Got to Hide Your Love Away "The History of British Rock"	Silkie (Sire)
+You've Got to Hide Your Love Away "Beach Boys' Party!"	The Beach Boys (Capitol)

YOUR ADDITIONAL SONGS

_____

_____

_____

_____

_____

"Unrequited Love"

Baby It's You "The Very Best of the Shirelles"	The Shirelles (United Artists)
+Baby It's You "Introducing the Beatles"	The Beatles (Vee Jay)
+Baby It's You (45 RPM Single)* "A Group Called Smith"*	Smith (ABC/Dunhill) (ABC/Dunhill)
A Case of You "Blue" "Miles of Aisles"	Joni Mitchell (Reprise) (Asylum)

"Unrequited Love"   (cont.)

Catch the Wind	Donovan
"Donovan's Greatest Hits"	(Epic)
"Like It Is"	(Hickory)
+Catch the Wind	Blues Project
"Reunion in Central Park"	(MCA)
+Catch the Wind	Johnny Rivers
"Rivers Rocks the Folks"*	(Imperial)
Cherish	The Association
"The Association's Greatest Hits"	(Warner Brothers)
+Cherish	Faith, Hope and Charity
"Life Goes On"	(RCA)
Crying	Roy Orbison
"The Very Best of Roy Orbison"	(Monument)
Glad to Be Unhappy	The Mamas and The Papas
"Golden Era Vol. II"	(ABC/Dunhill)
Hopelessly Devoted to You	Olivia Newton-John
"Grease" (Soundtrack)	(RSO)
How Can I Tell You	Cat Stevens
"Teaser and the Firecat"	(A&M)
+How Can I Tell You	Lani Hall
"Sundown Lady"	(A&M)
Hush	Deep Purple
"Shades of Deep Purple"	(Tetragrammaton)
"When We Rock, We Rock, and When We Roll, We Roll"	(Warner Brothers)
+Hush	Joe South
"Joe South's Greatest Hits"	(Capitol)
I Can't Help It If I'm Still in Love with You	Linda Ronstadt
"Heart Like A Wheel"	(Capitol)
+I Can't Help It If I'm Still in Love with You	Rick Nelson
"Ricky Nelson"	(United Artists)
If You Knew	The Young Rascals
"Groovin'"	(Atlantic)
I Will	The Beatles
"The Beatles" (White Album)	(Apple)
"Love Songs"	(Capitol)

"Unrequited Love"   (cont.)

Long Long Time "Greatest Hits" "Retrospective"	Linda Ronstadt (Asylum) (Capitol)
Lose Again "Hasten Down the Wind"	Linda Ronstadt (Asylum)
+Lose Again "Karla Bonoff"	Karla Bonoff (Columbia)
Love Has No Pride "Don't Cry Now" "Greatest Hits"	Linda Ronstadt (Asylum) (Asylum)
+Love Has No Pride "Give It Up"	Bonnie Raitt (Warner Brothers)
+Love Has No Pride "Fall into Spring"	Rita Coolidge (A&M)
+Love Has No Pride "American Flyer"	American Flyer (United Artists)
+Love Has No Pride "Libby Titus"	Libby Titus (Columbia)
+Love Has No Pride "Love Songs"*	Peter Yarrow (Warner Brothers)
Making Believe "Luxury Liner" "Profile: The Best of Emmylou Harris"	Emmylou Harris (Warner Brothers) (Warner Brothers)
Never Letting Go "Careless"	Steven Bishop (ABC)
+Never Letting Go "Never Letting Go"	Phoebe Snow (Columbia)
The Night Was So Young "Love You"	The Beach Boys (Brother/Reprise)
Over My Head "Fleetwood Mac"	Fleetwood Mac (Reprise)
Pretty Lady "Can You Feel It"	Lighthouse (Polydor)
Simple Man "Songs for Beginners"	Graham Nash (Atlantic)
+Simple Man "Live"	David Crosby/Graham Nash (ABC)

"Unrequited Love"   (cont.)

Since I Fell for You "Since I Fell for You"	Lenny Welch (Columbia)
+Since I Fell for You "Collections"*	The Young Rascals (Atlantic)
+Since I Fell for You "Bonnie Raitt"	Bonnie Raitt (Warner Brothers)
+Since I Fell for You "Mose Alive"	Mose Allison (Atco)
+Since I Fell for You "Spotlighting the Man"*	Bobby Bland (Duke)
Stubborn Kind of Fella "Anthology"	Marvin Gaye (Motown)
+Stubborn Kind of Fella "Hang On Sloopy"*	The McCoys (Bang)
+Stubborn Kind of Woman "Kate Taylor"*	Kate Taylor (Columbia)
To Know Him Is to Love Him "Phil Spector's Greatest Hits"	Teddy Bears (Warner-Spector)
+To Know Him Is to Love Him "Now We Are Six"	Steeleye Span (Chrysalis)
+To Know Him Is to Love Him (45 RPM Single)	Cilla Black (Capitol)
+To Know Him Is to Love Him "Bionic Gold"	Mick Farren (Big Sound)
+To Know Her Is to Love Her "My Own House"	David Bromberg (Fantasy)
To Love Somebody "Bee Gees' First" "Bee Gees' Gold"	The Bee Gees (Atco) (RSO)
+To Love Somebody "I Got Dem Ol' Kozmic Blues"	Janis Joplin (Columbia)
+To Love Somebody "Love Is . . ."	Eric Burdon and the Animals (MGM)
+To Love Somebody "Close Up the Honkey Tonks"	The Flying Burrito Brothers (A&M)
+To Love Somebody "The Union Gap"*	Gary Puckett and the Union Gap (Columbia)

"Unrequited Love" (cont.)

+To Love Somebody "Love, Peace and Happiness"	The Chambers Brothers (Columbia)
Turn Around, Look at Me "The Vogues' Greatest Hits"	The Vogues (Reprise)
What Do You Want the Boy to Do? "Home Plate"	Bonnie Raitt (Warner Brothers)
+What Do You Want the Girl to Do? "Silk Degrees"	Boz Scaggs (Columbia)
+What Do You Want the Girl to Do? "Thanks I'll Eat It Here"	Lowell George (Warner Brothers)
Willin' "Little Feat" "Waiting for Columbus"	Little Feat (Warner Brothers) (Warner Brothers)
+Willin' "Heart Like a Wheel"	Linda Ronstadt (Asylum)
+Willin' "Kindling"	Gram Parsons (Warner Brothers)
+Willin' "Commander Cody and His Lost Planet Airmen"	Commander Cody and the Lost Planet Airmen (Warner Brothers)

YOUR ADDITIONAL SONGS

_____

_____

_____

_____

_____

"Babe I'm Gonna Leave You" (partings)

Ain't That a Shame "Fats Domino"	Fats Domino (United Artists)
+Ain't That a Shame "Cheap Trick at Budokan"	Cheap Trick (Epic)

"Babe I'm Gonna Leave You" (partings)   (cont.)

Babe I'm Gonna Leave You "Led Zeppelin"	Led Zeppelin (Atlantic)
Breakaway "Breakaway"	Gallagher and Lyle (Columbia)
+Breakaway "Breakaway"	Art Garfunkel (Columbia)
By the Time I Get to Phoenix "Glen Campbell's Greatest Hits"	Glen Campbell (Capitol)
+By the Time I Get to Phoenix "Jim Webb Sings Jim Webb"	Jimmy Webb (Warner Brothers)
+By the Time I Get to Phoenix "The Union Gap"*	Gary Puckett and the Union Gap (Columbia)
+By the Time I Get to Phoenix "Changes"*	Johnny Rivers (United Artists)
+By the Time I Get to Phoenix "Honey"*	Bobby Goldsboro (United Artists)
+By the Time I Get to Phoenix "10-23"	José Feliciano (RCA)
+By the Time I Get to Phoenix "Hickory Holler Revisited"	O. C. Smith (Columbia)
Bye Bye Love "The Very Best of the Everly Brothers"	The Everly Brothers (Warner Brothers)
+Bye Bye Love "Bridge over Troubled Water"	Simon and Garfunkel (Columbia)
+Bye Bye Love "Love Me Again"	Rita Coolidge (A&M)
Crying Time "A Man and His Music"	Ray Charles (ABC)
Didn't Want to Have to Do It "The Very Best of the Lovin' Spoonful"	The Lovin' Spoonful (Kama Sutra)
Didn't We "His Greatest Performances"	Richard Harris (ABC/Dunhill)
+Didn't We "All by Myself"	Eddie Hendricks (Tamla)
+Didn't We "Sixteen Greatest Hits"	Dionne Warwick (Trip)

"Babe I'm Gonna Leave You" (partings)   (cont.)

Different Drum "Greatest Hits" "A Retrospective"	Linda Ronstadt (Asylum) (Capitol)
The Famous Final Scene "Stranger in Town"	Bob Seger and the Silver Bullet Band (Capitol)
Fool for You "Night on the Town"	Rod Stewart (Warner Brothers)
For the Good Times "Me and Bobby McGee"	Kris Kristofferson (Monument)
+For the Good Times "Transition"	Kenny Rogers (Reprise)
+For the Good Times "Welcome to My World"	Elvis Presley (RCA)
+For the Good Times "Al Green's Greatest Hits Vol. II"	Al Green (London)
Goodbye My Love "The History of the Searchers" "The Golden Hour of the Searchers"	The Searchers (Pye) (Golden Hour)
Hey, That's No Way to Say Goodbye "The Best Of"	Leonard Cohen (Columbia)
+Hey, That's No Way to Say Goodbye "First Take"	Roberta Flack (Atlantic)
+Hey, That's No Way to Say Goodbye "Wildflowers"	Judy Collins (Elektra)
+Hey, That's No Way to Say Goodbye "Touching You, Touching Me"	Neil Diamond (MCA)
I Can Almost See It "Don't Cry Now"	Linda Ronstadt (Asylum)
I'd Rather Leave While I'm in Love "Carol Bayer Sager"	Carol Bayer Sager (Elektra)
+I'd Rather Leave While I'm in Love "Phonogenic, Not Just Another Pretty Face"	Melanie (Midsong International)
+I'd Rather Leave While I'm in Love "I Could Have Been a Sailor"	Peter Allen (A&M)
I'll Follow the Sun "Love Songs" "Beatles '65"	The Beatles (Capitol) (Capitol)

"Babe I'm Gonna Leave You" (partings)   (cont.)

I'm Gonna Be Strong	Gene Pitney
"Greatest Hits of All Time"	(Musicor)
It Doesn't Matter Anymore	Buddy Holly
"The Buddy Holly Story"	(MCA)
"A Rock and Roll Collection"	(MCA)
+It Doesn't Matter Anymore	Linda Ronstadt
"Greatest Hits"	(Asylum)
"Heart Like a Wheel"	(Asylum)
It's Too Late	Carole King
"Tapestry"	(Ode)
"Her Greatest Hits"	(Ode)
+It's Too Late	The Isley Brothers
"The Best . . . Isley Brothers"	(Buddah)
I Will Always Love You	Linda Ronstadt
"Prisoner in Disguise"	(Asylum)
Leaving in the Morning	Barry Manilow
"Even Now"	(Arista)
Lover's Cross	Jim Croce
"Time in a Bottle"	(Lifesong)
"Photographs and Memories"	(ABC)
+Lover's Cross	Melanie
"Madrugada"*	(Neighborhood)
One Less Set of Foot Prints	Jim Croce
"Photographs and Memories"	(ABC)
Pretty Goodbyes	Souther, Hillman and Furay
"Souther, Hillman and Furay"	(Asylum)
Which Way to Nowhere	The Fifth Dimension
"Up Up and Away"	(Soul City)
Wild World	Cat Stevens
"Tea for the Tillerman"	(A&M)
"Greatest Hits"	(A&M)
+Wild World	Jimmy Cliff
"Best of Jimmy Cliff"	(Island)
+Wild World	Jimmy Cliff
"Reggae Spectacular" (Various Artists)	(A&M)
Without You	Harry Nilsson
"Nilsson Schmilsson"	(RCA)
"Greatest Hits"	(RCA)

"Babe I'm Gonna Leave You" (partings)   (cont.)

+Without You   Badfinger
  "No Dice"   (Apple)

You're Gonna Make Me Lonesome   Bob Dylan
  When You Go
  "Blood on the Tracks"   (Columbia)

YOUR ADDITIONAL SONGS

_____

_____

_____

_____

_____

"I Don't Wanna See You Again" (bitter partings)

Already Gone   The Eagles
"Their Greatest Hits 1971–1975"   (Asylum)
"On the Border"   (Asylum)

Another Girl   The Beatles
" 'Help!' (Soundtrack)"   (Capitol)

Bumble Bee   The Searchers
"The History of the Searchers Vol. II" (Pye)
"The Golden Hour of the Searchers"   (Golden Hour)

The Chain   Fleetwood Mac
"Rumours"   (Reprise)

Don't Think Twice, It's All Right   Bob Dylan
"Bob Dylan's Greatest Hits Vol. II"   (Columbia)
"The Freewheelin' Bob Dylan"   (Columbia)

+Don't Think Twice, It's All Right   Peter, Paul and Mary
"Ten Years Together"   (Warner Brothers)
"In the Wind"   (Warner Brothers)

+Don't Think Twice, It's All Right   Joan Baez
"The First Ten Years"   (A&M)
"Joan Baez in Concert Part II"   (Vanguard)

"I Don't Wanna See You Again" (bitter partings)   (cont.)

+Don't Think Twice, It's All Right
    "As I See It Now"

Melanie
(Neighborhood)

+Don't Think Twice, It's All Right
    "Darin 1936–1973"*

Bobby Darin
(Motown)

+Don't Think Twice, It's All Right
    "The Four Seasons Story"
    "The Four Seasons Sing the Hits"

The Four Seasons
(Private Stock)
(Philips)

+Don't Think Twice, It's All Right
    "Odetta Sings Dylan"

Odetta
(RCA)

+Don't Think Twice, It's All Right
    "The Essential Ramblin' Jack Elliot"

Ramblin' Jack Elliott
(Vanguard)

+Don't Think Twice, It's All Right
    "In the Wind"*

Jackie DeShannon
(Imperial)

+Don't Think Twice, It's All Right
    "All I Really Want to Do"*

Cher
(Imperial)

Gonna Send You Back to Walker
    "Best of the Animals"
    "The Animals"*

The Animals
(ABKCO)
(MGM)

Gotta Getaway
    "December's Children"

The Rolling Stones
(London)

Got to Get You Off My Mind
    "The Best of Solomon Burke"

Solomon Burke
(Atlantic)

+Got to Get You Off My Mind

    "I Don't Wanna Go Home"

Southside Johnny and the
    Asbury Jukes
(Epic)

+Got to Get You Off My Mind
    "Cut You Loose"*

James Cotton
(Vanguard)

Hit the Road Jack
    "A Man and His Music"

Ray Charles
(ABC)

+Hit the Road Jack
    "Animalism"

The Animals
(MGM)

I Hear You Knocking
    "Fats Domino Million Sellers"
    "Fats Domino"*

Fats Domino
(Liberty)
(United Artists)

+I Hear You Knocking
    "Rock Pile"

Dave Edmunds
(Mam)

+I Hear You Knocking
    "Live and Kicking"*

Kingfish
(United Artists)

"I Don't Wanna See You Again" (bitter partings)   (cont.)

I'll Feel a Whole Lot Better	The Byrds
"The Byrds' Greatest Hits"	(Columbia)
"Mr. Tambourine Man"	(Columbia)
+I'll Feel a Whole Lot Better	Johnny Rivers
"Blue Suede Shoes"	(United Artists)
It Ain't Me Babe	Bob Dylan
"Another Side of Bob Dylan"	(Columbia)
"Greatest Hits"	(Columbia)
"Before the Flood" (with The Band)	(Asylum)
+It Ain't Me Babe	Joan Baez
"Joan Baez"	(Vanguard)
+It Ain't Me Babe	The Turtles
"Happy Together Again"	(Sire)
+It Ain't Me Babe	Bryan Ferry
"Another Time, Another Place"	(Atlantic)
+It Ain't Me Babe	Johnny Cash
(45 RPM Single)	(Columbia)
It's All Over Now	The Rolling Stones
"12×5"	(London)
"Big Hits (High Tide and Green Grass)"	(London)
"More Hot Rocks (Big Hits and Fazed Cookies)"	(London)
+It's All Over Now	Rod Stewart
"Gasoline Alley"	(Mercury)
"The Best of Rod Stewart"	(Mercury)
"Faces Live—Coast to Coast"	(Mercury)
+It's All Over Now	Ducks Deluxe
"Don't Mind Rockin' Tonight"	(RCA)
+It's All Over Now	Johnny Rivers
"In Action"*	(Imperial)
+It's All Over Now	Johnny Winter
"Captured Live"	(Blue Sky)
+It's All Over Now	Ozark Mountain Daredevils
"It's Alive"	(A&M)
+It's All Over Now	Ry Cooder
"Paradise And Lunch"*	(Reprise)
It's Over	Boz Scaggs
"Silk Degrees"	(Columbia)

"I Don't Wanna See You Again" (bitter partings)   (cont.)

The Last Time	The Rolling Stones
"More Hot Rocks (Big Hits and Fazed Cookies)"	(London)
+The Last Time	Piper
"Piper"*	(A&M)
Most Likely You Go Your Way I'll Go Mine	Bob Dylan
"Blonde on Blonde"	(Columbia)
"Before the Flood"	(Asylum)
+Most Likely You Go Your Way I'll Go Mine	Rita Coolidge
"Nice Feeling"	(A&M)
+Most Likely You Go Your Way I'll Go Mine	Patti Labelle
"Patti Labelle"	(Epic)
+Most Likely You Go Your Way I'll Go Mine	Todd Rundgren
"Faithful"	(Bearsville)
No Time	The Guess Who
"The Best of the Guess Who"	(RCA)
One Less Set of Footprints	Jim Croce
"Photographs and Memories"	(ABC)
Run with the Pack	Bad Company
"Run with the Pack"	(Swan Song)
Think for Yourself	The Beatles
"Rubber Soul"	(Capitol)
You Better Run	The Young Rascals
"Time Peace"	(Atlantic)
"Groovin' "	(Atlantic)
You Keep Me Hanging On	The Supremes
"The Supremes' Greatest Hits"	(Motown)
"Anthology"	(Motown)
+You Keep Me Hanging On	Vanilla Fudge
"Vanilla Fudge"*	(Atco)
+You Keep Me Hanging On	Wilson Pickett
"Greatest Hits"	(Atlantic)
+You Keep Me Hanging On	Rod Stewart
"Foot Loose and Fancy Free"	(Warner Brothers)

YOUR ADDITIONAL SONGS

_____

_____

_____

_____

_____

"Please Don't Go" (unwilling partings)

Ain't Too Proud to Beg "The Temptations' Greatest Hits" "Anthology—Tenth Anniversary Special"	The Temptations (Gordy) (Gordy)
+Ain't Too Proud to Beg "It's Only Rock and Roll"	The Rolling Stones (Rolling Stone Records)
+Ain't Too Proud to Beg "David Ruffin at His Best"	David Ruffin (Motown)
+Ain't Too Proud to Beg "It's in There . . . And It's Got to Come Out"*	Kate Taylor (Columbia)
(Baby) Don't Do It "Rock of Ages"	The Band (Capitol)
+(Baby) Don't Do It "Nicolette"	Nicolette Larson (Warner Brothers)
Cara Mia "Greatest Hits"	Jay and the Americans (United Artists)
Don't Leave Me This Way "Anyway You Like It"	Thelma Houston (Tamla)
+Don't Leave Me This Way "Philadelphia Classics"	Harold Melvin (Philadelphia International)
D'yer Maker "Houses of the Holy"	Led Zeppelin (Atlantic)
Go Now "Moody Blues No. 1"	The Moody Blues (London)

"Please Don't Go" (unwilling partings) (cont.)

+Go Now
"Wings Over America"
Wings
(Capitol)

+Go Now
"The Original Billy Preston . . . Soul'd Out"
Billy Preston
(Crescent)

Hey Girl
"Livin' Inside Your Love"
George Benson
(Warner Brothers)

I Can't Turn You Loose
"The History of Otis Redding"
"Live in Europe"
Otis Redding
(Atco)
(Volt)

+I Can't Turn You Loose
"Live at Bill Graham's Fillmore East"
The Chambers Brothers
(Columbia)

If You Leave Me Now
"Chicago X"
Chicago
(Columbia)

(I Know) I'm Losing You
"Every Picture Tells a Story"
Rod Stewart
(Mercury)

+(I Know) I'm Losing You
"Anthology—Tenth Anniversary Special"
The Temptations
(Motown)

I've Been Loving You Too Long
"The History of Otis Redding"
"Otis Blue"
"Live in Europe"
Otis Redding
(Atco)
(Volt)
(Volt)

+I've Been Loving You Too Long
"Mad Dogs and Englishmen"
Joe Cocker
(A&M)

+I've Been Loving You Too Long
"Greatest Hits"
Ike and Tina Turner
(United Artists)

The Last Thing on My Mind
"Ramblin' Boy"*
Tom Paxton
(Elektra)

+The Last Thing on My Mind
"Shazam"*
The Move
(A&M)

+The Last Thing on My Mind
"See What Tomorrow Brings"
Peter, Paul and Mary
(Warner Brothers)

+The Last Thing on My Mind
"Recollections"
Judy Collins
(Elektra)

+The Last Thing on My Mind
"Go Away From My World"*
Marianne Faithful
(London)

"Please Don't Go" (unwilling partings)   (cont.)

+The Last Thing on My Mind
"Rainbow"

Neil Diamond
(MCA)

+The Last Thing on My Mind
"Carry It On"

Joan Baez
(Vanguard)

+The Last Thing on My Mind
"Feliciano"

José Feliciano
(RCA)

Love Me
"Children of the World"

The Bee Gees
(RSO)

Move Over
"Janis Joplin's Greatest Hits"
"Pearl"

Janis Joplin
(Columbia)
(Columbia)

Oh Darling
"Abbey Road"

The Beatles
(Apple)

+Oh Darling
"Sgt. Pepper's Lonely Hearts Club
  Band Soundtrack"

Robin Gibb
(RSO)

Overs
"Bookends"

Simon and Garfunkel
(Columbia)

Please Don't Go
"Fulfillingness' First Finale"

Stevie Wonder
(Tamla)

Please Don't Go
"Do You Wanna Go Party?"

K.C. and the Sunshine Band
(TK Records)

Pretty Little Baby
"Anthology"

Marvin Gaye
(Motown)

Think
"Aretha's Gold"

Aretha Franklin
(Atlantic)

Think It Over
"Hot Line"

J. Geils Band
(Atlantic)

Where Did Our Love Go?
"Where Did Our Love Go?"
"The Supremes' Greatest Hits"
"Anthology"

The Supremes
(Motown)
(Motown)
(Motown)

+Where Did Our Love Go?
"Blow Your Face Out"

J. Geils Band
(Atlantic)

+Where Did Our Love Go?
"Dry Your Eyes"

Brenda and the Tabulations
(Dionne)

+Where Did Our Love Go
"Pastiche"

Manhattan Transfer
(Atlantic)

YOUR ADDITIONAL SONGS

_____

_____

_____

_____

_____

"I Still Miss Someone"

Ain't No Sunshine	Bill Withers
"The Best of Bill Withers"	(Sussex)
"Just As I Am"	(Sussex)
Baby I Need Your Loving	The Four Tops
"Best of the Four Tops"	(Motown)
"Greatest Hits"	(Motown)
"Live"	(Motown)
"Anthology"	(Motown)
+Baby I Need Your Loving	Johnny Rivers
"Superpak"	(United Artists)
+Baby I Need Your Loving	Double Exposure
"Ten Percent"*	(Salsoul)
+Baby I Need Your Loving	O. C. Smith
"La La Peace Song"	(Columbia)
Bell Bottom Blues	Derek and the Dominos
"Layla and Other Assorted Love Songs"	(RSO)
Bring It On Home	Sam Cooke
"This Is Sam Cooke"	(RCA)
+Bring It On Home	Van Morrison
"It's Too Late to Stop Now"	(Warner Brothers)
+Bring It On Home to Me	The Animals
"Animal Tracks"*	(ABKCO)
"Best of the Animals"	(ABKCO)
+Bring It On Home	Dave Mason
"Dave Mason"	(Columbia)

"I Still Miss Someone"   (cont.)

+Bring It On Home/Send Me Some   John Lennon
     Lovin'
  "Rock and Roll"   (Apple)

+Bring It On Home/You Send Me   Rod Stewart
  "Smiler"   (Mercury)

+Bring It On Home to Me   Bill Haley
  "Rock and Roll"   (Crescendo)

+Bring It On Home to Me   Led Zeppelin
  "Led Zeppelin II"   (Atlantic)

+Bring It On Home to Me   Carla Thomas
  "The Best of Carla Thomas"   (Atco)

  Can't Smile Without You   Barry Manilow
  "Even Now"   (Arista)
  "Greatest Hits"   (Arista)

  Crying   Roy Orbison
  "The Very Best of Roy Orbison"   (Monument)

  Crying in My Sleep   Art Garfunkel
  "Watermark"   (Columbia)

  Dreamin' Again   Jim Croce
  "Time in a Bottle"   (Lifesong)

  The Great Pretender   The Platters
  "Encore of Golden Hits"   (Mercury)

+The Great Pretender   The Band
  "Moondog Matinee"   (Capitol)
  "Anthology"   (Capitol)

  I Call Your Name   The Beatles
  "Second Album"   (Apple)

+I Call Your Name   The Mamas and The Papas
  "Sixteen of Their Greatest"   (ABC/Dunhill)
  "If You Can Believe Your Eyes and   (ABC/Dunhill)
     Ears"

  I Can't Help It If I'm Still in Love   Linda Ronstadt
     with You
  "Heart Like a Wheel"   (Asylum)

+I Can't Help It If I'm Still in Love   Rick Nelson
     with You
  "Ricky Nelson"   (United Artists)

  I Can't Quit Her   Blood, Sweat and Tears
  "Child Is Father to the Man"   (Columbia)
  "Greatest Hits"   (Columbia)

"I Still Miss Someone"   (cont.)

+I Can't Quit Her "Al's Big Deal/Unclaimed Freight—An Al Kooper Anthology"	Al Kooper (Columbia)
I Can't See Nobody "Best of Bee Gees" "Bee Gees' First"	The Bee Gees (RSO) (Atco)
I Can't Stop Loving You "A Man and His Soul" "Modern Sounds in Country and Western"	Ray Charles (ABC) (ABC)
+I Can't Stop Loving You "Welcome to My World"	Elvis Presley (RCA)
I'm Sorry "Windsong" "Greatest Hits Vol. II"	John Denver (RCA) (RCA)
I Need You " 'Help!' (Soundtrack)"	The Beatles (Capitol)
I Need You "America" "History—America's Greatest Hits" "America Live"	America (Warner Brothers) (Warner Brothers) (Warner Brothers)
I Still Miss Someone "Linda Ronstadt"	Linda Ronstadt (Capitol)
+I Still Miss Someone "Joan Baez"	Joan Baez (Vanguard)
Jesse Come Home "Stars"	Janis Ian (Columbia)
+Jesse Come Home "Diamonds and Rust"	Joan Baez (A&M)
+Jesse Come Home "Killing Me Softly"	Roberta Flack (Atlantic)
Long and Winding Road "Let It Be" "The Beatles 1967–1970" "Love Songs"	The Beatles (Apple) (Apple) (Capitol)
+Long and Winding Road "Standing Ovation"	Gladys Knight and The Pips (Soul)
+Long and Winding Road "Come On Over"	Olivia Newton-John (MCA)

"I Still Miss Someone"   (cont.)

+Long and Winding Road | Leo Sayer
"All This and World War II" | (20th Century Records)
   (Soundtrack)

Love Has No Pride | Linda Ronstadt
"Greatest Hits" | (Asylum)
"Don't Cry Now" | (Asylum)

+Love Has No Pride | Libby Titus
"Libby Titus" | (Columbia)

+Love Has No Pride | American Flyer
"American Flyer" | (United Artists)

+Love Has No Pride | Bonnie Raitt
"Give It Up" | (Warner Brothers)

+Love Has No Pride | Peter Yarrow
"Love Songs"* | (Warner Brothers)

+Love Has No Pride | Rita Coolidge
"Fall Into Spring" | (A&M)

Mandy | Barry Manilow
"Barry Manilow II" | (Arista)
"Greatest Hits" | (Arista)

Miss You | The Rolling Stones
"Some Girls" | (Rolling Stone Records)

Miss You Nights | Cliff Richards
"I'm Nearly Famous" | (MCA)

+Miss You Nights | Art Garfunkel
"Fate for Breakfast" | (Columbia)

My World Is Empty Without You Babe | The Supremes
"The Supremes' Greatest Hits" | (Motown)
"Anthology" | (Motown)

+My World Is Empty Without You Babe | Mary McCaslin
"Old Friends"* | (Philo)

+My World Is Empty Without You Babe | José Feliciano
"Greatest Hits of José Feliciano" | (RCA)

Nights Are Forever | England Dan and John Ford Coley
"Nights Are Forever" | (Big Tree)

"I Still Miss Someone"   (cont.) •

Ooh Baby Baby	Smokey Robinson & the Miracles
"Greatest Hits Vol. II"	(Tamla)
"Anthology"	(Motown)
"Smokin' "	(Tamla)
+Ooh Baby Baby	Todd Rundgren
"A Wizard, a True Star"	(Bearsville)
"Back to the Bars"	(Bearsville)
+Ooh Baby Baby	Linda Ronstadt
"Living in the U.S.A."	(Asylum)
Photograph	Ringo Starr
"Ringo"	(Apple)
"Blasts from Your Past"	(Apple)
San Francisco Bay Blues	Richie Havens
"Mixed Bag"*	(MGM)
"Richie Havens On Stage"*	(Stormy Forest)
+San Francisco Bay Blues	Phoebe Snow
"Phoebe Snow"	(Shelter)
+San Francisco Bay Blues	Janis Joplin
"Janis" (Soundtrack)	(Columbia)
+San Francisco Bay Blues	Peter, Paul and Mary
"A Song Will Rise"	(Warner Brothers)
+San Francisco Bay Blues	Ramblin' Jack Elliott
"Ramblin' Jack Elliott"*	(Prestige)
+San Francisco Bay Blues	The Weavers
"Reunion At Carnegie Hall"	(Vanguard)
Tears on My Pillow	Little Anthony and the Imperials
"The Very Best of Little Anthony and the Imperials"	(United Artists)
+Tears on My Pillow	Sha Na Na
"Grease" (Soundtrack)	(RSO)
Tell Me	The Rolling Stones
"England's Newest Hit Makers"	(London)
"More Hot Rocks (Big Hits and Fazed Cookies)"	(London)
These Eyes	The Guess Who
"The Best of the Guess Who"	(RCA)
"Wheatfield Soul"	(RCA)

"I Still Miss Someone"   (cont.)

+These Eyes	Junior Walker and the All Stars
"Anthology"	(Motown)
Without Her	Blood, Sweat and Tears
"Child Is Father to the Man"	(Columbia)
+Without Her	Al Kooper
"Al's Big Deal/Unclaimed Freight—An Al Kooper Anthology"	(Columbia)
+Without Her	Harry Nilsson
"Aerial Pandemonium Ballet"	(RCA)
"Greatest Hits"	(RCA)

YOUR ADDITIONAL SONGS

_____

_____

_____

_____

_____

"Darling Be Home Soon" (temporarily apart)

All My Loving	The Beatles
"Meet the Beatles"	(Capitol)
"The Beatles at the Hollywood Bowl"	(Capitol)
"The Beatles 1962–1966"	(Apple)
And Settlin' Down	Poco
"Good Feeling to Know"	(Epic)
Babe	Styx
"Cornerstone"	(A&M)
Beth	Kiss
"Kiss Alive 2"	(Casablanca)
But You Know I Love You	Kenny Rogers
"Ten Years of Gold"	(United Artists)
"The First Edition '69"*	(Reprise)

"Darling Be Home Soon" (temporarily apart)   (cont.)

Come Home	The Dave Clark Five
"Glad All Over Again"	(Epic)
Coming Home	Delaney and Bonnie
"On Tour (with Eric Clapton)"	(Atco)
"The Best of Delaney and Bonnie"	(Atco)
Come Monday	Jimmy Buffett
"Living and Dying in ¾ Time"	(ABC)
"You Had to Be There"	(ABC)
Darling Be Home Soon	The Lovin' Spoonful
"The Very Best of the Lovin' Spoonful"	(Kama Sutra)
"The Best of the Lovin' Spoonful"*	(Kama Sutra)
"The Best . . . Lovin' Spoonful"	(Kama Sutra)
+Darling Be Home Soon	John Sebastian
"Real Live John Sebastian"	(Reprise)
Goodbye Again	John Denver
"John Denver's Greatest Hits"	(RCA)
Home Again	Carole King
"Tapestry"	(Ode)
+Home Again	Kate Taylor
"Sister Kate"*	(Cotillion)
Home on Monday	Little River Band
"Diamantina Cocktail"	(Harvest)
Leaving on a Jet Plane	John Denver
"John Denver's Greatest Hits"	(RCA)
"Rhymes and Reasons"	(RCA)
+Leaving on a Jet Plane	Spanky and Our Gang
"Spanky and Our Gang"*	(Mercury)
+Leaving on a Jet Plane	Peter, Paul and Mary
"Ten Years Together"	(Warner Brothers)
"1700 Album"	(Warner Brothers)
Long Way from Home	Foreigner
"Foreigner"	(Atlantic)
Nighteen Days	The Dave Clark Five
"Glad All Over Again"	(Epic)
Person to Person	Average White Band
"Average White Band"	(Atlantic)
"Person to Person"	(Atlantic)

"Darling Be Home Soon" (temporarily apart)   (cont.)

P.S. I Love You	The Beatles
"Introducing the Beatles"	(Vee Jay)
"Love Songs"	(Capitol)
Save Your Heart for Me	Gary Lewis and the Playboys
"Golden Greats"	(Liberty)
Sealed with a Kiss	Brian Hyland
"Brian Hyland's Greatest Hits"	(ABC/Paramount)
See You in September	The Tempos
"American Graffiti" (Soundtrack)	(MCA)
+See You in September	The Happenings
(45 RPM Single)	(B. T. Puppy)
Together Again	Chicago
"Chicago X"	(Columbia)
Traveling Prayer	Billy Joel
"Piano Man"	(Columbia)
Unchained Melody	The Righteous Brothers
"Phil Spector's Greatest Hits"	(Warner-Spector)
"The History of the Righteous Brothers"	(Verve)
+Unchained Melody	Sonny and Cher
"Look at Us"*	(Atco)
+Unchained Melody	The Stylistics
"Once Upon a Juke Box"	(H&L Records)
+Unchained Melody	George Benson
"Livin' Inside Your Love"	(Warner Brothers)
+Unchained Melody	Al Green
"Livin' for You"	(Hi)
+Unchained Melody	Elvis Presley
"Moody Blue"	(RCA)
Weekend in New England	Barry Manilow
"Live"	(Arista)
"Greatest Hits"	(Arista)
When I Get Home	The Beatles
"Something New"	(Capitol)
When I Need You	Leo Sayer
"Endless Flight"	(Warner Brothers)
Wishing You Were Here	Chicago
"Chicago IX Chicago's Greatest Hits"	(Columbia)
"Chicago VII"	(Columbia)

YOUR ADDITIONAL SONGS

_____

_____

_____

_____

_____

"Back Together Again"

Back Home Again	John Denver
"John Denver's Greatest Hits Vol. II"	(RCA)
Back in My Arms Again	The Supremes
"The Supremes at the Copa"*	(Motown)
"The Supremes' Greatest Hits"	(Motown)
"Anthology"	(Motown)
+Back in My Arms Again	Genya Ravan
"Urban Desire"	(20th Century Records)
Back in My Baby's Arms Again	Kris Kristofferson and Rita Coolidge
"Natural Act"	(A&M)
Deirdre	The Beach Boys
"Sunflower"	(Capitol)
+Deirdre	Bruce Johnston
"Going Public"	(Columbia)
Good Feeling to Know	Poco
"Good Feeling to Know"	(Epic)
"The Very Best of Poco"	(Epic)
Hold Me Tight	Johnny Nash
"Greatest Hits"	(Columbia)
I Don't Want to Be Alone Anymore	Billy Joel
"Glass Houses"	(Columbia)
It's a Miracle	Barry Manilow
"Barry Manilow II"	(Arista)
"Live"	(Arista)
"Greatest Hits"	(Arista)

"Back Together Again"   (cont.)

It's Gonna Work Out Fine
"Thoroughbred"

Carole King
(Ode)

It Won't Be Long
"Meet the Beatles"

The Beatles
(Capitol)

Lay Me Down
"Easter Island"

Kris Kristofferson
(Monument)

The Letter
(45 RPM Single)*

The Arbors
(Date)

+The Letter
"Super Hits"

Box Tops
(Bell)

+The Letter
"Mad Dogs and Englishmen"

Joe Cocker
(A&M)

+The Letter
"Darin 1936–1973"*

Bobby Darin
(Motown)

+The Letter
"Photograph"

Melanie
(Atlantic)

+The Letter
"Green Is Blue"

Al Green
(Hi)

+The Letter
"Dionne"

Dionne Warwick
(United Artists)

Mama Mia
"Greatest Hits"

ABBA
(Atlantic)

Reunited
"Too Hot"

Peaches and Herb
(Polydor)

So Close
"So Close, So Very Far to Go"

Jake Holmes
(Polydor)

+So Close
"So Close"

Helen Schneider
(Windsong)

Someday We're Gonna Love Again
"The History of the Searchers"
"The Golden Hour of the Searchers"

The Searchers
(Pye)
(Golden Hour)

Southwind
"JD"

John Denver
(RCA)

Together Again
"Elite Hotel"
"Profile: The Best of Emmylou
   Harris"

Emmylou Harris
(Warner Brothers)
(Warner Brothers)

"Back Together Again"   (cont.)

Wait	The Beatles
"Rubber Soul"	(Capitol)

YOUR ADDITIONAL SONGS

_____

_____

_____

_____

_____

"Here I Go Again" (love on the rebound)

First Cut Is the Deepest	Cat Stevens
"New Masters"	(Deram)
+First Cut Is the Deepest	Christine Perfect
"The Legendary Christine Perfect"	(Sire)
+First Cut Is the Deepest	Rod Stewart
"A Night on the Town"	(Warner Brothers)
Give Me Some Time	Dan Fogelberg
"Netherlands"	(Full Moon/Epic)
Help Me Rhonda	The Beach Boys
"The Beach Boys Today"	(Capitol)
"Dance, Dance, Dance"	(Capitol)
"Endless Summer"	(Capitol)
"In Concert"	(Brother/Reprise)
+Help Me Rhonda	Johnny Rivers
"New Lovers and Old Friends"	(Epic)
Here I Go Again	The Hollies
"The Very Best of the Hollies"	(United Artists)
"Here I Go Again"*	(Imperial)
I Just Want to Love You	Mary MacGregor
"Torn Between Two Lovers"	(Ariola/America)

"Here I Go Again" (love on the rebound)   (cont.)

If I Fell	The Beatles
"Love Songs"	(Capitol)
"'A Hard Day's Night' (Soundtrack)"	(United Artists)
"Something New"	(Capitol)
I'm Waiting for the Day	The Beach Boys
"Pet Sounds"	(Capitol)
I'm Ready	Martha Reeves and the Vandellas
"Anthology"	(Motown)
I'm Wonderin'	Stevie Wonder
"Greatest Hits"	(Tamla)
Is Your Love in Vain	Bob Dylan
"Street Legal"	(Columbia)
Running Scared	Roy Orbison
"The Very Best of Roy Orbison"	(Monument)
Seems So Long	Stevie Wonder
"Music of My Mind"	(Tamla)
So Good to Be in Love Again	Eddie Money
"Eddie Money"	(Columbia)
Take a Chance on Romance	J. Geils Band
"Ladies Invited"	(Atlantic)

YOUR ADDITIONAL SONGS

_____

_____

_____

_____

_____

"It's So Nice to See Old Friends" (reunion of old lovers)

Allison	Elvis Costello
"My Aim Is True"	(Columbia)

"It's So Nice to See Old Friends" (reunion of old lovers)   (cont.)

+Allison	Linda Ronstadt
"Living in the U.S.A."	(Asylum)
Caroline No	The Beach Boys
"Pet Sounds"	(Capitol)
"In Concert"	(Brother/Reprise)
"Good Vibrations—Best of the Beach Boys"	(Brother/Reprise)
Diamonds and Rust	Joan Baez
"Diamonds and Rust"	(A&M)
For Old Times Sake	Carly Simon
"Boys in the Trees"	(Elektra)
Funny How Time Slips Away	Willie Nelson
"Willie and Family Live"	(Columbia)
"Texas Country"	(United Artists)
+Funny How Time Slips Away	Joe Hinton
(45 RPM Single)*	(Back Beat)
+Funny How Time Slips Away	Al Green
"Call Me"	(Hi)
+Funny How Time Slips Away	Diana Ross and the Supremes
"Anthology"	(Motown)
+Funny How Time Slips Away	Bryan Ferry
"Another Time, Another Place"	(Atlantic)
I'd Really Like to See You Tonight	England Dan and John Ford Coley
"England Dan and John Ford Coley"	(Big Tree)
It's So Nice (to See Old Friends)	Minnie Riperton
"Perfect Angel"	(Epic)
Salon and Saloon	Jim Croce
"Time in a Bottle"	(Lifesong)
Scenes from an Italian Restaurant	Billy Joel
"The Stranger"	(Columbia)
Starting Again	Barry Manilow
"Even Now"	(Arista)
Still Crazy After All These Years	Paul Simon
"Still Crazy After All These Years"	(Columbia)
"Greatest Hits, Etc."	(Columbia)
Taxi	Harry Chapin
"Greatest Stories—Live"	(Elektra)
"Heads and Tales"	(Elektra)
We Just Disagree	Dave Mason
"Let It Flow"	(Columbia)

"It's So Nice to See Old Friends" (reunion of old lovers)   (cont.)

+We Just Disagree   Jim Krueger
  "Sweet Salvation"   (Columbia)
  W-O-L-D   Harry Chapin
  "Greatest Stories—Live"   (Elektra)
  "Short Stories"   (Elektra)

YOUR ADDITIONAL SONGS

_____

_____

_____

_____

_____

"Yesterday"/"Memories of Love"

  As Tears Go By   The Rolling Stones
  "December's Children (and   (London)
    Everybody's)"
  "Hot Rocks 1964–1971"   (London)
+As Tears Go By   Marianne Faithful
  "Greatest Hits"   (London)
  Back to the Island   Leon Russell
  "Best of Leon"   (Shelter)
  Brass Buttons   Poco
  "Crazy Eyes"   (Epic)
  Did She Mention My Name?   Gordon Lightfoot
  "The Very Best of Gordon Lightfoot" (United Artists)
  First Boy I Loved   Judy Collins
  "Who Knows Where the Time Goes"   (Elektra)
  Fountain of Sorrow   Jackson Browne
  "Late for the Sky"   (Asylum)
  High Flying Bird   Elton John
  "Don't Shoot Me I'm Only the Piano (MCA)
    Player"

"Yesterday"/"Memories of Love"   (cont.)

I Dreamed Last Night	Justin Hayward and John Lodge
"Blue Jays"	(Threshold)
If You See Her Say Hello	Bob Dylan
"Blood on the Tracks"	(Columbia)
Jealous Guy	John Lennon
"Imagine"	(Apple)
Last Time I Saw Her	Gordon Lightfoot
"The Very Best of Gordon Lightfoot"	(United Artists)
Long and Winding Road	The Beatles
"Let It Be"	(Apple)
"Love Songs"	(Capitol)
"The Beatles 1967–1970"	(Apple)
+Long and Winding Road	Gladys Knight and The Pips
"Standing Ovation"	(Soul)
+Long and Winding Road	Olivia Newton-John
"Come On Over"	(MCA)
+Long and Winding Road	Leo Sayer
"All This and World War II" (Soundtrack)	(20th Century Records)
Me and Baby Jane	Leon Russell
"Carney"	(Shelter)
Memories of Love	Chicago
"Chicago II"	(Columbia)
Memory Motel	The Rolling Stones
"Black and Blue"	(Rolling Stone Records)
Never Dreamed You'd Leave in Summer	Joan Baez
"Diamonds and Rust"	(A&M)
Once Upon a Time	Dan Fogelberg
"Netherlands"	(Full Moon/Epic)
Photographs and Memories	Jim Croce
"Photographs and Memories"	(ABC)
"Time in a Bottle"	(Lifesong)
Sad Memory	Buffalo Springfield
"Buffalo Springfield Again"	(Atco)
Sand in My Shoes	The Drifters
"Twenty-Four Original Hits"	(Atlantic)
Saturday Night	The Eagles
"Desperado"	(Asylum)

"Yesterday"/"Memories of Love"   (cont.)

Sometimes in Winter "Blood, Sweat and Tears Greatest Hits"	Blood, Sweat and Tears (Columbia)
Sunday Will Never Be the Same "Spanky's Greatest Hits" "Spanky and Our Gang"*	Spanky and Our Gang (Mercury) (Mercury)
These Dreams "Time in a Bottle" "Photographs and Memories"	Jim Croce (Lifesong) (ABC)
Traces "Oldies But Goodies, Volume 2"	The Classics IV (Original sound records)
Yankee Lady "Jesse Winchester"	Jesse Winchester (Bearsville)
+Yankee Man "As I See It Now"*	Melanie (Neighborhood)
Yesterday "Yesterday . . . and Today" "Love Songs"	The Beatles (Capitol) (Capitol)
+Yesterday "Wings Over America"	Wings (Capitol)
+Yesterday "Go Away From My World"	Marianne Faithful (London)
+Yesterday "Listen"	Ray Charles (ABC)
+Yesterday "All This and World War II" (Soundtrack)	David Essex (20th Century-Fox)

YOUR ADDITIONAL SONGS

_____

_____

_____

_____

_____

"Lessons Learned"

All in Love Is Fair "Innervisions"	Stevie Wonder (Tamla)
+All in Love Is Fair "Greatest Hits Vol. II"	Barbra Streisand (Columbia)
Funny How Love Is "Queen II"	Queen (Elektra)
Heart Like a Wheel "Heart Like a Wheel" "Greatest Hits"	Linda Ronstadt (Asylum) (Asylum)
+Heart Like A Wheel "Kate and Anna McGarrigle"	Kate and Anna McGarrigle (Warner Brothers)
I Threw It All Away "Nashville Skyline" "Hard Rain" (Soundtrack)	Bob Dylan (Columbia) (Columbia)
It's All in the Game (45 RPM Single)	Tommy Edwards (MGM)
+It's All in the Game "It's All in the Game"	Cliff Richards (Epic)
+It's All in the Game "Best of the Four Tops"	The Four Tops (Motown)
+It's All in the Game "Into the Music"	Van Morrison (Warner Brothers)
Learning the Game "The Best of Buddy Holly"	Buddy Holly (MCA)
+Learning the Game "What's Wrong with This Picture?"	Andrew Gold (Asylum)
Lemon Tree "Ten Years Together" "Peter, Paul and Mary"	Peter, Paul and Mary (Warner Brothers) (Warner Brothers)
Lessons Learned "Netherlands"	Dan Fogelberg (Full Moon/Epic)
Listen People "Herman's Hermits XX—Their Greatest Hits"	Herman's Hermits (ABKCO)
Love Is a Rose "Greatest Hits" "Prisoner in Disguise"	Linda Ronstadt (Asylum) (Asylum)
+Love Is a Rose "Decade"	Neil Young (Reprise)

"Lessons Learned" (cont.)

+Love Is a Rose   Nana Mouskouri
  "Roses and Sunshine"   (Cachet)

Love Takes Time   Orleans
  "Forever"   (Infinity)

Love Will Find a Way   Pablo Cruise
  "Worlds Away"   (A&M)

No Looking Back   Leo Sayer
  "Leo Sayer"   (Warner Brothers)

Only Love Can Break Your Heart   Neil Young
  "After the Gold Rush"   (Reprise)

+Only Love Can Break Your Heart   Elkie Brooks
  "Shooting Star"   (A&M)

The Things We Do for Love   10 CC
  "Deceptive Bends"   (Mercury)
  "Greatest Hits 1972–78"   (Polydor)

This Time Around   Peter Allen
  "Taught by Experts"   (A&M)

YOUR ADDITIONAL SONGS

_____

_____

_____

_____

_____

"Happy Together" (uptempo love songs)

Beginnings   Chicago
  "Chicago IX Chicago's Greatest Hits"   (Columbia)
  "Chicago Transit Authority"   (Columbia)

Darling   The Beach Boys
  "Good Vibrations—Best of the Beach   (Brother/Reprise)
    Boys"
  "In Concert"   (Brother/Reprise)
  "20/20"   (Brother/Reprise)

"Happy Together" (uptempo love songs)   (cont.)

+Darling   The Good Vibrations
  "The Good Vibrations"*   (Millennium)

Glad All Over   The Dave Clark Five
  "Glad All Over Again"   (Epic)
  "Glad All Over"*   (Epic)
  "History of British Rock"   (Epic)

+Glad All Over   Jeff Beck Group
  "Jeff Beck Group"   (Epic)

Heat Wave   Martha Reeves and the
                                              Vandellas
  "Anthology"   (Motown)
  "More American Graffiti"   (MCA)

+Heat Wave   The Who
  "A Quick One"   (MCA)

+Heat Wave   Pacific Gas & Electric
  "The Best of P G & E"   (Columbia)

+Heat Wave   Linda Ronstadt
  "Greatest Hits"   (Asylum)
  "Prisoner in Disguise"   (Asylum)

+Heatwave   The Jam
  "Setting Sons"   (Polydor)

How Sweet It Is   Marvin Gaye
  "Anthology"   (Motown)

+How Sweet It Is   James Taylor
  "Greatest Hits"   (Warner Brothers)
  "Gorilla"   (Warner Brothers)

+How Sweet It Is   Junior Walker and the All
                                              Stars
  "Anthology"   (Motown)

I Can Hear Music   The Beach Boys
  "Good Vibrations—Best of the Beach   (Brother/Reprise)
    Boys"
  "20/20"   (Capitol)

I Feel Fine   The Beatles
  "The Beatles 1962–1966"   (Capitol)
  "The Beatles '65"   (Capitol)

I Feel the Earth Move   Carole King
  "Tapestry"   (Ode)
  "Her Greatest Hits"   (Ode)

"Happy Together" (uptempo love songs)   (cont.)

I Only Want to Be with You "Dusty Springfield's Greatest Hits" "History of British Rock"	Dusty Springfield (Philips) (Sire)
+I Only Want to Be with You "Greatest Hits"	Bay City Rollers (Arista)
+I Only Want to Be with You "The Scratch Band"*	The Scratch Band (Big Sound)
I Should Have Known Better "'A Hard Day's Night' (Soundtrack)"	The Beatles (United Artists)
+I Should Have Known Better "In Action"*	Johnny Rivers (Imperial)
The More I See You (45 RPM Single)	Chris Montez (A&M)
+The More I See You "It's Time for Peter Allen" "Taught by Experts"	Peter Allen (A&M) (A&M)
More Than a Woman "Saturday Night Fever" (Soundtrack)	The Bee Gees (RSO)
+More Than a Woman "Saturday Night Fever" (Soundtrack) "Motel Shot"	Tavares (RSO) (Atco)
More Today Than Yesterday "More Today Than Yesterday"	Spiral Staircase (Columbia)
Never Ending Song of Love "The Best of Delaney and Bonnie"	Delaney and Bonnie (Atlantic)
Nothing's Too Good for My Baby "Greatest Hits"	Stevie Wonder (Tamla)
Rave On "The Buddy Holly Story" "Buddy Holly—A Rock and Roll Collection"	Buddy Holly (MCA) (MCA)
+Rave On "Hollydays"	Denny Laine (Capitol)
+Rave On "The Buddy Holly Story" (Soundtrack)	Gary Busey (MCA)
+Rave On "American Dream"	Jesse Colin Young (Elektra)

"Happy Together" (uptempo love songs)　(cont.)

+Rave On
　"Country Casanova"

Commander Cody and the
　Lost Planet Airmen
(Paramount)

+Rave On
　"Uncle Charlie"

Nitty Gritty Dirt Band
(United Artists)

She'd Rather Be with Me
"Happy Together Again"

The Turtles
(Sire)

She's a Woman
"Live at the Hollywood Bowl"
"Beatles '65"

The Beatles
(Capitol)
(Capitol)

+She's a Woman
　"Feliciano"

José Feliciano
(RCA)

Silly Love Songs
"Wings at the Speed of Sound"
"Wings Over America"
"Wings Greatest"

Wings
(Capitol)
(Capitol)
(Capitol)

So High
"Let It Flow"

Dave Mason
(Columbia)

Still the One
"Waking and Dreaming"

Orleans
(Asylum)

Sugar Magnolia
"American Beauty"
"Europe '72"
"Skeletons From the Closet"

The Grateful Dead
(Warner Brothers)
(Warner Brothers)
(Warner Brothers)

Sweet Caroline
"Gold"
"Hot August Night"

Neil Diamond
(MCA)
(MCA)

+Sweet Caroline
　"Bobby Womack's Greatest Hits"

Bobby Womack
(United Artists)

Thank You Girl
"The Beatles' Second Album"

The Beatles
(Capitol)

The Way You Do the Things You Do
"Greatest Hits"
"Anthology—Tenth Anniversary
　Special"

The Temptations
(Gordy)
(Motown)

+The Way You Do the Things You Do
"Streetheart"*

Dion
(Warner Brothers)

+The Way You Do the Things You Do
"Anytime . . . Anywhere"

Rita Coolidge
(A&M)

"Happy Together" (uptempo love songs)   (cont.)

The Wonder of You	Elvis Presley
"Worldwide 50 Gold Award Hits, Volume 2"	(RCA)
Wouldn't It Be Nice	The Beach Boys
"Pet Sounds"	(Capitol)
"Live in London"	(Capitol)
"Good Vibrations—Best of the Beach Boys"	(Brother/Reprise)
"The Beach Boys in Concert"	(Brother/Reprise)
You Baby	The Turtles
"Happy Together Again"	(Sire)
+You Baby	The Mamas and The Papas
"If You Can Believe Your Eyes and Ears"	(ABC/Dunhill)
+You Baby	Gary Lewis and the Playboys
"Hits Again"*	(Liberty)
You Make Lovin' Fun	Fleetwood Mac
"Rumours"	(Reprise)
You're So Good to Me	The Beach Boys
"Endless Summer"	(Capitol)
"Summer Days (and Summer Nights)"	(Capitol)
Your Smiling Face	James Taylor
"J.T."	(Columbia)

YOUR ADDITIONAL SONGS

_____

_____

_____

_____

_____

"And I Love You So" (ballad love songs)

And I Love Her	The Beatles
" 'A Hard Day's Night' (Soundtrack)"	(United Artists)
"Love Songs"	(Capitol)
"Something New"	(Capitol)
"The Beatles 1962–1966"	(Capitol)
+And I Love Her	Bobby Womack
"Understanding"	(United Artists)
+And I Love Her	José Feliciano
"Feliciano"	(RCA)
And I Love You So	Don McLean
"Tapestry"	(United Artists)
"Solo"	(United Artists)
+And I Love You So	Helen Reddy
"Greatest Hits"	(Capitol)
+And I Love You So	Elvis Presley
"Elvis in Concert"	(RCA)
Annie's Song	John Denver
"John Denver's Greatest Hits"	(RCA)
"Back Home Again"	(RCA)
As	Stevie Wonder
"Songs in the Key of Life"	(Tamla)
+As	Elkie Brooks
"Shooting Star"	(A&M)
Baby I Love You	Ronettes
"Phil Spector's Greatest Hits"	(Warner-Spector)
+Baby I Love You	Andy Kim
"Andy Kim's Greatest Hits"	(Steed)
+Baby I Love You	Terry Reid
"Rogue Waves"	(Capitol)
+Baby I Love You	Roberta Flack and Donny Hathaway
"Roberta Flack and Donny Hathaway"	(Atlantic)
+Baby I Love You	Dave Edmunds
"Subtle as a Flying Mallet"	(RCA)
+Baby I Love You	The Ramones
"End of the Century"	(Sire)
Baby I Love Your Way	Peter Frampton
"Frampton Comes Alive"	(A&M)

"And I Love You So" (ballad love songs)   (cont.)

Because	The Dave Clark Five
"Glad All Over Again"	(Epic)
"The Dave Clark Five's Greatest Hits"	(Epic)
"American Tour, Vol. I"	(Epic)
Betcha By Golly	The Stylistics
"The Best of the Stylistics"	(Avco)
Close to You	The Carpenters
"Close to You"	(A&M)
"The Carpenters' Collection"	(A&M)
+Close to You	Paul Williams
"The Best of Paul Williams"	(A&M)
Color My World	Chicago
"Chicago IX Chicago's Greatest Hits"	(Columbia)
"Chicago II"	(Columbia)
"At Carnegie Hall"	(Columbia)
Crazy Love	Van Morrison
"Moondance"	(Warner Brothers)
+Crazy Love	Rita Coolidge
"Rita Coolidge"	(A&M)
+Crazy Love	The Isley Brothers
"Sixteen Greatest Hits"	(Trip)
+Crazy Love	Helen Reddy
"I Don't Know How to Love Him"	(Capitol)
Dedicated to the One I Love	The Shirelles
"The Very Best of the Shirelles"	(United Artists)
+Dedicated to the One I Love	The Mamas and The Papas
"Sixteen of Their Greatest"	(ABC/Dunhill)
Devoted to You	The Everly Brothers
"The Very Best of the Everly Brothers"	(Warner Brothers)
+Devoted to You	The Beach Boys
"Beach Boys' Party!"	(Capitol)
+Devoted to You	Carly Simon
"Boys in the Trees"	(Elektra)
+Devoted to You	Fire and Rain
"Living Together"*	(20th Century Records)
Everything That Touches You	The Association
"The Association's Greatest Hits"	(Warner Brothers)
First Time Ever I Saw Your Face	Roberta Flack
"First Take"	(Atlantic)

"And I Love You So" (ballad love songs)   (cont.)

+First Time Ever I Saw Your Face
"See What Tomorrow Brings"
Peter, Paul and Mary
(Warner Brothers)

+First Time Ever I Saw Your Face
"Mary"*
Mary Travers
(Warner Brothers)

+First Time Ever I Saw Your Face
"Faithful Forever"*
Marianne Faithful
(London)

Forever My Love
"Hotcakes"
Carly Simon
(Elektra)

God Only Knows
"Live in London"
"Pet Sounds"
"Good Vibrations—Best of the Beach
Boys"
The Beach Boys
(Capitol)
(Capitol)
(Brother/Reprise)

+God Only Knows
"I'm Glad You're Here"
Neil Diamond
(MCA)

Here, There and Everywhere
"Revolver"
"Love Songs"
The Beatles
(Capitol)
(Capitol)

+Here, There and Everywhere
(45 RPM Single)
The Fourmost
(Capitol)

+Here, There and Everywhere
"Try Some of This"*
Jay and the Americans
(United Artists)

+Here, There and Everywhere
"Elite Hotel"
Emmylou Harris
(Warner Brothers)

How Deep Is Your Love
"Saturday Night Fever" (Soundtrack)
The Bee Gees
(RSO)

If Not for You
"Bob Dylan's Greatest Hits, Vol. II"
"New Morning"
Bob Dylan
(Columbia)
(Columbia)

+If Not for You
"All Things Must Pass"
George Harrison
(Apple)

+If Not for You
"Olivia Newton-John"
Olivia Newton-John
(MCA)

+If Not for You
"The End of the Beginning"
Richie Havens
(A&M)

I'll Have to Say I Love You in a Song
"Photographs and Memories"
"Time in a Bottle"
Jim Croce
(ABC)
(Lifesong)

In My Life
"Rubber Soul"
The Beatles
(Capitol)

"And I Love You So" (ballad love songs)   (cont.)

+In My Life — Judy Collins
  "In My Life" — (Elektra)

+In My Life — Keith Moon
  "Two Sides of the Moon" — (MCA)

+In My Life — José Feliciano
  "Feliciano" — (RCA)

In My Own Way — The Marshall Tucker Band
  "Where We All Belong" — (Capricorn)

I Only Have Eyes for You — The Swallows
  (45 RPM Single)* — (King)

+I Only Have Eyes for You — The Flamingos
  (45 RPM Single)* — (End)
  "American Graffiti" (Soundtrack) — (MCA)

+I Only Have Eyes for You — Art Garfunkel
  "Breakaway" — (Columbia)

Just the Way You Are — Billy Joel
  "The Stranger" — (Columbia)

+Just the Way You Are — Barry White
  "The Man" — (20th Century Records)

Lady of the Island — Crosby, Stills & Nash
  "Crosby, Stills & Nash" — (Atlantic)

Let It Be Me — The Everly Brothers
  "The Everly Brothers Original — (Barnaby/CBS)
    Greatest Hits"
  "Golden Hits of the Everly Brothers" — (Warner Brothers)

+Let It Be Me — Betty Everett/Jerry Butler
  (45 RPM Single)* — (Vee Jay)

+Let It Be Me — Peaches and Herb
  "Golden Duets" — (Date)

+Let It Be Me — Bob Dylan
  "Self-Portrait" — (Columbia)

+Let It Be Me — Sonny and Cher
  "Look at Us"* — (Atco)
  "The Best of Sonny and Cher" — (Atco)

+Let It Be Me — The Pointer Sisters
  "Live at the Opera House" — (Blue Thumb)

+Let It Be Me — Melanie
  "Phonogenic, Not Just Another Pretty — (Midsong)
    Face"

"And I Love You So" (ballad love songs)   (cont.)

+Let It Be Me "The Age of Aquarius"*	The Fifth Dimension (Soul City)
+Let It Be Me "Chapter II"	Roberta Flack (Atlantic)
Love Is All Around "History of British Rock"	The Troggs (Sire)
+Love Is All Around "Love Is All Around"	War Featuring Eric Burdon (ABC)
Love Me Tender "Worldwide 50 Gold Award Hits"	Elvis Presley (RCA)
+Love Me Tender "Living in the U.S.A."	Linda Ronstadt (Asylum)
+Love Me Tender "Someone Is Standing Outside"	Bill Medley (MGM)
+Love Me Tender "King Does the King's Things"	Albert King (Stax)
+Love Me Tender "Soul Folk"	Johnny Nash (Jade)
+Love Me Tender "B. J. Thomas' Greatest Hits"	B. J. Thomas (Scepter)
+Love Me Tender "Warm and Tender Soul"	Percy Sledge (Atlantic)
Loving You "Worldwide 50 Gold Award Hits"	Elvis Presley (RCA)
Marie "Good Old Boys"	Randy Newman (Reprise)
+Marie "Inside"	Kenny Rankin (Little David/Atlantic)
+Marie "Jericho Harp"*	Jericho Harp (United Artists)
+Marie "Hard Times for Lovers"	Judy Collins (Elektra)
Michelle "Love Songs" "Rubber Soul" "The Beatles 1962–1966"	The Beatles (Capitol) (Capitol) (Capitol)
+Michelle "All This and World War II" (Soundtrack)	Richard Cocciante (20th Century-Fox)

"And I Love You So" (ballad love songs)   (cont.)

More and More "Playing Possum"	Carly Simon (Elektra)
My Girl "The Temptations' Greatest Hits" "Anthology—Tenth Anniversary Special"	The Temptations (Gordy) (Motown)
+My Girl "Sixteen of Their Greatest"	The Mamas and The Papas (Dunhill)
+My Girl "Flowers"	The Rolling Stones (London)
+My Girl "The American Breed"*	The American Breed (Acta)
+My Girl "Here We Are Again"*	Country Joe and the Fish (Vanguard)
+My Girl "Outsiders"*	The Outsiders (Capitol)
+My Girl "I Was Made to Love Her"	Stevie Wonder (Tamla)
+My Girl "New Harvest . . . First Gathering"	Dolly Parton (RCA)
+My Girl "Otis Blue"	Otis Redding (Volt)
My Love "Red Rose Speedway" "Wings Over America" "Wings Greatest"	Wings (Capitol) (Capitol) (Capitol)
My Special Angel (45 RPM Single)*	The Duprees (Coed)
+My Special Angel "The Vogues' Greatest Hits"	The Vogues (Reprise)
+My Special Angel (45 RPM Single)*	Bobby Helms (Decca/MCA)
My Sweet Lady "Poems, Prayers and Promises"	John Denver (RCA)
Never My Love "The Association's Greatest Hits"	The Association (Warner Brothers)
Only You "Encore of Golden Hits"	The Platters (Mercury)

"And I Love You So" (ballad love songs)   (cont.)

+Only You   Ringo Starr
  "Blasts from Your Past"   (Apple)

Our House   Crosby, Stills, Nash & Young
  "Déjà Vu"   (Atlantic)

Something   The Beatles
  "Abbey Road"   (Apple)
  "Love Songs"   (Capitol)
  "The Beatles 1962–1966".   (Apple)

+Something   George Harrison
  "The Best of George Harrison"   (Apple)

+Something   Joe Cocker
  "Joe Cocker"   (A&M)

+Something   Elvis Presley
  "Aloha from Hawaii"   (RCA)

Songbird   Fleetwood Mac
  "Rumours"   (Reprise)

+Songbird   Rita Coolidge
  "Love Me Again"   (A&M)

A Song for You   Leon Russell
  "Best of Leon"   (Shelter)

+A Song for You   Donny Hathaway
  "The Best of Donny Hathaway"   (Atco)

Sunlight   Jesse Colin Young
  "On the Road"   (Warner Brothers)

+Sunlight   The Youngbloods
  "The Best of the Youngbloods"   (RCA)
  "Sunlight"   (RCA)

Time in a Bottle   Jim Croce
  "Time in a Bottle"   (Lifesong)
  "Photographs and Memories"   (ABC)

True Love   George Harrison
  "Thirty-Three & ⅓"   (Dark Horse)

Tupelo Honey   Van Morrison
  "Tupelo Honey"   (Warner Brothers)

+Tupelo Honey   Richie Havens
  "Richie Havens on Stage"*   (Stormy Forest)

Warm Ways   Fleetwood Mac
  "Fleetwood Mac"   (Reprise)

"And I Love You So" (ballad love songs)   (cont.)

We're All Alone "Silk Degrees"	Boz Scaggs (Columbia)
+We're All Alone "Anytime . . . Anywhere"	Rita Coolidge (A&M)
Wonderful Tonight "Slow Hand"	Eric Clapton (RSO)
Words of Love "The Buddy Holly Story" "Buddy Holly: A Rock and Roll Collection"	Buddy Holly (MCA) (MCA)
+Words of Love "Beatles '65" "Love Songs"	The Beatles (Capitol) (Capitol)
You and Me "The Alice Cooper Show"	Alice Cooper (Warner Brothers)
You Are So Beautiful "Greatest Hits" "I Can Stand A Little Rain"	Joe Cocker (A&M) (A&M)
+You Are So Beautiful "Tanya Tucker"	Tanya Tucker (Columbia)
+You Are So Beautiful "Kids and Me"	Billy Preston (A&M)
+You Are So Beautiful "The Kenny Rankin Album"	Kenny Rankin (Little David)
You Are the Sunshine of My Life "Talking Book"	Stevie Wonder (Tamla)
You're in My Heart "Foot Loose and Fancy Free"	Rod Stewart (Warner Brothers)
You're the Only One "Monkey Island"	J. Geils Bands (Atlantic)
Your Song "Elton John" "Greatest Hits"	Elton John (MCA) (MCA)
+Your Song "Golden Biscuits" "It Ain't Easy"	Three Dog Night (ABC/Dunhill) (ABC/Dunhill)
+Your Song "Live in Europe"	Billy Paul (Philadelphia International)

"And I Love You So" (ballad love songs)   (cont.)

You Send Me "This Is Sam Cooke"	Sam Cooke (RCA)
+You Send Me "Fly Like an Eagle"	Steve Miller (Capitol)
+You Send Me "Smiler"	Rod Stewart (Mercury)
+You Send Me "Lady's Choice"	Bonnie Bramlett (Capricorn)
+You Send Me "We Remember Sam Cooke"	The Supremes (Motown)
+You Send Me "Nicolette"	Nicolette Larson (Warner Brothers)

YOUR ADDITIONAL SONGS

_____

_____

_____

_____

_____

PART THREE

"Rock and Roll Is Here to Stay!"
(Guaranteed Argument Starters)

A BASIC ROCK LIBRARY

This section of albums, songs, and lists is comprised of the following:

1. Classic Albums
2. Landmark Albums
3. Important Live Albums
4. The Best of the Greatest Hits
5. "Sleeper" Albums (our individual choices of great albums that didn't make it commercially)
6. The Rock Music Source Book Top Forty

1. CLASSIC ALBUMS

In what was a close to impossible task, here is our attempt to list the fifty classic rock albums of all time. Although this list (like all the others in this book) is subjective, it should still provide the nucleus of a solid rock library.

We considered only original studio albums. The "Greatest Hits" collections and "Live" albums are listed and treated separately.

"Abbey Road," The Beatles, *1969* (Apple) . . . for Side Two alone.

"After the Gold Rush," Neil Young, *1970* (Reprise) . . . a most accurately named collection of songs.

"All Things Must Pass," George Harrison, *1970* (Apple/Capitol) . . . George's first post-Beatle effort, and by far his best.

"Alone Together," Dave Mason, *1969* (ABC/Blue Thumb) . . . Another case of an artist's first solo album also being his best.

"American Beauty," The Grateful Dead, *1970* (Warner Brothers) . . . almost a dead heat with "Workingman's Dead."

"Aqualung," Jethro Tull, *1971* (Chrysalis) . . . their first and finest "concept" album.

"The Band," The Band, *1969* (Capitol) . . . the successful follow-up to "Music from Big Pink."

"Band on the Run," Wings, *1973* (Apple/Capitol) . . . the classic McCartney album . . . so far.

"The Beatles" (White Album), The Beatles, *1968* (Capitol) . . . this double album is the most diverse of all the Beatles' albums, covering a wide array of musical styles.

"Beggars Banquet," The Rolling Stones, *1968* (London) . . . Brian Jones's last album with the Stones . . . contains "Sympathy for the Devil" and "Street Fighting Man," for starters.

"Blonde on Blonde," Bob Dylan, *1966* (Columbia) . . . "Just Like a Woman" . . . "I Want You" . . . "Rainy Day Women ⅜ 12 & 35" . . . "Sad Eyed Lady of the Lowlands" . . . "Memphis Blues Again" . . .

"Blood on the Tracks," Bob Dylan, *1975* (Columbia) . . . Dylan in the '70s, coming back to prove he's still got it.

"Blood, Sweat and Tears," Blood, Sweat and Tears, *1969* (Columbia) . . . the best and most successful of the jazz-rock albums.

"Bookends," Simon and Garfunkel, *1968* (Columbia) . . . an exquisite collection.

"Born to Run," Bruce Springsteen, *1975* (Columbia) . . . the first album where Bruce's writing, performing, and producing talents all came together.

"Bridge over Troubled Water," Simon and Garfunkel, *1970* (Columbia) . . . the album that truly bridged the music of the '60s and the '70s.

"Brothers and Sisters," The Allman Brothers, *1973* (Capricorn) . . . another tough choice, just squeezing out "Eat a Peach."

"Crosby, Stills & Nash," Crosby, Stills & Nash, *1969* (Atlantic) . . . their stunning debut album, featuring "Suite: Judy Blue Eyes" and nine other winners.

"Dark Side of the Moon," Pink Floyd, *1973* (Harvest) . . . a gigantic seller, and the epitome of the space-rock genre.

"Déjà Vu," Crosby, Stills, Nash & Young, *1970* (Atlantic) . . . equal to their first, plus Neil Young!

"The Doors," The Doors, *1966* (Elektra) . . . we could not think of a better first album by previously unknown musicians.

"Elton John," Elton John, *1970* (MCA) . . . Elton's ballad-oriented first American release . . . contains "Your Song."

"Emerson, Lake & Palmer," Emerson, Lake & Palmer, *1970* (Cotillion) . . . their debut album; includes the classic "Lucky Man."

"Every Picture Tells a Story," Rod Stewart, *1971* (Mercury) . . . "Wake up Maggie I think I've got something to say to you . . ."

"For Everyman," Jackson Browne, *1973* (Asylum) . . . much discussion went into this choice . . . with "Late for the Sky" a close second.

"Goodbye Yellow Brick Road," Elton John, *1973* (MCA) . . . one of the few double albums that warrants classic status.

"Heart Like a Wheel," Linda Ronstadt, *1974* (Capitol) . . . her usual batch of hit singles . . . and more. Her best album.

"Innervisions," Stevie Wonder, *1973* (Tamla) . . . the "innervision" of a musical genius.

"John Barleycorn Must Die," Traffic, *1970* (United Artists) . . . Traffic's masterpiece.

"Ladies of the Canyon," Joni Mitchell, *1970* (Reprise) . . . exquisite, bittersweet portraits of life and love. Our selection over "Blue" and "Court and Spark."

"Layla and Other Assorted Love Songs," Derek and the Dominos, *1970* (RSO) . . . another worthy double album, featuring Eric Clapton as Derek and Duane Allman as a Domino.

"Led Zeppelin II," Led Zeppelin, *1969* (Atlantic) . . . followed closely by "Led Zeppelin IV."

"Let It Bleed," The Rolling Stones, *1969* (London) . . . "Gimme Shelter" . . . "You Can't Always Get What You Want" . . . "Let It Bleed" . . . "Midnight Rambler" . . .

"Mixed Bag," Richie Havens, *1967* (Verve) . . . reestablished the artist as an interpreter—e.g., "Just Like a Woman" and "Eleanor Rigby."

"Moondance," Van Morrison, *1970* (Warner Brothers) . . . our choice over "Tupelo Honey" and "Astral Weeks."

"Night Moves," Bob Seger and the Silver Bullet Band, *1976* (Capitol) . . . A rock legend in his home town of Detroit for nearly a decade Bob broke nationally with this, his tenth release. Contains the could-be anthem for aging rock 'n' rollers: "Rock and Roll Never Forgets"!

"Pearl," Janis Joplin, *1970* (Columbia) . . . Janis' finest . . . and last moments.

"Pet Sounds," The Beach Boys, *1966* (Capitol) . . . Brian Wilson's masterpiece.

"Revolver," The Beatles, *1966* (Capitol) . . . classic Beatles! . . . "Eleanor Rigby" . . . "Taxman" . . . "Got to Get You into My Life" . . . "For No One" . . . "Good Day Sunshine" . . . etc. . . .

"Rubber Soul," The Beatles, *1965* (Capitol) . . . more classic Beatles! . . . "Michelle" . . . "I've Just Seen a Face" . . . "In My Life" . . . "Norwegian Wood" . . . "Run for Your Life". . . etc. . . .

"Rumours," Fleetwood Mac, *1977* (Warner Brothers) . . . and everyone wondered whether they could successfully follow up the "Fleetwood Mac" album!

"Sailor," Steve Miller, *1968* (Capitol) . . . pre-superstar Miller with the added talents of pre-superstar Boz Scaggs.

"Sittin' In," Loggins and Messina, *1971* (Columbia) . . . a pivotal album in the evolution of '70s "country rock."

"Songs in the Key of Life," Stevie Wonder, *1976* (Tamla) . . . "Sir Duke" . . . "I Wish" . . . "As" . . . "Isn't She Lovely" . . . and the rest: on key and on target, as usual.

"Sticky Fingers," The Rolling Stones, *1971* (Rolling Stone Records) . . . re-energized on this first outing for their own label . . . includes "Brown Sugar" . . . "Bitch" . . . "Wild Horses."

"Surrealistic Pillow," Jefferson Airplane, *1967* (RCA) . . . with this album the Airplane placed the budding "San Francisco sound" squarely on the musical map. Includes the hit singles "Somebody to Love" and "White Rabbit."

"Tapestry," Carole King, *1971* (Ode) . . . her masterpiece.

"Tea for the Tillerman," Cat Stevens, *1971* (A&M) . . . another tough choice, with "Teaser and the Firecat" as the runner-up.

"Who's Next," The Who, *1971* (MCA) . . . The Who at their rock and roll best . . . "Won't Get Fooled Again" . . . "Baba O'Reilly" . . . "The Song Is Over" . . . "Going Mobile" etc. . . .

"The Yes Album," Yes, *1971* (Atlantic) . . . a narrow pick over "Fragile" and "Close to the Edge."

2. LANDMARK ALBUMS

In addition to our classic albums, there are certain ones that were heralded for their uniqueness and for their contribution to a new musical direction. Over the course of time these "landmark" albums have earned a special niche in the evolution of rock music.

"Abraxis"—Santana, *1970* (Columbia)
> Led by Carlos Santana, this album represents the successful marriage of Latin music with rock. The album contains "Black Magic Woman" and "Oye Como Va," written by the "King of Latin Swing," Tito Puente.

"Are You Experienced?"—Jimi Hendrix, *1967* (Reprise)
> Combining psychedelic rock blues, spacy drug-oriented lyrics, and the most vociferous and experimental guitar playing of its time, this album stands as the epitome of the Psychedelic Era.

"Chicago Transit Authority"—Chicago, *1968* (Columbia)
"Child Is Father to the Man"—Blood, Sweat and Tears, *1968* (Columbia)
> Both released in 1968, these two albums serve as the first attempt to blend jazz qualities with rock music. With the addition of a brass section, extended instrumental solos, and experimental chord changes, they opened a musical path for the jazz/rock style that is an important part of our music today.

"Days of Future Passed"—The Moody Blues, *1967* (Deram/London)
> The Moody Blues enriched and expanded rock music through the use of a full orchestra, which at that time was unprecedented.

"Highway 61 Revisited"—Bob Dylan, *1965* (Columbia)
> The first whole album of electric guitar in the folk tradition. It captures Dylan at his best with "Like a Rolling Stone" and "Desolation Row."

"If You Can Believe Your Eyes and Ears"—The Mamas and The Papas, *1966* (ABC/Dunhill)
> This first album by The Mamas and The Papas was a precursor to the "Southern California sound." It featured slick, tight harmonies in a soft folk-rock setting.

"Meet the Beatles"—The Beatles, *1964* (Capitol)
> In addition to launching Beatlemania, "Meet the Beatles" focused attention on the album form itself, not just the singles on it.

"Music from Big Pink"—The Band, *1968* (Capitol)
> This album set a new standard and firmly re-established some of the lesser known roots of traditional American music.

"Sgt. Pepper's Lonely Hearts Club Band"—The Beatles, *1967* (Capitol)
> The quintessential rock album. A unique sequence of songs with stunning lyrics and varied musical styles bordering on perfection.

"Supersession"—Al Kooper (with Mike Bloomfield and Stephen Stills), *1968* (Columbia)
> A rock "jam" session which jelled into the first successful "super-group" collaboration.

"Sweet Baby James"—James Taylor, *1970* (Warner Brothers)
> This album heralded the age of the singer-songwriter—a return to folky, laid-back, acoustic music.

"Sweetheart of the Rodeo"—The Byrds, *1968* (Columbia)
> Rock goes country in this 1968 album that opened the floodgates for Poco, the Flying Burritos, the Eagles, et al.

"Talking Book"—Stevie Wonder, *1972* (Tamla)
> What was first attempted in "Music of My Mind" was perfected in this mix of "pop-oriented" rhythm and blues with electric funk. "Talking Book" also moved Black music from the predominantly "singles market" to the wider album-buying audience.

"Tommy"—The Who, *1969* (MCA/Track)
> "Tommy" is the brainchild of Pete Townsend and the first successful "rock opera."

3. IMPORTANT LIVE ALBUMS

We chose live albums based on three criteria:
    the quality of the musical performance
    the choice of material
    the documentation of an important moment or event
(N.B. If an album meets the criteria and is a part live/part studio recording, the letter (P) will follow the album title.)

Aerosmith—"Live Bootleg" (Columbia)

Peter Allen—"It's Time for Peter Allen" (A&M)

The Allman Brothers—"At Fillmore East" (Capricorn)

Atlanta Rhythm Section—"Are You Ready?" (Polydor)

Average White Band—"Person to Person" (Atlantic)

Kevin Ayers—"June 1, 1974" (Island)*

Joan Baez—"Joan Baez in Concert Vol. I" (Vanguard)
    "Joan Baez in Concert Vol. II" (Vanguard)
    "From Every Stage" (A&M)

The Band—"Rock of Ages" (Capitol)
    "The Last Waltz" (with various artists) (P) (Warner Brothers)

Be Bop Deluxe—"Live in the Air Age" (Harvest)

The Beach Boys—"Beach Boys in Concert" (Capitol)
    "In Concert" (Brother/Reprise)
    "Live in London" (Capitol)

The Beatles—"Live at the Star Club in Hamburg, Germany, 1962" (Lingasong)
    "The Beatles at the Hollywood Bowl" (Capitol)

The Bee Gees—"Here at Last . . . Bee Gees Live" (RSO)

Chuck Berry—"London Sessions" (P) (Chess)

Elvin Bishop—"Raisin' Hell" (Capricorn)

Blues Project—"Live at the Café Au Go-Go" (Verve)*
    "Blues Project at Town Hall" (Verve)*
    "Reunion at Central Park" (MCA)

David Bowie—"Stage" (RCA)

David Bromberg—"Wanted Dead or Alive" (Columbia)

Jackson Browne—"Running on Empty" (P) (Asylum)

Jimmy Buffett—"You Had to Be There" (ABC)

Paul Butterfield—"Live" (Elektra)

The Byrds—"Untitled" (P) (Columbia)

Johnny Cash—"At Folsom Prison" (Columbia)
   "At San Quentin" (Columbia)
John Cale—"Sabotage/Live" (A&M)
Harry Chapin—"Greatest Stories—Live" (Elektra)
Ray Charles—"Ray Charles Live—The Great Concerts" (Atlantic)
Eric Clapton—"Derek and the Dominos in Concert" (RSO)
   "Eric Clapton's Rainbow Concert" (RSO)
Jimmy Cliff—"In Person—The Best of Jimmy Cliff" (Reprise)
Climax Blues Band—"FM/Live" (Sire)
Joe Cocker—"Mad Dogs and Englishmen" (A&M)
Judy Collins—"The Judy Collins Concert" (Elektra)
Commander Cody and the Lost Planet Airmen—"Live from Deep in the
   Heart of Texas" (Paramount)
Ry Cooder—"Show Time" (Warner Brothers)
Cream—"Live Cream Vol. I" (RSO)
   "Live Cream Vol. II" (RSO)
Creedence Clearwater Revival—"Live in Europe" (Fantasy)
Crosby, Stills, Nash & Young—"Four Way Street" (Atlantic)
King Curtis—"Live at the Fillmore West" (Atco)
Deep Purple—"Made in Japan" (Tetragrammaton)
Delaney and Bonnie—"On Tour (with Eric Clapton)" (Atlantic)
Neil Diamond—"Hot August Night" (MCA)
Dion and the Belmonts—"Reunion—Live at Madison Square Garden
   1972" (Warner Brothers)
Donovan—"Donovan in Concert" (Epic)
The Doors—"Absolutely Live" (Elektra)
Bob Dylan—"Before the Flood" (with The Band) (Asylum)
   "Hard Rain" (Columbia)
Emerson, Lake & Palmer—"Pictures at an Exhibition" (Cotillion)
   "Welcome Back My Friends to the Show That Never Ends" (Man-
   ticore)
Focus—"Focus at the Rainbow" (Sire)
Foghat—"Live" (Bearsville)
Peter Frampton—"Frampton Comes Alive" (A&M)
Aretha Franklin—"Live at the Fillmore West" (Atlantic)
Marvin Gaye—"Live" (Tamla)
J. Geils Band—"Live—Full House" (Atlantic)
Genesis—"Seconds Out" (Atlantic)
Good Rats—"Live at Last" (Ratcity)

The Grateful Dead—"Live/Dead" (Warner Brothers)
"The Grateful Dead" (skull and cross bones album) (Warner Brothers)
"Europe '72" (Warner Brothers)
"Steal Your Face" (Grateful Dead Records)

Woody Guthrie—"A Tribute to Woody Guthrie" (various artists) Warner Brothers)

George Harrison—"Bangla Desh" (with various artists) (Apple)

"Havana Jam"—Various Artists (Columbia)

Richie Havens—"Live on Stage" (Stormy Forest) *
"Richard P. Havens, 1983" (P) (MGM) *

Jimi Hendrix—"Band of Gypsies" (Capitol)
"Monterey International Pop Festival" (with Otis Redding) (Reprise)

The Hollies—"Live" (Epic)

Hot Tuna—"Double Dose" (Grunt)

Humble Pie—"Performance—Rockin' the Fillmore" (A&M)

It's a Beautiful Day—"Live at Carnegie Hall" (Columbia)

Jefferson Airplane—"Bless Its Pointed Little Head" (RCA)
"Thirty Seconds over Winterland" (RCA)

Jethro Tull—"Jethro Tull Live—Bursting Out" (Chrysalis)

Elton John—"11-17-70" (Uni/MCA)

Janis Joplin—"In Concert" (Columbia)

Judas Priest—"Unleashed in the East—Live in Japan" (Columbia)

Kansas—"Two for the Show" (Kirshner)

B. B. King—"Live at the Regal" (ABC)
"Live and Well" (P) (ABC)
"Together, Live . . . for the First Time" (with Bobby Bland) (ABC)

The Kinks—"Live at the Kelvin Hall" (Reprise)
"Everybody's in Showbiz, Everybody's a Star" (P) (RCA)

Gladys Knight and The Pips—"Standing Ovation" (Buddah)

Al Kooper (with Mike Bloomfield)—"The Live Adventures of Al Kooper and Mike Bloomfield" (Columbia)

John Lennon—"The Plastic Ono Band—Live Peace in Toronto 1969" (Apple)

Little Feat—"Waiting for Columbus" (Warner Brothers)

Nils Lofgren—"Night After Night" (A&M)

Loggins and Messina—"On Stage" (Columbia)

Lynyrd Skynyrd—"One More from the Road" (MCA)

Marshall Tucker Band—"Where We All Belong" (Capricorn)

Bob Marley and the Wailers—"Live" (Island)
"Babylon by Bus" (Island)

Dave Mason—"Certified Live" (Columbia)

John Mayall—"Turning Point" (Polydor)

MC 5—"Kick Out the Jams" (Elektra)*

Don McLean—"Solo" (United Artists)

Ralph McTell—"Ralph McTell Live" (Fantasy)

Melanie—"Leftover Wine" (P) (Buddah)*

Bette Midler—"Live at Last" (Atlantic)

Joni Mitchell—"Miles of Aisles" (Asylum)

Moody Blues—"Caught Live + 5" (P) (Threshold)

Van Morrison—"It's Too Late to Stop Now" (Warner Brothers)

Mott the Hoople—"Live" (Columbia)

Mountain—"The Road Goes Ever On" (Windfall)

Rick Nelson—"In Concert" (MCA)

Willie Nelson—"Willie and Family Live" (Columbia)

Randy Newman—"Live" (Reprise)

New Riders of the Purple Sage—"Home, Home on the Road" (Columbia)

Nitty Gritty Dirt Band—"Stars and Stripes Forever" (United Artists)

"No Nukes"—Various Artists (Asylum)

Ted Nugent—"Double Live Gonzo" (Epic)

Phil Ochs—"Phil Ochs in Concert" (Elektra)
"Gunfight at Carnegie Hall" (A&M)

The Outlaws—"Bring It Back Alive" (Arista)

Graham Parker and the Rumour—"Parkerilla" (Mercury)

Tom Paxton—"The Compleat Tom Paxton" (Elektra)
"New Songs from the Briarpatch" (Vanguard)

Peter, Paul and Mary—"Peter, Paul and Mary in Concert" (Warner Brothers)

Poco—"Deliverin' " (Epic)

The Pointer Sisters—"Live at the Opera House" (ABC/Blue Thumb)

Elvis Presley—"On Stage: 1970" (RCA)
"As Recorded Live at Madison Square Garden"
"In Concert" (RCA)

Procol Harum—"In Concert with the Edmonton Symphony Orchestra" (A&M)

Pure Prairie League—"Takin' the Stage" (RCA)

Otis Redding—"Live in Europe" (Volt)
   "Monterey International Pop Festival" (with Jimi Hendrix) (Reprise)

Helen Reddy—"Live in London" (Capitol)

Lou Reed—"Rock and Roll Animal" (RCA)

Renaissance—"Live at Carnegie Hall" (Sire)

Smokey Robinson & the Miracles—"Smokin' " (Tamla)

Rolling Stones—"Got Live If You Want It" (London)
   "Get Yer Ya-Ya's Out" (London)
   "Love You Live" (Rolling Stone Records)

Todd Rundgren—"Back to the Bars" (Bearsville)

Leon Russell—"Live" (Shelter)

Santana—"Moonflower" (P) (Columbia)

John Sebastian—"The Real Live John Sebastian" (Reprise)*

Bob Seger and the Silver Bullet Band—"Live Bullet" (Capitol)

Paul Simon—"Live Rhymin' " (Columbia)

Spirit—"Spirit Live" (Potato)*

Bruce Springsteen—When Bruce finally gets around to releasing a live album [a double, we hope] it will take its place among the truly great live recordings, and will document one of the finest live and visual performers in the history of rock and roll.

Stephen Stills—"Live" (Atlantic)

Steeleye Span—"Live at Last" (Chrysalis)

Donna Summers—"Live and More" (Casablanca)

Thin Lizzy—"Live and Dangerous" (Warner Brothers)

Tower of Power—"Live and in Living Color" (Warner Brothers)

Traffic—"On the Road" (Capitol)

The Velvet Underground—"Live at Max's Kansas City" (Cotillion)

Tom Waits—"Nighthawks at the Diner" (Asylum)

The Weavers—"The Weavers at Carnegie Hall" (Vanguard)

"Volunteer Jam"—Various Artists (Capricorn)

Jerry Jeff Walker—"A Man Must Carry On" (MCA)

Muddy "Mississippi" Waters—"Live" (Blue Sky)

The Who—"Live at Leeds" (MCA)

Wings—"Wings Over America" (Capitol)

Edgar Winter—"Roadwork" (with White Trash) (Epic)

Johnny Winter—"Johnny Winter and Live" (Columbia)

"Woodstock" (Soundtrack) (Cotillion)

The Yardbirds—"Live Yardbirds" (Epic)

Yes—"Yessongs" (Atlantic)

Neil Young—"Live Rust" (Warner Brothers)

    —"Rust Never Sleeps" (P) (Warner Brothers)

4. THE BEST OF THE GREATEST HITS

The "Greatest Hits" or "Best of" packages are still the best buy for your record dollar. However, beware of rip-offs! Often a "Best of" collection is padded with non-hits and inferior new versions. We have attempted to select what we feel are the "Best of the Greatest Hits." To make it easier for you, we have listed them in the following categories, according to their time period or musical style. There are obvious overlaps from one decade to another.

A) Three Decades of Rhythm and Blues . . . and Rock
B) The 1950s//The Roots and Early Years of Rock and Roll
C) The 1960s//American Rock and Pop Bands and Artists
D) The British Invasion
E) The Wide and Assorted World of Rock and Roll in the 1970s
F) American Folk Music
G) English Folk Music

A) Three Decades of Rhythm and Blues . . . and Rock

Rock has its strongest roots in rhythm and blues music. The albums comprising this list span some twenty-five years.

Chuck Berry—"Golden Decade" (Chess)
   "Golden Decade Vol. II" (Chess)
The Blackbyrds—"Night Grooves" (Fantasy)
Bobby 'Blue' Bland—"The Best of Bobby 'Blue' Bland" (Duke)
James Brown—"Soul Classics" (Polydor)
Solomon Burke—"The Best of Solomon Burke" (Atlantic)
Jerry Butler—"The Very Best of Jerry Butler" (Mercury)
Ray Charles—"A Man and His Music" (ABC)
Chubby Checker—"Greatest Hits" (Atlantic)
The Coasters—"Greatest Hits" (Atco)
Commodores—"Commodores' Greatest Hits" (Motown)
Sam Cooke—"This Is Sam Cooke" (RCA)
Bo Diddley—"Golden Decade" (Checker)
"Got My Own Bag of Tricks" (Chess)
Fats Domino—"Legendary Masters—Fats Domino" (United Artists)
The Drifters—"Twenty-Four Original Hits" (Atlantic)
Earth, Wind and Fire—"Greatest Hits" (Columbia)

Four Tops—"Anthology" (Motown)

Aretha Franklin—"Greatest Hits" (Atlantic)
"Aretha's Gold" (Atlantic)

Marvin Gaye—"Anthology" (Motown)

Dobie Gray—"Greatest Hits" (MCA)

Al Green—"Greatest Hits" (Hi)

The Impressions—"Big Sixteen" (ABC)
"Big Sixteen Vol. II" (ABC)

The Isley Brothers—"The Isley's Greatest Hits" (T-Neck)
"The Best . . . Isley Brothers" (Buddah)

The Jackson Five—"Greatest Hits" (Motown)

Ben E. King—"Ben E. King's Greatest Hits" (Atco)

B. B. King—"The Best of B. B. King" (ABC)

Gladys Knight and the Pips—"Anthology" (Motown)
"The Best of Gladys Knight and the Pips" (Buddah)

Kool and The Gang—"Kool and The Gang Spin Their Top Hits" (De-lite)

Leadbelly—"Library of Congress" (Elektra)

Little Anthony and the Imperials—"The Very Best of Little Anthony and the Imperials" (United Artists)

Little Richard—"The Very Best of Little Richard" (United Artists)

The Marvelettes—"Anthology" (Motown)

Ohio Players—"Greatest Hits" (Westbound)

Johnny Otis—"The Best of Johnny Otis" (Savoy)

Billy Paul—"The Best of Billy Paul" (Philadelphia International)

Peaches and Herb—"Golden Duets" (Date)

Wilson Pickett—"The Best of Wilson Pickett" (Atlantic)
"Wilson Pickett's Greatest Hits" (Atlantic)

Lloyd Price—"Mr. Personality" (ABC)

Otis Redding—"History of Otis Redding" (Atco)
"The Best of Otis Redding" (Atco)

The Robins—"Best of The Robins" (Crescendo)

Smokey Robinson & the Miracles—"Anthology" (Motown)

Sam and Dave—"The Best of Sam and Dave" (Atlantic)

Percy Sledge—"The Best of Percy Sledge" (Atlantic)

Sly and the Family Stone—"Greatest Hits" (Epic)

The Spinners—"The Best of The Spinners" (Atlantic)

The Stylistics—"The Best of the Stylistics" (Avco)

Diana Ross and the Supremes—"Anthology" (Motown)

The Temptations—"Anthology" (Motown)

Ike and Tina Turner—"Sixteen Great Performances" (ABC)
 "The Very Best of Ike and Tina Turner" (United Artists)

The Tymes—"The Best of The Tymes" (ABKCO)

War—"Greatest Hits" (United Artists)
 "Music Band 2" (MCA)

Dionne Warwick—"The Very Best of Dionne Warwick" (United Artists)

Muddy Waters—"McKinley Morganfield a.k.a. Muddy Waters" (Chess)

Mary Wells—"Greatest Hits" (Motown)

Barry White—"Greatest Hits" (20th Century Records)

Jackie Wilson—"Greatest Hits" (Brunswick)

Bill Withers—"The Best of Bill Withers" (Sussex)

Stevie Wonder—"Looking Back" (Tamla)

Stevie Wonder—"Greatest Hits, Volume 1" (Tamla)
 "Greatest Hits, Volume 2" (Tamla)

B) The 1950s//The Roots and Early Years of Rock and Roll

Anthologies/Compilations:

Various Artists—"Echoes of a Rock Era—The Groups Volume 1" (Roulette)
 "Echoes of a Rock Era—The Groups Volume 2" (Roulette)
 "Echoes of a Rock Era—The Later Years" (Roulette)

Various Artists—"Oldies but Goodies Series: Volumes 1 Through 14" (Original sound recordings)

Paul Anka—"Vintage Years 1957–1961" (Sire)

Chuck Berry—"Golden Decade" (Chess)
 "Golden Decade Vol. II" (Chess)

The Coasters—"The Coasters' Greatest Hits" (Atco)

Eddie Cochran—"Very Best of Eddie Cochran" (United Artists)

Sam Cooke—"This Is Sam Cooke" (RCA)

Bobby Darin—"The Bobby Darin Story" (Atco)

Bo Diddley—"Golden Decade" (Chess)

Dion and the Belmonts—"Greatest Hits" (Laurie)

Duane Eddy—"Vintage Years" (Sire)

Fats Domino—"Legendary Masters—Fats Domino" (United Artists)

The Drifters—"Twenty-Four Original Hits" (Atlantic)

The Everly Brothers—"The Golden Hits of the Everly Brothers" (Warner Brothers)
"Everly Brothers Original Greatest Hits" (Barnaby)

Bill Haley and the Comets—"Bill Haley and His Golden Greats" (MCA)

Buddy Holly—"A Rock and Roll Collection" (MCA)
"Buddy Holly and the Crickets—Twenty Golden Greats" (MCA)

Jerry Lee Lewis—"Original Greatest Hits" (Sun)

Little Richard—"Grooviest 17 Original Hits" (Trip)

Rick Nelson—"Legendary Masters—Ricky Nelson" (United Artists)

Roy Orbison—"The All-Time Greatest Hits of Roy Orbison" (Monument)

Carl Perkins—"Original Golden Hits" (Sun)

The Platters—"Encore of Golden Hits" (Mercury)

Elvis Presley—"Worldwide 50 Gold Award Hits" (RCA)

Neil Sedaka—"Greatest Hits" (RCA)

Jackie Wilson—"Greatest Hits" (Brunswick)

Muddy Waters—"McKinley Morganfield a.k.a. Muddy Waters" (Chess)

C) The 1960s//American Rock and Pop Bands and Artists

The American groups of this era held their own amidst the surge of the English invasion, as evidenced by this list of fine music.

Anthologies/Compilations:

Various Artists: "Super Oldies of the Sixties Volume 1 Through 14" (Trip)

The Association—"Greatest Hits" (Warner Brothers)

The Beach Boys—"Endless Summer" (Capitol)
"Good Vibrations—Best of the Beach Boys" (Brother/Reprise)
"Spirit of America" (Capitol)

Blood, Sweat and Tears—"Greatest Hits" (Columbia)

Blues Project—"The Best of Blues Project" (Verve)

Booker T. and the MG's—"Greatest Hits" (Stax)

Box Tops—"Super Hits" (Bell)

The Buckinghams—"Made in Chicago" (Columbia)

Buffalo Springfield—"Retrospective" (Atco)

Paul Butterfield—"Golden Butter/The Best of the Paul Butterfield Blues Band" (Elektra)

The Byrds—"The Byrds' Greatest Hits" (Columbia)
   "The Best of the Byrds Greatest Hits Vol. II" (Columbia)

Glen Campbell—"Greatest Hits" (Capitol)

Canned Heat—"Cook Book" (Liberty)

Johnny Cash—"Greatest Hits" (Columbia)

Cher—"The Very Best of Cher" (United Artists)

The Chiffons—"Everything You Always Wanted to Hear by the Chiffons But Couldn't" (Laurie)

Creedence Clearwater Revival—"Chronicle" (Fantasy)

Delaney and Bonnie—"The Best of Delaney and Bonnie" (Atco)

Jackie DeShannon—"The Very Best of Jackie DeShannon" (United Artists)

Neil Diamond—"Double Gold" (Bang)

The Doors—"13" (Elektra)
   "Weird Scenes Inside the Gold Mine" (Elektra)

The Electric Flag—"The Best of the Electric Flag" (Columbia)

The Fifth Dimension—"Greatest Hits on Earth" (Arista)

Four Seasons—"The Four Seasons Story" (Private Stock)

Lesley Gore—"The Golden Hits of Lesley Gore" (Mercury)

Grand Funk—"Mark, Don and Mel 1969–71" (Capitol)

Grass Roots—"Their Greatest Hits" (ABC/Dunhill)

The Grateful Dead—"Skeletons from the Closet" (Warner Brothers)

The Guess Who—"The Best of the Guess Who" (RCA)

Jimi Hendrix—"Smash Hits" (Reprise)
   "The Essential Jimi Hendrix" (Warner Brothers)
   "The Essential Jimi Hendrix, Volume 2" (Warner Brothers)

The James Gang—"The Best of the James Gang" (ABC)

Tommy James and the Shondells—"The Best of Tommy James and the Shondells" (Roulette)

Jan and Dean—"Gotta Take That One Last Ride" (United Artists)

Jay and the Americans—"Greatest Hits" (United Artists)

Jefferson Airplane—"The Worst of the Jefferson Airplane" (RCA)
   "Flight Log" (RCA)

Janis Joplin—"Greatest Hits" (Columbia)

Gary Lewis and the Playboys—"Golden Greats" (Liberty)

Love—"Love Revisited" (Elektra)

The Lovin' Spoonful—"The Very Best of the Lovin' Spoonful" (Kama Sutra)
   "The Best . . . Lovin' Spoonful" (Kama Sutra)

The Mamas and The Papas—"Sixteen of Their Greatest Hits" (ABC/ Dunhill)

Country Joe and the Fish—"The Life and Times of Country Joe and the Fish—from Haight-Ashbury to Woodstock" (Vanguard)

Steve Miller Band—"Anthology" (Capitol)

Moby Grape—"Great Grape" (Columbia)

The Monkees—"Greatest Hits" (Arista)

The Mothers of Invention—"Mothermania" (Verve)

Mountain—"The Best of Mountain" (Windfall)

Gene Pitney—"Greatest Hits of All Time" (Musicor)

Gary Puckett and the Union Gap—"Greatest Hits" (Columbia)

Quicksilver Messenger Service—"Anthology" (Capitol)

Paul Revere and the Raiders—"All Time Greatest Hits" (Columbia)

The Righteous Brothers—"Greatest Hits, Volume 1"

Johnny Rivers—"The Very Best of Johnny Rivers" (United Artists)

Tommy Roe—"Greatest Hits" (ABC)

Mitch Ryder and the Detroit Wheels—"Greatest Hits" (Virgo)

Sam the Sham and the Pharaohs—"The Best of Sam the Sham and the Pharaohs" (MGM)

Shangri-las—"Greatest Hits" (Mercury)

The Shirelles—"The Shirelles Sing Their Very Best" (Springboard)

Simon and Garfunkel—"Greatest Hits" (Columbia)

Sonny and Cher—"The Best of Sonny and Cher" (Atco)

Joe South—"Greatest Hits" (Capitol)

Spanky and Our Gang—"Spanky's Greatest Hits" (Mercury)

Phil Spector—"Phil Spector's Greatest Hits" (Warner-Spector)

Steppenwolf—"Sixteen Greatest Hits" (ABC/Dunhill)

Three Dog Night—"Joy to the World" (ABC/Dunhill)

The Turtles—"Happy Together Again" (Sire)

The Velvet Underground—"Archetypes" (MGM)

The Youngbloods—"This Is the Youngbloods" (RCA)

The Young Rascals—"Time Peace" (Atlantic)

D) The British Invasion

Here are the bands/artists that were part of the "British Musical Invasion" of 1964, as well as the best of England's contribution to rock music in the 1960s.

Anthologies/Compilation:

Various Artists: "The History of British Rock—Volume 1" (Sire)
    "The History of British Rock—Volume 2" (Sire)
    "The History of British Rock—Volume 3" (Sire)

The Animals—"Best of the Animals" (ABKCO)

The Beatles—"The Beatles 1962–1966" (Apple)
    "The Beatles 1967–1970" (Apple)
    "Rock And Roll Music" (Capitol)
    (N.B.: Almost *any* Beatles album is a Greatest Hits album!)

The Bee Gees—"Bee Gees' Gold" (RSO)

Chad and Jeremy—"The Best of Chad and Jeremy" (Capitol)

The Dave Clark Five—"Glad All Over Again" (Epic)

Eric Clapton—"The History of Eric Clapton" (RSO)

Petula Clark—"Greatest Hits" (Warner Brothers)

Joe Cocker—"Greatest Hits" (A&M)

Cream—"Best of Cream" (RSO)

Spencer Davis—"Greatest Hits" (Island)

Donovan—"Greatest Hits" (Epic)

Marianne Faithful—"Greatest Hits" (London)

Gerry and the Pacemakers—"Greatest Hits" (Laurie)

Herman's Hermits—"Herman's Hermits XX—Their Greatest Hits" (ABKCO)

The Hollies—"Greatest Hits" (Epic)

The Kinks—"Greatest Hits" (Reprise)

Manfred Mann—"The Best of Manfred Mann" (Janus)

John Mayall—"Back to the Roots" (Polydor)

The Moody Blues—"This Is the Moody Blues" (Threshold)

The Move—"The Best of the Move" (A&M)

Peter and Gordon—"The Best of Peter and Gordon" (Capitol)

Procol Harum—"The Best of Procol Harum" (A&M)

The Rolling Stones—"Hot Rocks 1964–71" (London)
    "More Hot Rocks (Big Hits and Fazed Cookies)" (London)

The Searchers—"Golden Hour of the Searchers" (Golden Hour)
    "Golden Hour of the Searchers Vol. II" (Golden Hour)

The Seekers—"Greatest Hits" (Capitol)

Small Faces—"Vintage Years" (Sire)

Dusty Springfield—"Golden Hits" (Philips)

Them—"Them Featuring Van Morrison" (Parrot)

Traffic—"The Best of Traffic" (United Artists)

The Troggs—"Vintage Years" (Sire)

The Who—"Meaty Beaty Big and Bouncy" (MCA)

The Yardbirds—"Greatest Hits" (Epic)

The Zombies—"Time of the Zombies" (Epic)

E) The Wide and Assorted World of Rock and Roll in the 1970s

Rock music in the 1970s practically defies categorization. We have simply listed the "Best of the Greatest Hits" for the '70s in general.

ABBA—"Greatest Hits" (Atlantic)
    "Greatest Hits, Volume 2" (Atlantic)

The Allman Brothers—"The Road Goes On Forever" (Capricorn)

America—"History—America's Greatest Hits" (Warner Brothers)

Argent—"The Argent Anthology . . . A Collection of Greatest Hits" (Epic)

Bachman-Turner Overdrive—"Best of B.T.O. . . . (So Far)" (Mercury)

The Band—"Anthology" (Capitol)

Bay City Rollers—"Greatest Hits" (Arista)

Bee Gees—"Greatest Hits" (RSO)

David Bowie—"Changesonebowie" (RCA)

Bread—"Best of Bread" (Elektra)

Brewer and Shipley—"The Best of Brewer and Shipley" (Kama Sutra)

The Carpenters—"The Singles 1969–73" (A&M)

Harry Chapin—"Greatest Stories Live" (Elektra)

Cher—"Greatest Hits" (MCA)

Chicago—"Chicago IX" (Columbia)

Alice Cooper—"Greatest Hits" (Warner Brothers)

Jim Croce—"Photographs and Memories" (ABC)

Crosby, Stills, Nash & Young—"So Far" (Atlantic)

Mac Davis—"Greatest Hits" (Columbia)

Deep Purple—"When We Rock, We Rock, and When We Roll, We Roll!" (Warner Brothers)

John Denver—"Greatest Hits" (RCA)
    "Greatest Hits Vol. II" (RCA)

Neil Diamond—"Twelve Greatest Hits" (MCA)

The Doobie Brothers—"The Best of the Doobies" (Warner Brothers)

Dr. Hook—"The Best of Dr. Hook" (Columbia)

The Eagles—"Their Greatest Hits 1971–1975" (Asylum)

Electric Light Orchestra—"Olé ELO!" (United Artists)

England Dan and John Ford Coley "The Best of England Dan and John Ford Coley" (Big Tree)

Focus—"Dutch Masters" (Atco)

Free—"Best of Free" (A&M)

J. Geils Band—"Best of the J. Geils Band" (Atlantic)

Grand Funk—"Hits" (Capitol)

The Grateful Dead—"What a Long Strange Trip It's Been" (Warner Brothers)

Emmylou Harris—"Profile: The Best of Emmylou Harris" (Warner Brothers)

George Harrison—"The Best of George Harrison" (Capitol)

Hot Chocolate—"Ten Greatest Hits" (Big Tree)

Ian Hunter—"Shades of Ian Hunter—The Ballad of Ian Hunter" (Columbia)

Waylon Jennings—"Greatest Hits" (RCA)

Jefferson Starship—"Gold" (Grunt)

Jethro Tull—"M.U.—The Best of Jethro Tull" (Chrysalis)
"The Best of Jethro Tull Vol. II" (Chrysalis)

Elton John—"Greatest Hits" (MCA)
"Greatest Hits Vol. II" (MCA)

K.C. & The Sunshine Band—"Greatest Hits" (TK)

Carole King—"Her Greatest Hits" (Ode)

The Kinks—"Celluloid Heroes" (RCA)

Al Kooper—"Al's Big Deal/Unclaimed Freight—An Al Kooper Anthology" (Columbia)

Kris Kristofferson—"Songs of Kristofferson's" (Monument)

John Lennon—"Shaved Fish" (Apple)

Lighthouse—"The Best of Lighthouse" (Janus)

Loggins and Messina—"The Best of Friends" (Columbia)

Lynyrd Skynyrd—"Gold and Platinum" (MCA)

Barry Manilow—"Greatest Hits" (Arista)

Steve Miller Band—"Greatest Hits 1974–78" (Capitol)

Dave Mason—"Very Best of Dave Mason" (ABC)

Mott the Hoople—"Rock and Roll Queen" (Atlantic)*
   "Greatest Hits" (Columbia)

Johnny Nash—"Greatest Hits" (Columbia)

Nazareth—"Hot Tracks" (A&M)

New Riders of the Purple Sage—"The Best of the New Riders" (Columbia)

Harry Nilsson—"Greatest Hits" (RCA)

Nitty Gritty Dirt Band—"Dirt, Silver and Gold" (United Artists)

Danny O'Keefe—"The O'Keefe Files" (Warner Brothers)

Poco—"The Very Best of Poco" (Epic)

Raspberries—"Greatest Hits" (Capitol)

Renaissance—"In the Beginning" (Capitol)

The Rolling Stones—"Made in the Shade" (Rolling Stone Records)

Linda Ronstadt—"Greatest Hits" (Asylum)

Roxy Music—"Greatest Hits" (Atco)

Leon Russell—"Best of Leon" (Shelter)

Santana—"Greatest Hits" (Columbia)

Seals and Crofts—"Greatest Hits" (Warner Brothers)

Neil Sedaka—"Greatest Hits" (Rocket)

Carly Simon—"The Best of Carly Simon" (Elektra)

Paul Simon—"Greatest Hits, Etc." (Columbia)

Ringo Starr—"Blasts from Your Past" (Apple)

Steely Dan—"Greatest Hits" (ABC)

Cat Stevens—"Greatest Hits" (A&M)

Rod Stewart—"The Best of Rod Stewart" (Mercury)
   "Greatest Hits, Volume 1" (Warner Brothers)

Stephen Stills—"Still Stills—The Best of Stephen Stills" (Atlantic)

Strawbs—"The Best of Strawbs" (A&M)

Donna Summer—"On the Radio—Greatest Hits" (Casablanca)

James Taylor—"Greatest Hits" (Warner Brothers)

10 CC—"100 CC" (Mercury)
   "Greatest Hits 1972–78" (Polydor)

Ten Years After—"Classic Performances" (Columbia)

The Marshall Tucker Band—"Greatest Hits" (Capricorn)

Joe Walsh—"The Best of Joe Walsh" (ABC)

Frankie Valli—"The Very Best of Frankie Valli" (MCA)

Paul Williams—"Classics" (A&M)

...ngs Greatest" (Capitol)
...—"Decade" (Reprise)
...—"The Best of ZZ Top" (London)

F) American Folk Music

Folk music has always been an important political and social influence on rock, particularly in the '60s.

Anthologies/Compilations:

Various Artists: "Anthology of Folk Music, Volume 1" (Sine Qua Non)
"Anthology of Folk Music, Volume 2" (Sine Qua Non)

Various Artists: "The Bitter End Years" (Roxbury)

Various Artists: "Greatest Folksingers of the Sixties" (Vanguard)

Eric Andersen—"The Best of Eric Andersen" (Vanguard)
"The Best Songs" (Arista)

Joan Baez—"The First Ten Years" (Vanguard)
"Joan C. Baez" (A&M)

Leonard Cohen—"The Best Of" (Columbia)

Judy Collins—"Colors of the Day/The Best of Judy Collins" (Elektra)
"Recollections" (Elektra)

Country Joe and the Fish—"The Life and Times of Country Joe and the Fish from Haight-Ashbury to Woodstock" (Vanguard)

Bob Dylan—"Greatest Hits" (Columbia)
"Greatest Hits Vol. II" (Columbia)

Ramblin' Jack Elliott—"The Essential Jack Elliott" (Vanguard)

Richard and Mimi Fariña—"The Best of Richard and Mimi Fariña" (Vanguard)

Steve Goodman—"The Essential Steve Goodman" (Buddah)

Arlo Guthrie—"The Best of Arlo Guthrie" (Reprise)

Woody Guthrie—"Library of Congress" (Elektra)

Tim Hardin—"The Best of Tim Hardin" (Verve)

Ian and Sylvia—"Greatest Hits" (Vanguard)

The Kingston Trio—"Best of the Kingston Trio Vol. I" (Capitol)
"Best of the Kingston Trio Vol. II" (Capitol)

Jim Kweskin and the Jug Band—"The Best of Jim Kweskin and the Jug Band" (Vanguard)

Gordon Lightfoot—"The Very Best of Gordon Lightfoot" (United Artists)
"Gord's Gold" (Reprise)
Melanie—"From the Twelve Great Performances" (ABC)
Phil Ochs—"Chords of Fame" (A&M)
Odetta—"The Essential Odetta" (Vanguard)
Tom Paxton—"The Compleat Tom Paxton" (Elektra)
Peter, Paul and Mary—"Ten Years Together" (Warner Brothers)
John Prine—"Prime Prine" (Atlantic)
Tom Rush—"Classic Rush" (Elektra)
"The Best of Tom Rush" (Columbia)
Buffy Sainte-Marie—"The Best of Buffy Sainte-Marie" (Vanguard)
Peter Seeger—"The World of Pete Seeger" (Columbia)
"Greatest Hits" (Columbia)
"The Essential Pete Seeger" (Vanguard)
The Weavers—"Greatest Hits" (Vanguard)

G) English Folk Music

The Best of English folk music, both traditional and contemporary.

Fairport Convention—"Chronicles" (A&M)
Incredible String Band—"Relics of the Incredible String Band" (Elektra)
Steeleye Span—"Individually and Collectively" (Charisma)*
"Steeleye Span Almanack" (Charisma)*

5. "SLEEPER" ALBUMS (our individual choices of great albums that didn't make it commercially)

Everyone has some all-time favorite albums that did not make it commercially.

Bob Macken

Joy of Cooking—"Joy of Cooking" (Capitol)
> With vocals by Toni Brown and Terry Garthwaite, this 1970 debut album was a blend of good, funky rock with jazz overtones. Its consciousness-raising lyrics were built around the theme of women's identity and liberation.

Love—"Forever Changes" (Elektra)
> This minor classic from the fall of 1967 is a terrific album, whose music typified the "space rock" style of the "Psychedelic Era."

The Mark-Almond Band—"Mark-Almond '73" (Columbia)
> An exquisite collection of soft, jazz/rock pieces, this album remains the best work by ex-John Mayall members Jon Mark and Johnny Almond.

Laura Nyro (with Labelle)—"Gonna Take a Miracle" (Columbia)
> This venture, ahead of its time in 1970, joined the talents of Laura Nyro and Labelle and resulted in this exciting blend of soul, R & B, and rock.

Tom Pacheco—"Swallowed Up in the Great American Heartland" (RCA)
> Working in the folk and country traditions, Tom's moving lyrics reflect a "Woody Guthrie/Bob Dylan" look at life in America. His baritone voice is overpowering in this much ignored recording. The theme of "reunion with old lovers" is epitomized in the stirring "Song for Marilyn." A tough album to find, but worth the search.

Bonnie Raitt—"Home Plate" (Warner Brothers)
> Bonnie puts it all together on this, her fifth album. These songs reflect her rock and roll and blues influences.

Otis Redding—"Otis Blue—Otis Redding Sings Soul" (Volt)
> Highlighted by his classic "I've Been Loving You Too Long," this album is a true representative of the Rhythm and Blues genre . . . 1960s style. "Respect," "Shake," "My Girl," and the Rolling Stones' "Satisfaction" are all performed in the inimitable Otis Redding style.

Southside Johnny and the Asbury Jukes—"I Don't Want to Go Home" (Epic)
> One of my very favorite bands and albums. Drawing heavily from

the '50s and R & B, it features the rough, bluesy vocals of Johnny Lyons, backed by a brilliant horn section. It sounds even better on a weekend in the summertime!

Spirit—"Twelve Dreams of Dr. Sardonicus" (Epic)
A popular Los Angeles band in the late 1960s. Their distinctive music reached its apex in this 1970 masterpiece.

The Velvet Underground—"Loaded" (Atlantic)
Based around the talents and virtuosity of Lou Reed, this 1967 album is energetic and powerful rock and roll and contains the classic "Sweet Jane."

Peter Fornatale

The Byrds—"Younger Than Yesterday" (Columbia)
Putting aside the hit singles for a moment, this is probably their best and most cohesive work.

Bonnie Koloc—"You're Gonna Love Yourself in the Morning" (Ovation)
This gem of a record was hurt by a small label distribution. Worth looking for.

Magna Carta—"Magna Carta" (Vertigo)
This is a personal favorite that was released in 1970 and went nowhere. One side of the album contains a stunning piece of music about the passing of time called "Seasons."

Don McLean—"Tapestry" (United Artists)
This is his exquisite, pre-American Pie album. It remains my favorite.

The Move—"Shazam" (A&M)
Brilliant album by a much neglected group which spun off into ELO and Roy Wood's Wizard.

Thunderclap Newman—"Hollywood Dream" (Track)
A real oddball collection of wonderful songs with adventurous production by Pete Townsend.

Poco—"Good Feeling to Know" (Epic)
The best album by one of my favorite bands.

Bill Ayres

Henry Gross—"Love Is the Stuff" (Lifesong)
This is a fine album of rock and roll with at least four or five top-

notch songs. Gross is also a first-rate live performer. Maybe that is the missing element in his albums.

Kate and Anna McGarrigle—"Kate and Anna McGarrigle" (Warner Brothers)

Some of the most gorgeous vocal harmonies and delightful music on record.

Don McLean—"Tapestry" (United Artists)

This is McLean's first and, in my view, best record. There are several strong treatments of social themes.

Van Morrison—"Into the Music" (Warner Brothers)

This is the best album that Morrison has done in years, full of the joy of life and great rock and roll with a mixture of Irish music from the "rolling hills."

Randy Newman—"Sail Away" (Warner Brothers)

A collection of the most perceptive and biting pre-"Short People" Newman songs.

Andy Pratt—"Resolution" (Nemperor)

A whole album of engaging songs with effective performances. I thought it couldn't miss; it did.

John Prine—"John Prine" (Atlantic)

The first and still best bits of wit and wisdom from a man who has a disjointed, challenging, and often poignant view of life.

Bruce Springsteen—"Darkness on the Edge of Town" (Columbia)

This is *the* rock and roll album that I play over and over again. I wanted it listed as a CLASSIC album. I lost that battle, so I am sneaking it in here. Hopefully, by the time this book is out we will have a new album from Bruce.

Pete Townsend and Ronnie Lane—"Rough Mix" (MCA)

Another side of Pete Townsend, and a delightful side it is, a marvelously subtle approach to rock and roll.

Muddy Waters—"Hard Again" (Blue Sky)

B. B. King says that Muddy Waters is the "boss" when it comes to the blues. This album proves it.

6. THE ROCK MUSIC SOURCE BOOK TOP FORTY

In an attempt to pick forty songs, we reworked this list at least a dozen times. In the end, we could agree unanimously only on the thirty songs listed below. Bob swore we should include "Be My Baby" by the Ronettes. Bill made a strong case for The Stones' "You Can't Always Get What You Want." And Pete insisted that we were crazy for not including "I Can See for Miles" by The Who.

Since we failed to complete our Top Forty list, we're asking for your help in choosing another ten. If you do better than we did, send us your suggestions to the address found on page 644.

Good Luck!

Listed in *alphabetical* order:

1) Alice's Restaurant—Arlo Guthrie; "Alice's Restaurant" (Reprise)
2) American Pie—Don McLean; "American Pie" (United Artists)
3) Born to Run—Bruce Springsteen; "Born to Run" (Columbia)
4) Bridge over Troubled Water—Simon and Garfunkel; "Bridge over Troubled Water" (Columbia)
5) Fire and Rain—James Taylor; "Sweet Baby James" (Warner Brothers)
6) For What It's Worth—Buffalo Springfield; "Buffalo Springfield" (Atco)
7) Free Bird—Lynyrd Skynyrd; "Pronounced Leh-nerd Skin-nerd" (MCA)
8) Get Together—The Youngbloods; "Get Together" (RCA)
9) Gimme Shelter—The Rolling Stones; "Let It Bleed" (London)
10) Good Vibrations—The Beach Boys; "Smiley Smile" (Brother/Reprise)
11) Hey Jude—The Beatles; "Hey Jude" (Apple)
12) Johnny B. Goode—Chuck Berry; "Golden Decade" (Chess)'
13) Layla—Derek and the Dominos; "Layla and Other Assorted Love Songs" (RSO)
14) Light My Fire—The Doors; "The Doors" (Elektra)
15) Like a Rolling Stone—Bob Dylan; "Highway 61 Revisited" (Columbia)
16) Me and Bobby McGee—Janis Joplin; "Pearl" (Columbia)
17) Mr. Tambourine Man—The Byrds; "Mr. Tambourine Man" (Columbia)

18) Nights in White Satin—The Moody Blues; "Days of Future Passed" (London)

19) Rosalita—Bruce Springsteen; "The Wild, the Innocent and the E Street Shuffle" (Columbia)

20) Satisfaction—The Rolling Stones; "Through the Past Darkly" (London)

21) Stairway to Heaven—Led Zeppelin; "Led Zeppelin IV" (the runes album) (Atlantic)

22) Suite: Judy Blue Eyes—Crosby, Stills & Nash; "Crosby, Stills & Nash" (Atlantic)

23) Sunshine of Your Love—Cream; "Disraeli Gears" (RSO)

24) Sympathy for the Devil—The Rolling Stones; "Beggars Banquet" (London)

25) Truckin'—The Grateful Dead; "American Beauty" (Warner Brothers)

26) Whiter Shade of Pale—Procol Harum; "Procol Harum" (Deram)

27) Won't Get Fooled Again—The Who; "Who's Next" (MCA/Track)

28) Yesterday—The Beatles; "Yesterday . . . and Today" (Capitol)

29) Your Song—Elton John; "Elton John" (MCA)

30) You've Got a Friend—Carole King; "Tapestry" (Ode)
   +You've Got a Friend—James Taylor; "Mud Slide Slim and the Blue Horizon" (Warner Brothers)

Your Choices:

31) _____

32) _____

33) _____

34) _____

35) _____

36) _____

37) _____

38) _____

39) _____

40) _____

II. ROCK GOES TO THE MOVIES

1. ROCK-ORIENTED FILMS—a chronological listing by release date

There have been rock and roll movies for as long as there has been rock and roll. The following is a chronological* listing of all kinds of rock films—exploitative ones, terrible ones, great ones. There are comedies, documentaries, dramas, musicals, and performance films. All share one thing in common—each attempted to capture some aspect of the dynamism of rock on celluloid. (N.B. The list does not include films with rock stars in straight dramatic roles, e.g., James Taylor and Dennis Wilson in *Two Lane Blacktop*.)

1955 Blackboard Jungle

1956 The Girl Can't Help It
Rock Around the Clock
Shake, Rattle and R-O-C-K

1957 The Big Beat
Don't Knock the Rock
Jamboree
Mister Rock 'n' Roll
Rock Around the World
Rock Pretty Baby
Rock, Rock, Rock

1958 High School Confidential
Hot Rod Gang
Let's Rock

1959 College Confidential
Go Johnny Go

1960 All the Young Men
Because They're Young

1961 Hey Let's Twist
Teenage Millionaire
Twist Around the Clock

1962 Don't Knock the Twist

1963 Beach Party
Bye Bye Birdie
Live It Up

1964 Bikini Beach
Get Yourself a College Girl
A Hard Day's Night
Muscle Beach Party
Ride the Wild Surf
T.A.M.I. Show (Gather No
Moss)

1965 Beach Ball
Beach Blanket Bingo
Be My Guest
Ferry Cross the Mersey
The Girls on the Beach
Having a Wild Weekend
Help!
Hold On
How to Stuff a Wild Bikini

1966 The Big T.N.T. Show
Chappaqua
Fastest Guitar Alive
Good Times

1967 Don't Look Back
Festival
Magical Mystery Tour (ac-
tually a TV special)
Privilege
Tonight Let's All Make Love
in London

* Alphabetical within each year

1968 Head
Monterey Pop
Mrs. Brown You've Got a Lovely Daughter
Sympathy for the Devil/One Plus One
Wild in the Streets
Yellow Submarine
You Are What You Eat

1969 Alice's Restaurant
Farewell of the Cream

1970 Carry It On
Gimme Shelter
It's Your Thing
Jimi Plays Berkeley
Keep On Rockin'
Let It Be
Performance
The Strawberry Statement
Woodstock
Zachariah

1971 Celebration at Big Sur
Mad Dogs and Englishmen
Medicine Ball Caravan
Rainbow Bridge
Soul to Soul
200 Motels

1972 Concert for Bangla Desh
Fillmore
Groupies
The Pied Piper

1973 Born to Boogie
Catch My Soul
Jimi Hendrix
Journey Through the Past
Let the Good Times Roll
That'll Be the Day
Wattstax
Yessongs

1974 Janis

Ladies and Gentlemen, the Rolling Stones
Save the Children
Son of Dracula
Stardust
Tommy
Welcome Back My Friends to the Show That Never Ends

1975 Bound for Glory
Slade in Flame

1976 A Star Is Born
The Song Remains the Same

1977 The Grateful Dead Movie

1978 Almost Summer
American Hot Wax
The Buddy Holly Story
FM
Grease
I Want to Hold Your Hand
Renaldo and Clara
Sgt. Pepper's Lonely Hearts Club Band
Up in Smoke
The Last Waltz
The Wiz

1979 The Grateful Dead
Hair
The Kids Are Alright
Quadrophenia
Rock and Roll High School
Rust Never Sleeps

1980 The Blues Brothers
Can't Stop the Music
Coal Miner's Daughter
The Great Rock and Roll Swindle
Roadie
No Nukes
The Rose

2. Elvis Presley Films

Elvis Presley films get a special listing because they're . . . well, Elvis Presley films. Be advised, however, that with a few notable early exceptions, and the last two documentaries, these aren't really rock films after all.

The rock and roll movies are marked with an asterisk (*).

1956 Love Me Tender	1965 Girl Happy
1957 Loving You*	1965 Tickle Me
1957 Jailhouse Rock*	1965 Harum Scarum
1958 King Creole*	1966 Paradise—Hawaiian Style
1960 G.I. Blues	1966 Frankie and Johnny
1960 Flaming Star	1966 Spinout
1961 Wild in the Country	1967 Double Trouble
1961 Blue Hawaii	1967 Easy Come, Easy Go
1962 Follow That Dream	1967 Clambake
1962 Girls! Girls! Girls!	1968 Stay Away, Joe
1963 Kid Galahad	1968 Speedway
1963 It Happened at the World's Fair	1968 Live a Little, Love a Little
	1969 Charro!
1963 Fun in Acapulco	1969 The Trouble with Girls
1964 Kissin' Cousins	1969 Change of Habit
1964 Viva Las Vegas	1970 Elvis: That's the Way It Is*
1964 Roustabout	1972 Elvis on Tour*

3. Rock Soundtracks of Movies

In addition to the rock films listed above, many traditional Hollywood movies have been using rock on their soundtracks for years. The following is a partial alphabetical list of album soundtracks utilizing rock and roll music:

Across 110th Street—Bobby Womack   (United Artists)
Alice's Restaurant—Arlo Guthrie   (United Artists)
All This and World War II—Various Artists   (20th Century Records)
Almost Summer—Celebration with Mike Love   (MCA)
Americathon—Various Artists   (CBS)

American Graffiti—Various Artists (MCA)

American Hot Wax—Various Artists (A&M)

Can't Stop the Music—Village People (Casablanca)

Concert for Bangla Desh—George Harrison and Guests (Apple)

Black Caesar—James Brown (Polydor)

Blow-Up—Various Artists (MGM)

Book of Numbers—Sonny Terry and Brownee McGee (Brut)

Bound for Glory—David Carradine (United Artists)

Brewster McCloud—Various Artists (MGM)

Brothers—Taj Mahal (Warner Brothers)

The Buddy Holly Story—Gary Busey (Epic)

Bugsy Malone—Paul Williams (RSO)

Candy—Various Artists (ABC)

Carry It On—Joan Baez (Vanguard)

Car Wash—Various Artists (MCA)

Catch My Soul—Richie Havens/Tony Jo White (Metromedia)

Claudine—Gladys Knight and the Pips (Buddah)

Cleopatra Jones—Joe Simon/Millie Jackson (Warner Brothers)

Coal Miner's Daughter—Various Artists (MCA)

Cooley High—Various Artists (Motown)

Cruising—Various Artists (Casablanca)

Dusty and Sweets McGee—Various Artists (Warner Brothers)

Easy Rider—Various Artists (ABC)

The Electric Horseman—Willie Nelson (Columbia)

Fillmore—Various Artists (Columbia)

The Fish That Saved Pittsburgh—The Spinners (CBS)

The Flasher—Rupert Holmes (Green Bottle Record)

FM—Various Artists (MCA)

Fools—Kenny Rogers (Reprise)

Foxes—Various Artists (Casablanca)

Friends—Elton John (Paramount)

Godspell—Various Artists (Arista)

Goodbye Columbus—The Association (Warner Brothers)

Gordon's War—Various Artists (Buddah)

The Graduate—Simon and Garfunkel (Columbia)

Grease—Various Artists (RSO)

The Greatest—Various Artists (Arista)

Hair—Various Artists (RCA)

A Hard Day's Night—The Beatles (United Artists)

The Harder They Come—Jimmy Cliff (Mango/Capitol)

Having a Wild Weekend—The Dave Clark Five (Epic)

Heavy Traffic—Various Artists (Fantasy)

Hell Up in Harlem—Various Artists (Motown)

Help!—The Beatles (Capitol)

Here We Go Round the Mulberry Bush—Various Artists (United Artists)

A Hero Ain't Nothing but a Sandwich—Various Artists (Columbia)

Homer—Various Artists (Cotillion)

I Walk the Line—Johnny Cash (Columbia)

Janis—Documentary (Columbia)

Jesus Christ Superstar—Various Artists (MCA)

Jimi Hendrix—Documentary (Warner Brothers)

Jimi Plays Berkeley—Jimi Hendrix (Warner Brothers)

Jonathan Livingston Seagull—Neil Diamond (Columbia)

Journey Through the Past—Neil Young (Warner Brothers)

Jud—Various Artists (Ampex)

The Kids Are Alright—The Who (MCA)

The Last Waltz—Various Artists (Warner Brothers)

Let It Be—The Beatles (Apple) .

Let the Good Times Roll—Various Artists (Bell)

Lisztomania—Various Artists (A&M)

Live and Let Die—Paul McCartney (United Artists)

Looking for Mr. Goodbar—Various Artists (Columbia)

The Lords of Flatbush—Various Artists (ABC)

Mad Dogs and Englishmen—Joe Cocker (A&M)

The Magic Christian—Badfinger (Apple)

Mahogany—Diana Ross (Motown)

Mahoney's Last Stand—Ron Wood and Ronnie Lane (Atco)

The Main Event—Barbra Streisand (Columbia)

Meatballs—Various Artists (RSO)

Medicine Ball Caravan—Various Artists (Warner Brothers)

Midnight Cowboy—Original Soundtrack (United Artists)

Monterey Pop:

   The Monterey International Pop Festival—The Mamas and The Papas (Dunhill)

   Hendrix/Redding Live at Monterey—Jimi Hendrix/Otis Redding (Warner Brothers)

More—Pink Floyd   (Tower)

Mother, Jugs and Speed—Various Artists   (A&M)

The Naked Ape—Various Artists   (Playboy Records)

Nashville—Various Artists   (ABC)

Ned Kelley—Waylon Jennings/Kris Kristofferson   (United Artists)

Obscured by Clouds—Pink Floyd   (Harvest)

O Lucky Man—Alan Price   (Warner Brothers)

One on One—Seals and Crofts   (Warner Brothers)

Over the Edge—Various Artists   (Warner Brothers)

Pat Garrett and Billy the Kid—Bob Dylan   (Columbia)

Performance—Mick Jagger/Various Artists   (Warner Brothers)

Phantom of the Paradise—Paul Williams   (A&M)

Pipe Dreams—Gladys Knight and the Pips   (Buddah)

Privilege—Various Artists   (Uni/MCA)

Public Enemy Number One—Roger Daltry   (Polydor)

Quadrophenia—The Who   (Polydor)

Quincy Jones—Danny Hathaway   (Motown)

Rainbow Bridge—Jimi Hendrix   (Warner Brothers)

Roadie—Various Artists   (Warner Brothers)

Rock and Roll High School—Ramones   (Sire)

The Rocky Horror Picture Show—Various Artists   (Ode)

Roller Boogie—Various Artists   (Casablanca)

The Rose—Bette Midler   (Atlantic)

Rust Never Sleeps—Neil Young   (Warner Brothers)

Saturday Night Fever—The Bee Gees and Others   (RSO)

Sgt. Pepper's Lonely Hearts Club Band—Various Artists   (RSO)

Shaft—Isaac Hayes   (Stax)

Skatetown U.S.A.—Various Artists   (Columbia)

Skidoo—Harry Nilsson   (RCA)

Slade in Flame—Slade   (Warner Brothers)

The Song Remains the Same—Led Zeppelin   (Swan Song)

The Sorcerer—Tangerine Dream   (Epic)

Stardust—Various Artists   (Arista)

A Star Is Born—Streisand/Kristofferson   (Columbia)

Steal Your Face—The Grateful Dead   (United Artists)

Steelyard Blues—Various Artists   (Warner Brothers)

The Strawberry Statement—Various Artists   (MGM)

Superfly—Curtis Mayfield   (Curtom)

Together—Various Artists   (RCA)

Tommy—Various Artists   (Polydor)

Trouble Man—Marvin Gaye   (Tamla)

Up in Smoke—Cheech and Chong   (Warner Brothers)

Up Tight—Booker T. and the MG's   (Stax)

Vanishing Point—Various Artists   (Amos)

The Wanderers—Various Artists   (Warner Brothers)

Wattstax—Vol. I—Various Artists   (Stax)
          Vol. II—Various Artists   (Stax)

Welcome Back My Friends—Emerson, Lake & Palmer   (Manticore)

What's up, Tiger Lily?—The Lovin' Spoonful   (Kama Sutra)

White Rock—Rick Wakeman   (A&M)

Who Is Harry Kellerman?—Dr. Hook   (Columbia)

The Wiz—Various Artists   (MCA)

Woodstock—Various Artists   (Cotillion)

Woodstock II—Various Artists   (Cotillion)

Yellow Submarine—The Beatles   (Apple)

Yessongs—Yes   (Atlantic)

Youngbloods—War   (United Artists)

You Are What You Eat—Various Artists   (Columbia)

You Gotta Walk It Like You Talk It—Steely Dan   (Spark)

You're a Big Boy Now—The Lovin' Spoonful   (Kama Sutra)

Zabriskie Point—Various Artists   (MGM)

Zachariah—Various Artists   (ABC)

TV Soundtracks

Elvis in Concert—Elvis Presley   (RCA)

Hard Rain—Bob Dylan   (Columbia)

Love at the Greek—Neil Diamond   (Columbia)

Magical Mystery Tour—The Beatles   (Capitol)

The Music for UNICEF Concert—A Gift of Song—Various Artists
   (Polydor)

The Point—Harry Nilsson   (RCA)

Really Rosie—Carole King   (Ode)

The Rutles—The Rutles   (Warner Brothers)

The Secret Life of Plants—Stevie Wonder   (Tamla)

III. ROCK HISTORY

Important Dates in Rock and Roll

Unless otherwise specified, these are birth dates. Where helpful, the band or particular song the person is most identified with is indicated in parentheses.

JANUARY

1. Country Joe McDonald
   Hank Williams died, 1953
2. Roger Miller
   Chick Churchill (Ten Tears After)
3. Stephen Stills
   John Paul Jones (Led Zeppelin)
   George Martin (Producer)
   The "First Acid Test" held at Fillmore West, San Francisco
   (1966)
4. Volker Homback (Tangerine Dream)
5. Thom Mooney (Nazz)
   Charles Mingus died, 1979
6. Syd Barrett (formerly of Pink Floyd)
   Wilbert Harrison ("Kansas City")
7. Kenny Loggins
   Mike McGear (Paul McCartney's brother)
   Andrew Brown (The Fortunes)
   Paul Revere (Paul Revere and the Raiders)
   Cyril Davies (Blues Incorporated) died, 1964
8. Elvis Presley
   David Bowie
   Jimmy Page (Led Zeppelin)
   Robby Kreiger (The Doors)
   Shirley Bassey
   Lee Jackson (The Nice)
   Terry Sylvester (The Hollies)
9. Joan Baez
   Scott Walker (The Walker Brothers)
   Marcus Doubleday (The Electric Flag)

10. Rod Stewart
    Jim Croce
    Ronnie Hawkins
    Aynsley Dunbar (Journey)
    Martin Turner (Wishbone Ash)
    Donny Hathaway
    Johnnie Ray
    Howlin' Wolf died, 1976

11. Slim Harpo

12. Long John Baldry

13. John Lees (Barclay James Harvest)
    "London Rainbow Concert" with Eric Clapton, Pete Townsend

14. Allen Toussaint
    Tim Harris (The Foundations)
    First "Be-In," 1967, Golden Gate Park, San Francisco
    Donny Hathaway died, 1979

15. Captain Beefheart

16. Sandy Denny
    Raymond Phillips (Nashville Teens)
    "The Cavern Club" opened in Liverpool, England, 1957

17. Mick Taylor
    Muhammad Ali
    Chris Montez ("The More I See You")
    Billy Stewart died, 1970
    William Hart (The Delfonics)

18. Elmore James
    Bobby Goldsboro
    David Greenslade (Colosseum)
    David Ruffin (formerly of The Temptations)

19. Janis Joplin
    Phil Everly
    Dolly Parton
    Robert Palmer
    Rod Evans (Deep Purple)

20. Leadbelly (Huddie Ledbetter)
    Melvin Pritchard (Barclay James Harvest)
    George Grantham (Poco)
    Alan Freed died, 1965
    "Tribute to Woody Guthrie" concert at Carnegie Hall, 1968
    Beatles Release "Meet The Beatles" album, 1964

21. Edwin Starr
    Richie Havens

Jimmy Ibbotson (The Dirt Band)
Chris Britton (The Troggs)

22. Sam Cooke
Brian Keenan (The Chambers Brothers)

23. Bill Cunningham (Box Tops)
Jerry Lawson (The Persuasions)

24. Doug Kershaw
Neil Diamond
James "Shep" Shepherd (Shep and the Limelights) died, 1970

25.

26. Corky Laing (Mountain)

27. Nick Mason (Pink Floyd)
Bobby "Blue" Bland
Nedra Talley (The Ronettes)
Rudi Maugeri (The Crew Cuts)

28. Rick Allen (Box Tops)
Rick Wright (Pink Floyd)
Bobby Bloom died, 1974

29. David Byron (Uriah Heep)

30. Marty Balin (Jefferson Starship)
Steve Marriott (Humble Pie)
Joe Terranova (Danny and the Juniors)

31. Phil Collins (Genesis)
Phil Manzanera (Roxy Music)
Terry Kath (Chicago)

FEBRUARY

1. Don Everly
Bob Shane (The Kingston Trio)
Jimmy Carl Black (The Mothers of Invention)
Ray Sawyer (Dr. Hook and the Medicine Show)
Tommy Duffy (The Echoes)
"I Want to Hold Your Hand" by the Beatles becomes No. 1 song
in the United States, 1964

2. Graham Nash
Skip Battin (The Byrds)
Roberta Flack
Peter Macbeth (The Foundations)
Tom Smothers

   Derek Shulman (Gentle Giant)
   Sid Vicious died, 1979

3. Melanie
   Dave Davies (The Kinks)
   Johnny "Guitar" Watson
   Dennis Edwards (The Temptations)
   Buddy Holly, Ritchie Valens and the Big Bopper died, 1959
   Angelo D'Aleo (Dion and the Belmonts)

4. Jerry Shirley (Humble Pie)
   John Steel (The Animals)
   Alice Cooper
   Johnny Gamble (The Classics)

5. Al Kooper
   Alex Harvey
   Bob Marley
   Nigel Olsson (Elton John's band)
   Chuck Winfield (Blood, Sweat and Tears)
   Cory Wells (Three Dog Night)
   Ron Wilson (Joy of Cooking)
   Sven Johannson (Tangerine Dream)

6. Fabian
   Jessie Belvin died, 1960

7. Laurence Scott (Isotope)
   Beatles arrive in New York for first U.S. tour, 1964

8. James Dean
   Jim Capaldi (Traffic)
   Ted Turner (Wishbone Ash)
   Tom Rush
   Adolpho "Fito" dela Parra (Canned Heat)
   Max Yasgur, owner of "Woodstock Festival" site, died, 1973

9. Carole King
   Barbara Lewis
   Bruce Bennett (The Shadows)
   First Beatles appearance, The Ed Sullivan Show, 1964
   Mark Mathis (The Newbeats)

10.

11. Gene Vincent
    Josh White
    Earl Lewis (The Channels)

12. Stanley Knight (Black Oak Arkansas)
    Steve Hackett (Genesis)
    Gene McDaniels

Beatles played Carnegie Hall, 1964
Ray Mawzarek (The Doors)

13. Peter Tork (The Monkees)
The Rolling Stones appeared on The Ed Sullivan Show, 1966

14. Tim Buckley
Eric Andersen
Vic Briggs (original member of The Animals)

15. Brian Holland (Motown writer and producer)
Mick Avory (The Kinks)
Melissa Manchester

16. Sonny Bono
Lyn Paul (The New Seekers)

17. Gene Pitney
Tommy Edwards ("It's All in the Game")
Bobby Lewis ("Tossin' and Turnin' ")

18. Yoko Ono Lennon
Bon Scott (AC/DC) died, 1980

19. Smokey Robinson
Lou Christie ("Lightning Strikes")
Pierre Van Der Linden (Focus)
Tony Iommi (Black Sabbath)
Andy Powell (Wishbone Ash)
Phil Cracolici (The Mystics)

20. J. Geils
Buffy Sainte-Marie
Randy California (Spirit)
Alan Hull (Lindisfarne)
Barbara Ellis (The Fleetwoods)

21. Nina Simone
Florence Ballard (The Supremes) died, 1976
Janet Vogel Rapp (Skyliners) died, 1980

22. Bobby Hendricks (The Swallows)

23. Johnny Winter
Rusty Young (Poco)

24. Nicky Hopkins
Paul Jones (Manfred Mann, early lead singer)

25. George Harrison
Elkie Brooks

26. Fats Domino
Johnny Cash

Bob "The Bear" Hite (Canned Heat)
Sandy Shaw ("There's Always Something There to Remind Me")

27. Steve Harley

28. Joe South
    John Fahey
    Brian Jones

29. Gretchen Christopher (The Fleetwoods)

MARCH

1. Roger Daltrey
   Mike D'Abo (Manfred Mann)
   Sonny James
   Jim Edward Brown (The Browns)

2. Lou Reed
   Rory Gallagher
   Karen Carpenter
   Willie Chambers (The Chambers Brothers)

3. Chris Stainton
   Buzzy Linhart
   Tony S. McPhee (Groundhogs)
   Jance Garfat (Dr. Hook and the Medicine Show)
   Junior Parker

4. Mary Wilson (The Supremes)
   Bobby Womack
   Chris Squire (Yes)
   Eric Allendale (The Foundations)
   Miriam Makeba

5. Eddie Grant (The Equals)
   Tommy Tucker ("High Heeled Sneakers")
   Mike Jeffrey died, 1973 (Jimi Hendrix's manager)

6. Kiki Dee
   Randy Meisner
   Hugh Grundy (The Zombies)
   David Gilmore (Pink Floyd)
   Sylvia Vanderpool ("Pillow Talk")
   Doug Dillard (The Dillards)

7. Peter Wolf (J. Geils Band)
   Chris Taylor White

8. Ralph Ellis (The Swinging Blue Jeans)
   Charley Pride
   Rod "Pig Pen" McKernan (The Grateful Dead) died, 1973
   Little Peggy March ("I Will Follow Him")
   Shel Macrea (The Fortunes)

9. Robin Trower
   Lloyd Price
   Trevor Burton (The Move)
   James Fadden (The Dirt Band)
   Gary Leeds (The Walker Brothers)

10. Dean Torrence (Jan and Dean)
    Ted McKenna (The Sensational Alex Harvey Band)

11. Harvey Mandel
    Mark Stein (Vanilla Fudge)
    Mike Hugg (Manfred Mann Band)

12. James Taylor
    Paul Kantner (Jefferson Starship)
    Les Holroyd (Barclay James Harvest)
    Paul McCartney and Linda Eastman married, 1969
    Brian O'Hara (The Foremost)
    Charlie Parker died, 1955

13. Neil Sedaka

14. Jim Pons (The Turtles)
    Loretta Lynn
    Quincy Jones

15. Mike Love (The Beach Boys)
    Ry Cooder
    Phil Lesh (The Grateful Dead)
    Sly Stone
    Howard Scott (War)
    Allan Clarke (The Hollies)
    Lightnin' Hopkins
    Hughie Flint (McGuinness Flint)

16. Jerry Jeff Walker
    Tammi Terrell died, 1970

17. John Sebastian
    Harold Brown (War)
    Vito Picone (The Elegants—"Little Star")
    Dean Mathis (The New Beats)
    Clarence Collins (Little Anthony and the Imperials)

18. Wilson Pickett
    Robert Lee Smith (The Tams)
    Barry Wilson (early Procol Harum)

19. Mickey Dolenz (The Monkees)
    Derek Longmuir (Bay City Rollers)
    Paul Atkinson (The Zombies)
    Paul Kossoff died, 1976
    Gary Thain (Uriah Heep) died, 1976
    Jeff Neighbor (Joy of Cooking)

20. John Lennon and Yoko Ono married, 1969
    Carl Palmer (Emerson, Lake & Palmer)

21. The Beatles debuted at the Cavern Club in Liverpool, 1961

22. Keith Relf (The Yardbirds)
    Jeremy Clyde (Chad and Jeremy)
    Randy Hobbs (The Johnny Winter Band)
    Harry Vanda (The Easybeats)

23.

24. Mike Kellie (Spooky Tooth)
    Lee Oskar (War)
    Billy Stewart
    Colin Peterson (The Bee Gees)
    Holgar Czukay (Can)
    Dave Appell (The Appelljacks)

25. Aretha Franklin
    Elton John
    Johnny Burnette ("You're Sixteen")

26. Diana Ross
    Fred Parris (The Five Satins)
    Harold McNair (Ginger Baker/Air Force) died, 1971
    Steve Tyler (Aerosmith)

27.

28. Charlie McCoy
    John Evans (Jethro Tull)
    Arthur "Big Boy" Crudup died, 1974
    Dean Webb (The Dillards)
    Rufus Thomas ("Walking The Dog")

29. Lonnie Donegan
    John "Speedy" Keen (Thunderclap Newman)

30. Eric Clapton
    Graeme Edge (The Moody Blues)
    Sonny Boy Williamson
    Jim Dandy (Black Oak Arkansas)
    David Ball (Procol Harum)

31. Thijs Van Leer (Focus)
    Richard Hughes (The Johnny Winter Band)

Herb Alpert
Al Goodman (The Moments)

APRIL

1. Ronnie Lane
   Rudolph Isley (The Isley Brothers)
   Simon Crowe (Lindisfarne)
   Arthur Conley
   "Mar y Sol" Festival, Puerto Rico, 1972
   Alan Blakeley (The Tremeloes)
2. Marvin Gaye
   Leon Russell
   Larry Coryell
   Kerry Minnear (Gentle Giant)
3. Richard Manuel (The Band)
   Jan Berry (Jan and Dean)
   Dee Murray (Elton John band)
   Mel Schacher (Grand Funk Railroad)
   Tony Orlando
   Barry Pritchard (The Fortunes)
   Joe Vann (The Duprees)
4. Muddy Waters
   Berry Oakley (The Allman Brothers)
   Major Lance ("Um Um Um Um Um Um")
   Dave Hill (Slade)
   Christophe Franke (Tangerine Dream)
5. Dave Swarbrick (Fairport Convention)
   Tony Williams (The Platters)
   Crispian St. Peters ("The Pied Piper")
   Billy Bland ("Let the Little Girl Dance")
6. Merle Haggard
   Julie Rodgers ("The Wedding")
7. Janis Ian
   Billie Holiday
   Spencer Dryden (Jefferson Starship)
   Freddie Hubbard
   Mick Abrahams (Blodwyn Pig)
   Percy Faith
   Bobby Bare
   Charley Thomas (The Drifters)
   Steve Ellis (Love Affair)

8. Steve Howe (Yes)
   Roger Chapman (Family)
   Charley Chinn (Cat Mother and the All Night Newsboys)

9. Gene Parsons
   Carl Perkins
   Terry Knight (Grand Funk Railroad)
   Phil Ochs died, 1976
   Emil Stucchio (The Classics)

10. Glen Campbell
    Bobby Hatfield (The Righteous Brothers)
    Ricky Valence
    Nathaniel Nelson (The Flamingos)
    Stu Sutcliffe (almost a Beatle) died, 1962
    Chuck Willis ("Hang Up My Rock and Roll Shoes") died, 1958

11. Bob Dylan's first appearance at Gerde's Folk City, New York
    City, 1961
    Tony Victor (The Classics)

12. Tiny Tim
    John Kay (Steppenwolf)
    Herbie Hancock
    David Cassidy

13. Al Green
    Jack Cassady (Hot Tuna)
    Lester Chambers (The Chambers Brothers)
    Roy Loney (Flaming Groovies)
    Tim Field (The Springfields)
    Eve Graham (The New Seekers)
    Horace Kay (The Tams)

14. Ritchie Blackmore (Deep Purple and Rainbow)
    Buddy Knox
    Patrick Fairley (Marmalade)

15. Bessie Smith
    Wooley Wolstenholme (Barclay James Harvest)
    Dave Edmunds

16. Dusty Springfield
    Stefan Grossman (The Fugs)
    Bobby Vinton
    Herbie Mann
    Jimmy Osmond
    Roy Hamilton ("Unchained Melody")

17. Roy Ralph Estrada (The Mothers of Invention)
    Eddie Cochran died, 1960
    Vinnie Taylor (Sha Na Na) died, 1974
    Bill Kreutzmann (Grateful Dead)
    Bobby Curtola ("Fortune Teller")

18. Mike Vickers (Manfred Mann)

19. Alexis Korner
    Alan Price (The Animals)
    Mark Volman (The Turtles; Flo and Eddie)

20. Johnny Tillotson ("Poetry in Motion")

21. Alan Warner (The Foundations)
    Janis Joplin played Royal Albert Hall, London, 1969

22. Peter Frampton
    Charles Mingus
    Mel Carter ("Hold Me, Thrill Me, Kiss Me")

23. Roy Orbison
    Ray Peterson ("Tell Laura I Love Her")
    Peter Ham (Badfinger), 1975

24. Barbra Streisand
    Glen Cornick (Jethro Tull)
    Robert Knight
    Sandy Denny died, 1978

25. Albert King
    Ella Fitzgerald

26. Bobby Rydell
    Duane Eddy
    Pete Ham (Badfinger)
    Gary Wright
    Claudine Clark ("Party Lights")

27. Phil King (Blue Oyster Cult) died, 1972
    Maxine Brown (The Browns)

28. "Hair" opened on Broadway, 1968

29. Carl Gardner (The Coasters)
    Hugh Hopper (The Soft Machine)
    Tommy James (Tommy James and the Shondells)
    Duke Ellington
    Michael Karoli (Can)

30. Willie Nelson
    Bobby Vee ("Take Good Care of My Baby")
    Mike Deacon (Ox)

Johnny Horton
Richard Fariña died, 1966

MAY

1. Judy Collins
   Rita Coolidge
   Mimi Fariña
   Elvis Presley married Priscilla Beaulieu, 1967
   Little Walter ("Confess the Blues")
2. Link Wray ("Rumble")
   John Verity (Argent)
   Goldy McJohn (Steppenwolf)
   Lesley Gore
   Hilton Valentine (The Animals)
   Randy Cain (The Delfonics)
3. James Brown
   Pete Seeger
   Frankie Valli
   Mary Hopkins ("Those Were The Days")
   Peter Staples (The Troggs)
   John Richardson (The Rubettes)
   Les Harvey (Stone the Crows) died, 1972
4. Tammy Wynette
   Ed Cassady (Spirit)
   Ronnie Bond (The Troggs)
   Kent State Massacre, 1970
   Zel Cleminson (The Sensational Alex Harvey Band)
   Peggy Santiglia (The Angels—"My Boyfriend's Back")
5. Bill Ward (Black Sabbath)
   Jim King (Family)
   Johnnie Taylor ("Who's Making Love?")
   Buffalo Springfield broke up, 1968
   Rev. Gary Davis died, 1972
6. Herbie Cox (The Cleftones)
7. Jimmy Ruffin ("What Becomes of the Broken Hearted")
   Pete Wingfield ("Eighteen with a Bullet")
   Johnny Maestro (The Crests; The Brooklyn Bridge)
   Derek Taylor (The Beatles' publicity person)
   Mitch Jayne (The Dillards)
8. Rick Nelson
   Gary Glitter

Graham Bond (Graham Bond Organization)
Mark Bolan (T-Rex)
Euclid Sherwood (The Mothers of Invention)
Paul Samwell-Smith (The Yardbirds)
John Fred (John Fred and His Playboy Band—"Judy in Disguise")

9. Richie Furay
Steve Katz (Blues Project and Blood, Sweat and Tears)
Dave Prater (Sam and Dave)
Don Dannerman (The Cyrkle)
Billy Joel
Pete Birrell (Freddie and the Dreamers)
Mike Millward (The Fourmost)

10. Danny Rapp (Danny and the Juniors)
Dave Mason
Donovan
Jackie Lomax
Jay Ferguson (Spirit)
Larry Williams ("Bony Maronie")

11. Les Chadwick (Gerry and the Pacemakers)
Eric Burdon
Carla Bley (Jack Bruce Band)
Lester Flatt died, 1979

12. Steve Winwood
Ian McLagan (Small Faces)
Jayotis Washington (The Persuasions)
James Purify ("I'm Your Puppet")
Mick and Bianca Jagger married, 1971
Burt Bacharach
Bob Rigg (Frost)

13. Mary Welles
Stevie Wonder
Ritchie Valens
Danny Kirwin (Fleetwood Mac)
Peter Gabriel
Pete Watts (Mott the Hoople)

14. Bobby Darin
Jack Bruce
Al Ciner (The American Breed)
Gene Cornish (The Young Rascals)
Keith Relf (The Yardbirds) died, 1976
Art Grant (The Edgar Broughton Band)

15. Mike Oldfield
    Brian Eno
    Trini Lopez
    Tich (Dave, Dee, Dozy, Beaky, Mick and Tich—"Bend It")

16. Billy Cobham
    Barbara Lee (The Chiffons)

17. Taj Mahal
    Jesse Winchester
    Keith ("98.6")
    Bob Dylan's First London Concert: The Royal Festival Hall,
        1964

18. Rick Wakeman
    Joe Turner ("Corrina, Corrina")
    Albert Hammond ("It Never Rains in Southern California")
    George Alexander (Flaming Groovies)

19. Pete Townsend
    Jerry Hyman (Blood, Sweat, and Tears)

20. Joe Cocker
    Cher
    Jimmy Henderson (Black Oak Arkansas)
    Alex Broughton (The Edgar Broughton Band)

21. Ronald Isley (The Isley Brothers)
    Vincent Crane (The Crazy World of Arthur Brown)
    Marci Blane ("Bobby's Girl")

22. Bernie Taupin
    Ian Underwood (The Mothers of Invention)
    Kenny Ball ("Midnight in Moscow")

23.

24. Bob Dylan
    Steve Upton (Wishbone Ash)
    Elmore James died, 1963
    Leo Sayer
    Derek Quinn (Freddie and the Dreamers)
    Sarah Dash (LaBelle)

25. Miles Davis
    Brian Davidson (The Nice)
    Poli Palmer (Family)
    John Grimaldi (Argent)
    Sonny Boy Williamson II died, 1965
    Carole King Plays Central Park in New York City for 120,000,
        1973
    Tom T. Hall

26. Verden Allen (Mott the Hoople)
    Levon Helm (The Band)
    Jack Liebesit (Can)
    Ray Ennis (The Swinging Blue Jeans)

27. Cilla Black ("You're My World")
    Ramsey Lewis
    Marty Kristian (The New Seekers)

28. John Fogerty (Creedence Clearwater Rivival)
    Gladys Knight
    Ray Laidlaw (Lindisfarne)
    Prince Buster ("Al Capone")

29. Gary Brooker
    Mike Rossi (Status Quo)
    Irmin Schmidt (Can)
    Roy Crewsdon (Freddie and the Dreamers)

30. Lenny Davidson (The Dave Clark Five)
    First TV broadcast, 1939

31. John Bonham (Led Zeppelin)
    Charles Miller (War)
    Peter Yarrow (Peter, Paul and Mary)
    Mick Ralphs (Mott the Hoople)
    Augie Mayer (Sir Douglas Quintet)
    Junior Campbell (Marmalade)

JUNE

1. Ron Wood
   Johnny Bond ("Hot Rod Lincoln")
   Pat Boone
   "Sgt. Pepper's Lonely Hearts Club Band" released, 1967
   Sonny Boy Williamson died, 1948 ("Good Morning Little School Girl")

2. Charlie Watts
   Jimmy Jones ("Handy Man")
   William Guest (Gladys Knight and the Pips)

3. Ian Hunter
   Michael Clarke (The Byrds)
   Suzi Quatro
   The Rolling Stones began their first American tour, 1964

4. Gordon Waller (Peter and Gordon)
   Michelle Phillips (The Mamas and The Papas)

Alan White
Clifford Bennett (The Rebel Rousers)

5. Bill Hayes ("The Ballad of Davey Crockett")

6. Gary U.S. Bonds ("New Orleans," "Quarter to Three")
Edgar Froese (Tangerine Dream)
Peter Albin (Big Brother and the Holding Company)
Larry Taylor (Canned Heat)

7. Clarence White (The Byrds)
Tom Jones
The Who perform "Tommy" at the Metropolitan Opera House,
   New York, 1970
Gordy Garris (Frost)

8. Boz Scaggs
Julie Driscoll
Nancy Sinatra
Chuck Negron (Three Dog Night)
Mick Box (Uriah Heep)

9. Mitch Mitchell (Jimi Hendrix)
Jackie Wilson
Johnny Ace ("Pledging My Love")
Billy Hatton (The Fourmost)
Elvis Presley's first New York City concert, 1972

10. Howlin' Wolf
Shirley Alston (The Shirelles)
Rick Price (The Move)

11. Joey Dee (Joey Dee and the Starlighters—"Peppermint Twist")

12. Reg Presley (The Troggs)
The Beatles awarded "MBE" (Member of the Order of the Brit-
   ish Empire) by the Queen
Len Barry (The Dovells—"Bristol Stomp"; Solo—"1-2-3")
Roy Harper

13. Bobby Freeman ("Do You Wanna Dance?")
Clyde McPhatter (The Drifters) died, 1972
Dennis Locorriere (Dr. Hook and the Medicine Show)

14. Burl Ives
Rod Argent (The Zombies; Argent)
Jim Lea (Slade)
Muff Winwood (Spencer Davis Group)

15. Waylon Jennings
Harry Nilsson
Noddy Holder (Slade)

John Lennon meets Paul McCartney in Woolton, Liverpool, 1956

16. John Rostill (The Shadows)
    Lamont Dozier (Motown, composer)
    Monterey Pop Festival began, 1967

17. Chris Spedding
    Norman Kuhlke (The Swinging Blue Jeans)

18. Paul McCartney

19. Spanky McFarlane (Spanky and Our Gang)
    Tommy DeVito (Four Seasons)
    Al Wilson (The Rollers—"Continental Walk")

20. Brian Wilson (The Beach Boys)
    Anne Murray
    Alan Longmuir (Bay City Rollers)
    Billy Guy (The Coasters)
    Chet Atkins
    Jerry Keller ("Here Comes Summer")
    Nigel Morris (Isotope)

21. Ray Davies (The Kinks)
    Chris Britton (The Troggs)
    Joe Hiseman (Colosseum)
    O. C. Smith ("Little Green Apples")

22. Todd Rundgren
    Kris Kristofferson
    Peter Asher
    Howard Kaylan (The Turtles; Flo and Eddie)
    Alan Osmond

23. Adam Faith
    June Carter

24. Jeff Beck
    Arthur Brown (The Crazy World of Arthur Brown)
    Colin Blunstone (The Zombies)
    Charlie Whitney (Family)
    Chris Wood (Traffic)
    Mick Fleetwood
    Patrick Moraz

25. Carly Simon
    Eddy Floyd ("Knock on Wood")
    Clint Warwick (early Moody Blues)

26. Georgie Fame
    Richard McCracken (Taste)

27. Bruce Johnston (The Beach Boys)
    Denver Pop Festival, 1969
    Fillmore East closed, 1971

28. Bobby Harrison (Procol Harum)
    Dave Knights (Procol Harum)

29. Ian Paice (Deep Purple)
    Little Eva ("Locomotion")
    Tim Buckley died, 1975
    Shorty Long ("Here Comes the Judge") died, 1969
    Lowell George (Little Feat) died, 1979

30. Flo Ballard (The Supremes)
    Billy Brown (The Moments)
    Larry Hall ("Sandy")
    Larry Henley (The Newbeats)

JULY

1. Delaney Bramlett (Delaney and Bonnie)
   Marc Benno (Leon Russell)
   June Monteiro (The Toys)
   Eddie Bond (The Stompers)

2. Tom Springfield (The Springfields)

3. Matthew Fischer (Procol Harum)
   Fontella Bass ("Rescue Me")
   Brian Jones died, 1969
   Jim Morrison died, 1971
   Fred McDowell died, 1972
   Victor Unitt (The Edgar Broughton Band)
   Atlanta Pop Festival, 1970
   Newport Jazz Festival includes rock for the first time, 1969

4. Al Wilson (Canned Heat)
   Jeremy Spencer (Fleetwood Mac)
   Bill Withers ("Ain't No Sunshine")
   Donald McPherson (The Main Ingredient) died, 1971

5. Robbie Robertson (The Band)

6. Bill Haley (Bill Haley and the Comets)
   Jet Harris (The Shadows)
   Gene Chandler ("Duke of Earl")
   Richard Elswit (Dr. Hook and the Medicine Show)
   "A Hard Day's Night," Beatles' first film, debuted at London Pavilion, 1964

7. Ringo Starr
Rob Townsend (Family)
Jim Rodford (Argent)
Joe Zawinul (Weather Report)
Larry Rheinhardt (Iron Butterfly)

8. Jai Johnny Johanson (The Allman Brothers)

9. Donald McPherson (The Main Ingredient)
Van McCoy died, 1979

10. Arlo Guthrie
Dave Smally (Raspberries)

11. Terry Garthwaite (Joy of Cooking)

12. Christine McVie (Fleetwood Mac)
Minnie Riperton died, 1979

13. Roger McGuinn (The Byrds; solo artist)
Jay Uzzell (The Corsairs)

14. Woody Guthrie
The Everly Brothers announced their breakup, 1973
Bob Scholl (The Mello-Kings—"Tonight, Tonight")

15. Linda Ronstadt

16. Thomas Boggs (Box Tops)

17. Spencer Davis
Billie Holiday died, 1959
Geezer Butler (Black Sabbath)
Phoebe Snow

18. Brian Auger
Screamin' Jay Hawkins ("I Put a Spell on You")
Martha Reeves (Martha and the Vandellas)
Wally Bryson (Raspberries)
Dion (Dion and the Belmonts)
Tim Lynch (Flaming Groovies)

19. Clarence White (The Byrds)
Bernie Leadon (The Eagles)
Brian Harold May (Queen)

20. John Lodge (The Moody Blues)
Carlos Santana

21. Cat Stevens

22. Don Henley (The Eagles)
Estelle Bennett (The Ronettes)
Chuck Jackson

23. David Essex
Tony Joe White ("Polk Salad Annie")

Madeline "Maggie" Bell
Dino Danelli (The Rascals)
Cleveland Duncan (The Penguins)
Beatles released "Help!", 1965

24. Chris Townson (John's Children)

25. Steve Goodman
Jim McCarty (The Yardbirds)
Mark Clark (Uriah Heep)
Tom Dawes (The Cyrkle)

26. Roger Taylor (Queen)
Mick Jagger (The Rolling Stones)
Bob Dylan played Newport Folk Festival, 1963

27. Bobbie Gentry ("Ode to Billy Joe")
Nick Reynolds (The Kingston Trio)

28. Rick Wright (Pink Floyd)
Watkins Glen festival, 1973
Jonathan Edwards ("Sunshine")
Peter Boyle (The New Seekers)
George Cummings (Dr. Hook and the Medicine Show)

29. Cass Elliot died, 1974

30. Jeffrey Hammond (Jethro Tull)
Paul Anka
Glen Gains (Parliament Funkadelic) died, 1978
B. B. Dickerson (War)

31. Jim Reeves ("He'll Have to Go")

AUGUST

1. Dennis Payton (The Dave Clark Five)
George Harrison's "Concert for Bangla Desh," 1971
Johnny Burnette died, 1964

2. Garth Hudson (The Band)
Jim Capaldi (Traffic)
Andy Fairweather-Low
Andrew Gold
Edward Patten (Gladys Knight and the Pips)

3. John York (The Byrds)

4. Elsberry Hobbs (The Drifters)

5. Jimmy Webb
David LaFlamme (It's a Beautiful Day)
Rick Huxley (The Dave Clark Five)

6. Isaac Hayes
   Mike Elliot (The Foundations)

7. Andy Fraser (Free)
   Charles Pope (The Tams)

8. Joe Tex
   Jimmy Witherspoon
   Steve Perron (Children) died, 1973
   John David (Dr. Hook and the Medicine Show)

9. Lillian Roxon (Author of *Rock Encyclopedia*) died, 1973
   Barbara Mason ("Yes I'm Ready")

10. Ian Anderson (Jethro Tull)
    Bobby Hatfield (The Righteous Brothers)
    Ronnie Spector (The Ronettes)
    Eric Braunn (Iron Butterfly)
    Jimmy Dean ("Big Bad John")

11. Eric Carmen
    Jeff Hanna (The Dirt Band)
    Lou Reizner (The Skyliners)

12. Buck Owens
    Sam Andrew (Big Brother and the Holding Company)

13. King Curtis died, 1971

14. David Crosby
    Big Bill Broonzy ("See See Rider") died, 1958

15. Tommy Aldridge (Black Oak Arkansas)
    Peter York (Spencer Davis Group)
    Bobby Helms
    Woodstock festival began, 1969
    Floyd Ashton (The Tams)

16. Kevin Ayers
    Elvis Presley died, 1977
    The Beatles at Shea Stadium, 1965

17. Paul Williams (The Temptations)
    Gary Talley (Box Tops)

18. Carl Wayne (The Move)
    Nona Hendryx (LaBelle)
    Barbara Harris (The Toys)

19. Johnny Nash
    Billy J. Kramer (Billy J. Kramer and the Dakotas)
    John Deacon (Queen)
    Ginger Baker (Cream; Blind Faith)

20. Robert Plant (Led Zeppelin)
    Jim Pankow (Chicago)
21. Jackie DeShannon
22. Joe Chambers (The Chambers Brothers)
    John Lee Hooker
    Fred Milano (Dion and the Belmonts)
    Bob Flanigan (The Four Freshmen)
23. Keith Moon
    Rudy Lewis (The Drifters)
    The Beatles at Shea Stadium, 1966
24. John Cipollina (Quicksilver Messenger Service)
    David Freiberg (Jefferson Starship)
    William Winfield (The Harptones)
    Ernie Wright (Little Anthony and the Imperials)
    Ken Hensley (Uriah Heep)
25. Wayne Shorter (Weather Report)
    Stan Kenton died, 1979
26. Isle of Wight Festival, 1970
    Keith Allison (Paul Revere and the Raiders)
27. Tim Bogert (Vanilla Fudge)
    Simon Kirke (Free)
    Brian Epstein died, 1967
    Phil Shulman (Gentle Giant)
28. Dan Serephine (Chicago)
    Wayne Osmond
29. Dick Halligan (Blood, Sweat and Tears)
    Last Beatles performance, 1966, Candlestick Park, San Francisco
    Charlie Parker
    Chris Copping (Procol Harum)
30. John Phillips (The Mamas and The Papas)
    Chuck Colbert (American Breed)
31. Van Morrison

SEPTEMBER

1. Barry Gibb (The Bee Gees)
   Roy Head
2. Rosiland Ashford (Martha Reeves and the Vandellas)
   Joe Simon
3. Al Jardine (The Beach Boys)

Gary Walker (The Walker Brothers)
Mike Harrison (Spooky Tooth)
Don Brewer (Grand Funk Railroad)
Al Wilson (Canned Heat) died, 1970
George Biondo (Steppenwolf)

4. Gene Parsons (The Byrds)
Gary Duncan (Quicksilver Messenger Service)
Greg Elmore (Quicksilver Messenger Service)
Merald Knight (Gladys Knight and the Pips)

5. Buddy Miles
Freddie Mercury (Queen)
Loudon Wainwright III
Josh White died, 1969
Dave Clempson (Colosseum)
Dean Ford (Marmalade)

6. Roger Waters (Pink Floyd)

7. Buddy Holly

8. Ronald "Pigpen" McKernan (The Grateful Dead)

9. Otis Redding
Billy Preston
Inez Fox ("Mockingbird")
Jimmy Reed
Doug Ingle (Iron Butterfly)
Luther Simmons, Jr. (The Main Ingredient)

10. José Feliciano
Don Powell (Slade)
Barriemore Barlow (Jethro Tull)
Danny Hutton (Three Dog Night)
Arthur Tripp (Captain Beefheart's Magic Band)

11. Phil May (Pretty Things)
Bernie Dwyer (Freddie and the Dreamers)

12. Maria Muldaur
Gerry Beckley (America)

13. Peter Cetera (Chicago)
Plastic Ono Band played Toronto, 1969

14. Paul Kossoff (Free)

15. Les Braid (The Swinging Blue Jeans)
Lee Dorman (Iron Butterfly)
Jimmy Gilmer ("Sugar Shack")

16. B. B. King
Kenny Jones (Small Faces)
Bernie Calvert (The Hollies)

Marc Bolan died, 1977
Betty Kelly (Martha Reeves and the Vandellas)

17. Hank Williams

18. Frankie Avalon
Jimi Hendrix died, 1970

19. John Coghlan (Status Quo)
Brook Benton ("Rainy Night in Georgia")
David Bromberg
Cass Elliot (The Mamas and The Papas)
Bill Medley (The Righteous Brothers)
Gram Parsons died, 1973

20. Jim Croce died, 1973

21. Don Preston (The Mothers of Invention)
Dickey Lee ("Patches," "Laurie")
Leonard Cohen
Betty Wright

22. George Chambers (The Chambers Brothers)

23. Bruce Springsteen
Ray Charles
Roy Buchanan
Robbie McIntosh (Average White Band) died, 1974
Tim Rose
Barbara Allbut (The Angels—"My Boyfriend's Back")
Phyllis Allbut (The Angels—"My Boyfriend's Back")
Ross Busby (Iron Butterfly)

24. Linda McCartney
Gerry Marsden (Gerry and the Pacemakers)
Jerry Donahue (Fairport Convention)

25. John Locke (Spirit)
Joseph Russell (The Persuasions)

26. Bryan Ferry
Joe Bauer (The Youngbloods)
Olivia Newton-John
Bessie Smith died, 1937

27. Don Nix
Jimmy McCulloch (Wings) died, 1979

28. Ben E. King

29. Jerry Lee Lewis
Mark Farner (Grand Funk Railroad)
Mike Pinera (Iron Butterfly)
Freddie King

30. Dewey Martin (Buffalo Springfield)
    Gus Dudgeon (Elton John's producer)
    Mike Harrison (Spooky Tooth)
    James Dean died, 1955
    Marc Bolan
    Sylvia Peterson (The Chiffons)

OCTOBER

1. Scott McKenzie ("San Francisco [Be Sure to Wear Flowers in Your Hair]")
    Richard Harris ("MacArthur Park")
    Barbara Parritt (The Toys)
2. Don McLean
    Michael Rutherford (Genesis)
3. Eddie Cochran ("Summertime Blues")
    James Darren
    Chubby Checker
    Woody Guthrie died, 1967
4. Patti LaBelle
    Janis Joplin died, 1970
    Jim Fielder (Blood, Sweat and Tears)
5. Carlo Mastrangelo (Dion and the Belmonts)
    Steve Miller
6. Millie Small ("My Boy Lollipop")
7. Gary Puckett (Gary Puckett and the Union Gap)
    Johnny Kidd ("Shakin' All Over") died, 1966
8. Ray Rowyer (Procol Harum)
    Doc Green (The Drifters)
9. John Lennon
    John Entwhistle
    Jackson Browne
    Pat Burke (The Foundations)
10. Keith Reid (Procol Harum)
    Greg Lake
    John Prine
    Alan Cartwright (Procol Harum)
11. Darryl Hall
12. Rick Parfitt (Status Quo)
    Gene Vincent died, 1971
    Sam Moore (Sam and Dave)

13. Paul Simon
    Chris Farlowe
    Lenny Bruce
    Robert Lamm (Chicago)

14. Cliff Richard
    Justin Hayward (The Moody Blues)
    Robert Parker ("Barefootin' ")

15. Richard Carpenter
    Barry McGuire
    Tito Jackson (The Jackson Five)
    Mary Johnson ("You Got What It Takes")

16. Bob Weir (The Grateful Dead)
    Dave Lovelady (The Fourmost)

17.

18. Chuck Berry
    Russ Giguere (The Association)
    Ronnie Bright (The Coasters)

19. Peter Tosh
    Dave Guard (The Kingston Trio)

20. Ronnie Van Zandt, Steve Gaines, and Cassie Gaines (Lynyrd
    Skynyrd) died, 1977
    Ric Lee (Ten Years After)

21. Manfred Mann
    Steve Cropper
    Eric Faulkner (Bay City Rollers)
    Lee Loughnane (Chicago)
    Norman Wright (The Del-Vikings)

22. Leslie West
    Eddie Brigatti (The Young Rascals)
    Tommy Edwards died, 1969 ("It's All in the Game")

23. Ellie Greenwich
    Charlie Foxx ("Mockingbird")

24. Bill Wyman
    Dale Groffin (Mott the Hoople)
    Edgar Broughton (The Edgar Broughton Band)

25. Jon Anderson (Yes)
    Helen Reddy

26. Mahalia Jackson

27.

28. Wayne Fontana
    Curtis Lee
    Ricky Lee Reynolds (Black Oak Arkansas)

29. Peter Green (Fleetwood Mac)
    Denny Laine (Wings)
    Duane Allman died, 1971
30. Tim Schmidt (The Eagles)
    Eddie Holland (Motown composer)
    Grace Slick (Jefferson Starship)
31. Tom Paxton
    Kinky Friedman

NOVEMBER

1. Rick Grech (Blind Faith)
2. Keith Emerson
   Jay Black (Jay and the Americans)
   Dave Pegg (Fairport Convention)
   Earl Carroll (The Cadillacs)
3. Bert Jansch
   Lulu
   James Taylor and Carly Simon married, 1972
4.
5. Ike Turner
   Art Garfunkel
   Gram Parsons
   Miss Christine (The GTO's) died, 1972
   Peter Noone (Herman's Hermits)
   Johnny Horton died, 1960
6. P. J. Proby
   Doug Sahm (Sir Douglas Quintet)
   Glenn Frey (The Eagles)
   George Young (The Easybeats)
   Chris Glen (The Sensational Alex Harvey Band)
7. Joni Mitchell
   Johnny Rivers
   Mary Travers (Peter, Paul and Mary)
   Dee Clark ("Raindrops")
8. Roy Wood (The Move, early Electric Light Orchestra)
   Bonnie Bramlett (Delaney and Bonnie)
   Bonnie Raitt
   Minnie Riperton
9. Tom Fogerty (Creedence Clearwater Revival)
   Roger McGough (Scaffold)
   Lee Graziano (The American Breed)

10. Greg Lake
11. Mose Allison
    Jesse Colin Young
    Berry Oakley (The Allman Brothers) died, 1972
    Vince Martell (Vanilla Fudge)
12. Neil Young
    Booker T. Jones
    Leslie McKeown (Bay City Rollers)
    Jimmy Hayes (The Persuasions)
    Brian Hyland ("Sealed with a Kiss")
13. Terry Reid
14. Freddie Garrity (Freddie and the Dreamers)
    Keith Relf (The Yardbirds) died, 1976
15. Petula Clark
    Clyde McPhatter
16. Patti Santos (It's a Beautiful Day)
    Toni Brown (Joy of Cooking)
17. Gene Clark (The Byrds)
    Gordon Lightfoot
    Bob Gaudio (Four Seasons)
    Rod Clements (Lindisfarne)
    John Glasock (Jethro Tull) died, 1979
18. Danny Whitten (Crazy Horse) died, 1972
19. Ray Collins (The Mothers of Invention)
    Fred Lipsius (Blood, Sweat and Tears)
20. Duane Allman
    Gary Green (Gentle Giant)
    Norman Greenbaum ("Spirit in the Sky")
21. Dr. John
    Lonnie Jordan (War)
    Livingston Taylor
22. "Family Man" Barrett (The Wailers)
23. Freddie Marsden (Gerry and the Pacemakers)
24. Donald "Duck" Dunn
    Robin Williamson (Incredible String Band)
    Lee Michaels
25. Val Fuentes (It's a Beautiful Day)
    Roy Lynes (Status Quo)
26. John Rostil (The Shadows) died, 1973
    Tina Turner
    John McVie (Fleetwood Mac)

Olivia Newton-John
Burt Reiter (Focus)

27. Jimi Hendrix
Dozy (Dave, Dee, Dozy, Beaky, Mick and Tich)

28. Randy Newman
Hugh McKenna (The Sensational Alex Harvey Band)
R. B. Greaves ("Take a Letter, Maria")

29. John Mayall
Felix Cavaliere (The Young Rascals)
Jody Miller ("Queen of the House")

30. Paul Stookey (Peter, Paul and Mary)
Leo Lyons (Ten Years After)

DECEMBER

1. Billy Paul
Gilbert O'Sullivan
Bette Midler
Lou Rawls

2. Tom McGuiness (Manfred Mann)

3. John Wilson (Taste)
Ozzie Osbourne (Black Sabbath)

4. Dennis Wilson (The Beach Boys)
Freddie Cannon ("Tallahassee Lassie")
Chris Hillman (The Byrds)
Tommy Bolan died, 1976

5. Little Richard
Jim Messina
John Cale

6. "Gimme Shelter" (Movie by The Rolling Stones) opened in
New York City, 1970
Jonathan King ("Everyone's Gone to the Moon")
Leadbelly died, 1949
Keith West (Tomorrow)

7. Harry Chapin
Tom Waits

8. Jim Morrison
Gregg Allman
Jerry Butler
Graham Knight (Marmalade)

9. Junior Wells
   Rick Danko (The Band)
   Sam Strain (Little Anthony and the Imperials)
10. Chad Stewart (Chad and Jeremy)
   Otis Redding died, 1967
11. Brenda Lee
   David Gates (Bread)
   Sam Cooke died, 1964
12. Dionne Warwick
   Paul Rodgers (Bad Company)
   Jeff Lynne (Electric Light Orchestra)
   Mike Smith (The Dave Clark Five)
   Mike Herron (Incredible String Band)
   Dickey Betts
   Clive Bunker (Jethro Tull)
   Tony Williams
   Ray Jackson (Lindisfarne)
13. Davey O'List (Roxy Music)
14. Charlie Rich
15. Cindy Birdsong (The Supremes)
   Dave Clark
   Carmine Appice (Vanilla Fudge)
16. Tony Hicks (The Hollies)
17. John Bonfanti (Raspberries)
   Paul Butterfield
   Eddie Kendricks
   Carlie Barrett (The Wailers)
18. Keith Richards
   Chas Chandler (The Animals)
   Professor Longhair
19. Alvin Lee (Ten Years After)
   Phil Ochs
   John McEven (The Dirt Band)
20. Bobby Columby (Blood, Sweat and Tears)
   Bobby Darin died, 1973
21. Frank Zappa
   Carl Wilson (The Beach Boys)
22. Robin and Maurice Gibb (The Bee Gees)
23. Jorma Kaukonen (Hot Tuna)
   Tim Hardin
   Johnny Kidd (The Pirates)

24. Lee Dorsey
    Jan Akkerman
    Johnny Ace died, 1958
25. Merry Clayton
    Noel Redding (The Jimi Hendrix Experience)
26. Phil Spector
27. Tracy Nelson
    Mike Pinder (The Moody Blues)
    Les Maguire (Gerry and the Pacemakers)
28. Edgar Winter
    Johnny Otis
    "Pops" Staples (The Staple Singers)
29. Ray Thomas (The Moody Blues)
30. Del Shannon
    John Hartford
    Skeeter Davis ("End of the World")
    Bo Diddley
31. Odetta
    John Denver
    Patti Smith
    Burton Cummings

Rock Deaths

Johnny Ace, died December 25, 1954
Duane Allman, died October 29, 1971
Florence Ballard (The Supremes), died February 21, 1976
Jesse Belvin (Earth Angel), died February 6, 1960
Bobby Bloom, died January 28, 1974
Marc Bolan (T-Rex), died September 16, 1977
Tommy Bolan (Deep Purple), died December 4, 1976
Jacques Brel, died October 9, 1978
Lenny Bruce, died August 3, 1966
Tim Buckley, died June 29, 1975
Johnny Burnette, died August 1, 1964
Miss Christine, died November 5, 1972
Eddie Cochran, died April 17, 1960
Brian Cole (The Association), died August 2, 1972
Sam Cooke, died December 11, 1964

Jim Croce, died September 20, 1973

Arthur "Big Boy" Crudup, died March 28, 1974

King Curtis, died August 13, 1971

Bobby Darin, died December 20, 1973

Cyril Davies (Blues Incorporated), died January 7, 1964

Rev. Gary Davis, died May 5, 1972

James Dean, died September 30, 1955

Sandy Denny, died April 24, 1978

Tommy Edwards, died October 12, 1971

Mama Cass Elliot (The Mamas and The Papas), died July 29, 1974

Brian Epstein (The Beatles' manager), died August 27, 1967

Richard Fariña, died April 30, 1966

Lester Flatt, died May 11, 1979

Alan Freed (first rock and roll disc jockey), died January 20, 1965

Steven Gaines (Lynyrd Skynyrd), died October 20, 1977

Glen Gains (Parliament Funkadelic), July 30, 1978

Lowell George (Little Feat), died June 29, 1979

John Glasock (Jethro Tull), died November 17, 1979

Ralph Gleason (writer and contributor to *Rolling Stone*), died June 3, 1975

Woody Guthrie, died October 3, 1967

Pete Ham (Badfinger), died April 23, 1975

Les Harvey (Stone the Crows), died May 3, 1972

Donny Hathaway, died January 14, 1979

Jimi Hendrix, died September 18, 1970

Greg Herbert (Blood, Sweat and Tears), died January 31, 1978

Billie Holiday, died July 17, 1959

Buddy Holly, died February 3, 1959

Johnny Horton, died November 5, 1960

Howlin' Wolf, died October 10, 1976

Elmore James, died May 24, 1963

Mike Jeffreys (Jimi Hendrix's manager), March 5, 1973

Brian Jones, died July 3, 1969

Janis Joplin, died October 4, 1970

Terry Kath (Chicago), died January 23, 1978

Stan Kenton, died August 25, 1979

Johnny Kidd (The Pirates), died October 7, 1966

Phil King (Blue Oyster Cult), died April 27, 1972

Paul Kossoff (Free), died March 19, 1976

Van McCoy, died July 9, 1979

Jimmy McCulloch (Wings), died September 27, 1979

Fred McDowell, died July 3, 1972

Robbie McIntosh (Average White Band), died September 23, 1974

Rod "Pigpen" McKernan (The Grateful Dead), died August 8, 1973

Harold McNair (Ginger Baker), died March 26, 1971

Clyde McPhatter, died June 13, 1972

Donald McPherson (Main Ingredient), died July 4, 1971

Amos Milburn ("Chicken Shack Boogie"), died January 3, 1980

Charles Mingus, died January 5, 1979

Keith Moon (The Who), died September 8, 1978

Jim Morrison, died July 3, 1971

Johnny O'Keefe, died October 6, 1978

Berry Oakley (The Allman Brothers), died November 11, 1972

Phil Ochs, died April 9, 1976

Gram Parsons, died September 19, 1973

Elvis Presley, died August 16, 1977

Janet Vogel Rapp (Skyliners), died February 21, 1980

Otis Redding, died December 10, 1967

Keith Relf (The Yardbirds), died November 14, 1976

Minnie Riperton, died July 12, 1979

John Rostill (The Shadows), died November 26, 1973

Lillian Roxon (noted rock writer), died August 9, 1973

Bon Scott (AC/DC), died February 18, 1980

James "Shep" Shepherd (Shep and the Limelights), died January 24, 1970

Bessie Smith, died September 26, 1937

Billy Stewart, died January 17, 1970

Stu Sutcliffe, died April 10, 1962

Stacy Sutherland (13th Floor Elevator), died August 24, 1978

Vinnie Taylor (Sha Na Na), died April 17, 1974

Tammi Terrell, died March 16, 1970

Gary Thain (Uriah Heep), died March 19, 1976

Ronnie Van Zant (Lynyrd Skynyrd), died October 20, 1977

Gene Vincent, died October 12, 1971

Sid Vicious (Sex Pistols), died February 2, 1979

Clarence White (The Byrds), died July 19, 1973

Josh White, died September 5, 1969

Danny Whitten (Crazy Horse), died November 18, 1972

Chuck Willis ("Hang Up My Rock and Roll Shoes"), died April 10, 1958

Al "Big Bear" Wilson (Canned Heat), died August 3, 1973

Hank Williams, died January 1, 1953

Paul Williams (The Temptations), died August 17, 1973

Sonny Boy Williamson, died June 1, 1948

Sonny Boy Williamson II, died May 25, 1965

Max Yasgur (owned property where Woodstock took place), died February 8, 1973

IV. THE RECORD COMPANIES

The record companies in this list deal entirely or in part with rock and roll.

Many of them changed hands or disappeared almost as fast as we could list them. Some are owned by larger labels; some are distributed by larger labels. Recording artists are constantly switching record companies. Ideally this list should be written in pencil because of all the changes. Some of these addresses will be accurate for a long time; others will have changed by the time you read this. When in doubt, let your fingers do the walking.

A&M Records, 1416 North La Brea Avenue, Hollywood, California 90028
    also for: Horizon

ABC Records, 8255 Beverly Boulevard, Los Angeles, California 90048
    also for: ABC/Blue Thumb   ABC/Impulse
              ABC/Dot   ABC/Paramount
              ABC/Dunhill   ABC/Songbird

ABKCO Records, 1700 Broadway, New York, New York 10019

All Ears Records, 1420 North Beachwood Drive, Hollywood, California 90028

All Platinum Records, 96 West Street, Englewood, New Jersey 07631
    also for: Chess

Amherst Records, 355 Harlem Road, Buffalo, New York 14224

Angel, see Capitol

Apple, 1750 North Vine Street, Hollywood, California 90028

Ariola/America, 8671 Wilshire Boulevard, Beverly Hills, California 90211

Arista Records, 6 West 57th Street, New York, New York 10019
    also for: Freedom   Savoy   Morning Sky

Asylum, see Elektra/Asylum

Atco, see Atlantic

Atlantic Records, 75 Rockefeller Plaza, New York, New York 10019
    also for: Atco   Soul City
              Cotillion   Swan Song
              Rolling Stone Records   Lingasong
              Nemperor   Big Tree

ATV Music Corporation, 6255 Sunset Boulevard, Hollywood, California 90028

Avatar, see Capitol

Bang/Bullet Records, 2107 Faulkner Road, Atlanta, Georgia 30324

Barnaby Records, 816 North La Cienega Boulevard, Los Angeles, California 90069

Bearsville Records, 75 East 55th Street, New York, New York 10022

Bent Records, see Rounder

Beserkley Records, 1199 Spruce Street, Berkeley, California 94707

Big Sound Records, 175 Thompson Street, New York, New York 10012

Big Tree Records, see Atlantic

Bluebird, see RCA

Blue Horizon, see Sire

Blue Note, see United Artists

Blue River Records, 6223 Selma Avenue, Suite 125, Hollywood, California 90028

Blue Sky Records, 745 Fifth Avenue, Suite 1803, New York, New York 10022

Blue Thumb, see ABC Records

Broadside, see Folkways

Brunswick Records, 888 Seventh Avenue, New York, New York 10019

Buddah Records, 810 Seventh Avenue, New York, New York 10019
  also for: Kama Sutra Records

Butterfly Records, 900 Sunset Boulevard, Suite 617, Los Angeles, California 90069

Capitol Records, 1750 North Vine Street, Hollywood, California 90028
  also for: Angel   Harvest
           EMI   Avatar

Caprice Records, 907 Main Street, Nashville, Tennessee 37206
  also for: Checkmate

Capricorn Records, 535 Cotton Avenue, Macon, Georgia 31208

Caribou Records, 8500 Melrose Avenue, Los Angeles, California 09969

Casablanca Record and Film Works, 8255 Sunset Boulevard, Los Angeles, California 90046
  also for: Douglas

Casablanca Records, 8255 Sunset Boulevard, Los Angeles, California 90046
  also for: Chocolate City   Oasis

Cat Records, see T K Productions

CBS/Columbia Records, 51 West 52nd Street, New York, New York 10019

also for: Epic   Invictus
Portrait   Sweet City
Odyssey   T-Neck

Centurian Records, 3291 East 119th Street, Cleveland, Ohio 44120

Checkmate, see Caprice Records

Chess, see All Platinum

Chocolate City, see Casablanca

Chrysalis Records, 9255 Sunset Boulevard, Suite 212, Los Angeles, California 90069

Cleveland International Records, P.O. Box 783, Willoughby, Ohio 44094

Cotillion, see Atlantic

Cream Records, 8025 Melrose Avenue, Los Angeles, California 90046
also for: Hi Records

CTI, see Motown

Curtom Records, 5915 North Lincoln Avenue, Chicago, Illinois 60659

Dark Horse, see Warner Brothers

Dash, see T K Productions

Deram, see London

DJM Records, 119 West 57th Street, Suite 400, New York, New York 10019

Dot, see ABC Records

Douglas, see Casablanca

Dunhill, see ABC Records

Elektra/Asylum/Nonesuch Records, 962 North La Cienega Boulevard, Los Angeles, California 90069

EMI, see Capitol

Epic, see Columbia

Fania Records, 888 Seventh Avenue, New York, New York 10019

Fantasy/Prestige, Tenth & Parker Streets, Berkeley, California 94710
also for: Stax

Flying Fish Records, 3320 North Halstead, Chicago, Illinois 60657

Folkways Records, 43 West 61st Street, New York, New York 10023
also for: Broadside

Freedom, see Arista

Full Moon Records, 9126 Sunset Boulevard, Los Angeles, California 90069

Glenn Productions, 157 West 57th Street, New York, New York 10019
also for: Red Bird

G N P Crescendo Records, 8560 Sunset Boulevard, Suite 603, Los Angeles, California 90069

Gold Seal, see RCA

Gordy, see Motown

Great Gramophone, 240 West 55th Street, New York, New York 10019

Green Tree, see Rounder Records

Grunt, see RCA

GTD, see Surf City Records

Happy Tunes, see Springboard

Harvest, see Capitol

Hi, see Cream Records

Hickory Records, 2510 Franklin Road, Nashville, Tennessee 37204

Horizon, see A&M

Impulse, see ABC Records

Invictus, see CBS/Columbia

Island Records, 7720 Sunset Boulevard, Los Angeles, California 90046
    also for: True North

Janus Records, 8776 Sunset Boulevard, Los Angeles, California 90069

Jet Records, 2 Century Plaza, Suite 414, Los Angeles, California 90067

Kama Sutra, see Buddah

Kirshner Entertainment Corporation, 1370 Avenue of the Americas, New York, New York 10019
    also for: Kirshner Records

K-tel International Inc., 11311 K-tel Drive, Minnetonka, Minnesota 55343

Laurie Records, 20 F. Robert Pitt Drive, Monsey, New York 10977

Library of Congress, Recorded Sound Section, Washington, D.C. 20540

Lifesong Records, 488 Madison Avenue, New York, New York 10022

Lighthouse Records, 65 Lovel Avenue, San Rafael, California 94901

Lingasong, see Atlantic

Little David Records, 9229 Sunset Boulevard, Suite 901, Los Angeles, California 90069

London Records, 539 West 25th Street, New York, New York 10001
    also for: Deram   Parrot   Threshold

Marlin Records, see T K Productions

MCA Records, 100 Universal City Plaza, Universal City, California 91608
    also for: Track Records

Mercury, see Phonogram/Mercury

MGM, see Polydor

Midsong International Records, 1650 Broadway, New York, New York 10019

Millennium Records, 3 West 57th Street, New York, New York 10019

Monument Records Corporation, 21 Music Square East, Nashville, Tennessee 37203

Morning Sky, see Arista

Motown Records, 6255 Sunset Boulevard, Hollywood, California 90028
    also for: Gordy   Rare Earth
             Mowest   Tamla
             Prodigal   CTI

Mowest, see Motown

Muscadine Records, Advent Productions, P.O. Box 635 La Habra, California 90631

Mushroom Records, 8833 Sunset Boulevard, Los Angeles, California 90069

Musicor Records, 870 Seventh Avenue, Suite 348, New York, New York 10019

Nemperor, see Atlantic

New Wave Records, 10 North Third Street, Philadelphia, Pennsylvania 19106

Oasis, see Casablanca

Ode Records Inc., 1416 North La Brea, Hollywood, California 90028

Odyssey, see CBS/Columbia

Ovation Records, 1249 Waukegan Road, Glenview, Illinois 60025

Pacific Records, 9200 Sunset Boulevard, Hollywood, California 90069

Paradise Records Inc., 3300 Warner Boulevard, Burbank, California 91510

Paramount, see ABC Records

Paramount-West Enterprises, 8010 Second Street, Paramount, California 90723

Parrot, see London

Passport Records, 3619 Kennedy Road, South Plainfield, New Jersey 07080

Philadelphia International Records, 309 South Broad Street, Philadelphia, Pennsylvania 19107

Philo Records, The Barn, North Ferrisburg, Vermont 05473

Phonogram/Mercury, 1 IBM Plaza, Chicago, Illinois 60611
    also for: Fontana   Smash
             Philips   Vertigo

Pickwick Records, 135 Crossways Park Drive, Woodbury, New York 11797

Plantation Records, see Shelby Singleton Corporation

Playboy Records, 8560 Sunset Boulevard, Los Angeles, California 90069

Polydor Records, 810 Seventh Avenue, New York, New York 10019
    also for: MGM   Verve

Portrait, see CBS/Columbia

Prestige, see Fantasy/Prestige

Private Stock Records, 40 West 57th Street, New York, New York 10023

Prodigal, see Motown

Ram Records, c/o Max's Kansas City, 213 Park Avenue South, New York, New York 10003

Rare Earth, see Motown

Ratcity, see All Platinum Records

RCA Records, 1133 Avenue of the Americas, New York, New York 10036
    also for: Bluebird   Grunt
              Gold Seal   Windsong

Red Bird, see Glenn Productions

Reprise, see Warner Brothers

Rocket Records, 211 South Beverly Drive, Beverly Hills, California 90212

Rolling Stone Records, see Atlantic

Roulette Records, Inc., 17 West 60th Street, New York, New York 10023
    also for: Virgo

Rounder Records, 186 Willow Avenue, Somerville, Massachusetts 02144
    also for: Bent   Green Tree   Transatic

RSO Records, 8335 Sunset Boulevard, Los Angeles, California 90069

Savoy, see Arista

Scepter, see Springboard

Shelby Singleton Corporation, 3106 Belmont Boulevard, Nashville, Tennessee 37212
    also for: Plantation   Sun

Shelter Records, 5112 Hollywood Boulevard, Hollywood, California 90027

Sire Records, 165 West 74th Street, New York, New York 10023
    also for: Blue Horizon

Songbird, see ABC Records

Soul City, see Atlantic

Soul Train Records, 9200 Sunset Boulevard, Los Angeles, California 90069

Specialty Records, 8300 Santa Monica Boulevard, Los Angeles, California 90069

Springboard Records, 947 U.S. Highway 1, Rahway, New Jersey 07065
also for: Happy Tunes   Scepter   Trip

Stanyan Record Company, 8440 Santa Monica Boulevard, Hollywood, California 90069

Stax, see Fantasy/Prestige

Sun, see Shelby Singleton Corporation

Surf City Records, 5460 White Oak Avenue, Suite G-338, Encino, California 91316
also for: GTP

Swan Song, see Atlantic

Sweet City, see CBS/Columbia

Tamla, see Motown

Threshold, see London

T K Productions, 495 Southeast Tenth Court, Hialeah, Florida 33010
also for: Cat   Dash   Marlin

T-Neck, see CBS/Columbia

Tomato Music Company, 505 Park Avenue, New York, New York 10022

Track, see MCA

Transatlantic, see Rounder

Trip, see Springboard

True North, see Island

Twentieth Century, 8544 Sunset Boulevard, Los Angeles, California 90069

U K Records, 315 West 57th Street, Suite 3H, New York, New York 10019

Uni, see MCA

United Artists Records, 6920 Sunset Boulevard, Los Angeles, California 90028
also for: Blue Note

Vanguard Records, 71 West 23rd Street, New York, New York 10010

Vee Jay Records, 131 East Magnolia Boulevard, Burbank, California 91502

Vertigo, see Phonogram/Mercury

Verve, see Polydor

Virgin Records, 43 Perry Street, New York, New York 10014

Virgo, see Roulette

Warner Brothers Records, 3300 Warner Boulevard, Burbank, California 91510

> also for: Dark Horse   Warner-Curb
>   Paradise   Warner-Spector
>   Reprise

Warner-Curb, see Warner Brothers

Warner-Spector, see Warner Brothers

Windfall Records, 1790 Broadway, New York, New York 10019

Windsong, see RCA

Wing and a Prayer Records, 3 Patchin Place, New York, New York 10011

Yazoo Records, 245 Waverly Place, New York, New York 10014

N.B. Most folk and blues records may be obtained through two distributors:

> Rounder Records, 186 Willow Avenue, Somerville, Massachusetts 02144
>
> Muscadine Records, Advent Productions, P.O. Box 635, La Habra, California 90631

Rock Magazines and Publications

These are nine currently publishing rock and roll periodicals:

Billboard (weekly), 9000 Sunset Boulevard, Los Angeles, California 90069

Cash Box (weekly), 119 West 57th Street, New York, New York 10019

Circus (biweekly), 115 East 57th Street, New York, New York 10022

Creem (monthly), 187 South Woodward Avenue, Birmingham, Michigan 48011

Hit Parader (monthly), Charlton Publications, Derby, Connecticut 06418

Phonograph Record Magazine (monthly), P.O. Box 2404, Hollywood, California 90028

Record World (weekly), 1700 Broadway, New York, New York 10019

Rolling Stone (bimonthly), 745 Fifth Avenue, New York, New York 10022

Trouser Press (monthly, except March and September), 147 West 42nd Street, Room 801, New York, New York 10036

Rock Bibliography

In an earlier section of this book we dared to suggest a basic rock library of record albums. In this section we're going to attempt the equally difficult task of suggesting a basic rock library of books relating to the music and its people.

Belz, Carl. *The Story of Rock*. New York: Oxford University Press, 1969, second edition 1972; New York: Harper & Row, 1971, second edition 1973, paperback. This is one of the earliest "story of rock" books—and one of the best.

Carr, Roy. *The Rolling Stones: An Illustrated Record*. New York: Harmony Books, 1976. The Stones as depicted in a dazzling panorama of words and pictures.

Carr, Roy, and Tyler, Tony. *The Beatles: An Illustrated Record*. New York: Harmony Books, 1975. The "Fab Four" as depicted in a dazzling panorama of words and pictures.

Chapple, Steve, and Garofalo, Reebee. *Rock 'n' Roll Is Here to Pay*. Chicago: Nelson-Hall, 1977. This is not the definitive work it purports to be, but is nevertheless chock full of valuable information and interesting opinions.

Clark, Dick, and Robinson, Richard. *Rock, Roll and Remember*. New York: Thomas Y. Crowell Company, 1976. These are valuable reminiscences of the man who has seen it all—and overseen plenty of it!

Davies, Hunter. *The Beatles*. New York: McGraw-Hill, 1968; revised edition, 1978. Recently updated, this is the authorized biography and, as such, essential reading.

Eisen, Jonathan, ed. *The Age of Rock*. New York: Vintage Books, 1969. This is a brilliant anthology of articles and essays about many diverse facets of the rock and roll experience.

Friedman, Myra. *Buried Alive: The Biography of Janis Joplin*. New York: William Morrow & Co., 1973; New York: Bantam Books, 1974. Must reading—a National Book Award nominee.

Gillett, Charlie. *The Sound of the City: The Rise of Rock and Roll*. New York: Outerbridge & Dienstfrey, 1970; New York: Dell Publishing Co., 1972. Originally a master's thesis, this book is a studious examination of the origins and spread of rock and roll.

Goldstein, Richard. *The Poetry of Rock*. New York: Bantam Books, 1969. This book singlehandedly brought rock and roll into the classroom.

————. *Goldstein's Greatest Hits*. Englewood Cliffs, New Jersey: Prentice-Hall, 1970. Richard did more for early rock criticism than any other single individual, with the possible exception of Paul Williams. This book contains just what the title implies.

Hopkins, Jerry. *Elvis*. New York: Simon & Schuster, 1971. An essential, basic biography of the king of rock and roll.

Jenkinson, Philip, and Warner, Alan. *Celluloid Rock*. London: Lorrimer, 1974. This is an entertaining and informative survey of rock films from *Blackboard Jungle* through 1974.

Logan, Nick, and Woffinden, Bob. *The Illustrated Encyclopedia of Rock*. New York: Harmony Books, 1977. A marvelous, graphic counterpart and companion work to Lillian Roxon's original.

Lydon, Michael. *Rock Folk: Portraits from the Rock 'n' Roll Pantheon*. New York: The Dial Press, 1971. These are gripping portrayals of rock persons, places, and things which hold up remarkably well.

Marchbank, Pearce, and Miles, Barry. *The Illustrated Rock Almanac*. London: Paddington Press, 1977. This is a terrific day-by-day reference to rock events.

Marsh, Dave, with John Swenson. The Rolling Stone Record Guide. New York: Rolling Stone Press, 1979. An excellent compilation of reviews and ratings of over 10,000 rock, soul, country, blues, jazz, and gospel albums.

Marsh, Dave. *Born to Run*. New York: Dolphin Books/Doubleday, 1979. More than just a biography, this is a magnificent look at one of rock and roll's heralded performers: Bruce Springsteen.

McGregor, Craig, ed. *Bob Dylan: A Retrospective*. New York: William Morrow & Co., 1972. A marvelous collection of pre-1973 articles and essays.

Miller, Jim, ed. *The Rolling Stone Illustrated History of Rock and Roll*. New York: Rolling Stone Press/Random House, 1976. *Rolling Stone*'s thoroughly informative and entertaining survey of rock's first quarter of a century.

Nite, Norm N. *Rock On: The Illustrated Encyclopedia of Rock 'n' Roll*. New York: Thomas Y. Crowell Company, 1976. This is a solid reference work with particular appeal to the "oldies" buff.

Nugent, Stephen, and Gillett, Charlie. *Rock Almanac*. Garden City, New York: Anchor Press/Doubleday, 1978. Another excellent reference listing chart hits through the years.

Passman, Arnold. *The Deejays*. New York: The Macmillan Company, 1971. Though the definitive exploration remains to be done, this is an interesting history of a unique occupation.

Peelaert, Guy, and Cohn, Nik. *Rock Dreams*. New York: Popular Library, 1973. This book is a stunning and artistic evocation of the rock experience.

Pollock, Bruce, and Wagman, John. *The Face of Rock and Roll*. New York: Holt, Rinehart & Winston, 1978. The story of rock and roll told with an inspired selection of album covers. (See also *Album Cover Album* by Storm Thorgerson and Roger Dean.)

Propes, Steve. *Golden Goodies*. Radnor, Pennsylvania: Chilton Book Company, 1975. This, and two earlier volumes by Propes, are essential collections of rock biographies and discographies.

————. *Golden Oldies*. Radnor, Pennsylvania: Chilton Book Company, 1974.

————. *Those Oldies but Goodies*. New York: Collier Books, 1973.

Roxon, Lillian. *Rock Encyclopedia*. New York: Grosset & Dunlap, 1969. Revision by Ed Naha. New York: Grosset & Dunlap, 1978. Obviously dated, but the late Australian critic's book is still the best of its kind. (The revised edition tries hard, but check out the original if you can.)

Scaduto, Anthony. *Bob Dylan*. New York: Grosset & Dunlap, 1971. This is still a very good biography of the elusive, pre-'70s Mr. Dylan.

Somma, Robert, ed. *No One Waved Goodbye*. New York: Outerbridge & Dienstfrey, 1971. A sobering collection of essays exploring the harsh reality of rock death.

Stokes, Geoffrey. *Star-making Machinery: The Odyssey of an Album*. Indianapolis/New York: The Bobbs-Merrill Co., 1976. *The* definitive look at the business of rock and roll.

Thorgerson, Storm, and Dean, Roger. *Album Cover Album*. New York: A&W Visual Library, 1977. This is the best "album cover as art" book. (See also *The Face of Rock and Roll* by Bruce Pollock and John Wagman.)

Williams, Paul. *Outlaw Blues*. New York: E. P. Dutton & Co., 1969. These are somewhat dated, but nevertheless brilliant, observations about rock by one of its earliest serious critics.

AFTERWORD

In compiling THE ROCK MUSIC SOURCE BOOK, we realized that no matter how many themes and songs we listed, the book could never be judged complete. Our final cuffoff date for adding songs and albums was March 24, 1980. Those that we did choose to include may not all be on target or satisfactory to everyone. We do hope, however, that we have provided a source for informative and pertinent songs and a framework for your own additions.

Quite simply, we have tried our best. Now it is your turn.

If you know of songs we should have included, or disagree with some of the songs we did include, let us know! If there are specific topics or themes that you find interesting, tell us, and we will try to list them in future editions of THE ROCK MUSIC SOURCE BOOK.

Send your suggestions and thoughts—or gripes and complaints, for that matter—to:

THE ROCK MUSIC SOURCE BOOK
c/o Anchor Press
Doubleday & Company, Inc.
245 Park Avenue
New York, New York 10017

About the Authors

Bob Macken is a "rock and roll computer" who has made a hobby of documenting rock history and cataloging rock songs by their subject matter since 1967. His collection now includes over 40,000 songs, grouped by over 450 themes and topics. Born in New York City, Bob graduated from St. John's University with a degree in communication arts, and has done graduate work at the New School for Social Research. He has worked in various capacities for the NBC and ABC television networks. He currently produces the nationally syndicated radio show "Rock and Roll Never Forgets." He is a contributor to the BBC radio series "Twenty Five Years of Rock," and he provides thematic music for various television and radio programs. He also produces video projects for his production services company, Cracken Productions. THE ROCK MUSIC SOURCE BOOK is his first book.

Peter Fornatale has been a program host at WNEW-FM in New York since July 1969. He has taught communication arts on both the high school and college levels, and has lectured about the mass media at more than fifty colleges and universities in the Northeast. His articles about radio, television, and music have appeared in *TV Guide, Crawdaddy,* the New York *Daily News, Newsday,* and other publications. THE ROCK MUSIC SOURCE BOOK is Pete's first full-length book.

Bill Ayres has worked in the fields of religious education, pastoral counseling, community organization, social justice, and media. He has produced and appeared on over two thousand radio shows and over two hundred television shows. Bill is presently the host of a late-night telephone talk show, "Where's It All Going?" for WPLJ-FM in New York, and he interviews rock stars on a weekly show on WPLJ, KAUM-FM in Houston, WRIF-FM in Detroit, and WRQX in Washington, D.C. THE ROCK MUSIC SOURCE BOOK is his first book.